THE OFFICIAL® PRICE GUIDE TO

GLASSWARE

THE OFFICIAL® PRICE GUIDE TO

GLASSWARE

MARK PICKVET

SECOND EDITION

House of Collectibles

The Ballantine Publishing Group • New York

Copyright © 1998 by Mark Pickvet

 This is a registered trademark of Random House, Inc.

Published by: House of Collectibles
The Ballantine Publishing Group
201 East 50th Street
New York, NY 10022

Distributed by The Ballantine Publishing Group, a division of Random House, Inc., New York, and simultaneously in Canada by Random House of Canada Limited, Toronto.

Manufactured in the United States of America

ISSN: 0743-8699

ISBN: 0-676-60137-5

Text design by Holly Johnson

Cover photo by George Kerrigan

Second Edition: February 1998

10   9   8   7   6   5   4   3   2   1

CONTENTS

ACKNOWLEDGMENTS

A project of this magnitude is never completed alone. There are many people who helped along the way, and I sincerely hope that I do not forget anyone: Robin Rainwater, Kate Pickvet, Louis Pickvet, Jr., Leota Pickvet, Louis Pickvet III, Fairy Pickvet, Debbie Pickvet, Juli Pickvet, Andrea Pickvet, Michael Pickvet, Bill Willard, Kathy Willard, Tom Smith, Sandra Smith, David Smith, Ella Kitson, Robert Darnold, Sue Darnold, Rachel Moore, Ward Lindsay, Robert Davidson, Rick Patterson, Joe Renner, David Renner, Linda Renner, Paul Traviglia, Jennifer Hood, Robert Lutton, William Smola, Dr. Fred Svoboda, Dr. Arthur Harshman, Dr. David Churchman, Dr. Howard Holter, Dr. Mark Luca, Joy McFadden, Gail Grabow, Bonnie Van Sickle, Donna Williams, Jack Adamson, Gary Crossen, Joan Mogensen, Herbert Smith, David Hill, James Smith, George Nichols, Julie Barnett, Johanna Billings, Lori Whetzel, John and Karen Halsey, Sheryl Laub, Carol O'Laughlin, Nadine Wallenstein, Carol Buntrock, Brad and Vera Decker, Gordon Ferguson, Tammy and Forrest Kimble, John Lander, Carl Mann, Joan Lynn, Kathy Simon, Rita Erickson, Mary Blake, Larry Dearman, Ruth Bagel, Larry Mitchell, Connie DeAngleo, Brian Hill, Joseph Bourque, Don Kime, Virginia Scott, Wilma Thurston, Karen Skinner, Tom McGlauchlin, Adrienne Esco, Eunice Booker, Mary Sharp, Ellen Hem, Larry Branstad, Marie Heath, Kathy Harris, Marie McGee, Judy Maxwell, Barbara Hobbs, Harold Mayes, and members of the SGAC.

Of great help were librarians and personnel from the following libraries: the Carnegie Institute, the Chrysler Museum Library, the Corning Museum of Glass Library, the Detroit Public Library, the Fenton Art Glass Company Library, the Flint Public Library, the Harvard Widener Library, the Historical Society of Pennsylvania, the Library of Congress, the Milwaukee Public Library, the New York Public Library Annex, the Toledo-Lucas County Library, the Toledo Museum of Art Library, and the Libraries of the University of Michigan.

Finally, I wish to thank the following museum and company personnel: Christine Mack of the Allen Memorial Art Museum; Anndora Morginson of the Art Institute of Chicago; Barbara Anderson of the Bergstrom-Mahler

Museum; William Blenko, Jr., Richard Blenko, and Virginia Womack of the Blenko Glass Co.; M. E. Walter of the Block China Corp.; Bernard C. Boyd, Susan Boyd, and Luke Boyd of the Boyd Art Glass Co.; Sarah Nichols of the Carnegie Museum of Art; Donna Sawyer, Rosemary Dumais, Gary Baker, and Peter Dubeau of the Chrysler Museum; Jane Shadel Spillman, Jill Thomas-Clark, and Virginia Wright of the Corning Museum of Glass; Darlene Antonellis-LaCroix of the Currier Gallery of Art; Frank Fenton of the Fenton Art Glass Co.; Cathleen Latendresse of the Henry Ford Museum; Jack Wilkie of The Franklin Mint; Lisa Gibson of the Gibson Glass Co.; Jim Hill of the Greentown Glass Museum; Carrie Brankovich of the Lotton Art Glass Co.; Katherine McCracken of the National Heisey Glass Museum; Philip F. Hopfe of the New England Crystal Co.; Donna Baron of Old Sturbridge Village; Peter Moore of the Pilgrim Glass Corp.; Kirk Nelson of the Sandwich Glass Museum; Paula Belanger of the Showcase Antique Center; Sheila Machlis Alexander of the Smithsonian Institute; Sandra Knudsen of the Toledo Museum of Art; the Havenmeyer collection at the University of Michigan Museum of Art; William Hosley and Linda Roth of Wadsworth Athenum; and Dorothy Zyn of Bloomingdale's, Chicago.

INTRODUCTION

Glass is a fascinating substance. It may have first been discovered by a nomad of ancient Egypt, who started a simple wood fire in a sand pit. The two unlikely ingredients of glass—sand and ash—were soon combined to make decorative objects, some of which have been excavated in the tombs of pharaohs. Over the centuries the art of glassmaking evolved, and with it glassware became utilitarian. Cups, beakers, vases, bottles, mirrors, and windows reflected the glassmaker's skills. Glass eventually found its way into workplaces, houses of worship, and homes.

Today, we take glass for granted. Look around your home and you'll see glass windows, tumblers, doors, vases, eyeglasses, jars, coffee carafes, lightbulbs, aquariums, camera lenses, appliances, and a host of other useful items. Glass is certainly versatile.

What we are interested in here, though, is the collectibility of glassware and the state of the collector's market. This second edition of the *Official Price Guide to Glassware* expands on the first volume, offering price information on some of the more popular glassware available to collectors.

Along with updated and current pricing, the second edition includes at least a thousand more prices than the first, along with additional listings in the appendixes (more terms, references, clubs, manufacturer's marks, and even a few Web sites). It continues to be my goal to provide the most comprehensive listings for a broad range of categories in the field of collectible glassware. The prices listed here are intended only as a guide in evaluating glass items.

Generally, the bigger the piece, the higher the price. This is the old punch bowl to salt dip rule: if both are made in the same style and are of the same quality, the larger item will usually cost more. Of course, rarity and desirability play a large part in pricing. For instance, a small "Acorn Burrs" patterned Carnival glass vase whimsey outsells everything else in that pattern by at least a factor of six.

I received many letters in response to the first edition. The most frequently asked question concerned the cover photo of a small blue milk pitcher. This was the only photo that I did not take myself or arrange for the shooting, and so I was unable to identify it. Some collectors who wrote in about this particular piece noted that they had similar items for which they had paid from $25 to $40. One correspondent noted that she had purchased a creamer and sugar set in the same pattern for $40. To be honest, I've got an entire file of unidentified pieces that I hope to be able to eventually identify.

One item of note regards methods of measurement as given in this book. To clarify, I rely on two primary sources: one is the actual measurement that I do myself using rulers, templates, vernier calipers, graduated cylinders, measuring cups, beakers, and so on—a regular basement laboratory of equipment. The other is manufacturers' listings from company catalogs, advertisements, and trade journals. Due to mold variations or other slight changes made by manufacturers, expect variances up to a half inch as well as a few ounces in capacity. Especially where handmade glass is concerned, expect even more variance. This is particularly true for older art and other handmade styles of glass.

I wish to thank Sara Smith of Los Angeles, who provided measurement data for Depression glass tumblers. I also wish to note an error in Chapter 7 of the first edition regarding Cambridge swans. The measurements listed there are for length, not height.

Another item of note regards discrepancies in dating companies. I usually include the dates of production at the top of each price listing. For actual company histories, check the glossary. Errors in the glossary that had appeared in the first edition hopefully have all been addressed now. I thank all those readers who wrote in with clarifications and new information.

This second edition has been organized in the same way as the first. Pressed pattern and Depression glass are listed alphabetically by pattern name. Cut glass is alphabetized by company name since so many manufacturers produced the same patterns and basic cuttings. The section on Carnival glass includes a listing by pattern name as well as miscellaneous pieces made by particular companies. Modern, Art, and Foreign glassware sections include both manufacturers and pattern names; patterns are used when there is sufficient variety of pieces to list separately. The Modern section also includes some miscellaneous older listings that do not fit within the given categories (fruit or canning jars, for example).

Again, if you discover any mistakes, discrepancies, or inconsistencies, or if you have some new or interesting information or questions, please write to me at:

Mark Pickvet
5071 Watson Drive
Flint, MI 48506

Include a self-addressed stamped envelope and adequate postage for any photos you may include.

I wish you the best in your collecting endeavors and hope that you find the pieces of your dreams (at reasonable prices).

—*Mark Pickvet*

MARKET REVIEW, PRICING, AND CARE OF GLASSWARE

THE GLASS MARKETPLACE

In recent years, glass collecting has proliferated to an astounding degree. Much of this can be attributed to the rise in the popularity of reproduction Carnival glass in the 1960s, as well as the increasing popularity of Depression glass. Further proof of this can be found in the number of books published on the subject, the magazines devoted to glassware, the small art glass companies founded, the clubs organized, and the growing interest in the field. There are now frequent shows, auctions, and national advertising campaigns devoted to glass collecting.

For the most part, the hub of the glass world in the United States is still the East and Midwest. Historically, glassware factories sprang up in Massachusetts, Pennsylvania, New York, West Virginia, Ohio, and Indiana. With the exception of Bartlett-Collins in Oklahoma, all glass manufacturers in the United States through the Depression years were found east of the Mississippi River. As a result, prices and availability are adversely affected for those living in the western half of the country.

As the years go by, fewer pieces are available, which causes prices to soar. Pressed, cut, art, and Carnival glass are generally available only through auctions, choice shows, and exclusive dealers. Depression glass and even some modern glassware are slowly following this trend; however, both are still available through general shows and common dealers.

To recognize the best deals in glass, follow the dealers; that is, attend numerous auctions, know the value of patterns and styles in order to recognize a good deal when it comes along, answer advertisements in common newspapers by private collectors, check out rummage/garage sales for glassware, join a club in your area of interest, and attend large antique/flea markets.

At nearly every large show there is invariably a variety of dealers. Those that specialize in glass will usually sell it at or near the prices listed in popular price guides. It is the dealers that specialize in other merchandise who often offer the best bargains at shows. If these particular dealers have only a few glass items, they may not know the value of the pieces or may offer them at a lower markup.

IDENTIFYING GLASS

Glass now covers such a wide variety of forms and patterns that it is difficult to study them all. Most collectors focus on a certain category, color, style, manufacturer, or form. This book is divided into seven chapters covering the most popular categories.

There is no substitute for experience and education in collecting glass. Studying books, visiting museums and art galleries, speaking with dealers and visiting their shops, and attending auctions even as a nonbidding participant can all enhance one's knowledge of glassware.

Learn to recognize the *exact* marks and signatures of the various makers, particularly for the items or producers you are most interested in. By knowing these marks, you can be on the lookout for forgeries. Appendix 4 offers a directory of manufacturer's marks.

Glass that is considered highly collectible dates back to pressed items from the 1820s. Earlier pieces are usually found in museums. Pressed glass is identified by embossed or molded patterns. Such things as ribbing, arches, flutes, bull's-eyes, cables, thumbprints, and other geometrical or lacy designs are all common items on pressed glass. Cut glass often features similar designs, but these were cut by hand rather than applied by machine. As a result, cut glass is sharper, thicker, and brighter than pressed glass.

While pressed glass was done by hand-pressing machines, Depression glass was made by automated machines. The styles are very similar in that glass is pressed into a mold and the main pattern for it is built into the mold. The main difference is that Depression glass was made in greater quantities and the majority of it was produced in bright, vivid colors. Older pressed items occasionally contained colors, but they were generally duller and are easily distinguished from Depression glass.

Art glass features many unique qualities, such as color experimentation, opaque and opalescent styles, cameo or relief cut styles, gaudy objects and colors, ornamental styles, unique shadings, and a Victorian fondness for ostentation. The most popular art glass objects are vases. Vases range in height from a few inches to several feet, but most are found in the 6- to 20-inch range. Designs include trumpets, jack-in-the-pulpits, lilies, tulips, and rose bowls. Other common art glass objects are lamps, pitchers, baskets, and paperweights. Pieces generally were made to be displayed rather than used.

Carnival glass was originally considered a cheap version of art glass.

The glass was pressed into molds, then sprayed with metallic salts to produce an oily surface coloring. Carnival glass is usually fairly easy to identify, but it can be confused with reproduction iridescent forms. To make matters worse, some Depression glass includes light marigold iridescent forms. Carnival glass had a short history and was made from the turn of the century until the mid 1920s.

Other glass objects that have found their way into the hands of collectors are more specific, which simplifies identification. These include such collectibles as fruit jars, bottles, character glass, Christmas glass, Disney glass, Fire King ovenware, marbles, paperweights, souvenir glass, and thimbles.

PRICING

With the increase in the number of shows and auctions, prices are becoming more standardized for glass collectibles. The values listed in this book should serve as a general guide only and are not intended to set prices. They were gleaned from hundreds of shows, auctions, mail order listings, dealers, experts in the field, and private collectors. Neither the author nor the publisher assumes responsibility for any losses that might be incurred as a result of using this guide. The purpose of this book is to provide the most up-to-date and realistic prices for both rare and common collectible glassware.

Prices listed in this book are based on glass in excellent or mint condition. Glass that is chipped, heavily scratched, cracked, poorly finished, or with other major problems has very little value. Age, condition, demand, availability, and other factors are directly relevant to pricing. Take note that dealers pay only about half to two-thirds of the quoted prices. The categories themselves involve several different aspects regarding condition and are outlined as follows.

Pressed Glass

Pressed patterns are the oldest styles of glass priced in this guide. They are for the most part 19th-century hand-pressed items that vary a good deal in consistency. Further complicating matters is the general lack of patents; hence, numerous companies and individuals made the same designs in different molds. The end result are objects with wide variations in shape, pattern, type, and general formula. Ribbing may be thicker or thinner; vines may be single or double; gridding or checkering may be narrow or wide. Clear glass tends to tinge a pale purple with age. Manganese in the basic formula is responsible for amethyst coloring; a little too much coupled with prolonged exposure to the sun is responsible for this tinting.

Beware of tingeing as well as serious flaws within old pressed glass. Some clear Depression patterns and reproductions are at times confused with older and more valuable pressed designs. Thinner examples can be quite fragile, but for the most part, the formulas used in pressed glass have held together well. Also, look out for irregular, out of balance, or slightly stretched pieces, as well as pieces that appear off-center.

Art Glass

There is no other category of glass that requires as much attention as art glass. Pieces that run into the thousands and even the hundreds of thousands of dollars deserve the following 10-point guide.

1. *Mint condition.* The tiniest chip or crack, any missing portion, any part that is repaired or reground, discoloration, staining, internal bubbles that have burst, variations in cutting or enameling, or any other problems, no matter how minor, will reduce the prices listed in this guide. The only exception would be a few minor scratches on the underside of the base.

2. *The source or dealer.* A knowledgeable and reputable dealer is essential when purchasing art glass. A dealer should stand by the work, which might turn out to be a reproduction or even a fake. Be sure to request a signed certificate of authenticity from a dealer or auction house.

3. *Appraisal.* Get a second opinion if you have any doubt of the piece's authenticity. Museum personnel, licensed appraisers, or others with knowledge in the field should be called upon.

4. *Education.* Again, learn as much as you can about art glass by reading books, visiting museums and art galleries, speaking with dealers, and attending auctions.

5. *Marks and signatures.* Learn to recognize the marks and signatures of the various makers. Even then, be wary: marks of a well-known maker can be applied to unmarked objects of lesser quality and value, creating hard to recognize forgeries.

6. *Low prices.* Glass objects of rarity and significant value are rarely sold at low prices for fractions of their actual worth. Carder, Steuben, Tiffany, Galle, etc., are simply not found at flea markets and rummage sales. Remember that the majority of art glass in the past was purchased almost exclusively by the upper echelons of society.

7. *High prices.* Do not get caught up in bidding wars at auctions. At times, collectors searching for matching or highly desirable pieces may drive up prices. But by visiting a few galleries, signing up on "want lists" with specific dealers, and scouting patiently, you may get the piece you want.

8. *Age.* Older glass will usually have some telltale sign of wear. A slight bit of fading that does not detract from the item's overall appearance may

be evident. Tiny or random scratches on the base are common for art glass; most are present simply because the object has stood in one place for so long. A piece that appears brand new just might be.

9. *Color.* No matter how close it comes, the color of reproduction glassware always seems to differ from the original. Much of the difference is due to the original formulas and ingredients utilized in the glassmaking process. Sand, lead, and other additives are nearly impossible to duplicate, especially when they are obtained from different sources or regions. The raw materials and sandbanks of a hundred years ago no longer exist in some parts of the country. The slightest variation in color or hue from known examples can indicate a reproduction.

10. *Personal choice.* Occasionally an ill-formed, twisted, or unnatural shape, sometimes referred to as "grotesque," may look quite odd or lack value as compared to a graceful, free-flowing object, but it may meet your idea of beauty. A true object of beauty should capture your imagination and stir your emotions (unless you are buying strictly for investment purposes).

Cut Glass

Like art glass, cut glass was almost exclusively sold to the wealthy. Because of the extremely heavy lead content as well as the extensive hand-cutting, hand-engraving, and hand-polishing involved, reproductions of the original cut patterns have not been made using these methods. Some lead cut glass is thicker than 1/2 inch. One of the biggest mistakes you can make is assuming that thick glass is strong and durable. Cut glass is fragile because cutting weakens the glass structurally.

Quality and condition are the two most important factors when inspecting cut glass. Light refraction, a natural crystal gleam, is far superior to a cheaper acid finish. Uniform weight, balance, and thickness; true symmetrical cuts that are sharp and precise; a lack of cloudiness; and a resonating, bell-like sound when the piece is tapped with a fingernail are all determining factors of quality. Nicks, tiny chips, discoloration, a dull finish, and scratches all reduce the value of fine cut glass. Any major flaws, such as heavy scratching or chipping, render the object virtually worthless.

Carnival Glass

Originally, this type of glassware was produced as a cheap substitute for art glass; however, prices for some Carnival glass have easily reached the art glass level. Less expensive common items should be given the same general visual and hand inspection as that done with all glassware. Rare and more valuable items such as red Carnival should be evaluated more carefully. (Follow the 10-point guide outlined under art glass.)

Carnival glass is characterized by an iridescent metal flashing, which differentiates it from other glassware. The iridization should flow smoothly and consistently over the entire object. Gaps, discolorations, dull areas from excessive wear, or any incomplete flashing will lower the value. The base color in most pieces should be observed only on the underside; if it can be viewed in significant areas or portions on the outside, it may be a sign that the iridization has worn off or was incomplete.

Reproductions pose problems in Carnival glass. Some iridized Depression glass and later iridized examples resemble the original Carnival designs. Naturally, those that cause the most problems are new pieces made in the original molds. Fortunately, there are some manufacturers, like Imperial, who mark the new wares "IG" to distinguish them from the old.

Depression Glass

In no other category is the chip as much of a factor as in Depression glass. As a rule, most Depression glass was mass-produced cheaply in great quantities for the general public. Through constant everyday use, pieces became chipped. Foots, rims, lids, handles, joints, and so on should all be carefully inspected. With your eyes closed, run your finger around these areas to discover chips.

Minor flaws, such as an occasional air bubble, slight inconsistent coloring from piece to piece, and tiny trails of excess glass, do not detract from the value of Depression glass. A typical Depression mold might last for thousands of machine pressings, and it was impossible to match perfectly batch after batch of color. As a result, it is possible to accumulate a matching patterned set of over 50 pieces that vary slightly in color. Major flaws, such as excess scratching, large trails of glass, rough mold lines, chips, and missing pattern designs, render Depression glass virtually worthless.

Reproductions pose a few difficulties; however, there appear to be major differences in the new versions. The most prevalent difference is color. New reproduction colors appear washed out, dull, and not as attractive as the originals. Other differences involve dimensions and new colors that were not produced in the older original versions.

Modern Glass

Glass produced within the last 50 years or so should be in nothing less than new condition. Occasionally, enameling on cheaper advertising or character glass may fade or scratch easily; less than perfect items should be passed over unless they are highly desired and quite scarce. Even brand-new items should be inspected for any damage or flaws that may have occurred in the manufacture, shipping, or display stages.

CARE OF GLASS

There have been horror stories of glass shattering or spontaneously breaking from changes in temperature, from being in one place for too long, or from simple movement. Some of it is ground in myth; however, glass does require some minimal care. Machine and pressed glassware is generally sturdy and was designed for utilitarian purposes. Fancier items like art glass were designed for display purposes as true objects of art.

Glass will break with sudden temperature changes. Much depends on how fragile the piece is. A warm piece of glass at room temperature may break if suddenly exposed to cold temperatures. When being transported, glass should be wrapped carefully and remain wrapped for several hours until it gradually adjusts to the new temperature. Milk glass has been known to be especially vulnerable to temperature changes.

Never wash glassware until it has adjusted to room temperature. Lukewarm or warm water should be used; hot water can damage glass. Mild, nonabrasive cleaning solutions should be used on ordinary pressed wares like Depression glass. Some art glass pieces should not be washed at all. Anything beyond dusting may affect their finish. Avoid using a dishwasher for cleaning most collectible glass, since hot water and detergents can destroy or damage finishes.

Exposing older lead crystal to direct sunlight for lengthy periods of time can cause the manganese in the glass to react and turn the object a light shade of purple. Collectible glassware is best stored in sturdy cabinets or on well-secured shelves away from direct sunlight. Pieces should be cleaned and moved occasionally. There is some debate among chemists as to whether glass is a liquid or a solid. It appears to be a solid, but some low-quality forms have been known to run over time. Check out an abandoned home sometime and observe any remaining windows. Occasionally, you will find glass that has thickened and bulged at the bottom. Fortunately, the effect of gravity is a rarity in collectible glass; however, sitting in one spot for decades may cause a piece to run.

Older glass was not designed for the high pressure and extreme temperatures of dishwashers. Likewise, microwave use is not recommended, even though it has been proven that the lead in glass does not react to microwave energy. New glassware is acceptable for microwave use as long as it is recommended by the manufacturer.

Glass can survive the test of time. Just visit a major museum like the Corning Museum of Glass or the Chrysler Museum and you will find pieces that have survived for centuries. With a little careful attention, your pieces will last as well.

CHAPTER 1

FOREIGN GLASS
AND GLASSMAKING

A question that may never be answered fully is what led to the discovery of glass. Historians trace its development to Egypt, where surviving glass objects, such as small containers, have been found dating to 3500 years ago or 1500 B.C.

The prime ingredients of glass are silica, a form of sand, and ashes from plants and trees. Ash is an alkali that aids the sand in melting at lower temperature. Stabilizing substances like carbonate of soda and lime are crushed into fine powders and added to the batch. They not only assist in the fusion process but also protect against excessive moisture. Metals and other ingredients or additives have changed through the centuries, but the basic formula for glass has remained the same.

The technique of core forming was developed by Egyptian glassmakers and would not change for centuries until the rise of the Roman Empire. The first step in core forming was the construction of a base or core, ordinarily a mixture of clay and dung. Hot glass was then spun around the core. The core-formed glass was quite dark or opaque and was often decorated with brightly colored glass threads that were weaved around it.

The average citizens of ancient Egypt usually were not in possession of such ornaments. The new glassware was reserved for the wealthy such as high priests, the nobles, the pharaoh's assistants, and the pharaoh himself. Core-formed objects were usually made into containers for ointments, oils, and perfumes. These artistic items were present on thrones, buried with mummies in their cases, and even placed in the tombs of pharaohs.

Core forming was the exclusive method of early glassmaking, but advances and new ideas followed as the centuries passed. The Mesopotamians cast glass into moldlike containers. Simple clay molds may have lasted for only one good cast. Another innovation of the Mesopotamians was the addition of an extra step in the finishing process. After casting, the surface of the glass was polished by revolving wheels fed with abrasives.

These basic techniques of mold casting and polishing would be adopted later by European and American glassmakers.

The second significant step in the history of glassmaking was the development of the art of glass blowing. Around 50 B.C. the Romans developed the process, which involved blowing short puffs of air through a hollow metal tube into a gather or molten blob of glass. Glassmakers would heat glass to the melting point, inflate a bubble quickly at the end of the rod, then work it quickly while it was still warm to form many shapes and sizes. Glass blowing was the first significant alternative to the ancient methods of casting and core forming.

With the advent of blowing, glass was no longer a luxury product created exclusively for the wealthy. The Romans produced a variety of glassware, a good deal of which has survived. The most popular items blown were drinking vessels. Beakers depicting gruesome gladiator scenes, battles, heroes, chariots, and so on were designed for drinking wine. Glass was also blown into molds, and bottles were often decorated with the same scenery. Other popular shapes blown from glass included figureheads, gods and goddesses, and particularly grapes or grape clusters to celebrate wine and the vine it was derived from. The same grape patterns can be found in 19th-century, Carnival, and Depression wares.

The Romans experimented with many styles of decorating. The Greeks had borrowed cutting techniques from the Mesopotamians but learned to cut shallow grooves and hollows more precisely, similar to that applied to gemstones. The Romans advanced further with cutting, engraving, and polishing with the use of stone and wooden wheels. A glass object was held against a wheel and fed with an abrasive paste. Shallow, deep, and fancy cuts were made based for the most part on the cutter's skill.

Enameling developed long before glassware. The painting of cave walls, rocks, clay, pottery, and so on has been a part of every culture since the dawn of civilization. The Romans enameled glassware much like we do today. Colored glass was pulverized into a powder, mixed with oils like a paint, then applied to a glass article. The piece was then reheated to permanently fuse the enamel. Roman glassmakers for the most part manipulated cold glass and cold painting.

In the East, artisans in China delved into glassmaking in the form of beads, jewelry, and jadelike carved glass figurines about the same time as the Romans. Many of the pieces were traded since glass was not highly regarded. The Chinese would spend more time and effort creating the finest porcelain in the world. Not until the 18th century would glass become popular in China. Cut glass snuff bottles for inhaling opium and porcelain replicas of vases were made of glass. It would be in the Middle East, or the Islamic world, that new advances in glassmaking would take place.

Islamic glass dates to the 8th century A.D. The Romans had experimented with some cameo or relief cutting, but the Islamic cutters took it a step further. Relief cutting is a difficult, time-consuming, and expensive process. It involves outlining a design on a glass surface, then carefully cutting away part of the background to leave the original design raised in relief. Relief-cut glass was once again reserved for the upper echelons of society. Plants, geometric patterns, fish, quotations from the Koran, and a variety of other designs were highlighted on vases, perfume sprinklers, beakers, bottles, and many other articles.

Common items for ordinary people might include bowls, bottles, and drinking glasses primarily for wine consumption. Enameling was also done on oil lamps. The period of Islamic glass ended in 1401, when the Mongol conqueror Tamerlane destroyed Damascus and captured the city's glass artisans. He brought them and their skills to Samarkand.

Glassmaking in Europe faded during the Middle Ages. Only a few primitive vessels such as bowls and drinking vessels were created, but hardly anything of note. It was not until the 12th century that a new chapter in glassmaking history would be written.

Gothic architecture and the creation of the stained glass window brought glassmaking out of the Dark Ages. Stained materials from oils, plants, and vegetable matter were added to the basic ingredients of glass. The colored glass was then cast into flat cakes, cut into small pieces, and formed into mosaics. Brilliantly colored glass was included in some of the finest European architecture. Huge windows in shades of all colors adorned the greatest and most elaborate churches ever, such as Notre Dame and Westminster Abbey.

The hub of the glassmaking world in the 13th century was the city of Venice, a thriving trade center. Glassmakers there formed a guild to guard their trade secrets as commercial production of glass flourished once again.

Glassmakers in Venice were ordered by proclamation to move all operations to the nearby island of Murano. The reason was because the hazards associated with the great furnace fires could easily destroy the entire city if an accident occurred in one of the glassmaking houses. The glass trade was such an integral part of the commerce of Venice, that Venetian glassmakers were forbidden by law to leave Murano. The penalty for escape was death, although many did manage to do so.

It was not all that unfortunate a situation for the glass craftsmen living and working on Murano. Their skills and reputation were highly regarded, and their daughters were allowed to marry noblemen. For the most part, the city of Venice had a monopoly on the art of glassmaking. Their craftsmen held the secrets for furnace construction, glass formulas, including the ideal proportion of ingredients, and the use of tools and toolmaking.

Knowledge was passed down to the artisans' sons and those few outsiders who were admitted to the guild. The secrets were well guarded until 1612, when Antonio Neri made them available in his book *L'Arte Vetraria* (The Art of Glass). Neri was a master glass craftsman and understood the complete process involved in its production. His enjoyment of the trade is obvious in this quotation: "Glass is more gentle, graceful, and noble than any metal and its use is more delightful, polite, and sightly than any other material at this day known to the world."

The biggest impact the Venetians were to have on the evolution of glassmaking was the development of cristallo in the 16th century. Next to the discovery of glass and the invention of glass blowing, the development of a nearly colorless glass was a very significant innovation. The glass was adapted to the world's finest mirrors, far superior to those made of bronze, steel, or polished silver. Venetians produced glass beads for jewelry that rivaled gemstones. Glass jewelry was also used for barter in the African slave trade.

Venetian glass was produced in colors that would resurface in art glass in the 19th century and Depression glass in the United States in the early 20th. Emerald green, dark blue, amethyst, reddish-brown, and later milky-white all flowed steadily from the factories of Murano. The monopoly and production of fine Venetian glass dominated the world market through most of the 17th century.

Glass was a significant factor in science and technological advances. Clear optical lenses for microscopes, telescopes, test tubes, beakers, flasks, tubing, and a host of other laboratory apparatus were vital for scientific experimentation. The Venetian cristallo did not interfere with chemicals, and one could easily observe chemical reactions and the results through the clear glass.

As with most glass, the finest Venetian styles were created for the wealthy. Anyone of importance graced his or her table with glass wine goblets, fancy bowls, and vessels created in Venice. The Venetian glass cutters were the first to use diamond point engraving. Until the 17th century, India was the sole source of diamonds, and the majority of trade between East and West passed through Venice. With diamonds readily available, the glass artisans of Venice adapted them to their cutting wheels.

The one serious complaint with Venetian glass was that it was inherently frail. There was no question that the glass was exquisite and the best made in the world, but it was thin, fragile, and not easily transported. A more durable and stronger glass would be invented by the English.

Glassmaking houses soon sprang up around Northern Europe. Wood ash or potash was readily available and aided in the melting of the sand mixture. Heavy concentrations of iron in the soil produced glass of a pale or murky green color. These so-called forest glasshouses made windows and drinking vessels of poor quality; however, both were very practical items.

Huge drinking vessels were particularly popular in Germany, where beer was drunk in large quantities. Some vessels held several quarts and amazingly enough, drinkers often tried to drain them in a single gulp. The practice was frowned upon by Martin Luther, who referred to these vessels as "fool's glasses."

In the late 16th and early 17th centuries, German and Bohemian artisans began cutting and decorating glass. Their drinking glasses featured patriotic designs, coats of arms, biblical figures and references, mythological figures, and scenes of daily life. The German and Bohemian glassmakers experimented with formulas and developed a form of crystal that was easier to cut than the thin Venetian cristallo. In Bohemia and Brandenburg specifically, this new glass could be cut on rapidly rotating stone and copper wheels. The Germans were responsible for the perfection of wheel engraving.

This early history of glass is relevant to today's glassmaking. Sand and ash are still two primary ingredients and enameling, wheel cutting, cameo engraving, and other decorating techniques are still employed today. In 1571, Giacomo Verzelini and nine other Italian glassmakers escaped to London from Antwerp. Three years later, Verzelini received a patent from Queen Elizabeth to create glass in the Venetian style, with which he was well familiar. For the next 100 years, England would be the world leader in the production of practical glassware.

In 1615, English glassmakers were forced to switch from wood to coal as fuel for their furnaces. Because of a severe shortage, wood was reserved for shipbuilding. Coal posed special problems for glassmakers, however, because it was dirtier and the fumes produced could easily ruin molten glass during the blowing process.

The first significant item produced in England for export was the "black bottle" in the mid 17th century. It was actually a very dark green due primarily to iron and other elements present in the sand utilized in the glass formulas. Its deep color served to protect contents from light. Bottles made of this thick glass were durable and, unlike the thin Venetian glassware, rarely broke during transit. Throughout the 17th and 18th centuries, England was the largest supplier of bottles in the Western world.

A more important goal of English glassmakers was to find a cross between the delicate, clear Venetian glass and the strong, thick black bottle. The solution arrived in 1676 with George Ravenscroft. Ravenscroft was an English glassmaker who lived and studied for several years in Venice. He would forever etch his name in the history of glass development by perfecting a formula for heavy lead glass. The new glass held great advantages and was a significant factor in ending the Venetian dominance of glass-making. When heated, it remained in a workable condition for a lengthier period of time, which in turn allowed the glass artisan to indulge in fancier and more time-consuming endeavors. It was superior in clarity, weight, strength, and light-capturing ability. The workability of the first true lead crystal was responsible for a host of new stem formations, particularly in goblets. Airtwists, teardrops, knops or knobs, balusters, and others all refracted light as never before. With Ravenscroft's discovery, the English truly succeeded in their goal.

The English further experimented with refraction in their cutting techniques. Before this time, English crafters borrowed cutting techniques from German and Bohemian glassmakers. The new style developed in England covered the surface of a glass object with an orderly geometric pattern of facets. This technique, combined with the new crystal formula, maximized refraction, which in turn produced a brilliant, sparkling effect. This new beautifully patterned cut glass was applied to chandeliers, candlesticks, centerpieces, and drinking glasses. Previously, rooms in typical English homes were dark and candles were heavily taxed and, therefore, expensive. Glass served to lighten rooms and replaced candles, until it, too, became popular and was subject to taxation.

The new lead glass could be formed into thicker articles and was much easier to cut than the Venetian glass. Sturdier everyday items, such as firing and dram glasses, followed in the late 18th century. Firing glasses obtained their name from being slammed upon the table, since the resulting noise sounded like a group musket firing. The glasses were built with extremely thick bases and withstood the abuse inflicted upon them in taverns.

Durable glass products from England were exported in large quantities. Some items were shipped to the Far East in the 17th century, but much more in the 18th. The English East India Company exported significant amounts of glass to India, second only to what was shipped to America.

In 1780 Parliament lifted a 35-year ban on the exportation of Irish glass. Irish glass was tax free, and many of England's skilled glassworkers moved to Ireland. English and Irish glass was virtually identical in style and impossible to distinguish except for manufacturer's marks. Glassmaking cities such as Dublin, Belfast, Cork, and probably the most famous city for fine glass, Waterford, survived well into the 19th century. Some have been reorganized, such as Waterford, and continue to operate today.

British and Irish glassware was popular in the United States. Common pieces that were imported included water tumblers, decanters, firing glasses, wine glasses and other stemware, rummers, drams, fluted glasses, finger basins, bottles, punch jugs, liquors or cordials, salts, mustards, butter keelers, and globes.

While American glassmaking companies were gearing up in the 19th century, England and Ireland lost a significant share of their largest market; however, they still exported a good deal of glass to the United States. More glass found its way into domestic life and more decorations were applied to it. Landscapes, city views, and portraiture were all engraved, stained, or enameled on English glassware. Beakers often featured maps or scenes of famous battles.

In 1845 Parliament finally removed the excise tax on English glass. English artisans still were considered the source of some of the finest glassware in the world. In 1851 the World's Fair in London, dubbed "The Great Exposition of the Works of Industry of All Nations," exhibited a huge display of glass. One of the buildings from the fair was made of nearly 300,000 handblown panes. The displays and products at this exhibit could not but help stimulate the glass industry.

Complete matching table sets of glassware that would later be produced in quantity in the United States during the Great Depression had its roots in England. Table service items included stemmed drinking glasses in many different shapes and sizes, water beakers, beer tankards, decanters, bowls, sugar bowls and creamers, saltshakers, butter dishes, honey jars, flower vases, candlestick holders, bonbon dishes, carafes and pitchers. A variety of other glass items were also made in England, including jugs, water basins, powder boxes, jewelry dishes and boxes, toothbrush holders, and soap dishes.

The hand-pressing method first developed in the United States became popular in England. Also popular was cameo cut glass, which had not been available for centuries since the decline of Islamic glass. The glassmaker John Northward was credited for the revival of relief cutting in cameo colors. A blue or plum color cased in white with classic Greek and Roman themes was raised in relief on vases, flasks, plaques, and many other items.

Art glass developed in England in the late 19th century. One of the largest producers was Thomas Webb & Sons. Cameo, Burmese, Peachblow, and a variety of other designs were especially popular. Several English firms later adopted the cheaper Carnival glassmaking techniques from the United States. With the help of the English, Australian glassmaking houses were built and went on to produce Carnival glass. The late 19th century was a significant period for the entire European community as other countries joined in.

The biggest impact the French would have in the world of glassmaking was its leadership role in the Art Nouveau movement. Eugene Rousseau and Emille Galle were the premier French designer-artists of this period. Rousseau was especially influenced by Oriental art. The renewed interest in Orientalism, which followed Admiral Perry's opening of trade with Japan, was seen in rugs, porcelain pieces, prints, and paintings of this time. Rousseau and Galle did not limit themselves to Far Eastern influences, but rather combined them with traditional German and Italian Renaissance shapes. Galle more than Rousseau was the inspiration for this period. The new art form appeared not only in glass but in architecture, paintings, posters, book illustrations, furniture, wallpaper, fabric, embroidery, and jewelry. Unlike many of the cut glass manufacturers, Galle signed his works, which inspired others to do the same.

Art glass was richly ornamental and featured crackle effects, metal particles, asymmetrical designs, sinuous lines, weaving tendrils, flowing rhythms, and wild color effects. Colors and opaqueness were experimented with, and impractical items were made as works of art. Whimsies abounded and such things as insects, animals, and fruits were all re-created in glass. Rather than typical floral designs, thistles, pinecones, and simple plants were etched in glass. Rules and traditions were discarded in favor of innovation.

Galle went on to direct the highly acclaimed School of Art in Nancy, France. The institute dedicated itself to originality, innovation, and artistic achievement in glass. In the 1880s and 1890s, the city of Nancy became the hub of the Art Glass movement in Europe. Enameled, gilded, engraved, and bizarre color effects were all part of Galle's designs; however, he is most noted for his superb cameo relief creations in glass. Nancy attracted many other noted figures such as Jean Daum, second only to Galle in reputation. When Galle died in 1904, the quality of work in his factory suffered, and many believe that this event was the beginning of the decline of an era.

One other noteworthy French designer and artisan was René Lalique. Lalique began his career as a maker of art glass jewelry in the 1890s. He was commissioned by Coty Parfums to produce fancy decorative perfume bottles for Coty's various fragrances. From this point, the true artist was born and Lalique branched into glass sculpture. Figurals, nudes, vases, and even car hood ornaments were formed into frosted crystal works of art. Lalique experimented with colors but worked primarily with crystal. Many of his creations offer several separate views, such as a bowl formed by three kneeling nude figures.

Other figures in the Art Nouveau movement were the Austrian makers Johann Lutz, E. Bakalowits, and Moser and Sons; the artisans of Val St. Lambert, a famous glassware city in Belgium; and glassmakers of Venice, which continued to produce millefiori designs dating to the 13th century. Even famous American artists like Louis Comfort Tiffany and Frederick Carder visited Europe to gain firsthand knowledge of glassmaking trends.

The remaining chapter is a price guide to foreign glassware from the past two centuries. Refer to the section "Market Review, Pricing, and Care of Glassware" for an explanation of the pricing listed here.

ALEXANDRITE   THOMAS WEBB & SONS, ENGLAND, 1890s–EARLY 1900s

This English art glass features gradual shading from pale yellow or amber to a pinkish rose color and finally to blue. See additional material under Thomas Webb and Sons near the end of the chapter.

Bowl, 5″, finger, fluted, matching underplate $750
Bowl, finger with matching underplate, Honeycomb pattern $2250
Creamer, 3″ tall, pitcher style, Thumbprint pattern $2250
Goblet, 8¹/₂″, tall, wafer base, textured leaves on stem $2250
Match holder with square top, 3″ square, 2¹/₂″ tall, Diamond Quilted pattern ....
.... $800
Pitcher, 5¹/₂″ tall, petal top, applied handle $2000
Plate, 5¹/₂″, crimped, Thumbprint pattern $950
Plate, 6″, rippled $950
Tazza, 1¹/₂″ × 4¹/₂″, pedestal feet, Diamond Quilted pattern $850
Toothpick holder, 2¹/₂″ tall, dark or light color shading $950
Toothpick holder, 3″ tall, globe-shaped body, square top $750
Toothpick holder, 3″ tall, ruffled $675
Tumbler, 3″ tall, Honeycomb pattern $875
Vase, 4″ tall, Jack-in-the pulpit style, Honeycomb pattern $1100
Vase, 6″ tall, ruffled, Honeycomb pattern $850
Wine glass, 4¹/₂″ tall, Honeycomb pattern $1250
Wine glass, 4¹/₂″ tall, Thumbprint pattern $1350

ARGENTINIAN GLASS   1920s–PRESENT

Regolleau Christalerias was the first glassware company established in Buenos Aires. The company manufactured practical tableware and some Carnival glass items.

Ashtray, beetle-shaped, Carnival blue $500
Ashtray, R&C design, Carnival blue or Marigold $125

AUSTRALIAN CARNIVAL GLASS   1918–1930s

The most famous Australian factory to produce Carnival glass was Crystal Glass Works Ltd. of Sydney. The majority of glass was produced in marigold, purple, and amethyst. Native wildlife was a popular theme.

Bowl, 5″, Australian Swan pattern
    Marigold $75
    Purple $175
Bowl, 5″, banded Diamonds pattern, Marigold or amethyst $75
Bowl, 5″, Emu pattern, Marigold or amethyst $250
Bowl, 5″, Kangaroo pattern, Marigold or amethyst $125

Bowl, 5", Kingfisher pattern, Marigold or amethyst $125
Bowl, 5", Kookaburra pattern, Marigold or purple $125
Bowl, 5", Thunderbird pattern, Marigold or purple $100
Bowl, 5½", Australian Swan pattern
  Marigold $75
  Purple $115
Bowl, 6", Magpie pattern, Marigold or amethyst $300
Bowl, 8¾", Pin-Up pattern, Marigold or amethyst $150
Bowl, 9½", Australian Swan pattern
  Marigold $100
  Purple $250
Bowl, 9½", Kangaroo pattern, Marigold or amethyst $500
Bowl, 9½", Kingfisher pattern, Marigold or amethyst $250
Bowl, 9½", Thunderbird pattern, Marigold or amethyst $350
Bowl, 9", 12-sided, Kingfisher pattern
  Marigold $175
  Purple $225
Bowl, 9", Heavy Banded Diamonds pattern, Marigold or amethyst $125
Bowl, 9", Kangaroo pattern
  Marigold $95
  Purple $125
Bowl, 9", Thunderbird pattern, Marigold or purple $100
Bowl, 10", Banded Diamonds pattern, Marigold or amethyst $125
Bowl, 10", Emu pattern, Marigold or amethyst $1250
Bowl, 10", Kiwi pattern
  Amethyst $1250
  Marigold $350
Bowl, 10", Kookaburra pattern, Marigold or purple $350
Bowl, 10", Magpie pattern, Marigold or amethyst $500
Bowl, berry, Heavy Banded Diamonds pattern, Marigold or purple $95
Bowl, berry, Magpie pattern, Marigold $65
Bowl, octagonal, Emu pattern, Marigold, purple, or amber $110
Bowl, Pin-Up Square on Stem pattern, Purple $110
Butter dish, Triands pattern, Marigold $75
Cake plate, Butterfly Bower pattern, Marigold or purple $250
Cake plate, Flower Flannel pattern, Marigold $225
Cake plate, Ostrich pattern, Marigold, amethyst, or purple $350
Celery Vase, Triands pattern, Marigold $65
Compote, Butterflies and Bells pattern, Marigold or purple $250
Compote, Butterflies and Waratah pattern
  Amethyst $350
  Marigold $175
Compote, Butterfly Bower pattern, Marigold or purple $175
Compote, Flower Flannel pattern, Marigold or amethyst $175
Compote, Ostrich pattern, Marigold, amethyst, or purple $200
Compote, Rose Panels pattern, Marigold $150
Compote, S-Band pattern, Marigold or Amethyst $100
Compote, Wild Fern pattern
  Marigold $175
  Purple $250
Creamer, Australian Panels pattern, Marigold or Amethyst $85

Creamer, Australian pattern, Marigold or Amethyst $100
Creamer, Diamond Band pattern, Marigold or Amethyst $75
Creamer, Triands pattern, Marigold $65
Epergne, Sungold pattern
    Amethyst $500
    White $750
Mug, souvenir, Paneled Flute design, inscribed "Greetings from Mt. Gambier"
    Marigold $150
    White $450
Pitcher, water, Banded Diamonds pattern, Marigold, amethyst, or purple .. $1500
Pitcher, water, Beaded Spears pattern, Marigold, amethyst, or purple $325
Pitcher, water, blocks and arches, Marigold or amethyst $250
Pitcher, water, Vineyard Harvest pattern, Marigold $1500
Plate, 5¼", Golden Cupid pattern, Crystal with gold $90
Plate, 9", Golden Cupid pattern, Crystal with gold $110
Spooner, Triands pattern, Marigold $50
Sugar, Australian Panels pattern, Marigold or amethyst $85
Sugar, Australian pattern, Marigold or amethyst $100
Sugar, Banded Panels design, Marigold or amethyst $75
Sugar, Diamond Band pattern, Marigold or amethyst $75
Sugar, Triands pattern, Marigold $65
Tumbler, Banded Diamonds pattern, Marigold, amethyst, or purple $450
Tumbler, Beaded Spears pattern, Marigold, amethyst, or purple $110
Tumbler, blocks and arches, Marigold or amethyst $100
Tumbler, Vertical Grape pattern, Light marigold $35
Tumbler, Vineyard Harvest pattern, Marigold $250
Vase, shallow bowl with flower holder in center, 3-tiered Threaded design, Ice green $75
Vase, Tropicana pattern, Marigold $1750

AUSTRIAN GLASS   19TH CENTURY–PRESENT

Older Austrian glass from several factories can be difficult to distinguish from other European makers due to the country's historical association with Germany, Bohemia, and the Austro-Hungarian Empire. Austrian glass products are often combined with other miscellaneous European glassware.

Bowl, 4¾", Iridescent purple with pink and white threading $225
Brandy glass, 5¾" tall, Crystal $10
Compote, 3¾" tall, enameled black lattice design, Lime green with black foot ...
.... $275
Creamer, Banded Panels' design
Goblet, 8" tall, Iridescent light green, ... $250
Goblet, 8½" tall, curved stem, Kirkland design, Crystal $10
Lamp, 13" tall, metal base, 10" iridescent amber shade with pink threading, .. $1750
Paperweight, 1½" diameter, round, multicolor center with edelweiss and gentian floral design $65
Royal pumpkin coach (Cinderella's), 3" tall, drawn by two mice, mirrored base, gold crown, chain, wheel hubs, and visor $80

Austrian engraved beaker.
COURTESY OF THE CORNING MUSEUM
OF GLASS.

Shot glass, 2½" tall, Square-shaped 2 oz. crystal with etched floral pattern around glass $20
Shot glass, 2¾" tall, Crystal with gold rim and multicolored enamel flags and coat of arms $10
Vase, 3 ¼" tall, ruffled, iridescent blue with gold vines and jeweled butterflies $525
Vase, 4⅛" tall, Iridescent gold with amber spots $350
Vase, 6½" tall, Light orange with deep amethyst rim and handle $425
Vase, 7" tall, silver rim, iridescent green with applied serpent design $400
Vase, 8" tall, conch seashell-shaped, iridescent gold with green seashell foot $425
Vase, 9¾" tall, scalloped, iridescent yellow with orange design on base $525
Vase, 10⅜" tall, ruffled, iridescent purple with silver overlay $900
Vase, 12" tall, iridescent yellow with gilding $575

BACCARAT GLASS COMPANY   FRANCE, 1765–19TH CENTURY, 1953–PRESENT

The original Baccarat was most famous for high-quality millefiori and other paperweights in the mid-19th century; however, the company produced a variety of other art glass objects. Since 1953, Baccarat has resumed paperweight production and is noted for high-quality clear lead crystal products. Beware of imitation sulphide paperweights made in the United States, especially those of several presidents (e.g., Kennedy, Lincoln, Eisenhower, and Truman).

Angel with trumpet figure, 6" tall, crystal $175
Bottle, scent, 4½" tall, front label (Mitsonko) $110
Bottle, scent, 4¼" tall, Rose Tiente Swirl design $95
Bottle, scent, 4" tall, white and gold (cyclamen) $575

Bottle, scent, 6³/₄″ tall, Rose Tiente Swirl design $125
Bottle, scent, 7¹/₂″ tall, Rose Tiente Swirl design $150
Bowl, 5¹/₂″, 2″ tall, Amberina Swirl design $95
Bowl, rose, 5″, Rose Tiente Swirl design $75
Box with cover, 3″ × 2″, rectangular, Rose Tiente Swirl design $110
Candlestick, 7″ tall, footed, swirled amberina shading $85
Candlestick, 9″ tall, Crystal Bamboo Swirl design $125
Carafe, tumble-up, Rose Tiente swirl design $110
Cologne bottle with stopper, 5″ tall, swirled amberina shading $150
Compote, 4″ tall, amberina $200
Cordial, amber with gold geese decoration $30
Cougar head, 5¹/₂″ tall, 5″ wide, Crystal $425
Dachsund, 3 ¹/₄″ tall, 6″ long, Crystal $200
Decanter with stopper, 9¹/₂″ tall, Amber, gold geese decoration $200
Decanter with stopper, 13″ tall, Etched floral design $250
Decanter with stopper, 14″ tall, cut and etched (for JG Monnet & Co.) $250
Duck, 1⁵/₈″ tall, 2⁵/₈″ long, crystal, amethyst, amber, or emerald green $100
Epergne, 15″ tall, marbled base, swirled amberina shading $350
Epergne, bronze mounts, onyx footed plinth, amberina shading $350
Frog, 1³/₄″ tall, 1⁷/₈″ long, amber or moss green $90
Goblet, 5″ tall, Engraved Grape and Vine design, signed $200
Heart shape, 2³/₄″ long, Ruby red $100
Heart shape, 3″ long, Amethyst, blue, or green $100
Horse head, 4¹/₂″ tall, 5³/₄″ long, crystal $200
Inkwell with silver-plated lid, 2³/₄″ tall, square, Floral design $95
Ladybug, 1¹/₄″ tall, 2¹/₄″ long, Crystal, amber, light green, or yellow $90
Lamp, 4″ tall, Rose Tiente Swirl design, fairy figure, circular base $300
Lamp, hurricane, 22″ tall, bobeche with 4¹/₂″ prisms, Amberina $650
Lamp, peg, 8″ tall, ruffled shades, Rose Tiente Swirl design $525
Loch Ness monster, 3³/₄″ tall, 9″ long, 4 pieces, crystal $325
Mother with child figurine, 9¹/₄″ tall, crystal $250
Mug, swirled amberina shading, Thumbprint pattern $110
Paperweight, Double Clematis design $2000
Paperweight, 2¹/₂″, sulphide, Ben Franklin design (antique) $1500
Paperweight, 2¹/₂″, sulphide, crystal Patrick Henry design $275
Paperweight, 2³/₄″, sulphide, crystal Andrew Jackson design $275
Paperweight, 2³/₄″, sulphide, crystal James Monroe design $275
Paperweight, 2³/₄″, sulphide, Pope Pius XII design, signed "David," 1959,
Crystal $150
Paperweight, 2⁵/₈″, 10 twisted ribbons radiating from a millefiori center $550
Paperweight, 3¹/₄″, Queen Victoria design (antique) $550
Paperweight, 3¹/₄″, sulphide, faceted, outer canes, Queen Elizabeth design, 1977 .
.... $350
Paperweight, 3″, Multicolored Pansy Floral design $450
Paperweight, 3″, sulphide, faceted, crystal Abraham Lincoln $475
Paperweight, 3″, sulphide, faceted, Robert E. Lee design, 1955 .... $375
Paperweight, 4″, faceted, crystal Mount Rushmore design $450
Paperweight, Packed canes design, dated 1956 .... $300
Paperweight, scattered canes, muslin background, dated 1846 .... $1850
Paperweight, sulphide, faceted, crystal Alexander, the Great design $325
Paperweight, sulphide, faceted, John F. Kennedy design $550

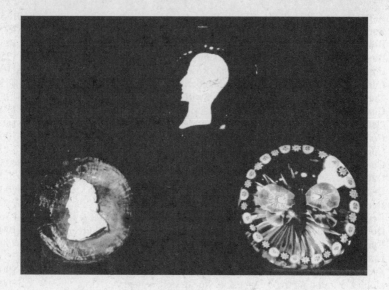

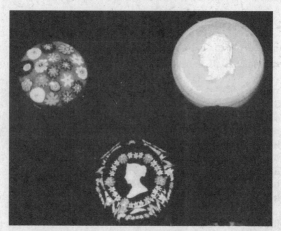

Baccarat paperweights. PHOTOS BY ROBIN RAINWATER.

Paperweight, sulphide, faceted, crystal Admiral DeGrasse design $375
Paperweight, sulphide, faceted, crystal Charlemagne design $450
Paperweight, sulphide, faceted, crystal Dwight D. Eisenhower design $475
Paperweight, sulphide, faceted, crystal George Washington design $550
Paperweight, sulphide, faceted, crystal Harry Truman design, gold base . . . $500
Paperweight, sulphide, faceted, crystal John F. Kennedy, Red and white overlaid .
. . . . $1750
Paperweight, sulphide, faceted, crystal Julius Caesar design $325

Paperweight, sulphide, faceted, crystal Martin Luther King, Jr., design $400
Paperweight, sulphide, faceted, crystal Napoleon design $375
Paperweight, sulphide, faceted, crystal Peter the Great design $375
Paperweight, sulphide, faceted, crystal Winston Churchill design $650
Paperweight, sulphide, faceted, crystal Woodrow Wilson design $450
Paperweight, sulphide, faceted, Pope John XXIII design $150
Paperweight, sulphide, faceted, crystal Thomas Paine design $400
Plate, Rose Tiente Swirl design $50
Rabbit, 3¼″ tall, crystal $75
Shaving brush holder, Rose Tiente Swirl design $100
Shot glass, 2¼″ tall, flared, millefiori, paperweight base $250
Soap dish, 4½″ across, 2″ tall, vaseline $60
Tumbler, 3¾″ tall, Rose Tiente Swirl and Gold Floral design $275
Tumbler, 4″ tall, Rose Tiente Swirl design $85
Vase, 7″ tall, cylindrical, crystal, cut ovals $95
Vase, 7″ tall, ovoid design, hexagonal top, crystal $225
Vase, 8″ tall, Coiled Snake design, signed $375
Vase, 8″ tall, French cameo, signed $450
Vase, 10″ tall, opalescent, Scenic View with Birds design $425
Vase, 12″ tall, Jack-in-the-Pulpit design, amethyst $300

BOHEMIAN GLASS   GERMANY, 17TH CENTURY–PRESENT

The original Bohemian Glass was characterized by heavy stone engraving overlaid with colored glass. A later design involved the cutting of two layers of colored glass. The object was then gilded or enameled. Individual items can be difficult to date because the glass has been continuously produced for over 300 years. Noted makers include Carl Goldberg, Count Arnost Harrach, Hartmann & Dietrichs, Carl Hosch, and H.G. Curt Schlevogt. Mantel lustres are decorative candleholders or vases for use above fireplaces.

Basket, 10½″ tall, milk white with transparent amber handle and base $350
Beaker, 5⅜″ tall, ruby red, deer and trees decoration $100
Bowl, 6″, Engraved Castle, Deer, and Foliage designs $100
Bowl, cranberry overlay, various enameled designs $150
Candlestick, 9″ tall, ruby and crystal cut, bird or deer decoration $75
Chalice, 6″ tall, fluted, footed, crystal to ruby coloring, stag design $125
Compote, 9″, white to green, Multicolored Floral design $175
Decanter with stopper, 12″ tall, narrow, etched and cut patterns $175
Decanter with stopper, 9″ tall, opaque shading of pink to white, cut floral design
.... $350
Decanter with stopper, ruby red, building and floral design $125
Goblet, 5½″ tall, ruby red scroll design $125
Goblet, 7¼″ tall, multicolored enameled floral cameo design (cameo enameling only) $150
Goblet, 7″ tall, ruby red, Battle Monument Baltimore decoration $525
Jar, 13″ tall, applied prunts, footed, enameled design of man with drinking cup, verse on reverse side. $300

Bohemian glass. PHOTO BY ROBIN RAINWATER.

Lamp shade, 5″ tall, 9″ diameter, milk glass with multicolored cameo design of bear on fallen log $2250
Mantel lustre, 12″ tall, tulip form top, hanging crystal prisms, green with white overlay, enameled floral design $425
Mantel lustre, 13″ tall, tulip form top, hanging crystal prisms, green with white overlay, enameled floral design $475
Mantel lustre, 14″ tall, ruby red with gilding and enameled floral design ... $475
Medallion, oval (2″ × 1½″), crystal, nude figure of woman with loincloth and basket on head. $375
Mug, beer, 5½″ tall, cranberry to clear etched $80
Plate, 12″, crystal, engraved building design in 4 views $575
Pokal, 16″ tall, ruby red, Niagara Falls and building decoration $2250
Pokal with cover, 8″ tall, ruby red and crystal, floral and building scenery $1350
Pokal with faceted finial, 24″ tall, green with multicolored shield and grape decoration $3750
Stein, 5½″ tall, ruby red, hunting dog and forest decoration $350
Stein, 5⅛″ tall, ruby red, floral paneled design $350
Stein, 5″ tall, ruby red, Niagara Falls decoration $350
Stein, 6¼″ tall, ruby red, castle scroll, and vine decoration $375
Tumbler, 3¾″ tall, ruby red, windmill decoration $80
Tumbler, 4″ tall, crystal, engraved chalet with heavy grass, lake, and bridge scene $200
Tumbler, 7″ tall, crystal with applied multicolored beading, multicolored knight and shield design $300
Tumbler, 7″ tall, crystal with multicolored enameled monastery design (various styles) $250
Urn with cover, 22″ tall, ruby red, stag and woodland scene $650
Vase, 5″ tall, crystal, engraved cameo face of woman $175

Bohemian glass. PHOTO BY MARK PICKVET, COURTESY OF THE CORNING MUSEUM OF GLASS.

Vase, 6″ tall, circular pedestal base, double loop handle, coralene $350
Vase, 7¹/₂″ tall, multicolored swirl design $110
Vase, 8¹/₄″ tall, cased with white, enameled floral design $125
Vase, 8¹/₄″ tall, scalloped, cobalt blue overlay $150
Vase, 9″ tall, emerald green with white and gold enameled floral design $225
Vase, 10¹/₂″ tall, cobalt blue encased in crystal $125
Vase, 10″ tall, cut windows, blue, yellow, and ruby red coloring $250
Vase, 11″ tall, crystal, many engraved miniature crescent moons design $150
Vase, 14″ tall, enameled butterfly design on white opal glass $1500
Wine glass, 6″ tall, crystal, engraved pinwheel design $50
Wine glass, knob stem, dark ruby red, monkey design $75

BRISTOL GLASS   EUROPE (ENGLAND, FRANCE, GERMANY, AND ITALY), 18TH–19TH CENTURIES

Bristol glass is usually characterized by an opaque or semi-opaque base color, which is further decorated by use of enamels. It originated in Bristol, England, and spread to other parts of Europe. Some pieces were produced in the United States by the New England Glass Co.

Basket, 10¹/₂″ tall, ruffled, pink opaline, bird design $225
Biscuit jar with silver-plated cover, 7¹/₂″ tall, tan birds and foliage with silver-plated handle and rim $250
Bowl, 7″, lily shape, amethyst color $65

Chandelier, 4-light, crystal bell and prism design $2000
Cologne bottle with gold ball stopper, 4″ tall, green with gold dot and star design
.... $110
Cologne bottle with stopper, 10″ tall, pink with gold band and foliage design ...
.... $160
Cologne bottle with stopper, 10″ tall, turquoise with gold band and enameled
floral design $95
Ewer, 10″ tall, clambroth with blue edging $95
Lamp, 10″ tall, square shade, shell-footed, enameled birds and floral designs .. $700
Pitcher, water, 8½″ tall, applied crystal handle, light green with enameled floral
and birds design $100
Salt dip, rectangular, white with multicolored enameled floral design $50
Sweetmeat jar, 5″ tall, silver-plated rim, cream with multicolored enameled floral
design $150
Urn with cover, 15″ tall, enameled floral design $175
Vase, 3¾″ tall, turquoise with gold band and enameled floral design $80
Vase, 6½″, turquoise with gold bands and floral design $90
Vase, 7¼″ tall, Opaque gray with multicolored enamel boy or girl $100
Vase, 8½″ tall, cylindrically-shaped, blue with multicolored enameled angel, Blue
.... $110
Vase, 9½″ tall, Green with gilded leaf design $75
Vase, 10″ tall, enameled gold and pink floral design $125
Vase, 10″ tall, handled, enameled green design $150
Vase, 11½″ tall, pink with multicolored enameled angel in chariot design ... $150
Vase, 11¾″ tall, opal, enameled floral design $150
Vase, 13½″ tall, amethyst tint, enameled floral design $150
Vase, 14½″ tall, dark gray with red and white floral design $250

Bristol glass. PHOTO BY ROBIN RAINWATER

Vase, 14½″ tall, cone shaped, blue with white floral design $250
Vase, 18″ tall, ruffled, enameled hydrangeas with gilding $300

CANADIAN GLASS   MID 1820s–PRESENT

Canadian glass is often ignored in the collector's field; however, a good deal of glass was made in Canada dating to the mid 1820s. The Mallorytown Glass Works in Ontario was the first to produce glass, and others followed pressed, art, and cut glass trends of Europe and the United States. Much of the glass made in Canada in the 19th century was very practical (e.g., bottles, tumblers, tableware, windows, fruit and canning jars). Dominion (which produced several pressed patterns, such as "Rayed Heart" and "Athenian") and Diamond were two successful companies that followed Mallorytown. Dominion eventually became Jefferson, a major producer of Art Nouveau lamps. Two other companies noted for pressed glasswares in the late 19th century were the O'Hara Glass Co. Ltd. and the Burlington Glass Works. There were also many noted Canadian cut glass manufacturers, including Gowans, Kent & Co., Ltd., Gundy-Clapperton Co., Lakefield Cut Glass Co., and the best known, Roden Brothers.

Bowl, 5″, Cut Hobster design (Gowans, Kent & Co.) $125
Bowl, 6″, Cut Buzzstar design (Gundy-Clapperton) $150
Bowl, 6″, Handled, Canadian pattern (Burlington Glass Works) $35
Bowl, 8″, footed, Athenian pattern (Dominion Glass Co.) $80
Bowl, 8″, Pressed Maple Leaf pattern $55
Bowl, 8″, Rayed Heart pattern (Dominion Glass Co.) $100
Bowl, Chandelier pattern (O'Hara) $30
Butter dish with cover, Canadian pattern (Burlington Glass Works) $90
Butter dish with cover, Chandelier pattern (O'Hara) $90
Butter dish with cover, Rayed Heart pattern (Dominion Glass Co.) $135
Butter dish with cover, Athenian pattern (Dominion Glass Co.) $125
Cake stand, Chandelier pattern (O'Hara) $75
Canning jar, 1 qt., embossed "Canadian Queen" (rare), Amber $375
Canning jar with glass lid, 1 pt., clear with embossed "Improved Gem" $6
Canning jar with glass lid, 1 pt., clear with embossed "Perfect Seal" $6
Canning jar with glass lid, 1 qt., clear with embossed "Improved Gem" $8
Canning jar with glass lid, 1 qt., clear with embossed "Perfect Seal" $8
Canning jar with zinc cover, 1 qt., embossed "Best" $3
Celery dish, 9″ oblong, Rayed Heart pattern (Dominion Glass Co.) $100
Celery dish, Canadian pattern (Burlington Glass Works) $55
Celery dish, Chandelier pattern (O'Hara) $45
Compote, 6¾″ diameter, Canadian pattern (Burlington Glass Works) $40
Compote, 6″ or 7″, Chandelier pattern (O'Hara) $45
Compote, 7″ diameter, Pressed Maple Leaf pattern $60
Compote, 9″ diameter, 6½″ tall, cut diamond and hobstar design
 (Roden Brothers) $200
Compote with cover, 7″ or 8″, Canadian pattern (Burlington Glass Works) $100
Compote with cover, 8″, Chandelier pattern (O'Hara) $75
Cookie jar with silverplated lid and top handle, 10½″ tall, silverplated beaver finial on handle, enameled grape decoration $350
Cordial, Canadian pattern (Burlington Glass Works) $35

Canadian glass. reproduced from an early 20th century trade catalog.

Canadian glass. reproduced from an early 20th century trade catalog.

Creamer, 4″ tall, pitcher-style, 2-handled, Cut Maple Leaf pattern $175
Creamer, Athenian pattern (Dominion Glass Co.) $60
Creamer, Canadian Pattern, (Burlington Glass Works) $55
Creamer, Chandelier Pattern, (O'Hara) $35
Creamer, Rayed Heart pattern, (Dominion Glass Co.) $80
Goblet, 5½″ tall, Pressed Honeycomb pattern with faceted design within combs (copper wheel engraved, Diamond Glass Co., 1890s) $150
Goblet, 6″ tall, Pressed Rasberry pattern (1890s) $75
Goblet, Canadian pattern, (Burlington Glass Works) $45
Goblet, Etched, Chandelier pattern, (O'Hara) $35
Hat, 2¾″ tall, Canadian Pillar pattern, (Lamont Glass Co., 1890s) $65
Heart shape, 1″ thick, 2″ long, various iridized colors, 1890s, (Robert Held) $25
Inkwell, Chandelier pattern, (O'Hara) $400
Jam jar with cover, ribbed lid, Canadian pattern, (Burlington Glass Works) $75
Lamp, 14″ tall, Bronze base, Cobalt Blue with enameled Palm Trees design, (Jefferson Glass Co.) $1500
Lamp, 18″ tall, opal with enameled water scene with two sailing ships, (Jefferson Glass Co.) $750
Lamp, kerosene, 16″ tall, emerald green base and globe, #102 style, (Dominion Glass Co., 1880s) $300
Nappy, 4″, Athenian pattern, (Dominion Glass Co.) $35
Paperweight, 2½″ tall, 10⅜″ circumference, opal 5-petal lily on multicolored chips background, cobalt blue writing, "Souvenir de Wallaceburg, Ont." (1910s), ... $325
Paperweight, 3⅛″ tall, 10⅛″ circumference, cased 5-petal lily on bubble stem, opal glass petals with emerald green and multicolored chips background (1890s) ... $350
Pitcher, milk, 6½″ tall, Cut Buzzstar pattern, (Roden Brothers) $300
Pitcher, milk or water, Canadian pattern, (Burlington Glass Works) $100
Pitcher, water, 10⅜″ tall, footed, handblown crystal (Excelsior Glass Co., 1880s)
....$200
Pitcher, water, 11½″ tall, footed, Pressed Maple Leaf pattern $250
Pitcher, water, Chandelier pattern, (O'Hara) $55
Plate, 6″, Canadian pattern, (Burlington Glass Works) $30
Powder jar with cover, 3½″ tall, 4″ diameter, Cut Regina pattern (Roden Brothers) $150
Salt and pepper shakers, 3″ tall, milk glass, Pressed Butterfly and Tassel pattern $95
Salver, 9″ diameter, 5½″ tall, Athenian pattern, (Dominion Glass Co). $100
Spooner, Chandelier pattern, (O'Hara) $40
Spooner, Rayed Heart pattern (Dominion Glas Co.) $65
Sugar, 3½″ tall, 2-handled, Cut Maple Leaf Pattern. $125
Sugar shaker, Chandelier pattern (O'Hara) $100
Sugar with cover, Chandelier pattern (O'Hara) $50
Sugar with cover, Athenian pattern (Dominion Glass Co.) $85
Sugar with cover, Canadian Pattern, (Burlington Glass Works) $75
Sugar with cover, Rayed Heart pattern (Dominion Glass Works) $125
Toothpick holder, 2¼″ tall, Pressed Canadian beaded oval and fan pattern ... $65
Tray, celery, 11½″ × 4″ oval, Cut Aster pattern (Roden Brothers) $350
Tumbler, 5½″ tall, Cut Buzzstar pattern $85
Tumbler, 5″ tall, Diamond Crosscut pattern $75
Vase, 8″ tall, slender form, ruffled, 4 Long Fluted design $50

Vase, 9″ tall, ruffled, crystal to cranberry shading (Chalet Artistic Glass, Ltd.) . . . .
. . . . $250
Vase, 11″ tall, footed, ruffled, long flutes with pressed floral band at top (Jefferson
Glass Co.) $90
Wine glass, Canadian pattern (Burlington Glass Works) $45

CLICHY   FRANCE, 1840s–1880s 1950s–PRESENT

The French classic period of paperweight manufacturing ran from about 1845 to
1860. The factories in the town of Clichy, including Baccarat and St. Louis, produced many examples, then closed during the later Art Nouveau period. In the
1950s paperweight production was revived by these glassmaking companies.

Paperweight, 2½″, multicolored densely packed millefiore design, signed $3750
Paperweight, 2¾″, sulphide, white cameo of Comte de Chambord on deep cobalt
blue ground $575
Paperweight, 2½″, cin mill, turquoise with cane gar and florets $750
Paperweight, 2½″, multicolored densely packed millefiore design, hexagon-
shaped, signed $4000
Paperweight, 2¼″, 30 pink and white swirled threads $1500
Paperweight, 2¼″, con mill, 4 rows in blue and white basket $1750
Paperweight, 2¾″, multicolored mill canes with pink and green rose $900
Paperweight, 2¾″, pattern mill, faceted, canes with rose and 5 rings $900
Paperweight, 2⅝″, Checkered Barber Pole design with 18 canes, twists, and fili-
gree rods $3000
Paperweight, 2⅝″, two-tone green and white spiral design $375
Paperweight, 2″, white mill canes with pink and green floral design $800
Paperweight, 3½″, multicolored florettes separated by varied threaded white strips
. . . . $850
Paperweight, 3⅛″, crystal with dark emerald green 4-leaf clover $2500
Paperweight, 3⅛″, large dark pink Chamomile design $750
Paperweight, 3¾″, con mill, cane gar, 7-rose design (1 in center) $850
Paperweight, 3⅜″, translucent ground, Alfred de Musset design $625
Paperweight, 3″, con mill, 8-point star cane in basket $2000
Paperweight, 3″, con mill, star cane cluster with 3 rings and rose $1400

*Clichy swirl paperweight. DRAWING BY MARK
PICKVET.*

Clichy paperweight. PHOTO BY ROBIN RAINWATER.

Paperweight, 3″, pinwheel, 44 amethyst rods, white tubes and turquoise floret $1750
Paperweight, 3″, scattered mill, pink rose in center $950

CRYSTAL MINIATURES   VARIOUS COMPANIES, 1970s-PRESENT

These pieces have been around only since the 1970s yet are highly collectible. They are made throughout Europe (Austria, Germany, Sweden, France, Ireland, etc.). The largest producer is Swarovski of Austria. A few pieces are made in the United States. Most pieces are faceted and animals are the most popular image, although new and larger items are appearing constantly. Colors are primarily used for accents, although a few pieces exhibit more surface area color.

Airplane, 2⅛″ long, 2¼″ wingspan, Crystal $125
Airplane, F-14 Tomcat, 1″ tall, 2⅝″ long, Crystal $115
Airplane, F/A-18 hornet, 1″ tall, 1¾″ long, Crystal $100
Airplane, Stealth fighter, 2″ long, Crystal $40
Anchor, ship's, 1½″ tall, gold chain, Crystal $50
Angel fish, 1¾″ long, frosted fins, Crystal $50
Apple, 1¼″ tall, rainbow colors $55
Balloon, hot air, 1½″ tall, red basket, Crystal, red $75
Basket of violets, 1¼″ tall, Crystal $70
Bear, 1½″ tall, red heart and "I love you" disk, Crystal, red $40
Bear, 1½″ tall, with captain's hat and stern wheel, Crystal $60
Bear, 1¼″ tall, Grandma or Grandpa with spectacles, Crystal $60
Bear, 1⅛″ tall, holding pink balloon, black eyes and nose, Crystal $35
Bear, 1¾″ tall, with baseball bat, Crystal $75
Bear, 1¾″ tall, with party hat, cake, and horn, Crystal $50
Bear, 1¾″ tall, with tennis racket, Crystal $75
Bear, 1⅛″ tall, scuba diving bear with treasure fish and swimming fish, Crystal $95

Crystal miniatures. PHOTO BY ROBIN RAINWATER.

Bear, 1⅝" tall, with gold club, green cap, amethyst ball, and red feet. $85
Bear, 2⅛" tall, with golf club and ball, Crystal $120
Bears, 2⅜" tall, two at candlelight dinner on circular base, moonlit window in background, Crystal $150
Bee, ½" tall, ⅝" long, Crystal $25
Butterfly, 1" long, octagonal base with pink flower, Crystal $45
Cable car or trolley, 1¼" long, Crystal $40
Cable car or trolley, 4" long, Crystal $175
Candle, Christmas, 1½" tall, holly berries on base, Crystal $30
Cannon, 2" tall, 2⅝" long, 3" round mirror base, 3 black cannonballs, Crystal $175
Car, 1⅝" long, red taillights, Crystal $60
Carousel, 2½" tall, 3 horses, Crystal $150
Carousel, 2¼" tall, 1⅛" diameter, 2 horses $100
Carousel horse, 2½" tall, 3 horses, Crystal $150
Carousel horse with bear holding balloon, 2⅜" tall, Crystal $100
Castle, 2½" tall, with changing color base, rainbow stairway on base, Crystal . . . $225
Castle, 2¼" tall, with changing color base, rainbow stairway at base, Crystal . . . $150
Castle, 3" tall, slender, amber base, 2" wide, Crystal, amber $70
Castle, 4³⁄₁₆" tall, with changing color base, Camelot, Crystal $550
Castle on green base, 1" tall, Crystal, green $35
Cat, 1⅜" tall, Siamese mother, black ears and feet, Crystal, black $50
Cat, 1" tall, kitten with red ball, Crystal $65
Cat, ¾" tall, 1¾" long, crouched, Crystal $35
Cat, ⅝" tall, Siamese kitten, black ears and feet, Crystal, black $25
Cat sitting in rocking chair, 3" tall, Crystal $90
Cat staring at fish in fishbowl, 1¾" tall, Crystal $100

Cats, 1½″ tall, mother with kitten, Crystal $75
Cats, 1½″ tall, 1″ across, 2 kittens together, Crystal $45
Cats in a basket, 1″ tall, 2½″ long, 2 sleeping, Crystal $60
Chick, 1″ tall, chubby, silver feet and beak, Crystal, silver $35
Chickens, 1″ tall, circular base, 2 chicks and red hearts, Crystal $50
Christmas Tree, 2″ tall, with tiny kitten and present, Crystal $60
Christmas Tree, 3⅜″ tall, with tiny kitten and present, Crystal $90
Christmas tree with presents, 6″ tall, 6″ diameter, colorful accents, limited edition
(1,000), Crystal $950
Church, 2¾″ tall, ¾″ square base, rainbow colors, Crystal $160
Cocker Spaniel, ½″ tall, puppy, Crystal $15
Cocker Spaniel, ¾″ tall, Crystal $20
Cottage, honeymoon, 1¾″ tall, multicolored accents, Crystal $125
Crab, 1⅛″ tall, 1½″ long, claws up, Crystal $50
Crab, hermit, 1½″ long, Crystal $50
Dice, pair (actual size), red or black dots, Crystal $50
Dog, ⅞″ tall, puppy, black eyes and nose, Crystal $30
Dog with doghouse, 1″ tall, Crystal $65
Dolphins, 2¼″ tall, 2 (1 with ball), rainbow base, Crystal $45
Dragonfly, 1⅝″ long, thin silver thread bones, Crystal $65
Dragster, 4″ long, red exhaust vents, Crystal $100
Duck, ¾″ long, black eyes and yellow beak, Crystal $30
Elephant, 3¼″ tall, 4½″ long, frosted tusks, Crystal $325
Fire engine, 1½″ long, Crystal $75
Fish, puffer, ¾″ tall, 1⅝″ long, Crystal $50
Frog, ½″ tall, Crystal $15
Gingerbread house, 2½″ tall, on square mirrored base, Crystal, multicolored .. $175
Hippopotamus, 1¼″ long, black eyes, red mouth, Crystal $30
Horse, rocking, 2″ tall, 2¼″ long, Crystal $70
House, Victorian, 3″ tall, multicolored accents, Crystal $250
Hummingbird, ⅝″ tall, 1″ long, Crystal $50
Ice cream sundae, 1″ tall, multicolored accents, Crystal $40
Jack-in-the-box, 1⅜″ tall, multicolored accents, Crystal $50
Jukebox, 2″ tall, 1¾″ wide, Crystal $100
Knight, 3″ tall, with shield and sword, Crystal $65
Koala bears, 1½″ tall, on mirrored base, 2 bears sharing a heart, Crystal $75
Lighthouse, 2½″ tall, gold circular base, Crystal $55
Lighthouse with changing color base, 2½″ tall, rainbow stairway on base, Crystal
.... $125
Lobster, 3″ long, gold feelers, Crystal $55
Meadowlark, 1⅜″ tall, Crystal $45
Moose, 1″ tall, 1½″ long, Crystal $50
Moose, ⅞″ tall, Crystal $30
Motorcycle, 2″ tall, 3″ long, Crystal $200
Mouse, 1¾″ tall, Grandpa or Grandma on rocking chair, Crystal $75
Mouse, ½″ long, Crystal $10
Octopus, 1½″ wide, Crystal $30
Octopus, 2½″ wide, Crystal $45
Otter, ½″ tall, 1¼″ long, Crystal $55
Owl, 1″ tall, Crystal $20
Panda bear, ¾″ tall, black ears, arms, and legs, Crystal $25

Penguin, 1 1/2″ tall, Crystal $45
Pig, 7/8″ tall, black eyes and pink nose, Crystal $30
Pigs in race car, 1 1/4″ tall, 2 1/2″ long, 2 pigs, Crystal $85
Pineapple, 1 1/4″ tall, gold top, Crystal $40
Pineapple, 2 1/4″ tall, gold top, Crystal $60
Pineapple, 3″ tall, gold top, Crystal, gold top $100
Rabbit, 1 1/2″ tall, skiing, Crystal $60
Rabbit, 1/2″ tall, 3/4″ long, lop-eared, Crystal $20
Rabbit in basket, 2″ tall, red bow and base, Crystal $45
Rabbit with pool table, 1 1/8″ tall, cue stick and balls, Crystal $85
Rabbits, 1″ tall, 2″ across, 2 bunnies sharing a heart, Crystal $55
Rabbits on beach under palm tree, 1 7/8″ tall, Crystal $125
Raccoon, 1″ tall, black eyes, nose, and tail $125
Red wagon (Flyer) with bunnies, 1 1/2″ long, Crystal $75
Sailboat, 1 1/8″ tall, 1″ square base, Crystal $30
Scorpion, 2 3/4″ long, tail up, Crystal $75
Seal, baby, 1/2″ tall, 3/4″ long, silver whiskers, Crystal $15
Sheep, 1 1/4″ tall, black legs and face, Crystal $40
Shell with faux pearl, 1″ tall, 1″ long, Crystal $40
Shell with faux pearl, 2″ tall, Crystal $100
Ship, cruise, 2 1/4″ long, 1″ tall, Crystal $110
Slot machine, 1 3/4″ tall, gold and red accents, Crystal $125
Slot machine, 2 1/4″ tall, gold and red accents, black ball on handle, Crystal $175
Snail, 3/4″ tall, Crystal $12
Snail, 1″ tall, Crystal $15
Snowman on skis, 1 1/8″ tall, red scarf, Crystal $45
Space shuttle, 3″ tall, on green globe base, Crystal $400
Squirrel, 1 1/2″ tall, black eyes, holding acorn, Crystal $40
Starship Enterprise, Star Trek, red and yellow accents, Crystal $150
Stork, 3″ tall, with baby in beak, Crystal $75
Swan, 3/4″ tall, 1″ long, Crystal $40
Taj Mahal, 4 1/2″ tall, 4″ square, limited edition (200), Crystal $850
Tank, M-1A, 1 3/8″ tall, 2 1/4″ long, Crystal $90
Telephone, 3/4″ tall, red or black buttons, Crystal $45
Train engine, 1 1/4″ tall, 2″ long, Crystal $110
Tunnel of love sculpture, 2″ tall, 2″ wide, 2 doves on boat in arch, Crystal $150
Turkey, 1 5/8″ long, Crystal $70
Turtle, 1 1/8″ long, Crystal $15
Tweety Bird sculpture, 2 3/8″ tall, (Looney Tunes), Crystal $150
Vase, 2″ tall, 6 red roses with green stems, Crystal $65
Wishing well with bucket of flowers, 2″ tall, Crystal $65
Yosemite Sam on wooden base, 3 1/2″ tall, (Looney Tunes), Crystal $150

CZECHOSLOVAKIAN GLASS 1918–1992

Much of this glassware is simply marked "Czechoslovakia" or "Made in Czechoslovakia," but older items are stamped with a variety of manufacturer's marks. The glass comes in many styles, including colored art (especially orange), Carnival, and engraved crystal. The most famous name in Czechoslovakian glass is that of Moser (see separate listing for "Moser Glass"). Beware of cheaper Victorian figures that are similar to the older and more expensive Mary Gregory glass produced by Boston & Sandwich in the United States. The newer Czechoslovakian pieces are generally worth only about one-fourth to one-third of the original Mary Gregory items.

Basket, 5¹/₂″ tall, crystal thorn handle, red with streaking $175
Basket, 8″ tall, black with ruffled yellow top, black handle $150
Bell, 5″ tall, ruby red with crystal ball finial and gilded filigree design $40
Biscuit jar with cover, 6¹/₂″ tall, 4³/₄″ diameter, crystal, Diamond pattern, (Ceska) $85
Bottle, Inca pattern, Carnival marigold or amethyst $250
Bowl, 12″, flared, red $70
Bowl, 5¹/₂″, footed, Cameo Cut, dark green on light orange $450
Bowl, 8¹/₂″, 4³/₄″ tall, crystal, striped pattern, (Ceska) $50
Bowl, 8″, Fleur-De-Lys pattern, Carnival marigold $400
Bowl, rose, Classic Arts pattern, Carnival marigold $550
Box with cover, 4″ across, ruby red with cut floral design $80
Candlestick, 10¹/₂″ tall, orange with multicolored base $50
Compote, 6³/₄″, footed, ruby red with gold gilding $125
Compote, 6³/₄″, footed, ruby red with gold gilding, enameled cameo design . $100
Cordial, barber bottle design, Carnival marigold $50
Cordial, Zipper Stitch pattern, Carnival marigold $125
Decanter with stopper, green with gold trim $65
Decanter with stopper, cone-shaped, ruby red handle, Opalescent Crackle design $250
Decanter with stopper, Zipper Stitch pattern, Carnival marigold $1250
Goblet, ruby red with heavy gold gilding $35
Ice bowl with insert, 7″ diameter, 5¹/₂″ tall, crystal, Vertical Ribbed design, (Ceska) $100
Lamp, 9″ tall, crystal bubble sphere on pedestal with Art Deco dancer $500
Nude statue, 8¹/₂″ tall, 2 nude women, Light Blue and Frosted Opalescent design $1750
Perfume bottle, 5¹/₂″ tall, with frosted pink floral dome stopper, crystal with frosted nude applicator connected to stopper $1500
Perfume bottle with crystal figural stopper, 5¹/₂″ tall, amber $250
Perfume bottle with frosting, 11¹/₂″ tall, loving couple stopper, crystal with engraved floral design $750
Perfume bottle with nude figural stopper, 6¹/₂″ tall, amethyst $450
Perfume bottle with stopper, 6¹/₄″ tall, crystal with blue Art Deco design ... $250
Perfume bottle with stopper, 7¹/₂″ tall, crystal, Cut Hobstar design $85
Perfume bottle with stopper, 7″ tall, crystal, daffodils design $150
Perfume bottle with stopper, Horizontal Ribbed design, Carnival marigold $125
Pin box, Horizontal Ribbed design, Carnival marigold $80
Pitcher, water, 10″ tall, topaz with green streaking and blue threading $175
Pitcher, water, 11¹/₂″ tall, black handle, orange with colorful Jungle Bird design $175
Powder jar with cover, Classic Arts pattern, Carnival marigold $750
Puff box, Horizontal Ribbed design, Carnival marigold $100
Ring tree, Horizontal Ribbed design, Carnival marigold $75
Soap dish, Horizontal Ribbed design, Carnival marigold $65

Tray, Barber Bottle design, Carnival marigold $75
Tray, Zipper Stitch pattern, Carnival marigold $250
Tumbler, Horizontal Ribbed design, Carnival marigold $85
Vanity set, 4-piece (small water bottle with stopper, oval dish, and tray), crystal, Beaded Medallion pattern $90
Vase, 4½″ tall, Cobalt blue Spatter design $60
Vase, 4″ tall, hexagonal, footed, multicolored Spatter design $60
Vase, 5½″ tall, ruffled, white with rose interior $80
Vase, 6½″ tall, 4 blown applied crystal feet, orange curved figure 6 design ... $85
Vase, 6¼″ tall, orange with silver-deposit floral design $55
Vase, 6″ tall, ruffled, cased blue with white interior $200
Vase, 7½″ tall, Crystal Crackle with Embossed Floral design $45
Vase, 7⅛″ tall, Jack-in-the-pulpit style, orange with black spots $85
Vase, 7″ tall, Classic Arts pattern, Carnival marigold $750
Vase, 7″ tall, frosted with horses raised in relief $110
Vase, 7″ tall, Horizontal Ribbed design, Carnival marigold $75
Vase, 7″ tall, Inca pattern, Carnival marigold or amethyst $1000
Vase, 8½″ tall, goddess design, Carnival marigold $1500
Vase, 8½″ tall, ruffled, blue with pink interior $125
Vase, 8½″ tall, black-lined rim, orange with enameled black medallions $85
Vase, 8″ tall, Fleur-de-Lys pattern, Carnival marigold $750
Vase, 8″ tall, ruffled, tangerine blue design $125
Vase, 8″ tall, ruffled, yellow with black snake $225
Vase, 9½″ tall, fan style, amber with blue threading $125
Vase, 9″ tall, tricornered top, gloss black over orange design $90
Vase, 10″ tall, Classic Arts pattern, Carnival marigold $1000
Vase, 11¼″ tall, Pebble and Fan design, Carnival blue iridized amber $1000
Vase, 11″ tall, square-shaped, emerald green with floral design in relief $275
Vase, 13″ tall, canary yellow with black handles $150
Vase, 13″ tall, ruby red with heavy gold gilding $150
Vase, 15½″ tall, 3⅞″ diameter, tapers in at top, crystal with 12 interlocking circles $375
Vase, fish-shaped, Carnival or iridized colors $500
Whiskey tumbler, 2½″ tall, green with gold trim (matches decanter above) .. $12

DAUM, NANCY GLASS   DAUM GLASS, FRANCE, 1880s–1910s

Daum was one of the most important French factories producing art glass. It specialized in cameo designs, intaglio, inlaid, enameled, acid cutting, and copper wheel engraving. Almaric Walter was one of the artisans who worked at the Verreries Artistiques des Frères factory in Nancy.

Beaker, 4½″ tall, footed, green with gold flowers $175
Bowl, 3¾″, translucent blue, green, and yellow, butterfly design $2500
Bowl, 6″, yellow, orange, and blue enameled Mulberry and Floral Cameo design $1250
Bowl, 10″, pedestal base, cameo $1500
Bowl, 12″, amber, etched triangles in panels $1000
Box with hinged cover, 3″ diameter, leaves and berries with grasshopper on cover, signed "A. Walter" $5500

Box with hinged cover, 6″ tall, green and blue, pyramid on cover, signed "A. Walter" $3500

Box, square with hinged domed cover, 6″ diameter, cameo river scene $4000

Cat figurine, 10½″ tall $750

Decanter with red stopper, 11″ tall, crystal with gray streaking $450

Egg, glass with glass base, 5″ tall, gilded pedestal foot, opalescent, acid etched with cameo engraved ducks $2000

Lamp, 7½″ diameter shade, amber base, red floral cameo design $10500

Lamp, 7″ tall, marble base, green and brown, forest lake scene $2500

Lamp, 19¼″ tall, 3-arm iron mounted, multicolored winter landscape $8000

Lamp, 30½″ tall, 2-piece (lighted base and dome), opaque blue and yellow with multicolored floral design $20000

Paperweight, 10″, sea nymph rising from surface, signed "Cheret" $6500

Pitcher, water, Tortoise Shell Cameo design, signed $500

Powder box with sterling silver cover, multicolored floral design $1000

Salt dip, 2″ square, 1″ tall, yellow floral cameo design, enameled $1750

Sherbet, 4¼″ tall, apricot with gold mica $150

Tray, 7½″ long, triangular, gray with mallard duck faces, signed "A. Walter" . . . $3000

Tray, 7″ long, salamander with ivy leaves and yellow blossoms, signed "A. Walter" $4750

Tumbler, 4¾″ tall, green leaves and purple violets design $1750

Tumbler, wooded winter snow scene, signed $400

Vase, 4¾″ tall, pale green with large air bubbles $300

Vase, 4″ tall, amber, Sailing Ship design $1250

Vase, 5½″ tall, green to purple shading, Sunflower and Daisy Floral design . . . $1250

Vase, 5¼″ tall, red millefiori design $950

Vase, 5″ tall, pedestal foot, Cameo Ducks design $2750

Vase, 5″ tall, violet pedestal foot, yellow and turquoise color $1100

Vase, 6½″ tall, frosted with pine forest and lake scene $500

Vase, 6¾″ tall, 3-layered cameo $600

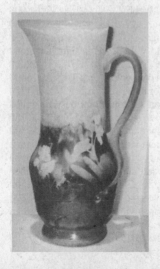

Daum pitcher. PHOTO BY MARK PICKVET, COURTESY OF THE CORNING MUSEUM OF GLASS.

Vase, 7″ tall, 5″ diameter, cameo red and yellow on aqua, floral, signed"A. Walter" $2250
Vase, 8″ tall, 8″ diameter, flared, vertical ribs, gray $1200
Vase, 9″ tall, light blue to cobalt blue shading, gold mica $2750
Vase, 10¼″ tall, enameled Joan of Arc design $2500
Vase, 10″ tall, slender, blue, orange, and yellow, Cameo Berry Cluster design $2000
Vase, 13½″ tall, cone-shaped, footed, yellow with enameled flower blossoms $6750
Vase, 13″ tall, ovoid shape, yellow with etched leaves $2500
Vase, 14″ tall, gold gilded on amethyst, Cameo Iris and Dragonfly design $2250
Vase, 15¼″ tall, mottled, shaded gray, Enameled Cornflower design $5500
Vase, 15½″ tall, white with green holly berries $1250
Vase, 16″ tall, green and gold gilt on yellow, cameo $2000
Vase, 16″ tall, multicolored cameo iris with gilded leaves and dragonfly ... $7500
Vase, 18″ tall, red and yellow spatter with gold mica $2000
Vase, 27″ tall, amethyst with yellow center, autumn woodland cameo scene .. $1000
Wine Goblet, engraved and enameled Lily design, signed $375
Woman figurine, 7″ tall, seated with head in hands, yellow, signed, "A. Walter" .. $2250

ENGLISH CAMEO GLASS   1850s–1890s

Cameo glass consists of at least two layers: the inner layer is usually a dark color, and the outer layer, or casing, is white. Classic, floral, natural, and other scenes can be carved into as many as five layers. The most popular English makers were Thomas Webb & Sons and Stevens & Williams. Cameo glass was also produced by other manufacturers, including some in France. See the entry "French Cameo Glass."

Bowl, 4″ tall, 6″ diameter, ruffled, pink on white satin with apple blossoms, signed "Stevens & Williams" $900
Bowl, 5″, 2″ tall, white on cranberry, floral, signed "Webb" $900
Bowl, 6″ tall, white on blue, dragon design (Webb) $2750
Bowl, 7″ tall, aqua on blue, Seaweed and Shell design $2750
Bowl, rose, 3½″, white on rose mother-of-pearl, Wild Rose design, Diamond Quilted pattern $2000
Cup, loving, 7½″ tall, 3 applied handles, light gold on dark gold (Webb) $400
Epergne, 10½″ tall, white on red, mirrored base, floral $4750
Perfume bottle with cut stopper, 4″ tall, white on saffron, floral design, signed "Webb" $1750
Perfume bottle with Faberge stopper, 3¾″ tall, white on blue, floral $7500
Plate, 13″ round, white on amber, winged horse and rider (Stevens & Williams) $3500
Platter, 14″ round, 4-color (white, red, light blue, and tan florals) on green cameo (Webb) $8500
Saucer, 6″, white circular floral design on rust (Stevens & Williams) $800
Sweetmeat jar with silver cover, 6″ tall, white on light blue, fancy leaf design $2250
Vase, 5″ tall, white on yellow, Violets and Leaves design $2000

English cameo glass. PHOTO BY MARK PICKVET.

Vase, 5″ tall, 5″ diameter, white on blue mother-of-pearl, Apple Blossom design, Diamond Quilted pattern $2250
Vase, 5″ tall, white on blue, floral, signed "Stevens & Williams" $1750
Vase, 6½″ tall, white on amber to rose shading, Ovoid Geranium design, signed "Webb" $1500
Vase, 6″ tall, white on amethyst, Beetle and Nasturtiums design, signed "Stevens & Williams" $3750
Vase, 6″ tall, white on blue, floral design $2250
Vase, 6″ tall, white on citron, signed "Webb" $2250
Vase, 7½″ tall, tan with white figure, signed "Woodall & Webb" $9000
Vase, 7″ tall, blue with white figure, signed "Woodall" $8000
Vase, 7″ tall, rose on white, Scroll design, signed "Webb" $1750
Vase, 7″ tall, white on tan, signed "Stevens & Williams" $1750
Vase, 8¼″ tall, classic 2-handled style, white child on black (Joseph Northwood) $8000
Vase, 8″ tall, white on blue, Rose design, signed "Stevens & Williams" $2250
Vase, 8″ tall, white on red mother-of-pearl (Webb) $5500
Vase, 8″ tall, white on yellow, Tall Grass design, signed "Woodall" $3750
Vase, 8″ tall, white woman with harp (siren) on brown, signed "Geo. Woodall" $8000
Vase, 9¾″ tall, white on reddish-orange, Bird, Dragonfly, and Iris design, signed "Webb" $3500
Vase, 9″ tall, white on blue, floral design on body and neck $3500
Vase, 9″ tall, white on peachblow, floral, signed "Webb" $5500

Assorted English cameo glass. PHOTO BY ROBIN RAINWATER. COURTESY OF THE CORNING MUSEUM OF GLASS

Vase, 10″ tall, white on red, signed "Webb" $3500
Vase, 11½″ tall, white on red, signed "Webb" $3750
Vase, 11¾″ tall, classic 2-handled style, white floral and stork design on dark blue $4000
Vase, 11¾″ tall, opalescent white on blue (Webb) $4000
Vase, 12½″ tall, mother-of-pearl, signed "Webb" $4250
Vase, 12″ tall, banded neck, white on peach, floral, signed "Stevens & Williams" $3750
Vase, 12″ tall, gourd-shaped, white on yellow, horsemen design $4250
Vase, 12″ tall, white on red, Floral and Plums design, signed "Stevens & Williams" $3750

English cameo glass.
PHOTO BY ROBIN
RAINWATER, COURTESY
OF THE CORNING
MUSEUM OF GLASS.

Vase, 13″ tall, tan with white figures, signed "Woodall & Webb" $10500
Vase, 23¹/₂″ tall, white on red, Foxgloves design (Webb) $8500

ENGLISH CARNIVAL GLASS   1910-EARLY 1930s

Carnival glass was first introduced in England from the United States and soon caught on. The most noted English producers were Davisons of Gateshead, Guggenheim Ltd. of London, and the Sowerby Company of Gateshead-on-Tyne. There are many serving items available such as butter dishes, creamers, bowls, and water sets. As in the United States, the fad quickly died and production was phased out by the early 1930s.

Banana dish, Cut Arches pattern, Marigold $100
Banana dish, Moonprint pattern, (Sowerby), Marigold $175
Basket, thin handle, alternating diamonds with floral design, (Davisons of Gateshead), Marigold $75
Bean pot with cover, Fruit and Berries design, Marigold or blue $550
Boat (used for holding pens/pencils), Daisy Block pattern, (Sowerby) Aqua opalescent $750
   Marigold or amethyst $300
Bonbon dish, Illinois Daisy pattern, (Davisons of Gateshead), Marigold $60
Bowl, 7¹/₂″, Intaglio Daisy design, (Sowerby), Marigold $75
Bowl, 4¹/₂″, Intaglio Daisy design, (Sowerby), Marigold $50
Bowl, 4¹/₂″, Mitered Diamonds and Pleats pattern, Marigold and blue $45
Bowl, 4″, Intaglio Daisy pattern, (Sowerby), Marigold $35
Bowl, 4″, Modern pattern, Marigold $50
Bowl, 4″, Pineapple pattern, (Sowerby), Carnival colors $50
Bowl, 5″, Lattice Heart pattern, (Sowerby), Carnival colors $45
Bowl, 5″, Prism and Cane pattern, (Sowerby), Carnival colors $75
Bowl, 6″, footed, Thistle and Thorn pattern, Marigold $65
Bowl, 7³/₄″, Intaglio Daisy pattern, (Sowerby), Marigold $60
Bowl, 7″, English Hob and Button pattern, Carnival colors $75
Bowl, 7″, Pineapple pattern, (Sowerby), Carnival colors $75
Bowl, 8¹/₂″, Feathered Arrow pattern, (Guggenheim), Marigold $65
Bowl, 8¹/₂″, Mitered Diamonds and Pleats pattern, Marigold and blue $55
Bowl, 8″, Illinois Daisy pattern, (Davisons of Gateshead), Marigold $75
Bowl, 8″, Moonprint pattern, (Sowerby), Marigold $60
Bowl, 8″, Pinwheel pattern, Carnival colors $85
Bowl, 9″, Petals and Prisms pattern, Marigold $75
Bowl, 10″, English Hob and Button pattern, Carnival colors $100
Bowl, 10″, Grape and Cherry pattern, (Sowerby)
   Blue $225
   Marigold $95
Bowl, 10″, Lattice Heart pattern, (Sowerby), Carnival colors $75
Bowl, 14″, Moonprint pattern, (Sowerby), Marigold $100
Bowl, oval or round, Finecut Rings pattern, (Guggenheim), Marigold $150
Bowl, Flora pattern, (Sowerby), Marigold or blue $150
Bowl, Fruit, Petals and Prisms pattern, Marigold $100
Bowl, Hobstar and Cut Triangles design

Green or amethyst $100
Marigold $80
Bowl, oval or round, footed, Lea pattern, (Sowerby), Marigold or amethyst $65
Bowl, Prism and Cane pattern, (Sowerby)
Marigold $75
Purple $125
Bowl, rose, Classic Arts pattern, (Davisons of Gateshead), Marigold $175
Bowl, rose, footed, Kokomo pattern, (Sowerby), Marigold, green, or blue ... $75
Bowl, rose, Hobstar and Cut Triangles Design
Green or amethyst $100
Marigold $80
Bowl, rose, Intaglio Daisy pattern, (Sowerby), Marigold $70
Bowl, rose, Pineapple pattern, (Sowerby), Carnival colors $150
Bowl, rose, Sea Thistle pattern, Marigold $75
Bowl, rose, Vining Leaf Variant design, Marigold $325
Bowl with cover, Diamond Pinwheel pattern, (Davisons of Gateshead), Marigold
.... $50
Butter dish, 10″ diameter, Cathedral pattern, (Davisons of Gateshead)
Clear $50
Amethyst or blue $70
Butter dish, Diamond Pinwheel pattern, (Davisons of Gateshead), Marigold ... $100
Butter dish, Hobstar Reversed pattern, (Davisons of Gateshead), Marigold, blue,
or amethyst $70
Butter dish, Moonprint pattern, (Sowerby), Marigold $150
Butter dish, Pineapple pattern, (Sowerby), Carnival colors $95
Butter dish, Split Diamond pattern, (Davisons of Gateshead), Marigold or
amethyst $90
Butter dish, Triands pattern, Marigold $75
Butter dish with cover, Beaded Swirl pattern, (Sowerby), Marigold $125
Butter dish with cover, Finecut Rings pattern, (Guggenheim) $175
Butter dish with cover, Rose Garden pattern
Blue, green, amethyst, or purple $350
Marigold $175
Butter dish with cover, Shooting Star pattern, Marigold $175
Cake plate, footed, Diamond Ovals pattern, (Sowerby), Marigold $175
Cake plate, footed, Thistle and Thorn pattern, Marigold $175
Cake stand, Finecut Rings pattern, (Guggenheim), Marigold $175
Candleholder, Victorian Crown or Coronation pattern, Marigold $300
Candlestick, Moonprint pattern, (Sowerby), Marigold $55
Carafe, Daisy and Cane pattern, (Sowerby), Marigold $115
Casserole dish with cover, Fruit and Berries pattern
Clear $325
Blue $375
Celery dish, Finecut Rings pattern, (Guggenheim), Marigold $125
Celery vase, Heavy Prisms pattern, (Davisons of Gateshead)
Blue or purple $150
Marigold $125
Celery vase, Triands pattern, Marigold $75
Chalice, 7″ tall, Cathedral pattern, (Davisons of Gateshead)
Amethyst or blue $125
Marigold $100

Cheese dish, Moonprint pattern, (Sowerby), Marigold $150
Coaster, Rayed Star design, Marigold $45
Compote, 5″, War Dance pattern, Marigold $100
Compote, Beaded Swirl pattern, (Sowerby), Marigold or blue $75
Compote, Cathedral pattern, (Davisons of Gateshead)
   Amethyst or blue $70
   Marigold $55
Compote, Daisy and Cane pattern, (Sowerby), Marigold $40
Compote, Diamond Pinwheel pattern, (Davisons of Gateshead), Marigold ... $75
Compote, Diamond Prisms pattern, Marigold $75
Compote, footed, Diamond Ovals pattern, (Sowerby), Marigold $50
Compote, Hobstar and Cut Triangles design
   Green or amethyst $100
   Marigold $85
Compote, Lattice Heart pattern, (Sowerby), Carnival colors $85
Compote, Moonprint pattern, (Sowerby), Marigold $55
Compote, Pineapple pattern, (Sowerby), Carnival colors $80
Compote, Stippled Diamond Swag design, Marigold, blue, or green $85
Cookie jar, Illinois Daisy pattern, (Davisons of Gateshead), Marigold $100
Cordial, Star and Fan pattern, Marigold $125
Cordial, Zipper Stitch pattern, Marigold $50
Cracker jar with metal cover, Fans pattern, (Davisons of Gateshead), Marigold ..
.... $250
Creamer, Apple Panels pattern, (Sowerby)
   Blue $75
   Marigold $50
Creamer, Beaded Swirl pattern, (Sowerby), Marigold or blue $75
Creamer, Catherdral pattern, (Davisons of Gateshead), Marigold $55
Creamer, Diamond Ovals pattern, (Sowerby), Marigold $65
Creamer, Diamond Top pattern, Marigold $55
Creamer, Diamond Vane pattern, Marigold $50
Creamer, English Button Band pattern, Marigold $65
Creamer, Finecut Rings pattern, (Guggenheim), Marigold $125
Creamer, footed, Lea pattern, (Sowerby), Marigold or amethyst $60
Creamer, Hobstar Panels pattern, Marigold $60
Creamer, Moonprint pattern, (Sowerby), Marigold $60
Creamer, Petals and Prisms pattern, Marigold $75
Creamer, Pineapple pattern, (Sowerby), Carnival colors $75
Creamer, Rose Garden pattern
   Blue, green, amethyst, purple $100
   Marigold $60
Creamer, Sea Thistle pattern, Marigold $65
Creamer, Shooting Star pattern, Marigold $65
Creamer, Split Diamond pattern, (Davisons of Gateshead), Marigold or amethyst
.... $60
Creamer, Sunken Daisy pattern
   Blue $65
   Marigold $50
Creamer, Thistle and Thorn pattern, Marigold $75
Creamer, Triands pattern, Marigold $60
Creamer, Zipper Stitch pattern, Marigold $65

Decanter with stopper, Daisy and Cane pattern, (Sowerby), Marigold or blue $275
Decanter with stopper, Star and Fan pattern, Marigold $750
Decanter with stopper, Zipper Stitch pattern, Marigold $400
Epergne, Cathedral pattern, (Davisons of Gateshead), Marigold $550
Epergne, with metal base, English Hob and Button pattern, Marigold colors $225
Flower holder, Cathedral pattern, (Davisons of Gateshead), Marigold $100
Frog, flower with base, Hobstar Reversed pattern, (Davisons of Gateshead), Marigold $70
Frog, flower, Flower Block design, (Sowerby), Carnival colors $75
Frog, flower, Zip Zip pattern, Marigold $85
Hen dish with cover, (Sowerby), Marigold $175
Hen dish with cover, miniature, (Sowerby), Marigold $225
Jam jar, Finecut Rings pattern, (Guggenheim), Marigold $150
Jam jar with cover, Moonprint pattern, (Sowerby)
  Blue $150
  Marigold $100
Lamp, Fountain pattern, (Sowerby), Marigold $350
Nut dish, Bow and English Hob pattern, Marigold $60
Nut dish, Thistle and Thorn pattern, Marigold $85
Paperweight, Sphinx design, Amber $750
Pitcher, milk, Fans pattern, (Davisons of Gateshead), Marigold $150
Pitcher, milk, Moonprint pattern, (Sowerby), Marigold $150
Pitcher, milk, Rose Garden pattern
  Blue, green, amethyst, or purple $750
  Marigold $475
Pitcher, water, Banded Grape and Leaf pattern, Marigold $525
Pitcher, water, Beaded Swirl pattern, (Sowerby), Marigold or blue $250
Pitcher, water, Fans pattern (Davisons of Gateshead), Marigold $250
Pitcher, toy (miniature), Fancy Cut pattern, Marigold $250
Plate, Hobstar and Cut Triangles design
  Green or amethyst $125
  Marigold $85
Powder box with cover, paneled, sculptured lady handle on lid, (Davisons of Gateshead), Marigold $150
Powder jar, Classic Arts pattern, (Davisons of Gateshead), Marigold $175
Punch Bowl, Cathedral Arches pattern, Marigold $550
Punch cup, Cathedral Arches pattern, Marigold $55
Sauce dish, Split Diamond pattern, (Davisons of Gateshead), Marigold or amethyst $45
Spittoon, Daisy and Cane pattern, (Sowerby), Blue $350
Spooner, Diamond Top pattern, Marigold $45
Spooner, Hobstar Reversed pattern, (Davisons of Gateshead), Marigold $75
Spooner, Rose Garden pattern
  Blue, green, amethyst, or purple $90
  Marigold $60
Spooner, Triands pattern, Marigold $60
Sugar, Apple Panels pattern, (Sowerby)
  Blue $75
  Marigold $50

Sugar, Beaded Swirl pattern, (Sowerby), Marigold or blue $75
Sugar, Diamond Ovals pattern, (Sowerby), Marigold $65
Sugar, Diamond Top pattern, Marigold $55
Sugar, Diamond Vane pattern, Marigold $50
Sugar dish with cover, Beaded Swirl pattern, (Davisons of Gateshead) $80
Sugar dish with cover, Finecut Rings pattern, (Guggenheim), Marigold ... $150
Sugar dish with cover, Signet pattern, Marigold $95
Sugar dish with cover, Zipper Stitch pattern, Marigold $100
Sugar, English Button band pattern, Marigold $65
Sugar, footed, Hobstar Panels, Marigold $60
Sugar, Moonprint pattern, (Sowerby), Marigold $65
Sugar, Petals and Prisms pattern, Marigold $75
Sugar, Pineapple pattern, (Sowerby), Carnival colors $75
Sugar, Rose Garden pattern
  Blue, green, amethyst, or purple $65
  Marigold $65
Sugar, Sea Thistle pattern, Marigold $65
Sugar, Shooting Star pattern, Marigold $65
Sugar, Split Diamond pattern, (Davisons of Gateshead), Marigold or amethyst ...
.... $60
Sugar, Sunken Daisy Pattern, Marigold $50
Sugar, Thistle and Thorn pattern, Marigold $75
Sugar, Triands pattern, Marigold $65
Swan dish with cover, (Sowerby)
  Amethyst, purple, or blue $350
  Marigold $225
Toothpick holder, African Shield pattern, Marigold $150
Toothpick holder, Banded Diamond and Fans pattern, Marigold $100
Tray, serving, Star and Fan pattern, Marigold $250
Tray, serving, Zipper Stitch pattern, Marigold $175
Tumbler, Banded Grape and Leaf pattern, Marigold $150
Tumbler, Beaded Swirl pattern, (Sowerby), Marigold or blue $75
Tumbler, Fans pattern, (Davisons of Gateshead), Marigold $100
Tumbler, toy (miniature), Fancy Cut pattern, Marigold $75
Vase, 5″ tall, Thin Rib and Drape design, (Sowerby), Carnival colors $175
Vase, 6¹/₂″ tall, Pinwheel pattern, Carnival colors $125
Vase, 6″ tall, Thistle design, Marigold $75
Vase, 7″ tall, Classic Arts pattern, (Davisons of Gateshead), Marigold $200
Vase, 8″ tall, Pinwheel pattern, Carnival colors $175
Vase, 10″ tall, Classic Arts pattern, (Davisons of Gateshead), Marigold $250
Vase, 13¹/₂″ tall, Fine Prisms and Diamonds pattern, Marigold, blue, green, or
purple $100
Vase, 14″ tall, Thin Rib and Drape design, (Sowerby), Carnival colors $275
Vase, Daisy and Cane pattern, (Sowerby), Marigold or blue $125
Vase, Finecut Rings pattern, (Guggenheim), Marigold $125
Vase, Flora pattern, (Sowerby), Marigold or blue $150
Vase, Footed Prisms pattern, (Sowerby)
  Blue or green $150
  Marigold $100
Vase, Moonprint pattern, (Sowerby), Marigold $75

Vase, Pebble and Fan pattern
  Cobalt blue or amber $550
  Vaseline $150
Vase, Rose Garden pattern, Blue, green, amethyst, or purple $275
Vase, seagull design, Marigold $900
Vase, Spiralex pattern, Marigold, blue, green, or amethyst $100
Vase, Square Diamond pattern, Blue $150
Vase, Sunflower and Diamond pattern
  Blue $125
  Marigold $85
Vase, Tropicana pattern, Marigold $1400
Vase, Vining Leaf variant pattern, Marigold $350

FINNISH GLASS   20TH CENTURY

Finnish companies produced some Carnival glass in the 1930s after the fad had faded in the United States, England, and Australia. The largest factory was located in Riihimakei. A contemporary art glass company is Notsjo Glassworks of Nuutajarvo.

Decanter, with multicolored transparent rooster stopper, Light bluish-gray $350
Decanter with stopper, Banded Diamonds and Bars pattern, Carnival
marigold $750
Lollipop Isle sculpture, Crystal base with multicolored lollipop stems, (Notsjo) .
.... $550
Pitcher, water, Grand Thistle pattern, Carnival blue or amethyst $750
Tumbler, 2¼" tall, Banded Diamonds and Bars pattern, Carnival marigold .. $500
Tumbler, 4" tall, Banded Diamonds and Bars pattern, Carnival marigold ... $500
Tumbler, Grand Thistle pattern, Carnival blue or amethyst $250
Vase, 5½" tall, Heavy Crystal with controlled air buble design, (Notsjo) $150
Vase, 13½" tall, orchid, bullet design with oval center hole, Heavy crystal $250

FRENCH CAMEO GLASS   1850s–EARLY 20th CENTURY

Like the English version, French cameo glass consists of at least two layers: a darker inner layer and a white outer layer. Classic, floral, natural, and other scenes are carved in as many as five layers. The chief French manufacturers were Galle and Daum. Beware of "French" cameo glass that has been produced by Romanian companies since the 1960s; much of it is signed with the older French marks. For other examples, see the entries "Daum, Nancy Glass" and "English Cameo Glass."

Ashtray, 6" across, Pate de Verre design, (A. Walter) $800
Basket, 7" tall, floral design (Daum), Black, red, and yellow $675
Bowl, 2½", Berries and Leaves design, signed (Galle), Crystal on orange .. $1000
Bowl, 3" tall, rose, Lake and Forest scene, (De Vez), Black on gold and pink satin
.... $1250
Bowl, 13½", bun feet, Flower Cluster design, (La Verre Français), Wine on rust ..
.... $2250

French Gallé cameo. PHOTO BY MARK
PICKVET, COURTESY OF THE CORNING
MUSEUM OF GLASS.

Chandelier, 13″ tall, Trumpet Flower design on conical shade (La Verre Français),
Burgundy to brown on yellow $3250
Compote, 4″, clear interior village scene with river and mountains (De Vez), Brown
and rust on yellow $1400
Ewer, 9″ tall, Thistle design (Roux Chalon) $600
Goblet, 8″ tall, blue floral design (Galle) $1250
Lamp, 15″ tall, dark red shade and base, Egyptian scene (Degue) $3750
Lamp, 19″ tall, floral design, Green and pink $1400
Lamp, 21″ tall, signed "LeMaitre," blue, amber, and green on translucent white
. . . . $2500
Perfume bottle with stopper, 6¹/₂″ tall, Floral and Bird design (D'Argental),
Orange and brown on amber $1500
Pitcher, 6″ tall, (Schneider), Shaded orange and white $475
Powder jar with cover, 6″ tall, Red carved flowers on green ground, signed (Galle)
. . . . $2250
Tumbler, 4″ tall, signed (Galle) $500
Vase, 3¹/₂″ tall, Rose and Thorn design (Weis), Purple on white $750
Vase, 3″ tall, Orchid design (Verrerie D'Art), Amethyst and crystal $1000
Vase, 4¹/₄″ tall, multicolor enameled landscape scene (Legras) $875
Vase, 4″ tall, lakeside scene, signed "De Vez," Rust on amber $550
Vase, 5¹/₂″ tall, Purple sweet peas on frosted ground, signed (Galle) $800
Vase, 5″ tall, Maple Leaves and Pod design (Legras), Green on light yellow $400
Vase, 6″ tall, Floral and Foliage design (D'Argental), Amethyst on frosted ground
. . . . $500
Vase, 6″ tall, Morning Glory design (Arsall), Green on chartreuse $1500
Vase, 6″ tall, violet and crystal foliage (Vessiere) $700
Vase, 7″ tall, enameled floral (St. Louis), Blue $950
Vase, 8″ tall, blue foot (Richard), Red to black $400
Vase, 8″ tall, matte crystal and enamel (Baccarat) $700
Vase, 8″ tall, Winding River and Trees design (De Vez), Burgundy on amber . . . . .
. . . . $1500

Vase, 9½″ tall, footed, urn-shaped, Swag design (La Verre Français), Purple on pink and orange $1200
Vase, 9″ tall, Pâte de Verre design (Argy-Rousseau) $1750
Vase, 10″ tall, 3-color, signed (Galle), Olive green to blue to rose floral ... $2500
Vase, 10″ tall, slender bottle form, red and green on light green to red shading (D'Argental) $1750
Vase, 11½″ tall, (Monthoye), Red and amethyst floral $600
Vase, 11½″ tall, (Arsall), Light pink with purple and green irises $2250
Vase, 11″ tall, Brown and red floral $950
Vase, 11″ tall, (De Vez), Shaded red and yellow mums $800
Vase, 11″ tall, floral design (Degue), Purple on multicolored ground $1250
Vase, 12″ tall, Ship design (D'Argental), Brown and red $850
Vase, 13″ tall, elongated feet, Trees and Fence design (D'Argental), Dark brown on green rust $1750
Vase, 14″ tall, enameled floral design, Green $750
Vase, 15″ tall, footed, Cherry Branch design (Ledoux), Gray, orange, and red ....
.... $1250
Vase, 15″ tall, purple columbine blossoms on frosted gray, signed (Galle) .. $5000
Vase, 16″ tall, bulbous, Grapevine design (Legras), Pink on gray $2000
Vase, 17″ tall, Grapevines design (D'Argental), Burgundy on amber $2500
Vase, 17″ tall, mottling, Grape and Leaf design, Light orange with brown and green
.... $2250
Vase, 18″ tall, footed, Art Deco Floral design (La Verre Français), Multicolored on yellow and rust $2000
Vase, 19″ tall, footed, Geese design (La Verre Français), Brown on yellow . $2750
Vase, 22″ tall, cylindrically shaped (La Verre Français), Orange on light green floral top $3500
Vase, 33½″ tall, floral, signed (Galle), Dark tan to light orange $5500
Whiskey Tumbler, 2″ tall, floral $50
Wine glass, 8½″ tall, bell-shaped, Double Teardrop design (D'Argental), Cranberry to clear $450
Wine glass, teardrop stem Cut Hobstar and Fern pattern, Amethyst to clear $550

GALLE, EMILE   FRANCE, 1874–EARLY 1900s

Emile Galle was a designer, innovator, and leader of the Art Nouveau movement in Europe. He was noted most for helping to revive the art of cameo engraving in multiple layers. Galle was careful to sign all of his creations, which inspired others to do so. Occasionally, his signature is hidden within the design of the object. (See "French Cameo Glass" for additional listings.)

Biscuit jar with cover, 8″ tall, footed, Flower Blossom design, signed, Purple on light gray cameo $2250
Bowl, 4½″, dark green with enameled tropical flowers, signed $2000
Bowl, 8½″, pedestal base, signed $575
Bowl, 8″, ruffled, amber with enameled flowers and dragonflies, signed "Emile Galle Fecit," Amber $700
Bowl with cover, 6″, Seascape and Floral design, Swirled green $2500
Bowl, 7″ × 5″, oblong boat-shaped, brown design on peach to green cameo, tree and stream scene, signed $1750

Gallé glass. PHOTO BY MARK PICKVET. COURTESY OF THE CORNING MUSEUM OF GLASS.

Gallé bowl. COURTESY OF THE CORNING MUSEUM OF GLASS.

Champagne glass, 5¼″ tall, etched and enameled, signed $350
Chandelier, 9″ diameter, Dragonfly and Tulip design, signed, Cameo orange on light blue $7750
Compote, 4″, enameled pink flowers interior, Carved Leaf design exterior $1100
Compote, 6½″, enameled pink pods interior, frosted exterior with maple leaves $1250
Cup, footed, enameled, Thistle design, signed, Light amber $650
Decanter with handle and stopper, 8″ tall, amber with enameled Pink Thistle design, signed $1750
Decanter with stopper, 8¼″ tall, enameled lady in dress, signed "Galle" $2000
Decanter with stopper, 11¼″ tall, Apple Blossom and Dragonfly design $1500
Ewer, 8″ tall, amber with giliding and multicolored floral design, signed $2500
Ewer, 11¼″ tall, olive green with floral design $3500
Inkwell, 5¾″, layered amber with foliage design $1750
Lamp, 19¼″ tall, pelican design on bronze base, sprayed flower blossoms on shade, signed $11500

Lamp, 27″ tall, circular base, long stem, mushroom dome top with brass fixtures, shaded woodland scene, Red to white $12500

Lamp, candle, 7″ tall, pedestal stand, cameo floral design, signed, Multicolored $13000

Medallion, Napoleon profile, 3½″ diameter, signed $300

Perfume bottle with frosted stopper, 4½″ tall, Green Fern design, signed, Cameo green $2500

Perfume bottle with stopper, 4¾″ tall, enameled scene of man in boat on lake, signed $2250

Pitcher, 3″ tall, frosted handle, enameled Bleeding Hearts design, signed $1500

Pitcher, 3″ tall, green serpent handle, enameled red and brown floral design ... $2000

Ring tree, 11¾″ tall, crystal tree with enameled insects on base $1150

Saucer, enameled Thistle design, signed, Light amber $350

Shot glass, 2½″ tall, Maple Seed design, signed, Pink and green on frosted cameo $800

Tumbler, 4½″ tall, enameled Arabesques design, signed $275

Vase, 2″ tall, miniature, pinecone decoration, signed $250

Vase, 3¾″ tall, miniature, Floral design, signed, Blue and green $800

Vase, 4½″ tall, dark red with enameled green and gold lizard, signed "Galle" $600

Vase, 5″ tall, cabbage-shaped, signed $375

Vase, 5″ tall, scalloped, pinched sides, Oriental Algae and Starfish design, signed $8500

Vase, 6½″ tall, cameo violet on frosted to yellow shading, signed $1500

Vase, 7½″ tall, applied stems and flower blossoms, signed, Light mauve to pink shading $650

Vase, 7″ tall, frosted burnt orange and foliage design, signed $500

Vase, 8″ tall, signed, Light and dark mauve $750

Vase, 9½″ tall, various applied ceramic decorations, signed $550

Vase, 10″ tall, light tan with enameled floral design, signed $2000

Vase, 11½″ tall, hexagonal shape, brown and tan cameo foliage, signed ... $3750

Vase, 13¼″ tall, flask-shaped, Poppy Blossoms design, signed $8000

Vase, 14″ tall, Leaves, Berries, and Foliage design, signed $4500

Vase, 16¾″ tall, Chestnuts and Foliage design, signed $5000

Vase, 19½″ tall, Falling Maple Leaves design, signed $3250

Vase, 19″ tall, inverted cylinder, Lily design, signed, Tan on ice blue cameo .. $2250

Vase, 20¼″ tall, jack-in-the-pulpit style, Foliage and Flower Blossoms design, signed $9000

Vase, 20″ tall, circular base, Lilac Floral design, signed, Dark amethyst to yellow shading $4000

Vase, 24¾″ tall, Butterflies and Iris Blossoms design, signed $9500

Whiskey tumbler, 2¾″ tall, white, blue, and green cameo on crystal and pink background, 4-Petal Flower design, signed $800

GERMAN GLASS   20TH CENTURY

The listings below are for modern examples of German glass. Older items can be found in the entry "Bohemian Glass." Popular items include thimbles, crystal Hummels, and fancy steins.

Apple, 3¹/₂″ tall, 3″ diameter, long stem $25
Bowl, 5¹/₂″, 4¹/₄″ tall, crystal with a transparent blue and yellow bird figurine attached to rim $45
Bowl, salad, 10″, 5¹/₂″ tall, silver-plated base, Diamond and Oval pattern, Crystal ..
.... $30
Brandy snifter, 6¹/₂″ tall, Crystal $5
Candy dish with cover, 6³/₄″ tall, 5³/₄″ diameter, canopy-shaped, frosted embossed carousel horses, transparent gold ball finial on cover $50
Cat paperweight, 2″ tall, 3″ long, Amethyst $35
Egg, 3¹/₄″ tall, 12 oz., all-over floral design, Crystal with frosted blue finish $35
Hummel figurines, 2″ tall, (For Mother, Little Sweeper, March Winds, Sister, Soloist, or Village Boy) (Goebel), Frosted crystal $65
Hummel figurines, 3⁵/₈″ tall, (Apple Tree Girl, Merry Wanderer, The Postman, Visiting an Invalid) (Goebel), Frosted crystal $75
Hummel figurines, 3″ tall, (Apple Tree Girl, The Botanist, Meditation, Merry Wanderer, The Postman, Visiting an Invalid) (Goebel), Frosted crystal $75
Mug, barrel-shaped, Etched Grape and Leaf pattern, green handle, Crystal ... $10
Pear, 4″ tall, 2¹/₂″ wide, long stem $25
Photo frame, 11¹/₄″ × 9¹/₂″ rectangle, crystal with diamond and shell border .. $45
Pilsner glass, 9¹/₂″ tall, 14 oz., Crystal $6
Pitcher, water, Targon pattern, Carnival marigold $2000
Spittoon, Targon pattern, Carnival marigold $4000
Stein, 6¹/₂″ tall, pewter lid and finial on handle, engraved block cameos of various woodland wildlife, barrel-shaped, limited edition (500), Ruby red $275
Stein, 8¹/₂″ tall, pewter lid and finial on handle, with engraved fisherman in water and ducks, limited edition (250), Deep blue $300
Stein, 9¹/₂″ tall, pewter lid and finial on handle, with engraved stag and woodlands, Ruby red $225

German Edelweiss bird trinket box. PHOTO BY ROBIN RAINWATER.

Stein, 9¹/₂″ tall, pewter lid and finial on handle, Crystal with Engraved Royal Blossom, and Diamond pattern $125

Stein, 10¹/₂″ tall, pewter lid and finial on handle, with engraved floral design, limited edition (250) $250

Stein, 10³/₈″ tall, pewter lid and finial on handle, with etched Apple Tree and Garden design, Crystal $140

Thimble, 2″ tall, blown within a miniature antique milk bottle, Crystal $12

Thimble, Cut Diamond pattern, Crystal $20

Thimble, Cut Diamond pattern, gold base, Crystal $25

Thimble, gold-plated, etched floral design, Crystal $25

Thimble, lavender, light blue, ruby red, yellow, or amethyst with etched floral and grape design $20

Thimble, ruby-flashed crystal with etched hummingbird $25

Thimble, stein-shaped with gold-plated lid and handle, with Etched star design, Ruby-red or emerald green $20

Thimble, stein-shaped with gold-plated lid and handle, with etched star design and enameled gold floral design, Cobalt blue $20

Thimble, with 22 kt. gold floral design, Cobalt blue $30

Thimble, with engraved owl design, Crystal $25

Thimble, with engraved Swan design, Crystal $30

Thimble, with etched edelweiss flower, Crystal $17

Thimble, with handpainted Amish symbol, Crystal $25

Thimble, with handpainted floral design, Crystal $20

Thimble, with handpainted heart and leaves, Crystal $25

Thimble, with rainbow-colored glass decorations, Crystal $20

Tumbler, Targon pattern, Carnival marigold $500

Vase, 5¹/₄″ tall, with embossed swallows around glass, Opaque teal $45

Vase, 6¹/₂″ tall, heart-shaped top, grooved sides, (Gorham), Crystal $35

Vase, 8¹/₂″, fan-shaped, star and lovebird cuts, Crystal $35

Wine Glass, 6 oz., green base and stem, crystal bowl with gold rim and gold Leaf and Grape design $10

HUNGARIAN GLASS   20TH CENTURY

The most notable modern Hungarian products are colored cut crystal dinnerware, such as goblets, wine glasses, tumblers, bowls, and plates. Typical cut colors include ruby red, cobalt blue, emerald green, and amethyst. The colors are strong and sharp. Horchow is one current manufacturer of cut glass. Products can be found in boutiques and jewelry stores, and by mail through Bloomingdale's and Fifth Avenue Crystal.

Bell, 7¹/₂″ tall, 3¹/₂″ wide, Diamond and Fan cased cut crystal, Ruby red or cobalt blue $35

Bowl, 9¹/₄″, 6 scallops with 6 cut floral and leaf designs, Ruby red in cased crystal $150

Bowl, 9″, Cut Palmette pattern (diamond hex dots with large fans), Cobalt blue or ruby red $175

Bowl, rose, 5¹/₂″ diameter, 4¹/₂″ tall, Cut Astor pattern, emerald green, cobalt blue, amethyst, or ruby red $50

Cordial, 2 oz., Cut Essex pattern (Diamond and Fan variation), emerald green, cobalt blue, amethyst, or ruby red $25
Goblet, 8¼″ tall, with green stem, frosted wavy leaves on Bowl, Crystal $12
Goblet, 10 oz., crystal cut fluted stem, cut cased crystal and cobalt blue floral patterned bowl $100
Tumbler, 5½″ tall, Cut Fan pattern, Various colors $35
Tumbler, 8″ tall, Cut Fan pattern, Various colors $40
Wine glass, 6½ oz., crystal cut fluted stem, cut cased crystal and cobalt blue floral patterned bowl $100

IRISH GLASS   18TH CENTURY–PRESENT

Glassware has been produced in Ireland for centuries, and much has been exported to the United States. The most famous manufacturer is Waterford (see separate listing), but the cities of Cork and Dublin also boast large factories. A few of the newest rivals to Waterford's cut crystal are Tipperary, Galway, and Kerry Glass.

Apple, 3¼″ tall, crystal with 40 shades of green (Kerry) $40
Bell, 6″ tall, green with crystal handle, engraved Claddagh design (Duiske of Ireland) $35
Biscuit jar with cover, 8″ tall, crystal with diamond cuts (Galway) $90
Bowl, 4¾″, crystal with diamond cuts (Tipperary) $40
Candleholder, 6″ long, Aladdin's lamp style, crystal with diamond and straight cuts (Tipperary) $40
Candy dish, 4⅛″ tall, footed, crystal cut diamond and fan design (Tipperary) $25
Chandelier, 24″ tall, 21″ wide, crystal with cut diamonds, 5 light, brass fittings ...
.... $1750
Clock, miniature grandfather, 4½″ tall, crystal diamond cuts (Galway) $70
Cornucopia nut dish, footed, crystal with diamond and oval cuts (Galway) .. $75
Creamer, 4″ tall, 10 oz., Pitcher style, crystal with cross cuts, (Tipperary) ... $40
Dolphin figure, 5″ long, 2½″ tall, crystal and sapphire blue swirled design ... $35
Football, 3¾″ long, crystal with cut threads (Tipperary) $100
Globe, 4¾″ tall, crystal with etched continents, diamond cut crystal base (Cavan Crystal) $140
Mug, coffee, 5½″ tall, 8 oz., low handle, crystal with etched harp, shamrocks, and "Irish Coffee" $20
Paperweight, 3½″ tall, oval-globe shape, ocean blue swirled design (Kerry) .. $30
Paperweight, 4½″ tall, oval-globe shape, crystal with 40 shades of green swirls (Kerry) $30
Paperweight, 4″ tall, slender oval egglike shape, crystal with 40 shades of green and a stone from Blarney $50
Pig figurine, 3½″ long, 2″ tall, crystal with 40 shades of green swirls $40
Pinecone, 3¾″ tall, crystal, rough-edged faceted diamond cuts $100
Pitcher, water, 7¾″ tall, 20 oz., crystal with fan cuts (Tipperary) $75
Plate, 8¼″, diamond cuts with etched Claddagh coat of arms (Galway) $85
Sherbet, 4¾″ tall, crystal with etched shamrocks $35
Slipper, 3″ tall, 6⅛″ long (Tipperary) $45
Tumbler, 12 oz., old-fashioned style, crystal with etched shamrocks $8
Tumbler, 3″ tall, 9 oz., Cashel pattern (Tipperary) $25
Tumbler, 4¾″ tall, 5 oz., footed, crystal with fan cuts (Tipperary) $30

Irish Kerry glass paperweight. PHOTO BY
ROBIN RAINWATER.

Vase, 3″ tall, crystal with diamond and oval cuts (Tipperary) $25
Vase, 5″ tall, crystal with diamond and fan cuts (Tipperary) $40
Vase, 7″ tall, castle-shaped, crystal cut diamond and fan cuts (Tipperary) $75
Vase, 8″ tall, crystal with cut diamonds and leaves (Galway) $70
Wine Goblet, 8 oz., crystal with etched harps $10

LALIQUE GLASS RENÉ LALIQUE, FRANCE, LATE 19TH CENTURY–PRESENT

René Lalique worked in the 1890s as a jeweler making paste glass jewelry. He was
contracted by the perfumer M.F. Coty to design perfume bottles. As a result of his
innovative glass creations, Lalique soon became France's premier designer.
Lalique's figure glass is usually made of quality lead crystal and is frosted or enameled, although a few rare items were produced in black. The figures are often
formed into useful objects and may be molded or blown in several identical views.
Figures also may be cameo engraved, heavily etched, and contain smooth acidized
or pearlized finishes. Dating is a big problem with Lalique glass. Older molds have
been reused, but some signed marks are helpful. Until his death in 1945, most were
marked "R. Lalique." The "R″ was dropped later. Other pieces may be signed
"R. Lalique, France."

Ashtray, 4½″ long, 8 girls' faces around the edge $125
Ashtray, 5½″ long, Fish with Bubbles design, signed "R. Lalique" $250
Ashtray, mouse in center, signed "R Lalique, France," Yellow $425
Beaker, 4″ tall, 6 panels of classical standing figures $175
Bell with finch finial $175
Birds, flying, 12″ tall, framed, signed "R. Lalique." $2750
Birds, love, menu holder, framed, signed "R. Lalique" $275
Bowl, 8″, berry foot, gray, Mistletoe design, signed "R. Lalique" $350
Bowl, 8″, opalescent blue, nude design in relief $775
Bowl, 8″, opalescent, mermaids design $1600
Bowl, 9½″, Dahlias design, signed "R. Lalique, France," Opal $950
Bowl, 9½″, Fish and Waves design, signed "R. Lalique, France," Opal $975
Bowl, 9½″, footed, Dog and Foliage design, signed "R. Lalique, France" $975

Bowl, 10″, Opal Peacock Feather design, signed "R. Lalique, France" $1000

Bowl, 10″, amber finish, Black Flower design, signed "R. Lalique, France" ... $1100

Bowl, 12″, Fish and Bubbles design $750

Bowl, 14¼″, calypso, nude maidens in the sea $1750

Bowl, ivy, 14″ diameter, globe-shaped, frosted and Green Maple Leaf design ....
.... $1000

Bowl, rose, 5¾″, frosted, ball-shaped, flower blooms and stems $300

Box, 4″ diameter, Black Rooster and Wheat design, signed "Lalique" (without original box $4250) $6500

Box with cover, 5½″, enameled black with molded Dahlia cover, signed .. $1500

Buffalo figurine, 4½″ tall, frosted $275

Candelabrum, 4-light, Brown Pheasants design $2250

Candlestick, 6″ tall, embossed geometric designs, signed $275

Cat, crouching, 9″ long, satin frosted finish, signed $600

Cat, sitting, 8¼″ tall, satin frosted finish $250

Lalique glass.
PHOTO BY MARK
PICKVET.

Lalique glass. PHOTO BY
MARK PICKVET.

Lalique glass. PHOTO BY ROBIN RAINWATER.

Lalique angel fish. PHOTO BY ROBIN RAINWATER.

Chalice, 9¹/₂″ tall, oval bowl with foliage design, signed. $325
Chandelier, 14″ diameter, bowl form with 4 chains framed design, signed "R. Lalique" $3750
Clock, pendulum, 4¹/₂″ square, nudes, signed "R. Lalique" $2750
Cockatoo Figurine, 11³/₄″ tall, satin frosted finish $2250
Falcon mascot, 6″ tall, framed, signed "R. Lalique" $1100
Fish, 2″ tall 2¹/₈″ long, various frosted colors, signed "Lalique France" $110
Fish, 5″ tall, polished crystal $80
Gazelle Bookends, 4″ × 4″, leaping gazelles $400
Girl, 4″ tall, nude with goat, signed "Lalique" $350
Hood ornament, 3⁷/₈″ tall, fish design, frosted, signed "R. Lalique France" $4000
Hood ornament, 4⁵/₈″ tall, eagle's head $1750
Hood ornament, 5¹/₄″ long, kneeling nude with flowing hair $3500
Hood ornament, 5″ tall, Rearing Horse design $5000
Hood ornament, 6¹/₄″ long, Frosted Dragonfly design $5500
Hood ornament, 7¹/₂″ tall, Frosted Nude design $7500
Hood ornament, 7¹/₄″ long, light amethyst Rooster design $6000
Hood ornament, 7³/₄″ long, Greyhound design $2000
Hood ornament, 8″ long, frosted yellow Dragonfly design $6000
Inkwell, 6″ diameter, spiraled serpents, signed "R. Lalique" $4000

Jardiniere, 5¼″ diameter, 2 antelope-designed handles $2750
Lamp, 16½″ tall, square base and stem, brown to light tan peacock design, light tan floral shade, signed "Lalique" $7500
Lizard figurine, 6½″ tall, green $275
Mascot, 5″ tall, kneeling nudes bending backward, signed "R. Lalique, France" . .
. . . .$4500
Nude woman figurine, 13½″ tall, satin frosted finish, signed $450
Owl figurine, 3″ tall $130
Paperweight, eagle head, 4½″, amber $1350
Paperweight, owl, 3½″, frosted $155
Perfume bottle, 10 ½″ tall, with kneeling nude garlanded stopper, light amber floral design $1000
Perfume bottle with ball stopper, 8″ tall, disk form, Nina Ricci brand $275
Perfume bottle with stopper, 3½″ tall, framed crystal, Deux Fleurs brand, signed "R. Lalique" $450
Perfume bottle with stopper, 4½″ tall, 4 paneled turtles with heads back $6500
Perfume bottle with stopper, 6″ tall, footed, framed design, Roses brand, signed "R. Lalique" $750
Perfume bottle with stopper, 6″ tall, transparent brown finish, Coty Amber Antique brand, signed "R. Lalique" $1350
Perfume bottle with stopper, 7″ tall, black enamel, Forvil Le Parfum brand, signed "R. Lalique, France" $850
Plate, 8″, engraved hunting dog, signed "Lalique" $525
Plate, 9″, Opalescent Seashell design $1100
Plate, collector, 1965 . . . . $1100
Plate, collector, 1967 . . . . $250
Plate, collector, 1968 through 1976 . . . . $135
Plate, collector, 8½″, 1966, Dream Rose pattern $375
Powder box with cover, 3⅝″ diameter, dancing Nudes and Garland design $400
Rooster mascot, 8″ tall, framed, signed "R. Lalique, France" $725
Seal, 5¼″ tall, frosted on jagged clear crystal base $1000
Sparrow, 4¼″ long, satin frosted finish $135
Tray, 15½″, oval, clear and frosted carnation blossoms design $1100
Vase, 4¾″ tall, 4″ wide, Dampierre design $400
Vase, 5¼″ tall, male nudes in base "holding up" vessel $3000
Vase, 5″ tall, bulbous, Fish design $875
Vase, 5″ tall, footed, frosted swirled body with 2 applied doves $250
Vase, 6¾″ tall, globe-shaped, swimming fish with lengthy fins and tails $375
Vase, 6″ tall, black on opal coloring, Band of Rabbits design, signed "R. Lalique"
. . . . $1600
Vase, 7¼″ tall, 6 Nudes Holding Urns design $2500
Vase, 7″ tall, frosted, Nesting Birds design $400
Vase, 7″ tall, globe-shaped, blue, Fern Leaf design, signed "R. Lalique" . . . $1350
Vase, 7″ tall, globe-shaped, frosted, Antelope design, signed $400
Vase, 8½″ tall, blue opal, Snail Shell design, signed "R. Lalique, France" $2500
Vase, 8″ tall, 2 Doves design, signed "Lalique" $425
Vase, 8″ tall, gray, Ibex and Floral design, signed "R. Lalique, France" $1850
Vase, 9½″ tall, 6 alternating panels of female nudes $4500
Vase, 9½″ tall, globe-shaped, dark gray, Large Fish design, signed "R. Lalique"
. . . . $20500
Vase, 9½″ tall, opal, 4 pairs of lovebirds, signed "R. Lalique, France" $3500

Vase, 9¼" tall, globe-shaped, All-over Molded Fish design $2000
Vase, 10" tall, bulbous, amber, Coiled Serpent design, signed "R. Lalique" ... $18500
Vase, 10" tall, frosted, Naked Maidens design around vase $5500
Vase, 10" tall, ovoid shape, Framed Archers design $4500
Vase, 10" tall, smoke-colored Eagles and Feathers design $3750
Vase, 11" tall, tapered neck, frosted, Mythological Creatures design $1750
Vase, 13¼" tall, black, Alligator and Pineapple Branch design, signed "R. Lalique,"
.... $13500
Wine glass, 6" tall, crystal and frosted, dancing nudes on stem $200
Yorkshire terrier, 2½" tall, frosted $350

LISMORE　　WATERFORD CRYSTAL LTD., IRELAND, 1951–PRESENT

"Lismore" is one of Waterford's most popular cut patterns. For other items, see the Waterford listings near the end of this chapter. A recently introduced item is the Village Collection, including cottages, schoolhouses, churches, and other buildings (more are planned for the future).

Bell, 3" tall, ring handle $50
Biscuit jar with cover, 7" tall $150
Bowl, 4", 2¼" tall $40
Bowl, 5" $70
Bowl, 9½" $140
Brandy snifter $50
Cake shop, Village Collection, 2" tall, 2½" long $75
Carafe, wine, 22 oz. $150
Champagne glass $40
Church, Village Collection, 4" tall, 4" long $85
Claret glass $40
Cordial glass $30
Cottage, Village Collection, 2" tall, 3½" long $75
Creamer, pitcher-style, 3" tall $50
Decanter, ship with faceted stopper, 9½" tall $275
Decanter, whiskey, 10" tall $275
Decanter, wine $225
Honey jar with cover, 4⅛" tall $85
Hotel, Village Collection, 3" tall, 3" long $75
Perfume bottle with brass top and atomizer, 4½" tall $80
Pitcher, milk, 24 oz. $140
Post office, Village Collection, 1½" tall, 2¼" long $75
Salt and pepper shakers, 6" tall, round feet, silver-plated tops $125
Sauce boat, 8 oz., small cup-pitcher style $60
Schoolhouse, Village Collection, 2½" tall $75
Sherbet $50
Shot glass, 1.6 oz., 2½" tall $30
Sugar Bowl, 1¾" tall $35
Sugar shaker with silver-plated top, 8" tall $70
Surgery, Village Collection, 2" tall $75
Tumbler, 5 oz. $30

Tumbler, 9 oz., old-fashioned style $35
Tumbler, 10 oz. $40
Tumbler, 10 oz., iced tea, footed $50
Tumbler, 12 oz., old-fashioned style $40
Vase, 8¹/₂″ tall, round base $100
Vase, 9″ tall, wedge and olive cuts $175
Vase, bud, 4″ tall $45
Wine glass, 10 oz. $60
Wine glass, oversized $95
Wine glass, red or white $40

LOETZ GLASS   AUSTRIA, 1840s–EARLY 1900s

The original Loetz Glassworks was founded in 1840 in Western Austria (Kloster-
mule). The company earned a reputation early on as a maker of high-quality glassware. During the Art Nouveau period, it produced iridescent glass similar to that of
Carder at Steuben and Tiffany. Other Loetz originals include threaded glass and
cameo designs. Identification can be difficult since much of Loetz's work was not
signed. Cheaper imitation iridescent glass has sometimes been attributed to Loetz.

Basket, 9″ tall, lilac and green spotted design with flower prunts $225
Basket, 10″ tall, amber with iridescent blue threading, prunt handle $875
Basket, bride's, red with enameled designs, silver holder $775
Biscuit jar with cover, square shape, Iridescent pink $500
Bowl, 2¹/₂″, miniature, green papillon with silver deposit $375
Bowl, 6¹/₂″, ruffled, 3 applied purple handles $125
Bowl, 9¹/₂″, scalloped, iridescent gold leaf design $525
Bowl, 9″, ruffled, Iridescent purple $400
Bowl, 12″, applied glass decoration, Iridescent gold $600
Bowl, rose, 4¹/₂″, staghorn base, green with purple threading $400
Bowl, rose, 4″, iridescent shades of red $100
Candlestick, 10″ tall, Red and Green Fern design $300

Loetz glass. PHOTO BY ROBIN RAINWATER.

Chalice, 5½" tall, Teardrop design, Iridescent blue-green $2750
Cookie jar with silver-plated cover, Pink Florette design $400
Epergne, 4 Green Trumpet Style Lilies and Small Baskets design $625
Ewer, 6" tall, iridescent green with applied handles $550
Jar with cover, 8" diameter, cameo floral design, signed "Loetz" $775
Lamp, candle, 12" tall, gold spotted shade and base, red and green leaves design
. . . . $775
Lamp, table, 20" tall, bronze serpent base, iridescent threaded green globe shade
. . . . $5250
Perfume bottle with stopper, 5½" tall, silver accents, iridescent green with white
threading $500
Pitcher, 5½" tall, square top, ribbed handle, iridescent white crackle $575
Pitcher, syrup with silver-plated lid, 8" tall, Iridescent cobalt blue $1050
Toothpick holder, silver overlay $225
Vase, 4½" tall, signed "Loetz," Iridescent silver to blue $575
Vase, 5" tall, signed "Loetz," Iridescent gold $350
Vase, 6½" tall, Blue and Platinum Wave design, Iridescent yellow to gold $1850
Vase, 6½" tall, green with blue serpent around neck $500
Vase, 6" tall, Iridescent green $175
Vase, 6" tall, Lily Pad design, signed "Loetz," Iridescent blue to gold $600
Vase, 6" tall, pinched sides, Iridescent blue $600
Vase, 6" tall, signed "Loetz," Iridescent gold $375
Vase, 6" tall, signed "Loetz," Iridescent purple to silver $400
Vase, 7" tall, bottle form, Applied Iridescent Grape design $200
Vase, 7" tall, 13" diameter, 3-lobed rim, Swirls and Spots design, Iridescent green to
silver to blue $1600
Vase, 8" tall, pedestal base, Iridescent bronze $250
Vase, 8" tall, pinched sides, Iridescent Blue Swirl Design $625
Vase, 8" tall, ruffled, opalescent green swirl $200
Vase, 9¼" tall, Bronzed Leaf and Floral design on green cameo $1850
Vase, 9¾" tall, pinched, ribbed, Iridescent gold $850
Vase, 9" tall, bronze holder, ruffled, Iridescent Gold Wavy design $1750
Vase, 9" tall, pinched sides, iridescent blue to gold with pink highlights $675
Vase, 10½" tall, swirled onyx design $1000
Vase, 10" tall, iridescent gold with silver overlay $1200
Vase, 11" tall, iridescent bronze with purple threading $1250
Vase, 12½" tall, Iridescent blue to green $675
Vase, 12" tall, Iridescent dark blue to light blue $775
Vase, 12" tall, floral decoration, Iridescent gold $625
Vase, 12" tall, ruffled, Blue with pink interior $325
Vase, 12" tall, ruffled, Iridescent crystal with pink interior $300
Vase, 13¼" tall, bronzed leaves on yellow $2250
Vase, 13" tall, amber with gold and rose decoration $350
Vase, 14" tall, Butterfly and Floral design, Green on gray cameo $1750
Vase, 19" tall, Iridescent Blue and Silver Peacock design $1750

MEXICAN GLASS   1920s–PRESENT

One factory known to produce a little Carnival glass was Cristales de Mexico. The company's products usually have an "M" within a "C" mark on the underside. The Oklahoma and Ranger water sets appear to be a close copy of Imperial Glass Company's original designs. Modern Mexican designs include chili peppers, and transparent colored trims, such as emerald green and cobalt blue.

Candleholder, footed, 4¹/₂″ tall, Cross and Bleeding Heart pattern, Carnival marigold and green $500
Cruet, 4¹/₄″ tall, 6″ diameter, crystal, ruby or chili pepper stopper with green stem, crystal applied handle, pitcher-shaped $30
Cruet, crystal, ruby or emerald green chili pepper stopper with green stem, no handle, carafe-shaped $30
Decanter with dolphin finial stopper, 11¹/₂″ tall, Crystal $60
Donkey and cart, 9³/₈″ long, 4¹/₈″ tall, milk glass reproduction $35
Goblet, 16 oz., circular base, thick stem, Cobalt blue $10
Pitcher, water, crystal with emerald green rim and lip, applied emerald green handle $30
Pitcher, water, Oklahoma pattern, Carnival marigold $500
Shot glass, 2³/₄″ tall, crystal with emerald green or cobalt blue trim $10
Stirrer (for crystal pitcher above with emerald green accents), green cactus at end $10
Tumbler, emerald green rim, green saguaro cactus stem (matches pitcher and stirrer above) $20
Tumbler, water, Oklahoma pattern, Carnival marigold $250
Tumbler, water, Ranger pattern, Carnival marigold $125

MID-EASTERN GLASS   1980s–PRESENT

Although glassmaking first developed in Egypt thousands of years ago, older pieces, particularly ancient glass of the region, are rarely offered for sale. Modern examples are now available in the collector's market. The Israeli pieces listed here are made by David Barak in his studio in Herzlia, Israel.

Bowl, 3″, silver decoration at top, cinnamon red, dark green, or ultramarine, Israel $55
Bowl, 5″, silver decoration at top, cinnamon red, dark green, or ultramarine, Israel $100
Creamer, 4¹/₂″ tall, silver handle and decoration at top, cinnamon red, dark green, or ultramarine, Israel $75
Menorah, crystal ice sculpture with mountainous Jerusalem landscape, slots for 9 candles $100
Perfume bottle, with red and blue female figural stopper, handblown, fluted, blue and red diamond design, Egypt $35
Perfume bottle with amethyst and crystal stopper, handblown, amethyst with gold lines and etched vining $40
Perfume bottle with gold stopper, 4¹/₄″ tall, handblown, Egypt, Amber with gold accents $35

Egyptian perfume bottle. PHOTO BY ROBIN RAINWATER.

Perfume bottle with gold stopper, 5½" tall, handblown, Egypt, Amber with gold accents $35

Perfume bottle with gold stopper, 5½" tall, handblown, Egypt, Rose red with gold accents $40

Perfume bottle with gold stopper, 5" tall, handblown, Egypt, Ruby red with gold floral accents $35

Perfume bottle with gold stopper, 6½" tall, handblown, Egypt, Aquamarine with gold accents $40

Salt cellar, 2" tall, silver overlay decoration, cinnamon red, dark green, or ultramarine, Israel $55

Sugar, 5" tall, silver lid and decoration at top, cinnamon red, dark green, or ultramarine, Israel $75

Vase, 6½" tall, silver stem and trailings, cinnamon red, dark green, or ultramarine, Israel $80

Vase, 6" tall, silver stem and trailings, cinnamon red, dark green, or ultramarine, Israel $75

Vase, 8" tall, silver stem and trailings, cinnamon red, dark green, or ultramarine, Israel $95

Vase, 9½" tall, silver stem and trailings, cinnamon red, dark green, or ultramarine, Israel $125

Vase, 9" tall, 2-handled, opaque frosted blue with seals on the handles, Tehran, Iran $50

Vase, 12" tall, silver stem and trailings, cinnamon red, dark green, or ultramarine, Israel $275

MILLEFIORI GLASS Venice, Italy, 19th Century–Present

Millefiori (Italian for "thousand flowers") is a glass technique in which tiny multi-colored glass disks are embedded in the surface of an object to produce a mosaic effect. The disks are made by slicing fused glass canes or cylindrical rods. These cross sections are in turn arranged in a pattern, refired, and shaped into the desired item. The pieces listed below are Venetian from the late 19th to mid 20th centuries. Very few America pieces are made in this way (Carder's "Tessera" is one example).

Basket with red and white twist handle, 4¹/₄" diameter, solid millefiori
(no capacity) $750
Bowl, 4", 2 applied crystal handles, Blue and white canes $90
Bowl, 6", brass holder $225
Bowl, finger, 2", 2 applied crystal handles, Pink, green, and white canes $65
Bowl, finger, 3", Blue ground $100
Creamer, 4" tall, scattered design on white ground $225
Cruet with stopper, 5" tall, all-over millefiori including handle and stopper . . . $425
Cup, 2¹/₄" tall $85
Egg shape, 3" tall, multicolored millefiori $50
Epergne, 16" tall, bowl with 3 ruffled trumpet style vases $325
Goblet, 7¹/₂" tall, crystal stem and base, multicolored canes $225
Lamp, 7" tall, dome shade, millefiori shade and base $350
Lamp, 10" tall, shade and base in lavender cane form $450
Lamp, 19" tall, 9" diameter dome shade, millefiori shade and base $850
Letter opener, glass, 6³/₄" long, multicolored millefiori handle, silver blade $75
Magnifying glass, 5" long, multicolored millefiori handle, crystal lens enclosed in
silver circle $85
Paperweight, 2¹/₂" diameter, multicolored millefiori black Rosone design $75
Paperweight, 2¹/₂" diameter, multicolored millefiori Fish design $75
Paperweight, 3", all-over Crowned design $125
Paperweight, 3", pink center with turquoise canes, Gold Dust design $75
Pitcher, water, 8" tall, crystal circular base and applied crystal handle with gold
leafing, multicolored millefiori $200
Saucer (matches cup above) $55

Millefiore glass. COURTESY OF THE CORNING MUSEUM OF GLASS.

Sugar with cover, 4″ tall, Blue $275
Toothpick holder, 2³/₄″ tall, Blue ground $100
Tumbler, 4″ tall, blue and green millefiori design $175
Tumbler, 4″ tall, 9 oz., multicolred millefiori design (matches pitcher above) ... $65
Vase, 4¹/₂″ tall, handkerchief style, multicolored canes $150
Vase, 4″ tall, miniature, Blue ground $175
Vase, 6¹/₄″ tall, cobalt blue with multicolored canes $250
Vase, 8″ tall, Blue ground $775
Vase, 8″ tall, 2-handled, millefiori in curving rows $400
Vase, 8″ tall, ruffled, applied crystal handle, multicolored canes $275
Vase, 15″ tall, Assymetrical Tilted design, pierced hole, polychrome patchwork ..
.... $4000
Vase, Dragonfly with Netting design, signed $875
Vase, ruffled, Violet ground $225

Millefiore paperweights. PHOTO BY ROBIN RAINWATER.

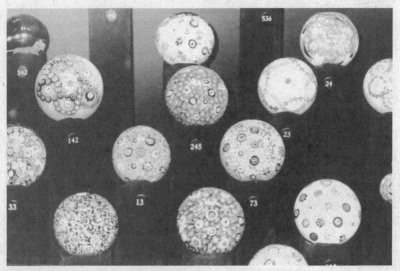

Millefiore paperweights. PHOTO BY ROBIN RAINWATER.

MOSER GLASS   CZECHOSLOVAKIA, 1850s–PRESENT

The original Moser Glass was founded by Leo Moser in Karlsbad (Karlovy-Vary), Czechoslovakia. Moser began his career by doing commissioned portrait engraving on glass for wealthy patrons of health spas. In his own factory, he further developed artistic forms, including Alexandrite colored glass (separate from Webb's), carved animal forms (especially birds in flight), carved floral designs, and gold leaf and other enameling. Items marked "Malachite" are characterized by swirled layers of dark green shades.

Basket, 5½" tall, Green Cherub design, Malachite $400
Basket, 6" tall, 6½" diameter, Woman and Cherubs design, marked "Moser/Carlsbad," Malachite $250
Bowl, 5", cut panels, signed "Moser-Alexandrite" $275
Box with hinged cover, 3" tall 4" diameter, nude woman on cover, marked "Moser/Carlsbad," Malachite $200
Box with hinged cover, 5¾", gold vines, Cranberry $200
Candlestick, 4" tall, signed, Amethyst $125
Candlestick, 14" tall, cranberry overlay with gilded scrolls $750
Chalice, 6¾" tall, gold leaves design, Amethyst to crystal $725
Compote, blue and crystal floral decoration, gold rim $175
Cruet with stopper, 5" tall $325
Decanter with stopper, 12½" tall, gold grapes, Cranberry $675
Decanter with stopper, 16" tall, applied prunts and glass jewels $600
Ewer, 6" tall, green with multicolored enameled Fern design $625
Ewer, 9" tall, cornucopia-shaped, pedestal base $1200
Ewer, 11½" tall, multicolored beads, enameled floral design $850
Ewer, 12" tall, multicolored leaves on amber base, blue handle $950
Perfume bottle with cut stopper, 3" tall, amethyst Prism Cut design $325
Perfume bottle with stopper, 4½" tall, cobalt blue with gold figures $200
Perfume bottle with stopper, 10" tall, crystal with heavy gold decoration $575
Pitcher, water, 7" tall, crackle glass with multicolored enameled Fish and Seaweed design $350
Pitcher, water, 8¼" tall, footed, amber with blue trim $475
Pitcher, water, 10" tall, 4 gilded feet, green with multicolored (including gold) floral and scroll design $650
Tumbler, 4 ¼" tall, cranberry with gold floral design $125
Urn, 14" tall, white to cranberry cut, enameled floral with gold $850
Vase, 3½" tall, miniature, Amethyst $150
Vase, 3" tall, gold bands, enameled Oriental Woman design, Cobalt blue ... $200
Vase, 5" tall, gold foliage with enameled acorns and oak leaves $275
Vase, 5" tall, nude woman and floral design, marked "Moser/Carlsbad," Malachite
.... $175
Vase, 6½" tall, gold rim, Engraved Tulips design, Amethyst $400
Vase, 7" tall, Enameled Floral design, Amber and blue $775
Vase, 8¾" tall, smoke crackle, enameled Orchid design $850
Vase, 8" tall, 6" diameter, 4-footed, blue floral design with gold scrolling $1200
Vase, 9½" tall, ruffled, pink flowers with gilding $250
Vase, 9½" tall, Nude Woman and Grapes design, marked "Moser/Carlsbad," Malachite $275
Vase, 10" tall, gold trim, birds and lily pads design, Amethyst $550

Vase, 10″ tall, bulbous, signed, Cobalt blue $200
Vase, 10″ tall, dark amber with enameled Elephant design $750
Vase, 10″ tall, handled, overall enamel design, signed $700
Vase, 10″ tall, 3″ diameter, Cameo Poppy design $2750
Vase, 11¹/₂″ tall, crystal with intaglio engraved purple flowers $825
Vase, 11″ tall, gold rim, engraved elephants and palm trees, Cobalt blue ... $2250
Vase, 12¹/₂″ tall, blue with multicolored enameled flowers, butterflies, and bees ...
....$325
Vase, 12¹/₂″ tall, Raised Scroll design with applied metal bees, signed $625
Vase, 13″ tall, cobalt blue to white shading, multicolored enameled floral design,
gold trim $750
Vase, 15″ tall, flared, crystal to green with Engraved Floral design $925
Vase, 16″ tall, green with multicolored enameled pink and blue floral design .....
....$1150
Vase, 20″ tall, trumpet form, gold feet and border, light purple with enameled nude
design $1200
Vase, 22″ tall, handled, emerald green with gold leaves, Dutchman in Reserve
design $1750
Whiskey tumbler, 3″ tall, cranberry with gold grapes $125

NAILSEA GLASS   ENGLAND, LATE 18TH CENTURY–PRESENT

This glass obtained its name from the small town of Nailsea, England. Although
there is a Nailsea Glass House, other companies also produced the style. The style
is characterized by colored or crystal glass decorated with contrasting loops, swirls,
or spirals. It spread to other parts of England and even to the United States.

Bottle, bellows, 11″ long, crystal with pink and white loopings $125
Bowl, 4¹/₄″ tall, 2¹/₄″ tall, citron with white looping $125
Bowl, finger, 4″, crystal with blue and white streaking $100
Bowl, finger, 4¹/₂″, 4-fold rim, chartreuse with white loopings $90
Candlestick, 10″ tall, bulb stem, cone-shaped base, crystal with white loopings ...
.... $175
Cologne bottle, 5³/₈″ tall, milk white with blue and cranberry loopings, crystal
stopper with blue, pink, and white loopings $525
Flask, 6¹/₂″ tall, milk white with dark blue loopings $150
Flask, 7¹/₄″ tall, crystal with cranberry and white loopings $175
Flask, 7³/₈″ tall, cobalt blue with white loopings $175
Lamp, 6″ tall, ruffled base, blue with white loopings $525
Lamp, 7″ tall, blue shade with white loopings $650
Mug, 5¹/₂″ tall, crystal with blue and white loopings $350
Pitcher, water, 9¹/₂″ tall, applied crystal handle and feet, cranberry with white
loopings $1250
Powder horn novelty, 12″ long, light and dark blue shading with white loopings .
....$225
Rolling pin, 19″ long, crystal with pink loopings $200
Rolling pin, blue with white loopings $300
Salt dip, 3²/₄″ diameter, footed, crystal with white loopings $175
Vase, 4¹/₂″ tall, rolled edge, blue with white loopings $150
Witch ball, 4¹/₂″ diameter, crystal with thin white loopings $225

Nailsea glass. PHOTO BY ROBIN RAINWATER.

PEACHBLOW   THOMAS WEBB & SONS, ENGLAND, 1890s– EARLY 1900s

Peachblow was originally made in the United States and usually shades from a rose pink at the top to a white or grayish-white at the bottom. See the entry "Webb, Thomas & Sons."

Biscuit jar with cover, 6″ tall, Pine Needles and Butterfly design with gold decoration $1050
Bowl, 2¹/₂″, 3³/₄″ tall, Gold Butterfly and Pine Needles design $300
Bowl, rose, 2³/₄″, 3″ tall, 8-crimped $275
Cologne bottle with stopper, 5″ tall $625
Vase, 3³/₄″ tall, 2³/₄″ diameter, Gold Prunus design $375
Vase, 4¹/₂″ tall, Gold Flowers With Silver Centers design $525
Vase, 5³/₄″ tall, coralene Seaweed design $375
Vase, 5³/₄″ tall, 3″ diameter, Gold Floral and Insect design $375
Vase, 5″ tall, footed, applied crystal flowers and leaves $550
Vase, 6¹/₂″ tall, 3¹/₂″ diameter, Gold Prunus and Bee design $525
Vase, 6″ tall, ruffled, blue interior, Enameled Floral design $375
Vase, 7¹/₂″ tall, Gold and Purple Floral design $325
Vase, 7¹/₂″ tall, gold bands, Floral and Butterfly design $850
Vase, 7¹/₄″ tall, Gold Prunus design $375
Vase, 7″ tall, Gold Floral, Leaves, and Dragonfly design $775
Vase, 7″ tall, 4″ diameter, Gold Prunus design $375
Vase, 8¹/₂″ tall, Gold Branches with Blossoms and Leaves design $500
Vase, 8¹/₄″ tall, horizontal ribbing, white interior $350
Vase, 8″ tall, pinched sides, acid-cut $800
Vase, 8″ tall, slender, lined $725
Vase, 9⁷/₈″ tall, bottle-shaped, Gold Floral and Leaves design $550
Vase, 10″ tall, 6″ diameter, Gold Prunus design $775
Vase, 11³/₄″ tall, 5³/₄″ diameter, Clear Feet and Floral design $825
Vase, 15″ tall, 7″ diameter, rose shaded to pink, Gold Floral and Birds design . . . .
. . . .$1350

PEKING GLASS   CHINA, 1680–EARLY 20TH CENTURY

Glassware in China was made to resemble the more desirable porcelain. Glass was considered inferior to porcelain; however, Chinese artisans experimented with opaque glassware, including cameo designs. The name "Peking" is also atrributed to glassware made in other cities in China (such as Po-shan) whose final finish was applied in Peking factories. Look for modern glass that is reverse painted. In reverse painting, the mirror image is painted on the inside of the piece. Traditional Oriental themes (mountains, waterfalls, pagodas, bamboo stands, etc.) are common. Note that it is not a good idea to keep live plants or flowers, especially in water, in reverse painted objects. Natural materials can destroy the finish.

Bowl, 7″, Floral design, Blue on white cameo $250
Bowl, 7″, multicolored Flowers, Leaves, and Butterfly design on white cameo ....
....$350
Bowl with cover, 7¹/₂″, Bird on Floral Branches design, Red on white cameo .. $425
Bowl, 11″, ribbed, multicolored Floral Cameo design $375
Bowl, rose, 3³/₄″ tall, 4¹/₂″ diameter, frosted, reverse painted with multicolored Oriental designs $50
Candlestick, 6″ tall, dragon foot, green cased center with oak leaf top $150
Cup, 3¹/₂″ tall, flared, dragon and cloud design, Blue on white cameo $275
Snuff bottle, 2¹/₄″ tall, white with green Floral design $125
Snuff bottle, 3″ tall, sailing ship with painted peony, Green on white cameo ... $375
Tumbler, Shanghai pattern, Carnival marigold color $75
Urn with cover, teakwood stand, blue and white floral stand $275
Vase, 3¹/₂″ tall, pink floral design on white cameo $1000
Vase, 6″ tall, Butterflies and Peony design, Red on white cameo $200
Vase, 7″ tall, reverse painted with multicolored Oriental scenery, Frosted $75
Vase, 8¹/₂″ tall, bulbous, Floral design, Red on white cameo $300
Vase, 8″ tall, cameo yellow floral design on white $275
Vase, 8″ tall, Dragonfly and Water Lily design, Teal on white cameo $300
Vase, 9¹/₄″ tall, butterfly and peony design, Yellow on white cameo $325
Vase, 9¹/₄″ tall, Monkey in Pine Tree design, Red on white cameo $325
Vase, 9″ tall, Raven and Pine Tree design, Green on white cameo $325

Chinese reverse painted rose bowl.
PHOTO BY ROBIN RAINWATER.

Peking glass. PHOTO BY ROBIN RAINWATER.

Vase, 9″ tall, Birds and Pine Tree design, Red on white cameo $325
Vase, 10¼″ tall, hexagonal, Floral Panel design, Red on white cameo $400
Vase, 10″ tall, Bird in Floral Tree design, Blue on white cameo $375
Vase, 10″ tall, gourd shape, peony design, Red on white cameo $375
Vase, 10″ tall, Monkey in Pine Tree design, Yellow on white cameo $375
Vase, 12½″ tall, Floral design, Red on white cameo $625
Vase, 12″ tall, bulbous, white with dark red Floral design $400
Vase, 12″ tall, Butterflies and Peonies design, Red on white cameo $550

PELOTON GLASS BOHEMIA (WESTERN CZECHOSLOVAKIA), 1880–EARLY 20TH CENTURY

This design was first patented by Wilhelm Kralick in 1880 and is characterized by short, random lengths and shapes of colored streaks (or threads) on an opaque base. The base is most often opal white. The streaking was added by rolling the threads directly into the base when the article was removed from the oven. Pieces were also further decorated by enameling.

Biscuit jar with cover, 6″ tall, multicolored threading on opal white $525
Biscuit jar with silver-plated cover and handle, 7¾″ tall, pink ribbed with white interior and multicolored strands $1250
Biscuit jar with silver-plated cover and handle, 7″ tall $650
Bowl, rose, 2½″, 6-crimped, multicolored threading on opal white $225
Bowl, rose, 2½″, 6-crimped, crystal feet, multicolored threading on lavender ... $225
Bowl, rose, 2½″, 6-crimped, wishbone feet, multicolored strings on cased pink ...
.... $225
Cruet with crystal stopper, 7″ tall, pastel filaments on light blue ground ... $325
Pitcher, water, 7½″ tall, clear and white threading, enameled Leaves and Floral design $450

Pitcher, water, 8″ tall, Blue and Green Shaded Butterfly design $1000
Pitcher, water, 8″ tall, crystal overshot style $400
Plate, 7″, single colors on a translucent ground $350
Vase, 3¹/₈″ tall, crystal with white threading $225
Vase, 3³/₄″ tall, 6-petal feet, 4-corner top, Multicolored Threaded design $325
Vase, 3″ tall, miniature, applied legs, Violet $300
Vase, 4″ tall, bulbous, ribbed, pastel strings on pink shading $575
Vase, 4″ tall, folded tricornered top, multicolored threading on opal white .. $400
Vase, 5³/₈″ tall, ruffled, yellow and white threading $350
Vase, 5″ tall, tricornered top, blue and white threading $350
Vase, 6³/₄″ tall, yellow with white interior and threading $400
Vase, 6″ tall, crimped, multicolored threading on crystal to lavender shading ... $450
Vase, 7″ tall, 5 wishbone feet, ribbed, multicolored threading on opal white $500
Vase, 8″ tall, tiny multicolored flaking on opal white $500
Vase, 9″ tall, multicolored threading on opal white $525
Vase, 13″ tall, multicolored threading on opal white $725

PERTHSHIRE PAPERWEIGHTS LTD.   CRIEFF, SCOTLAND, 1970–PRESENT

Although Perthshire has been in business only since 1970, already many of its limited editions are valued at over $500. It is only one of many companies that have sparked a revival in paperweight making and collecting.

Bowl, 4¹/₂″, blue rim, white vertical latticino bands, millefiori base $125
Inkwell, 7¹/₂″ tall, millefiori base and stopper $450
Paperweight, 2⁷/₈″, mill heart on red ground $200
Paperweight, 2⁷/₈″, opal blue ground, multicolored butterfly within a millefiori circle $775

Perthshire paperweights. PHOTO BY ROBIN RAINWATER, COURTESY OF THE BERGSTROM-MAHLER MUSEUM.

Paperweight, 3¹/₂″, seahorse and 2 fish, pink seaweed, crab, and shell $350
Paperweight, 3¹/₄″, thistles within stardust canes $400
Paperweight, 3¹/₈″, 86-petal dahlia in canes $675
Paperweight, 3″, pattern mill, central cane with ribbon twist and other canes $125
Paperweight, Panda, 3″, limited edition (300), Translucent blue $850
Perfume bottle with glass swirl threaded stopper, millefiori base $175
Shot glass, 2⁷/₈″ tall, 5-petal yellow lampwork flower on translucent blue ground ..
.... $85
Tumbler, millefiori base $100

POLISH GLASS   20TH CENTURY

The most notable modern Polish products are handcut crystal dinnerware, such as goblets, wine glasses, tumblers, bowls, jars, and plates. Occasionally, a colored piece can be found, but most of the work is completed with a good-quality shiny 24% lead crystal. Look for Polish products in fine gift stores, boutiques, and jewelry stores, and by mail order through such companies as Tyrol's and Fifth Avenue Crystal.

Basket, 9″ tall, crimped base, shell edge, cut crystal, Lily and Fan pattern ... $40
Bowl, 6″ tall, 8″ diameter, crimped base, shell edge, Cut Crystal Lily and Fan pattern $35
Bowl, 11″ oval, vertical line and hexagon-cube cuts, crystal $50
Bowl, rose, 5″ diameter, cut crystal Diamond and Fan pattern $25
Champagne glass, 7¹/₄″ tall, 2¹/₂″ width Bowl, crystal with Cut Optic pattern in lower bowl $10
Creamer, 6″ tall, pitcher style with handle and lip, circular base, crystal faceted and frosted design (matches sugar below) $25
Decanter with crystal ball stopper, 14″ tall, 6¹/₂″ wide, circular hole in center $50
Lamp, 13″ tall, 6¹/₂″ diameter circular base, brass accents, brass shell electric switch, cut diamonds and fluted circular base, large cut fans on lamp $125
Lamp, 29″ tall, cut diamonds and fluted circular base, fluted stem with hanging faceted prisms, 7¹/₂″ diameter globe with Engraved Floral design, crystal chimney
.... $300
Sherbet, 6″ tall, 4″ diameter bowl, teardrop stem $10
Sugar dish with cover, 7″ tall, no handles, ball stopper on cover, Crystal Faceted and Frosted design (matches creamer above) $25
Vase, 9″ tall, crimped base, shell edge, Cut Crystal Lily and Fan pattern $35
Vase, bud, 7″ tall, tapers wide at top, Cut Crystal Diamond design with engraved grape leaves $30
Vase, bud, 8″ tall, Crystal with Cut Spiral Pinwheel design $30

SABINO ART GLASS   FRANCE, 1920s–1930s, 1960s–1970s

Marius-Ernest Sabino first created a variety of Art Glass items (mostly figurines) in the 1920s. When the Art Nouveau period ended in the 1930s, Sabino stopped production. He resurfaced in the 1960s with his own handmade molds and a special formula for gold opalescent glass. Sabino died in 1971; his family continued exporting the glass but was unable to duplicate his original formula.

Bird, perched $70
Bird, wings down $80
Birds figure, 2 babies perched on branch $30
Birds figure, 3½″ tall, 4½″ across, 2 birds $235
Birds figure, 5 birds perched on branch $1275
Bowl, 5″, Fish design $80
Bunny rabbit, 2″ tall $40
Butterfly, 2¾″ tall, small, wings open $55
Butterfly, 6″ tall, (large) $35
Cat, 2¼″ tall, sitting $50
Cat, 2″ tall, sleeping $35
Cherub, 2″ tall $45
Chick, baby, 3¾″ tall, jumping, wings up $70
Chick, baby, drinking, wings down $55
Collie, 2″ tall $60
Dove, small, head up $40
Dragonfly, 6″ tall, 5¾″ long $160
Elephant $35
Figurine, Isadora Duncan $775
Figurine, nude with long flowing hair, 6¼″ tall $250
Figurine, Venus de Milo (large) $90
Fish, 2″ long $35
Fish, 4″ tall, 4″ long $85
Fox $35
Gazelle $110
German shepherd, 2″ tall $45
Hand, either left or right $250
Hen $40
Knife rest, Bee or Fish design $30
Mockingbird, large $110
Mouse, 3″ long $65
Owl, 4½″ tall $75
Pekingese, 1¼″ tall $40
Perfume bottle, 6¼″ tall, frivolities, Opal Women and Swans design $80
Perfume bottle, 6″ tall, loosely draped figures around bottle $80
Pigeon, 6¼″ tall $135
Poodle, 1¾″ tall $40
Rabbit, 1⅞″ long $40
Rooster, 3½″ tall $45
Rooster, large $500
Scottish terrier, 1½″ tall $100
Snail, 1″ tall, 3″ long $45
Squirrel, 3½″ tall, oval base $50

Stork, 7¼″ tall $150
Tray, shell (small) $45
Tray, swallow (small) $40
Turkey bookends (2 turkeys—one upright and one sitting on each bookend), pair
.... $500
Turtle $40
Vase, Oval and Pearl design $275
Vase, oval, Colombes design $525
Woodpecker $75
Zebra, 5½″ tall, 5½″ long $160

ST. LOUIS, FRANCE   1840s–EARLY 1900s, 1950s–PRESENT

The French classic period of paperweight manufacturing lasted from about 1845 to 1860. The factories in the town of St. Louis, such as Baccarat and Clichy, produced many items, then closed during the later Art Nouveau period. A revival in the 1950s of paperweight production occurred here and in other French glassmaking towns.

Bear cub, 5¼″ tall, frosted with clear ball base $100
Paperweight, 2½″ 15-petal blue clematis, red and white ground $2000
Paperweight, 2½″, dark pink chamomile with 4 green leaves and one bud .. $425
Paperweight, 2¾″, 2 red and 2 white turnips in swirled basket $1750
Paperweight, 2¾″, 45-petal dahlia, star base, blue and amber cane stamen $3750
Paperweight, 2¾″, chamomile with 52 blue petals, cane center $475
Paperweight, 2¾″, double pink clematis, double swirl on white lattice
ground $375
Paperweight, 2⅜″, 10 red and green spiral twists, alternating with 10 white spiral twists, blue and white millefiori center $575
Paperweight, 2⅜″, hollow white canes (honeycomb effect) with green interior, millefiori center $2500
Paperweight, 2⅝″, 2 strawberries with 5 blossoms $1750
Paperweight, 2⅞″, 9-petaled red clematis with 3 green leaves, millefiori center, Blue and white jasper ground $2000
Paperweight, 2⅞″, marbleized turquoise and white swirls $525

St. Louis glass (France). PHOTO BY
ROBIN RAINWATER.

Paperweight, 2⁷/₈″, multicolored butterfly with millefiori wings and circular border $2750
Paperweight, 3¹/₈″, 3 apples and 3 pears in white lattice bowl $2000
Paperweight, 3¹/₈″, 5-petaled blue, white, and red flowers with Millefiori centers, green leaves $850
Paperweight, 3¹/₈″, millefiori mushroom, green stem, blue and white filigree base $2250
Paperweight, 3″, red and white flower bouquet $650
Paperweight, sulphide, faceted, Pope John Paul II design $175
Paperweight, sulphide, 2″, King Edward VIII plaque design $275
Paperweight, sulphide, 3″, faceted, Marquis de Lafayette design $275
Seal with ball, 6″ tall, frosted with clear ball base and clear ball on seal's nose $125
Vase, 13³/₄″ tall, 3¹/₄″ square base, cobalt blue encased in crystal $175
Vase, 14″ tall, 3″ square base, Crystal or burgundy $175

STEVENS & WILLIAMS   ENGLAND, 1830s–1920s

Stevens & Williams produced glass in the village of Stourbridge, England, Although the factory was called the Brierly Hill Glassworks, many of the products are signed "Stevens & Williams." The company developed several art glass styles (alexandrite, engraved crystal, silver decorating, etc.), as well as an inexpensive method of manufacturing cameo glass. See additional listings under "English Cameo Glass."

Basket, 13¹/₂″, amber footed, thorn handle, Draped Leaf design $750
Bell, 6¹/₂″ tall, pink and white overlay $425
Biscuit jar with sterling silver cover, 7¹/₂″ tall, ruffled leaves design with pink lining $450
Bowl, 3³/₄″, 2¹/₂″ tall, ruffled, Pale orange $200
Bowl, 7¹/₂″, 6″ tall, crimped, amber rim, Floral design $375
Bowl, rose, 2³/₄″, Thumbprint pattern, Blue $225
Bowl, rose, 3¹/₂″, crimped, Opaque white $175
Bowl, rose, 4¹/₄″, Cranberry $250
Candlestick, 10″ tall, Moss agate $175
Compote, 6″, honeycomb stem, Engraved Poppies and Pods design $250
Ewer, 5¹/₄″ tall, amber branch handle, Cherry design $175
Goblet, 7″ tall, crystal foot and stem, red cut overlay bowl $250
Goblet, 8¹/₂″ tall, Gold Cut Overlay Floral design on green ground $275
Lamp, miniature, 5¹/₄″ tall, ruffled rim on base, Stripe pattern $750
Perfume bottle, 13″ tall, swirled, blue with gold and enameled berries $375
Perfume bottle with stopper, 4¹/₂″ tall, Moss agate $150
Perfume bottle with stopper, 9″ tall, Green and Crystal Swirl design $225
Salt dip, white threading, Enameled Berry design $175
Vase, 5³/₄″ tall, Loop and Berry design, Amber and gold $300
Vase, 5³/₄″ tall, 4″ diameter, dark pink with opal interior and ruffled amber leaves $200
Vase, 5″ tall, 3″ diameter, pink with white leaves and engraved grass $450
Vase, 6¹/₂″ tall, opaque cream with pink cherries $200

Vase, 6¹/₂″ tall, 3³/₄″ diameter, 8-crimped rim, pink with Ruffled Leaves design . . .
. . . .$250
Vase, 7¹/₂″ tall, ruffled, amber feet, pink with apple leaves $275
Vase, 8³/₄″ tall, Silveria pattern $300
Vase, 11¹/₂″ tall, ruffled, Amber and cranberry Floral design $425
Vase, 12″ tall, 5″ diameter, clear opal rim and leaves, Coral with white interior . . .
. . . .$475
Vase, 13″ tall, pear-shaped, multicolored Floral design $350
Vase, 15¹/₄″ tall, jack-in-the-pulpit style, Pink and white $425

SWEDISH GLASS 20TH CENTURY

One of the oldest Swedish glass firms noted for quality glass products was Kosta, founded in 1742. Much of the company's contemporary art pieces of the early to mid 20th century are highly collectible. The Eda Glassworks in the Varmland region also produced some glass, including Carnival items, in the early 20th century. Other Swedish firms experimented later with crystal art forms and engraving; the Orrefors Glasbruck (established in 1898) is noted for engraving, particularly for its spectacular "Graal" line. Mats Jonasson is a contemporary designer of crystal animal sculptures.

Angelfish ice sculpture, 4¹/₄″ tall (Jonasson) $95
Bear ice sculpture, 6³/₄″ long, grizzly (Jonasson) $250
Bird figurine, 3″ tall, early 1980s, Ruby red $20
Bowl, 4¹/₂″, Corona design (Orrefors), Crystal $45
Bowl, 5¹/₄″, 3″ tall (Kosta), Blue crystal $550
Bowl, 5″, crystal with etched mother and child (Orrefors) $225
Bowl, 5″, 3¹/₂″ tall, bulbous, flared (Kosta), Cranberry with white gridding $225
Bowl, 6¹/₄″, 5″ tall, crystal cased to green, brown swirls, etched "Kosta Sweden" . .
. . . .$425
Bowl, 6″, Rose Garden pattern, Carnival colors $100
Bowl, 6″, 3³/₈″ tall, crystal faceted cuts (Orrefors) $75
Bowl, 8³/₄″, Rose Garden pattern, Carnival colors $85
Bowl, 10″, Cathedral or Curved Star pattern, Carnival blue or marigold $75
Bowl, berry, 5″, Grand Thistle pattern, Carnival marigold $25
Bowl, berry, 5″, Grand Thistle pattern, Green, Carnival purple, or smoke $45
Bowl, rose, 5″ tall, 6¹/₄″ diameter, crystal cased to green, green and brown internal swirling (Kosta) $0
Bowl, rose, Rose Garden pattern, Carnival colors $750
Buffalo ice sculpture, 6″ long (Jonasson) $125
Butter dish, Rose Garden pattern, Carnival colors $450
Butter dish with cover, Cathedral or Curved Star pattern, Carnival
blue or marigold $250
Cardinals ice sculpture, 6¹/₄″ long, pair (Jonasson) $150
Chalice, Cathedral or Curved Star pattern, Carnival blue or marigold $200
Clock, 3¹/₈″ octagon, beveled (Orrefors), Crystal $100
Compote, 474 pattern variant, Carnival green $125
Compote, Cathedral or Curved Star pattern, Carnival blue or marigold $100

Creamer, footed, Cathedral or Curved Star pattern, Carnival blue or marigold . . . .
. . . . $100
Decanter with melon-ribbed decanter, 11″ tall, (Orrefors) $100
Decanter with stopper, 11³/₄″ tall, crystal with engraved underwater fisherman
(Orrefors) $200
Dolphin ice sculpture, 2″ long, (Jonasson) $40
Dolphins ice sculpture, 5³/₄″ long, pair (Jonasson) $130
Eagle ice sculpture, 7³/₄″ long, bald eagle (Jonasson) $175
Elephant ice sculpture, 6″ long, (Jonasson) $55
Elephant ice sculpture, 8″ long, (Jonasson) $125
Epergne, Cathedral or Curving Star pattern, Carnival blue or marigold $350
Foal ice sculpture, 4³/₄″ long, (Jonasson) $90
Goats ice sculpture, 6″ long, pair of mountain goats (Jonasson) $165
Golfer ice sculpture, 6″ tall, golfer swinging (Nybro) $95
Horse ice sculpture, 4³/₄″ long, foal (Jonasson) $100
Ice sculpture, jagged outer edge, engraved reindeer drinking from a pool of water
(Kosta) $1850
Kitten ice sculpture, 2″ long, (Jonasson) $40
Kitten ice sculpture, 3³/₄″ long, (Jonasson) $65
Lion and lioness ice sculpture, 6¹/₄″ long, (Jonasson) $325
Lion cub ice sculpture, 4³/₄″ long, (Jonasson) $90
Loon ice sculpture, 5¹/₄″ long, (Jonasson) $175
Lynx ice sculpture, 6″ long, (Jonasson) $125
Owl ice sculpture, 5¹/₂″ long, 3 owls (Jonasson) $110
Owl ice sculpture, 3³/₄″ long, owlet (Jonasson) $70
Owl ice sculpture, 6¹/₄″ long, barn owl (Jonasson) $130
Owl ice sculpture, 7¹/₄″ long, eagle owl (Jonasson) $235
Owls ice sculpture, 5″ long, 5 owlets (Jonasson) $95
Paperweight, 3″ round, crystal, cat, dove, eagle, koala, mouse, or wren (Jonasson)
. . . .$50
Pitcher, water, 38 oz., (Orrefors), Crystal $100
Pitcher, water, Cathedral or Curved Star pattern, Carnival blue or marigold . . . . . .
. . . .$2000
Pitcher, water, Grand Thistle pattern, Carnival blue $2750
Pitcher, water, Rose Garden pattern, Carnival colors $750
Plate, 8″, crystal with copper wheel engraved head of Greek goddess Helena, 1940s
. . . . $575
Polar bear ice sculpture, 6″ long, (Jonasson) $125
Polar bear cub ice sculpture, 2″ long, (Jonasson) $40
Rabbit ice sculpture, 3³/₄″ long, (Jonasson) $70
Seal ice sculpture, 2¹/₂″ long, baby seal (Jonasson) $50
Seal ice sculpture, 3¹/₄″ long, baby seal (Jonasson) $75
Seals ice sculpture, 8″ tall, pair, limited edition (975) (Jonasson) $525
Sugar, footed, Cathedral or curved star pattern, Carnival blue or marigold $100
Swans ice sculpture, 4″ long, swan and cygnet (Jonasson) $100
Tiger ice sculpture, 7″ tall, (Jonasson) $175
Tumbler, Cathedral or curved star pattern, Carnival blue or marigold $450
Tumbler, Grand Thistle pattern, Carnival blue $625
Urn with cover, 10¹/₂″ tall, crystal with engraved Garden of Eden design (Orrefors)
. . . . $1250

Vase, 4³/₄″ tall, globe-shaped, crystal with internal fish and seaweed design (Orrefors) $600

Vase, 4⁷/₈″ tall, globe-shaped, crystal with green and black swimming fish, Orrefors "Graal" design $1250

Vase, 4″ tall, crystal with etched woman viewing moon and stars (Orrefors) ... $350

Vase, 5″ tall, crystal with engraved bird in flight (Orrefors) $125

Vase, 6³/₄″ tall, cylindrical, blue and amber gondolier $2000

Vase, 6³/₄″ tall, flattened oval shape, blue and green spiral striping (Kosta) $450

Vase, 7¹/₈″ tall, engraved male nude diver (Orrefors) $750

Vase, 7⁵/₈″ tall, Prism "Thousands Windows" Cut Crystal pattern (Orrefors) $300

Vase, 8¹/₂″ tall, thick crystal base, vertically striped in Lila, Orrefors "Graal" design
.... $1500

Vase, 8¹/₄″ tall, engraved gondolier and woman on reverse, signed, Orrefors "Graal" design $2500

Vase, 8¹/₄″ tall, square base (Orrefors), Crystal $150

Vase, 8³/₄″ tall, crystal with interior decoration of amorphic figures playing games, inscribed "Orrefors 1938 Graal" $7500

Vase, 9″ tall, Rose Garden pattern, Carnival colors $250

Vase, 10¹/₄″ tall, frosted slim female archer, signed "Orrefors" $150

Vase, 12″ tall, Teardrop form, cased crystal to red (Kosta) $300

Vase, 13″ tall, cut crystal twist design, black-lined interior (Kosta) $625

Vase, 14″ tall, crystal with white interior, seaweed design (Kosta) $650

Vase, crystal with separate base, copper wheel engraved Egyptian dancer, 1940s ..
....$725

Vase, Seagull design, Carnival marigold $1250

Vase, letter, Rose Garden pattern, Carnival colors $200

Vase, Cathedral or Curved Star pattern, Carnival blue or marigold $100

Whale sculpture, 5³/₄″ tall, 9¹/₄″ long, blue whale (Jonasson) $250

Wolf ice sculpture, 6″, (Jonasson) $110

VAL ST. LAMBERT   BELGIUM, 1880s–PRESENT

The original company was established in 1825 by Kemlin and Lelievre. The firm followed the Art Nouveau movement of the late 19th century and produced cameo glass as well as glass similar to that of Lalique. Although the quality of the pieces was outstanding, the company never achieved the same reputation as its French counterparts.

Bowl, 6″, blue rim, crystal overlay, engraved design, signed $175

Bowl, 8″, scalloped, applied teardrops $225

Bowl, 12″, Cranberry to crystal shading $400

Candlestick, 6¹/₄″ tall, Crystal Elysee pattern $100

Candlestick, 11″ tall, 4-footed, Bird design $85

Candlestick, 11″ tall, Crystal Elysee pattern $125

Perfume bottle with stopper, 5¹/₄″ tall, signed, Cranberry to crystal $250

Perfume bottle with stopper, 5″ tall, Embossed Frosted Blue design $250

Puff box with cover, Opalescent blue $125

Tumbler, 5¹/₂″ tall, signed, Translucent pink $110

Val St. Lambert engraved oval platter. PHOTO BY MARK PICKVET.

Tumble-up, signed (includes tumbler and matching underplate), Cameo cranberry
....$850
Vase, 5³/₄″ tall, multicolored enamel on cameo, Olive green base $850
Vase, 6″ tall, multicolored on opal gray cameo, Sailboat design $1350
Vase, 6″ tall, Sweet Gum Leaves and Balls pattern, Green $400
Vase, 7³/₄″ tall, gray with scrolled foliage bands $375
Vase, 7″ tall, 3 notches on collar, Crystal $175
Vase, 7″ tall, 3″ diameter, notched collar, Floral design, Light green on frosted
cameo $800
Vase, 8″ tall, Cameo cranberry $575
Vase, 9″ tall, ovoid shape, amber with embossed acanthus leaves $275
Vase, 9″ tall, red floral design on yellow cameo $900
Vase, 10¹/₂″ tall, red floral and branch cameo design on white $1350
Vase, 10″ tall, double gourd shape, Lavender Floral design $650
Vase, 16¹/₂″ tall, cameo with multicolored enameled floral design $975
Vase, 17¹/₂″ tall, silver, green, and yellow cameo floral design on cream base .....
....$1600

VENETIAN GLASS   VENICE, ITALY, 18TH CENTURY–PRESENT

Venetian glass is characterized by millefiori designs on very thin soda- or lime-based glass. For centuries, Venetian artisans dominated the world of glass, producing clear glass objects such as mirrors and tableware. The items priced below are from the late 18th century to the present; older items do not surface often (most are in museums or permanent private collections). Newer items are generally thicker than the thin cristallo of old. Venetian glass is still made on the island of Murano near Venice today. Glassmakers incorporate many of the same designs and techniques employed for centuries. Of particular interest today are the encased fish sculptures. See "Millefiori Glass" and "Venini Art Glass" for additional listings.

Aquarium sculpture, 5½″ tall, 5″ diameter, crystal with multicolored tropical fish and plants encased in bowl, transparent sapphire rim $325

Basket, 5″ tall, rúby red with crystal base, rim, and handle $150

Bird figurine, 3½″ tall, latticino design, gold-flecked beak $75

Birds in tree sculpture, 20 birds in large tree, 20″ tall $225

Birds, figural pair, 10″ tall, Ruby red to clear shading $175

Bottle, water, 9″ tall, enameled decoration, Cranberry $150

Bowl, 6½″, green and gold ribbons with latticino bands, flower finial $225

Bowl, 7″, Red and white stripes $175

Bowl, 9″ oval, 3¾″ tall, Cranberry with opalescent ribbing $175

Candleholder, 6″ tall, ovoid design, seated female figure $900

Candlestick, 5¾″ tall, ruby red bowl, holder, and circular base, crystal stem with grape bunch $100

Candlestick, 5″ tall, dolphin stem, gold flecks with berry prunts $35

Candlestick, 10½″ tall, crystal angel shape, amber halo $55

Candlestick, 12″ tall, crystal with gold dust $150

Compote, 6″ tall, green with white and gold decorations $175

Creamer, 4″ tall, pitcher-style, red clover design $400

Decanter with cone-shaped stopper, 20″ tall, multicolored vertical bands $375

Decanter with stopper, 13″ tall, silver speckled amber with star canes $450

Decanter with stopper, 18″ tall, ruby red with heavy gold gilding, gilded foot, handle, and stopper $300

Epergne, 15½″ tall, bowl with 3 vases, ruby red with applied crystal accents $500

Fish figurine, 9¾″ tall, ruby red with gold-flecked fins $125

Flask with ruby red stopper, 11½″ tall, crystal with enameled red and green floral decoration $60

Goblet, water, 9″ tall, ruby red bowl and base, crystal dolphin stem with gold flecks $200

Venetian glass. PHOTO BY ROBIN RAINWATER.

Venetian glass candy. PHOTO BY ROBIN RAINWATER.

Goblet, water, 9″ tall, tall stem, white and red latticino design $225
Lamp, 8″ tall, miniature, millefiori mushroom styled shade and base $425
Lamp, 20″ tall, 11″ millefiori mushroom shade with matching base $475
Lamp, 20″ tall, 4-arm stand, 11″ swirled silver, gold, and silver shade $475
Paperweight, car-shape, 1½″ tall, 5½″ long, Amethyst, blue, cobalt blue $35
Paperweight, dome-shaped, millefiori floral design $75
Paperweight, pear-shaped, pale yellow glass with hollow red center, green stem
and leaf, Air bubble pattern $225
Pelican sculpture, 14½″ tall, crystal footed base, crystal to bright sapphire blue
body, orange gold fish encased in crystal beak $300
Perfume bottle with ruby red stopper, 3¼″ tall, crystal with enameled red and
green floral design $50
Plate, boomerang shape, 10″ long, yellow with internal slices of murrhine ......
.... $100
Rooster figurine, 9¾″ tall, standing position, amber with gold dust $150
Swan figurine dish, 7½″ long, ruby red with crystal wings and accents $55
Tumbler, water, 4″ tall, millefiori purple shades $110
Vase, 6″ tall, multicolored spatter on ruby red $55
Vase, 8½″ tall, cornucopia style with circular base, ruby red with applied crystal
flowers $150
Vase, 8″ tall, blue with red lines and millefiori Floral design $700
Vase, 8″ tall, handled, millefiori vertical bands $400
Vase, 8″ tall, handled, red and white floral design $250
Vase, 8″ tall, millefiori floral and net design $725

Vase, 11″ tall, 5″ diameter, mouth-blown, edelweiss green with etched dark green and white Birch Forest design $300
Vase, 12″ tall, ruby red with applied crystal swan handle $200
Vase, 12″ tall, scalloped, inverted ribbing on neck, Ruby red $200
Wine glass, 4″ tall, clear with encrusted gold band $125
Wine glass, 6½″ tall, ruby red with heavy gold gilding, gilded foot $50
Wine glass, 6″ tall, sea serpent-shaped stem $55

VENINI ART GLASS   MURANO, ITALY, 1940s–PRESENT

Contemporary art glass is still being made on the famous island of Murano using ancient methods combined with modern technology. Most items listed below are signed "Venini" or "Venini Murano" or even "Murano Made in Italy." Venini (named for Paulo Venini, who died in 1959) is the most recognizable name in the modern Venetian glass world.

Bell, 5″ tall, alternating pink and white filigree swirls $75
Bird figurine, 12″ tall, signed "Murano Made in Italy," Transparent iridescent ....
.... $1600
Bottle with white stopper, 13″ tall, white lower half, olive green upper half $500
Bowl, 4½″, alternating white and turquoise filigree swirls $350
Bowl, 7¾″, 3½″ tall, moss green with bubbles $125
Bowl, 10″, crystal with colored (amethyst, gold, and white) spiral stripes ... $175
Candy dish, 2¼″ tall, 5″ diameter, light green and white ribbon design $175
Candy dish with cover, 6″ tall, Pinecone pattern, Frosted $90
Decanter with stopper, 8″ tall, clear cased amber with incised surface $1250
Decanter, clown figurine design, 14″ tall, multicolored body with cobalt blue hat and tie $350
Hourglass, 7″ tall, signed, Blue and green $650
Musician figurine with gown and headpiece, 9″ tall $400
Perfume bottle with stopper, 6″ tall, alternating scarlet and teal stripes $750
Vase, 4″ tall, 6″ diameter, egg form, 2 rim openings, cameo, 3 color layers $5500
Vase, 8½″ tall, black circular base, alternating black and yellow laced stripes .....
.... $1000
Vase, 10½″ tall, double neck design, opaque blue with multicolored peacock design
.... $1000
Vase, 12″ tall, crystal with amber and tan interior and 2 holes that completely pass through the body $975
Vase, 14″ tall, cylindrical, red and blue swirled stripes design $575
Vase, 24″ tall, classic form, Crystal cased to white $675
Vase, bottle, 10″ tall, dark green with red and white band $1250
Vase, handkerchief, 3¾″ tall, pink and white latticino design $300
Vase, handkerchief, 5¾″ tall, crystal with blue and white latticino design $350
Vase, handkerchief, 6″ tall, white cased in crystal $400
Vase, handkerchief, 8″ tall, White with yellow interior $625
Vase, handkerchief, 9″ tall, Tan cased to white $675

WATERFORD GLASS COMPANY   IRELAND, 1783–1851, 1951–PRESENT

Waterford is known for its fine grade of crystal. New items, including tableware, functional products, and some novelty pieces, are also made of quality lead crystal and are becoming quite collectible. Since the 1970s, Waterford has been the largest producer of handmade crystal in the world. Of particular note are the handmade limited edition Masterpiece Collection items. More Waterford listings can be found under "Lismore."

Angelfish figurine, 3″ tall $60
Baseball, 3″ diameter, (regulation size) $100
Baseball, 3″ diameter, (regulation size), engraved with New York Yankees' logo ..
.... $125
Bell, 4¾″ tall, etched crest design $70
Biscuit jar with cover, 6″ tall, diamond and slender leaf cuts $175
Block, ABC baby style, 2″ dimensions, beveled crystal $65
Bookends, 5¼″ diameter ¼″, circle wedges, 1⅛″ thick, diamond and fan cuts, pair
.... $175
Bootie, baby, 4″ long $65
Bowl, 6¼″ oblong, 3½″ wide, 1½″ tall, vertical ribbed sides and diamond base $60
Bowl, 7″, 3½″ tall, leaf and diamond design $85
Bowl, 8″, Calais pattern $70
Bowl, 8″, 3½″ tall, Colleen pattern $135
Bowl, 9″, 6½″ tall, round base, leaf and diamond cuts $400
Bowl, 10″, 7½″ tall, footed, diamond and wedge cuts $1250
Bowl, 11″, Cut Apprentice pattern $650
Bowl, heart-shaped, 4½″ across, wedge cut $55
Bowl, oval, (11″ × 7″), notched, Diamond and Fan design $150
Bowl, potpourri, 4⅝″, 2¼″ tall, leaf design $55
Bowl, rose, 5½″ tall, 5¼″ diameter, Calais pattern $85
Box with hinged lid, shell-shaped $100
Brandy glass, Alana pattern $55
Brandy glass, Colleen pattern $60
Brandy glass, Kylemore pattern $60
Brandy glass, Patrick pattern $55
Bride and groom figurine, 7″ tall $150

Waterford crystal. PHOTO BY ROBIN RAINWATER.

Brush, makeup, 6″ long, crystal handle $45
Butter dish with cover, ¼ lb. size, 7¼″ long, 2½″ tall, Open Diamond Cut design
.... $160
Butterfly figure, 3½″ across $50
Candelabra, 9¼″ tall, 2-tiered candleholder, diamond and wedge cuts with
teardrops $775
Candleholder, 2-piece, base bowl and small shade, diamond cuts $150
Candleholder, 3⅝″ tall, scalloped, round base $70
Candlestick, 4½″ tall, Palladia pattern $70
Candlestick, 5½″ tall, stemmed, diamond cuts $50
Candlestick, globe-shaped, 2½″ diameter, Diamond pattern $40
Candy dish, heart-shaped, 7¾″ × 7½″ $65
Cat figure, regal cat, 5″ tall $100
Centerpiece stemmed bowl, 9″ tall, diamond and vertical cuts $850
Champagne glass, Alana pattern $45
Champagne glass, Castletown pattern $75
Champagne glass, Colleen pattern $55
Champagne glass, Kylemore pattern $55
Champagne glass, Patrick pattern $45
Champagne glass, Powerscourt pattern $65
Chandelier, 22″ tall, 15″ wide, 5 large teardrops $2250
Chandelier, 23″ tall, 22″ wide, 57 teardrops $2500
Chandelier, 30″ tall, 30″ wide, 9 large teardrops $3000
Claret glass, Alana pattern $45
Claret glass, Castletown pattern $75
Claret glass, Colleen pattern $55
Claret glass, Kylemore pattern $55
Claret glass, Patrick pattern $45
Claret glass, Powerscourt pattern $65
Clock, 2¾″ tall, crystal shell shape $60
Clock, 2⅝″ tall, 4″ long, Kensington pattern $70
Coaster, 5″ diameter, diamond cuts $55
Creamer, footed, pitcher-style, leaf cuts $75
Creamer, pitcher-style, cut ovals, gold rims $45
Cruet, 4¼″ tall, (no stopper), diamond cut $50
Decanter, claret with faceted stopper, 12½″ tall, old-fashioned style, diamond cut
.... $700
Decanter, cut with etched Christmas tree $225
Decanter, ship with faceted stopper, 9½″ tall, diamond cuts $325
Decanter, whiskey, Kylemore pattern $200
Decanter, whiskey, Patrick pattern $175
Decanter, wine, Alana pattern $225
Decanter, wine, Castletown pattern $350
Decanter, wine, Colleen pattern $225
Decanter, wine, Patrick pattern $200
Decanter, wine, Powerscourt pattern $375
Dove figure, 1¾″ tall, 5″ long $75
Dreidel spinning shape, 5″ tall, 2½″ square, prism faceted cut $125
Duck, mallard, 2½″ tall, 3¾″ long, wedge cut feathers $100
Egg, 3½″ tall, 2¼″ wide, Diamond and Sunburst pattern $100
Egg, 3¼″ tall, 2¼″ wide, annual editions beginning in 1991 (price is for each) .. $125

Egg, 5½″ tall, pedestal stand, diamond cuts $115
Fish, leaping salmon figure, 8½″ tall $125
Frame, photo, heart-shaped, 4½″ tall, 4¼″ wide $55
Frog figure, 2⅜″ tall $75
Gavel, 5½″ long $75
Ginger jar with cover, 8″ tall Diamond and Rosette pattern $175
Globe sculpture, 6½″ diameter, 14″ tall, with mahogany base, diamond cut continents $2750
Goblet, Alana pattern $50
Goblet, Castletown pattern $75
Goblet, Colleen pattern $55
Goblet, cut with etched Christmas tree $50
Goblet, Kylemore pattern $55
Goblet, Patrick pattern $50
Goblet, Powerscourt pattern $65
Golf Ball, regulation size, 2½″ diameter $85
Golf Club Head, 3″ tall $75
Golf shoe, 6″ long $75
Harp, 5″ tall, 2″ wide $70
Heart-shaped box, 2¾″ × 2¾″, 2-piece $65
Horse figure, rearing, 3¾″ tall, 2¾″ wide $55
Ice bucket, 5⅜″ tall, silver-plated handle, diamond cut $160
Lamp, 13″ tall, Diamond pattern $500
Lamp, 18″ tall, Diamond pattern $800
Lamp, 20″ tall, brass base, crystal part 8¾″ tall $250
Leprechaun figurine with pot of gold, 3″ tall, 3½″ wide $75
Madonna figure with child, 7″ tall $150
Mug, christening, 3″ tall $70
Mug, tankard style, 4½″ tall, 13 oz., diamond and long slender leaf cuts $85
Mustard pot with cover, 3″ tall, perpendicular cuts $40
Napkin ring, oval, open diamond cut design $40
Owl figure, 3⅛″ tall $75
Paperweight, 3¼″, globe-shaped, various engraved floral designs $75
Paperweight, 3½″ diameter, diamond and star cuts $75
Paperweight, 3½″ long, 2¾″ wide, strawberry-shaped $75
Paperweight, 4″, shamrock design $125
Paperweight, 4½″ long, 1¾″ tall, open diamond cuts, turtle design $75
Paperweight, 5″ tall, number ″1″ shape, diamond cuts $75
Perfume atomizer, 4″ tall, diamond cuts $85
Pitcher, water, 24 oz., cut design with etched Christmas tree $150
Pitcher, water, 32 oz., long, slender oval cuts $175
Plate, 8″, cut diamonds and etched golfer in center $100
Ram, 2″ tall, 3¼″ long $65
Ring holder, 2¾″ tall, heart base (3″ across) $45
Sailboat, 5½″ tall, 4¾″ long, cut ovals $115
Salt and pepper shakers, 6″ tall, round feet, silver-plated tops, diamond and leaf cuts $100
Salt cellar, 2⅝″ tall, stemmed, boat-shaped, tiny diamond cuts $85
Sconce, 2-light, 11¼″ tall, 12½″ wide, 2 4½″ diamond cut plates, each with 8 teardrops $850
Sea horse figure, 3½″ tall $45

Sea horse figure, 6³/₄″ tall $200
Sherbet, Alana pattern $50
Sherbet, Castletown pattern $85
Stein, 6″ tall, diamond and narrow leaf cuts $100
Sugar, cut ovals, gold rim $45
Sugar, footed, leaf cuts $65
Sugar shaker with silver-plated top, 6¹/₂″ tall, stemmed, diamond and leaf cut ...
.... $65
Teddy bear figure, 3″ tall $55
Thimble, 1¹/₂″ tall $40
Tray, oval, (8″ × 6″), central star, vertical flutes $65
Tray, shell-shaped, 5″ × 4¹/₂″, 1″ tall $55
Tumbler, 9 or 10 oz., cut with etched Christmas tree $40
Tumbler, 9 oz., Castletown pattern $70
Tumbler, 9 oz., Colleen pattern $45
Tumbler, 9 oz., old-fashioned style, Alana pattern $40
Tumbler, 9 oz., old-fashioned style, Kylemore pattern $50
Tumbler, 9 oz., Patrick pattern $35
Tumbler, 9 oz., Powerscourt pattern $55
Tumbler, 9 oz., Wide Diamond pattern $35
Tumbler, 12 oz., Colleen pattern $55
Tumbler, 12 oz., Powerscourt pattern $60
Tumbler, 12 oz., old-fashioned style, Patrick pattern $45
Vase, 4″ tall, diamond and flute design $55
Vase, 7⁵/₈″ tall, Prism "Thousand Windows" pattern $275
Vase, 7″ tall, slender, diamond and vertical cuts $60
Vase, 9″ tall, Calais pattern $60
Vase, 10″ tall, round base, wide neck, wedge and diamond cuts $200
Vase, 12″ tall, round base, flared top, all-over cut pattern, Masterpiece Collection .
.... $925
Wine glass, Alana pattern $40
Wine glass, Castletown pattern $75
Wine glass, Colleen pattern $50
Wine glass, Kylemore pattern $50
Wine glass, oversize, Colleen pattern $100
Wine glass, Patrick pattern $40
Wine glass, Powerscourt pattern $60

WEBB, THOMAS & SONS   STOURBRIDGE, ENGLAND, 1880s–1930s

Webb is the most famous English name in the Art Glass world. The company was a major part of the European Art Nouveau movement and followed American trends as well. It borrowed Peachblow and Burmese designs from America but also produced Alexandrite, Cameo, and a host of other designs. Additional listings for Webb can be found under "Alexandrite," "English Cameo Glass," and "Peachblow."

Biscuit jar with cover, 7¹/₂″ tall, pink satin with floral design on body and cover $600
Biscuit jar with cover, 8″ tall, signed, Frosted yellow $1500

Webb glass. PHOTO BY ROBIN RAINWATER, COURTESY OF THE CORNING MUSEUM OF GLASS.

Bowl, 3¹/₂″, ruffled, enameled floral and butterfly design, signed $400
Bowl, 4⁷/₈″, crimped, mother-of-pearl, Diamond Quilted pattern $675
Bowl, 5³/₄″, pink with white lining, intaglio flowers and branches $850
Bowl, 5″, ruffled, Burmese $175
Bowl, 6¹/₄″, applied rim, Burmese with floral design $1500
Bowl, rose, 6″, 5″ tall, yellow to cream satin with white interior $375
Centerpiece, 12¹/₂″ diameter, 7″ tall, ruffled, blue overlay with enameled floral design $575
Creamer, 2⁵/₈″ tall, fluted, Burmese with green leaves design $750
Epergne, 21″ tall, center trumpet design with 3 hanging baskets, Cranberry and vaseline $1250
Ewer, 3³/₄″ tall, 5³/₄″ diameter, ivory handle, green to white satin, apples and leaves design $575
Flask with threaded silver stopper, 5³/₄″ tall, swan's head design $2500
Perfume bottle with silver top, 6″ tall, red to yellow to dark amber shading $350
Perfume bottle with sterling silver stopper, 3¹/₂″ tall, Burmese with purple floral design $750
Perfume bottle with sterling silver stopper, 4³/₄″ tall, Burmese with gold branches design $850
Perfume bottle with stopper, 5¹/₂″ tall, ivory satin with gold bamboo and multicolored floral design $550
Perfume bottle with stopper, citron, vine, and floral decoration $850
Pitcher, water, 6¹/₂″ tall, loop handles, blooming bamboo plant design, Ivory $1750
Pitcher, water, 7¹/₂″ tall, Red to white shading $625
Plate, 6¹/₂″, ruffled, Diamond Quilted pattern, Butterscotch $110
Salt dip, rectangular, Red $650
Toothpick holder, 2⁵/₈″ tall, hexagonal collared top, Burmese $375

Tumbler, 5″ tall, Red to white shading $200
Vase, 2½″ tall, miniature, blue with enameled butterfly and floral design $650
Vase, 3½″ tall, vertical ribs, Burmese $175
Vase, 3¾″ tall, hexagonal top, Burmese with lavender floral and leaves design ...
....$425
Vase, 3⅜″ tall, ivory with gold butterfly and floral design $250
Vase, 3″ tall, miniature, Red with carved white fuchsias $375
Vase, 4½″ tall, green with gold leaves and hydrangea blossoms $425
Vase, 5″ tall, pink interior, Gold Floral and Butterfly design $400
Vase, 5″ tall, 2¾″ diameter, Floral and Bees design, Gold on coral $300
Vase, 6½″ tall, Red to pink shading $425
Vase, 6″ tall, footed, cut crystal, red and white Trumpet Floral design $3000
Vase, 6″ tall, ruffled, satin, Diamond Quilted pattern $375
Vase, 7″ tall, urn-shaped, 2 applied handles, ribbed, Iridescent gold $1750
Vase, 8½″ tall, amber with Enameled Butterflies and Cattails design $550
Vase, 8½″ tall, ribbed, Fishscale and Vine design, signed $3250
Vase, 8¼″ tall, Burmese with green leaves and coral flower buds $850
Vase, 9″ tall, Butterfly and Floral design, Burmese $2000
Vase, 10½″ tall, gourd-shaped, blue with white floral design $2750
Vase, 10″ tall, Amethyst Cameo design, signed $1350
Vase, 10″ tall, bottle-shaped, Burmese with Mums and Leaves design $1250
Vase, 11″ tall, gourd-shaped, footed, yellow satin with cream interior $450
Vase, 12″ tall, ruffled, coral design with cream interior $525
Vase, 14″ tall, red with enameled floral decorations $675
Vase, 15″ tall, flared, multicolored floral design $700

CHAPTER 2

PRESSED GLASS

The American glass industry experienced a shaky start, but it was not for lack of ambition. As early as 1607, the Jamestown Colony settlers included glassblowers. America had an abundance of all the necessary ingredients: excellent sources for ash, plenty of sand, and massive forests for fuel. A small glasshouse was built the very next year but closed without producing any useful items. The Germans with very limited success would be the next immigrants to attempt glassmaking in the New World.

In 1739 a German immigrant named Caspar Wistar built a factory in New Jersey. He hired skilled German glassworkers and became the first commercially successful glass manufacturer in the United States. He began

Pressed glass decanters; from left to right, patterns are Flute & Pine Tree, Baroque Shell, Diamond Quilted, and Vertically Ribbed. PHOTO COURTESY OF THE SANDWICH GLASS MUSEUM.

Pressed glass lacy salt dishes. PHOTO COURTESY OF THE SANDWICH GLASS MUSEUM.

by meeting the immediate need for bottles and windows. Wistar also made some crude tableware and a few scientific glass vessels for Benjamin Franklin. It was surprising that any glass was made at all at this time since England had banned the manufacture of glass in the Colonies. The Wistar house, however, did not survive for long.

From 1763 to 1774 another German by the name of Henry W. Stiegel operated a glassmaking enterprise in Manheim, Pennsylvania. Stiegel acquired some of the former employees of Wistar's business and hired a few other experienced workers from both Germany and England. Although he went bankrupt in 1774, he did manage to create some window and bottle glass. The American Revolution forced his business to shut down permanently.

One year after the revolution, another German immigrant opened a glass factory in America. In 1784 John Frederick Amelung produced a fair amount of hand-cut tableware, much of it engraved. Amelung's factory also made a pair of bifocals for Benjamin Franklin. The company, however, could not operate consistently at a profit and shut down in 1795.

Although there was a great demand for glass, these early ventures failed. The reasons were numerous. First, foreign competition and pressure from the English government were significant. Manufacturing plants were well established in England and Ireland and were capable of producing large quantities of cheap glass. Second, American entrepreneurs lacked the capital and many of the skills necessary to manufacture glass. Third, transportation problems resulted in shipping that was too difficult and costly.

The Alleghenies, in particular, were a disadvantage to Eastern manufacturers but a boon to those living in eastern Ohio, northern West Virginia, and western Pennsylvania. The mountains served as a barrier to foreign and Eastern glass long before the great canals were built. In 1797 the first frontier glassmaking factory was constructed by Albert Gallatin, an immigrant from Switzerland, about 60 miles south of Pittsburgh. Later that year, a bottle factory was built in Pittsburgh by James O'Hara and Isaac Craig. This factory, named the Pittsburgh Glass Works, merged with Gallatin's New Geneva Glass Works in 1798. The combined works did manage to produce handblown windows, bottles, and a bit of tableware, but the owners were unable to operate profitably. They sold out to Edward Ensell soon after.

Pittsburgh and the surrounding area was an ideal place to manufacture glassware. Wood for fuel was readily available; later, massive coal deposits were discovered in the region. Large sand or sandstone deposits lay along the numerous riverbeds, and red lead for fine crystal production was available nearby in the Illinois territory. The commercial markets were wide open in every direction except back East. North to Canada, west to the Pacific, and south to the major trading centers of New Orleans and the Gulf of Mexico were all available by easy river transport. With these strategic advantages, early attempts still ended in failure.

Early successes in glassmaking can be traced to many individuals, but one figure stands out in particular. Deming Jarves not only founded many companies, but attracted knowledgeable foreign workers, obtained the proper ingredients and good formulas, and wrote an important trade volume in 1854 titled *Reminiscences of Glassmaking*. Most importantly, he was able to obtain enough financial backing to keep businesses operating long enough to achieve consistent profit margins.

In the 1790s the Boston Crown Glass Company was chartered to produce window glass. The company was the first to introduce lead crystal in the United States. Many of the workers left and went on to form the Boston Porcelain and Glass Company in 1814. They built a factory in 1815 and made a few limited lead glass products before failing in 1817. Deming Jarves, with three associates (Amos Binney, Daniel Hastings, and Edmund Monroe), purchased the holdings of the company and incorporated it into a new business in 1818. It was dubbed the New England Glass Company and was established in East Cambridge, Massachusetts.

From the beginning, the business operated profitably, and the owners continuously reinvested in new equipment and recruited skilled workers from Europe. Jarves assumed a leading role as first agent and then manager. He was a prosperous businessman and held a monopoly on red lead production. Jarves left New England Glass in 1826 and went on to form the Boston & Sandwich Glass Company, another successful operation.

What Jarves accomplished in the East, the team of Bakewell, Ensell, and Pears was attempting in the West. In 1807 Edward Ensell founded a small glass company in Pittsburgh. The business was purchased the following year by Benjamin Bakewell and associates. Bakewell sent his son Thomas and a trusted clerk named Thomas Pears on numerous trips to Europe to hire experienced glassworkers. Pears left in 1818 to start a bottle factory, which subsequently failed. He then rejoined the Bakewells. Pears quit again in 1825 and moved to Indiana, but returned a year later. He died soon after. His son, John Palmer Pears, became manager of the glass factory and later changed the name to Bakewell, Pears, and Company.

The Early Period of American glass history lasted from 1771 to 1830. During this time, several glass companies were founded east and west of the Alleghenies, but nearly all ended in failure. Cheap European glass and lack of protective tariffs hurt Eastern glassmakers. Out West, skilled workers were difficult to find, and the capital necessary to establish a business was not available to sustain long-term growth and operation. Economic depressions such as the one after the War of 1812 also led to the shutdowns. Except for the rare successes of a few enterprising men like Jarves, this first period in American glass history was marked by unprofitability and failure.

The Middle Period of American glass history dates from 1830 to about 1880. To help struggling U.S. manufacturers, the Baldwin Bill in 1830 placed duties and high tariffs on foreign imports. The new tariffs worked, and the glass industry in the United States was given a much needed boost. Along with the imposition of taxes, the invention of a mechanical pressing machine in the late 1820s led to the mass production of glassware. The invention of the handpress was America's greatest contribution to glassmaking. It was as important as the discovery of lead crystal, glassblowing, and the invention of glass itself. Mechanical handpresses revolutionized the industry; they were fast, efficient, and could be run by less-skilled workers.

Pressed glass was made by forcing melted glass into shape under pressure. A plunger was used to force or press molten glass into an iron mold. The mold, made up of two or more parts, imparted lines or seams where the mold came apart. With each piece the mold was reassembled and filled once again. Some of the marks left by the mold were hand finished to remove them. Molds might include patterns, were usually hinged, and could be full-size, single-piece forms or separate pieces for more complicated objects. Candlesticks, vases, common table items, and especially matched sets of tableware were easily manufactured in this way.

Pressed items were made in great quantities, especially in the factories opened by Jarves. The New England Glass Company, which eventually became Libbey, and the Boston & Sandwich Glass Company were two of the most successful factories producing pressed glass in the United States. Many followed in the mid 19th century, including Adams & Company; Bakewell, Pears & Company; McKee Brothers; Bryce Brothers; Hobbs, Brocunier & Company; and King & Son.

Individual patterns were rarely patented by any one company. Even when patents were obtained, designs were copied. Ashburton or Hex Optic,

Bull's-Eye, Cable, Thumbprints, Hamilton, Comet, Grapes, Pineapples, Ribs, Sunbursts, Pillars, Flutes, and so on are at times difficult to distinguish from one company to the next.

One other American invention was the discovery of a cheap lead substitute in 1864 by William Leighton. Leighton was employed by Hobbs, Brocunier & Company at the time and developed a glass formula that substituted lime for the much more expensive lead. The glass products manufactured with lime still maintained a good degree of clarity. Although the brilliance was not as sharp as lead crystal, the price savings and practicality of it more than made up for the difference in quality. Most companies were forced to switch to lime in order to remain competitive.

Pressed glass remained somewhat affordable as compared to art and cut glass in the late 19th and early 20th centuries. Fire polishing, which was developed in England in 1834, was adopted in the United States. Fire polishing removed mold and tool marks by reheating and gave glass a shinier finish that was a little closer to fine cut crystal.

Simple clear pressed glass articles were combined with other design features and decorating techniques. Pressed glass was made in many colors, flashed, cut occasionally like simple fluting, cased, enameled, and might contain applied blown accessories such as handles and feet. All still qualify as pressed glass items, but the quality and dull colors were still far behind cut crystal and art glass items. Then again, the lower cost allowed glassware to be within the reach of the average American.

Other makers in the late 19th and early 20th centuries included the conglomerate U.S. Glass Company, George Duncan & Sons, Central Glass Company, and Indiana Tumbler & Goblet Company. Many later pressed patterns were more elaborate, patented, and not easily copied, a great aid in identification.

ACTRESS   LABELLE GLASS COMPANY, 1870s

Actors and actresses are formed on this pattern in portrait with light ridges. The pieces are also framed by stippled shell forms rising off the sides of the glass.

Bowl, 8″, footed $45
Bowl, flat $30
Butter dish with cover $125
Cake stand, 7″ tall $150
Candlestick $100
Celery dish, Pinafore design $175
Cheese dish with cover, "The Lone Fisherman" design $200
Compote with cover, 8″ tall $175
Compote with cover, low $150
Creamer $75

Pressed glass. Left: "Actress" pattern. Right: "Alabama" pattern. DRAWINGS BY MARK PICKVET.

Goblet	$100
Honey dish with cover	$100
Jam jar with cover	$125
Mustard jar with cover	$75
Pickle dish, embossed "Love's Request Is Pickles"	$65
Pitcher, milk (small)	$225
Pitcher, water (large)	$250
Platter, oval, Pinafore design	$150
Platter, round, Miss Nielson design	$175
Salt and pepper shakers	$75
Sauce bowl, flat	$35
Sauce bowl, footed	$45
Spooner	$70
Sugar	$100
Tray, embossed "Give Us This Day"	$125

ALABAMA   U.S. GLASS COMPANY, EARLY 1890s

"Alabama" was the first of U.S. Glass's state series. It is also known as "Beaded Bull's Eye" "Drape" pattern. Green pieces are priced the same as the clear items listed below, while a few rare ruby flashed items should be doubled.

Bowl, 5″	$20
Butter dish with cover	$80
Cake stand	$55
Celery holder, upright	$50
Compote with cover	$150
Compote, open, 5″ tall	$40
Creamer	$45
Honey dish with cover	$100
Nappy with handle	$30
Pitcher, milk	$75
Pitcher, syrup, with lid	$75
Pitcher, water	$80

Relish dish, oblong, 3 varieties $25
Spooner $30
Sugar with cover $75
Toothpick holder $75
Tumbler $30

AMERICA   AMERICAN GLASS COMPANY AND RIVERSIDE GLASS WORKS, EARLY 1890s

This pattern is also referred to as "Swirl and Diamond" and is sometimes confused with other similar patterns.

Bowl, 8½" $20
Butter dish with cover, pedestal base $50
Carafe $35
Celery vase $25
Compote, 8" tall, 8" diameter $50
Creamer, tankard-style, applied handle $30
Goblet $20
Pitcher, tankard-style, 64 oz., applied handle $50
Relish dish $15
Sauce dish, 4½", flat $10
Spooner $15
Sugar with cover (large) $35
Sugar with cover, individual (small) $25
Tumbler $15

AMERICAN   FOSTORIA GLASS COMPANY, 1915–1970s

Fostoria's "American" pattern is sometimes confused with block optic or cubist patterns of the Depression era. Some colors were added during the Depression, including amber, green, and yellow (increase prices by 50%), as well as blue and some iridized or Carnival colors (double the prices). "American" is a relatively inexpensive pattern because of its long production history; however, some pieces were discontinued early on and have increased in value.

Ashtray, 2⅞" square $10
Ashtray, 3⅞" oval $15
Ashtray, 5½" oval $30
Ashtray, 5" square $25
Banana dish, 9" oblong, 3½" width, 1 tab handle $25
Basket, reed handle $80
Bell (rare) $300
Bonbon dish, 7", 3-footed $50
Bottle, catsup, with stopper $100
Bottle, water, 9¼" tall, 44 oz. $75
Bowl, 3½" $10
Bowl, 4¼" $10

Bowl, 5″ $12
Bowl, 5″, flared $12
Bowl, 6″ $14
Bowl, 7″ $15
Bowl, 8″ $17
Bowl, 8″, 3-footed $32
Bowl, 9″ $20
Bowl, 10½″, 3-footed $25
Bowl, 10″ $22
Bowl, 11″, centerpiece $55
Bowl, 12¼″ $75
Bowl, 16″, centerpiece $150
Bowl, rose $50
Butter dish with cover, 5¾″ dome diameter, 7¼″ underplate diameter $100
Cake plate, 7½″ $15
Cake salver, 10″ round $75
Cake salver, 10″ square $115
Cake stand, 12″ $65
Candelabra, 2-light $150
Candlestick, 3″ tall $15
Candlestick, 6″ tall $45
Candlestick, 7″ tall $50
Candy dish with cover, hexagonal, footed $40
Celery vase, 6″ tall, 3½″ diameter $25
Cheese dish with cover, dome and underplate $100
Cigarette box with cover $50
Coaster, 3½″ $8
Cocktail glass, 2⅞″ tall, 3 oz., footed $15
Cologne bottle with stopper, 7½″ tall, 8 oz. $35
Comport, 4″, open $15
Comport, 5¼″, open, no stem $16
Comport, 8½″, open, no stem $20
Comport, 9½″, open, no stem $22
Compote, 5″, open $15
Compote, 7″, open $17
Cookie jar with cover, 8⅞″ tall $250
Cordial, 2⅞″ tall, footed $8
Cracker jar with cover, 8¾″ tall, 5¾″ diameter $200
Cracker jar with cover, 10″ tall, 5¾″ diameter $300
Creamer, 4¼″ tall (large) $12
Creamer, individual, 5 oz. (small) $10
Cruet with stopper, 6½″ tall, 5 oz. $60
Cruet with stopper, 7″ tall, 7 oz. $65
Cup, 8 oz. $7
Cup, custard, 6 oz., 2 styles $7
Decanter with sterling silver stopper, 10″ tall $125
Decanter with stopper, 2 styles, metal holder and chain, engraved tabs ("Scotch" or "Rye") $150
Fernery, 3-footed $10
Flowerpot with cover (rare) $1000
Glove box with cover, rectangular, (9½″ × 3½″) $90

Goblet, 5½″ tall, 9 oz. $12
Goblet, 6¾″ tall, 9 oz. $15
Hairpin box with cover, rectangular, (3½″ × 1½″) $90
Handkerchief box with cover, rectangular, (5½″ × 4½″) $75
Hat, 2½″ tall $15
Hat, 3″ tall $20
Ice bucket, 7″ tall, 10″ diameter, metal handle $85
Ice tub, 5½″ $40
Jelly dish with cover, 4½″ diameter, 7″ tall $100
Jewel box with cover, rectangular, (5¼″ × 2¼″) $75
Lamp, hurricane $175
Lamp, perfume $60
Mayonnaise set, 3-piece (dish, plate, & 1 spoon) $40
Mayonnaise set, 3-piece (divided dish & 2 spoons) $50
Molasses, can, 2 styles $275
Mug, beer, 4½″ tall $40
Mustard jar with cover and spoon, 3¾″ tall $40
Napkin ring, 2″ $15
Nappy, 4¼″, 1 handle $12
Nappy, 5¼″, 1 handle $14
Nappy, 5¼″, 2 handles $15
Nappy, triangular-shaped with loop handle $15
Nut dish, 4½″ oval $15
Nut dish, oval (3¾″ × 2¾″) $10
Olive dish, oval (6″ × 3½″) $12
Pickle dish, oval (8″ × 4″) $15
Pin tray, 5¼″ oval $100
Pitcher, 44 oz., 7½″ tall $75
Pitcher, 69 oz., jug-style $125
Pitcher, syrup with metal lid, 5¼″ tall, 6 oz. $80
Pitcher, syrup with metal lid, 6¾″ tall, 11 oz. $90
Pitcher, water, 55 oz., 8″ tall $100
Pitcher, water, 58 oz., 7¼″ tall $100
Pitcher, water, 71 oz. $110
Plate, 7″ $8
Plate, 8½″ $10
Plate, 9½″ $12
Plate, 9″ $10
Plate, 10½″ $12
Plate, 10″, square-shaped, pedestal base $15
Plate, 11 ½″ $15
Plate, torte, 14″ $40
Platter, 10½″ oval $50
Platter, 12″ round $100
Platter, 13″ round $100
Platter, 18″ torte $125
Platter, 20″ torte $150
Platter, 24″ torte $175
Puff box with cover, (3″ × 3″ × 2⅞″), cube-shaped $125
Punch bowl with stand, 14″, 10″ tall, 2 gallon $350
Punch bowl with stand, 18″, 12″ tall, 3¾ gallon $450

Punch cup, several styles $10
Relish dish, 8¹/₂″ oval, 2-section $25
Relish dish, 9¹/₂″ oval, 3-section $35
Relish dish, 10¹/₂″ oval, 3-section $40
Relish dish, 11″ oblong, 2-section $35
Relish dish, 11″ square, 4-section $175
Ring holder $20
Salt and pepper shakers, 2-styles, (3″ or 3¹/₄″ tall) $25
Sandwich server with center handle $40
Saucer, 6″ $4
Sherbet, 31/″ tall, 4¹/₂ oz. $8
Sherbet, 3¹/₂″ tall, 4¹/₂ oz., with handle $10
Sherbet, 4¹/₄″ tall, flared, hexagonal stem $12
Spoon, serving $35
Spooner, 3³/₄″ tall $8
Sugar shaker with chrome top, 4³/₄″ tall $25
Sugar with cover, 6¹/₄″ tall, (large) $15
Sugar, open, individual, 6 oz., 2-handled (small) $12
Tidbit, 7″ tall, 3-footed $22
Toothpick holder, 2¹/₄″ tall $20
Tray, boat, 12″ oblong, 4¹/₂″ wide $70
Tray, boat, 8¹/₂″ oblong, 3¹/₂″ width $50
Tray, celery, oval, (10″ × 4¹/₂″) $35
Tray, fruit, 16″ round, 4″ tall $95
Tray, ice cream, oval, (13¹/₂″ × 10″) $70
Tray, oval, (10″ × 5″), 2-handled $40
Tray, oval, (6³/₄″ × 3″) $12
Tray, serving, oval, (11¹/₂″ × 8″) $60
Tumbler, 4 ″ tall, 8 oz. $15
Tumbler, 4¹/₄″ tall, 8 oz. $16
Tumbler, 5¹/₄″ tall, 8 oz. $18
Vase, 8″ tall, bud, footed $20
Vase, 8″ tall, cylindrically shaped, 3¹/₂″ diameter $55
Vase, 9¹/₂″, flared $40
Vase, 9″ tall, square-footed $40
Vase, 10″ tall, 4″ diameter, cylindrically shaped $65
Vase, 10″ tall, 6″ diameter $100
Vase, 10″ tall, 8 ″ diameter $100
Vase, 12″ tall, 4¹/₂″ diameter, cylindrically shaped $80
Vase, 15″ tall, narrow $65
Vase, 20″ tall, narrow $85
Vase, 25″ tall, narrow $115
Vase, bud, 6″ tall, footed $40
Vase, 6″ tall, flared $20
Whiskey tumbler, 2 oz. $15
Wine glass, 4¹/₄″ tall, 2¹/₂ oz. $12

APOLLO   ADAMS & COMPANY, 1870s

There was also an "Apollo" pattern made by McKee, which was quite different from Adam's style.

Bowl, 7″
Crystal $25
Frosted $35
Ruby-flashed $50
Bowl, 8″
Crystal $30
Frosted $40
Ruby-flashed $60
Butter dish with cover
Crystal $40
Frosted $50
Ruby-flashed $75
Cake stand, 10″
Crystal $70
Frosted $80
Ruby-flashed $110
Celery with base, upright
Crystal $25
Frosted $35
Ruby-flashed $50
Cheese dish with cover
Crystal $85
Frosted $110
Ruby-flashed $140
Compote with cover, 8″
Crystal $55
Frosted $70
Ruby-flashed $95
Compote, open, 5″
Crystal $35
Frosted $45
Ruby-flashed $65
Creamer
Crystal $40
Frosted $50
Ruby-flashed $70
Egg holder
Crystal $25
Frosted $35
Ruby-flashed $50
Goblet
Crystal $35
Frosted $45
Ruby-flashed $65
Pickle dish
Crystal $25

Frosted $35
Ruby-flashed $45

Pitcher, syrup with lid
Crystal $75
Frosted $85
Ruby-flashed $115

Pitcher, water
Crystal $55
Frosted $77
Ruby-flashed $100

Sauce dish, flat
Crystal $8
Frosted $10
Ruby-flashed $15

Sauce dish, footed
Crystal $10
Frosted $15
Ruby-flashed $20

Spooner
Crystal $25
Frosted $35
Ruby-flashed $50

Sugar shaker
Crystal $35
Frosted $45
Ruby-flashed $60

Tray
Crystal $35
Frosted $45
Ruby-flashed $60

Tumbler
Crystal $25
Frosted $35
Ruby-flashed $50

Wine
Crystal $35
Frosted $45
Ruby-flashed $65

ARCHED GRAPE BOSTON & SANDWICH GLASS COMPANY, 1870s–1880s

One of the many typical "Grape" patterns produced throughout the 19th century.

Butter dish with cover $65
Celery vase $45
Compote with cover (high) $75
Compote with cover (low) $60
Creamer $30

Pressed glass, "Arched Grape" pattern. DRAWING BY MARK PICKVET.

Pitcher, water	$85
Sauce dish, 4″	$10
Spooner	$25
Stemware, cordial	$45
Stemware, wine goblet	$35
Sugar dish	$30
Sugar with cover	$45

ASHBURTON   VARIOUS COMPANIES, 1840s–1880s

"Ashburton" is a large thumbprint pattern that was made in some quantity by Boston & Sandwich, New England, McKee, and many others. There are a few rare pieces, such as the toddy jar, butter dish, and creamer. Prices steadily increased over the past few years, especially for the larger and rarer pieces. Double the prices below for any colored items (a few flashed ruby red pieces have been found). The creamer, sugar, wine glass, and goblet have all been reproduced, which is cause for some concern.

Ale glass, 5″ tall, Crystal	$65
Bitters bottle	$75
Butter dish with cover	$175
Candy dish (no cover)	$75
Celery dish	$85
Celery dish, scalloped	$100
Cordial, 4¹/₂″ tall	$100
Creamer	$225
Decanter with stopper, 16 oz.	$100
Decanter with stopper, 32 oz.	$125
Decanter with stopper, 48 oz.	$150
Egg holder	$75
Goblet, barrel-shaped cup, flared, Crystal	$40
Goblet, straight sides	$40
Lamp	$175
Mug	$25

Pitcher, milk, 32 oz. $250
Pitcher, syrup with lid, 16 oz., jug-style $250
Pitcher, water, 48 oz. $275
Sauce dish (large) $25
Sauce dish (small) $15
Spooner $45
Sugar with cover $175
Toddy jar with cover, handled, matching underplate $425
Toddy jar with cover, matching underplate $375
Tumbler, water $75
Tumbler, water, footed $125
Tumbler, whiskey, with handle $125
Wine glass $40

BALDER   U.S. GLASS COMPANY, 1890s–EARLY 1900s

A few pieces of this pattern were trimmed in gold (add 25% to the prices below for any not listed), but it is difficult to find those with the gold lining or trim completely intact. Note that gold trim can usually be removed from clear or colored glass with a pencil eraser, but be careful with flashed items: the flashing could easily be scraped or rubbed off. "Balder" is also known as the U.S. Glass Company's "Pennsylvania" pattern in that company's state series.

Bowl, 8″
  Crystal $20
  Emerald-green $30
  Ruby-red $35
Butter dish with cover
  Crystal $75
  Emerald-green $125
  Ruby-red $175
Carafe
  Crystal $35
  Emerald-green $45
  Ruby-red $60
Carafe, water
  Crystal $65
  Emerald-green $75
  Ruby-red $85
Compote, ruffled
  Crystal $35
  Emerald-green $45
  Ruby-red $60
Creamer (large)
  Crystal $30
  Emerald-green $40
  Ruby-red $50
Creamer, individual (small)
  Crystal $20

Emerald-green $30
Ruby-red $35

Cup
Crystal $10
Emerald-green $12
Ruby-red $15

Goblet
Crystal $25
Emerald-green $35
Ruby-red $40

Goblet with gold trim
Crystal $30
Emerald-green $40
Ruby-red $50

Pitcher, syrup with metal lid
Crystal $60
Emerald-green $85
Ruby-red $115

Plate, 8″
Crystal $25
Emerald-green $35
Ruby-red $40

Punch cup
Crystal $10
Emerald-green $12
Ruby-red $15

Sauce dish
Crystal $10
Emerald-green $12
Ruby-red $15

Spooner
Crystal $20
Emerald-green $30
Ruby-red $35

Sugar with cover (large)
Crystal $35
Emerald-green $45
Ruby-red $60

Sugar, handled (small)
Crystal $15
Emerald-green $20
Ruby-red $25

Tumbler
Crystal $25
Emerald-green $35
Ruby-red $40

Whiskey tumbler
Crystal $60
Emerald-green $80
Ruby-red $115

Wine glass
Crystal $20
Emerald-green $30
Ruby-red $35

Wine glass with gold trim
Crystal $25
Emerald-green $35
Ruby-red $40

BARRED OVAL GEORGE DUNCAN & SONS AND U.S. GLASS COMPANY, 1890s–EARLY 1900s

The frosted items can be found more often than the rare ruby red. The pattern is characterized by five horizontal bars that pass through the center of the ovals in each object.

Bottle, water
Crystal $50
Frosted $75
Ruby-red $125

Butter dish with cover
Crystal $100
Frosted $150
Ruby-red $250

Celery dish
Crystal $35
Frosted $60
Ruby-red $85

Compote, open
Crystal $40
Frosted $70
Ruby-red $100

Creamer
Crystal $40
Frosted $60
Ruby-red $85

Cruet with faceted stopper
Crystal $75
Frosted $175
Ruby-red $300

Goblet
Crystal $25
Frosted $40
Ruby-red $60

Pitcher, water
Crystal $100
Frosted $175
Ruby-red $250

Plate, 5″
Crystal $25

Frosted $40
Ruby-red $60
Sauce dish
Crystal $15
Frosted $25
Ruby-red $40
Spooner
Crystal $25
Frosted $40
Ruby-red $60
Sugar with cover
Crystal $60
Frosted $85
Ruby-red $175
Tumbler
Crystal $25
Frosted $40
Ruby-red $60

BASKET WEAVE   VARIOUS COMPANIES, 1880s–1890s

Colored pieces include amber, blue, green, and yellow. Beware of modern reproductions of pitchers, tumblers, and goblets.

Bowl with cover
Colors $55
Crystal $35
Bowl, berry
Colors $40
Crystal $25
Bowl, finger
Colors $45
Crystal $30
Butter dish
Colors $55
Crystal $35
Cake plate
Colors $75
Crystal $50
Compote with cover
Colors $75
Crystal $50
Cordial
Colors $50
Crystal $35
Creamer
Colors $40
Crystal $30

Cup
　Colors $35
　Crystal $25
Egg holder, double
　Colors $40
　Crystal $30
Goblet
　Colors $40
　Crystal $30
Lamp
　Colors $75
　Crystal $50
Mug
　Colors $35
　Crystal $25
Pickle dish
　Colors $40
　Crystal $30
Pitcher, milk
　Colors $85
　Crystal $60
Pitcher, syrup with metal lid
　Colors $100
　Crystal $75
Pitcher, water
　Colors $100
　Crystal $75
Plate, 8 ³/₄″, 2 handles
　Colors $30
　Crystal $20
Salt and pepper shakers
　Colors $60
　Crystal $40
Salt dip
　Colors $22
　Crystal $15
Sauce dish, round
　Colors $40
　Crystal $22
Saucer
　Colors $18
　Crystal $12
Spooner
　Colors $35
　Crystal $25
Sugar
　Colors $45
　Crystal $35
Tray, 12″ diameter
　Colors $65
　Crystal $45

Wine glass
Colors $40
Crystal $30

BEADED MEDALLION GRAPE   BOSTON SILVER GLASS
COMPANY, LATE 1860s–1870s

The feet of certain objects may be plain or banded. The traditional grape design is in a cameo or medallion form. Color flashed versions were made during the Depression era.

Bowl, oval (large), $8^{1}/_{2}''$ $40
Bowl, oval (small) $30
Butter dish, acorn finial $70
Castor bottle $85
Celery vase $45
Champagne glass $50
Compote with cover (high), oval, $(10'' \times 7'')$ $95
Compote with cover (low), oval $75
Cordial $80
Creamer, applied handle $50
Egg holder $30
Goblet $35
Honey dish $30
Lamp, handled $100
Pickle dish $40
Pitcher, water $150
Plate, 6″ $45
Salt dip, footed $35
Salt dip, oval, flat $30
Salt dip, round, flat $30
Spooner $30
Sugar bowl with cover, acorn finial $85

Pressed glass, "Beaded Grape Medallion" pattern. DRAWING BY MARK PICKVET.

BEDFORD   FOSTORIA GLASS COMPANY, 1901–1905

"Bedford" was one of Fostoria's first lines of glass and was referred to as "Line No. 1000."

Bonbon dish, 5″, 1 handle	$25
Bonbon dish, 6″, 1 handle	$30
Bowl, 9″ oval	$40
Bowl, 10″ oval	$45
Bowl, berry, 7″	$30
Bowl, berry, 8″	$35
Butter dish with cover	$100
Celery vase	$40
Claret glass	$40
Compote, 6″, open	$40
Compote, 7″, open	$45
Compote with cover, 6″	$85
Cracker jar with cover	$175
Creamer (large)	$40
Creamer, individual (small)	$30
Cruet with hollow stopper	$60
Cup, custard	$30
Goblet	$40
Ice cream tray, rectangular	$55
Pitcher, jug-shaped	$75
Salt dip, individual	$22
Spooner	$35
Sugar (large)	$60
Sugar shaker	$65
Sugar with cover, individual (small)	$55
Toothpick holder	$50
Tumbler, water	$35
Whiskey tumbler	$20
Wine glass	$40

BELLFLOWER   VARIOUS COMPANIES, 1840s–1880s

Also known as the "Ribbed Leaf and Bellflower," this pattern boasts some of the oldest, rarest, and most valuable early pattern glass made in America. It is also characterized by fine vertical ribbing. Some pieces may have a single or double vine within the pattern. A few rare colors, such as amber and cobalt, also exist (double the prices below). Boston & Sandwich Glass Company was the original maker of this pattern, but others, such as McKee Brothers, also produced it.

Bowl, 6″	$105
Bowl, 8″	$130
Bowl, flat, scalloped and pointed edge	$175
Bowl, flat, with scalloped edge	$130
Bowl, oval, 7″ × 5″	$55
Bowl, oval, 9″ × 6″	$65

Pressed glass, "Bellflower" pattern. DRAWING BY MARK PICKVET.

Butter dish with cover, beaded edge $150
Butter dish with cover, plain edge $125
Butter dish with cover, rayed edge $175
Cake stand $2000
Celery vase $225
Champagne glass $125
Compote with cover (high), 8″ $175
Compote with cover (low), 8″ $150
Compote, open (high), 8¹/₂″ tall, 9³/₄″ diameter $125
Compote, open (high), 8″ $110
Compote, open (low), 6³/₄″ $100
Cordial, several styles $75
Creamer $150
Cruet with stopper $100
Decanter, with bellflower-patterned stopper, 16–32 oz. $550
Decanter with stopper, 16 oz. $275
Decanter with stopper, 32 oz. $325
Egg holder, flared sides $55
Egg holder, straight sides $50
Goblet (several styles) $55
Honey dish, 3¹/₄″ × 2¹/₂″ $30
Lamp, bracket, all glass $375
Lamp, marble base $200
Mug, applied handle $275
Pickle dish $60
Pitcher, milk $750
Pitcher, syrup with lid, 10-sided $1100
Pitcher, syrup with lid, round $850
Pitcher, water, 2 styles $325
Plate, 6″ $125
Salt dip, footed $50
Salt dip with cover, footed $200
Sauce dish, various styles $30
Spooner $50
Sugar with cover $175
Sugar, octagonal $400
Tumbler, footed $250
Tumbler, water $125
Whiskey tumbler $200
Wine glass, several styles $125

BERRY OR BARBERRY BOSTON & SANDWICH GLASS
COMPANY, 1860s; MCKEE BROTHERS, 1880s.

The berries on this pattern may be round or oval, and the number varies (particularly on the goblets). A few pale green pieces have been found (same price as the clear), as well as amber and blue (double the prices below).

Bowl with cover, 8″	$65
Bowl, oval, (8″ × 5½″)	$70
Butter dish with cover, 8″	$90
Cake stand	$150
Celery dish	$50
Compote with cover (high)	$65
Compote with cover (high), shell finial	$85
Compote with cover (low)	$55
Cordial	$60
Creamer	$45
Egg holder	$40
Goblet	$35
Honey dish, 3½″	$22
Pickle dish	$28
Pitcher, syrup, with pewter lid	$175
Pitcher, water, applied handle	$150
Plate, 6″	$22
Salt dip, footed	$30
Sauce dish	$30
Sauce dish, footed	$35
Spooner	$35
Sugar with cover	$60
Wine glass	$35

BLEEDING HEART BOSTON & SANDWICH GLASS COMPANY,
1860s–1870s; KING, SON AND COMPANY, 1870s.

This pattern, originally known as "Floral," features a floral design that is usually separated by a vertical line above the halfway point. King, Son and Company also produced this pattern in white opaque (milk) glass (increase the prices below by 25%).

Bowl with cover	$75
Bowl, oval	$60
Bowl, waste	$50
Butter dish	$95
Cake plate with stand, 9″ - 9½″ tall	$80
Cake stand, 11″ tall	$100
Compote with cover, high-footed	$95
Compote with cover, low-footed	$85
Compote with cover, oval	$110
Creamer, applied handle	$65

Pressed glass. Left: "Bleeding Heart" pattern. Right: "Block and Fan" pattern. DRAWINGS BY MARK PICKVET.

Egg holder, barrel-shaped	$50
Egg holder, straight-sided	$45
Goblet, knob on stem (several styles)	$40
Mug	$50
Pickle dish, oval	$35
Pitcher, milk	$225
Pitcher, water	$175
Plate (several styles)	$75
Platter, oval	$85
Relish dish, 4 divisions	$125
Salt dip, oval	$40
Salt dip, round, footed	$30
Sauce dish, oval	$28
Sauce dish, round, flat	$22
Spooner	$40
Sugar with cover	$75
Tray, oval	$50
Tumbler, footed	$50
Tumbler, water	$75
Wine glass	$50

BLOCK AND FAN RICHARDS & HARTLEY GLASS COMPANY, 1880s

This design, also known as the "Romeo" pattern, is characterized by horizontal bands of fans that circle the top and bottom of each object. Between the fans are horizontal rows of blocks. There are a few rare ruby-flashed pieces (double the listed prices).

Bowl, 8″	$40
Butter dish with cover	$75
Cake stand, 10″	$55
Celery vase	$45
Compote, open	$45

Cordial $55
Creamer $45
Cruet without stopper (large) $50
Cruet without stopper (small) $40
Goblet $50
Jam jar without cover $85
Lamp $150
Pickle dish $30
Pitcher, water, pedestal base $85
Plate, 10½″ $30
Salt and pepper shakers $55
Sauce dish, 4″, circular, footed $25
Sauce dish, square, flat $20
Spooner $35
Sugar with cover $60
Sugar, open $45
Tumbler $45
Wine glass $50

BROKEN COLUMN   VARIOUS COMPANIES, 1880s–1890s

This pattern, also referred to as "Irish Column" and "Notched Rim," is characterized by raised columns that project outward from the object. Known producers
were the Columbia Glass Company, The Portland Glass Company, and the U.S.
Glass Company. Some pieces have ruby notches or flashing (double the prices below); others are trimmed in gold (increase the prices by about a third). Beware of
reproductions—both the goblet and compotes have been reproduced.

Banana dish, flat $55
Banana stand $200
Basket with handle, 13½″ long $110
Bottle, water $85
Bowl, 6″, with cover $45
Bowl, 7″, with cover $50
Bowl, 8½″ $50

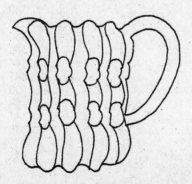

Pressed glass, "Broken Column" pattern.
DRAWING BY MARK PICKVET.

Bowl, 8″, with cover $55
Bowl, finger $25
Butter dish with cover $95
Cake stand, 9″ $100
Celery dish $50
Celery tray $50
Compote with cover $100
Compote, open $60
Creamer $50
Cruet with stopper $85
Cup, custard $25
Goblet $45
Pitcher, syrup with lid, jug-shaped $100
Pitcher, water $100
Plate, 7³/₄″ $35
Salt and pepper shakers with pewter tops $60
Sauce dish, flat $20
Spooner $35
Sugar $50
Sugar shaker $75
Tumbler $50
Wine Glass $45

BUCKLE   VARIOUS COMPANIES, 1850s–1870s

The original "Buckle" pattern is attributed to Boston & Sandwich, but others followed. Those listed "with band" are identical in pattern except for an extra horizontal band at the top of each piece. The pattern is also sometimes referred to as
"Oaken Bucket." Some pieces were made in a finer grade of crystal (add 25% to the
prices below); also, a few light blue pieces have been foound (double the prices).
Water pitchers are very rare in this pattern.

Bowl, 6″, rolled rim $65
Bowl, 6″, with band, flat rim $30
Bowl, 7″, with band, flat rim $35
Bowl, 7″, rolled rim $70
Bowl, 8″, rolled rim $75
Bowl, 8″, with band, flat rim $40
Butter dish with cover $110
Champagne glass $50
Compote with cover, with band $60
Compote, open $45
Compote, open, with band $45
Cordial, with band $50
Creamer, pedestal foot, applied handles $60
Creamer, with band $45
Egg holder $35
Egg holder, with band $35
Goblet $35

Pressed glass, "Buckle" pattern. COURTESY OF THE SANDWICH GLASS MUSEUM.

Goblet, with band $35
Pickle dish, oval $40
Pitcher, water, applied handle $775
Pitcher, water, with band $525
Salt dip, footed $20
Salt dip, footed, with band $18
Salt dip, oval, flat, pattern in base only $16
Spooner, scalloped $35
Spooner, with band $25
Sugar with cover $70
Sugar with cover, with band $55
Tumbler $50
Tumbler, with band $40
Wine glass $40

BULL'S-EYE   VARIOUS COMPANIES, 1850s–1870s

The original "Bull's-Eye" pattern was made by both the New England Glass Company and the Boston & Sandwich Glass Company. A few pieces were produced in green, red, and milk white (double the prices below). Several variations of the basic "Bull's-Eye" pattern were produced by the U.S. Glass Company, the Union Glass Company, Dalzell, Gilmore & Leighton, and others. These include "Bull's-Eye and Daisy," "Bull's-Eye and Fan," "Bull's-Eye with Fleur-de-Lis," "Bull's-Eye and Pillar," and "Bull's Eye and Star." The prices are comparable for all basic pattern variants.

Bitter's bottle $85
Bottle, water, tumble-up $200
Butter dish with cover $175

Pressed glass, "Bull's Eye" pattern. Reproduced from a 19th century McKee Brothers catalog.

Pressed glass, "Bull's Eye" pattern. PHOTO BY MARK PICKVET.

Castor bottle with stopper $75
Celery vase $90
Champagne glass $125
Cologne bottle with stopper $125
Compote, open (high) $85
Compote, open (low), footed $65
Creamer $150
Cruet with stopper $65
Decanter with stopper, 16 oz. $200
Decanter with stopper, 32 oz. $350
Egg cup with cover $225
Egg holder $55
Goblet $80
Goblet, with knobbed stem $95
Jam jar with cover $100
Jelly dish $40
Lamp $150

Pickle dish, oval $50
Salt dip with cover, oblong, footed $125
Salt dip, footed $40
Spooner $45
Sugar with cover $175
Toothpick holder $35
Tumbler (small), 3¹/₂" $50
Tumbler, water $100
Wine glass $50

BUTTON ARCHES   DUNCAN & MILLER GLASS COMPANY, 1890s

The arched button design of this pattern appears on the lower quarter or fifth of most objects. "Button Arches" was a popular pattern for souvenirs. Most pieces can be found with ruby red, ruby flashed, etched, engraved, and frosted band designs. The prices below are for plain crystal. Increase the prices by 50% for ruby or ruby flashed and by 25% for any etching, engraving, or frosted bands. There are a few clambroth or off-white opaque pieces in this pattern as well (double the listed prices).

Bowl, 8" $30
Cake stand, 9¹/₄" $50
Compote $30
Creamer $30
Cruet with stopper $75
Cup $20
Goblet $20
Mug (large), 4" $25
Mug (small), 3" $20
Pitcher, syrup $175
Pitcher, water $100
Punch cup $15
Salt and pepper shakers $50
Spooner $20
Sugar dish with cover $45
Toothpick holder $20
Tumbler, water $30
Wine glass $20

CABBAGE ROSE   CENTRAL GLASS COMPANY, 1880s–1890s

The pattern is usually on the lower half to two-thirds of each object and is separated from the clear unpatterned portion by a horizontal band.

Bowl, oval, 7¹/₂" $35
Butter dish with cover $85
Cake stand, 9¹/₄" $50
Cake stand, 11" $75

Cake stand, 12½″ $88
Celery vase $50
Compote with cover, 6″ $65
Compote with cover, 7″ $70
Compote with cover, 8″ $75
Compote with cover, 9″ $85
Compote with cover, 10″ $100
Cordial $50
Creamer, applied handle $60
Egg holder $45
Goblet $40
Pickle dish $30
Pitcher, 32 oz. $150
Pitcher, 48 oz. $175
Salt dip, footed, beaded rim $35
Sauce dish, several varieties $20
Spooner $40
Sugar $45
Sugar with cover $75
Tumbler, water $50

CABLE   BOSTON & SANDWICH, 1850s

Color pieces are very rare and include opaque blue and opaque green. Some pieces can also be found with amber panels. "Cable" was produced to commemorate the laying of the Transatlantic cable linking Europe to America. A few pattern variations were introduced later by other companies.

Butter dish with cover
   Colors $275
   Crystal $125
Compote, 5¾″ tall, 11″ diameter
   Colors $225
   Crystal $100
Compote, 9¾″ tall, 10″ diameter
   Colors $275
   Crystal $125
Cordial
   Colors $275
   Crystal $125
Creamer
   Colors $750
   Crystal $350
Decanter with stopper, 16 oz.
   Colors $450
   Crystal $225
Decanter with stopper, 32 oz.
   Colors $525
   Crystal $275

Egg holder
Colors $125
Crystal $55
Goblet
Colors $150
Crystal $65
Honey dish
Colors $100
Crystal $55
Lamp, all glass
Colors $375
Crystal $175
Lamp, with marble base
Colors $300
Crystal $125
Mug
Colors $225
Crystal $100
Pitcher, syrup
Colors $750
Crystal $350
Pitcher, water
Colors $1250
Crystal $500
Plate, 6″
Colors $225
Crystal $100
Salt dip, footed
Colors $75
Crystal $35
Salt dip, individual, flat
Colors $70
Crystal $30
Sauce dish
Colors $75
Crystal $35
Spooner
Colors $85
Crystal $40
Sugar with cover
Colors $250
Crystal $110
Tumbler, footed
Colors $400
Crystal $175
Wine glass
Colors $100
Crystal $50

CALIFORNIA   U.S. GLASS COMPANY, 1880s–1890s

The "California" pattern, also known as "Beaded Grape," features a horizontal line of beading at the top as well as vertical bands that frame the grape design. Some pieces were trimmed in gold (add 25% to the prices below if the gold is completely intact).

Bowl, oblong
Crystal $25
Green $40
Bowl, 5¼″ square
Crystal $20
Green $35
Bowl, 6¼″ square
Crystal $25
Green $40
Bowl, 7¼″ square
Crystal $30
Green $45
Bowl, 8¼″ square
Crystal $35
Green $50
Butter dish with cover
Crystal $70
Green $90
Cake stand
Crystal $55
Green $75
Celery tray, oblong
Crystal $35
Green $45
Compote with cover, 7″ tall
Crystal $40
Green $55
Compote with cover, 8″ tall
Crystal $45
Green $60
Compote with cover, 9″ tall
Crystal $50
Green $65
Compote, open, 4″ tall
Crystal $25
Green $35
Compote, square, 6″
Crystal $30
Green $40
Cordial
Crystal $45
Green $65
Creamer
Crystal $40
Green $55

Cruet with swirl stopper
Crystal $85
Green $110
Goblet
Crystal $30
Green $45
Jelly dish with cover, 4″ tall
Crystal $40
Green $55
Pickle dish
Crystal $30
Green $40
Pitcher, 32 oz., (round)
Crystal $75
Green $100
Pitcher, 32 oz., (square)
Crystal $80
Green $110
Pitcher, 48 oz., (round)
Crystal $85
Green $125
Pitcher, 48 oz., (square)
Crystal $90
Green $135
Pitcher, 64 oz., (round)
Crystal $125
Green $175
Plate, 8½″ square
Crystal $25
Green $35
Platter, 10¼″ × 7¼″, oblong
Crystal $50
Green $65
Salt and pepper shakers
Crystal $50
Green $75
Salt and pepper shakers with metal tops
Crystal $60
Green $80
Salt dish, 4½″
Crystal $16
Green $20
Sauce dish, 3½″
Crystal $12
Green $15
Sauce dish, 4″
Crystal $14
Green $18
Sauce dish with 2 handles
Crystal $16
Green $22

Spooner
 Crystal $25
 Green $35
Sugar shaker
 Crystal $60
 Green $85
Sugar with cover
 Crystal $60
 Green $80
Toothpick holder
 Crystal $40
 Green $55
Tumbler, water
 Crystal $35
 Green $50
Vase, 6″ tall
 Crystal $25
 Green $35
Wine glass
 Crystal $30
 Green $45

COLORADO   U.S. GLASS COMPANY, 1890s–EARLY 1900s

"Colorado" is part of the state series by U.S. Glass. There are several color variations associated with this pattern. For green, cobalt blue, and ruby red, increase the
prices below by 50%. For clambroth, double the prices. For the rare amethyst-
stained glass in this pattern, triple the prices. Finally, increase the prices by 25% for
engraved pieces. Note that some pieces may also contain enameled decorations
(same prices) and some gold trimming (increase price by 25% if the gold is completely intact).

Bowl, triangular $25
Butter dish with cover $75
Cheese dish, footed $40
Compote, 9¹/₄″ $75
Creamer $40
Nappy, 7¹/₄″ $25
Pitcher, water $60
Plate, 6³/₄″ $35
Salt and pepper shakers, 3-footed $50
Spooner $30
Sugar with cover (large) $55
Sugar, individual, 2 open handles (small) $25
Toothpick holder $40
Tray, 4″, crimped $25
Tray, 4″, flared $20
Tray, 8″, crimped $35
Tray, 8″, flared $30

Tumbler	$30
Tumbler, souvenir	$35

CORD AND TASSEL   CENTRAL GLASS COMPANY, 1870s

Several items in this pattern (creamer, cruet, lamp, mug, pitcher, and sugar) have handles that were either applied or pressed. The price is the same for either method.

Bowl, oval	$35
Butter dish with cover	$75
Cake stand	$55
Celery vase	$45
Compote with cover, 8″	$75
Cordial	$30
Creamer	$40
Cruet with stopper	$65
Egg holder	$40
Goblet	$40
Lamp, low pedestal	$95
Mug	$45
Pitcher, water	$125
Sauce dish, flat	$20
Spooner	$30
Sugar with cover	$60
Wine glass	$40

CORD DRAPERY   INDIANA TUMBLER & GOBLET COMPANY, 1890s–EARLY 1900s

Colors include amber, canary yellow, cobalt blue, emerald and opaque nile green, and white. Chocolate pieces are far more valuable than these colors (2–3 times) and are listed under "Chocolate" in Chapter 4.

Pressed glass. Left: "Cord and Tassel" pattern. Right: "Cord Drapery" pattern.
DRAWINGS BY MARK PICKVET.

Bowl, berry
Colors $40
Crystal $25

Bowl, oval, deep
Colors $60
Crystal $40

Butter dish with cover
Colors $100
Crystal $60

Cake stand
Colors $85
Crystal $55

Compote with cover, 8″
Colors $200
Crystal $125

Compote, open, fluted
Colors $110
Crystal $65

Creamer
Colors $80
Crystal $50

Cruet with dewey stopper (amber only) $350

Goblet
Colors $75
Crystal $45

Jelly dish with cover
Colors $85
Crystal $55

Pitcher, syrup with lid
Colors $175
Crystal $100

Pitcher, water
Colors $175
Crystal $100

Plate, 6″
Colors $75
Crystal $40

Punch cup
Colors $35
Crystal $20

Relish dish, $9^{1}/_{4} \times 5^{1}/_{4}$″
Colors $75
Crystal $40

Salt and pepper shakers
Colors $85
Crystal $50

Sauce dish
Colors $40
Crystal $25

Spooner
    Colors $55
    Crystal $35
Sugar
    Colors $80
    Crystal $50
Tumbler
    Colors $70
    Crystal $40
Wine glass
    Colors $75
    Crystal $45

CROESUS   RIVERSIDE GLASSWORKS, 1890s

"Croesus" is characterized by curves, shells, and diamonds. Double the prices below for emerald green and triple them for the rare amethyst color. For intact gold trimming, increase the prices by 25%. Beware of reproductions. Toothpick holders and tumblers have been reproduced in America, while the 4-piece table set has been reproduced in Japan.

Bowl with cover, 7" $60
Bowl, scalloped rim $35
Butter dish with cover $85
Celery dish $35
Compote with cover $75
Creamer, small (individual) $25
Creamer, medium (berry) $35
Creamer, large (regular table size) $45
Cruet with stopper $150
Pitcher, water $75
Salt and pepper shakers $60
Sauce dish $25
Spooner $25
Sugar bowl with cover $75
Table set, 4-piece $175
Toothpick holder $55
Tray $50
Tumbler, water $35

CRYSTAL WEDDING   ADAMS GLASS COMPANY, 1880s

"Crystal Wedding" was also produced in amber, blue, yellow, and ruby-stained (double the prices below). For any frosted, engraved, or banded designs, increase the prices by 25%. Beware of reproductions, particularly the compotes.

Banana stand $125
Basket, fruit $125

Bowl, 7″, scalloped rim $50
Butter dish with cover $85
Cake stand, 9″, square-shaped $100
Celery dish $50
Claret glass $50
Compote with cover (high) $50
Compote with cover (low) $35
Creamer $60
Cruet with square stopper $100
Goblet $45
Lamp, 9″ $275
Pickle dish, oblong $50
Pitcher, water, square-shaped $225
Salt and pepper shakers $80
Salt dish $40
Spooner $40
Sugar bowl with cover $75
Tumbler, water $45
Vase $75

CUPID AND VENUS   Richards & Hartley Glass Company, 1870s–1880s

This pattern is sometimes referred to as "Guardian Angel." The mythological figures appear in beaded medallion form. Amber and a few vaseline items have been found (double the listed prices for colors).

Bowl, oval $75
Butter dish with cover $100
Cake plate, 11″ $75
Celery vase, scalloped rim $65
Champagne glass $125
Compote with cover (high) $90
Compote with cover (low) $75

*Pressed glass, "Cupid and Venus"
pattern. DRAWING BY MARK PICKVET.*

Compote, open $50
Cordial $80
Creamer $50
Goblet $75
Marmalade jar with cover $150
Mug, 2″ $30
Mug, 2½″ $35
Mug, 3½″ $40
Pickle castor $25
Pickle castor in frame, metal lid $225
Pitcher, milk, 7½″ $75
Pitcher, water $100
Plate, 10½″ $45
Plate, 10½″, handled $50
Sauce dish, 3½″, footed $18
Sauce dish, 4″, footed $20
Sauce dish, 5″, footed $25
Sauce dish, round, flat $15
Spooner $40
Sugar with cover $85
Wine glass $100

DAISY AND BUTTON   GILLINDER & SONS, 1876; HOBBS, BRO-CUNIER AND COMPANY, 1880s; GEORGE DUNCAN & SONS, 1880s; RICHARDS & HARTLEY, 1890s; BRYCE BROTHERS, 1890s; U.S. GLASS COMPANY, 1890s; DUNKIRK GLASS COMPANY, EARLY 1900s.

This is a fairly common pressed pattern manufactured by many companies. The original "Daisy and Button" was created by Gillinder & Sons and was displayed at the Philadelphia Centennial Exhibition of 1876. The pattern is a geometric design consisting of spoked circles (daisies) and open or plain circles (buttons). The design is much like a cut glass look-a-like. There are several design variations as noted below, along with some unique and rare dishes. Crossbars, ovals, panels, narcissus floral designs, prisms, ornaments, and others can all be found with the basic pattern. Colors include amber, yellow, light and dark blue, rose, red, and green; increase prices below by 50%. For vaseline, double the prices. For intact gold trimming, increase prices by 25%. Beware of reproductions, especially of smaller pieces (toothpick holders, tumblers, etc.). L.G. Wright Company reproduced some pieces, including a 6″ boat-shaped dish.

Ashtray, 3-footed $10
Bowl, 7″, crossbars in pattern $25
Bowl, 7″, paneled pattern $25
Bowl, 8¾″, hexagonal $45
Bowl, 8″, crossbars in pattern $30
Bowl, 8″, paneled pattern $30
Bowl, 8″, triangular $65
Bowl, V-ornament design $35
Bowl with cover, 7½″, paneled pattern $50

Pressed glass, "Daisy & Button" pattern. Reproduced from a U.S. Glass Co. catalog.

Bowl with cover, 8½″, paneled pattern $65
Bowl, finger, crossbars in pattern $20
Butter dish with cover $100
Butter dish with cover, flat or footed, crossbars in pattern $75
Butter dish with cover, narcissus flower design $85
Butter dish with cover, oval medallion in pattern $75
Butter dish with cover, paneled pattern $100
Butter dish with cover, V-ornament design $75
Butter dish with Spartan helmet-shaped cover (rare) $250
Celery dish, oval medallion in pattern $35
Celery dish, thumbprints in pattern $35
Celery dish, V-ornament design $35
Celery vase, narcissus flower design $40
Compote, 8″, paneled pattern $50
Compote, 9½″, scalloped rim $40
Compote, narcissus flower design $50
Compote with cover, 7″, crossbars in pattern $50
Compote with cover, 8″, crossbars in pattern $60
Creamer $50
Creamer, crossbars in pattern $35
Creamer, narcissus flower design $40
Creamer, oval medallion in pattern $35
Creamer, paneled pattern $50
Creamer, prisms in pattern $40
Creamer, thumbprints in pattern $35
Creamer, V-ornament design $35
Cruet with square stopper, paneled pattern $175
Cruet with stopper, crossbars in pattern $65
Cup, V-ornament design $25
Decanter with stopper, narcissus flower design $125
Dish with fly-shaped cover (rare) $200
Dish, fan-shaped $20
Dish, oblong, V-ornament design $30
Goblet, crossbars in pattern $40
Goblet, narcissus flower design $40
Goblet, oval medallion in pattern $45
Goblet, thumbprint panels $55
Lamp, crossbars in pattern $100
Mug, crossbars in pattern $35
Pickle castor in frame, V-ornament design $100
Pitcher, milk, 1 qt., crossbars in pattern $75
Pitcher, milk or water, oval medallion in pattern $75
Pitcher, syrup, crossbars in pattern $75
Pitcher, water, 2 qt., crossbars in pattern $75
Pitcher, water, narcissus flower design $75
Pitcher, water, paneled pattern $125
Plate, 5″ $75
Platter, oval, 2-handled $50
Platter, oval, paneled pattern $65
Salt and pepper shakers, crossbars in pattern $55
Salt and pepper shakers, narcissus flower design $55

Salt and pepper shakers, pewter tops $65
Sauce dish, 4½″, footed, paneled pattern $25
Sauce dish, 4½″, paneled pattern $20
Sauce dish, narcissus flower design $20
Sauce dish, oval medallion in pattern $25
Spooner, crossbars in pattern $20
Spooner, narcissus flower design $25
Spooner, oval medallion in pattern $25
Spooner, V-ornament design $25
Sugar dish, V-ornament design $50
Sugar dish with cover $75
Sugar dish with cover $60
Sugar dish with cover, crossbars in pattern $50
Sugar dish with cover, narcissus flower design $60
Sugar dish with cover, oval medallion in pattern $50
Sugar dish with cover, paneled pattern $75
Sugar dish with cover, thumbprints in pattern $50
Toothpick holder $25
Toothpick holder, V-ornament design $35
Tray, water, crossbars in pattern $40
Tray, water, narcissus flower design $50
Tumbler, water $50
Tumbler, water, crossbars in pattern $40
Tumbler, water, narcissus flower design $40
Tumbler, water, paneled pattern $50
Tumbler, water, V-ornament design $40
Wine glass, crossbars in pattern $40
Wine glass, narcissus flower design $40

DAKOTA   U.S. GLASS COMPANY, 1890s

"Dakota" is also known as "Baby Thumbprint" or "Thumbprint Band" because of
the single band of thumbprints that make up the pattern. Colors include ruby-
flashed (increase prices by 50%) and the rare cobalt blue (triple prices). Some
pieces have been etched or engraved (increase prices by 25%).

Basket with metal handle $250
Bowl, 8″ $45
Butter dish with cover $100
Cake stand, 10″ $85
Celery vase, flat base $50
Compote with cover, 5″ $55
Compote with cover, 6″ $65
Compote with cover, 7″ $75
Compote with cover, 8″ $85
Creamer, pedestal base $60
Goblet $35
Jug, 1 qt. $90
Pitcher, water $100

Salt and pepper shakers	$85
Spooner, pedestal base	$35
Sugar dish with cover	$75
Tray, 13", ruffled edge	$100
Tumbler, water	$50
Wine glass	$35

DELAWARE U.S. GLASS COMPANY, BRYCE BROTHERS, AND KING GLASS COMPANY, LATE 1890s–EARLY 1900s

"Delaware," also called "New Century" and "Four Petal Flower," is characterized by long, thin leaves and 4-petaled flowers. The pattern was made in a variety of colors, including a pale red or rose stain and green (increase prices by 50%), and the rarer opaque green and milk glass (double prices). Gold trim was also applied to many of the pieces (increase prices by 25% for complete, intact gold trim).

Banana bowl, boat-shaped	$75
Bowl, 8", with or without flutes	$35
Bowl, 9", with or without flutes	$40
Butter dish with cover	$85
Celery vase	$45
Creamer	$50
Cup	$15
Pitcher, milk, (jug-shaped)	$125
Pitcher, water	$125
Punch cup	$15
Spooner	$35
Sugar dish with cover	$75
Tankard, 9¼"	$75
Toothpick holder	$60
Tumbler	$35

DIAMOND HORSESHOE THE BRILLIANT GLASS WORKS, LATE 1880s; GREENSBURG GLASS COMPANY, 1880s–1890s

This design is sometimes referred to as "Aurora." A few pieces were engraved (increase prices by 25%) and ruby-flashed (double prices).

Butter dish with cover	$85
Cake stand	$60
Compote with cover	$60
Compote, open	$35
Creamer	$45
Decanter with stopper	$85
Goblet	$35
Pitcher, water	$75
Salt and pepper shakers	$40
Spooner	$30

Pressed glass. Left, "Aurora" or
"Diamond Horseshoe" pattern.
Right: "Diamond Point" pattern.
DRAWINGS BY MARK PICKVET.

Sugar $45
Wine glass $30

DIAMOND POINT   VARIOUS COMPANIES, 1830s–1880s

The original "Diamond Point" was produced by the Boston & Sandwich Glass
Company as early as 1830. Bryce, Richards & Company produced pieces in the
1850s, and other companies followed. There are many rare pieces, and some colors
were produced (triple the prices for color). Note that these prices are for full lead
crystal (or flint glass) pieces. For cheaper lime formulas, decrease the prices by
about a third.

Ale glass $65
Bowl, 7″ oval $40
Bowl, 8″ oval $45
Bowl, 9″ oval $50
Bowl, 10″ oval $60
Butter dish with cover $150
Celery vase $75
Champagne glass $100
Compote, 6″, open $65
Compote, 7″, open $70
Compote, 8″, open $75
Compote with cover, 6″ $125
Compote with cover, 7″ $150
Compote with cover, 8″ $175
Cordial $65
Creamer, scalloped, footed $150
Cruet with stopper $150
Decanter with stopper, 16 oz. $225
Decanter with stopper, 32 oz. $275
Egg holder $45
Goblet, knob stem $60

Pressed glass, "Diamond Point" pattern. PHOTOS BY MARK PICKVET.

Honey dish	$40
Lamp	$200
Mug	$85
Pitcher, milk, 32 oz.	$175
Pitcher, milk, 32 oz., footed	$200
Pitcher, syrup, 16 oz.	$250
Pitcher, syrup, 16 oz., footed	$275
Pitcher, water, 48 oz.	$275
Pitcher, water, 48 oz., footed	$300
Plate, 3″–3¼″	$30
Plate, 5½″	$40
Plate, 6″	$45
Plate, 7″	$50
Plate, 8″	$55
Plate, Pie, 6″, (deep)	$65
Plate, Pie, 8″, (deep)	$75
Salt dip with cover, footed	$90
Sauce dish	$40
Spooner	$45
Sugar with cover, footed	$125
Tumbler, water	$75
Whiskey tumbler	$75

Pressed glass, "Dot" or "Beaded Oval and Scroll" pattern. DRAWING BY MARK PICKVET.

DOT   BRYCE BROTHERS, 1870s–1880s

"Dot" is also known as "Beaded Oval and Scroll" because of the large beaded vertical ovals that alternately enclose the scroll design.

Bowl, 6¼″ $30
Bowl, 8″ $35
Butter dish with cover $75
Cake stand $50
Compote with cover $60
Compote, open $35
Cordial $40
Creamer $35
Goblet $35
Pickle dish $30
Pitcher, water $75
Salt and pepper shakers $50
Sauce dish, flat $15
Spooner $30
Sugar with cover $60
Sugar, open $35
Wine glass $35

Pressed glass, "Excelsior" pattern. DRAWING BY MARK PICKVET.

EXCELSIOR VARIOUS COMPANIES, 1850s–1870s

"Excelsior" was made primarily by the Boston & Sandwich Glass Company, McKee Brothers, and C. Ihmsen and Company. A few other companies also produced it. Pale green items are found occasionally (increase prices by 25%). The pattern variant referred to below was produced exclusively under McKee Brothers and is sometimes referred to as "Tong." The ovals have a wider diameter (nearly circular) but converge at the bottom to what is nearly a point.

Ale glass $75
Bitters bottle $65
Bowl, 10″ $55
Bowl with cover $85
Butter dish with cover $150
Butter dish with cover (McKee Pattern variant) $100
Candlestick $150
Celery Vase (McKee Pattern Variant) $50
Celery Vase, scalloped (McKee Pattern Variant) $65
Champagne glass $60
Cordial (McKee Pattern variant) $60
Creamer (McKee Pattern variant) $125
Creamer, 2 styles $125
Decanter, 16 oz., with or without foot $75
Decanter, 32 oz. $85
Egg holder, single $45
Egg holder, double $55
Goblet (McKee Pattern variant) $50
Goblet, barrel-shaped bowl, Maltese Cross design (Boston & Sandwich) $80
Lamp, whale oil, Maltese Cross design (Boston & Sandwich) $250
Mug, applied handle $75
Pitcher, milk $400
Pitcher, syrup with lid $400
Pitcher, water (McKee only) $400
Salt dip, footed $35
Spooner (McKee Pattern variant) $40
Spooner, 4³/₄″ $45
Sugar with cover (McKee Pattern variant) $100
Sugar with cover, 6¹/₂″ $175
Sugar with cover, 8¹/₂″ $225
Sugar with pagoda-style cover $125
Tumbler, bar $50

Tumbler, footed (McKee Pattern variant) $50
Tumbler, water, various styles $45
Wine glass $50

FAN AND FLUTE　　U.S. GLASS COMPANY, 1890s

This pattern was also referred to as "Millard." The fluted panels may be stained with amber (increase the listed prices by 50%) or with ruby red (double the prices). The panels might also be engraved rather than pressed (increase prices by 25%).

Bowl, 7″ $16
Bowl, 8″ $20
Bowl, 9″ $25
Butter dish $50
Cake stand $50
Celery tray $25
Celery vase $30
Compote, 6″, open $22
Compote, 7″, open $25
Compote, 8″, open $30
Compote, 9″, open $35
Creamer $30
Cruet with stopper $50
Cup $20
Goblet $30
Pitcher, milk $75
Pitcher, syrup with lid $75
Plate, 7″ $16
Plate, 9″ $20
Plate, 10″ $22
Salt shaker $25
Sauce dish, 4″, flat $12
Sauce dish, 4″, footed $14
Sauce dish, 4½″, flat $14
Sauce dish, 5″ $16
Spooner $22
Sugar $30
Toothpick holder $40

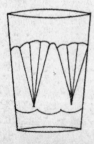

Pressed glass, "Fan and Flute" pattern. DRAWING BY MARK PICKVET.

Tray, 7″, oblong $20
Tray, 8″, oblong $25
Tray, 9″, oblong $30
Tray, 10″, oblong $35
Tumbler, water $25
Wine glass $30

FEATHER   MCKEE GLASS COMPANY, 1890s

"Feather" goes under many names, including the original "Doric" as well as "Fine-cut and Feather" and "Indiana Swirl." Like so many pressed designs, this one resembles cut glass with alternating panels of rosette points and beaded flutes. Colors are very scarce and valuable. For green, double the prices; for amber or ruby red, triple the prices; for chocolate, quadruple the prices. Wine glasses made in cranberry or pink stain were reproduced in the 1950s by the Jeannette Glass Company, which had purchased McKee.

Banana dish $70
Bowl, 7½″ $30
Bowl, 8½″ $35
Bowl, berry, square $35
Bowl, oval, 9″ $35
Butter dish with cover $75
Cake stand, 8″–8½″ $50
Cake stand, 9½″ $55
Cake stand, 11″ $65
Celery vase $40
Compote with cover, 7″ $125
Compote, open, 8″ $50
Cordial $75
Creamer, scalloped $45
Cruet with stopper $85
Goblet $35
Jam jar with cover $100
Pickle dish $35
Pitcher, milk $75
Pitcher, water $85
Plate, 7″ $30
Plate, 8″ $35
Plate, 9½″ $40
Plate, 10″ $45
Platter $45
Relish dish, 8″ $35
Sauce dish, flat $20
Sauce dish, footed $25
Spooner, scalloped $35
Sugar with cover $75
Toothpick holder $65
Tumbler, water $50
Wine glass, scalloped band $45

FINE RIB   NEW ENGLAND GLASS COMPANY, 1850s–1870s

Other ribbed designs were produced, but this pattern features very fine ribbing that extends from the top to the bottom of each piece. Nearly all of the pieces have scalloped bottom panels. Some bowls and compotes also have wavy rims.

Ale glass $65
Bitters bottle $75
Bottle, water, tumble-up $85
Bowl, 7″ oval $50
Bowl, 8″ oval $55
Bowl, 9″ oval $60
Bowl, 10″ oval $65
Bowl with cover, 7″ $75
Butter dish with cover $150
Celery vase $75
Champagne or claret glass $65
Compote with cover, 7″, footed $125
Compote with cover, 8″ footed $150
Compote, open, 7″, footed $75
Compote, open, 8″, footed $80
Compote, open, 9″, footed $85
Compote, open, 10″, footed $90
Creamer $100
Cruet with stopper $125
Cup, custard $65
Decanter with stopper, 16 oz. $125
Decanter with stopper, 32 oz. $150
Egg holder $50
Goblet $55
Honey dish $30
Lamp, handled $200
Mug $70
Pitcher, milk, 32 oz. $225
Pitcher, syrup with lid, 16 oz. $350
Pitcher, water, 48 oz. $275
Plate, 6″ $60
Plate, 7″ $70
Salt dip with cover, footed $125
Salt dip, flat $45

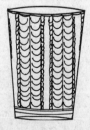

Pressed glass. Left: "Fine Rib" pattern. Right: "Fishscale" pattern. DRAWINGS BY MARK PICKVET.

Sauce dish	$35
Tumbler, water	$60
Whiskey taster with handle	$60
Whiskey tumbler	$60
Wine glass	$55

FISHSCALE   BRYCE BROTHERS, 1880s–1890s

"Fishscale" also known as "Coral," features vertical bands of half-circles that resemble the scales of a fish.

Ashtray, Daisy and Button Slipper design (slipper is amber, blue, crystal, or topaz) attached to rectangular tray (tray features the fishscale pattern)	$50
Bowl, 6″	$25
Bowl, 7″	$30
Bowl, 8″	$35
Bowl with cover, 7″ square, round base	$55
Bowl with cover, 8″ square, round base	$65
Butter dish with cover	$75
Cake stand, 10″	$40
Cake stand, 11″	$45
Cake stand, 8³⁄₄″ - 9″	$35
Celery vase	$50
Compote with cover, 6″	$60
Compote with cover, 7″	$70
Compote with cover, 8″	$80
Compote, open, 10″	$45
Compote, open, 7″	$30
Compote, open, 8″	$35
Compote, open, 9″	$40
Creamer	$40
Goblet	$40
Lamp, handled	$100
Mug	$75
Pickle dish	$25
Pitcher, 1 gal.	$100
Pitcher, 32 oz.	$60
Pitcher, 64 oz.	$80
Plate, 7″	$25
Plate, 8″	$30
Plate, 8″ square	$35
Plate, 9″ square, round corners	$40
Salt and pepper shakers	$70
Sauce dish, 4″, flared, footed	$20
Sauce dish, 4″, flat	$15
Spooner	$25
Sugar with cover	$60
Tray, oblong, scalloped edge (for shakers)	$45
Tray, water, round	$55
Tumbler	$35

FLEUR-DE-LYS   ADAMS & COMPANY, 1880s–1890s

"Fleur-de-Lys" is also referred to as "Fleur-de-Lys and Drape" or "Fleur-de-Lys and Tassel." For green and opal colors, increase the prices by 50%. The basic design is in relief and includes upright fleur-de-lys with upside-down tassels (or drapes).

Bottle, water	$60
Butter dish with cover	$75
Cake stand	$60
Celery vase	$40
Claret glass	$50
Compote with cover	$75
Compote, open	$50
Cordial	$60
Creamer	$50
Goblet	$40
Lamp	$150
Mustard jar with ribbed cover	$85
Pitcher, milk	$75
Pitcher, syrup with lid	$100
Pitcher, water	$100
Sauce dish, 4½", flat	$22
Sauce dish, 4", flat	$20
Spooner	$22
Sugar with cover	$85
Tumbler	$40
Wine glass	$45

FLUTE   VARIOUS COMPANIES, 1850s–1880s

The original "Flute" patterns usually were 6 or 8 large rounded flutes that encompassed the object. Most pieces feature a plain band across the top. Many companies had their own pattern names, such as "Bessimer Flute," "Brooklyn Flute," "New England Flute," "Reed Stem Flute," and "Sandwich Flute," "

Ale glass	$35
Berry set, children's, 7-piece	$55
Bitters bottle	$50
Bowl, scalloped	$40
Candlestick	$30
Champagne glass	$30
Compote, 8" diameter	$45
Creamer	$35
Cup, custard	$40
Decanter, 32 oz.	$85
Egg holder, double	$35
Egg holder, single	$25
Goblet	$35

Honey dish $25
Lamp, whale oil $125
Mug, applied handle $50
Mug, toy, 2 oz., with handle $25
Pitcher, water $100
Salt dip, footed $25
Sauce dish, flat $20
Spooner $25
Tumbler, 4 oz. $25
Tumbler, 6 oz. $30
Tumbler, 8 oz. $35
Tumbler, bar, 12 oz. $40
Whiskey tumbler, 2 oz. $15
Wine glass $30

HAMILTON   BOSTON & SANDWICH GLASS COMPANY, 1860s–1880s

The leaf pattern variant is sometimes referred to as "Hamilton with Leaf." The horizontal diamond band in the middle of each piece in the original "Hamilton" is replaced by leaves in the pattern variant. The "Hamilton with Leaf" pattern was also produced by other companies in the 1890s. Occasionally the leaves can be found frosted (add 25% to prices).

Butter dish with cover $125
Butter dish with cover (Leaf pattern variant) $150
Castor bottle with stopper $75
Celery vase $55
Celery vase (Leaf pattern variant) $65
Compote, 7″, scalloped rim $50
Compote with cover, 6″ $80
Compote, open (high foot) $50
Compote, open (Leaf pattern variant) $55
Compote, open (low foot) $45

Pressed glass, "Hamilton" pattern. DRAWING BY MARK PICKVET.

Cordial (Leaf pattern variant) $50
Creamer $50
Creamer, molded handle (Leaf pattern variant) $65
Decanter with stopper $200
Egg holder $40
Egg holder (Leaf pattern variant) $65
Goblet $45
Honey dish $25
Lamp, 7" tall, 2 styles (Leaf pattern variant) $175
Pitcher, syrup with metal lid $275
Pitcher, water $250
Pitcher, water (Leaf pattern variant) $200
Plate, 6" $100
Salt dip, footed (Leaf pattern variant) $40
Sauce dish, 4" $15
Sauce dish, 5" $20
Spooner $35
Spooner (Leaf pattern variant) $45
Sugar with cover (Leaf pattern variant) $100
Sugar, open $50
Tumbler, bar (Leaf pattern variant) $100
Tumbler, water $90
Whiskey tumbler $125
Wine glass $90
Wine glass (Leaf pattern variant) $100

HEART WITH THUMBPRINT   VARIOUS COMPANIES, 1880s–1900s

There are several rare and valuable pieces in this pattern, especially those in color. For green, double the prices. For the rare custard or ruby-stained, triple the prices.

Banana dish, 10" long $125
Bowl, 9" $50
Bowl, rose $60
Butter dish with cover $100
Carafe $100
Celery vase $75
Compote, ruffled rim $225
Cordial $150
Creamer $50
Creamer, individual (small) $35
Cruet with stopper $100
Goblet $50
Nappy, 6¼" $25
Pitcher, water $100
Salt dish $35
Sauce dish, crimped $35
Spooner $40
Sugar bowl with cover $75

Sugar bowl, individual, handled	$35
Toothpick holder	$150
Tumbler, water	$60
Vase, 10″	$60
Wine glass	$50

HONEYCOMB   VARIOUS COMPANIES, 1860s–1880s

"Honeycomb" is also known as "Cincinnati," "Vernon," and "Hex Optic." Bakewell, Pears, & Company, Lyons Glass Company, McKee Brothers, and others manufactured this pattern. Colors include amber, cobalt blue, green, opal, and topaz (double the listed prices). "Honeycomb" variations were also made during the Depression.

Ale glass	$50
Bitters bottle	$75
Bowl, 6″	$30
Bowl, 7″	$35
Bowl, 8″	$40
Bowl, 9″	$45
Bowl, 10″	$50
Bowl with cover, 6″	$55
Bowl with cover, 7″	$65
Bowl with cover, 8″	$75
Bowl, oval	$40
Butter dish	$50
Castor bottle with stopper	$75
Celery vase	$70
Champagne glass	$45
Compote with cover, 7″	$65
Compote with cover, 7″, low foot	$60
Compote with cover, 8″	$75
Compote with cover, 8″, low foot	$70
Compote, open, 7″	$40
Compote, open, 7″, low foot	$35
Compote, open, 8″	$45
Compote, open, 8″, low foot	$40
Compote, open, 9″	$50
Compote, open, 10″	$55
Cordial	$60

Pressed glass, "Honeycomb" pattern. DRAWING BY MARK PICKVET.

Creamer, 5¹/₂″ tall $50
Cup, custard $45
Decanter with stopper, 16 oz. $75
Decanter with stopper, 32 oz. $100
Egg holder $40
Goblet, barrel-shaped bowl $50
Honey dish $25
Jelly glass, pedestal base $75
Jug, 8 oz. $45
Jug, 16 oz. $50
Jug, 32 oz. $60
Jug, 48 oz. $65
Lamp, all glass $100
Lamp, marble base $125
Mug, 8 oz. $50
Pitcher, water, applied handle $125
Plate, 6″ $40
Plate, 7″ $50
Salt and pepper shakers $60
Salt dip with cover, footed $65
Salt dip, footed $25
Sauce dish $25
Spooner $35
Sugar $55
Tumbler, 5¹/₂ oz. $50
Tumbler, 8 oz. $50
Tumbler, 8 oz., footed $70
Wine glass $40

HORN OF PLENTY   VARIOUS COMPANIES, 1830s–1870s

"Horn of Plenty" and "Comet" are virtually identical; however, "Comet" is attributed solely to the Boston & Sandwich Glass Company. "Horn of Plenty" was also
made by Boston & Sandwich, as well as Bryce Brothers, McKee Brothers, and possibly others. This is a rare and valuable pattern. A few pieces were made in amber,
canary yellow, cobalt blue, and an opalescent white (double listed prices). The lamp
is completely glass. The water tumbler and goblet have been reproduced in amber
and crystal.

Bottle, bar, with stopper $125
Bowl, 8 ¹/₂″ $225
Bowl, oval, (8″ × 5¹/₂″) $225
Butter dish with cover, George Washington's head finial $750
Butter dish with cover, 6″ diameter $175
Cake stand, 9¹/₂″, (frosted—same price) $100
Celery vase $175
Champagne glass $175
Compote, 8″ tall, open $125
Compote, 12″ tall, open $150
Compote with cover, 6″ $125

Pressed glass, "Horn of Plenty" pattern. DRAWING BY MARK PICKVET.

Compote with cover, 13″	$150
Cordial	$150
Creamer (Comet pattern, Boston & Sandwich)	$225
Creamer, 5¹/₂″ tall	$200
Creamer, 7″ tall	$225
Decanter with stopper, 16 oz.	$150
Decanter with stopper, 32 oz.	$175
Decanter with stopper, 64 oz.	$225
Egg holder	$65
Goblet (Comet pattern, Boston & Sandwich)	$150
Honey dish, 3¹/₄″	$25
Lamp, marble base	$275
Lamp, all glass, 15″	$250
Mug, applied handle	$175
Pickle dish	$110
Pitcher, milk	$750
Pitcher, water	$650
Pitcher, water (Comet pattern, Boston & Sandwich)	$650
Plate, 6″	$100
Salt dip, oval	$60
Sauce dish, 4¹/₂″	$25
Sauce dish, 5″–5¹/₄″	$30
Sauce dish, 6″	$40
Spooner	$55
Spooner (Comet pattern, Boston & Sandwich)	$85
Sugar with pagoda cover	$225
Tumbler, water (Comet pattern, Boston & Sandwich)	$175
Whiskey tumbler	$110
Whiskey tumbler (Comet pattern, Boston & Sandwich)	$160
Wine glass	$175

JACOB'S LADDER   BRYCE BROTHERS, 1870s–1880s

The original name for "Jacob's Ladder" was "Maltese" because of the cross design on many pieces. A few rare amber and yellow pieces were also made (double the prices).

Bowl, 6″	$30
Bowl, 7″ oval	$35

Pressed glass, "Jacob's Ladder" pattern.
DRAWING BY MARK PICKVET.

Bowl, 8″ oval $40
Bowl, 9″ oval $45
Bowl, 10″ oval $50
Bowl, 10³/₄″–11″ oval $50
Butter dish with cover, Maltese Cross finial $85
Cake stand, 8″ $45
Cake stand, 9″ $50
Cake stand, 11″ $60
Cake stand, 12″ $65
Castor bottle with stopper $50
Celery dish $35
Celery vase, 9″ tall $40
Compote with cover $90
Compote, dolphin $325
Compote, open, with silver-plated holder $125
Compote, open, scalloped edge, 9³/₄″ $55
Cordial $65
Creamer, footed $45
Cruet with Maltese Cross stopper $110
Goblet $60
Marmalade dish, Maltese Cross finial $95
Mug $55
Pickle dish $40
Pitcher, syrup with metal lid, 2 styles $125
Pitcher, water, applied handle $175
Plate, 6″–6¹/₄″ $30
Salt dip, master, footed $50
Salt dip, master, round, flat $40
Sauce dish, 3¹/₂″, flat, footed $15
Sauce dish, 4¹/₂″, footed $18
Sauce dish, 4″, flat, footed $18
Sauce dish, 5″, flat, footed $20
Spooner, 6″ $40
Sugar with cover, Maltese Cross finial $95
Tray, oval $35
Tumbler, 8 oz. $50
Wine glass $45

Pressed glass, "Lattice" pattern. DRAWING BY MARK PICKVET.

LATTICE   KING, SON AND COMPANY, 1880s

"Lattice," also known as "Diamond Bar," is characterized by occasional vertical diamond bands that resemble latticework. There are usually horizontal diamond bands at the top and bottom of each object.

Bowl, 8″ oval	$30
Butter dish with cover	$70
Cake stand, 8″	$50
Celery vase	$40
Compote with cover, 8″	$70
Cordial	$55
Creamer	$35
Goblet	$35
Lamp	$125
Marmalade jar	$150
Pickle dish	$30
Pitcher, syrup with lid	$80
Pitcher, water	$100
Plate, 6¼″	$20
Plate, 7¼″	$25
Plate, 10″	$35
Platter, oval, (11½″ × 7½″), embossed "Waste Not, Want Not"	$55
Salt and pepper shakers	$60
Sauce dish, flat	$12
Sauce dish, footed	$15
Spooner	$20
Sugar with cover	$55
Tray	$75
Wine glass	$35

*Pressed glass, "Madora (Arrowhead in Oval)" pattern. DRAWING
BY MARK PICKVET.*

MADORA   HIGBEE GLASS COMPANY, 1880s–1890s

"Madora" is sometimes referred to as "Arrowhead" or "Arrowhead in Oval" because of the large arrowhead design in the center of the pattern. A few pieces were
embossed "Bee" (the company trademark) and are a little more valuable than those
without it (increase prices by 25%).

Basket, 7″ long $60
Bowl, rose, with foot and stem $40
Cake stand $50
Celery dish with handles $45
Creamer $35
Plate, 7″ square $25
Punch cup $20
Salt and pepper shakers $50
Salt dip, individual $20
Sherbet $25
Sugar with cover $50
Wine goblet $30
Butter dish with cover, children's miniatures $45
Creamer, children's miniatures $30
Spooner, children's miniatures $25
Sugar with cover, children's miniatures $45
Complete set of 6 pieces, children's miniatures $150

MASSACHUSETTS   U.S. GLASS COMPANY, 1898–1900s

Colors in this pattern are somewhat rare and include emerald green, ruby stain, and
cobalt blue (double the prices). Note that the butter dish with cover has been reproduced in crystal, pink, and light green.

Banana stand $150
Basket $60
Bonbon dish, 5″, handled $25
Bottle, water $100
Butter dish with cover $85

Cologne bottle, 7¹/₂″ tall $65
Compote $25
Creamer $40
Cruet with stopper, 3¹/₂″ tall (small) $100
Goblet $50
Jug, shaped like a teapot $125
Lamp $100
Pitcher, water $125
Plate, 8″ $25
Salt and pepper shakers $60
Shot glass $25
Spooner, handled $25
Sugar dish with cover, handled $65
Toothpick holder $75
Vase, 6¹/₂″ $40
Vase, 10″ $60

MICHIGAN   U.S. GLASS COMPANY, 1890s

Another in U.S. Glass Company's state series, "Michigan" is also known as "Loop and Pillar," which more adequately describes the basic pattern. The series also includes some miniature or toy pieces originally designed for children. For ruby-stained pieces, double the prices. For any additional decorations (i.e., gold trim, etching, or enameling), increase the prices by 25%.

Bowl, 7¹/₂″ $35
Bowl, 8¹/₂″ $40
Bowl, 10″ $50
Butter dish with cover $85
Butter dish with cover, miniature (toy) $60
Creamer $45
Creamer, individual (small) $25
Creamer, miniature (toy) $75
Cruet with stopper $85
Cup $15
Goblet $35
Pitcher, water, miniature (toy), tankard style $50
Pitcher, water, tankard style $100
Punch cup $15
Salt and pepper shakers $60
Sauce dish, handled $20
Spooner $25
Spooner, miniature (toy) $50
Sugar bowl with cover $65
Sugar bowl with cover, miniature (toy) $75
Sugar dish, individual (small) $25
Toothpick holder $100
Tumbler, water $45
Wine glass $40

Pressed glass, "Moon & Stars" pattern.
PHOTO BY ROBIN RAINWATER.

MOON AND STARS   WILSON GLASS COMPANY, 1890; PIONEER GLASS COMPANY, 1892; IMPERIAL GLASS COMPANY, 1890s; COOPERATIVE FLINT GLASS COMPANY, 1890s; PHOENIX GLASS COMPANY, 1930s

"Moon and Stars" is characterized by large round orbs (moons) inscribed with stars. This pattern is probably one of the most reproduced pressed patterns out there. Some of the original molds were sold to Phoenix in 1937; the company continued to produce pieces in this pattern. The original series was crystal, while most reproductions boast a variety of color (greens, reds, blues, yellows, etc.). The price is the same for all colors with the exception of frosted pieces and milk glass (increase the prices by 25% to 35%).

Ashtray	$20
Bowl, 6″	$25
Bowl, 12 ½″	$40
Butter dish with cover	$85
Cake stand	$75
Celery dish	$20
Compote	$25
Compote with cover, 7″	$35
Compote with cover, 8″	$40
Compote with cover, 10″	$50
Creamer	$60
Goblet	$45
Lamp shade	$25
Lamp, table	$100
Pitcher, water	$150
Salt and pepper shakers	$40
Sugar bowl with cover	$80

Toothpick holder	$20
Tumbler, water	$55
Tumbler, water, footed	$60
Wine glass	$45

NEW ENGLAND PINEAPPLE   BOSTON & SANDWICH GLASS COMPANY, 1860s

The pineapple of this pattern is pressed into large oval shapes that encompass the object. Many pieces are quite scarce and are therefore valuable.

Bowl, fruit	$175
Butter dish with cover	$225
Castor bottle	$100
Celery vase	$225
Champagne glass	$175
Compote with cover, 6″	$225
Compote, open	$75
Cordial	$150
Creamer	$200
Cruet with stopper	$150
Decanter with stopper, 16 oz.	$275
Decanter with stopper, 32 oz.	$325
Egg holder	$65
Goblet, 2 styles	$75
Honey dish	$30
Mug	$150
Pitcher, water	$350
Plate, 6″	$150
Salt dip, footed	$85
Sauce dish	$30
Spooner	$75
Sugar with cover	$225
Tumbler, water	$125
Tumbler, water, footed	$150
Whiskey tumbler, 2 oz.	$110
Wine glass	$75

Pressed glass, "New England Pineapple" pattern. DRAWING BY *MARK PICKVET.*

OREGON   U.S. GLASS COMPANY, EARLY 1900s

"Oregon," also known as "Beaded Loop" or "Skilton," is characterized by oval beading and diamonds that resemble cut glass. The beading intersects, as do the ovals along the top. Prices should be increased by one-third to one-half for green. Flashed pieces were made during the Depression years and sell for about the same price as below. Note that some partial flashing is present on some pieces (flashed feet on the footed tumbler, for instance).

Bowl with cover, 6"	$55
Bowl with cover, 7"	$65
Bowl with cover, 8"	$75
Butter dish (2 styles)	$75
Cake stand, 6", (small)	$40
Cake stand, 7³/₄", (medium)	$50
Cake stand, 9¹/₂", (large)	$60
Celery vase	$35
Compote, 5¹/₂"	$25
Compote with cover	$55
Cordial	$40
Creamer	$40
Goblet	$40
Jelly dish	$40
Mug	$45
Pickle dish, boat-shaped	$45
Pitcher, milk	$85
Pitcher, syrup with lid	$100
Pitcher, water, 64 oz.	$100
Relish dish, 7¹/₂" oval	$20
Salt and pepper shakers	$50
Sauce dish, 3¹/₂"	$15
Sauce dish, 4"	$20
Sugar shaker	$40
Sugar with cover	$65
Sugar, open	$40
Toothpick holder	$80
Tray, 7¹/₂" oval	$30
Tray, 9¹/₂" oval	$45
Tray, 10¹/₂" oval	$50
Tray, bread	$50
Tumbler, footed	$45
Tumbler, water	$40
Vase	$40
Wine glass	$45
Wine glass, pedestal base	$55

Pressed glass, "Paneled Dewdrop" pattern. DRAWING BY *MARK PICKVET.*

PANELED DEWDROP CAMPBELL, JONES, & COMPANY, 1870s–1880s

This pattern, sometimes referred to as "Striped Dewdrop," is characterized by vertical strips or panels of dewdrops. Some pieces may have rows of dewdrops on the base.

Butter dish with cover	$75
Celery vase	$45
Champagne glass	$40
Cheese dish with cover	$90
Compote, open, 8″, footed	$65
Cordial	$40
Creamer, applied handle	$45
Goblet, dewdrops on base	$40
Goblet, plain base	$35
Honey dish with cover, 11″	$150
Marmalade jar	$75
Mug, applied handle	$40
Pickle dish	$60
Pitcher, water	$75
Plate, 7″	$35
Plate, 11″	$65
Platter, oblong, handles	$60
Platter, oval	$45
Relish	$20
Sauce dish, flat	$12
Sauce dish, footed	$15
Spooner	$20
Sugar with cover	$60
Tumbler, water	$35
Wine glass	$35

PANELED GRAPE   D.C. JENKINS GLASS COMPANY, EARLY 1900s

This pattern is also known as "Heavy Paneled Grape." Note that the listed prices are for clear glass only. The pattern was heavily reproduced in milk glass, Carnival glass, and other colors.

Ale glass $70
Bowl with cover $65
Bowl, oval $40
Butter dish $75
Celery vase $50
Compote with cover $85
Compote, open $55
Cordial $60
Creamer, 4½" tall $55
Cup $45
Goblet $75
Pitcher, milk $150
Pitcher, syrup $175
Pitcher, water $175
Sauce dish, 4¼" round $25
Sauce dish, footed $35
Sauce dish, oval $25
Spooner $30
Sugar dish, open $40
Sugar with cover $65
Toothpick holder $60
Tumbler, water $65
Wine glass $75

PANELED THISTLE   VARIOUS COMPANIES, 1910s–EARLY 1920s

The original maker, the Higbee Glass Company, referred to this pattern as "Delta." The Jefferson Glass Company of Toronto and the Dominion Glass Company also produced items in this pattern. Some pieces have Higbee's "Bee" mark (increase

Pressed glass. Left: "Paneled Grape" pattern. Right: "Paneled Thistle" pattern. DRAWINGS BY MARK PICKVET.

prices by 25%). A few reproductions have been made, including colored salt dips, clear salt dips that are taller than 1", and a slim, flared toothpick holder.

Basket, various styles $100
Bowl, 6½" $35
Bowl, 7" $40
Bowl, 8½" $50
Bowl, 9" $55
Bowl, footed $50
Butter dish, flanged, with cover $75
Cake stand, 9¾" diameter $50
Celery dish $30
Celery vase, handled $45
Compote, 5", open $35
Compote, 8", open $45
Cordial $40
Creamer, knob feet $45
Cruet (without stopper) $40
Cup, custard $35
Goblet, flared $40
Goblet, straight $35
Honey dish with cover, square, footed $85
Pickle dish, 8¼" $25
Pitcher, milk, 32 oz. $75
Pitcher, water, 64 oz. $90
Plate, 6" $30
Plate, 7¼" $30
Plate, 8¼" $35
Plate, 9½" $40
Plate, 10¼" $45
Salt and pepper shakers $65
Salt dip, individual, 1" tall, footed $20
Sauce dish, several styles $20
Spooner, 2-handled $35
Sugar bowl with cover, 2-handled $65
Toothpick holder $60
Tray, celery $45
Tumbler, water $35
Wine glass, flared $35
Wine glass, straight $30

PENNSYLVANIA   U.S. GLASS COMPANY, 1890s

Colors include green, ruby or ruby-stained, and blue (double the prices). Increase the prices by 25% for any fully intact gold trimming.

Butter dish with cover $90
Carafe $75
Creamer $40
Cup $20

Pressed glass, "Pineapple and Fan" pattern. DRAWING BY
MARK PICKVET.

Goblet	$30
Punch cup	$20
Shot glass	$50
Spooner	$25
Sugar dish with cover	$65
Toothpick holder	$50
Wine glass	$35

PINEAPPLE AND FAN   ADAMS AND COMPANY, 1880s; U.S. GLASS COMPANY, 1890s

This pattern is also referred to as "Cube with Fan" because of the cube or pineapple design on the lower half of each piece. The fan design is on the top portion and the cubes are flat, beveled squares. A few objects have been found in color. For green, increase the listed prices by 50%; for ruby-stained, double the prices.

Bowl, 8″	$30
Bowl, 9″	$35
Butter dish with cover	$75
Cake stand	$55
Celery vase	$45
Creamer	$40
Custard cup	$25
Goblet	$35
Mug	$25
Piccalilli jar with cover	$65
Pitcher, 16 oz.	$50
Pitcher, 32 oz.	$60
Pitcher, 64 oz., tankard style	$75
Pitcher, 96 oz., tankard style	$100
Salt dip, individual	$15
Sauce dish, 4¹/₂″	$15
Sauce dish, 4″	$15
Spooner	$30
Sugar with cover	$55
Tumbler, water	$25
Wine glass	$35

POINTED THUMBPRINT BAKEWELL, PEARS AND COMPANY, 1860s; BRYCE BROTHERS, 1890s

The thumbprints on this pattern are pointed on the ends to resemble almonds; hence the alternative "Fingerprint" and "Almond Thumbprint" labels. Bryce Brothers produced a cheaper lime glass in the early 1890s in the same pattern; the prices here are for lead glass (reduce by two-thirds for nonlead).

Butter dish with cover, cable edge $125
Celery vase $65
Compote with cover, 4³/₄″ tall $60
Compote with cover, 7″ tall $70
Compote with cover, 10″ tall $90
Creamer $50
Egg holder $35
Goblet $35
Pitcher, water $125
Sugar with cover $75
Tumbler $50
Wine glass $35

PRIMROSE CANTON GLASS COMPANY, 1880s

This flower and leaf design also includes vertical panels and horizontal ribbing. Several items were made in a variety of colors besides the usual crystal. For amber, green, and yellow, increase the listed prices by 50%. For amethyst (slag), cobalt blue, vaseline, and black, double the prices.

Bowl, berry $25
Bowl, waste $30
Butter dish with cover $65
Cake stand $50
Celery vase $35
Compote with cover, 6″ $40

Pressed glass, "Primrose" pattern. DRAWING BY MARK PICKVET.

Compote with cover, 7½" $50
Compote with cover, 8" $60
Compote with cover, 9" $75
Cordial $40
Creamer $35
Egg holder $35
Goblet, knob stem $35
Goblet, plain stem $30
Marmalade jar $60
Pickle dish $25
Pitcher, 7½" tall $60
Plate, 4½" $20
Plate, 6" $25
Plate, 7" $25
Plate, 8¾", cake, handled $35
Platter, oval, (12½" × 8"), flower handles $45
Sauce dish, 4", footed $16
Sauce dish, 5½", footed $20
Sauce dish, flat $15
Spooner $25
Sugar with cover $50
Tray, water $50
Wine glass $30

RIBBED GRAPE   BOSTON & SANDWICH GLASS COMPANY, 1850s–1860s

This pattern is characterized by grape clusters, leaves, vines, and vertical ribbing. Colors include an aqua or bluish-green and opaque white (double the listed prices).

Bowl, berry $75
Butter dish with cover $125
Celery vase $85

Pressed glass, "Ribbed Grape" pattern. PHOTO COURTESY OF THE SANDWICH GLASS MUSEUM.

Compote, 8″, open, footed $85
Compote with cover, 6″ $175
Cordial $125
Creamer $150
Goblet, 2 styles $75
Pitcher, water $225
Plate, 6″ $50
Plate, 7½″ $60
Sauce dish, flat $30
Spooner $50
Sugar with cover $125
Tumbler, water $80
Whiskey tumbler $100
Wine glass $50

RIBBED PALM   MCKEE BROTHERS, 1860s–1870s

The palm leaves in this pattern are quite large and usually begin at the bottom and nearly reach the top. The remaining portion consists of vertical ribbing. There are quite a few rare pieces, such as the creamer and pitcher. A few odd colors, such as green and ruby-stained, have been found (double the listed prices).

Bowl, 6″, flat rim $40
Bowl, 6″, oblong, scalloped $50
Bowl, 7″, oblong, scalloped $55
Bowl, 8″, oblong, scalloped $60
Bowl, 9″, oblong, scalloped $65
Butter dish with cover $125
Celery vase $75
Champagne glass $100
Compote, 7″, open, scalloped $80
Compote, 8″, open, scalloped $100
Compote, 10″, open, scalloped $150
Compote with cover, 6″ $150
Cordial $100
Creamer, applied handle $200
Egg holder $40
Goblet $50
Lamp, 3 styles $150
Pickle dish $55
Pitcher, 9″ tall, applied handle $250
Plate, 6″ $45
Salt dip, pedestal base $45
Sauce dish, 4″ $25
Spooner $35
Sugar with cover $125
Tumbler, 8 oz. $100
Whiskey tumbler $100
Wine glass $75

ROMAN ROSETTE BRYCE, WALKER & COMPANY, 1870s; U.S. GLASS COMPANY, 1890s

The rosettes in this pattern are large and encircle each object. The pattern is a typical "Sandwich" design in that many similar patterns have been reproduced and referred to as "Old Sandwich" glass. A few odd colors and ruby decorations have been found in the original pattern (double the listed prices).

Bowl, 5"	$20
Bowl, 6"	$25
Bowl, 7"	$30
Bowl, 8"	$35
Bowl with cover, 9"	$75
Butter dish with cover	$75
Cake stand, 9"	$50
Cake stand, 10"	$60
Castor bottle with stopper	$50
Castor stand (holds 3 castor bottles)	$30
Celery vase	$40
Compote with cover, 5"	$55
Compote with cover, 6"	$65
Compote with cover, 7"	$75
Compote with cover, 8"	$85
Cordial	$50
Creamer, 16 oz.	$40
Goblet	$35
Mug	$40
Mustard jar	$55
Pickle dish	$30
Pitcher, milk, 32 oz.	$175
Pitcher, syrup with metal lid	$100
Plate, 7¼"	$70
Platter, oval (11" x 9")	$40
Salt and pepper shakers	$50
Sauce dish, flat, 4½"	$20
Sauce dish, flat, 4"	$15
Sauce dish, footed	$25
Spooner	$30

Pressed glass, "Roman Rosette" pattern.
DRAWING BY MARK PICKVET.

Sugar with cover	$60
Tumbler, water	$75
Wine glass	$60

SAWTOOTH   BOSTON & SANDWICH GLASS COMPANY, 1860s; NEW ENGLAND GLASS COMPANY, 1860s

A sawtooth design is a little sharp for pressed glass but is still easily distinguished from cut glass. The teeth usually begin at the bottom of each object and proceed about three-quarters of the way up. Original pieces usually have sawtooth rims, knobbed stems, and applied handles (reduce the prices by 25% if any of these are lacking). For any colored pieces, double the listed prices.

Bowl, 5″	$20
Bowl with cover, 7″	$65
Bowl, berry, 8″	$45
Bowl, berry, 9″	$50
Bowl, berry, 10″	$55
Butter dish with cover	$75
Butter dish, miniature (children's)	$75
Cake stand, 9″	$110
Cake stand, 10″	$125
Celery vase, pointed edge	$60
Celery vase, rolled edge	$75
Champagne glass	$75
Compote, 6″, open	$40
Compote, 7″, open	$50
Compote, 8″, open	$60
Compote, 10″, open	$75
Compote with cover, 6″	$70
Compote with cover, 7″	$75
Compote with cover, 8″	$80
Compote with cover, 9″	$90
Compote with cover, 10″, knob on stem	$175
Compote with cover, 11″, knob on stem	$200
Compote with cover, 12″, knob on stem	$225
Cordial	$50
Creamer	$60
Creamer, miniature (children's)	$75

Pressed glass, "Sawtooth" pattern. DRAWING BY MARK PICKVET.

Cruet with stopper	$125
Decanter with stopper, 32 oz.	$100
Egg holder	$40
Goblet, knob on stem	$45
Honey dish	$25
Jar with cover, Acorn finial	$100
Lamp	$125
Pitcher, water, 64 oz.	$175
Salt dip	$25
Salt dip with cover, footed	$45
Sauce dish, 4″	$20
Sauce dish, 5″	$25
Spooner	$40
Spooner, miniature (children's)	$50
Spooner, octagonal	$55
Sugar dish with cover	$65
Sugar dish, miniature (children's)	$75
Tray, 10″ oval	$45
Tray, 11″ oval	$50
Tray, 12″ oval	$60
Tray, 14″ oval	$75
Tumbler, juice, 3½″ tall	$30
Tumbler, water	$40
Tumbler, water, footed	$50
Wine glass, knob on stem	$40

STAR-IN-BULL'S-EYE   U.S. GLASS COMPANY, EARLY 1900s

The eyes of this "Bull's-Eye" pattern are large and the circles overlap at the edges. The star pattern is within the bull's-eye, as the pattern name suggests. A few other pieces besides the water tumbler may be found trimmed in gold (add 25% to the listed prices if the gold is completely intact). For ruby-stained pieces, double the listed prices.

Bowl, berry	$35
Butter dish	$55
Cake stand	$55
Celery vase	$35
Compote, 6″, open, flared	$35
Compote with cover	$60
Creamer	$35
Cruet with stopper, 4″ tall	$55
Goblet	$30
Pickle dish, diamond-shaped	$25
Pitcher, water	$75
Spooner	$25
Sugar with cover	$50
Toothpick holder, double	$50
Toothpick holder, single	$40

Tumbler, water, gold band	$30
Whiskey tumbler, 2 oz.	$50
Wine glass	$30

SUNBURST   D.C. JENKINS GLASS COMPANY, EARLY 1900s

The original "Sunburst" pattern by Jenkins was also referred to as "Squared Sunburst." It is a fairly common pattern with the exception of the toothpick holder.

Bowl, oblong (deep)	$30
Butter dish	$30
Cake plate	$35
Celery vase	$30
Compote with cover	$50
Cordial	$30
Creamer, 4½″ tall, (large)	$20
Creamer, individual (small)	$15
Cup	$15
Egg holder	$20
Goblet	$20
Marmalade jar	$50
Pickle dish, 8″, 2 divisions	$35
Pickle dish, 10″, 2 divisions	$45
Pickle dish, single	$25
Pitcher, milk	$40
Pitcher, water	$50
Plate, 6″	$25
Plate, 7″	$30
Plate, 11″	$40
Salt shaker	$25
Sauce dish, 1 handle	$20

Pressed glass. From left to right: "Star-in-Bull's Eye" pattern, "Sunburst" pattern, and "Teardrop and Thumbprint" pattern. DRAWINGS BY MARK PICKVET.

Spooner $15
Sugar with cover (large) $30
Sugar, open, individual (small) $15
Toothpick holder $75
Tumbler, water $15

TEARDROP   RIPLEY & COMPANY, 1870s–1880s; U.S. GLASS COMPANY, 1890s

The basic "Teardrop" is sometimes referred to as "Teardrop and Thumbprint" because of the band of thumbprints above the teardrops. There are many variations of this pattern. Some pieces may be engraved (increase prices by 25%). Other colors include ruby-flashed and cobalt blue (double the prices). A few ruby-flashed items in this pattern were produced and may include engraving or enameling.

Bowl, oval $30
Butter dish with cover $75
Cake stand $60
Celery dish $40
Compote, open $50
Creamer $40
Goblet $35
Pitcher, syrup with metal lid $100
Pitcher, water $100
Salt shaker $40
Sauce dish, 4″, flat $15
Sauce dish, footed $20
Spooner $30
Sugar with cover $60
Sugar, open $35
Tumbler, water $30
Wine glass $30

TEARDROPS AND DIAMOND BLOCK   ADAMS & COMPANY, 1870s; U.S. GLASS COMPANY, 1890s

This pattern is characterized by large teardrops at the bottom of each object. The remaining portion is in the block diamonds. It is also referred to as "Job's Tears" and "Art." Some pieces have been found with ruby flashing (increase prices by 50%).

Banana dish, oblong, flat $75
Basket, 10″ tall $75
Bowl, 8″ $50
Butter dish with cover $75
Cake stand, 9″ $65
Cake stand, 10″ $75
Celery vase $50
Compote, 8″, open $45

Pressed glass, "Teardrops and Diamond Block" pattern. DRAWING BY MARK PICKVET.

Compote, 9″, open	$50
Compote, 10″, open	$55
Compote with cover, 7″, footed	$75
Cracker jar with cover	$85
Creamer, 2 styles	$45
Cruet with stopper	$75
Goblet	$40
Mug	$40
Pitcher, water, 64 oz.	$100
Relish dish	$35
Sauce dish, 4″, shallow	$25
Spooner	$35
Sugar with cover	$75
Tumbler	$40
Wine glass	$40

TEASEL   BRYCE BROTHERS, 1870s; NEW MARTINSVILLE GLASS COMPANY, EARLY 1900s

The original design was made by Bryce Brothers and was modeled after the teasel herb, which is used to comb wool. The New Martinsville version was originally called "Long Leaf Teasel"; a few extra pieces (butter dish and cruet) were produced that were not part of the Bryce set.

Bowl, 8″, pedestal base	$35
Bowl, oval, (9″ × 5″)	$30
Butter dish with cover (New Martinsville)	$60
Cake stand	$50
Celery dish	$35
Compote, open	$35
Cracker jar with cover	$75
Creamer	$40
Cruet with stopper (New Martinsville)	$60
Goblet, several styles	$35

Honey dish with cover, oblong $75
Pitcher, water $75
Plate, 7″ $25
Plate, 9″ $30
Sauce dish, round, flat $15
Spooner $30
Sugar with cover $55
Toothpick holder $65
Tumbler, water $40
Whiskey tumbler $50

TEXAS   U.S. GLASS COMPANY, LATE 1890s–EARLY 1900s

One of the rarest of the state patterns from U.S. Glass, "Texas" is also referred to as
"Loop with Stippled Panels." For ruby or red stained items, double the listed prices.
For crystal pieces with gilded tops, increase the prices by 25%; for colored pieces
with gilded tops, increase the prices by 150%.

Bowl with cover, 6″ $60
Bowl with cover, 7″ $70
Bowl with cover, 8″ $80
Bowl, berry $40
Butter dish with cover $150
Celery dish $65
Celery vase $75
Compote, 5½″ diameter, open $50
Compote, 6″, scalloped rim $75
Creamer (large) $65
Creamer, individual (small) $30
Cruet with stopper, Inverted pattern $225
Goblet $85
Horseradish dish with opening for spoon $75
Pitcher, 48 oz., Inverted pattern $275
Pitcher, pattern variant $425
Pitcher, syrup with metal lid $350
Plate, 8¾″ $65
Preserve dish, oval $55
Salt and pepper shakers (small) $125
Salt and pepper shakers (large) $150
Saltshaker $75
Spooner $60
Sugar with cover, individual (small) $125
Sugar with cover, individual (large) $150
Sugar, open $30
Toothpick holder $50
Tray, 11¼″ × 6½″ $65
Tumbler, water, Inverted pattern $55
Tumbler, water, pattern variant $55
Vase, 6½″ tall, (straight or cupped) $30

Vase, 8″ tall, (straight or cupped) $45
Vase, 9″ tall, (straight or cupped) $55
Vase, 10″ tall, (straight or cupped) $65
Wine glass $75

THUMBPRINT   BAKEWELL, PEARS & COMPANY, 1860s

The original "Thumbprint" pattern was first named "Argus" by Bakewell, Pears. It has also been referred to as "Early Thumbprint." Colors in this pattern are extremely scarce (triple the prices listed below).

Ale glass, 7½″ tall $150
Bowl with cover $200
Butter dish, 2 styles $150
Cake plate $125
Castor bottle $150
Celery vase, 2 styles $135
Champagne glass $90
Claret glass $150
Compote with cover, 6″, hexagonal $125
Compote with cover, 7″, hexagonal $150
Compote with cover, 8″, hexagonal $175
Compote with cover, 10″, hexagonal $225
Compote, open, 6″ $75
Compote, open, 8″ $85
Compote, open, 9″ $95
Cordial $85
Creamer, applied handle $100
Decanter with stopper, 32 oz. $175
Egg holder $55
Goblet, barrel-shaped $60
Goblet, ring stem $75
Honey dish $30
Lamp, 10″ tall $75
Mug, applied handle, 8 oz. $100
Pickle dish $45
Punch bowl with stand, 12″ diameter, 23½″ tall $1500
Salt dip, individual (small) $25
Salt dip, master (large) $35

Pressed glass, "Thumbprint" pattern. DRAWING BY MARK PICKVET.

Pressed glass, "Thumbprint" pattern. DRAWING BY MARK PICKVET.

Sauce dish, 4½″, flat	$35
Sauce dish, 4″, flat	$30
Spooner	$50
Sugar with cover	$150
Tumbler, bar	$90
Tumbler, footed	$65
Vase, 9½″ tall	$80
Whiskey tumbler, 2 oz.	$85
Wine glass	$65

TULIP WITH SAWTOOTH BRYCE, RICHARDS & COMPANY, 1850s

The original pattern name was "Tulip," but the "Sawtooth" was added because of the design at the bottom of the pattern. The original pieces were primarily crystal, but some cheaper lime substitutes have been found (reduce the prices by 50% for noncrystal).

Bowl, berry	$65
Butter dish with cover	$150
Celery vase	$85
Champagne glass	$125
Compote, 8″, open	$55
Compote with cover (low)	$75
Compote with cover (small)	$85
Compote with cover (large)	$100
Cordial	$75
Creamer	$125
Decanter with patterned stopper, 32 oz., handled	$275

Pressed glass, "Tulip with Sawtooth" pattern. DRAWING BY MARK PICKVET.

Decanter with stopper, 8 oz. $150
Decanter with stopper, 16 oz. $200
Egg holder with cover $225
Goblet, 7″ tall, knob stem $75
Honey dish $45
Pitcher, water $300
Plate, 6″ $75
Pomade jar $100
Salt dip, master $40
Salt dip, petal rim, pedestal base $55
Spooner $40
Sugar dish, open $75
Tumbler, bar $75
Tumbler, water $70
Tumbler, water, footed $75
Whiskey tumbler $75
Wine glass $75

VERMONT U.S. GLASS COMPANY, LATE 1890s–EARLY 1900s

Another of U.S. Glass Company's state patterns, "Vermont" is also known as "Honeycomb with Flower Rim" and "Inverted Thumbprint with Daisy Band." There are a few color variations. For gold trimming or gilding, increase the prices by 25%; for amber and green, increase the prices by 50%; for cobalt blue and decorated custard, double the prices. The reproduced toothpick holder in chocolate or opalescent is valued at $65.00. The candlestick that was produced in custard only was originally referred to as "Jeweled Vermont."

Basket (several varieties) $50
Bowl $35
Bowl, waste $45
Butter dish with cover $75
Candlestick, Custard only $80
Celery tray $30
Celery vase $40
Compote with cover $65
Compote, open $45

Creamer $35
Goblet $40
Pickle dish $25
Pitcher, water $100
Relish dish $30
Saltshaker $30
Sauce dish $25
Spooner $25
Sugar $35
Sugar with cover $50
Toothpick holder $45
Tumbler, water $40
Vase $35

VIRGINIA OR BANDED PORTLAND   U.S. GLASS COMPANY, 1901

This is another item in U.S. Glass Company's state series and is sometimes referred to as "Maiden Blush." Flashed on colors of blue, green, ruby red, and yellow have been discovered (double the prices).

Bottle, water $55
Bowl, 6" $30
Bowl, 8" $40
Bowl with cover, 8" $100
Butter dish with cover $75
Celery dish $40
Compote with cover $100
Creamer $40
Cruet with stopper $75
Cup $20
Dish, sardine, oblong $25
Goblet $40
Jelly dish with cover $110
Pitcher, syrup with lid $75
Pitcher, water $100
Relish dish $30
Salt and pepper shakers $75
Sugar shaker $40
Sugar with cover $60
Toothpick holder $40
Tumbler $35
Vase, 6" tall $35
Wine glass $40

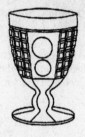

Pressed glass, "Waffle and Thumbprint" pattern. DRAWING BY MARK PICKVET.

WAFFLE AND THUMBPRINT VARIOUS COMPANIES, 1850s–1870s

Here is one variation of the "Waffle" pattern in which the rectangles are interspersed with thumbprints. For noncrystal pieces, reduce the listed prices by 50%. The Boston & Sandwich Glass Company, the New England Glass Company, and Curling, Robertson & Company were the primary producers of this pattern.

Bowl, rectangular, (7″ × 5″) $45
Bowl, rectangular, (8″ × 6″) $55
Butter dish with cover $150
Celery vase $100
Champagne glass $85
Claret glass $85
Compote with cover, 6″ $125
Compote with cover, 7″ $150
Compote with cover, 8″ $175
Cordial $75
Creamer $150
Decanter with stopper, 16 oz. $150
Decanter with stopper, 32 oz., (pointed paneled stopper) $200
Egg holder $65
Goblet $85
Goblet, knob stem $90
Lamp $150
Pitcher, water $550
Spooner $65
Sugar with cover $200
Tumbler, water $100
Tumbler, water, footed $110
Whiskey tumbler $100
Wine glass $85

WAFFLE   BOSTON & SANDWICH GLASS COMPANY 1850s–1860s; BRYCE, WALKER & COMPANY, 1850s–1860s

Since there is some confusion as to which company produced the pattern first, records are sketchy. A few colors, including opaque white, have been found (double the listed prices). The simple square "Waffle" design has been reproduced in a variety of forms.

Butter dish with cover	$150
Celery vase, 9″ tall	$90
Champagne glass	$125
Claret glass	$135
Compote, 6″, open	$75
Compote, 8″, open	$85
Compote with cover, 7″	$125
Compote with cover, 9″	$150
Cordial	$65
Creamer, 6³/₄″ tall	$150
Decanter with stopper, 16 oz.	$125
Decanter with stopper, 32 oz.	$175
Egg holder	$55
Goblet, knob stem	$65
Lamp, applied handle, marble base	$200
Lamp, complete glass	$200
Pitcher, water, 9¹/₂″ tall	$500
Plate, 6″	$90
Relish dish, oval, (6″ × 4″), scalloped	$60
Salt dip with cover	$125
Salt dip, footed	$50
Sauce dish, 4″	$25
Spooner	$75
Sugar with cover	$200
Toy mug, applied handle	$150
Tumbler, water	$85
Whiskey tumbler	$85
Wine glass	$65

WILDFLOWER   ADAMS & COMPANY, 1870s; U.S. GLASS COMPANY, 1890s

This pattern is characterized by six-petaled flowers with leaves, stems, and berries that form a continuous design around each object. There is also vertical flutelike ribbing at the bottom and vertical trapezoidal bands at the top. Colors include amber, cobalt blue, green, and yellow (double the prices). The goblet, flat sauce dish, water tumbler, wine glass, and a 10″ plate have all been reproduced in this pattern.

Bowl, 7¹/₂″	$40
Bowl, waste	$60
Butter dish with cover	$65

Butter dish with cover, footed	$75
Cake plate with metal handle	$100
Cake stand (large)	$60
Cake stand (small), 8½″	$50
Celery dish	$40
Compote with cover, 6″	$60
Compote with cover, 8″	$75
Compote, open	$45
Compote, open, 8″, (low)	$35
Cordial	$60
Creamer	$35
Goblet	$30
Pickle dish, 5¾″ square	$25
Pickle dish, 6¼″ square	$30
Pickle dish, 7¾″ square	$35
Pickle dish with cover, 7¾″ square	$65
Pitcher, syrup with metal lid	$125
Pitcher, water	$100
Plate, 9¾″, square	$40
Plate, 10″	$75
Platter, 10″ oblong	$75
Salt and pepper shakers	$60
Sauce dish, 3½″, round, footed	$30
Sauce dish, 4″, round, footed	$35
Sauce dish, round, flat	$15
Sauce dish, square, flat	$20
Spooner	$25
Sugar with cover	$50
Tray, oval, (13″ × 11″)	$50
Tray, round	$40
Tumbler, water	$35
Wine glass	$40

WISCONSIN   U.S. GLASS COMPANY, 1898–EARLY 1900s

The last of U.S. Glass Company's state patterns, "Wisconsin" is also known as "Beaded Dewdrops." It is characterized by vertical teardrops that section off oval beaded designs.

Bowl, 7″	$40
Bowl, 8″	$45
Butter dish with cover	$85
Cake stand	$65
Candy dish	$30
Celery dish	$40
Celery vase	$45
Compote with cover, 6″ tall	$50
Compote with cover, 7″ tall	$60
Compote with cover, 8″ tall	$70

Compote, open, 5″ $40
Creamer (large) $50
Creamer, individual (small) $35
Cruet with stopper $75
Goblet $40
Jelly dish, handled $35
Lamp $100
Marmalade jar $85
Mug $35
Pickle dish $35
Pitcher, 32 oz. $60
Pitcher, 48 oz. $75
Pitcher, syrup with lid $100
Punch cup $35
Salt and pepper shakers, short $50
Salt and pepper shakers, tall $60
Sauce dish, 4″, flat $15
Spooner $35
Sugar with cover $75
Sugar, individual (small) $35
Sweetmeat dish $30
Toothpick holder, 3-footed base $50
Tray, 6″ oval, handled, with cover $50
Tumbler $45
Wine glass $40

CHAPTER 3

CUT GLASS

The Brilliant period of American glassmaking history lasted from 1880 to 1915. Pieces made during this time are characterized by deep cutting, exceptional brilliance or sparkle, heavy lead crystal formulas, and very elaborate and ornate designs.

Cut glass was made using steel or iron wheels that revolved in a trough while a stream of water mixed with abrasives dripped down on the wheel from above. This initial process, known as roughing, was responsible for the first cut. Heavier wheels were used to make deeper and sharper cuts. In the next step, glass proceeded to a hard stone wheel, where the rough cut was smoothed out. At this point, a polisher would work on the glass on a softer wooden wheel, and a buffer would further smooth it out on a buffing wheel. Buffing was eventually replaced by acid polishing in the 1890s, but true craftsmen argued that acid polishing was inferior since it wasn't permanent and could gradually wear away. Acid polishing also left a somewhat dull finish, hiding the brilliance of the piece.

The aim of a cutter was to remove imperfections and impart facets to capture light. Several inventions from this period improved on cutting. The flat-edged wheel made square-ended cuts and the convex-edged wheel made hollowed cuts. The miter-edged wheel, which made curved or V-shaped cuts, was invented in the 1870s and freed cutters from the dependence on straight line cuts. Wheels were made not only of stone and steel, but also of copper and carborundum. Electricity when available was used to power the wheels as well as to provide the craftsmen with better lighting. Additional steps were added to the cutting process as finer wheels and milder abrasives made cutting more precise.

Copper wheel cutting or engraving was the end in the evolutionary process for the finest cut glass. Up to 150 wheels of different diameters were utilized. A copper wheel engraver held the final pattern in his mind without outlining it on the glass. Glass objects were pressed to the revolving wheel, which instantly cut through or roughened the surface. It was then rubbed repeatedly with oils using one's fingers as it was placed on and off the wheel. Before the introduction of lathes, wheels were operated by foot-powered treadles and were somewhat limited in size. An electrically

Cut glass snowflake by Nehemiah Packwood. PHOTO BY MARK PICKVET.

Cut glass. PHOTO BY MARK PICKVET, COURTESY OF THE BERGSTROM-MAHLER MUSEUM.

operated lathe made heavier wheels possible, including large diamond-point cutting wheels. It might take weeks, months, even years to finish a single piece on copper wheels.

Elaborate carving, such as cameo engraving, was also completed on copper wheels. Stone wheels were used primarily for depth, while copper was best for more detailed work. Copper wheel engravers were compensated more than cutters and were some of the most highly skilled artisans in the glassmaking business.

Along with blowers, copper wheel engravers commanded salaries as high as $6.00 a day in the 1880s, common cutters about $3.50 to $4.00 a day, and ordinary general workers about $14.00 to $20.00 a week based on a six-day workweek. The higher wages provided incentive to foreign workers to migrate to the United States. In Europe, English and Irish glassmakers earned $7.00 to $9.00 a week. U.S. wages were typically three to four times higher than European. One disadvantage of this wage system was that European glassmakers produced cheaper glass products. Even after a 45% tariff was added to imported glass in 1888, European glassware was still highly competitive.

To make fine cut glass, a quality handblown blank was necessary. Many decorating companies purchased blanks of high-quality lead glass from major glass companies for their cutters to work. Traditionally, blowers had to be very skilled artisans. Years of training, hard work, and an ability to perform effectively under pressure as well as in poor working conditions were all prerequisites for a successful blower. A blower typically had to work near a blinding furnace with roasting heat, eye-watering smoke, and coal dust. Under such pressures, the glassblower had to exercise the utmost skill, control, patience, steady nerve, and judgment, all mixed with creativity and occasional bouts of spontaneity. In short, glassblowing was an art.

There were many positions in the glassmaking trade. A gatherer would gather a blob of molten glass at the end of a blowpipe, pontil, or gathering iron for the blower. A cutter ordinarily apprenticed for three years at a small salary after completing eight grades of formal education. A good cutter might work up to copper wheel engraver after years of practice.

At the turn of the 20th century, women held some jobs in the field, although glassmaking was primarily a man's business. Women dusted glass in showrooms and salesrooms, distributed glass to cutters, updated catalogs, made drawings of blanks, waxed the glass before an acid dip, and washed or dried glass before packing it. Some enamelers and cutters may have been women.

The production of glass was not easy or safe. The basic ingredients of sand, potash, and lead were mixed in a huge clay pot and heated to extreme temperatures. The best batches had the highest lead content. Molten glass had to be gathered by a worker to press into a mold or simply for the blower to work. Several tools were available, including a pontil, which was used to remove expanded glass objects from the blowing iron. However, the pontil would leave a mark. It was later replaced with a special rod called a gadget. A gadget had a spring clip on the end of it to grip the foot of a glass piece and hold it while another worker trimmed the rim and applied what finishing touches were needed.

Ovens were important, especially those with a special opening called a "glory hole." A glory hole was a small opening in the side of the oven where objects could be reheated and reworked without destroying the original shape. A lehr was an annealing oven that toughened glass through gradual cooling. A muffle kiln was a low-temperature oven for firing or permanently fusing enamels.

Various terms are associated with the glassmaking process. Moil is waste glass left on the blowpipe or pontil. Pucellas are tonglike tools that are used to grasp glass objects. Arrissing is the process of removing sharp edges from glass. Cracking off involves removing a piece of glass from the pontil by cooling, gently tapping, and then dropping it into a soft sand tray. Fire polishing is the process of reheating objects at the glory hole to remove tool marks.

Glass did not always turn out perfectly and imperfections resulted. Such "sick" glass usually was not tempered or annealed properly and showed random cracks, flaking, and possible disintegration. Another problem was seeds, tiny air bubbles in glass that indicated an underheated furnace or impurities caused by flecks of dirt.

Other techniques were used to make glass. Cutting was done primarily in geometrical patterns. Pictorial, cameo, and intaglio (heavily engraved) designs were all cut regularly. Acid etching was the process of covering glass with an acid-resistant layer, scratching on a design, then permanently etching the design with acids. Acid polishing, which gave cut glass a polished surface, involved dipping the entire object into a mild solution of sulfuric or hydrofluoric acid. Hand painting and firing of enamels were two other common techniques.

Sandblasting was a distinct American process. A design was coated with a protective layer, then the exposed surfaces were sandblasted with a pressurized gun. Trimming with enamels like silver, gold, and platinum were in use in the early 1900s. Staining, gilding, monogram imprinting, rubber stamping, and silk screening were other popular methods of decorating glass.

In 1913 the gang-cut wheel was introduced, which allowed workers to make several parallel incisions at once. The wheel made rapid and inexpensive cutting possible, such as crosshatching and blunt-edged flower petals. For the most part, cut glass was simply that: undecorated crystal except for the elaborate cutting.

The decline of superb cut crystal picked up momentum as World War I neared. The exclusive market it catered to faded as the wealthy preferred Art Deco styles and European imports. Cheaper glass formulas, labor troubles, increased imports, more and more machine-made glass, and lead shortages were all factors leading to the end of the Brilliant Period in American glass.

Some of the biggest names in the cut glass world were Libbey, T.G. Hawkes, C. Dorflinger, Mt. Washington/Pairpoint, John Hoare, T.B. Clark, H.P. Sinclaire, and Tuthill. Hundreds of cut glass patterns were made and although many were patented, they were still copied or similar variations were produced by others. There were also many common designs or combinations shared by all, including rosettes, hobstars, fans, strawberry diamonds, geometric cuts, flutes, buzzstars, blocks, and hobnails. Fortunately, more distinct marks and signatures were applied to cut glass products than any other category of glass (see Appendix 4, "Manufacturer's Marks").

ALFORD, C.G. & CO.   1872-1918

Alford was a jeweler and watch repair company that operated in New York City. There is some debate as to whether the company cut any glass or simply applied its mark to pieces done by others.

Bonbon dish, Hobstar bottom, signed "Alford" $200
Celery dish, 12″ oval, 4 hobstars in each corner, signed "Alford" $300
Cruet with faceted ball stopper, Brunswick pattern $275
Decanter with faceted stopper, 9½″ tall, 32 oz., no handle, Hobstar and Fan design, Viola pattern $800
Nappy, 6″, Trieste pattern $225
Plate, 7¼″, large center hobstar surrounded by 8 smaller hobstars, signed "Alford" $150
Vase, 14″ tall, Brunswick pattern, signed "Alford" $400

ALMY & THOMAS   1903-1918

Although they were not a large maker of cut glass, the team of Charles H. Almy and G. Edwin Thomas cut good-quality blanks provided by the Corning Glass Works.

Bowl, 8″, notched rim, Alternating Star and Hobstar design $225
Decanter with faceted stopper, 7″ tall, notched handle, Fan and Star pattern .....
.... $725
Decanter with faceted stopper, 8¾″ tall, Brunswick pattern $850
Whiskey tumbler, 3″ tall, Fan and Star pattern $150

AVERBECK CUT GLASS COMPANY   1892-1923

Averbeck first operated as a jewelry store. In 1892, the company began selling cut glass by mail order. Its name appeared on some of what it shipped and it is possible that it owned a small cutting shop; however, the company most likely purchased glass wholesale from small, relatively unknown cutting shops.

Bowl, 6″ nappy, Boston, Frisco, Occident, Paris, Puck, Saratoga, and Spruce patterns
.... $175
Bowl, 7″ nappy, Boston, Frisco, Occident, Paris, Puck, Saratoga, and Spruce patterns $200
Bowl, 8″, Azalia pattern $250
Bowl, 8″ nappy, Boston, Frisco, Occident, Paris, Puck, Saratoga, and Spruce patterns $225
Bowl, 9″ nappy, Boston, Frisco, Occident, Paris, Puck, Saratoga, and Spruce patterns $250
Bowl, 10″ nappy, Boston, Frisco, Occident, Paris, Puck, Saratoga, and Spruce patterns
.... $275
Bowl, banana, 10″ oval, Genoa pattern $500
Decanter with stopper, 9¼″ tall, Acme pattern $850
Decanter with stopper, 10″ tall, Electric pattern $1100

Decanter with stopper, 12″ tall, Alabama pattern $1250
Jug with stopper, 6″ tall, Liberty pattern $350
Jug with stopper, 8″ tall, Genoa pattern $375
Plate, 6″, Spruce pattern $175
Spoon holder, 4″ tall, prism $150
Spoon holder, 5½″ tall, 2-handled, Logan pattern $175
Tray, 7″ oval, Canton, Lady Curzon, Marietta, Priscilla, Ruby, and Saratoga patterns $350
Tray, 8″ oval, Canton, Empress, Marietta, Royal, Ruby, and Saratoga patterns .. $400
Tray, 12″ oblong, Diamond, Frisco and Liberty patterns $450
Tray, 14½″ oval, Cape Town pattern $525
Tray, 14″ oblong, ruffled edge, Acme pattern $475

BERGEN, J.D. COMPANY 1880–1916

James D. Bergen operated a cut glass business under a variety of names and, like so many others in the 19th and early 20th centuries, recruited relatives to work in his cutting shop. Other names included the Bergen Cut Glass Company, Bergen-Phillips Cut Glass Company, Bergen & Son, Bergen Glass Works, and the Bergen Glass Company.

Basket, large, straight cuts $100
Basket, small, straight cuts $75
Bonbon dish, 6″, Pilgrim pattern $125
Bonbon dish, heart-shaped, Emblem pattern $375
Bottle, wine with straight cut stopper, 12¾″ tall, Tasso pattern $600
Bowl, 6″ oval, ripple pattern $175
Bowl, 7″ oblong, Keystone pattern $225
Bowl, 7″ oval, Caprice pattern $200

J. D. Bergen Co. ad in the February 6, 1901, JEWELER'S CIRCULAR WEEKLY.

Bowl, 8″, 6 circles, notched edge, Azalia design $300
Bowl, 8″, Goldenrod pattern $225
Bowl, 9″, Bermuda pattern $250
Celery dish, 2-handled, Logan pattern $525
Cheese dish with domed cover, 9″ tall, Glenwood pattern $800
Compote with cover, Arcadia pattern $2250
Decanter with stopper, 8″ tall, Bedford pattern $475
Glove box with hinged cover, Harvard pattern with engraved floral design ... $2250
Goblet, star base, three 16-point hobstars, strawberry diamond and fan vesicas, signed $125
Hairpin Box with cover, 3 applied feet, chair bottom design, Harvard pattern, signed "Bergen" $1500
Humidor with cover, 8″, Glenwood pattern, signed "Bergen" $875
Plate, 7″, Sunflower pattern $150
Plate, 7″, White Rose pattern $175
Powder jar with cover, Swirled Comet pattern, signed "Bergen" $500
Punch bowl with stand, 14″, Glenwood pattern $2750
Punch bowl with stand, Wabash pattern $2500
Saucer, 5″, Bedford, Bermuda, Corsair, Frisco, Golf, Kenwood, Magnet, Progress, and Webster patterns $75
Saucer, 6″, Bedford, Bermuda, Corsair, Frisco, Golf, Kenwood, Magnet, Progress, and Webster patterns $100
Tray, 6½″ oblong, straight sides, Magnet pattern $175
Tray, 6″ oblong, slanted, Key West pattern $150
Tray, 7½″ oblong, short handle, Emblem pattern $250
Tray, 7″ oval, Laurel pattern $200
Tray, 9″ oblong, circular center, 5″ wide, Dariel pattern $475
Tray, oval, 9″ × 5″, Hawthorne pattern $300
Tray, rectangular, (11½″ × 7″), Hobstars and Diamonds pattern $425
Vase, 6″ tall, notched prism $225
Vase, 21″ tall, 9″ diameter, 2-part, Sunbeam pattern $600

BLACKMER CUT GLASS COMPANY   1894–1916

Arthur L. Blackmer was a salesman for his company and employed others to make the glass. Like so many other glassmaking enterprises, the business did not survive World War I.

Bowl, 7″, Starling pattern $175
Bowl, 7″, Troy pattern $150
Bowl, 9″, Columbia pattern $250
Compote, 9″ diameter, 6½″ tall, Celtic or Medina pattern $200
Creamer, Eudora or Ruby pattern $125
Cruet with faceted stopper, 6″ tall, Oregon pattern $325
Decanter with cut stopper, Concord pattern $525
Ice tub, angled cradle shape, Columbia pattern $850
Nappy, 6″, notched edge, Troy pattern $150
Nappy, 6″, Regal pattern $225
Plate, 7″, Newport pattern $175

Plate, 8″, Doris pattern $200
Platter, 12″ round, Crescendo pattern $600
Relish dish, 7″ across, tab handle, Sultana pattern $225
Sugar dish, Eudora or Ruby pattern $125
Tray, 10″ round, Emerson pattern $250
Tray, 12″ oval, Plymouth pattern $375
Tumbler, 8″ tall, Constellation pattern $175
Vase, 11″ tall, 12″ diameter, Sultana pattern $550

CLARK, T.B. & COMPANY   1884–1930

Thomas Byron Clark operated the second-largest cut glass operation in Pennsylvania (Dorflinger was first). Clark actually used Dorflinger's blanks early on, and the quality of his company's products rank with the best.

Bonbon dish, Adonis, Arbutus, Dorrance, Jewel, Manhattan, St. George, Venus, and Winola patterns $125
Bonbon dish with handle, Irving, Jefferson, and St. George patterns $150
Bowl, 6″, footed, Manhattan pattern $225
Bowl, 8″, Adonis, Arbutus, Desdemona, Magnolia, Manhattan, Priscilla, Venus and Winola patterns $275
Bowl, 8″, Prima Donna pattern, signed "Clark" $400
Bowl, 8″ square, Corinthian pattern $300
Bowl, 9″, Adonis, Arbutus, Desdemona, Magnolia, Manhattan, Priscilla, Venus, and Winola patterns $300
Bowl, 10″, Adonis, Arbutus, Desdemona, Magnolia, Manhattan, Priscilla, Venus, and Winola pattern $325
Bowl, 12″, notched edge, Strawberry Diamond pattern, signed "Clark" $375

T. B. Clark & Company, cut glass, from a Clark period catalog.

T. B. Clark & Company, cut glass, 1892 patent, "Sea Shell" pattern.

Bowl, oval, (11½" × 9"), Quatrefoil Rosette pattern, signed "Clark" $500
Bowl, rose, 7", Manhattan pattern $250
Cheese dish with dome cover, Manhattan pattern $800
Claret jug with sterling silver stopper, Arbutus pattern, signed "Clark" $1350
Cologne bottle with stopper, 6 oz., globe-shaped, Jewel or Venus pattern $500
Compote, 5" diameter, 5½" tall, hobstars, signed "Clark" $325
Compote, 8" tall, Harvard pattern variant $450
Compote, 10" diameter, Arbutus pattern $400
Creamer, 3½" tall, Cut Thistle design $150
Creamer, 4" tall, Strawberry Diamond and Star pattern $350
Decanter with stopper, 32 oz., no handle, Winola pattern $500
Decanter with stopper, 32 oz., with handle, Strawberrry Diamond and Fan pattern
.... $450
Decanter with stopper, 32 oz., with handle, Winola pattern $525
Goblet, Winola pattern $100
Mug, Jewel and Winola patterns $150
Nappy, 5", Jewel, Manhattan, and Winola patterns $125
Nappy, 6", Jewel, Manhattan, and Winola pattern $150
Nappy, 7", Arbutus, Desdemona, Jewel, Manhattan, and Winola patterns ... $175
Nappy, 8", Arbutus, Desdemona, Manhattan, and Winola patterns $200
Nappy, 9", Arbutus, Desdemona, and Manhattan patterns $225
Nappy, 10", Arbutus, Dedemona, and Manhattan patterns $250
Pitcher, milk, 32 oz., Venus pattern $400
Pitcher, water, 48 oz., Venus pattern $450
Pitcher, water, Triple Square pattern, signed "Clark" $550
Plate, 6", Harvard pattern variant $100
Plate, 7", Prima Donna pattern, signed "Clark" $175
Plate, 7", Venus pattern $150
Plate, 12", Pinwheel pattern, signed "Clark" $475
Platter, 12" round, Waldorf pattern $475
Punch bowl, 12", Desdemona pattern $1000
Punch bowl with stand, 14" diameter, Desdemona pattern $1750
Relish, 9" diameter, 4-part, 2-handled, 4 hobstars $275
Sugar dish, 3½" tall, Cut Thistle design $150

Sugar shaker with sterling silver top, Henry VIII pattern $275
Sugar with cover, 4½" tall, Strawberry Diamond and Star pattern $450
Tray, 11½" × 8" rectangular, Jewel Pattern $650
Tray, 12" oval, Baker's Gothic pattern $375
Tray, 13 ", Adonis, Manhattan, Venus, and Winola patterns $450
Tray, bread, 12½", Hobstars and Fans with engraved leaves $400
Tray, celery, 11", Adonis, Desdemona, Dorrance, Manhattan, Nordica, and Winola
patterns. $350
Tray, celery, 11⅞" oval, Pinwheels and Hobstars design $350
Tray, celery, Pinwheel design, signed "Clark" $250
Tumbler, 8 oz., Coral pattern $150
Tumbler, 8 oz., Strawberry Diamond and Fan design $125
Vase, 4" tall, notched rim, wide-style, Henry VIII pattern $225
Vase, 8" tall, circular base, Jewel pattern $200
Vase, 10¼" tall, 8½" wide, Mistletoe pattern $1250
Vase, 10" tall, circular base, Jewel pattern $250
Vase, 12" tall, circular base, Jewel pattern $275
Vase, 18" tall, circular base, Palmetto pattern $575
Whiskey tumbler, Strawberry Diamond and Fan design $85
Wine glass, Winola pattern $85

DITHRIDGE AND COMPANY   1881–1891

Dithridge was a large supplier of lead blanks and did a little cutting of its own.

Pitcher, 10" tall, corset-shaped, scalloped, sunburst and geometric design .. $425
Tray, oval, 6⅞" long, angled cut squares, alternating with diamond cross-cut
squares $200
Wine glass, 4¾" tall, Strawberry Diamond and Fan pattern $175

DORFLINGER, CHRISTIAN & SONS   1852–1921

Fine cut glass by Dorflinger & Sons graced the table of many U.S. presidents. Dorflinger spared no expense in finding excellent workmen and obtaining the best lead
and other ingredients. Above all, he demanded quality workmanship. The company
was one of the largest producers of cut crystal glassware prior to World War I.

Bowl, 6½" square, Strawberry Diamond pattern $175
Bowl, 8", Gladys pattern $225
Bowl, 8", notched edge, Amore pattern $200
Bowl, 9", Alternating Small and Large Diamond-Checkered pattern (Pattern #28)
.... $250
Bowl, 9" diameter, 7" tall, Prince of Wales design, Plumes pattern with hobstar foot
.... $525
Bowl, 9", Large Leaf (6 leaves) design, Paola pattern $175
Bowl, 10" oval, Strawberry pattern $325
Bowl, finger, with underplate, Picket Fence pattern $100
Bowl, rose, Brilliant pattern $250

*Christian Dorflinger & Sons,
Rattan pattern.*

Carafe, 8¹/₄″ tall, Split pattern $325
Cheese dish with dome cover, 7″, Russian pattern $825
Cologne bottle with stopper, 7¹/₂″, Princess pattern $500
Cookie jar with cover, 6¹/₄″ tall, hobstar base, sterling silver cover marked
"Gorham," Sussex pattern $550
Creamer, notched prism handles, Colonial pattern $150
Creamer, Russian pattern $150
Cruet, Fan and Star design (Pattern #80) $250
Cruet with stopper, 8″ tall, globe-shaped, Gladys pattern $375
Cruet with stopper, 10¹/₄″ tall, Marlboro pattern $400
Decanter, Renaissance pattern $325
Decanter with silver stopper, 12″ tall, Parisian pattern $850
Fernery, Picket Fence pattern $85
Goblet, 5¹/₂″ tall, mitered stem, Parisian pattern $275
Ice bucket with underplate, handle tabs, Marlboro pattern $2000
Lamp, banquet oil, 4-part, matching cut chimney, paper label $750
Lamp, Gone with the Wind, 20″ tall, 12″ base diameter, Hobstar and Diamond
design $1400
Parfait, 6″ tall, Kalana Lily pattern $150
Perfume with stopper, hobstar base, Marlboro pattern $250
Pitcher, cereal, 5″ tall, diamond and fern cuts (Dorflinger's Pattern #80) . . . $300
Pitcher, cream, 4¹/₂″ tall, Parisian pattern $275
Pitcher, cream, 6″ tall, Parisian pattern $275
Pitcher, water, 7¹/₂″ tall, Colonial pattern $350
Pitcher, water, 7¹/₄″ tall, globe-shaped, applied handle, Strawberry Diamond and
Fan pattern $350
Pitcher, water, 8¹/₂″ tall, globe-shaped, scalloped, sunburst base, paneled neck,
Strawberry Diamond and Fan pattern $450
Pitcher, water, 8″ tall, Colonial pattern $350
Plate, 6¹/₄″, Picket Fence pattern $75
Plate, 7¹/₂″, scalloped and serrated rim, American pattern $100

Plate, 7″, Parisian pattern $125
Plate, 7″, Russian pattern $200
Plate, 8″, Gladys pattern $175
Punch bowl ladle, cranberry to clear, Montrose pattern $3250
Punch bowl with stand, 14⅛″ diameter, 11½″ tall, 24-point hobstar on center and base, twelve 8-point hobstars, Marlboro pattern $2250
Salad set, 3-piece, 10″ handled square bowl, Parisian pattern, sterling silver fork and spoon $2250
Salt dip, paperweight style, Parisian pattern $125
Sugar dish, no handles, Russian pattern $150
Sugar dish, notched prism handles, Colonial pattern $150
Tray, 11″ oval, Middlesex pattern $300
Tray, 12½″ oval, ice cream, pinwheels $575
Tumbler, juice, 3¾″ tall, Old Colony pattern $175
Tumbler, juice, 3⅞″ tall, Parisian pattern $200
Vase, 6″ tall, Kalana Pansy pattern $125
Vase, 7½″ tall, Kalana Geranium pattern $150
Vase, 10″ tall, hobstars with 5 large bull's-eyes $300
Vase, 10″ tall, Kalana Wild Rose pattern with Amethyst Flowers design $325
Vase, 10″ tall, 7″ diameter, Russian pattern $375
Vase, 12″ tall, circular base, diamond and horizontal step cutting $400
Vase, 12″ tall, flared top and bottom, Kalana Pansy design $375
Vase, 14″ tall, circular base, notched top edge, Parisian pattern $450
Vase, 14″ tall, Cosmos pattern $375
Vase, 15″ tall, Inverness pattern $325
Wine glass, knobbed stem, Colonial pattern $125

EGGINTON, O.F. COMPANY   1899–1920

Oliver F. Egginton was once a manager of T.G. Hawkes's cutting department and went on to establish the Egginton Rich Cut Glass Company with Walter F. Egginton. Egginton purchased blanks from the Corning Glass Works and patented a few patterns, such as "Magnolia" and "Trellis."

Bowl, 5¾″, notched edge, Cluster pattern $150
Bowl, 7½″, Lotus pattern $250
Bowl, 7¼″, Trellis pattern $225
Bowl, 8″, chain of hobstars, triple bands $250
Bowl, 8″, Cluster pattern $275
Bowl, 9″, Marquise or Roman pattern $225
Bowl, 10″, Calve pattern, signed $250
Bowl, finger, 5″, Bull's-Eye and Hobstar pattern, signed "Egginton" $85
Butter dish with cover, 5″ dome cover, 7″ plate, Lotus pattern, signed $600
Celery dish, 11¾″ × 4¾″ oval, Arabian pattern $400
Creamer, 4″ tall, Trellis pattern variation, signed $250
Decanter with matching stopper, Creswick pattern $3250
Ice bucket, 8″ tall, tab handles, Creswick pattern $475
Nappy, 6″, notched edge, Lotus pattern $100
Nappy, 7″, notched edge, 1 handle, Lotus pattern $150
Pitcher, water, 10″ tall, Thistle pattern, signed "Egginton" $275

Plate, 7″, Lotus pattern, signed $125
Plate, 7″, Prism pattern $150
Plate, 8″, Magnolia pattern, signed "Egginton" $175
Platter, 12″ diameter, Trellis pattern, signed "Egginton" $475
Punch bowl with stand, 14″ diameter, 13″ tall, Arabian pattern, signed ... $1500
Punch cup, stemmed, Arabian pattern $125
Relish, 8″ oval, Arabian pattern $225
Spooner, 8″, Star and Hobnail design $85
Spooner, oval, 8″ × 4″, flat, Lotus pattern $100
Sugar, 4″ tall, rose bowl–shaped, Trellis pattern variation, signed $250
Tray, celery, 12″ oval, Lotus pattern $250
Tray, ice cream, 12″ oval, Calve pattern $250
Tumbler, Thistle pattern, signed "Egginton" $125
Vase, 12″ tall, Victoria pattern $550
Vase, 14″ tall, urn-shaped, 4 Hobstars with Comet Swirls design $2500

EMPIRE CUT GLASS COMPANY 1890s–1925

Empire was founded in the early 1890s by Harold Hollis in New York City. In 1902, Hollis sold it to his employees, who operated it as a cooperative until 1904. The company was then sold to Henry C. Fry, who continued producing cut glass under the Empire name into the 1920s.

Bonbon dish, applied curled up handle, Atlantic pattern $225
Bowl, 6″, notched edge, Saxonia pattern $175
Bowl, 8″, Dupont, Isabella, Manhattan, Nelson, or Typhoon pattern $250
Bowl, 8″, Kremlin pattern $275
Bowl, 8″, shallow, Japan pattern $225
Bowl, 9″, Berkshire or Iorio special pattern $300
Carafe, water, 7³/₄″, Peerless pattern $200
Celery dish, 11¹/₂″ oval, Princeton pattern $300
Decanter with faceted ball stopper, Diamond and Fan design $400
Nappy, 6″, notched edge, Prince pattern $125
Plate, 8″, notched edge, Plymouth pattern $175
Relish dish, 8″, 2 applied handles, 4 divisions, Madame pattern $225
Tray, 12″ oblong, notched edge, Atlantic pattern $375
Tray, 14″ oblong, notched edge, Elsie pattern $425
Vase, 9″ tall, Waldorf pattern $300
Vase, 12″ tall, circular base, Viola pattern $650

ENTERPRISE CUT GLASS COMPANY 1905–1917

Enterprise actually obtained a good deal of blanks for cutting from Belgium; others were purchased from the Union Glass Works. The advent of World War I cut off supplies, and the company was out of business by 1917.

Bowl, 7¹/₂″, Buzz Star pattern $150
Bowl, 7¹/₂″, notched edge, Star pattern $175

Decanter with stopper, 13″ tall, large hobstar on globe-shaped base,
vertically cut neck $625
Pitcher, 7″ tall, tankard-style, Daisy pattern $350
Pitcher, milk, 8″ tall, Sunburst pattern $375
Pitcher, water, 13½″ tall, Imperial pattern $525
Plate, 8¼″, notched edge, Daisy pattern $150
Punch bowl with stand, 11″ diameter, 10″ tall, Majestic pattern $3000
Punch bowl with stand, 14″ diameter, 16½″ tall, 8½″ deep, Royal pattern $4250
Tray, celery, 12½″ oval, notched edge, Rose pattern $500
Tray, ice cream, 14″ × 7½″ oval, Buzz Star pattern $600
Tumbler, Sunburst pattern $75
Vase, 13″ tall, circular diamond cut base, Large Hobstar design $1350

FRY, H.C. AND COMPANY   1901–1934

Henry C. Fry worked for a variety of glass firms before establishing his own business in 1901. The company's product line included not only cut glass, but also pressed and etched glass, ovenware, and blown blanks.

Bonbon dish, 5″ square, King George pattern $150
Bowl, 4″, Wheat pattern $125
Bowl, 6″, 4 ovals with crosscuts and chains of stars $175
Bowl, 6″, Wheat pattern $175
Bowl, 8″, 2 circular handles, Trojan pattern $275
Bowl, 8″, Cleo pattern, signed "Fry" $225
Bowl, 8″, Nelson or Wheat pattern $200
Bowl, 9″, rayed base, chain hobstars and fans, signed "Fry" $300
Bowl, 10″, Frederick, Keystone, or Wheat patterns $250
Decanter with faceted stopper, 10″ tall, Genoa pattern $625
Lamp, 20″ tall, Notched Prism pattern with hobtars $1500
Mayonnaise bowl, 5″ diameter, circular pedestal base, Swirled Wheat pattern ....
.... $200
Plate, 7″, Brighton pattern $200
Plate, 8″, Wheat pattern $150
Platter, 12″ oblong, Atlantic pattern $475
Platter, 12″ round, Frederick pattern, signed "Fry" $700
Sandwich server with center handle, 10″ diameter, Asteroid pattern $450
Seving dish, 9¾″, tricornered, Flaring Notched Prism pattern $725
Tray, 14″ oblong, notched edge, Elsie pattern $400
Tray, 14″ oval, Sciota pattern $500
Tray, 14″ rectangular, Leman pattern $575
Tray, bread, 12″ oval, Elba pattern $450
Tray, bread, 12″ oval, Typhoon pattern $475
Tumbler, 6″ tall, Georgia pattern $150
Tumbler, highball, 5½″ tall, pinwheel center, hobstar on base $125
Umbrella stand, 24″ tall, Star, Diamond, and Bull's-Eye design $5000
Wine glass, Supreme pattern, signed "Fry" $75

HAWKES, T.G. COMPANY   1880-1903

Thomas Gibbon Hawkes was an Irish immigrant with a long family history of glass artistry. He was a direct descendant of the Hawkes family of Dudley, England, and the Penrose family of Waterford, Ireland. Hawkes came to America in 1863 and fell in with such famous glassmakers as John Hoare, Henry Sinclaire, and Oliver Eggington. He purchased blanks from the Corning Glass Works through 1904. He then teamed up with several relatives and Frederick Carder to form Steuben Glass Works. Hawkes's painstaking attention to details and his patented patterns, including "Russian," "Louis XIV," "Brazilian," and "Nautilus," established him as one of the elite cut glass manufacturers.

Basket, 9″ tall, 8″ diameter, 3 thumbprints on applied handle, hobstar base, Hobstar and Fans pattern $1250
Basket, 10″ diameter, Russian pattern $600
Basket, 12″ tall, 8½″ diameter, barrel-shaped, notched handle, cut horizontal rows with vertical divisions $800
Bonbon dish, 5″ round, Russian pattern $125
Bonbon dish, 5″, Strawberry Diamond and Fan pattern $100
Bowl, 4½″, Harvard pattern $125
Bowl, 6″, Festoon pattern $150
Bowl, 7″, 2″ tall, Kohinoor and Hobstar pattern, signed "Hawkes" $350
Bowl, 7″, Gladys pattern $175
Bowl, 7″ oblong, Panel pattern $300
Bowl, 7″, straight sides, Venetian pattern $275
Bowl, 8″, crimped, Russian pattern $350
Bowl, 8″, footed, Russian pattern $375
Bowl, 8″, Nautilus pattern $525
Bowl, 8″ square, notched edge, Festoon pattern $225
Bowl, 9¼″, scalloped, engraved dahlias and swirls $500
Bowl, 9″, hobstars and bull's-eye clusters (Queen's pattern variant) $550
Bowl, 9″, Russian pattern $375

T. G. Hawkes cut glass. PHOTO BY MARK PICKVET.

T. G. Hawkes cut glass.
COURTESY OF THE CORNING
MUSEUM OF GLASS.

Bowl, 10″, Comet pattern, signed "Hawkes" $450
Bowl, 10″, Devonshire pattern $450
Bowl, 10″, footed, Russian pattern $450
Bowl, 10″, Harvard pattern $325
Bowl, 12″, Chrysanthemum or Russian pattern, signed "Hawkes" $825
Bowl, centerpiece, 9″ diameter base, 4″ diameter bowl, scalloped, 24-point hobstar bottom, Hobstar pattern, signed "Hawkes" $600
Bowl, fruit, 9″, Millicent pattern $325
Bowl, rose, 7¹/₂″, 8″ tall, Queen's pattern, signed "Hawkes" on bottom and liner ..
....$725
Butter dish with cover, 5″ cover diameter, Jersey pattern $750
Candelabra, 17″ tall, 3-light, Brazilian pattern $3250
Candleholder, 3¹/₂″ tall, hollow bulb stem, Intaglio Floral design $100
Candlestick, 12″ tall, swirled pillar stem, Russian patterned square foot $375
Candlestick, rayed base, faceted ball, paneled stem $300
Carafe, water, Devonshire pattern $800
Celery dish, boat-shaped, Harvard pattern $600
Cheese dish with cover, Aberdeen pattern $475
Cocktail shaker with cover, 9″, Diamond Cut design $325
Cologne with stopper, bell-shaped, Gravic desgin, signed "Hawkes" $475
Compote, 7″ diameter, 7″ tall, open, Venetian pattern $250
Compote, 13″ diameter, 10″ tall, Panel pattern, signed "Hawkes" $675
Compote, large, hobstar and thumbprints enclosed in diamonds $575
Cordial, 1 oz., square base, Cut Diamond design $75
Cruet with stopper, 6″ tall, Venetian pattern $550
Cruet with stopper, 9″ tall, Dundee pattern $1250
Decanter with silver-hinged stopper, Chrysanthemum pattern $675
Decanter with stopper, 12″ tall, Brunswick pattern $750
Decanter with stopper, 12″ tall, Grecian pattern $750
Globe, rose, 6¹/₂″ tall, circular pedestal base, Brunswick pattern $175
Goblet, 5³/₄″ tall, Gravic Floral design, signed "Hawkes" $125
Goblet, 6³/₄″ tall, Intaglio 3-Fruit design $175

Humidor, tobacco, 8″ tall, large cut oval ball on cover, Brunswick pattern .. $775
Humidor, tobacco, 8¹/₂″ tall, large cut oval ball on cover, Marlboro pattern ... $875
Ice bowl, 7″ round, 5″ tall, 2 tab handles, Iceland pattern $500
Ice cream tray, oval (15¹/₂″ × 10¹/₂″), Chrysanthemum pattern $800
Ice tub, 5″ tall, 6″ across, rayed base, Strawberry Diamond and Fan pattern $375
Knife rest, 5″ long, faceted $75
Napkin ring, 1³/₄″ tall, Hobstar design $85
Nappy, 6″, handled, engraved flowers between hobstars $85
Nappy, 8″, Russian pattern, signed "Hawkes" $275
Olive dish, 9″, acorn-shaped, Strawberry Diamond pattern $425
Pitcher, cocktail, 16″ tall, silver-plated stirrer, Cut Band design $300
Pitcher, milk, 6¹/₂″ tall, 7¹/₂″ wide, Intaglio and Chrysanthemum pattern, signed
"Hawkes" $2000
Pitcher, syrup with sterling silver lid, 4¹/₂″ tall, St. Regis pattern $500
Pitcher, syrup with sterling silver lid, 7″ tall, Brunswick pattern, signed .. $1500
Pitcher, water, 10″ tall, Panel pattern, signed "Hawkes" $1000
Pitcher, water, 11¹/₂″ tall, Chrysanthemum pattern $1250
Pitcher, water, 11″ tall, pedestal base, Queen's pattern, signed "Hawkes" .. $1500
Pitcher, water, 12″ tall, Intaglio cut and Chrysanthemum pattern, signed "Hawkes"
.... $1750
Plate, 7¹/₂″, Napoleon pattern $275
Plate, 7¹/₂″, Queen's pattern $375
Plate, 7″, Astor, Cambridge, Grecian, and Venetian patterns $225
Plate, 7″, Chrysanthemum pattern $250
Plate, 8¹/₂″, Venetian pattern $300
Plate, 8″, notched edge, Russian pattern $300
Plate, 9″, Venetian pattern, signed "Hawkes" $325
Plate, 10″, Constellation or Holland pattern $225
Plate, 11″, Cardinal pattern, signed "Hawkes" $375
Plate, 12″, Constellation or Panel pattern $325
Plate, 12″, Venetian pattern, signed "Hawkes" $425
Plate, 13 ¹/₂″, scalloped, 8-pointed hobstar, stamped "Hawkes" $1250
Plate, 13″, Kensington pattern $1250
Platter, 11¹/₂″ round, Panel pattern, signed "Hawkes" $750
Platter, 12¹/₂″ oval, Albany pattern $675
Platter, 13″ round, Venetian pattern $725
Platter, 14″ round, Constellation pattern $425
Platter, 14″ round, North Star pattern $900
Platter, 15¹/₂″ round, King's pattern $900
Platter, 16″ round, Constellation pattern $500
Powder box with hinged cover, Chrysanthemum pattern, signed $575
Punch bowl with stand, 12″ diameter, 12″ tall, Queen's pattern, signed "Hawkes"
.... $3000
Salt and pepper shakers, Alberta pattern $275
Tray, 11″ oval, Devonshire, Naples, and Wild Rose patterns $475
Tray, dresser, 10″ oval, Sheraton pattern $300
Tray, ice cream, 14″ (nearly rectangular), ruffled edge, Mars pattern $425
Tray, ice cream, 14″ oval, Russian pattern $725
Tray, oblong, 15″ × 8″, Nautilus pattern, signed "Hawkes" $1500
Vase, 4¹/₂″ tall, 3 engraved medallions, Gracia pattern, signed "Hawkes" $275
Vase, 11¹/₂″ tall, sterling silver foot, knob stem, Millicent pattern $350

Vase, 11″ tall, globe-holder, globe knob stem, circular base, Russian pattern . $450
Vase, 12″ tall, Brunswick pattern $400
Vase, 12″ tall, engraved ferns and roses with bands of hobstars $450
Vase, 12″ tall, globe-top, circular base, Franklin pattern $425
Vase, 13″ tall, globe-holder, globe knob stem, circular base, Russian pattern . $525
Vase, 14″ tall, flared, notched rim, circular base, Brighton pattern $775
Vase, 14″ tall, 6″ diameter, Lattice and Rosette pattern, signed "Hawkes" ... $800
Vase, 18″ tall, pedestal base, Queen's pattern, signed "Hawkes" $900
Whiskey Tumbler, 2¾″ tall, Monarch pattern, signed "Hawkes" $125
Wine glass, 5½″ tall, double knob, circular foot, Engraved Iris design $100
Wine glass, 6½″ tall, square base, Cane and Queen's patterns $125

HOARE, J. & COMPANY   1853–1890s

John Hoare was one of the early leaders of the Brilliant Period in glassmaking. He and his father, James, were both born in the famous glassmaking town of Cork, Ireland. The Hoare family was associated with Thomas Webb & Sons and other firms in England. John Hoare also paid the boat fare for Thomas G. Hawkes, who was employed briefly by the Hoares. The company's cut glass products were some of the best ever produced. This is evidenced by the numerous awards it received at various expositions (e.g., the gold medal at the Columbian Exposition in Chicago, 1893).

Basket (small), 2¾″ diameter, 5″ tall, applied thumbprint handle, Crosby
pattern $175
Basket, 18″ tall, flared top, Diamond, Fan, and Hobstar cuts $900
Bell, 6″ tall, Monarch pattern $125
Bonbon dish, 5″ round, Croesus pattern $125
Bowl, 7″, rolled side, Creswick pattern $275

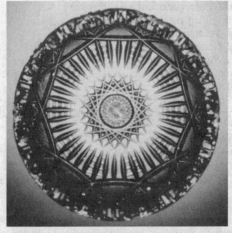

J. Hoare cut glass. PHOTO BY ROBIN RAINWATER.

Bowl, 8¼″ diameter, 2½″ tall, scalloped, serrated rim, 8 oval miteres with 6 rows of hobstars between the ovals, marked "J. Hoare & Co./1853/Corning" $625

Bowl, 8″, Croesus pattern $225

Bowl, 8″ square, Pebble pattern $375

Bowl, 8″, Strawberry Diamond and Fan pattern, signed "Hoare" $225

Bowl, 9″, footed, Corning pattern $300

Bowl, 9″ square, Croesus pattern $350

Bowl, 10″ square, Corning pattern $400

Bowl, 11″ square, Marquise pattern $475

Bowl, 14″, shallow, Diamond and Bar design (Pattern #5336) $725

Bowl, centerpiece, 11½″ diameter, 5½″ tall, Scalloped and Swirled Leaves with Alternating Strawberry and Diamond pattern $1500

Bowl, rose, 7″, 6″ tall, Wedding Ring pattern $675

Butter pat, Hobstar and Crossed Oval pattern, signed "Hoare" $75

Candlestick, 8″ tall, Crosshatched Diamond design $350

Candlestick, 10″ tall, Colonial pattern $175

Carafe, Queen's pattern, signed "J. Hoare and Company" $550

Celery dish, 11¼″ long, Harvard pattern, signed "Hoare" $225

Centerpiece, canoe-shaped, 12½″ long, 4″ tall, scalloped, Quarter Diamond pattern $1250

Champagne glass, Sunburst base, circular foot, fluted and notched hourglass stem, hobstars between mitered cuts $125

Creamer, Swirled Hobstar and Fan design $150

Cruet with stopper, 6″ tall, Strawberry Diamond and Fan pattern, signed "Hoare" $425

Decanter with sterling silver stopper, 9″ tall, Wheat and Thistle design ... $950

Decanter with stopper, 8½″ tall, Prism pattern $300

Decanter with stopper, 8″ tall, 16 oz., Hindoo pattern $400

Decanter with stopper, 13½″ tall, Wedding Ring pattern $825

Goblet, 8½″ tall, wafer base, textured leaves on stem $2250

Handkerchief box with hinged cover, Nassau pattern, silver overlay by Birks $1250

Ice cream tray, 13″ long, scalloped hobstar and strawberry diamond border, oval hobstar and fans on center, marked "J. Hoare and Company" $850

Jug, whiskey with stopper, 10″ tall, 7″ diameter, 1gal., Monarch pattern, signed $2750

Pitcher, water, 9¼″ tall, applied handle, notched rim, Hindoo pattern $500

Pitcher, water, 9¼″ tall, flared bottom, sunburst base, scalloped, large hobstars, signed "J. Hoare & Co./1853/Corning" $525

Pitcher, water, 12″ tall, Eleanor pattern $2500

Pitcher, water, 12″ tall, Wheat pattern $675

Plate, 6″, Acme pattern $150

Plate, 7″, hexagonal, Nassau pattern $200

Plate, 7″ square, Corning pattern $200

Plate, 8″ square, Corning pattern $225

Platter, 12″, circular, Carolyn pattern $500

Platter, 14″, circular, Creswick pattern $575

Platter, 14″, circular, Hindoo pattern $600

Punch bowl, 12½″, Newport pattern $2750

Punch bowl, 12″, 6″ tall, Wheat pattern $3000

Punch bowl with base, oval (20″ × 13″), 10″ tall, Croesus pattern $4250

Punch bowl with stand, 12″ diameter, 13″ tall, Limoges pattern $3750
Punch cup, handled, Croesus pattern $125
Relish dish, 6″ long, 3-lobed, Hobstar and Facets design $125
Relish dish, 7″ long, Brighton pattern $150
Sachet jar with cover, 4″ tall, Hindoo pattern $500
Sugar dish, Swirled Hobstar and Fan design $150
Tobacco Jar with cover, 7¹/₈″ tall, hobstars, swags, and facets $700
Tray, celery, oval (11″ × 5″), Eclipse pattern $425
Tray, celery, oval (10¹/₂″ × 5″), Large Hobnail design $375
Tray, celery, oval (12″ × 4¹/₂″), Victoria pattern $475
Tray, celery, oval (9¹/₂″ × 4″), Strawberry Diamond and Fan pattern $275
Tray, ice cream, 13¹/₂″ oval, Wheat pattern $925
Tray, ice cream, 17¹/₂″, Hobstar design $1500
Tray, ice cream, 17″ oval, Meteor design $1500
Tumbler, 3³/₄″, Croesus pattern $175
Vase, 12″ tall, 2-handled, Monarch pattern $1500
Vase, 12″ tall, 5″ diameter, trumpet shape, prism with button squares $375
Vase, 14″ tall, 6¹/₂″ diameter, Comet pattern, signed $1750
Whiskey tumbler, 2³/₄″ tall, Monarch pattern $125
Wine glass, Monarch pattern $100

HOPE GLASS WORKS   1872–1923

This small manufacturer of cut glass had trouble operating profitably and went through several changes in ownership, although the company name was never altered. The firm made glass globes, knobs, and shades, along with some tableware.

Bowl, 7″, shallow, notched edge, large star cut surrounded by 6 small hobstars .. $150
Creamer, 4¹/₂″ tall, handle and spout (pitcher style), notched rim, applied notched handle, vertically cut with mitered diamond band at top $225
Cruet with stopper, 5″ tall, Hobstar and Diamond pattern $525
Plate, 7″, cut star surrounded by engraved carnations $550
Sugar, 4¹/₄″ tall, 2 notched handles, notched rim, vertically cut with mitered diamond band at top $200

HUNT GLASS COMPANY   1895–1973

In 1880, Thomas Hunt, along with his son, Harold, came to the United States from England. The elder Hunt first worked for T.G. Hawkes before establishing his own operation in 1895. Hunt's cut glass was made prior to World War I. The company's "Royal" pattern is the most common.

Bonbon dish, 3³/₄″ square, Royal pattern $100
Bowl, 9″, Cut Bar and Circle design $225
Bowl, rose, 7¹/₂″, Royal pattern $500
Creamer, Royal pattern $175
Punch bowl with stand, Royal pattern $1750

Sandwich server, engraved fruit, signed $375
Sugar dish, Royal pattern $175
Tray, 7³/₄″ oval, Royal pattern $225
Tray, bread, 11¹/₂″, Royal pattern $325
Tray, ice cream, 10¹/₂″, Hobstar and Fan design $275
Tray, ice cream, 14¹/₂″, Stafford pattern $500
Tumbler, juice, Royal pattern $75

IDEAL CUT GLASS COMPANY   1904–1934

Ideal was another small company that made very few products. It did, however, patent six-petaled flower and sailing ship patterns.

Lamp, 18″ tall, Hobstar and Fluted design $1500
Pitcher, 14¹/₂″ tall, corset-shaped, serrated lip, cut vertical rows alternating with hobstars $850
Plate, 8″, engraved sailing ship (Constitution) $1500
Tumbler, Diamond Poinsettia pattern $275
Vase, 12″ tall, notched edge, Diamond Poinsettia pattern $1250

IRVING CUT GLASS COMPANY   1910–1933

Irving was formed by George Reichenbacher, Eugen Coleman, William Hawken, William Seitz, George Roedine, and John Gogard, six glass cutters who had previously worked for others. The company survived World War I, but closed during the Depression.

Bonbon dish, butterfly shape, 6″, Elk pattern $150
Bowl, 8″, Pinwheel pattern $200
Butter dish with cover, 6″ diameter dome, 8″ diameter underplate, Rose Combination pattern $750
Butter dish with cover, 8″ diameter, 5¹/₂″ tall, Zella pattern $750
Creamer, pitcher-style, applied handle, notched rim, Large Hobstar design $275
Goblet, 4¹/₂″ tall, White Rose pattern $150
Lamp, 22″ tall, dome shade, Zella pattern $2750
Nappy, 11″ diameter, 6″ tall, 2-sectioned, center top handle, Hobstar and Diamond Cut design $525
Pitcher, water, 9″ tall, applied handle, Carnation pattern $575
Plate, 7″, White Rose pattern $150
Plate, 10″, Victrola pattern $450
Relish tray, 9″ × 4″ oval, 2 divisions, Iowa pattern $500
Sugar, 2 applied handles, notched rim, Large Hobstar design $275
Tray, boat-shaped, 9″ oblong, Iowa pattern $625
Tumbler, 4″ tall, Signora pattern $75

Jewel cut glass, 1912 patent, "Primrose" pattern.

JEWEL CUT GLASS COMPANY 1907–1928

The firm began as the C.H. Taylor Glass Company in 1906 but changed the name to Jewel the following year. It patented a few patterns, but as the market for fine cut glass declined, the company stopped cutting glass and began selling greeting cards in 1928.

Bonbon dish, 6″, 2 tab handles, Engraved Floral design $275
Bowl, 8″, shallow, notched edge, Engraved Primrose pattern $350
Bowl, 11″, rolled rim, Bishop's Hat design, Aberdeen pattern $450
Creamer, 3¹/₂″ tall, Aberdeen pattern $300
Handkerchief box with cover, 7″ square-shaped, Aberdeen pattern $1350
Plate, 7″, Regency pattern $125
Plate, 8″, Empire pattern $200
Plate, 8″, Fluted and Hobnail design $150
Platter, 16″ circular, Aberdeen pattern $1250
Punch bowl with stand, 14″ diameter, 14″ tall, Aberdeen pattern $3000
Sugar, open, 3¹/₂″ tall, Aberdeen pattern $300
Tray, oval, (15¹/₄″ × 9¹/₂″), Aberdeen pattern $500

KEYSTONE CUT GLASS COMPANY 1902–1918

Keystone purchased its blanks from the Corning Glass Works and Dorflinger. The business closed just after the end of World War I.

Bowl, 9″, 4¹/₂″ tall, notched edge, Rose pattern $325
Butter dish with cover, 6″ tall, Rose pattern $900
Creamer, 2 applied handles, double spout, Romeo pattern $475
Creamer, 2-handled, double spout, signed "Keystone Cut Glass Company" . . . $525

Goblet, 6″ tall, Pluto pattern $150
Lamp, 22″ tall, Branning's Fan Scallop pattern $2850
Pitcher, water, 10¼″ tall, applied handle, Pluto pattern $475
Sugar, 2 applied handles, notched edge, Romeo pattern $475
Sugar, 2-handled, signed "Keystone Cut Glass Company" $525

LAUREL CUT GLASS COMPANY 1903–1920

Laurel was another of those small companies with a limited distribution network. It produced some cut glass and briefly joined with Quaker City directly after World War I. The two separated by 1920, when Laurel ended cut glass production.

Bowl, 6″, Amaranth pattern $150
Bowl, 8″, Cypress, Everett or Triumph pattern $225
Compote, 8″ tall, 8″ diameter, notched edge, Hobstar design $225
Creamer, single handle and single spout, Eunice pattern $200
Plate, 8″, central hobstar surrounded by 6 smaller hobstars $175
Sugar, 2-handled, Eunice pattern $200
Tray, 8″ oblong, ruffled edge, Audrey pattern $275
Tumbler, whiskey, Crescent pattern $125

LIBBEY GLASS COMPANY 1888–1936

You will find more listings for Libbey than any other cut glass manufacturer and for good reason: Libbey was the largest producer of cut glass in the world. Its products rivaled the best anywhere, and the company won numerous awards at various expositions.

Basket, oval (12¼″ × 7¼″), 17″ tall, Intaglio and Brilliant pattern, signed "Libbey"
.... $1000
Bell, 4½″ tall, faceted handle, Puritana pattern $575
Bell, 5⅜″ tall, faceted handle, Hobstar, Diamond and Fan design $350
Bottle, water, Imperial pattern, signed "Libbey" $325
Bottle, whiskey, 14″ tall, cut stopper, Intaglio Rye design $375
Bowl, 4½″, flared, ruffled, Foliage design, signed "Libbey" $200
Bowl, 7″, Colonna pattern, signed "Libbey" $250
Bowl, 8½″, hobstars with fans and diamond panels, signed "Libbey" $275
Bowl, 8″, 2 tab handles, Sunset pattern $375
Bowl, 8″, Corinthian pattern $275
Bowl, 8″, Delphos pattern, signed "Libbey" $325
Bowl, 8″, Gloria or Isabella pattern $275
Bowl, 8″, Star and Feather pattern $225
Bowl, 9″, Colonna or Greek Key pattern $300
Bowl, 9″, Columbia pattern $300
Bowl, 9″, Empress pattern $325
Bowl, 9″, Finely Detailed Snowflake pattern, signed "Libbey" $1100
Bowl, 9″, Glenda pattern, signed "Libbey" $325
Bowl, 9″, Harvard or Senora pattern $425

Libbey cut glass, 1889 patents. Left: "Florence" pattern; right: "Stratford" pattern.

Bowl, 10¹/₈″, Stratford pattern $625
Bowl, 10″, 16-point hobstar on base, Sultana pattern, signed "Libbey" $450
Bowl, 10″, Aztec or Florence pattern $350
Bowl, 10″, fluted, Kimberly pattern $425
Bowl, 10″, tricornered, Marcella pattern, signed "Libbey" $750
Bowl, 10″, 5″ tall, Intaglio and Leaves pattern, signed "Libbey" $475
Bowl, 11¹/₂″ × 4¹/₂″ oval, Russian Ambassador pattern $950
Bowl, 12″, Geometric pattern, signed "Libbey" $750
Bowl, 13 ¹/₂″, Russian ambassador pattern $1250
Bowl, 14″, shallow, Libbey pattern, signed "Libbey" $750
Bowl, fan and hobstars, Eulalia pattern $525
Bowl, finger, 5″, Etched Floral design $150
Bowl, finger, 5″, Intaglio Grape and Leaf design $200
Bowl, fruit, hat-shaped, Thistle pattern, signed "Libbey" $600
Bowl, fruit with base, 13″, hobstar and trellis cutting $2000
Bowl, rose, 5¹/₂″ tall, Senora pattern $750
Bowl, rose, 6¹/₂″ tall, 4¹/₂″ top opening, ribbed, signed "Libbey" in circle $175
Box, powder, 6″ diameter, hinged lid, Florence pattern $650
Butter dish with domed cover, matching underplate, Columbia pattern $850
Butter dish with domed cover, matching underplate, hobstar and Strawberry
Diamond design, Gloria pattern $850
Butter dish with domed cover, Rajah pattern $850
Cake plate, 12″, Aztec pattern, signed "Libbey" $550
Candlestick, 6″ tall, fluted, teardrop stem, signed "Libbey" $200
Carafe, Elsmere pattern, signed "Libbey" on flute $325
Carafe, fan, hobstar, and miter cut, signed "Libbey" $275
Carafe, New Brilliant pattern $300
Celery dish, 11″ long, Harvard pattern $200
Chalice, 11″ tall, Colonna pattern $1000
Champagne glass, Embassy pattern, signed "Libbey" $100
Champagne glass, Fern and Flower design, signed "Libbey" $100
Champagne glass, Imperial pattern, signed "Libbey" $100

Cheese dish with dome cover, matching underplate, Columbia pattern, signed "Libbey" $950

Cologne bottle with stopper, 6″ tall, 6″ diameter, globe-shaped, Columbia pattern $650

Cologne bottle with stopper, 8″ tall, globe-shaped, Columbia pattern $675

Compote, 8½″ diameter, Ozella pattern $550

Compote, 10½″ diameter, knobbed stem with teardrop, geometric design, signed "Libbey" $850

Cordial, 24-ray base, fluted, faceted knob, Harvard pattern, signed "Libbey" ..$125

Cordial, 3½″ tall, Sultana pattern, signed "Libbey" $125

Cordial, Embassy pattern, signed "Libbey" $125

Cordial, Princess pattern, signed "Libbey" $125

Creamer, hobstars and strawberry diamond, signed "Libbey" $175

Creamer, raised lip, Eulalia pattern $175

Creamer, Star and Feather design $175

Decanter, side handle, Corinthian pattern $500

Decanter with stopper, 18″ tall, pedestal base, Herringbone pattern, signed "Libbey" $3500

Decanter with stopper, 19⅛″ tall, cut circular foot, applied cut handle, tapering shape, small pouring lip, Sunburst pattern variant, signed "Libbey" $5250

Goblet, Columbia pattern $150

Goblet, water, Princess pattern, signed "Libbey" $100

Ice cream dish, 17½″ long, Senora pattern $1350

Ice cream tray, 12″ diameter, Somerset pattern $300

Ice cream tray, 14″ × 7½″, Kimberly pattern $400

Ice cream tray, 16″ × 9¾″, 4-sectioned cut flowers, flashed, Ivernia pattern, signed "Libbey" $1350

Ice cream tray, 18″ diameter, Princess pattern $800

Jug, 7″ tall, with handle, stopper on side spout, Sultana pattern, signed "Libbey" $2750

Nappy, 7″, Heart-Shaped Heart pattern, signed "Libbey" $200

Nappy, hobstars, Strawberry Diamond, and Fan design, signed "Libbey" ...$150

Pitcher, champagne, 11½″ tall, Iola pattern $675

Pitcher, milk, 7¾″ tall, Corinthian pattern $425

Pitcher, milk, Harvard pattern $425

Pitcher, water, 8½″ tall, Corinthian pattern $475

Pitcher, water, 8″ tall, tankard-style, New Brilliant pattern $400

Pitcher, water, 8″ tall, tankard-style, rayed base, sunburst with bands of hobstars $400

Pitcher, water, 9″ tall, Columbia pattern, signed "Libbey" $575

Pitcher, water, 9″ tall, Kingston pattern $500

Pitcher, water, 11″ tall, Imperial pattern, signed "Libbey" $650

Pitcher, water, 12″ tall, Aztec pattern, signed "Libbey" $775

Pitcher, water, 13″ tall, Kingston pattern $700

Pitcher, water, Scotch Thistle pattern $475

Plate, 6″, Columbia pattern $150

Plate, 6¾″, Ellsmere pattern, signed "Libbey" $175

Plate, 7″, Aztec pattern, signed "Libbey" $200

Plate, 7″, Colonna or Kimberly pattern $200

Plate, 7″, Prism pattern, signed "Libbey" $175

Plate, 7″, Spillane pattern, signed "Libbey" $175

Plate, 10″, Columbia or Corinthian pattern $275
Plate, 10″, Kingston pattern, signed "Libbey" $300
Plate, 10″, Princess pattern $350
Plate, 11¹/₂″, 6-paneled, Thistle design, signed "Libbey" $400
Plate, 11³/₄″, Sultana pattern, signed "Libbey" $425
Plate, ice cream, 6³/₄″, Prism pattern, signed "Libbey" $200
Platter, 12″, circular, Neola pattern $775
Platter, 12″, circular, Ozella pattern $625
Platter, 16″, circular, Diana pattern, signed "Libbey" $1850
Punch bowl with stand, Spillane pattern, signed "Libbey" $4250
Relish, 6″ diameter, 2¹/₂″ tall, signed "Libbey" $250
Salt dip, pedestal base, signed "Libbey" $150
Saucer, 5″, hobstars with asymmetrical center star $125
Sherry glass, Moonbeam pattern, signed "Libbey" $75
Spooner, 6″ tall, Sultana pattern $175
Sugar, 2-handled, Star and Feather design $175
Sugar, flared rim on 2 sides, Eulalia pattern $150
Sugar, hobstars and strawberry diamond, signed "Libbey" $175
Tankard, 11¹/₂″ tall, hobnail and cross cutting, signed "Libbey" $850
Tray, 10¹/₂″ oblong, Puritan pattern, signed "Libbey" $650
Tray, 10″ oval, Senora pattern, signed "Libbey" $525
Tray, 11¹/₄″ × 4¹/₂″, Wisteria or Lovebird pattern $1500
Tray, 12″ diameter, scalloped, 6-paneled, diamond point with star $1350
Tray, 12″ diameter, Senora pattern, signed "Libbey" $725
Tray, 15³/₄″ oblong, 9¹/₂″ wide, fishtail-shaped, Prism pattern, signed "Libbey" ....
.... $1000
Tray, 17¹/₂″ oval, Wedgemere pattern, signed "Libbey" $2000
Tray, heart-shaped, Florence Star pattern $575
Tray, celery, 12″ × 4³/₈″, eight 12-pointed hobstars, fan center, diamond and
fan cuts, Gem pattern $225
Tray, ice cream, 14″ oval, 2 tab handles, Prism pattern, signed "Libbey" ... $825
Tray, pickle, 8″ oval, Regis pattern $200
Tumbler, New Brilliant pattern $75
Tumbler, Scotch Thistle pattern $100
Tumbler, Strawberry Diamond design, signed "Libbey" $100
Tumbler, juice, Corinthian pattern $100
Vase, 5¹/₂″ tall, sawtooth rim, Bull's-Eyes and Fern design $200
Vase, 10″ tall, fine ribbed cuts $225
Vase, 12″ tall, corset-shaped, signed "Libbey" $675
Vase, 12″ tall, Radiant pattern $500
Vase, 16″ tall, rose cutting, signed "Libbey" $425
Vase, 16″ tall, Star and Feather pattern, signed "Libbey" $1350
Vase, 18″ tall, 2 notched handles, Hobstars and Hobnails design $2750
Vase, 18″ tall, Wedgemere pattern $2500
Vase, 20″ tall, 7¹/₂″ diameter, pedestal base, Kensington pattern variation, signed
"Libbey" $2350
Wine glass, cut stem only, signed "Libbey" $175
Wine glass, 5³/₄″ tall, circular foot, double knob, signed "Locke Art" $150
Wine glass, 7¹/₄″ tall, Cornucopia pattern $100
Wine glass, Embassy pattern, signed "Libbey" $100

LUZERNE CUT GLASS COMPANY   1910s–LATE 1920s

Luzerne was a small, obscure company with few surviving products. They were established some time before World War I and were out of business by 1930.

Tray, 14½″ oval, notched edge, Electra pattern $400
Tray, 14″ oblong, notched edge, 2 tab handles, Myron pattern $350

MAPLE CITY GLASS COMPANY   1910–1920s

Maple City purchased a factory in Hawley, Pennsylvania, that was formerly run by John S. O'Connor. What few cut glass products the company made were marked with an etched maple leaf.

Banana boat, 10″ long, strawberry diamond and hobstars, marked with maple leaf $350
Bowl, 7″, crossed oval design $175
Bowl, 8″, Fenmore pattern $200
Bowl, 9″, notched edge, Emerald pattern $225
Celery dish, boat-shaped, marked inside with maple leaf $1000
Mustard dish with cover and matching underplate, 3½″ tall, Panel and Notched Prism design, signed $325
Punch bowl, 12¼″ diameter, 11½″ tall, Temple pattern $3750
Tobacco jar with cover, 6″ tall, 5″ diameter, hemispherical cut finial, Hobstar and Fan design $1300
Tray, 12″ oval, notched edge, Manchester pattern $300
Tray, 14″ oval, notched edge, Gloria pattern $350
Tray, ice cream, 14½″ × 8″, Cane, Fan, Hobstar, and Strawberry design, marked with maple leaf $750
Vase, 7½″ tall, Pansy pattern $375

MERIDEN CUT GLASS COMPANY   1895–1923

Meriden, Connecticut, was a relatively unknown glassmaking town that featured several small companies. The Meriden Cut Glass Company was one such business that produced blanks for cutting as well as some cut products of its own. It was noted for the "Alhambra" pattern, also known as "Greek Key."

Bottle, worcester with stopper, 8″ tall, Alhambra pattern $725
Cake Salver, 10″ diameter, stemmed, Alhambra pattern $525
Cheese dish with domed cover, Plymouth pattern $475
Cruet with stopper, 8″ tall, Albany pattern $650
Cruet with stopper, 9½″ tall, Alhambra pattern $775
Decanter with stopper, 6″ tall, Wheeler pattern $575
Decanter with stopper, 12½″ tall, Alhambra pattern $1250
Decanter with stopper, Plymouth pattern $725
Fern dish with metal liner, 8½″ diameter, Alhambra pattern $1000

Pitcher, water, 9″ tall, large heavy sterling silver top, including pouring lip, Alhambra pattern $1250
Pitcher, water, 12¹/₂″ tall, tankard-style, sterling silver top, Alhambra pattern $1750
Plate, 7″, Alhambra pattern $150
Plate, 7″ square, notched edge, hobstars and circles inscribed in squares $225
Plate, 10″, Alhambra pattern $300
Tray, 12¹/₂″, Hobstar design $1000
Tray, 13″ oval, Alhambra pattern $1250
Tumbler, 4¹/₂″ tall, Thalia pattern $375
Vase, 16″ tall, Alhambra pattern $4000

MONROE, C.F. COMPANY   1880–1916

C.F. Monroe was better known as an art glass company; however, it did employ glass cutters (refer to Chapter 4 for additional Monroe listings).

Bowl, 7″, Rockmere pattern $225
Bowl, 8″, notched edge, Monroe pattern $200
Bowl, 9¹/₂″, footed, central hobstar with chain of smaller hobstars, silver rim $575
Carafe, 9¹/₂″ tall, Nevada pattern $250
Fernery, 8″ tall, silver rim, all-over Hobstar and Fan pattern $575
Hairpin box with lid, 4″ diameter, brass rim at top of box and bottom of lid, fluted base, Hobstar and Fan pattern $550
Pitcher, syrup with silver-plated lid and handle, Hobstar and Fan pattern ... $775
Powder box with cover, 5¹/₂″ diameter, silver rim at top of box and bottom of cover, Hobstar, Fan, and Strawberry Diamond design on base and cover $725
Powder box with cover, 6″ diameter, brass rim at top of box and bottom of cover, central hobstar with Star and Fan design on base and cover $725
Powder box with cover, 6″ diameter, silver rim at top of box and bottom of cover, fluted base, large center hobstar on cover $675
Powder box with cover, 8″ diameter, silver rim at top of box and bottom of cover, fluted base, central hobstar with several small hobstars on cover $750
Vase, 14″ tall, Ariel pattern $750

C. F. Monroe cut glass. Reproduced from a 1902 patent.

Watch box with cover, 3″ diameter, brass rim at top of box and bottom of cover, fluted base, pinwheel design on cover $475

MT. WASHINGTON GLASS WORKS   1837–1894

Mt. Washington is noted for its famous art glass products, although it was also a significant producer of cut glass. The company patented many designs, including several floral patterns such as "Rose" and "Rose" variations and "Daisy." In 1894, Mt. Washington became part of the Pairpoint Manufacturing Company, which continued with several of Mt. Washington's cut lines (see the listings under "Pairpoint Glass Corporation").

Bonbon dish, 5″, finger-hold handle, Priscilla pattern $175
Bowl, 6″, Bedford pattern $150
Bowl, 8³⁄₄″, picket fence with 24-point star base, acid finish $275
Bowl, 8″, Magnolia pattern $225
Bowl, 8″, Russian pattern $275
Bowl, 10″, Princess pattern $375
Butter tub with cover, 2-handled (cover has indentation for handles), 5″ diameter, 8″ diameter matching underplate, Diamond and Star pattern $2750

Handled Bon Bon, Priscilla.	Bon Bon, Priscilla.	Bon Bon, Priscilla.
No. 205, 5 inches, $3.00.	No. 235, 6 inches, $5.00.	No. 221, 6 inches, $5.00.
Plate, Priscilla.	Saucer, Priscilla.	Bon Bon, Priscilla.
No. 267, 7 inches, $5.00.	No. 205, 6 inches, $4.00.	No. 231, 6 inches, $5.00.
Bon Bon, Priscilla.	Bon Bon, Priscilla.	Bon Bon, Priscilla.
No. 253, 6 inches, $5.50.	No. 295, 8 inches, $6.00.	No. 215, 6 inches, $5.50.

Mount Washington cut glass, reproduced from a late 19th-century catalog.

Champagne glass, 5″ tall, Diamond and Star pattern with hobstar base $150

Cheese dish, with 9¼″ matching underplate, Nevada pattern $750

Cracker jar with cover, Strawberry Diamond and Fan pattern $800

Creamer, Bedford, Corinthian, Regent, Strawberry Diamond and Fan, and West patterns $200

Decanter with stopper, no handle, Corinthian pattern $650

Decanter with stopper, right-angle handle, Bedford pattern $625

Decanter with stopper, Westminster pattern $675

Jam jar with hinged cover, handled, Strawberry Diamond and Hobstar pattern, marked "M.W." on cover $450

Mug, 8 oz., Regent, Westminster, or Wheeler pattern $150

Mustard jar with cover, 1 handle, Strawberry Diamond and Fan and Westminster patterns $325

Pitcher, water, Regent, Strawberry Diamond and Fan, and West patterns ... $375

Pitcher, water, 8″ tall, Radiant pattern $400

Pitcher, water, Corinthian pattern $300

Plate, 5½″, Hortensia pattern $125

Plate, 6″, Corinthian, Priscilla, Strawberry Diamond and Fan, and West patterns $150

Plate, 7″, Bedford, Corinthian, Priscilla, Regent, and Westminster patterns .. $175

Plate, 7″ square, Madora pattern $250

Plate, 8″, Bedford, Butterfly and Daisy, Corinthian, and Westminster patterns $200

Platter, 14½″ circular, silver rim, Daisy pattern $1600

Platter, 15″ oval, large diamond with octagon cuts $575

Punch bowl with base, 14″ diameter, Regent pattern $3750

Punch ladle, Regent pattern $550

Relish dish, 3 divisions, Strawberry Diamond and Fan pattern $225

Salt and pepper shakers, ribbed, Pillar pattern, metal holder with handle .. $375

Spoon holder, 6″ oblong, Strawberry Diamond and Fan Pattern $100

Spoon holder, 7″ oblong, Strawberry Diamond and Fan pattern $125

Sugar, Bedford, Corinthian, Regent, Strawberry Diamond and Fan (without cover), and West patterns $200

Sugar shaker, egg-shaped, metal top, Corinthian, Strawberry Diamond and Fan, and Wheeler patterns $550

Sugar with cover, Strawberry Diamond and Fan pattern $250

Tray, 12″ × 5½″ rectangular, Block Diamond and Strawberry Diamond and Fan patterns $300

Tray, 9″ square, Corinthian pattern $475

Tray, 14½″ × 7¾″ rectangular, diamond with fans on edges $750

Tray, 14″ oblong, Strawberry Diamond and Fan pattern $325

Tray, dresser, Tulip pattern $250

Tray, irregular, 1 large semicircle for pitcher, 2 smaller semicircles for tumblers, Strawberry Diamond and Fan pattern $425

Tumbler, 3¾″ tall, Block Diamond design $75

Whiskey tumbler, 2½″ tall, Westminster pattern $125

Wine glass, 6⅛″ tall, fluted stem, Angular Ribbon pattern with star base $150

PAIRPOINT GLASS CORPORATION 1880–1938

As noted in the entry for Mt. Washington, Pairpoint purchased that company in 1894 and continued production of cut glass. It also patented several lines, including "Tulip" and "Anemone."

Bonbon dish, 5″, 2 tab handles, Salem pattern $175
Bottle, whiskey with stopper, 10″ tall, 1qt., Old English pattern $1750
Bowl, 8″, notched edge, Montrose and Wisteria patterns $350
Bowl, 9″, notched edge, Montrose pattern $375
Bowl, 11″, Myrtle pattern $525
Bowl, 12″, Berwick pattern $675
Bowl, 12″, notched edge, Wisteria pattern $675
Bowl, 14″, notched edge, Wisteria pattern $875
Cheese dish with cover, Strawberry Diamond pattern $1250
Cologne bottle with stopper, 2 oz., Arbutus pattern $250
Comport, 6½″ tall, Diamond-Hob design $200
Comport, 8″ tall, Diamond-Hob design $250
Compote, 10″ tall, teardrop stem, hobstar base, Avila pattern $375
Compote, 10″ tall, Hobstar and Fan design, Uncatena pattern $375
Creamer, domed base, Colias pattern $100
Cruet with flower cut stopper, Ramona pattern $325
Flower holder, 13½″ diameter, Butterfly and Daisy pattern $500
Mug, 4″ tall, Tyrone pattern $275
Nappy, 5½″, heart-shaped, Fairfax pattern $200
Nappy, 5″, "+" shaped, Block Diamond design $100
Nappy, 7¾″, Essex pattern $150
Nappy, 8″, Bombay and Montank patterns $175
Plate, 8″, Clarina pattern $100
Spoon holder, 2 handles, Malden pattern $150
Spoon holder, 7¾″ oval, Canton pattern $125
Sugar tray, Domino, rectangular with tab handles $225
Sugar, domed base, Colias pattern $100
Tray, 8½″ × 4″ rectangular, Wakefield pattern $225
Tray, 9¼″ oval, Kingston pattern $275
Tray, 9″ oval, Essex pattern $250
Tray, 10″ oval, Russian pattern (Persian variation) $325
Tray, 10″, triangular, Russian pattern $400
Tray, 14″ oblong, ruffled edge, Silver Leaf pattern $500
Vase, 6″ tall, Fan Scroll pattern $200
Vase, 8″ tall, Fan Scroll pattern $225
Vase, 12″ tall, Fan Scroll pattern $300
Whiskey tumbler, 2½″ tall, Butterfly and Daisy pattern $100

PITKIN & BROOKS   1870s–1920

Edward Pitkin and Jonathan Brooks, Jr., formed a wholesale glass and china business in 1872. They later opened several cutting shops and employed cutters to produce products with their P&B mark. The pair sold glassware through their
wholesale business and patented several lines (e.g., "Korea," "Wild Daisy," and
"Heart and Hobstar").

Bowl, 6½″, Venice pattern $125
Bowl, 8″, Athole and Border patterns $200
Bowl, 8″, Plymouth pattern $200
Bowl, 8″, shallow, Belmont pattern $175
Bowl, 8″, 3½″ tall, notched edge, Hobstar and Diamond pattern $175
Bowl, 9″, notched edge, Heart pattern $275
Candlestick, 14″ tall, Heart pattern $375
Celery dish, 12″ tall, Plaza pattern $350
Compote, 7″ tall, Border pattern $425
Compote, 11¾″ tall, 10½″ diameter, 2-part, floral design, Plymouth pattern, signed
.... $775
Creamer, Rajah pattern $175
Fernery, 7¾″ diameter, Paneled Floral and Diamond design, signed $200
Lamp, 23″ tall, 12″ diameter shade, Plymouth pattern, signed $1850
Nappy, 6″, Seymour pattern $150
Nappy, 6″, tab handle, Heart pattern $225
Nappy, 7½″, 2 tab handles, Phena Star pattern $225
Nappy, 7″, Corsair, Meadville, Mikado, and Myrtle patterns $200
Nappy, 8″, Corsair, Meadville, and Myrtle patterns $250
Nappy, 9″, Corsair or Meadville pattern $275

*Pitkin & Brooks cut glass. Reproduced
from a late 19th-century advertisement.*

Pickle dish, 7″, Nellore pattern $200
Pitcher, 12″ tall, Heart pattern $1000
Plate, 7″, Hexagonal, Star pattern $225
Plate, 7″, Mars and Wild Daisy patterns $125
Plate, 7″, Rosette and Buzz Star pattern $125
Plate, 9″, Roland pattern $175
Plate, 12″, Roland pattern $225
Plate, 14″, Roland pattern $275
Punch bowl, 12″, Korea pattern with engraved floral design $1000
Punch cup (matches bowl), Korea pattern with engraved floral design $75
Relish tray, 7″, Osborn pattern $250
Saucer, 5″, Corsair, Meadville, Mikado, and Myrtle patterns $150
Saucer, 6″, Corsair, Meadville, Mikado, and Myrtle patterns $175
Spoon boat, 11⅝″ × 4⅝″, canoe shape, Hobstar design $500
Spoon tray, 7½″ oblong, Cortez pattern $250
Sugar, 2-handled, Rajah pattern $225
Tray, 10″, hobstar center, Myrtle pattern $300
Tray, 10″ oval, Nellore pattern $300
Tray, 11″ oblong, 5 large hobstars, Cortez pattern $350
Tray, 12″ oval, Athole pattern $325
Tray, 12″ oval, notched edge, Bowa pattern $300
Tray, 13½″ across, oak leaf–shaped, notched prisms and vesicas $775

QUAKER CITY CUT GLASS COMPANY   1902–1927

Quaker City was also known as the Cut Glass Corporation of America. Few examples of the company's products have been found that are easily identified. It did use paper labels with a bust of William Penn, but the gummed labels easily fell off or were removed. The most impressive and valuable items are the vases, which typically were made in three separate pieces that screwed together.

Bonbon dish, 5½″ oval, notched edge, Mystic pattern $150
Bowl, 4½″ tall, footed, notched edge, Whirlwind pattern $225
Bowl, 4″ tall, footed, ruffled edge, Berlyn pattern $300
Bowl, 9″, notched edge, Columbia and Marlborough patterns $225
Compote, Angora pattern $575
Cup, 4″ tall, Eden pattern $300
Plate, 11″, Du Barry pattern $325
Punch bowl with stand, 14″ diameter, 15″ tall, Majestic pattern $5000
Punch cup (matches bowl), Majestic pattern $250
Vase, 20″ tall, 3-part, Empress pattern $5500
Vase, 24″ tall, 3-part, Empress pattern $6000
Vase, 36″ tall, 3-part, Riverton pattern $7500

SINCLAIRE, H.P. COMPANY   1904–1930s

The Sinclaires were associated with several famous glassmakers. Henry P. Sinclaire, Sr., was the secretary of the Corning Glass Works from 1893 until he died in 1902. Henry P. Sinclaire, Jr., was the secretary of T.G. Hawkes from 1893 to 1903, when he went on to establish his own business. He purchased blanks from the Corning Glass Works and patented several cut patterns before being forced to close during the Depression.

Bonbon dish, 7″ rectangular, Strawberry Diamond and Assyrian patterns ... $175
Bowl, 9″ top diameter, 4″ tall, Assyrian pattern $425
Bowl, 9″, 2³/₄″ tall, hobstar and mitered cuts, signed "Sinclaire" $275
Bowl, fruit, 8″ diameter, 5″ tall $350
Butter dish, 6″ rectangular, open, Strawberry Diamond pattern $175
Champagne glass, Ivy pattern, signed "Sinclaire" $100
Children's miniature cereal set, 2-piece, pitcher and bowl, Queen Louise pattern, signed "Sinclaire" $475
Clock, mantle, 8″ tall, copper wheel engraved, signed "Sinclaire" $550
Cologne bottle with stopper, 6″ tall, floral design, signed "Sinclaire" $275
Cordial, star base, Greek Key pattern, signed "Sinclaire" $100
Creamer, 6″ tall, Vintage pattern, signed "Sinclaire" $250
Creamer, Queen Louise pattern, signed "Sinclaire" $175
Cup, loving, 9¹/₄″ tall, 8¹/₂″ diameter, 2-handled, signed "Sinclaire" $1500
Decanter with stopper, 5″ tall, Bengal pattern, signed "Sinclaire" $375
Decanter with stopper, Queen's pattern, signed "Sinclaire" $600
Epergne, 2-part, 14″ tall, 10¹/₂″ diameter, engraved floral and foliage design, signed "Sinclaire" $1350
Flower pot, intaglio border, geometric design, signed "Sinclaire" $325
Ice cream tray, rectangular (14″ × 9″), Assyrian pattern, signed "Sinclaire" $1200
Lamp, 17″ tall, Flower basket pattern $1350
Nappy, 3¹/₄″, triangular-shaped, Cumberland pattern $150
Olive dish, 7¹/₄″ × 4″, sixteen 12-point hobstars in a chain, etched floral and foliage design $175
Pitcher, 7″ tall, Westminster pattern, signed "Sinclaire" $350
Pitcher, 8¹/₂″ tall, barrel-shaped, scalloped, strawberry and diamonds above vertical panels $475
Pitcher, 9″ tall, pedestal base, signed "Sinclaire" $2500
Plate, 10″, Adam pattern $375
Plate, 12″, Stars and Garlands pattern, signed "Sinclaire" $450
Plate, 5″, 32-point star on base, diamond crosscut, signed "Sinclaire" $125
Plate, 7″, Assyrian pattern, signed "Sinclaire" $275
Platter, 15″, circular, Hiawatha pattern, signed "Sinclaire" $775
Platter, 13¹/₄″, circular, Assyrian pattern, signed "Sinclaire" $700
Punch bowl with stand, 18″ diameter, 11¹/₂″ tall, Constellation pattern $2500
Sugar with cover, Queen Louise pattern, signed "Sinclaire" $225
Sugar, open, Vintage pattern, signed "Sinclaire" $250
Teapot with lid, 8″ tall, Intaglio and Damascus pattern, signed "Sinclaire" ... $3000
Tray, 12″ × 5″, Assyrian pattern $375
Tray, 12″ × 5″, flared ends, scalloped sides, geometric cutting with hobstars, signed "Sinclaire" $350

Tray, 14″ oval, 2 tab handles, diamond and threading with engraved floral design in center $800
Tray, 15″ circular, Cornwall pattern $850
Tray, 7″ × 4¾″, Hobs in Chain design, engraved border, signed "Sinclaire" ... $175
Tray, oval (10″ × 7″), crosscut, Fans and Hobstars pattern $300
Tray, rectangular (12″ × 5″), Adam pattern, signed "Sinclaire" $425
Vase, 6½″ tall, flower center, Bengal pattern $900
Vase, 11″ tall, flower center, flute and panel border $425
Vase, 12″ tall, 5″ diameter, Assyrian pattern, signed "Sinclaire" $525
Vase, 14″ tall, 5″ diameter, Assyrian pattern, signed "Sinclaire" $825
Vase, 15½″ tall, Queen Louise pattern, signed "Sinclaire" $450
Vase, 16″ tall, Stratford pattern, signed "Sinclaire" $550
Wine glass, Ivy pattern, signed "Sinclaire" $100

STERLING CUT GLASS COMPANY   1904–1950

The firm was established by Joseph Phillips in 1904 as the Sterling Glass Company. In 1913 Joseph Landenwitsch joined the company. Sterling was briefly known as Joseph Phillips & Company. Apparently, what little cut glass it produced was in the early teens, because in 1919 Phillips became a salesman for the Rookwood Pottery Company and Landenwitsch became president of Phillips Glass Company, another offshoot. Later, the company reorganized as the Sterling Cut Glass Company. Pieces made by Sterling are scarce; however, those that exist feature exquisite cutting and elegant engraving and are quite valuable.

Plate, 10″, engraved floral border, Regal pattern $1250
Plate, 10″, Fruits and Butterfly design, Eden pattern $1750
Tray, 11″ oval, Arcadia pattern $550

STRAUS, L. & SONS   1888–EARLY 1900s

In 1852, Lazarus Straus, a Bavarian immigrant, came to the United States with his wife, Sara, and two sons, Isidor and Nathan. He opened an import business selling china and glassware and began cutting glass products around 1888. The pieces are usually marked "Straus Cut Glass" and feature a faceted gem within a circle.

Bowl, 10″, Warren pattern $275
Bowl, 11½″ oval, Imperial pattern $325
Bowl, 12″ square, Venetian pattern $375
Bowl, 6″, Bijoux pattern $125
Bowl, 7″, Rex pattern $150
Bowl, 8″, Norma pattern $200
Bowl, 8″, notched ovals edge, Daisies and Diamonds pattern $175
Bowl, 9″, Hobstar design with hobnail and miter cuts, sawtooth rim $225
Bowl, 9″, notched edge, Americus pattern $200
Bowl, 9″, Tassel pattern $225
Bowl, rose, 5½″, Electra pattern $450
Carafe, water, Drape pattern, signed "Straus" $325

Celery dish, Encore pattern, signed "Straus" $250
Cheese dish with dome cover, 9″ diameter underplate, 6″ diameter dome, Corinthian pattern $750
Compote, 12″ tall, Corinthian pattern $750
Creamer, 3″ tall, notched handle, Prism and Bull's-Eye design $150
Decanter with cut stopper, 11″ tall, Americus pattern $500
Pitcher, water, 12″ tall, Drape pattern $1250
Plate, 7″, Antoinette and Rex patterns $125
Plate, 7″, Inverted Kite pattern $125
Plate, 8″, notched edge, Lily of the Valley and Pansy patterns $150
Plate, 8″, Venetian pattern $175
Plate, 10″, Maltese Urn pattern $375
Platter, 12″ round, Maltese Urn pattern $625
Punch bowl, 12½″ diameter, Corinthian pattern $1250
Sugar, 3″ tall, notched handles, Prism and Bull's-Eye design $150
Tray, celery, 11″ oblong, 2 hobstars and crosscuts $325
Tray, celery, acorn-shaped, rosettes and crosscuts $450
Wine glass, Encore pattern $125

TAYLOR BROTHERS COMPANY   1902–1915

In 1902 Albert and Lafayette Taylor joined with John H. Williams to form Taylor Brothers and Williams. Williams moved on soon after and was dropped from the company's name. The brothers managed to stay afloat for only a short period of time and filed for bankruptcy in 1911. They hung on a little longer until World War I forced them out permanently. Some of the more interesting pieces from the company were casserole dishes; not many other factories produced these.

Bowl, 9″ diameter, 4½″ tall, ferns, hobstars, and stars $325
Bowl, 9″, pentagonal, Palm pattern $525
Casserole dish with cover, 2 handles, pedestal base, Hobstar and Diamond pattern, signed $2500
Casserole dish with cover, 8½″, 7″ tall, Palm pattern, signed $2000
Casserole dish with cover, 9″, 2 handles, Palm pattern, signed $2250
Compote, 13½″ tall, 10″ diameter, Fine Diamond and Fan pattern $1350
Nappy, 5″, 1 handle tab, large fluted star in center, small hobstars and crosscuts $225
Nappy, 6″, 1 tab handle, large star surrounded by 6 smaller stars $200
Platter, 12″ round, ruffled edge, Palm pattern, signed $425
Toothpick holder, 2¼″ tall, Geometric pattern $125
Tray, 10½″ oval, ruffled edge, Arcadia pattern $525
Tray, ice cream, 10″ oval, scalloped, hobstar rings within a crystal band ... $650
Tray, oval, 11½″ × 6½″, hobstars, stars and diamonds $450

THATCHER BROTHERS 1886–1907

George Thatcher worked at the Boston & Sandwich Glass Company, the Mt. Washington Glass Company, and Smith Brothers before joining his brother Richard to form Thatcher Brothers. The company produced some cut glass before going out of business during the panic of 1907.

Bowl, 8¼", notched edge, Rosette and Foliage design $175
Vase, 10½" tall, cylindrical, Diamond and Fan design (alternating large diamonds and tiny diamond sections) $425
Vase, 13" tall, circular base, stemmed, vertically ribbed bulbous midsection, Rosette and Foliage design $575

TUTHILL CUT GLASS COMPANY, 1900–1923

Charles Guernsey Tuthill formed C.G. Tuthill & Company in 1900. His brother James and sister-in-law Susan joined with him in 1902, and the name was amended to the Tuthill Cut Glass Company. The quality of their products was outstanding, and much of it was attributed to Susan, who served as an inspector, constantly measuring depth, observing details, and not allowing glass to leave the factory that was in less than perfect condition. As a result, Tuthill won numerous awards and its products rivaled those of the best cut glass producers in the country. The company patented many patterns, including "Tomato," "Tiger Lily," "Grape," "Cosmos," "Orchid," and "Grapefruit."

Basket, 21" tall, Vintage pattern $2850
Basket, oval, 9" long, 5" tall, Poppy pattern $925
Basket, rectangular, Intaglio and Brilliant pattern $1150
Bottle, whiskey with stopper, 12" tall, Cornell pattern $750
Bowl, 8", Hobstar and Fan design $450
Bowl, 8", Rose pattern $400
Bowl, 8", 2½" tall, rolled rim, Bishop's Hat design, Vintage pattern $1350
Bowl, 9½", Rex pattern $350
Candlestick, 12" tall, Rosemere pattern, signed "Tuthill" $625
Candy box with cover, 6" round, 3" tall, Vintage pattern $1750
Charger, 12½", Intaglio Strawberry Leaf and Vine design $475
Cologne bottle with sterling silver stopper, Wild Rose pattern, signed "Tuthill" .
.... $525
Compote, 6½" diameter, 14½" tall, Intaglio Vintage pattern $225
Compote, 8¼" top diameter, 3½" tall, Rosemere pattern $325
Creamer, 4" tall, Large Hobstar design $200
Cruet with stopper, 8" tall, Poppy pattern, signed "Tuthill" $475
Cruet with stopper, 10" tall, pedestal base, Vintage pattern, signed "Tuthill" .....
.... $525
Decanter with stopper, 11" tall, 6" diameter, Intaglio and Brilliant pattern, signed "Tuthill" $950
Decanter with stopper, 12" tall, handled, Primrose pattern $575
Lamp, 22" tall, 12" diameter shade, Rex pattern, signed "Tuthill" $5750

Mayonnaise set, 2-piece, 5″ bowl with 6″ matching underplate, Stars and Arcs pattern, signed "Tuthill" $525
Mayonnaise set, 2-piece, 6″ hexagonal bowl with matching 6″ hexagonal underplate, Phlox pattern, signed "Tuthill" $700
Mug, Dawson pattern $150
Pitcher, 9″ tall, Rose pattern, signed "Tuthill" $1000
Plate, 7″, Rex pattern, signed "Tuthill" $325
Plate, 9″, Quilted Diamond pattern $350
Plate, 10″, Rosemere pattern $700
Plate, 10″, Silver Rose pattern $750
Plate, 10″, Wild Rose pattern $475
Plate, oval (5⅞″ × 4½″), Rosemere pattern, signed "Tuthill" $275
Platter, 12″, circular, Vintage pattern, signed "Tuthill" $700
Platter, 13″, circular, Vintage pattern, signed "Tuthill" $775
Platter, 14¼″, circular, Wild Rose pattern, signed "Tuthill" $875
Punch bowl, 13″ diameter, 16″ tall, scalloped, footed, engraved grape clusters and leaves, alternating crosscuts and hobstars, signed "Tuthill" $6500
Punch cup, 3½″ tall, flared, circular foot, stemmed, Vintage pattern $175
Sugar, 3¾″ tall, 2-handled, Large Hobstar design $200
Toothpick holder, 4″ tall, stemmed, Wild Rose pattern, signed "Tuthill" ... $225
Tray, 8½″ oval, scalloped, Intaglio Floral design $300
Tray, 12″, circular, Engraved Blackberry design $500
Tray, celery, Pinwheel design, signed "Tuthill" $475
Vase, 10″ tall, cylindrically shaped (4″ diameter from top to bottom), Rex pattern, signed "Tuthill" $3250
Vase, 11″ tall, urn shape, 2 handles, Vintage pattern $875
Vase, 16½″ tall, slender form, Vintage pattern $575

UNGER BROTHERS   1901–1918

Another small company with limited production, Unger Brothers produced some silver housewares and cut glass before closing for good just after World War I.

Bowl, 8″, Pinwheel design with hobstar center $150
Bowl, 8″, shallow, notched edge, Fontenoy pattern $175
Nappy, 6″, applied handle, Floradora pattern $175
Perfume bottle with sterling silver screw top, 4″ tall, Russian pattern $900
Pitcher, water, notched handle, ruffled ridge, Hobart pattern $575
Plate, 7″, six hobstars in a circular pattern $125
Plate, 12″, notched edge, La Voy pattern $425
Tankard, 11″ tall, Hobart pattern $325
Tray, 14″ rectangular, Duchess pattern $400

WESTMORELAND SPECIALTY COMPANY   1889–1930s

Westmoreland was established by brothers George Robinson West and Charles Howard West in Grapeville, Pennsylvania. The company was reorganized as the Westmoreland Glass Company in 1924 and lasted until 1985. Westmoreland was not known as a huge cut glass producer; however, some have argued that it produced more cut glass in the 1920s and the 1930s than any other glass manufacturer in America. Of course, the 1920s and 1930s was a time of colored Depression glass and the Brilliant Period of American cut glass had ended over a decade before. Westmoreland cut glass products tend to feature more engraving than cutting. A few pieces are found marked with Westmoreland's Keystone W.

Candlestick, 7″ tall, Engraved Floral design $62
Candlestick, 8″ tall, Bead and Reel design $75
Cigarette bowl with cover, 6″ × 3½″ rectangular, Engraved Floral and Irish setter design $250
Pitcher, water, 2 qt., Colonial pattern, sunburst and Grecian cut $150
Relish dish, 8¼″ diameter, 4-divisions, 2 tab applied handles, Engraved Butterfly and Floral design $125
Salt dip, hexagon-shaped, cut stars on each side $50
Salt dip, round, Hobstar design $40
Sandwich tray with center handle, 6″ diameter, Crosshatched Diamond Design with engraved grape clusters $50
Tray, 10″ octagon, Engraved Floral design $0
Tumbler, Colonial pattern, Sunburst and Grecian cut $50
Vase, 7″ tall, hexagonal base, Sunburst and Grecian cut $75
Vase, 9″ tall, hexagonal base, Grecian cut with Engraved Thistle design $100
Vase, 12″ tall, hexagonal base, Sunburst and Grecian cut $100

CHAPTER 4

AMERICAN ART GLASS

In the midst of the Brilliant Period, a new form of glass arose. This new "Art Nouveau" or "art glass" was developed in the 1880s, and its popularity lasted well into the early 20th century. Artists, designers, and other creative people who had not previously worked in glass turned their talents to producing some of the most spectacular glass objects ever composed.

Some experts point to the Philadelphia Centennial Exhibition of 1876 as the introduction of art glass in the United States. As with the expositions taking place in Europe, the event allowed glassmakers to display some of their finest pieces to date. The Centennial Exhibition featured a massive cut glass chandelier and a glass fountain that was 17 feet high. The fountain was an ornamental design with cut crystal prisms lit by 120 gas jets and surmounted by a glass figure of liberty.

The Art Nouveau movement had its beginnings in France with Rousseau and Galle (see Chapter 1, "Foreign Glass and Glassmaking"); however, the United States produced its own share of world-class designers. Two of the most famous American art glass sculptors were Louis Comfort Tiffany and Frederick Carder.

Tiffany was an American painter who visited Paris in 1889 and observed Galle's work in person at the Exposition Universelle. He was also the son of the jewelry magnate who had founded Tiffany & Co., the famous jewelry store. Louis Comfort Tiffany began his work in glass by producing stained glass windows without using stains or paints. The color, detail, and illusion were created within the glass itself by plating one layer of glass over another. Tiffany broadened his work to include lamps and was one of the first to experiment with iridescent glass. He named his iridescent products "Favrile" or "Tiffany Favrile." The term was derived from the word "fabrile," which means "belonging to a craftsman or his craft."

Iridescence is produced by firing on combinations of metallic salts that in turn create a wide variety of coloring effects. Luminous colors and metallic luster produced a silky smooth or delicate patina on Tiffany's glass. According to Tiffany, his main inspiration was the decayed objects from Roman glass discovered in archeological excavations.

With the success following the presentation of his works at the World's

Exposition in Chicago in 1893, orders poured in and Tiffany expanded his work to other art forms. Tableware, vases, flowers, unique shapes, and many other table items came from Tiffany's skilled hands. His designs were never decorated or painted; they were made by combinations of different colored glass during the blowing operation. His goods were displayed throughout Europe, including the 1900 Paris Exposition, which in turn inspired young European artists to copy his style.

Frederick Carder was an apprentice of the famous English glass artisan John Northwood. He emigrated from Stourbridge, England, and founded the Steuben Glass Works in Corning, New York. Carder created several varieties of lustrous lead glass such as Aurene, an ornamental iridescent form. In 1918 he sold Steuben to the Corning Glass Works but continued to produce some of the finest crystal forms in the world through 1936 for Corning. Carder's glass was also exhibited at numerous national and international expositions, galleries, and museums.

Many others followed in the footsteps of Tiffany and Carder. So much experimentation took place that America invented more distinctive styles than all of Europe combined. Many American firms copied or attempted to reproduce popular designs of others and at times, the experimentation led to new creations.

In 1883 Joseph Locke, an Englishman employed by the New England Glass Company, was the first to obtain a patent for Amberina. In 1885 another Englishman named Frederick Shirley patented Burmese for the Mt. Washington Glass Company. Burmese products were sent to Queen Victoria of England as gifts; she was so impressed with the style, that she ordered more. Mt. Washington shared the formula with Thomas Webb & Sons of England, which also produced Burmese products. In 1886 Shirley also patented Pearl Satin Glass for Mt. Washington. In 1887 Locke patented Agata Glass for New England.

More patents followed for a variety of art glass patterns, including Amethyst, Aurora, Cintra, Cluthra, Cranberry, Crown Milano, Custard, Intarsia, Lava, Mercury, Peach Blow, Rubina, Satin, Slag, and Spatter, to name a few. See the individually priced categories as well as the glossary for descriptions of these particular designs.

AMBERINA   NEW ENGLAND, LIBBEY, MT. WASHINGTON, TIFFANY, AND OTHERS, 1880s–1920

"Amberina" is a single-layered style of glass created by the New England Glass Company in 1883. Joseph Locke was responsible for much of its development. The style is characterized by an amber color at the bottom of an object that gradually shades into red at the top. The shading changes with each object. The red might be a brilliant ruby red or a deep violet or purple referred to as fuchsia. Genuine gold was at times mixed with the transparent amber. The New England Glass Company placed a high-quality, vibrantly colored Amberina plating on some wares. These particular items are very rare and valuable. "Amberina" was used for both art objects and functional tableware. The style was continued under Edward Libbey when the company was purchased by him and moved to Toledo, Ohio. Both the New England Glass Works and Libbey can be found on many examples. "Amberina" was most popular in the 1880s and was revived by Libbey from 1917 to 1920, but it flopped after World War I. In the meantime, Libbey sold some patent rights, including "Amberina," to other companies. Varieties of "Amberina" have been reproduced by several companies and individuals. Reproductions as well as less valuable flashed-on and enameled examples are found. Flashed-on and enameled items usually include metal oxides that produce an iridescent finish or enamel that flecks or eventually peels. The original "Amberina" has no such iridescence and was rarely enameled.

Basket, 7 1/2" tall, signed "Libbey" $2000
Bonbon dish, 7" oval, shallow, Daisy and Button pattern (Hobbs Brocunier) $550
Bottle, perfume with stopper, signed "Libbey" $925
Bowl, 2 3/4", 4 1/2" tall, Plated Amberina $3750
Bowl, 3", fluted, Plated Amberina $3750
Bowl, 3", scalloped, fine coloring, Plated Amberina $5500
Bowl, 5 1/4", Plated Amberina, ruffled top (New England Glass Co.) $2250
Bowl, 5 3/8", 2 3/4" tall, with scalloped rim $275
Bowl, 7 1/2", 3 1/2" tall, Plated Amberina, scalloped rim, white lining, paper label "Aurora/NEGW" (New England Glass Co.) $3000
Bowl, 8", scalloped, Plated Amberina $5750
Bowl, 10" oval, Daisy and Button pattern (Hobbs Brocunier) $375
Bowl, footed, lustrous rose, Old Iron Cross mark (Imperial) $250
Bowl, finger, 5 3/8", 2 1/2" tall (New England Glass Co.) $250
Bowl, melon, 7" tall, ribbed, 4-footed $475
Bowl, rose, 6", hobnail $375

Fenton plated "Amberina." PHOTO BY ROBIN RAINWATER, COURTESY OF THE FENTON ART GLASS MUSEUM.

Butter dish, 4³/₄″, ribbed, silver-plated base with unicorn in center, Plated Amberina $2750

Carafe, 6³/₄″ tall, ruffled tricornered top (New England Glass Co.) $350

Carafe, 8″ tall, hobnail $375

Castor set, 2 cruets with stoppers, salt and pepper shakers with pewter tops, and silver-plated tray (New England Glass Co.) $1750

Celery Vase, 6¹/₂″ tall, light color, Diamond Quilted pattern $275

Champagne glass, 6″ tall, with hollow stem (New England Glass Co.) $325

Cheese dish with cover, 9¹/₂″ diameter, 8″ tall, large circles in cover and round knob, flared rim (New England Glass Co.) $700

Compote, 4¹/₄″ diameter, 7″ tall, crimped rim, Diamond Quilted pattern (New England Glass Co.) $700

Compote, 5″ diameter, signed "Libbey" $750

Cordial (Gunderson-Pairpoint) $55

Creamer, 2¹/₂″ tall, Plated Amberina (New England Glass Co.) $3750

Creamer, 2⁵/₈″ tall, amber handle, scalloped, Inverted Thumbprint pattern (New England) $450

Creamer, 4³/₄″ tall, ribbed, ribbed feet, hollow knobby stem, signed "Libbey" $1350

Creamer, 5″ tall, pitcher-style, ribbed, Plated Amberina $5500

Cruet, 6¹/₂″ tall, with faceted stopper, amber handle, Plated Amberina $2750

Cup, punch, Diamond Quilted pattern (New England Glass Co.) $350

Cup, punch, Plated Amberina (New England Glass Co.) $2000

Dish, canoe-shaped, 8″ long, Daisy and Button pressed design $900

Goblet, rose amber (Mt. Washington Glass Co.) $275

Hat, 6″ wide $125

Lamp shade, 14″, Plated Amberina (New England Glass Co.) $4000

Lemonade, Plated Amberina $1500

Mug, 7¹/₂″ tall, reverse color, Inverted Thumbprint pattern $450

Mug, amber handle, ribbed, Plated Amberina $2500

Mug, barrel-shaped, 2¹/₂″ tall, Thumbprint pattern $225

Parfait, Plated Amberina (New England Glass Co.) $1500

Pitcher, 7¹/₂″ tall, ribbed, Inverted Thumbprint pattern, reverse Amberina color, signed "Libbey" $750

Pitcher, 7″ tall, cornered spout, Plated Amberina (New England Glass Co.) $7500

Pitcher, 7″ tall, square top, Inverted Thumbprint pattern (New England Glass Co.) $300

Pitcher, 9¹/₂″ tall, ruffled, amber handle, Inverted Thumbprint pattern $350

Pitcher, 10″ tall, amber handle, Inverted Thumbprint pattern, signed "Libbey" $475

Pitcher, 12″ tall, engraved Otus and Ephialtes holding Mars captive, title panel, signed "J. Locke" $1250

Pitcher, syrup with pewter top, Inverted Thumbprint pattern (New England Glass Co.) $500

Pitcher, syrup with top, 6″ tall, Plated Amberina (New England Glass Co.) ... $7500

Pitcher, water, 8″ tall, Reverse Color design $500

Punch cup, 2¹/₂″ tall, Diamond Quilted pattern (New England) $175

Punch cup, 2³/₄″ tall, ribbed, amber handle, Plated Amberina $2250

Salt and pepper shakers, Plated Amberina $5500

Salt and pepper shakers, Diamond Quilt pattern $250

Salt and pepper shakers, Inverted Thumbprint pattern (Mt. Washington Glass Co.) $400

Saltshaker, pewter top, Reverse Amberina Color pattern $250

Sauce dish, 5¹/₂″ square, Daisy and Button pattern (Hobbs Brocunier) $300

Spittoon, hourglass-shaped with ruffled edge $375

Spooner, 5″ tall, Plated Amberina $2250

Spooner, round with scalloped top and square mouth, Venetian Diamond pattern (New England Glass Co.) $600

Sugar, 2¹/₂″ tall, Plated Amberina (New England Glass Co.) $3750

Sugar, 4¹/₂″ tall, ribbed, ribbed feet, hollow knobby stem, signed "Libbey" $1500

Sugar shaker, 4″ tall, butterfly on lid, Inverted Thumbprint pattern $500

Swan, 5″ tall (Pairpoint-Bryden) $75

Toothpick holder, 2¹/₂″ tall, 3-footed, Daisy and Button pattern (Hobbs Brocunier) $300

Toothpick holder, 2¹/₂″ tall, round with square rim, Diamond Quilted pattern (New England Glass Co.) $175

Toothpick holder, 2″ tall, ribbed, Plated Amberina $3000

Toothpick holder, Reversed Color pattern $200

Tumbler, Diamond pattern, Fuchsia shading at the top (New England Glass Co.) $250

Tumbler, Inverted Thumbprint pattern $125

Tumbler, Inverted Thumbprint pattern, signed "Libbey" $150

Tumbler, Plated Amberina (New England Glass Co.) $2250

Tumbler, ribbed, 5″ tall, Plated Amberina $2250

Tumbler, swirled $150

Tumbler, swirled, 3³/₄″ tall, gold amber (New England Glass Co.) $175

Vase, 4¹/₈″ tall, Plated Amberina (New England Glass Co.) $3000

Vase, 4⁵/₈″ tall, pressed Stork pattern, scalloped top (New England Glass Co.) $625

Vase, 4″ tall, cylindrically shaped (New England) $175

Vase, 7³/₄″ tall, applied swirled circular domed foot, drinking horn shaped with coiled tail (Libbey) $1400

Vase, 7″ tall, cylindrically shaped, ruffled, Inverted Thumbprint pattern $175

Vase, 7″ tall, jack-in-the-pulpit style, Fuchsia to amber shading $500

Vase, 7″ tall, with tricornered top (New England Glass Co.) $525

Vase, 8¹/₈″ tall, applied crystal spiral stem $275

Vase, 8³/₄″ tall, cylindrically shaped, swirled $200

Vase, 8″ tall, lily-shaped, Plated Amberina $2750

Vase, 9¹/₂″ tall, 2-handled, signed "Libbey" $775

Vase, 10¹/₂″ tall, lily-shaped, metal stand, Plated Amberina $4500

Vase, 10¹/₂″ tall, swirled, Amber Rigaree, footed $250

Vase, 10″ tall, jack-in-the-pulpit style, signed "Libbey" $800

Vase, 11″ tall, signed "Libbey" $1250

Vase, 23¹/₂″ tall, ribbed, knob stem (New England Glass Co.) $1750

Vase, swirled, satinized, Reverse Amberina Color pattern, enameled gold flowers $1750

Vase, lily, 6¹/₄″ tall, Plated Amberina (New England Glass Co.) $2500

Vase, lily, 7¹/₂″ tall, signed "Libbey" $625

Whiskey glass, 2⁵/₈″ tall, Diamond Quilted pattern (New England Glass Co.) ... $150

AURENE   STEUBEN GLASS WORKS, 1904–1933

"Aurene" was produced in five basic colors: blue, brown, gold, green, and red. It remains among Steuben's most desirable and popular colored glass designs, although pieces are quite scarce today. The style is characterized by an iridescent sheen applied by spraying on various metallic salts and other chemical mixtures. Base colors were ordinarily clear, amber, or topaz. Matte finishes were applied by spraying on tin or iron chloride solutions. Alabaster and calcite were necessary for the green and red colors.

Atomizer, 5″, ribbed, Iridescent gold $275
Basket, 5″ tall, ruffled, Gold with light green highlights $1400
Basket, 12½″ tall, crimped rim, Gold with applied berry prunts $1250
Bowl, 9″, 3½″ tall, footed, Gold $500
Bowl, 10″, Blue $650
Bowl, oval (4″ × 2″), Calcite and gold $175
Bowl, finger, 4″, signed "F. Carder," Red $5250
Candlestick, 4¾″ tall, Gold $525
Candlestick, 8″ tall, marked "Aurene 686," Gold $575
Candlestick, 10″ tall, air twist stem, Blue $850
Candlestick, 12″ tall, tulip-shaped, Gold $775
Cologne bottle with stopper, 5½″ tall, bell-shaped, marked "Aurene 1818", iridescent gold $700
Cologne bottle with stopper, 6½″ tall, ribbed, Iridescent gold $900
Compote, 6″, Blue $1250
Compote, 8″, Gold $1100
Cordial, 3½″ tall, twisted stem, Gold $250
Cordial, 7″ tall, Blue $575
Darner, stocking, Gold $625

"Aurene" art glass. COURTESY OF THE CORNING MUSEUM OF GLASS.

Darner, stocking, Blue $775
Decanter with stopper, 10³/₄″ tall, dimpled body, circular foot, marked "Aurene
2759", Gold $675
Goblet, 6¹/₄″ tall, twisted stem, Gold $350
Goblet, 8″ tall, Venetian style, Gold $550
Perfume bottle with stopper, 5⁷/₈″ tall, Blue $775
Perfume bottle with stopper, 8″ tall, signed, Blue $775
Salt dip, 2″ tall, pedestal foot, signed, Gold $250
Salt dip, 8 ribs, Blue $425
Shade, 4¹/₂″ tall, Iridescent green with calcite interior, platinum foliage design ....
.... $1250
Shade, 4¹/₂″ tall, tulip-shaped, Gold $275
Shade, 6¹/₂″ × 6″, Green with calcite interior, platinum foliage design $1250
Shade, iridescent brown with calcite lining, blue drape design $525
Shade, iridescent light brown with gold leaves and threading, gold lining ... $375
Sherbet with matching underplate, Gold $425
Tray, oblong stretched border, footed, signed "Carder," Blue $850
Vase, 5¹/₂″ tall, iridescent gold with green and white floral design $2100
Vase, 5″ tall, signed, Blue $625
Vase, 6¹/₂″ tall, 3-stemmed, Blue $1000
Vase, 6¹/₄″ tall, stump-shaped, 3-pronged, signed, Gold $650
Vase, 6³/₄″ tall, iridescent gold with calcite interior $550
Vase, 6″ tall, Iridescent gold $500
Vase, 6″ tall, jack-in-the-pulpit style, Gold $1500
Vase, 6″ tall, stick style, Iridescent blue $525
Vase, 7″ tall, gold with green foliage and white flowers $3500
Vase, 8¹/₂″ tall, Blue $250
Vase, 9″ tall, 3-handled, Gold $850
Vase, 9″ tall, 9″ diameter top, ruffled, Iridescent gold $1250
Vase, 10¹/₂″ tall, green with gold interior, rim, heart and vine decoration ... $3750
Vase, 10″ tall, blue button design, signed "F. Carder" $1600
Vase, 10″ tall, paneled design, Blue $1350
Vase, 11″ tall, fan-shaped, Iridescent gold $1350
Vase, 12¹/₂″ tall, blue with white floral design $1500
Vase with holder, 4″ tall, Gold $550
Wine glass, 6″ tall, air twist stem, Gold $575

BOSTON & SANDWICH GLASS COMPANY   1820s–1880s

One of the early successful glassmaking businesses, Boston & Sandwich was noted
most for "Sandwich," or pressed glass, from which its name is derived. The company manufactured hand-pressed glass but occasionally created objects of art in the
form of lacy glass in the French style, paperweights, opal wares, and engraved
glass. See additional listings under "Mary Gregory Glass."

Basket, bride's, 9″ diameter, overshot, twisted handle, Crystal $250
Bottle, 8″ tall, triple cased with cut windows $200
Bottle with screw-on cap, 2¹/₂″ tall, marbleized cobalt and white $150
Bowl, 9″, Lacy design, peacock eye coloring $150

Boston and Sandwich Co. art glass.
PHOTO BY MARK PICKVET.

Threaded art glass by Lutz for Boston and Sandwich Glass Co. PHOTO COURTESY OF
THE SANDWICH GLASS MUSEUM.

Bowl with matching underplate, 3″ tall, ruffled, Canary yellow $150
Candlestick, 1⅞″ tall, miniature, crystal $40
Candlestick, 6¾″ tall, hexagonal base, clambroth, Dolphin design $475
Candlestick, 7½″ tall, hexagonal base, Amethyst $500
Candlestick, 7½″ tall, hexagonal, Amber $400
Candlestick, 7¼″ tall, hexagonal base, green socket, clambroth foot and stem ....
.... $675
Candlestick, 7″ tall, circular diamond point base, petal socket, Canary yellow ....
.... $325
Candlestick, 7″ tall, circular base, petal socket, Canary yellow $275
Candlestick, 7″ tall, clambroth, Petal and Loop design $200

Candlestick, 7″ tall, hexagonal, Amber $375
Candlestick, 9¼″ tall, hexagonal base, Light blue $375
Candlestick, 9¾″ tall, cobalt socket, clambroth base and stem, Acanthus Leaf design $425
Candlestick, 9″ tall, cobalt petal socket, clambroth column $275
Candlestick, 10¼″ tall, single step base, blue socket, gilded, clambroth, Dolphin design $800
Candlestick, 10¼″ tall, single step base, clambroth, Dolphin design $475
Candlestick, 10¼″ tall, single step base, Dolphin design, Green $675
Candlestick, 10¾″ tall, double step base, clambroth, Dolphin design $425
Candlestick, 11½″ tall, Crucifix design, Canary yellow $375
Candlestick, 11½″ tall, Crucifix design, Green $575
Candlestick, 12″ tall, hexagonal, Dark blue $425
Candlestick, clambroth with translucent blue acanthus leaves $650
Cheese dish with cover, 8″, crystal overshot $325
Claret glass, 4½″ tall, craquelle finish with ruby threading $85
Claret glass, 5″ tall, Canary yellow with threading $175
Cologne bottle with ball stopper, 8″ tall, square-shaped, crystal overshot .. $225
Epergne, 12″ tall, ruffled bowl with ruby threading, cut circular tray $275
Fishbowl, 16½″ tall, ruffled crystal base with dolphin's tail, crystal bowl with etched fish and plants $675
Ice cream dish, 4¼″ diameter, 4¼″ tall, circular pedestal base, white casing with ruby threads $200
Ice cream tray, 13″ long, crystal overshot $175
Jam jar, 3½″ tall, Bear design, Opaque blue $425
Jug, 6¾″ tall, barrel-shaped, Etched Bees and Floral design, crystal with ruby threading $200
Lamp, kerosene, jade green with white overlay $5250
Paperweight, 2½″ diameter, blue poinsettia, green stem, jeweled leaves on white latticino $775
Paperweight, 2½″ diameter, white latticino basket with multicolored flowers and green leaves $1100
Paperweight, 2¾″ diameter, 12-ribbed blue dahlia petals, latticino basket, yellow cane, emerald green stem $375
Paperweight, 2¾″ diameter, 6-petaled flower and leaves $675
Paperweight, 2⅜″ diameter, latticino with pears, cherries and green leaves $575
Paperweight, 2⅝″ diameter, latticino with pink poinsettia and green leaves $325
Paperweight, 2⅝″ diameter, white latticino with flowers, green leaves, blue and white canes $500
Paperweight, 2⅞″ diameter, Candy Cane design $200
Paperweight, 3″ diameter, jasper with Jenny Lind sulphide bust $250
Paperweight, 3″ diameter, Sulphide Bird design, Red, white, and blue $300
Pipe, 15″ long, crystal with white loopings $425
Pitcher, 6½″ tall, amber overshot, green reeded handle $275
Pitcher, 8½″ tall, Tortoise Shell design, amber handle $400
Pitcher, 10½″ tall, blue overshot, amber lip and handle $475
Pitcher, 11″ tall, pink overshot with crystal handle $525
Pitcher, 12″ tall, pear-shaped, fluted rim, Crystal Crackle design $375
Punch bowl with cover, 11″ tall, overshot, globe-shaped, fruit stem finial .. $525
Salt dip, rectangular (2⅞″ × 1⅞″), 4-footed, gothic arches on feet, Opalescent blue $250

Salt dip, rectangular (2$^7/_8''$ × 1$^7/_8''$), oval knobs on base, scrolled, stippled, transparent green, French Lacy design $250

Salt dip, boat-shaped, 3$^1/_2''$ long, blue paddle wheeler, marked "Lafayet" on wheels, signed "B. & S. Glass Co." $575

Saltshaker, 2$^3/_4''$ tall, barrel-shaped, threaded rim with pewter top, sunburst on base, marked "patented December 25, 1877," Dark blue $200

Tankard, 7$^1/_2''$ tall, engraved cattails, water lilies, and crane, crystal with ruby threading $325

Tankard, 7$^1/_4''$ tall, engraved cattails and lilies, amber with threading $350

Tankard, 9'' tall, dark amber overshot $525

Tankard, 11'' tall, crystal overshot, reeded handle $175

Tieback knob, cobalt to clear coloring over mercury $110

Tieback knob, cranberry to clear coloring over mercury $110

Tumbler, 3$^1/_4''$ tall, engraved cattails and lilies, crystal with ruby threading .. $135

Tumbler, 3$^3/_4''$ tall, engraved foliage, crystal with ruby threading $135

Tumbler, 5$^1/_2''$ tall, canary yellow with threading $200

Tumbler, 5$^1/_2''$ tall, crystal with blue threading $200

Tumbler, 6'' tall, engraved floral design on top, cranberry threading on bottom ....
.... $150

Vase, 4'' tall, enameled floral design $150

Vase, 6$^1/_2''$ tall, floral design, Bluerina (blue to amber shading) $325

Vase, 8$^1/_2''$ tall, celery, scalloped, hourglass $125

Vase, 9$^1/_4''$ tall, flared, 3 scrolled gilded feet, opaque white with red enameled leaves
.... $325

Vase, 10'' tall, cranberry cut to clear roundels $375

BURMESE   MT. WASHINGTON WORKS AND PAIRPOINT MANUFACTURING COMPANY, 1880s–1950s

"Burmese" is characterized by a gradual shading of bright or canary yellow at the base to a salmon pink at the top. It is also thin and rather brittle. The colors were created by the addition of gold and uranium. The most common decorations applied were gold enamels (real gold mixed with acid) and popular cut patterns. Mt. Washington obtained an exclusive patent on this pattern in 1885. The technique of creating "Burmese" continued when Pairpoint purchased Mt. Washington, including reissues in the 1950s. Reproductions are difficult if not impossible to make because of the federal government's restrictions on the use of uranium.

Basket, thorn handle, 1950s (Gunderson) $350

Bell, 11$^3/_4''$ tall, emerald green handle $2600

Biscuit jar, barrel-shaped, silver-plated top, Oak Leaves and Acorn design, Paper Label $1250

Bowl, 4$^3/_4''$, ice cream, ruffled $325

Bowl, 4'', fluted edge $300

Bowl, 6$^1/_2''$, footed, applied Burmese decoration $1500

Bowl, 7'', curled feet (Gunderson) $350

Bowl, 12'', scalloped $1000

Bowl, rose, 2$^1/_2''$, hexagonal top $250

Bowl, rose, gold handles, ivy decoration, Dickens verse $2750

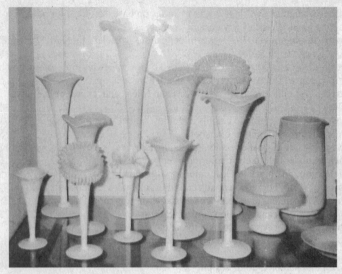

Burmese art glass. PHOTO BY MARK PICKVET.

Castor set, 5-piece, salt and pepper shakers with silver-plated tops, 2 globe-shaped cruets with pointed stoppers, footed silver-plated stand $3000
Cracker jar with cover, 6¹/₂″ tall, acidized finish, applied handles $1500
Creamer, 4″ tall, 3¹/₂″ diameter, footed $1250
Creamer, 5¹/₂″ tall, pitcher style, Hobnail pattern $2250
Cruet with stopper, 7″ tall, acid or gloss finish $1250
Cup, satin shading $250
Epergne, 2 circular bowls, 4″ tall, ruffled, enameled flowers, 4-footed silver-plated stand $3750
Ewer, 9″ tall, squat dome, enameled decoration $2000
Hat, 3¹/₂″ × 2³/₄″, Upside Down (Bryden) $150
Lamp, crimped top and plate, Fairy (Gunderson) $525
Mustard pot, silver cover, acidized, ribbed $275
Perfume bottle with cut stopper $300
Pig, miniature, ⁷/₈″ long, (Gunderson) $175
Pitcher, 4³/₄″ tall, square lip, yellow reeded handle, enameled mums $750
Pitcher, 5″ tall, Inverted Thumbprint pattern, Egyptian with Bow in Chariot design $1350
Pitcher, 6³/₄″ tall, acidized, Ivy design, Dickens verse $3750
Pitcher, 9″ tall, acidized, gold-outlined foliage design $3750
Pitcher, syrup with silver lid, 6″ tall, enameled decoration $1600
Pitcher, tankard style, acidized, gloss finish $1250
Pitcher, water, satin finish $2250
Plate, 6″ $150
Plate, acidized, floral design $350
Salt and pepper shakers, barrel-shaped, pewter tops $475
Saucer, satin shading $200

Shade, 5¼″ × 3¾″, satin finish $275
Sugar shaker, 4″ tall, globe-shaped, Leaves and Berries design $875
Toothpick holder, bowl-shaped, hexagonal top, satin finish $350
Toothpick holder, circular base, square top, enameled floral design $575
Toothpick holder, Diamond Quilted pattern $450
Top hat, 1⅝″ tall, gloss finish $625
Tumbler, 3⅞″ tall, satin finish $225
Tumbler, 4″ tall, dull or shiny finish (Gunderson) $225
Tumbler, Thomas Hood verse $1600
Vase, 3″ tall, bulbous, 3-petal folded rim $275
Vase, 4″ tall, ruffled, acidized, enameled foliage design, 4-footed silver-plated holder $825
Vase, 4″ tall, ruffled, fluted base $350
Vase, 5″ tall, enameled yellow handles, pink and yellow enameled floral design $2100
Vase, 5″ tall, ruffled, footed $350
Vase, 6¾″ tall, Jack-in-the-Pulpit design, enameled $750
Vase, 6″ tall, lily-shaped, paper label $775
Vase, 7″ tall, acidized, Hobnail pattern (Gunderson) $350
Vase, 7″ tall, lily-shaped, paper label $825
Vase, 8″ tall, lily-shaped, paper label $900
Vase, 9″ tall, crimped, Jack-in-the-Pulpit design $850
Vase, 10¾″ tall, enameled Daisy and Butterfly design, Verse $2750
Vase, 10″ tall, lily-shaped, paper label $950
Vase, 11¾″ tall, acidized, enameled Scroll and Floral design $2750
Vase, 11¾″ tall, enameled Daisy and Butterfly design $3000
Vase, 11¾″ tall, enameled Daisy and Butterfly design, Montgomery verse $3000
Vase, 12″ tall, lily-shaped, paper label $1250
Vase, 12″ tall, crimped, folded rim, floral stem, Jack-in-the-Pulpit design .. $1500
Vase, 12″ tall, enameled Daisy and Butterfly design, Montgomery verse ... $3250
Vase, 12″ tall, gloss finish, Jack-in-the-Pulpit design $1500
Vase, 12″ tall, Ibis and Pyramid design $4250
Vase, 13½″ tall, ruffled foot and top $1500
Vase, 14″ tall, lily-shaped, paper label $1250
Vase, 15″ tall, 2-handled, enameled yellow to pink $6500
Vase, 17½″ tall, Egyptian Man with Staff design $5750
Vase, 24″ tall, lily-shaped, paper label $1600
Vase, 26″ tall, slender, yellow to pale pink coloring $1350

Fenton "Chocolate" art glass. PHOTO BY ROBIN RAINWATER, COURTESY OF THE FENTON
ART GLASS MUSEUM.

CHOCOLATE   INDIANA TUMBLER & GOBLET COMPANY, 1900–1903; FENTON GLASS COMPANY, 1907–1910

"Chocolate" refers to the color of this earthy opaque glass. Variances are from light
tan to caramel to deep chocolate brown. The dark chocolate color is most desirable
and may sell for 10% to 20% premium above lighter colors. Lighter "Chocolate"
articles are sometimes incorrectly referred to as "Caramel Slag Glass." Aside from
a few novelty items such as glass animals, "Chocolate" was used in numerous patterns, such as "Austrian," "Cactus," "Dewey," "Geneva," "Melrose," and "Shuttle,"
as well as several floral and leaf designs. Jacob Rosenthal created the formula for
the Indiana Tumbler & Goblet Company of Greentown, Indiana, and shared it with
a few other select factories, including Fenton.

Berry, 4″, Waterlily and Cattails design (Fenton) $125
Berry set, 8″ diameter, Fruit bowl with 6 sauce dishes, Leaf pattern $575
Bowl, 9¹/₂″, footed, Panther pattern (Fenton) $150
Bowl, fruit, 8″ diameter $175
Bowl, fruit, 9¹/₄″ diameter, Cactus pattern $125
Bowl, oval, 8¹/₄″ × 5¹/₄″, Geneva pattern $110
Butter dish with cover, 4″ diameter, Dewey pattern $225
Butter dish with cover, Cactus pattern $275
Butter dish with cover, pedestal, Cactus pattern $475
Butter dish with cover, Waterlily and Cattails design (Fenton) $200
Compote, 4¹/₂″ diameter, 3¹/₂″ tall, Geneva pattern $200
Compote, 5¹/₄″ diameter, 5″ tall, Cactus pattern $210
Compote, 6″ diameter, Melrose pattern with scalloped rim $375
Compote, 8¹/₄″ diameter, Cactus pattern $275
Creamer, 6″ tall, Stirgil pattern $135
Creamer, Cactus pattern $125
Creamer, Cord Drapery pattern $135
Creamer, Shuttle pattern $100
Creamer, Waterlily and Cattails design (Fenton) $125

Creamer, Leaf pattern $110
Cruet with stopper, Cactus pattern $250
Cruet with stopper, Leaf pattern $225
Fernery, 3-footed, Fenton Vintage pattern $250
Hatpin box, Orange Tree pattern $350
Jelly dish with cover, Cord Drapery pattern $250
Lamp, kerosene, Wild Rose pattern $350
Mug, Cactus pattern $125
Mug, Herringbone pattern $100
Mug, Shuttle pattern $125
Nappy, handled, Masonic pattern $150
Nappy, triangular, handled, Leaf pattern $100
Pitcher, syrup with lid, Cactus pattern $200
Pitcher, syrup with lid, Cord Drapery pattern $375
Pitcher, water, Cord Drapery pattern $375
Pitcher, water, Deer pattern $550
Pitcher, water, Feather pattern $850
Pitcher, water, Heron pattern $450
Pitcher, water, Ruffled Eye pattern $650
Pitcher, water, Squirrel pattern $550
Pitcher, water, Waterlily and Cattails design (Fenton) $550
Pitcher, water, Wild Rose pattern $525
Relish, oval (8″ × 5″), Leaf pattern $125
Saltshaker, Leaf pattern $175
Sauce dish, Cactus pattern $100
Sauce dish, Dolphin pattern $375
Sauce dish, Geneva pattern $80
Sauce dish, Leaf pattern $75
Sauce dish, Tassel pattern $200
Sauce dish, Wild Rose pattern $150
Spooner, 2-handled, Waterlily and Cattails design (Fenton) .. $125
Spooner, Australian pattern $250
Spooner, Austrian pattern $225
Spooner, Cactus pattern $150
Spooner, Cord Drapery pattern $125
Spooner, Dewey pattern $125
Spooner, Leaf pattern $175
Spooner, Wild Rose pattern $200
Sugar, Cord Drapery pattern $150
Sugar with cover, Cactus pattern $225
Sugar with cover, Chrysanthemum pattern $475
Sugar with cover, Leaf pattern $175
Sugar with cover, Waterlily and Cattails design (Fenton) $200
Sweetmeat dish with cover, Cactus pattern $550
Toothpick holder, Cactus pattern $150
Toothpick holder, Geneva pattern $200
Toothpick holder, Picture Frame design $875
Tray, 11″ long, Leaf pattern $175
Tray, oval (10³/₄″ × 5¹/₂″), Leaf pattern $150
Tray, serpentine, Dewey pattern $90
Tumbler, Biscuit pattern $250

Tumbler, Cactus pattern $125
Tumbler, Cord Drapery pattern $375
Tumbler, Leaf pattern $100
Tumbler, Sawtooth pattern $125
Tumbler, Shuttle pattern $150
Tumbler, Waterlily and Cattails design (Fenton) $150
Tumbler, Wild Rose pattern $175
Vase, 5¹/₄″ tall, Fleur-de-lys pattern $325
Vase, Scalloped Flange pattern $125

COIN GLASS   CENTRAL GLASS COMPANY, 1890s

The first "Coin Glass" was made in 1892, the centennial year of the United States Mint. Silver dollars, half dollars, quarters, twenty-cent pieces, dimes, and half dimes were reproduced in glass relief, then placed on each article. The coins in relief were usually frosted on clear crystal glass, but clear, amber, red, and gold examples were also produced. The patterns were not identical to the actual minted coins; however, five short months after production, they were outlawed by the U.S. government as being a form of counterfeiting. Other medallions were allowed, such as Christopher Columbus ("Columbian Coin Glass"), coats of arms, and other foreign explorers ("Foreign Coin Glass"). Numerous coin examples have been made since by such companies as Fostoria and Avon (see Chapter 7).

Bowl, 8″, oval, frosted coins $350
Bread tray, frosted half dollars and silver dollars $450
Butter dish with cover, half dollars and silver dollars $725
Cake stand, 10″ diameter, clear silver dollars $400
Cake stand, 10″ diameter, frosted silver dollars $550
Champagne glass, frosted dimes $475
Compote, 5¹/₂″ diameter, 5¹/₂″ tall, frosted dimes and quarters $325
Compote, 6 ¹/₂″ diameter, 8″ tall, frosted dimes and quarters $350
Compote, 7″ diameter, 5³/₄″ tall, frosted dimes and quarters $550
Compote, 8″ diameter, 11¹/₄″ tall, frosted coins $725
Compote with cover, 6⁷/₈″ tall, frosted coins $675
Compote with cover, 6″ diameter, 9¹/₂″ tall, silver dollar $525
Compote with cover, 8″ diameter, high pedestal, 1892 quarters and half dollars ...
.... $600
Compote with cover, 8″ diameter, 11¹/₂″ tall, frosted coins $725
Compote with cover, 9″ diameter, frosted coins $750
Creamer, frosted coins in base, 1 handle $450
Cruet with stopper, 5¹/₂″ tall, frosted coins $750
Epergne, frosted silver dollars $1750
Goblet, frosted dimes $375
Lamp, kerosene, handled, clear quarters in base $500
Lamp, kerosene, pedestal base, amber stained silver dollars $850
Lamp, kerosene, pedestal base, frosted quarters $700
Lamp, milk glass, 8″ tall, Columbian coin $500
Mug, frosted coins $475
Pickle dish, oval, 7¹/₂″ × 3³/₄″, clear coins $275

Pitcher, water, frosted coins $750
Pitcher, water, gilded Columbian coins in base $500
Preserve tray, single crystal silver dollar in center $350
Relish, frosted coins $300
Saltshaker with pewter top $200
Sauce dish, 4″ diameter, frosted quarters $225
Spooner, frosted quarters $400
Sugar with cover, frosted coins $550
Toothpick holder, clear or frosted coins $275
Tumbler, frosted coins around base $200
Tumbler, frosted dollar in base $250
Vase, clear dimes $225
Vase, clear quarters $350
Vase, frosted quarters $400
Wine glass, frosted half dimes $650

CORALENE   MT. WASHINGTON GLASS WORKS, 1880s–1890s

"Coralene" is sometimes referred to as "Mother-of-Pearl" for its pearly or coral-like sheen. Small beads of clear, colored, or opalescent glass are applied to an object, then fired on. There were several pattern styles, but most include coral, seaweed, and floral designs. Beware of reproductions or remakes where the beading is not fired on. Pieces can easily chip and flake.

Bowl, rose, 3″ tall, 4½″ diameter, crimped, amber foot, pink with yellow seaweed design $425
Decanter with stopper, 10″ tall, yellow seaweed decoration $500
Mug, 2″ tall, orange seaweed with turquoise handle $150
Pitcher, 7½″ tall, orange and green coral, orange handle $325
Pitcher, 8″ tall, blue and yellow coral design $650
Pitcher, water, 9½″ tall, blue and yellow seaweed, white handle, blue inner casing $850
Toothpick holder, yellow seaweed with white shading $350
Tumble-up, carafe with lid, White coral on light pink cranberry $375
Tumbler, 4″ tall, yellow seaweed with pink shading $250
Vase, 5¾″ tall, blue with beaded yellow seaweed, white inside $600
Vase, 5″ tall, yellow and green coral on a dark brown background $275
Vase, 6″ tall, floral and sprayed beading design, Mother-of-pearl $575
Vase, 6″ tall, ruffled, blue coral design with white floral beading $225
Vase, 7″ tall, footed, tan satin design $775
Vase, 8½″ tall, flared rim, yellow seaweed $400
Vase, 9″ tall, Orange on white coloring $1100
Vase, 9″ tall, urn-shaped, vertical rainbow colors $900
Vase, 10¼″ tall, reeded and scrolled feet, gold rim, green leaves and pink and blue floral beading on a cranberry background $450

"Cranberry" art glass. PHOTO BY
MARK PICKVET.

CRANBERRY   VARIOUS PRODUCERS, 1820s–1880s

"Cranberry," sometimes referred to as ruby or rose red, is a transparent glass the color of dark pink or light red cranberries. It was created by adding tiny amounts of gold oxide as the primary coloring agent. Larger amounts of gold oxide produce a darker, true ruby red. "Cranberry" glass was a popular item with many glass and decorating companies, including T.B. Clark, T.G. Hawkes, Mt. Washington, New England, Northwood, and Steuben. It is also one of the oldest forms of art glass produced in the United States. Beware of cheaper flashed, coated, and stained articles in a similar color. Pieces may chip and scratch if the color is not consistent throughout the entire glass, both inside and out. "Cranberry" has been reproduced by several modern companies in a wide variety of items.

Basket, 6″ tall, vertical ribbing, scalloped, clear handle, circular foot $200
Basket, 8″ tall, ruffled, crystal handle $200
Bell, 5″ tall, dark coloring $125
Bell, 7½″ tall, swirled with crystal handle $375
Bell, 7″ tall, gold tracing $550
Bell, 12″ tall, clear handle, green clapper $300
Bottle, perfume with cut stopper, 8¼″ tall, brass ormolu at base $275
Bottle, perfume with stopper, 3¼″ tall $150
Bottle, square, 8½″ tall, vertical ribbing $175
Bowl, 4″ diameter, with hinged cover $200
Bowl, 7½″ diameter, enameled flowers $250
Bowl, finger, 3¼″ diameter, ruffled $125
Bowl, flower, 3″ tall, ruffled $125
Box with hinged lid, 3″ tall, 3½″ square, ribbed, gold decoration $300
Castor set, pickle dish in silver-plated frame with lid and tongs (several designs) .
.... $425
Chalice with cover, 16″ tall, gilded with enameled figure of girl $350
Cheese dish, cranberry dome with crystal ball handle and crystal underplate
(Hobbs Brocunier) $250
Cologne bottle with stopper, 6″ tall, silver overlay $425
Cordial, 4″ tall, gold paneled, clear stem and base $125

Creamer, 4¼" tall, ruffled, clear handle, shell feet $150
Creamer and sugar set in silver-plated holder (several varieties) $375
Cruet with cut crystal stopper, 6½" tall, clear handle $325
Cruet with silver-plated stopper, 5½" tall $150
Cruet with stopper, 6" tall, clear handle $275
Cup, loving, 3½" tall, 3-handled, silver overlay $750
Cup, punch, clear handle, enameled flowers $75
Decanter with clear stopper, 10½" tall, clear handle, enameled floral design .....
.... $300
Decanter with clear stopper, 11" tall, clear handle, Inverted Thumbprint pattern ..
....$325
Decanter with crystal cut stopper, 10" tall $250
Decanter without stopper, 6" tall $175
Epergne, 12" tall, double trumpet style $400
Epergne, 13½" tall, 3 trumpets, crystal base, enameled floral design $450
Hat, 2½" tall $175
Lamp, kerosene, 8½" tall, brass base with cranberry shade $475
Lamp, kerosene, swirled shade, brass frame for hanging $475
Lamp, oil, 18" tall, Thumbprint patterned globe, enameled design $650
Mug, 4" tall, clear handle, Inverted Thumbprint pattern $125
Nappy, 6½", Cut Strawberry and Diamond pattern (C. Dorflinger & Sons) $650
Pitcher, 7½" tall, ruffled, clear handle, enameled floral design $350
Pitcher, 9" tall, Swirl pattern with enameled flowers $300
Pitcher, square top, Bull's-Eye pattern $375
Pitcher, syrup, 6¾" tall, silver-plated handle and spout $400
Pitcher, water, 8" tall, Inverted Thumbprint pattern $200
Plate, 6" diameter $75
Plate, 8" diameter $85
Salt and pepper shakers, metal tops, enameled floral design $225
Sugar bowl with cover, Guttate pattern (Consolidated) $225
Sugar bowl with cover, shell feet $175
Sugar shaker with silver top, 6½" tall, Drape pattern $150
Toothpick holder, barrel-shaped, Inverted Thumbprint pattern $175
Tumbler, 3½" tall, clear pedestal foot, enameled floral design with gold decoration
.... $100
Tumbler, 4¾" tall, Small Thumbprint pattern $100
Vase, 5¼" tall, 5¼" diameter, footed, silver leaves and gold floral and butterfly
design $475
Vase, 6¾" tall, flared, clear pedestal base $150
Vase, 7½" tall, enameled gold and white flowers $175
Vase, 7½" tall, ruffled, clear circular foot $200
Vase, 8½" tall, enameled gold and white flowers $225
Vase, 8" tall, ruffled $200
Vase, 10" tall, slender form, enameled floral design $250
Vase, 12" tall, bubble connector (Pairpoint) $300
Vase, 12" tall, cylindrical, 3-footed $250

Crown Milano art glass. PHOTO BY ROBIN RAINWATER.

CROWN MILANO   MT. WASHINGTON GLASS WORKS, 1890s

"Crown Milano" is another of Mt. Washington's patented Art Glass patterns. It is characterized by heavy gold enameling on an opal or earth-toned background. Some pieces feature jewel work or settings for glass beads. The name was derived from the signature, which typically is a crown within a wreath. For the most part, "Crown Milano" is identical in design to that of the older but less popular "Albertine" glass which was originally created by Albert Steffin.

Basket, bride's, 9″ tall, folded rim, white with enameled floral design $550
Basket, bride's, 14¼″ tall, ruffled, yellow with enameled floral design, footed silver-plated stand, signed $1100
Biscuit jar with cover, 6″ tall, thistle and gold enameled design, signed on bottom and cover $1850
Biscuit jar with cover, 8¼″ tall, white, enameled desert scene, cover has silver decoration, Pairpoint stamp $1350
Biscuit jar with cover, 9″ tall, floral and foliage design, signed $1000
Bowl, 6″, crimped, gold rim, Pansy design $175
Bowl, 8″, fan-shaped, shallow, White Pansy design $200
Bowl, rose, 4″, yellow with gold lines and enameled floral design $250
Cracker jar with cover, gold and green foliage design, signed $800
Creamer, 3¼″ tall, ribbed, white with gold decoration, signed $500
Ewer, 10″ tall, twisted handle, paneled design $1750
Ewer, Shepherd, Flock and Church enameled design $3250
Jar with cover, white opal with gold beading $800
Lamp, 16¾″ tall, Asian man and Camel on shade, elephants on base globe, metal base $5750
Pitcher, water, 12″ tall, white floral design, signed $1600
Pitcher, water, 13½″ tall, bulbous, rural scene, gold decoration $1850
Powder jar with cover, 3″ tall, ribbed, enameled floral design, signed $750
Sugar shaker, 3″ tall, ribbed, orange to yellow shading, foliage design $575
Sugar with cover, 6″ tall, ribbed, handled, white with gold decoration $525

Sweetmeat jar with cover, 5″ tall, embossed, gold wash design, signed $800
Tumbler, gloss finish, 3³/₄″ tall, enameled floral and wreath design $1100
Urn with crown-shaped cover, 16¹/₂″ tall, foliage decoration $4000
Vase, 3″ tall, enameled Leaf design $650
Vase, 5¹/₂″ tall, Scroll and Floral design, signed $1850
Vase, 7″ tall, swirled, bulbous, Cactus and Foliage design $3500
Vase, 8¹/₂″ tall, swirled, Wild Fowl design, signed $3000
Vase, 9″ tall, globular, scrolls on neck, gold and tan Fern design $1250
Vase, 10¹/₂″ tall, Duck design $3250
Vase, 11″ tall, baluster-shaped, gloss finish, gilded handles, "The Courting Couple"
design, scrolled ribbons, signed $2500
Vase, 11″ tall, bulbous, Chrysanthemum design, signed $1500
Vase, 13″ tall, Angel design $2750
Vase, 13″ tall, white to green shading, gold enamel $1350
Vase, 14″ tall, handled, Acorn design with gold trim, signed $1850
Vase, 14″ tall, handled, floral design $1600
Vase, 15″ tall, Gold Dragon design, signed $2150
Vase, 17″ tall, Duck design, signed "Frank Guba" $5000

CUSTARD   VARIOUS PRODUCERS, 1890s–1915

"Custard" refers to the milky white to deep yellow opaque coloring like that of custard pudding. It is sometimes referred to as "Buttermilk" because it resembles yellow buttermilk. Uranium salts are often added to produce a vibrant yellow opalescence that is very mildly radioactive (safe for one to handle!) and reacts to black light. As with most art glass, a variety of decorations and colors were applied to the base custard-colored glass. These include flashing or enameling of blue, brown, green, pink, and red, as well as gilding and painting. Flower enameling is the most common design, but the basic glass was produced in numerous patterns by a host of companies. Northwood is recognized as the most prolific producer of "Custard" glass, but a good deal was also made by Adams, Cambridge, Diamond, Dugan, Fenton, Greenberg, Heisey, Jefferson, Labelle, and McKee.

Bowl, 8″, Banded Ring pattern $175
Bowl, 8¹/₂″, Maple Leaf pattern $175
Bowl, 10¹/₂″, Argonaut Shell pattern $275
Bowl, 11¹/₂″, Fan and Feather pattern $475
Bowl, 11″, ruffled, footed, Grape pattern $575
Bowl, 12″, 3-footed, Maple Leaf pattern $575
Butter dish with cover, beaded circle, Cherry and Scale, Diamond, Grape, and
Maple Leaf patterns $375
Butter dish with cover, gold decoration, Argonaut pattern $450
Butter dish with domed cover, Gold Louis XV pattern (Northwood) $375
Cologne bottle with stopper, 5¹/₂″ tall, Grape pattern $700
Cologne bottle with stopper, 6¹/₄″ tall, scrolled design $400
Compote, footed, gold Louis XV pattern (Northwood) $175
Creamer, Argonaut Shell, Banded Ring, Beaded Circle, Chrysanthemum, Maple
Leaf, Scrolled, and Victoria patterns $175
Creamer, gold Louis XV pattern (Northwood) $225

Cruet with stopper, 5½″ tall, Banded Ring, Chrysanthemum, Grape, and Scrolled patterns $450
Cruet with stopper, 6¼″ tall, intaglio design $475
Cruet with stopper, 6″ tall, Beaded Circle pattern $825
Cruet with stopper, gold Louis XV pattern (Northwood) $450
Humidor with cover, 8″ tall, grape design $750
Jelly dish, Everglade and Maple Leaf patterns $475
Jelly dish, Inverted Fan and Feather pattern $525
Mug, souvenir (several varieties) $100
Napkin ring, souvenir (several varieties), Diamond pattern $175
Nappy, 6½″, ruffled $100
Pickle dish, 7½″ long, Beaded Swag pattern $325
Pitcher, syrup with lid, Scroll pattern $500
Pitcher, water, 8″–10″ tall, Argonaut Shell, Beaded Circle, Chrysanthemum, Diamond, Grape, Maple Leaf, Drape, and Scrolled patterns $475
Pitcher, water, gold Louis XV pattern (Northwood) $525
Punch bowl, footed, Fan and Feather pattern $3750
Salt and pepper shakers, with pewter tops, pink and gold trim, Fan and Feather pattern $575
Salt and pepper shakers, with tops, Geneva pattern $200
Sauce dish, various styles and patterns $90
Spooner, Argonaut Shell, Banded Ring, Beaded Circle, Everglade, Fan and Feather, Geneva, Grape, Maple Leaf, and Scrolled patterns $150
Sugar with cover, Argonaut Shell, Banded Ring, Beaded Circle, Chrysanthemum, Maple Leaf, Scrolled, and Victoria patterns $250
Sugar with cover, gold King Louis XV pattern (Northwood) $275
Toothpick holder, 2¾″ tall, Chrysanthemum and Fan and Feather patterns ....
.... $575
Toothpick holder, 3″ tall, Ribbed Drape pattern $225
Toothpick holder, Wild Bouquet pattern $800
Tumbler, Banded Ring, Beaded Circle, Chrysanthemum, Everglade, Intaglio, Maple Leaf, Prayer Rug, Scrolled and Victoria patterns $175
Tumbler, gold Louis XV pattern (Northwood) $200
Vase, 7½″ tall, Banded Ring and Scrolled patterns $250
Vase, 6″ tall, Georgia Gem pattern $400
Vase, hat-shaped, ruffled, Grape and Arch pattern $125
Vase, souvenir (several varieties) $125
Wine glass, Diamond pattern $100

CUT VELVET   VARIOUS PRODUCERS, 1880s–EARLY 1900s

"Cut Velvet" is characterized by two separate layers fused together that are blown into a mold. It comes in a variety of colors and was made by many manufacturers in several patterns. The glass is most often found in the "Diamond Quilted" pattern.

Bottle, 8¼″ tall, blue with white lining, Diamond Quilted pattern $250
Bowl, 7″, ribbed, Tan $325
Bowl, finger, 3½″ diameter, pink with white lining $225
Bowl, flower, 4¼″ tall, pink and white or blue and white shading, Diamond Quilted pattern $250

Bowl, flower, 4″ diameter, blue with white lining $225
Bowl, rose, 3¹/₂″, crimped (4 or 6), Diamond Quilted pattern, Blue or pink $225
Creamer, 3¹/₂″ tall, Diamond Quilted pattern $325
Cup, punch, pink with white lining, Diamond Quilted pattern $150
Ewer, 12″ tall, pink and white shading, Diamond Quilted pattern $350
Pitcher, 4¹/₂″ tall, pink with white lining, amber handle, Honeycomb pattern ... $500
Pitcher, 7¹/₂″ tall, Diamond Quilted pattern, Blue $400
Pitcher, water, Diamond Quilted pattern, Yellow $650
Tumbler, 3¹/₂″ tall, Diamond Quilted pattern, Pink $350
Tumbler, 5″ tall, Diamond Quilted pattern, Pink or blue $125
Vase, 11″ tall, Diamond Quilted pattern, Amethyst $550
Vase, 11″ tall, Herringbone pattern, Pink $300
Vase, 6¹/₂″ tall, pleated top, Diamond Quilted pattern, Dark blue $550
Vase, 6¹/₄″ tall, green with white lining, Diamond Quilted pattern $175
Vase, 6″ tall, ribbed, Butterscotch color $350
Vase, 7″ tall, ruffled, footed, pink to white shading, Diamond Quilted pattern ... $275
Vase, 8″ tall, blue satin, Diamond Quilted pattern $475
Vase, 8″ tall, blue with vertical ribbing $250
Vase, 9¹/₄″ tall, flared, ruffled, Diamond Quilted pattern $225
Vase, 9″ tall, ruffled, Diamond Quilted pattern, Blue $550

DE VILBISS   DE VILBISS COMPANY, 1880s–1920s

The De Vilbiss Company purchased blank vases from other companies such as Cambridge, Fenton, Steuben, and so on. They added such things as bulbs, collars, decorations, gilding, etc. Many were signed, stamped, or labelled with the "De Vilbiss" or "De Vilbiss—Made in U.S.A." trademark. They were most famous for perfume spray bottles referred to as atomizers.

Bottle, perfume, 5″ tall, footed, gold trim $225
Bottle, perfume, 7″ tall, gold crackle with black trim $175
Bottle, perfume, metallic black with chrome neck $125
Dresser set, 7-piece, gold trim with enameled flowers, signed "De Vilbiss" $950
Hairpin box, hinged lid, iridescent with gilding $175
Lamp, perfume, 7″ tall, glass insert with nude figure $300
Lamp, perfume, 12″ tall, glass insert with nude figure $375
Perfume atomizer, 4³/₄″ tall, gold crackle design with beaded flower at top $100
Perfume atomizer, 6¹/₄″ tall, tasseled bulb, Black $110
Perfume atomizer, 6″ tall, crystal base, orange stain $100
Perfume atomizer, 7¹/₄″ tall, gold draped woman on stem, Crystal $325
Perfume atomizer, 7³/₄″ tall, signed "De Vilbiss," Iridescent orange $375
Perfume atomizer, 9¹/₄″ tall, Black and gold $225
Perfume atomizer, blue with black enameling $125
Perfume atomizer, gilded with black enameling $150
Perfume atomizer, gilded, tapered top, amber jewel set in cap $325
Perfume atomizer, green with cut leaves, signed "De Vilbiss" $225
Perfume atomizer, signed "De Vilbiss," Iridescent amber $275
Pin tray, black with gold trim $60
Pin tray, rectangular (5¹/₂″ × 3¹/₄″), black and gold decoration, orange stain $60
Tray, iridescent with gilding $90

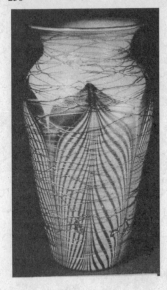

Durand art glass. PHOTO BY ROBIN RAINWATER.

DURAND ART GLASS COMPANY   1912–1935

Victor Durand came from the famous glassmaking town of Baccarat, France, and began producing art glass in the United States in 1912. His company was one of the few to make fancy blown art glass during the Depression years. The Durand Art Glass Company made a variety of objects in various colors and patterns but it is noted for vases. Most of its products feature a silver and black label with "Durand" on it or an engraved silver signature in script. The script may also have a wide V shape beneath it.

Bowl, 6″, ruffled, signed "Durand," Iridescent gold $475
Bowl, 10″ diameter, Orange and gold $650
Bowl, King Tut pattern, signed "Durand," Blue and silver $750
Bowl with cover, Moorish Crackle pattern, Red and white $350
Bowl, flower, 7½″ diameter, signed "Durand," Iridescent blue $1000
Box with cover, King Tut pattern, signed "Durand," Green and gold $1250
Candlestick, 9″ tall, amber with blue feathering $175
Candlestick, 10″ tall, King Tut pattern, Green $775
Compote, 5½″, Amethyst $400
Compote, 7″ diameter, numbered and signed "Durand," Gold and iridescent $525
Cup, signed "Durand," Iridescent gold $250
Jar with cover, 7″ tall, iridescent red with silver threading $3750
Jar with cover, 11″ tall, calcite with gold feathers, signed $1750
Jar with cover, 11″ tall, signed "Durand 1994-8", Green with white iridescence ...
.... $1600
Jar with cover, vertical ribs, green triple overlay, signed "Durand" $3000
Lamp, 24″ tall, Pulled Leaf design with threaded overlay $750
Lamp, electric, 7½″ tall $850
Light with iron holder, 9¾″ tall, King Tut pattern, Green $700

Perfume with stopper, 6″ tall, Gold $775

Plate, 8″, blue with feathering $375

Plate, 8″, engraved "Bridgeton Rose," Red and white $425

Plate, 8″, red with white feathers $400

Saucer, signed "Durand," Iridescent gold $200

Shade, 5¹/₂″ tall, blue, white, and gold design (2 styles) $200

Sherbet, green with white feathering, signed "Durand" $350

Sherbet with matching underplate, 2-piece set, King Tut pattern $450

Tazza, 7³/₄″ × 6³/₄″, signed "Durand," Iridescent gold $925

Tumbler, signed "Durand," Amber $150

Vase, 4″ tall, iridescent blue feathering $400

Vase, 4″ tall, signed "Durand," Iridescent amber $225

Vase, 5¹/₂″ tall, Egyptian Crackle pattern, Green and gold on opal $850

Vase, 6¹/₂″ tall, signed "Durand," Blue and black cameo $2500

Vase, 6¹/₄″ tall, gold luster, Heart and Vine design $575

Vase, 6¹/₈″ tall, flared, iridescent blue with silver threading, signed "Durand 1710-6" $1000

Vase, 6″ tall, green with iridescent gold and platinum $1000

Vase, 6″ tall, inverted rim, Raindrop pattern, signed "Durand 1968–6," Transparent yellow $750

Vase, 7¹/₂″ tall, iridescent blue with white hearts and vines $1500

Vase, 7¹/₄″ tall, signed "Durand," Iridescent gold $550

Vase, 7″ tall, Iridescent blue $550

Vase, 7″ tall, intaglio cut, signed "Durand" $1850

Vase, 7″ tall, oiled luster with opal, signed "Durand" $525

Vase, 8″ tall, handled, iridescent yellow and gold with blue edge, engraved "Durand 1974–15" $1500

Vase, 8″ tall, intaglio cut with iridescent gold, signed "Durand 20161–8" .. $1300

Vase, 8″ tall, King Tut pattern, signed "Durand," Iridescent green with silver $1600

Vase, 8″ tall, urn-shaped, King Tut pattern, Green and gold $1100

Vase, 9¹/₄″ tall, blue and ivory with gold interior $1100

Vase, 9¹/₄″ tall, urn-shaped, white exterior with blue color and gold threading, yellow interior, signed "Durand" $800

Vase, 9³/₄″ tall, cut vertically, red and clear overlay $975

Vase, 9³/₄″ tall, white with red collar and foot $1250

Vase, 9″ tall, green with white interior and silver swirls, King Tut pattern, signed "Durand" $1250

Vase, 9″ tall, King Tut pattern, Green and gold $950

Vase, 10¹/₂″ tall, frosted glass with blue and white overlay, signed "Durand" ... $1000

Vase, 10³/₄″ tall, intaglio cut with 4 layers, signed "Durand 1911–70″ $1250

Vase, 10″ tall, intaglio cut, crystal with red casing, signed "Durand" $1000

Vase, 10″ tall, iridescent gold with silver, King Tut pattern, signed "Durand 1910″ $850

Vase, 10″ tall, signed, Iridescent cobalt blue $1600

Vase, 10″ tall, white, orange, and gray with heart-shaped leaves $750

Vase, 11¹/₂″ tall, blue exterior with silver interior, signed "Durand" $1100

Vase, 12¹/₂″ tall, green with pink highlights, King Tut pattern, signed "Durand" $1350

Vase, 12¹/₂″ tall, red with silver exterior, gold interior, King Tut pattern, signed "Durand" $1350

Vase, 12″ tall, iridescent blue with gold crackle, signed "Durand" $750
Vase, 13″ tall, green with white feathers $600
Vase, 15½″ tall, ivory on gold, King Tut pattern, signed "Durand 1974–15" $1250
Wine glass, yellow with feathering $300

FAVRILE   LOUIS COMFORT TIFFANY, 1892–1920s

Developed and patented in 1892, "Favrile" is characterized by multicolored iridescent base colors decorated with applied or embedded designs. "Favrile" was one of
the major movements in the Art Nouveau period, as other companies sought to copy
or create similar color effects.

Candlestick, 20″ tall, gold with bronze base, Lily Pad design, stamped "27466" ..
.... $950
Candy jar with cover, 9¾″ tall, circular foot, iridescent blue, marked "X236 L.C.
Tiffany-Favrile" $2250
Chandelier, 50″ tall, alamander leaded glass, 6 chains, 6 gold favrile shades
marked "L.C.T.," multicolored floral design $35000
Compote, 5¼″ tall, ruffled, signed "L.C. Tiffany–Favrile," Gold $750
Compote, 5″ tall, signed "L.C.T. Favrile," Blue $1500
Floriform, 11¼″ tall, gold ribbing, signed "L.C. Tiffany Favrile–455H" ... $1250
Flower bowl with frog, 10¾″ diameter, blue floral design, bowl signed
"Louis C. Tiffany–Furnaces Inc. Favrile," frog signed "L.C. Tiffany–Favrile"
.... $2500

Collection of Favrile art glass vases. COURTESY OF THE CORNING MUSEUM OF GLASS.

Frog, flower, 3³/₄″ tall, double, signed "L.C. Tiffany Favrile–5678K" $600

Jar, ginger with cover, 8¹/₂″ tall, yellow with green glaze, signed "L.C. Tiffany–Favrile" $2500

Jug with handle, 4″ tall, signed "L.C. Tiffany-Favrile," Blue $1000

Lamp, 17³/₄″ tall, Venetian style, gilded shade in bronze mount, signed "L.C.T.," Iridescent gold $3750

Lamp, 28″ tall, 22″ diameter, cabochon jewels, iridescent amber, blue, and green, dragonfly border $45000

Perfume with stopper, 4¹/₄″ tall, iridescent blue with blue highlights, signed "L.C. Tiffany Favrile-923OG" $850

Sherbet, 3¹/₂″ tall, intaglio engraved grapes, signed "1225 L.C.T. Favrile," Gold $850

Vase, 2¹/₂″ tall, urn-shaped, red exterior, yellow interior, signed "1611K L.C. Tiffany Favrile' $1750

Vase, 4″ tall, flared, signed "1027-883 GM–L.C. Tiffany Favrile" $500

Vase, 5″ tall, ovoid form, yellow with cobalt, signed $17500

Vase, 6¹/₄″ tall, inverted rim, multicolored cameo floral design, signed "L.C. Tiffany-Favrile" $4500

Vase, 6″ tall, crystal with multicolored morning glories, signed "L.C. Tiffany-Favrile" $3250

Vase, 7¹/₄″ tall, flask-shaped, lava, signed "L.C. Tiffany-Favrile" $20500

Vase, 9¹/₄″ tall, floriform, gold with green lily pads, signed "L.C. Tiffany-Favrile" $1500

Vase, 9″ tall, urn-shaped, cameo foliage, signed "Louis C. Tiffany Favrile 6368N," Iridescent gold $2750

Vase, 10″ tall, intaglio floral design, signed "1153-3643K L.C. Tiffany Favrile," Iridescent gold $2500

Vase, 11¹/₄″ tall, jack-in-the-pulpit style, signed "L.C. Tiffany–Favrile," Blue $3500

Vase, 12″ tall, floriform, blue with trailing green lily pads, signed "L.C. Tiffany–Favrile" $3500

Vase, 15¹/₂″ tall, green with amber lily pads and millefiore flowers, signed "L.C. Tiffany–Favrile" $4500

Vase, 16¹/₂″ tall, jack-in-the-pulpit, iridescent gold, foot inscribed "7841B L.C. Tiffany Favrile" $4500

Vase, 19¹/₂″ tall, jack-in-the-pulpit style, signed "L.C. Tiffany–Favrile," Blue $37500

Vase, 19¹/₄″ tall, urn-shaped, gold foot, iridescent blue on gold with blue and amber bands, signed "5622G L.C. Tiffany–Favrile" $4500

Wine glass, 8″ tall, circular foot, opalescent pink bowl, green stem, signed "L.C.T. Favrile" $475

FRY, H.C. GLASS COMPANY   1900–1934

Fry Glass is usually found in fine cut and ovenware examples. Like other glass-makers, the company experimented with color effects. Its most noteworthy artistic products were opal or opaline "Foval" and "Pearl Art" styles. Both are character-ized by a white opalescence with color accents. Some products were also decorated with silver and colored threading.

Basket, 7½″ tall, 7½″ diameter, opal with blue handle $425
Bowl, 10″, white opal with blue trim $300
Bowl, 12″, centerpiece, green base, opalescent $400
Bread pan, opalescent, Fry ovenware $50
Candlestick, 10″, white opal with blue threading $150
Candlestick, 12″ tall, white opal with blue handle $175
Casserole dish with cover, 1½ qt., oval, blue finial, Fry ovenware, dated 1925-6
.... $75
Casserole dish, miniature (children's), 4″ diameter, Fry ovenware $85
Coffee pot with cover, white opal with blue handle and finial $550
Compote, 7″, opalescent white with blue threading $375
Creamer, opal with blue handle $225
Cruet, opal with cobalt blue handle and cobalt blue stopper $400
Cup, opal with jade green $85
Cup, white opal with cobalt blue handle $95
Cup with underplate, handled, Opaque blue $110
Custard cup, Fry ovenware, dated 1919 .... $25
Measuring cup, ½ cup, 3-spout, Fry ovenware $110
Nappy, handled, opaline $85
Pie plate, Fry ovenware $40
Pitcher with cover, clear craquelle with jade green handle $200
Pitcher, water, 8″ tall, blue and white opal with amethyst handle $450
Reamer, juice, opaline $75
Saucer, opal with jade green $55
Saucer, white opal $40
Sherbet, opal with blue stem and foot $110
Sugar, opal with blue handles $110
Teapot with cover, opaline with green spout and handle $275
Toothpick holder, 2¼″ tall, opal with blue handles $85
Vase, 8″ tall, white opal with lavender top, signed "Fry" $275
Vase, 11″ tall, opaline with blue spiral twist and blue rim $275
Vase, clear craquelle with applied amethyst rosettes $100
Vase, opal with blue pedestal base $375

GILLINDER & SONS   1870s–EARLY 1890s

The Gillinders built a small glass factory and presented many of their products dur-ing the 1876 Centennial Exposition in Philadelphia. Some pieces are even marked "Centennial 1876" or "Gillinder and Sons, Centennial Exhibition." The family also gave away small novelty items as souvenirs, such as glass hats and slippers. Many of their products are frosted, cut, and pressed into various shapes. Lion refers to a head finial, while the frosted lion appears on the objects as a frosted design. The cameo vases are particularly rare and valuable.

Bowl with cover, oval ($6^7/8'' \times 3^7/8''$), frosted lion $175
Bowl with cover, oval ($7^1/2'' \times 4^3/4''$), frosted lion $200
Bowl with cover, oval ($9'' \times 5^1/2''$), frosted lion $225
Bust, Abraham Lincoln, 6" tall, Opaque white $550
Bust, George Washington, 5" tall $400
Bust, William Shakespeare, 5" tall, frosted bust $300
Butter dish with cover, lion $200
Celery vase, etched lion design $125
Cheese dish with cover, lion $450
Children's miniature set, 5-piece lion (creamer and sugar, covered compote, stemmed glass, stemmed covered compote) $575
Compote, $7^3/4''$ diameter, frosted lion $150
Compote, 8" oval, frosted lion $175
Compote, 9" oval, frosted lion $200
Compote with cover, $6^3/4''$ oval, 7" tall, lion $200
Compote with cover, $7^3/4''$ oval, lion $225
Compote with cover, 7" diameter, 11" tall, lion $225
Compote with cover, 8" diameter, 13" tall, lion $250
Creamer, frosted lion $125
Duck dish (duck cover), Amber $90
Egg cup, frosted lion $150
Figurine, Buddha, 6" tall, Amber $100
Goblet, $6^1/4''$ tall, frosted lion $125
Jar, marmalade, with cover, lion $175
Paperweight, frosted lion $200
Paperweight, intaglio portrait of Abraham Lincoln $175
Paperweight, Ruth the Gleaner $175
Paperweight, Challinor, 3" diameter, faceted, concentric colored rings $375
Pitcher, milk, $6^1/2''$ tall, frosted lion $475
Pitcher, syrup with metal lid, frosted lion $350
Pitcher, water, $8^1/4''$ tall, frosted lion $375
Pitcher, water, hexagonal, alternating draped women in gothic arches $500
Plate, $10^1/2''$, handled, frosted lion $125
Plate, 10", Blaine design, signed "Jacobus" $250
Plate, 10", warrior, signed "Jacobus" $200
Platter, $12^1/4''$ oval, frosted lion center $150
Platter, oval ($10^1/2'' \times 9''$), lion handles $150
Relish dish, $8^1/2''$ long, frosted lion $100
Salt dip, rectangular, $3^1/2''$ long, frosted lion $450
Sauce dish, 5" diameter, footed, frosted lion $75
Slipper, lady's glass, marked "Gillinder & Sons Centennial Exhibition" $90
Spooner, frosted lion $100
Sugar dish, $3^1/2''$ tall, frosted lion $125
Toothpick holder, $2^1/2''$ tall, baby chick $150
Vase, $6^1/2''$ tall, frosted lion $150
Vase, frosted, pressed "Gillinder Centennial" $90
Vase, cameo, $6^3/4''$ tall, white leaves on blue background $2250
Vase, cameo, $7^3/4''$ tall, floral design on yellow background, flared $2250

Vase, cameo, 8½″ tall, floral design on blue background, flared $2750
Vase, cameo, ruffled, footed, floral design on a ruby red background $2350
Wine glass, 5¾″ tall, frosted lion $250

HANDEL & COMPANY 1890s–1930s

Some of the most exquisite lamps ever made in America were fabricated by Handel and signed by numerous individual artists working in the company. Chipped glass effects, hand-decorated interiors, bent inserts, metal or leaded shades, fired-on metallic stains, gilding, cameo engraving, and etchings can all be found on these famous lamps. Even the bases were quite elaborate; copper, brass, bronze, and white plated metals were used. Handel also produced some tableware, opal glass, and a few nonglass products (wood, metal, procelain, and pottery items).

Bowl, 8″, enameled trees design, signed $225
Candlestick, 8½″ tall, footed, frosted with enameled landscape and windmills ...
....$800
Candlestick, 9″ tall, amber with etched floral design $325
Cigar holder with hinged lid, 6″ × 3¼″, Bear design $325
Humidor with cover, Shriner's fez and printed "Cigars" on cover, gold and white trim, Man Riding Camel design, Brown and green $800
Humidor with pewter cover, 5″ tall, opal, Owl and Branch design, signed and numbered $475
Humidor with pewter cover, Horse and Dog design, signed "Braun," Opal with brown and green $600
Lamp, 6¾″ tall, double green and yellow mica shades $1500
Lamp, 7¼″ tall, cone shade, blue and white globe, metal base $650
Lamp, 7″ tall, crystal flecked design, bronze base, signed $1250
Lamp, 8½″ tall, glass base, blue floral design $1350
Lamp, 9½″ tall, brass base, amber and brown swirled shade $1250
Lamp, 9¼″ tall, 3-footed, shaded amber to blue $1250
Lamp, 9″ tall, multicolored floral design on red background $6750
Lamp, 9″ tall, multicolored Parrots and Tropical Foliage design $4750
Lamp, 10½″ tall, green and red floral design on a yellow background, signed ....
.... $1500
Lamp, 10″ tall, green and yellow floral design on a white background, brass base, signed $2250
Lamp, 11¼″ tall, green and white lily design, signed "Handel" $6750
Lamp, 11″ tall, red and white floral design on a brown background, signed $4500
Lamp, 12″ tall, light ice blue mica shade with birds and foliage, brass base ......
.... $10500
Lamp, 12″ tall, multicolored Lake and Trees on yellow background, signed ... $6750
Lamp, 12″ tall, Windmill design, dark bronze base $2250
Lamp, 14″ tall, bronze base, orange Wavy Pattern with yellow domed shade ......
....$1150
Lamp, 15″ tall, reverse painted shade, multicolored landscape with tan trees and orange water on a green background $3000
Lamp, 22½″ tall, green domed shade, multicolored Storm at Sea design ... $3500
Lamp, 22½″ tall, red domed shade, Pine Needle design $3000

Lamp, 28" tall, leaded blue domed shade, bronze base, Egyptian (Sphinx) design
.... $11000
Lamp, 29" tall, leaded blue domed shade, metal base, Tree and Foliage design ....
.... $13000
Lamp, wall globe, cobalt blue bird on floral background $650
Pitcher, 9½", pink roses and white carnations $375
Plate, cake, 10", 2 handles, pink floral design with gold edge $175
Vase, 10" tall, green and brown Forest design, signed $2250
Vase, 12" tall, multicolored Floral and Scrolled design, signed $800
Vase, 5½" tall, 4" diameter, white floral design on green background $475
Vase, 7½" tall, green trees and foliage on yellow background $725

HOBBS, BROCUNIER AND COMPANY   1860s–1891

The most popular art glass created by this company was "Frances Ware." It is characterized by an amber color, fluted rims, a hobnail pattern, and an all-over camphor staining. The stain produced a dull or flat finish.

Bonbon dish with cover, 6", amber finial "Frances Ware" $200
Bowl, 14¼" × 4¾", boat-shaped, Daisy and Button pattern $500
Bowl, 4", "Frances Ware," Hobnail pattern $60
Bowl, 7½", "Frances Ware," Hobnail pattern $85
Bowl, 8" square, "Frances Ware" $150
Bowl, 9", "Frances Ware" $125
Butter dish with cover, amber rim, frosted, Hobnail pattern $200
Butter dish with cover, frosted, "Frances Ware" $200
Carafe, water, frosted with amber flashing, Block design $200
Cheese dish with cover, blue ball handle and crystal underplate, Circle pattern,
Bluerina color $1000
Creamer, amber rim, frosted, "Frances Ware," Hobnail pattern $115
Creamer, amber rim, frosted, Hobnail pattern $135
Creamer, amber rim, Hobnail pattern $85
Pitcher, milk, 5½" tall, frosted, "Frances Ware" $275
Pitcher, milk, 5" tall, amber rim, Hobnail pattern $250
Pitcher, syrup with pewter lid, frosted, "Frances Ware," Hobnail pattern ... $225
Pitcher, water, 8" tall, globe-shaped, amber neck and rim, Hobnail pattern .. $325
Pitcher, water, 9" tall, Cranberry Crackle design with applied crystal handle. $350
Pitcher, water, Hexagon Block pattern, ruby stained with engraved Leaf design,
applied crystal handle $350
Plate, 5¾" square, frosted, "Frances Ware," Hobnail pattern $50
Sauce dish, "Frances Ware" $60
Spooner, amber rim, frosted, Hobnail pattern $90
Sugar with cover, amber rim, Frosted, Hobnail pattern $175
Sugar with cover, amber rim, Hobnail pattern $125
Toothpick holder, 2" tall, "Frances Ware" $125
Toothpick holder, Daisy and Button pattern $275
Tray, 12" × 7", "Frances Ware" $150
Tray, 14" × 9½", frosted, "Frances Ware" $325
Tumbler, 4" tall, frosted, "Frances Ware" $85

Tumbler, amber ribbon, Hobnail pattern $500
Vase, 7″ tall, fluted rim, opalescent pink with white hobnails $375

HOLLY AMBER   INDIANA TUMBLER & GOBLET COMPANY, 1903

Holly Amber is a rare pressed art design featuring holly leaves on colored glass that shades from a light creamy opalescent to a darker brown-amber. The color is sometimes referred to as golden agate. It was made only from January 1 to June 13, 1903.

Bowl, 10″ rectangular $950
Bowl, berry, 7½″ oval, 4½″ tall $650
Bowl, berry, 8½″, 3½″ tall $800
Butter dish with cover, domed with tapered top $1350
Cake salver, 9½″ diameter $2000
Compote with cover, 6½″ diameter $1500
Compote with cover, 8½″ diameter $1750
Creamer, 3″ tall $950
Cruet with stopper, 6¼″ tall $1850
Cup, handled, 5″ tall $575
Dolphin dish with cover, 7″ $1350
Mug, handled, 4½″ tall, amber white handle $550
Mug, handled, 4″ tall, amber white handle $525
Parfait, 6″ tall $650
Pickle dish, 6½″ × 4″, 2-handled $500
Pitcher, syrup with tin lid $1100
Pitcher, water, 8¾″ tall $2600
Plate, 7½″ square $850
Plate, 9¼″ $2350
Relish dish, 7½″ oblong $675
Salt and pepper shakers $1500
Sauce dish $275
Spooner $500
Sugar dish with cover $1750
Toothpick holder, 2½″ tall $1000
Toothpick holder, 5″ tall, pedestal base $1500
Tumbler, 4″ tall, holly branch panels, transparent amber rim $450
Tumbler, water, wreath in base $450
Vase, 6″ tall, footed $725

HONESDALE DECORATING COMPANY   EARLY 1900s–MID 1930s

Honesdale was a branch of C. Dorflinger & Sons. The company produced decorated glass vases and other articles featuring enameling, engraving, etching, gilding, and silver and gold trims. It also employed fired-on iridescent colors.

Bowl, 8″, cameo design with green scrolls $350
Goblet, 7″ tall, gold design and border (Heisey Blank) $85

Plate, 8¹/₂″, amethyst with gold rim $115
Tumbler, 6¹/₄″ tall, crystal with gold trim $55
Vase, 5″ tall, light iridescent with blue cameo scrolls $375
Vase, 6¹/₂″ tall, multicolored floral design on a blue base $450
Vase, 7″ tall, flared, yellow cameo mums outlined in blue $400
Vase, 8¹/₂″ tall, green, purple, and red floral design outlined in gold, gold beaded rim, signed $525
Vase, 9″ tall, green acid cutback design, crystal base with gold trim, signed $500
Vase, 9″ tall, green cameo scrolls with gold $475
Vase, 10³/₄″ tall, blue cameo with gold, gilded rim $600
Vase, 10″ tall, green and gold cameo, signed $550
Vase, 10″ tall, yellow cameo outlined in crystal $525
Vase, 11¹/₂″ tall, blue cameo on crystal base $850
Vase, 11″ tall, amethyst cameo on crystal, gilded, signed $500
Vase, 11″ tall, red cameo with hunting scene $1350
Vase, 12¹/₂″ tall, blue cameo on frosted crystal, gilded outline, etched floral and scroll designs, signed "Honesdale" $850
Vase, 12″ tall, green cameo with gold outline, Geese and Cattails design $750
Vase, 12″ tall, red cameo on frosted crystal, gold outline, flared $800
Vase, 13¹/₂″ tall, blue and yellow floral design on a crystal base, gilded outline $475
Vase, 14¹/₂″ tall, gilded, etched, Versailles pattern $300
Vase, 14″ tall, crystal with gilding, signed "Honesdale" $375
Vase, 14″ tall, emerald green background with gilding, floral design $250
Vase, 17¹/₂″ tall, crystal with gold tracing, Basketweave design $1150

IMPERIAL GLASS COMPANY   1901–1920s

Imperial, a major manufacturer of Carnival and Depression glass, experimented with iridescent art forms such as vases. "Imperial Jewels" was a pressed and blown colored glass introduced in 1916.

Bowl, 9″, ribbed, signed, Amber $200
Bowl, rose, jewels, signed, Amethyst $175
Candlestick, 10″ tall, crystal with ruby red holder and base $125
Candy dish with cover, jewels, Pink $60
Pitcher, water, 8¹/₂″ tall, Hobnail pattern, Cobalt blue $425
Sweetmeat jar with cover, jewels, Blue $175
Vase, 6¹/₂″ tall, green loops on blue oval $275
Vase, 6″ tall, iridescent blue with white foliage $275
Vase, 6″ tall, jewels, Amethyst $200
Vase, 6″ tall, ruffled, Ruby red $225
Vase, 7³/₄″ tall, flared, footed, iridescent green ground, silver designs $450
Vase, 7″ tall, gold loops, Iridescent white $325
Vase, 8¹/₂″ tall, Imperial Jewels, Blue $400
Vase, 8″ tall, frosted ground, iridescent blue designs $225
Vase, 9″ tall, blue loops on opal $400
Vase, 9″ tall, white foliage on green background, orange neck $250
Vase, 10″ tall, blue loops, Opaque white $350

Vase, 10″ tall, green scrolling, orange interior $250
Vase, 11¼″ tall, green leafing on white, orange interior $450

KEW BLAS   UNION GLASS COMPANY, 1893–1924

W.S. Blake (superintendent at Union Glass) created the name "Kew Blas" by re-arranging the letters of his name. "Kew Blas" was made in a variety of colors such as brown, cream, green, tan, and white. "Kew Blas" is fairly scarce and is often confused with other art glass produced in the same colors by other companies. "Kew-Blas" is sometimes found etched or signed on the underside of the company's glassware.

Bowl, 6½″, Zipper pattern, signed, Iridescent gold and green $775
Bowl, 6″, 3-footed, flared, white interior, signed, Light blue opal $425
Candlestick, 8″ tall, iridescent gold with swirled stem, signed $325
Candlestick, 9″ tall, calcite and gold with green Feather design, signed $375
Compote, 5″ tall, 4″ diameter, 3-footed, Iridescent gold $375
Compote, 6″ tall, 4½″ diameter, iridescent gold $450
Creamer, 3¼″, signed, Iridescent gold $500
Cup, applied handle, Feather design, signed, Iridescent green, gold, and ivory ....
.... $475
Decanter with enameled stopper, 15″ tall, ribbed, Gold $1100
Pitcher, 4½″ tall, gold with green Feather design, gold interior, swirled handle ....
.... $850
Saucer, Feather design, signed, Iridescent green, gold, and ivory $275
Tumbler, 3½″ tall, 4-sided, Iridescent gold $525
Tumbler, 4″ tall, gold with Feather design $475
Vase, 12″ tall, Cat Tail design, Iridescent gold $1350
Vase, 5½″ tall, Iridescent gold on white $550
Vase, 5¾″ tall, flared, ruffled, Fishscale pattern, Iridescent amber $550
Vase, 6½″ tall, green and gold feathers on an iridescent gold background, signed ..
.... 1050
Vase, 6″ tall, calcite, Wavy Gold design, gold interior $650
Vase, 7″ tall, gold and green with diagonal stripes, signed $625

"Kew Blas" bowl.
PHOTO BY ROBIN RAINWATER.

Vase, 8¹/₂" tall, Iridescent gold $450
Vase, 9" tall, calcite, gold and green Feather design, signed $1000
Wine glass, 4³/₄" tall, twisted stem, signed, Iridescent gold $225

KIMBLE GLASS COMPANY   1930s

"Cluthra" art glass was Kimble's only popular product. It is characterized by brilliant, gloss-finished colors with cloud formations and multiple air bubbles of varying sizes. It is often confused with Steuben's "Cluthra," which usually has a higher concentration of bubbles. Some pieces are signed in silver with the "Kimble" name or a "K" and a date and number code. Also, a few can be found with the "Durand-Kimble" signature, indicating a brief partnership between the two companies.

Bowl, globe-shaped, blue with streaked orange and brown, Cluthra design, signed, numbered $275
Vase, 10" tall, Cluthra design, Blue $350
Vase, 10" tall, crystal with green to white shading, enameled floral design, signed $225
Vase, 11¹/₂" tall, Cluthra design, signed, Blue and white $375
Vase, 12" tall, Cluthra design, signed, numbered, Jade green and white $475
Vase, 12" tall, white with enameled design, signed "Durand-Kimball" $475
Vase, 18" tall, Cluthra design, signed, Blue and yellow $650
Vase, 4¹/₄" tall, Cluthra design, signed, Light blue and orange $275
Vase, 6¹/₂" tall, Cluthra design, signed, Green, orange, white, and yellow $1050
Vase, 6¹/₂" tall, flared, triple-hued, Cluthra design $750
Vase, 6" tall, Cluthra design, signed, White $200
Vase, 7³/₄" tall, signed, White $275
Vase, 8¹/₂" tall, footed, Cluthra design, Orange and white $300
Vase, 8" tall, green with white enameling, signed $275
Vase, 5" tall, Cluthra design, signed, Blue $475

LIBBEY ART GLASS   1870s–1930s

Although Libbey is noted more for brilliant cut crystal, the company did continue some of the traditions of the New England Glass Company, which William L. Libbey purchased. "Amberina" was its most popular form of art glass. Other pieces include souvenir items (from the 1893 World's Fair), glassware featuring the "Maize" (corncob design), ornamental glassware, and experimental forms with shading (see additional entries under "Amberina" and "Peachblow").

Bowl, 2¹/₂", cream-colored satin, signed $950
Bowl, 8³/₄", opaque white with green leaves, "Maize" pattern $250
Bowl, flared, pink with trapped bubbles, Swirl pattern, signed $300
Box, 4¹/₄", Cream satin finish, enameled daisies, marked "World's Fair 1893," signed "Libbey Cut" $475
Candlestick, 6" tall, crystal foot and stem, opalescent cup with pink interior, signed "Libbey" $925
Candlestick, 6" tall, crystal stem and foot, red feather top, signed $875

Candlestick, 8″ tall, air twist stem $225
Celery vase, clear iridescent, "Maize" pattern $225
Champagne glass, squirrel stem, signed "Libbey" $225
Cocktail glass, crow stem, signed "Libbey $110
Cocktail glass, opalescent kangaroo stem, signed "Libbey" $200
Compote, 3³/₈″ tall, 5³/₄″ diameter, circular foot, gold knob, blue to iridescent gold
shading $575
Cruet, clear iridescent, "Maize" pattern $225
Cup, marked "World's Fair 1893" $100
Cup, vaseline, marked "World's Fair 1893" $150
Goblet, 6¹/₄″ tall, raised blown opalescent drops over bowl, low circular foot, Morn-
ing Mist pattern $200
Goblet, 9¹/₄″ tall, cut circular foot, rub knob on stem, cased pink and white Victo-
rian cameo cut design, 4 lady cameos separated by columns $5750
Goblet, 9¹/₈″ tall, circular foot, 4 globe-shaped bubbles in stem, ruby-flashed bowl
with engraved scroll, foliage, and ribbons, Campanille pattern $775
Goblet, 10³/₄″ tall, engraved circular foot, spiral engraved stem with ruby threading,
engraved fruit baskets and scrolls on bowl $775
Paperweight, frosted, Lady's head, marked "Columbian Exposition 1893" . $375
Paperweight, Lady's head, marked "World's Fair 1893" $275
Pitcher, syrup with pewter lid, 6″ tall, iridescent gold corn cob, blue husks,
"Maize" pattern $575
Plate, 7³/₄″ tall, ship ("Santa Maria"), sepia-hued $575
Salt and pepper shakers, brass tops, "Maize" pattern $275
Salt and pepper shakers, egg design, marked "1893 Exposition," Blue $350
Saucer, leaf-shaped, marked "World's Fair 1893" $80
Saucer, vaseline, marked "World's Fair 1893" $100
Tazza, 6″ tall, opalescent bowl and foot, crystal stem, blue swirled threading $900
Toothpick holder, pink shading to white, blue and green floral design, gold
inscribed "Little Lob" $150
Toothpick holder, yellow with green leaves outlined in gold, "Maize" pattern . . . .
. . . . $450
Tumbler, 3″ tall, crystal foot, dark green prunts, signed "Libbey" $200
Tumbler, iridescent gold ear with blue leaves, "Maize" pattern $275
Vase, 4¹/₂″ tall, mushroom-shaped, signed "Libbey" $925
Vase, 6¹/₂″ tall, domed circular foot, engraved sitting gazelle, Modern America
Series $275
Vase, 10⁷/₈″ tall, flared, 3 bubble round strawberry-shaped feet, crystal, Modern
American Series $275
Vase, 10″ tall, opalescent rabbit base $250
Vase, 11¹/₄″ tall, circular foot, amber stem, signed "Libbey" $675
Vase, 12¹/₂″ tall, circular foot, ribbed, signed "Libbey" $925
Vase, opaque white with green husks, "Maize" pattern $250
Wine glass, 5″ tall, opalescent monkey stem, crystal bowl, signed "Libbey" . $175
Wine glass, 6″ tall, kangaroo stem, crystal, signed "Libbey" $150
Wine glass, opalescent polar bear stem, crystal bowl, signed "Libbey" $175

LOCKE ART GLASS   1891–1920s

After leaving the New England/Libbey Glass Companies in 1891, Joseph Locke founded his own cutting and decorating shop. Blanks were purchased from Dorflinger; as a result, some Locke Art Glass pieces are similar to Dorflinger's Kalana designs. Locke's knowledge and original designs were instrumental in New England/Libbey's production of Amberina, Pomona, Peachblow, and so on. He continued those fine traditions with his own company.

Brandy glass, 3¼″ tall, etched floral design, paper sticker $150
Champagne glass, 6″ tall, Poppy pattern $150
Goblet, 6¼″ tall, etched vines, signed $150
Goblet, 6¾″ tall, etched floral design, signed $150
Parfait, footed, etched Kalana poppy, signed $175
Pitcher, 8½″ tall, tankard-style, ornate handle, Grape and Vine design $1100
Pitcher, 8″ tall, etched Vintage pattern, signed $550
Pitcher, 8″ tall, etched Rose pattern, signed $350
Plate, 7″, etched poinsettias, signed $250
Punch cup, Poppy pattern, signed "Locke Art" $100
Salt dip, rectangular (2¼″ × 1¼″), pedestal foot, Vintage pattern $100
Sherbet, 3½″ tall, etched grapes and vines $125
Sherbet, 3¾″ tall, etched vines, signed $250
Sherbet, etched with various fruit, signed $250
Tray, rectangular, 15¾″ × 8″, etched floral design $400
Tumbler, 5¼″ tall, ribbed, etched Vintage pattern $150
Tumbler, 5¾″ tall, etched Grape and Vine pattern $125
Vase, 5″ tall, flared, poppies and flower buds $550
Vase, 5″ tall, ruffled, etched floral design, signed $750
Vase, 6¼″ tall, flared, etched roses, signed $600
Vase, 6″ tall, engraved poppies $275
Vase, 10½″ tall, crimped folded rim, ribbed, etched fern design $175
Vase, 10¾″ tall, gold tinted roses and leaves, signed "Locke Art—Mount Oliver, Pennsylvania" $1250
Whiskey tumbler, 2⅝″ tall, engraved Wheat pattern $175
Wine glass, ribbed, Poppy design $100

MARY GREGORY GLASS   BOSTON & SANDWICH GLASS
COMPANY, 1870s–1910

This crystal and colored glassware (most commonly pastel pink) is commonly decorated with white enameled designs of one or more boys and/or girls playing in Victorian scenes. Mary Gregory worked as a decorator for the Boston & Sandwich Glass Company from 1870 to 1880, but it is unclear whether she actually painted the glass. Beware of cheaper Victorian figures made in Czechoslovakia before 1992. The newer Czechoslovakian pieces are generally worth about one-fourth to one-third of the original Mary Gregory items. Westmoreland produced some ruby red Mary Gregory–styled glassware in the early 1980s before going out of business (refer to Chapter 7). Fenton is also producing glass in the 1990s in this style as well.

Mary Gregory art glass. PHOTO BY MARK PICKVET.

Bottle, wine, 9¹/₂″ tall, sapphire blue with enameled white Girl design $225
Bottle, wine with amber faceted stopper, 9″ tall, Boy design, Amber $250
Bottle, wine with crystal bubble stopper, 10‴ tall, Girl design, Cranberry . . $275
Bottle, wine with crystal bubble stopper,, 7¹/₈″ tall, Boy design, Cranberry $225
Bowl, 5″, Girl Fishing design, Cranberry $100
Box with hinged cover, 3³/₄″ × 3³/₄″, brass foot, Boy design, Lime green . . . $275
Box with hinged cover, 4″ × 3⁵/₈″, Girl with Scarf design, Amber $375
Candy dish with cover, 7¹/₂″ tall, 3-footed, Girl and Boy design $275
Cheese dish with dome cover, 9″, Two Girls and Boy design, Cranberry . . . $400
Cookie jar with cover, Girl Sitting on Fence design, Cranberry $550
Cruet with amber stopper, 9¹/₂″ tall, 3-petal top, Boy design, Amber $325
Cruet with crystal stopper, blue with crystal handle, Boy with Flower design . . .
. . . . $375
Decanter with stopper, 10″ tall, 3-petal top, Young Girl design, Lime green $250
Decanter with stopper, 13¹/₂″ tall, Boy in Riding Outfit design, Amber . . . $375
Goblet, 4³/₄″ tall, cranberry with crystal pedestal foot, Girl with Hat design . . . $125
Goblet, 5³/₄″ tall, Boy Feeding Birds design, Cranberry $150
Mug, 3⁷/₈″ tall, Boy and Girl design, Amber $150
Mug, 4″ tall, Boy with Balloons design, Blue $150
Pitcher, 5″ tall, green with gold trim, Boy and Floral design $225
Pitcher, water, 10″ tall, tankard-style, blue, Girl Tending Sheep design $350
Pitcher, water, 9¹/₂″ tall, crimped, crystal, Girl Chasing Butterfly design $250
Pitcher, water, 9″ tall, cranberry with crystal spout, Boy design $500
Plate, 8″, Girl in Swing design, Black $75
Tumbler, 2¹/₂″ tall, Girl and Boy design, Cranberry $150
Tumbler, 3¹/₂″ tall, 2 girls, 1 boy, and 3 Trees design, Green $125
Vase, 4¹/₄″ tall, cranberry with crystal pedestal foot, Girl design $150
Vase, 4³/₄″ tall, Girl Sitting with Flower basket design, Cobalt blue $200
Vase, 4″ tall, Boy in Garden design, Blue $125
Vase, 6¹/₄″ tall, Boy and Girl design, Sapphire blue $175
Vase, 6¹/₄″ tall, Boy or Girl design, Cranberry $250
Vase, 7¹/₂″ tall, Boy with Hat and Oars design, Cobalt blue $175
Vase, 7³/₄″ tall, pink with white interior, Girl with Butterfly Net design $175
Vase, 9¹/₈″ tall, Girl with Umbrella design, Cranberry $300
Vase, 9³/₄″ tall, Girl with Hat design, Black amethyst $250

Vase, 9″ tall, pedestal foot, Boy Blowing Bubbles design, Cranberry $350
Vase, 10³/₄″ tall, Boy or Girl design, Black amethyst $325
Vase, 10″ tall, Boy or Girl design, Cranberry $225
Vase, 10″ tall, scalloped, Boy or Girl design, Amber $300
Vase, 11¹/₄″ tall, scalloped, pedestal base, gold trim $350
Vase, 11³/₄″ tall, Boy Kneeling Offering Heart to Girl design, Blue $500
Vase, 12″ tall, 5¹/₂″ diameter, Girl Sitting on Branch design, Pink $325
Vase, 15″ tall, Boy Chasing Butterfly with Net design, Black amethyst $500
Vase, 17″ tall, Boys and Girls Gathering Apples design, Cranberry $600
Vase, 17″ tall, Girl with Hat, Umbrella, and Basket design, Black amethyst $600

MONROE, C.F. COMPANY   KELVA, NAKARA, AND WAVE CREST

C.F. Monroe was a small art decorating company in Meriden, Connecticut. It applied opal enamels in both satin and brightly colored finishes to blanks provided by Pairpoint as well as French factories. The company produced only three products that are not easily distinguished. Most pieces are either signed or stamped "KELVA," "NAKARA," or "WAVE CREST."

Ashtray, 4¹/₂″, opal scrolls and pink apple blossoms $300
Bonbon tray, swirled with beading, signed "NAKARA" $450
Box, 8¹/₂″ wide, picture of 2 women in garden, signed "NAKARA" $950
Box, hinged lid, gold decoration and opal flowers, signed "WAVE CREST" ... $900
Box, glove, rectangular 8¹/₂″ × 4¹/₂″, hinged cover, signed "WAVE CREST" ... $850
Box, hexagonal, 4″ across, hinged cover, signed "NAKARA" $450
Box, hexagonal, 4″ tall, hinged cover, signed "NAKARA" $450
Box, jewelry, 7″, signed "WAVE CREST" $300
Box, octagonal, hinged cover, signed "KELVA" $750
Box, ring, 3¹/₂″, gray and blue floral design, signed "KELVA" $450
Box, ring, 3¹/₂″, signed "WAVE CREST" $225
Box, round, 6″ diameter, hinged cover, signed "NAKARA" $600
Box, trinket, signed "NAKARA" $275
Cigarette holder, hexagonal $500

C.F. Monroe art glass.
PHOTO BY MARK
PICKVET.

Cracker jar with silver-plated cover, 6″ tall, silver-plated handle, enameled scroll design, Wave Crest $400

Creamer, Swirl pattern with silver-plated mounts $175

Cruet with brass handle and stopper, Angel design Wave Crest $450

Ewer, 14″ tall $225

Ewer, melon, 15½″ tall, ribbed $275

Fernery, 7″ wide, gold and white design, Wave Crest (unsigned) $400

Fernery, 11″ tall, 8″ wide, scalloped, beading, Wild Rose and Foliage design, signed "WAVE CREST" $1000

Hair receiver, diamond-shaped with cover, white beading and blue enamel, signed "NAKARA" $525

Hair receiver with cover, 4″ tall, small floral decoration, signed "KELVA" $350

Hairpin dish, 3¼″ diameter, signed "WAVE CREST" $150

Ice bucket, 11″ tall, 6″ diameter, silver cover and handle, Wild Rose design, Wave Crest $800

Ice bucket, 13¼″ tall, Wild Rose design, signed "WAVE CREST," Light blue $1000

Jar, biscuit with silver-plated cover and handle, 8″ tall, Lilac design, Wave Crest $525

Jar, biscuit with silver-plated cover, 10″ tall, Swirl pattern $575

Jar, blown-out with cover, 3″ tall, Wave Crest (unsigned) $375

Jar, tobacco with metal cover, 6¾″ tall, lettered "Tobacco," signed "NAKARA" $925

Jar, toothpowder with embossed brass cover, signed "WAVE CREST" $550

Jardiniere, 7″ tall, straight sides, ring feet, enameled floral design with gold trim, Wave Crest $550

Jardiniere, 12″ tall, gold decoration, Nakara, White $650

Lamp base, blown-out, 17″ tall, frosted crystal shade, Wave Crest (unsigned) $850

Lamp, table, signed "WAVE CREST" $525

Letter holder, footed base, Wave Crest (unsigned) $400

Perfume bottle, 3½″ tall, with brass stopper and double handles, pink and purple floral design, Wave Crest $300

Pitcher, syrup, swirled with silver-plated top and handle, enameled pink roses $650

Pitcher, syrup with silver-plated lid, 4″ tall, raised paneled floral design, Wave Crest $800

Planter, 7½″ tall, beaded brass rim, 2 brass handles, floral design, Wave Crest $525

Platter, rectangular (11″ × 8″), scrolled edge, enameled roses, Wave Crest $575

Salt and pepper shakers with pewter tops, 3″ tall, enameled floral design, Kelva, Moss green $425

Salt and pepper shakers with pewter tops, signed "WAVE CREST" $475

Salt dip, brass rim, 2 brass handles, floral design, Wave Crest $125

Sugar shaker with silver-plated top, 4″ tall, floral design, Wave Crest $200

Sugar, swirl pattern with silver-plated mounts $175

Toothpowder jar with brass cover, 3½″ tall, white and pink floral design .. $375

Vase, 5″ tall, with bronze-footed holder $225

Vase, 11¼″ tall, blue with Burmese shading, enameled orchids, Nakara ... $1100

Vase, 12″ tall, 9″ wide, handles, footed, signed "WAVE CREST" $775

Vase, 13″ tall, hexagonal, marbled background with white rim, signed "KELVA"
.... $725
Vase, 14″ tall, green background with silver-plated feet, signed "KELVA" .. $850
Vase, 17½″ tall, 4-footed brass base, 2 brass handles connected with brass rim, cartouche hand-painted maiden outlined in gold and mauve, Wave Crest $1750
Whisk broom holder, 8½″, signed "WAVE CREST" $825

MOTHER-OF-PEARL   VARIOUS COMPANIES, 1880s–EARLY 1900s

"Mother-of-Pearl" is characterized by two or more layers of glass in a satin, pearl-like finish and internal indentations that purposefully trap air bubbles. The two major producers of this pearlized glass were the Mt. Washington Glass Works and the Phoenix Glass Works, but others like Steuben, Tiffany, and Libbey also created glass in this manner. A host of decorating techniques and coloring effects were applied, including beading, cameo engraving, enameling, and gold leafing. Colors are much like those of pearls: shaded light blues, light pinks, light purples, light yellows, and sparkling off-whites. These colors were applied to numerous popular cut patterns of the 19th century, including "Diamond Quilted," "Herringbone," "Raindrops," "Ribbed," and "Thumbprints."

Basket, 5½″ tall, ruffled, pink with frosted handle, Herringbone pattern $275
Basket, 12″ tall, thorn handle, Moire pattern with enameled decoration $750
Bottle, cologne, 4½″ tall, apricot with silver stopper, Drape design $250
Bowl, 4″ tall, ruffled, frosted feet, ribbon pattern, Blue $500
Bowl, bride's, 10″ diameter, scalloped, ribbed, Amber with gold floral design, Diamond Quilted pattern $1000
Bowl, bride's, 11″ diameter, ruffled, blue and white with gold highlights, Herringbone pattern $475
Bowl, rose or flower, 4″ tall, 3½″ diameter $675
Box with hinged cover, 4¼″ tall, brass handle, blue with white lining, gold leaves and scrolls $350
Cookie jar with cover, green with silver-plated cover, handle, and rim, enameled chrysanthemum $275
Creamer, 4½″ tall, blue frosted handle and white lining, Teardrop pattern .. $325
Creamer, frosted handle, Raindrop pattern, Apricot $175
Cruet with stopper, 6½″ tall, blue with frosted handle $600
Cruet with stopper, 6″ tall, pink with white interior, Diamond Quilted pattern ...
.... $225
Ewer, 10½″ tall, 2 frosted handles, pink with white interior $1250
Ewer, 12″ tall, shaded rose, Swirl pattern $850
Lamp, 9¾″ tall, 3-footed, brass base, Raindrop patterned shade $850
Lamp, 12¼″ tall, brass base, pink and white floral design, signed $1200
Lamp, 20½″ tall, brown, brass foots and mounts, Swirl pattern $1350
Mug, 3½″ tall, frosted handle, pink to white floral design, Diamond Quilted pattern
.... $325
Perfume bottle with stopper, 5″ tall, Diamond Quilted pattern, Blue $400
Pitcher, cream, 5½″ tall, ruffled, frosted handle, Herringbone pattern $450
Pitcher, syrup with lid, Beaded Drape pattern, Red $525

Pitcher, water, 9¹/₄″ tall, oval top, frosted handle, enameled blue foliage design ...
....$425
Salt and pepper shakers with pewter tops, 3¹/₂″ tall, pink to white shading, Raindrop pattern $375
Sugar shaker, 5″ tall, cranberry floral and stork design, Inverted Thumbprint pattern $800
Sugar with dome cover, Raindrop pattern, Apricot $225
Tumbler, 3³/₄″ tall, Herringbone pattern, Apricot $175
Tumbler, 4″, enameled daisies and leaves, Diamond Quilted pattern $275
Vase, 3″ tall, miniature, Diamond Quilted pattern, Salmon $250
Vase, 4³/₄″ tall, enameled floral design, Diamond Quilted pattern, Blue $250
Vase, 5¹/₂″ tall, folded-in square top, Hobnail pattern, Blue $325
Vase, 5³/₄″ tall, Rose design, Acorn pattern $525
Vase, 5″ tall, ruffled, Diamond Quilted pattern, Pink $325
Vase, 6¹/₂″ tall, white ground with gold design, Ribbon pattern $1250
Vase, 6³/₄″ tall, ruffled, rose, Herringbone pattern $275
Vase, 6″ tall, yellow to white shading, Hobnail pattern $775
Vase, 7¹/₄″ tall, Drape pattern, Dark pink $275
Vase, 7¹/₄″ tall, ruffled, ribbed, Raindrop pattern, Light caramel $300
Vase, 8″ tall, enameled Peacock Tail (eye) design, White $650
Vase, 9″ tall, ruffled, yellow with white lining, enameled floral design, silver-plated holder, ribbon handles $325
Vase, 9″ tall, triple-ring neck, Diamond Quilted pattern, Peach $275
Vase, 10″ tall, ruffled, green with white lining, Diamond Quilted pattern $575
Vase, 11¹/₂″ tall, ruffled, Loop and Teardrop pattern, Blue $550
Vase, 11″ tall, shaded apricot, Raindrop pattern $575
Vase, 13″ tall, ruffled, Herringbone pattern, Blue $500
Vase, 16″ tall, ribbed, chartreuse lining, Zipper pattern $675

MT. WASHINGTON GLASS WORKS   1870–1894

With such influences as Deming Jarves, Libbey, and A.H. Seabury, Mt. Washington became a major producer of Art Glass tableware and vases in the late 19th century. A variety of styles and designs, including "Amberina," "Burmese," "Crown Milano," "Mother-of-Pearl," and "Peachblow" were all part of Mt. Washington's output. Additional listings can be found under these designs. Note that "Royal Flemish" refers to a Mt. Washington design that resembles stained windows (individual pieces of glass separated by lead borders).

Basket, bride's, 6″ tall, 5¹/₂″ diameter, cameo, blue and white floral design, silver-plated holder $875
Basket, bride's, 12″ tall, cameo, flared, 4-footed, pink and white design, silver-plated holder $1350
Bowl, 7¹/₂″, cameo, floral design with winged griffins, Red and white $1100
Bowl, 8¹/₂″, cameo, blue and white floral design $650
Bowl, 9¹/₂″, cameo, pink and white floral designs $1100
Bowl, rose, 6″, 5¹/₄″ tall, pink and blue enameled floral design $325
Bowl, rose, cameo, white and yellow daisies $375
Candlestick, 7¹/₄″ tall, silver holder, enameled pink floral design $275
Cookie jar with cover, 6¹/₄″ tall, Gold Thistle design $850

Mount Washington Burmese lamp. PHOTO BY ROBIN RAINWATER.

Cookie jar with cover, 6″ tall, Royal Flemish design, Pink $1850
Cracker jar, 6½″ tall, pastel floral design, Albertine $800
Cracker jar, 6″ tall, crystal with enameled brownies, signed "Napoli" $1250
Cracker jar with cover, 6½″ tall, Royal Flemish Leaf design $800
Cruet with stopper, 5¾″ tall, Inverted Thumbprint pattern, Rose amber $650
Ewer, 11⅜″ tall, twisted handle and neck, Royal Flemish design $575
Ewer, 15½″ tall, rope handle, overlaid Royal Flemish design $2250
Ewer with cover, 16″ tall, rope handle, Royal Flemish, Coat of Arms decoration ..
....$5750
Hatpin holder, mushroom-shaped, lusterless, satin finish, Fern and Flower design
.... $325
Lamp, 19¾″ tall, kerosene, milk shade, pink and yellow floral design, globular
glass base, footed (Shells and Ram's head) $1850
Lamp, 42″ tall, electric, crystal shade, gold lions and shields, red accents, Royal
Flemish design, Blue aqua $7750
Mustard jar with hinged cover, Leaf design on pink and white background ... $375
Paperweight, 4⅛″ diameter, blue and white shaded rose, green stem, serrated green
leaves $2500
Pitcher, syrup with lid, multicolored floral design outlined in gold $2250
Pitcher, syrup with metal lid, barrel-shaped, ribbed, metal handle, floral design ..
.... $550
Pitcher, syrup with metal lid, barrel-shaped, ribbed, metal handle, floral design ..
.... $550
Pitcher, water, 9″ tall, tan and brown with red scrolls, Royal Flemish design .....
.... $3000
Pitcher, water, 10″ tall, crystal, crab decoration $850
Plate, 10″, lusterless, enameled pansies $100
Plate, 12″, lusterless, enameled portrait of woman $150
Salt and pepper shakers, 2½″ tall, egg-shaped, pewter tops, opaque white with
various enameled floral designs $500

Salt dip, 4-footed, ribbed, pink and yellow pansies with gold highlights $225
Saltshaker, egg-shaped, white with enameled foliage, metal chick's head top ....
.... $450
Saltshaker, Inverted Thumbprint pattern, Rose amber $225
Sugar shaker, cream white with pink and blue enameled floral design $475
Sugar shaker, ribbed, Purple Violet design $325
Toothpick holder, 2⅛" tall, lusterless, white with enameled leaves $350
Vase, 3¾" tall, lava with white outlines, multicolored mica chips $2250
Vase, 4½" tall, lava, applied handles, acidized $2250
Vase, 4¾" tall, satin finish, enameled Forget-Me-Not design $725
Vase, 5¼" tall, rolled rim, Venetian diamond, enameled floral design $700
Vase, 6½" tall, lava, multicolored imbedded glass flecks $3750
Vase, 6" tall, pink ground, gilded rings, enameled bird on branch, Opaque white ..
.... $200
Vase, 7½" tall, 2-handled, Royal Flemish, tan and brown Medallion design $2250
Vase, 7¼" tall, gold tracing and edging, floral design $2500
Vase, 8¼" tall, pear-shaped, floral design, inscribed "Progressive/Fuchre/November
16, 1886" $2250
Vase, 8" tall, brown shading, gold outlining, Royal Flemish design with winged
gargoyle $3750
Vase, 9" tall, 7½" diameter, yellow opal, Chrysanthemum design $675
Vase, 9" tall, globe base, gold trim, Frog and Reeds design, signed "Napoli" ... $1100
Vase, 10½" tall, enameled Dragonflies and Floral design $850
Vase, 10½" tall, tan and red panels, gold beading at top and base, red top, Royal
Flemish design, gold serpent and falcon on front and back $4750
Vase, 10" tall, enameled floral design, signed "Napoli" $775
Vase, 11" tall, gourd-shaped, brown to gold satin, Seaweed design $575
Vase, 13" tall, Royal Flemish, Camel and Rider Paneled design $5750
Vase, 15" tall, Royal Flemish, duck decorations $3500
Vase, 16" tall, Boy on front and foliage on back, signed "Verona" $1500

NASH, A. DOUGLAS CORPORATION   EARLY 1900s–1931

The Nash family, including Arthur J., A. Douglas, and Leslie, all worked for various glass companies in England and the United States. Under the A. Douglas Nash
Corporation, the family produced art glass products in the style of Tiffany (Leslie
Nash once managed the Tiffany Glass Furnace at Corona, New York). "Chintz"
glass is the most recognizable form of Nash's designs and is characterized by a
spoked, rayed, or striped pattern emanating from the center of an object. Multiple
colors on iridescent backgrounds are also characteristic of Nash's products. Some
pieces also were decorated in gold or platinum luster or trims.

Bowl, 10¼", ruffled, signed, Iridescent green $775
Bowl, 4", red with silver stripes, Chintz design $600
Bowl with underplate, signed, numbered, Iridescent gold and platinum $450
Box with hinged cover, 5" diameter, Chintz design, signed, Blue $425
Candlestick, 4" tall, ball stem, Chintz design, Red and gray $350
Chalice, 4½" tall, fluted, signed, numbered, Gold, pink, and platinum $675
Cologne bottle with stopper, 5" tall, alternating stripes of green and blue, Chintz
design $675

Compote, 7¹/₄″ diameter, 4¹/₂″ tall, Chintz design, signed, Green $350
Compote, 8″ diameter, 5″ tall, green with red and gray spiraled rim, Chintz design
. . . . $500
Cordial, 4″ tall, Chintz design, Blue and green $150
Goblet, 5″ tall, pedestal foot, Chintz design, signed, Blue and silver $200
Goblet, twisted stem, wafer foot, pink threaded bowl, signed "Libbey-Nash" . . . $200
Nut dish, 1¹/₄″ × 4″, ruffled, Iridescent gold $275
Perfume bottle with stopper, 8″ tall, blown-out bottom, Iridescent gold . . . $825
Plate, 6¹/₂″, chartreuse and orchid spirals from center, Chintz design $200
Salt dip, 4″ diameter, blue and violet highlights, signed, Iridescent bronze . . $250
Vase, 4¹/₄″ tall, flared, signed "Nash-544," Iridescent amber $575
Vase, 5¹/₂″ tall, stretched iridescent gold $500
Vase, 5³/₄″ tall, red ground with silver stripes, Chintz design, signed $850
Wine glass, 6″ tall, Chintz design, signed, Green and lavender $225

NEW ENGLAND GLASS COMPANY   EARLY 1800s-1880s

New England Glass was blessed with many gifted designers, including Joseph
Locke, Henry Whitney, and Louis Vaupel. The company's output was huge and
spanned all lines of glass from early pressed practical wares to fancy art glass. New
England's art examples include "Agata," "Amberina," and "Pomona."

Bowl, finger 4¹/₂″, scalloped, Agata style $900
Bowl, 7″, opaque blue $825
Bowl, 8″, opaque green $1350
Bowl, 8¹/₂″, ruffled, amber rim, Pomona style $275
Creamer, Agata style $1350
Cruet with stopper, 5¹/₂″ tall, opaque green $1650
Cruet with white stopper, 5¹/₂″ tall, globe-shaped, ruffled, pink handle, Agata style
. . . . $1650
Paperweight, 2⁵/₈″ diameter, latticino ground, 3 red and white flower buds, green
leaf tips $3500
Paperweight, 2³/₄″ diameter, pink poinsettia with white center and green stem and
leaves, white latticino basket $850
Paperweight, apple with cut slice, 3″ diameter, crystal base (François Pierre) . . $3250
Pitcher, 4¹/₄″ tall, square top, white reeded handle, Agata style $1750
Pitcher, 6¹/₄″ tall, square top, Pomona style, Cornflower design $650
Pitcher, 8¹/₄″ tall, amber top, Pomona style, Cornflower design $550
Pitcher, 10″ tall, pear-shaped, crystal with vertical cleats below the waist . . . $425
Plate, 6¹/₂″, fluted rim, Agata style $900
Punch bowl, 9¹/₄″, amber trim, Pomona style $1500
Punch cup, amber trim, Pomona style $125
Salt dip, 3″ long, 2¹/₈″ tall, 4-footed, floral design, signed $250
Saltshaker, 3³/₄″ tall, Agata style $525
Spooner, 4¹/₂″ tall, opaque green with gold band $1000
Sugar, 3″ tall, 2 handles, gold band of berries and leaves, Pomona style $450
Sugar, 4″ tall, flared, square neck, 2 handles, gold decoration, Agata style . . $1850
Sugar shaker, 4″ tall, ribbed, fig form, lime opal with pink floral design $875
Toothpick holder, square top, Agata style $675
Toothpick holder, gold-stained collar, Pomona style $375

Tray, 12½″ × 7½″, ruffled, gold rim, Stained Cornflower design, Pomona style . . $800
Tumbler, 3¾″ tall, Agata style $750
Tumbler, 3¾″ tall, opaque green with gold band (several styles) $1000
Tumbler, 3¾″ tall, amber top, Pomona style, Cornflower design $250
Tumbler, 4″ tall, Agata style $850
Vase, 4½″ tall, 4 pinched sides, ruffled, crimped, Agata style $2500
Vase, 5¾″ tall, Agata style $2250
Vase, 6″ tall, circular foot, Agata style $2750
Vase, 7″ tall, trumpet-shaped, footed, Amethyst Molded Ovals design $200

ONYX GLASS　　VARIOUS COMPANIES, 1889–EARLY 1900s

The first patent was obtained by George Leighton in 1889 while he worked for Dalzell, Gilmore, and Leighton Company. The design was referred to as "Findlay Onyx." The company experienced difficulties in perfecting a durable formula; the onyx products were brittle and cracked easily. Onyx glass is characterized by parallel layers of colors, at times thin enough to be translucent, as well as lustrous forms of platinum or silver, opal forms, concentric rings on the base, and varying degrees of relief.

Bowl, 4″, red and white floral design $1250
Bowl, 8″, white with silver flowers $1100
Butter dish with cover, 6″ diameter, 4½″ tall, platinum design on cream background $1850
Creamer, raised white opalescent design on red background $1250
Muffineer, 5″, White $550
Paperweight, pig (Findlay) $275
Pitcher, syrup with silver-plated lid, 7½″ tall, metal handle, silver design on ivory background $650
Pitcher, syrup with silver-plated lid, 7″ tall, ivory with gold decoration . . . $650
Sugar shaker, 5″ tall, Light brown $675
Sugar shaker with metal cover, 5¾″ tall, silver flowers on cream background $550
Sugar with cover, 6″ tall, platinum flowers on cream background $750
Sugar with cover, raised white opalescent design $1250
Toothpick holder, raised silver design on ivory background $300
Tumbler, 3½″ tall, white with silver floral design $450
Tumbler, 3¼″ tall, barrel-shaped, silver design on cream background $400
Tumbler, 4″ tall, dark red and white floral design $1250
Vase, 5″ tall, cream with silver floral design $675
Vase, 6½″ tall, raised silver flowers on cream background (Findlay) $750

PAIRPOINT MANUFACTURING COMPANY　　1894–1957

Pairpoint merged with Mt. Washington in 1894. The company produced a variety of items from functional tableware and lamps to fancy art glass and cut designs. Robert Gunderson and Robert Bryden were active with the firm in the mid 20th century.

Bowl, 12″, footed base, Ruby and Blue Twist design $350
Bowl, 14″, footed base, Ruby and Blue Twist design $400

Bowl, 16″, footed base, Ruby and Blue Twist design $450
Bowl, footed, green with crystal swan handles (large) (Gunderson-Pairpoint) ... $375
Bowl, green with crystal swan handles (small) (Gunderson-Pairpoint) $175
Bowl with cover, 8″, 6½″ tall, 2 handles, fish with Chrysanthemum design, signed "Pairpoint Limoges 2502/50" $875
Bowl, bride's, 9″, cut rim, medallion design, footed, silver-plated frame $325
Bowl, bride's, Daisy and Bluebell design, silver-plated holder, signed "Pairpoint" .
.... $775
Bowl, centerpiece, turned down rim, amber with silver overlay $350
Box with hinged cover, oval, cream with gold foliage, signed "Pairpoint" .. $600
Box with hinged cover, oval, scalloped, cream with gold foliage, signed "Pairpoint" $600
Candlestick, 4½″ tall, mushroom top, green with crystal bubble in stem $90
Candlestick, 5″ tall, Ruby and Blue Twist design $250
Candlestick, 10″ tall, engraved floral holder, air twist stem, Veneti design .. $275
Candlestick, 16″ tall, Emerald green $325
Candlestick, prism cut, ball connector, Emerald green $225
Candy dish with cover, engraved Dew Drop design, Canaria pattern, crystal bubble finial $250
Compote, 4¼″ tall, 6″ diameter, ruby with crystal bubble in stem $150
Compote, 4⅝″ tall, 8″ diameter, Ruby and Blue Twist design $225
Compote, 4″ tall, 6″ diameter, Aurora pattern $150
Compote, 5″ tall, ruby with crystal bubble in stem $250
Compote, 6½″ tall, 10½″ diameter, green with crystal bubble in stem $200
Compote, 6½″ tall, 12″ diameter, paperweight base, amber with crystal bubble in stem $200
Compote, 7½″ tall, black with silver overlay $400
Compote, 7¼″ tall, 6¼″ diameter, amber with crystal bubble in stem $200
Compote, 8″ tall, 8″ diameter, floral design, green with crystal ball stem, silver overlay, marked "Rockwell" $300
Compote, upturned foot, Colias pattern, light green with crystal ball connector ...
....$300
Compote with cover, green with crystal bubble connector $175
Cracker jar with cover, melon with gold tracings, signed "Pairpoint" (cover signed "M.W.") $500
Goblet, engraved Grape design, Canaria pattern $150
Hat, 3¼″ tall, opaque pink to blue coloring $90
Lamp, 13¾″ tall, 4-sectioned shade, metal base (tree), enameled apples and apple blossoms $5750
Lamp, 15¾″ tall, frosted domed shade, enameled desert scene (sunset) $3000
Lamp, 21″ tall, metal base, multicolored Leaf design, Grape pattern, shade stamped "The Pairpoint Corp." $3750
Lamp, 21″ tall, 14″ diameter shade, brass base, Floral and Butterfly design, Papillon pattern $4750
Lamp, 24¼″ tall, red domed shade, green and black flower blossoms in relief ....
.... $2000
Lamp, 9¼″ tall, miniature, kerosene, blue and white Windmill design, signed "Delft" $550
Lamp, boudoir, 5″ diameter shade, Rose Bouquet design, tree trunk base, signed "Pairpoint" $2500
Lamp, floor, metal base, signed shade "Garden of Allah" (on reverse) $5000

Lamp, table, 8″ diameter shade, brass base, Dogwood border, signed "Pairpoint" .
. . . . $2750
Paperweight, 7″ tall, crystal fish with bubbles design $90
Paperweight, crystal cut base, yellow Rose design (Bryden-Pairpoint) $225
Pitcher, miniature, 3″ tall, Violet with White design, paper label "Pairpoint-Bryden" $125
Plate, 12″, enameled floral, Spanish galleon, or whale decoration $175
Plate, 8″, enameled floral, Spanish galleon, or whale decoration $110
Powder jar with hinged cover, 6″ diameter, crystal, Viscaria pattern $275
Swan, 12″ tall, crystal head and neck, ruby red body $575
Tumbler, 8″ tall, enameled floral, Spanish galleon, or whale decoration $175
Urn with cover, 6½″ tall, Osiris design, Amethyst, blue, green, and yellow $300
Urn with cover, 6″ tall, Osiris design, Amethyst, blue, green, and yellow . . . $300
Vase, 5″ tall, ruffled, cobalt with crystal bubble in stem $225
Vase, 8″ tall, enameled floral, Spanish galleon, or whale decoration $375
Vase, 8″ tall, Osiris design, various styles and colors (Amethyst, blue, green, and yellow) $225
Vase, 8″ tall, rolled rim, ruby with crystal bubble in stem $225
Vase, 9¾″ tall, cut green to crystal design, Colias pattern $350
Vase, 9″ tall, Osiris design, various styles and colors (Amethyst, blue, green, and yellow) $275
Vase, 9″ tall, ruby cornucopia design with crystal bubble in stem $250
Vase, 9″ tall, village scene, signed "Ambero" $1100
Vase, 10″ tall, Osiris design, various styles and colors (Amethyst, blue, green, and yellow) $325
Vase, 10″ tall, ruby with crystal bubble in stem $350
Vase, 12″ tall, flared, ruby with crystal ball connector $375
Vase, 14½″ tall, Cameo Vintage design, signed $1350
Vase, 15″ tall, amethyst with cover $375
Wine glass, black foot and stem, red bowl, with or without silver overlay . . $125

PEACHBLOW   VARIOUS COMPANIES, 1880s–1950s

"Peachblow" is similar to "Burmese," but the uranium oxide is replaced with cobalt or copper oxide in the general formula. The shading varies from a light grayish-blue at the base to a rose pink or peach at the top. Cobalt generally produces a slightly darker shade than copper. Also like "Burmese," "Peachblow" is found in numerous finishes, patterns, and enamels, tends to be thin and fragile, and is valuable. Unlike "Burmese," it was produced by several companies, including Mt. Washington/Pairpoint/Gunderson, Hobbs, Brocunier, New Martinsville, and New England/Libbey. See Chapter 1 for items produced by Thomas Webb & Sons.

Bottle banjo, 6¼″ tall (Gunderson) $250
Bottle, water, 7″ tall, pyramid shape (Wheeling) $1350
Bowl, 3½″, Applied Leaf design (Gunderson) $150
Bowl, 4½″ diameter, 3″ tall, ruffled, 3-footed, (Mt. Washington) $1600
Bowl, 4″, pinched edge (Mt. Washington) $2600
Bowl, 4″, scalloped, Diamond Quilted pattern (Mt. Washington) $2350
Bowl, 5½″ diameter, 2½″ tall, 10 pleated sides, Wild Rose pattern (New England) .
. . . . $425

Bowl, 8″ diameter, ruffled (New Martinsville) $175
Bowl, 10″, ruffled, ribbed, yellow interior, gilded (Mt. Washington) $650
Bowl, ruffled, sharp, vibrant color (Boston & Sandwich) $450
Bowl, bride's, 10³/₄″ diameter, fluted (New Martinsville) $275
Bowl, finger, 2¹/₂″, crimped, acid finish (New England) $775
Bowl, rose, 5″, floral decoration (New England) $625
Bowl, rose, gold design, marked "World's Fair 1893" (Libbey) $575
Celery dish, 4³/₄″ tall, square top, scalloped (New England) $675
Creamer, cased white interior (Wheeling) $650
Creamer, handled (Mt. Washington) $3250
Cruet with cut stopper, tricornered spout, crystal handle (Wheeling) $1850
Cruet with stopper, 7″ tall, acid finish (Wheeling) $1350
Cup, satin finish (Gunderson) $175
Darner, stocking (New England) $175
Decanter with amber stopper, 9″ tall, amber handle, acid finish (Wheeling) .....
.... $1750
Ewer, 6″ tall (Gunderson) $250
Ewer, 8″ tall, Rigaree decoration (Wheeling) $1600
Hat, 2⁷/₈″, Diamond Quilted pattern (Gunderson) $150
Lamp, 21″ tall, Gone with the Wind style, crystal chimney (Hobbs Brocunier) ....
.... $12500
Lamp, hall, brass frame $1750
Muffineer, 5¹/₂″, (Hobbs Brocunier) $675
Pear, 4¹/₂″ tall, blown, curved stem (New England) $425
Perfume bottle with stopper, enameled apple blossoms (Mt. Washington) $2750
Pitcher, 5″ tall, square top, amber handle (Wheeling) $1250
Pitcher, acidized, yellow handle (Mt. Washington) $3250
Pitcher, syrup with pewter lid, 7″ tall, (Wheeling) $1500
Pitcher, water, 7″ tall, amber handle (Hobbs Brocunier) $1750
Pitcher, water, 8¹/₂″ tall, acid finish (Wheeling) $1500
Pitcher, water, 10″ tall, amber ring handle (Wheeling) $1750
Powder jar with silver-plated lid, 4″ tall, Floral and Leaf design $325
Punch cup, 2″ tall, dull acid finish (New England) $450
Punch cup, amber handle, opaque white handle (Wheeling) $500
Punch cup, gloss finish (New England) $450

"Peachblow" art glass. COURTESY OF THE CORNING
MUSEUM OF GLASS.

"Peachblow" art glass. COURTESY OF THE CORNING MUSEUM OF GLASS.

Saltshaker, 3″ tall $500
Saucer, satin finish (Gunderson) $125
Spooner, 5″ tall, ruffled (New England) $325
Sugar, 2¹/₂″ tall, handled, label (Mt. Washington) $2500
Sugar, enameled "World's Fair 1893" (Libbey) $650
Sugar shaker, 5¹/₂″ tall (New England) $1000
Sugar shaker, 5¹/₂″ tall, ringed neck (Wheeling) $650
Sugar shaker with silver-plated top, 5″ tall, dull acid finish (Wheeling) ... $575
Toothpick holder, 2¹/₂″ tall, square rim, silver-plated holder 5¹/₂″ tall (New England) $825
Toothpick holder, 2¹/₄″ tall, tricornered top, satin finish (New England) $675
Toothpick holder, 2³/₄″ tall, enameled floral design (Mt. Washington) $3750
Tumbler, 3³/₄″ tall, (New England) $700
Tumbler, 4″ tall, acid finish, daisy decoration (Mt. Washington) $2350
Tumbler, dark gloss cobalt finish (Hobbs Brocunier) $425
Vase, 2¹/₄″ tall, miniature, acid finish, gold decoration (Wheeling) $775
Vase, 3 turned-down sides, ruffled (Mt. Washington) $4750
Vase, 3″ tall, applied prunts (Mt. Washington) $300
Vase, 4¹/₂″ diameter, 2¹/₂″ tall, white interior (Hobbs Brocunier) $325
Vase, 4¹/₂″ tall, ruffled, fold-over rim, 5 frosted feet (Boston & Sandwich) $350
Vase, 4¹/₂″ tall, scalloped, flared, ribbed (Mt. Washington) $2750
Vase, 4¹/₄″ tall, crimped (New England) $375
Vase, 6¹/₄″ tall, trumpet-shaped (Mt. Washington) $1750
Vase, 8″ tall, gourd-shape (Wheeling) $850
Vase, 9¹/₄″ tall, trefoil-shaped (Gunderson) $425
Vase, 9″, barrel-shaped, ruffled, enameled birds and leaves and insects (Boston & Sandwich) $375
Vase, 10¹/₂″ tall, crimped, Jack-in-the-Pulpit design (Mt. Washington) $7750
Vase, 10¹/₂″ tall, ruffled, footed (Mt. Washington) $4500
Vase, 10¹/₂″ tall, spangled, 2 applied crystal reeded handles (Hobbs Brocunier) ....
.... $3500
Vase, 10¹/₄″ tall, oval, narrow neck, amber holder with 5 griffins (Hobbs Brocunier)
.... $1850
Vase, 11″ tall, bulbous, dull finish $1250
Vase, 12″ tall, trumpet-shaped, rose to white shading (New England) $1500

Vase, 18″ tall, trumpet shape (New England) $2000
Whiskey tumbler, 2″ tall, acid finish (New England) ....~...... $375

PHOENIX GLASS COMPANY 1880–1950s

Much of the art glass of Phoenix Glass Company is similar to products from
Lalique. Figures have a smooth, satiny, acidized finish and are sometimes colored.
Cameo engraving, pearlized finishes, and heavy etching are also part of Phoenix's
designs. Glass made by Phoenix is also very similar to certain styles produced by
Consolidated, although the colors of Phoenix are limited and more common.

Ashtray, 5½″ long, pearl floral design on coral background $100
Banana dish, Pearl opalescent $200
Bowl, 11″, Tiger Lily design, Yellow $150
Bowl, ruffled, divided, gilded floral design on satin background, Opaque pink ....
.... $425
Bowl, berry with cover, Pearl opalescent $200
Bowl, flower, floral design on pink background $200
Bowl, powder, blue Hummingbird design $150
Candleholder, strawberry shape, 4¼″ tall, Tan $100
Candleholder, water lily shape, 4¾″ tall, green on crystal $125
Candlestick, 6¾″ tall, Bird of Paradise design, Green $150
Candy box, 6½″ diameter, crystal with white violets on a light blue background ..
.... $225
Candy dish with cover, 6¾″ tall, periwinkle blue cameo $175
Centerpiece bowl, footed, diving nudes, crystal $275
Compote, 6″, pedestal base, amethyst pastel, Dolphin design $250
Compote, Fish design, Amber $125
Compote with cover, Pearl opalescent $250
Creamer, Pearl opalescent $150
Lamp, 10½″, Foxglove pattern, Yellow, green, and white $150
Lamp, 14″ tall, Foxglove pattern, marble base, Aqua, orange, and white $250
Pitcher, water, Pearl opalescent $650
Plate, 6¼″, yellow, green, and white chrysanthemums $85
Sugar, Pearl opalescent $150
Sugar with cover, Lacy Dewdrop pattern, Blue $125
Tumbler, Pearl opalescent $275
Vase, 5½″ tall, Hummingbird design, Brown and white $75
Vase, 5″ tall, pearl floral design on light blue background $100
Vase, 6½″ tall, rectangular, frosted, Pair of Lovebirds design $125
Vase, 7″ tall, Fern design, Blue $135
Vase, 8¼″ tall, fan-shaped, bronze-colored grasshopper $250
Vase, 8¾″ tall, milk glass on tan background, Primrose design $225
Vase, 8″ tall, Freesia, flared, crystal satin, sea green background $150
Vase, 8″ tall, frosted, Katydid pattern $125
Vase, 8″ tall, Preying Mantis pattern, Pink $150
Vase, 9½″ tall, two-toned apricot $200
Vase, 9¼″ tall, Fish design, Blue $250
Vase, 9¼″ tall, milk glass, Wild Geese design on blue background $225
Vase, 9¼″ tall, opalescent satin, Wild Geese design $225

Vase, 9$^1/_2$″ tall, 12″ diameter, frosted, Flying Geese design $225
Vase, 10″ tall, frosted Madonna pattern, Dark blue $325
Vase, 11″ tall, brown and green Dogwood design $300
Vase, 11″ tall, bulbous, red ground with iridescent flowers $275
Vase, 11″ tall, cream ground, dancing nudes $550
Vase, 12$^1/_4$″ tall, pink peonies with Turquoise Leaves design $250
Vase, 12″ tall, dancing females in relief, White $275
Vase, 14$^1/_2$″ tall, nudes, Blue and white $650
Vase, 17″ tall, blue ground, Thistle design $575

PIGEON BLOOD   VARIOUS COMPANIES,
LATE 1880s–EARLY 1900s

"Pigeon Blood" is characterized by a transparent deep scarlet red (or blood red). Pieces produced in "Pigeon Blood" tend to have a glossy or shiny finish. Note that the red coloring characteristic of this style was applied to many cut glass patterns.

Bowl, 6″ diameter, gold floral design $100
Bowl, 8$^1/_2$″ tall, 3-footed, crystal feet and handles $200
Butter dish with cover, enameled white floral design $550
Cookie jar with cover, silver-plated cover, handle, and rim, Florette pattern (Consolidated) $325
Creamer, 3$^1/_2$″ tall, enameled floral design $200
Cruet with stopper, 5$^3/_4$″ tall, enameled scrolls $250
Lamp, 10$^1/_2$″ tall $750
Pitcher, 7$^1/_4$″ tall, gilded, ribbed handle, ruffled top (Consolidated) $350
Pitcher, 7″ tall, clear handle $300
Pitcher, milk, 7$^1/_4$″ tall $225
Pitcher, syrup with lid, 4$^3/_4$″ tall $450
Pitcher, tankard-style, 10″ tall, Diamond Quilted pattern $250
Pitcher, water, 11″ tall $500
Salt and pepper shakers (Consolidated) $200
Salt and pepper shakers, several styles $200
Spooner, several styles $100
Sugar dish, 3$^1/_2$″ tall, enameled floral design $200
Sugar shaker, several styles $350
Toothpick holder, Loop pattern $175
Toothpick holder, ribbed $90
Tumbler, enameled design, several styles $90
Vase, 8$^1/_4$″ tall, enameled floral design $225
Vase, 10$^1/_2$″ tall, enameled floral design $250
Wine glass, 6″ tall $50

PINK SLAG   INDIANA TUMBLER & GOBLET COMPANY,
1880s–EARLY 1900s

"Pink Slag" was an opaque pressed glass with swirled or marbleized shading from white to pink. It was used primarily in tableware. The rarest and most valuable pattern was Indiana's "Inverted Fan and Feather." The color is also referred to as "Agate" or "Marble." Offshoots of this marbleized design were produced by other companies in various shades, although the style is not that common. Swirling is not an easy effect to achieve since colors tend to blend together rather than remaining separate or partially mixing.

Bowl, 6½", Inverted Fan and Feather pattern $875
Butter dish with cover, 6" diameter, Inverted Fan and Feather pattern $1250
Compote, 5", Inverted Fan and Feather pattern $750
Creamer, 3½" tall, handled, Inverted Fan and Feather pattern $725
Creamer, 4½" tall, pitcher-style, Inverted Fan and Feather pattern $750
Creamer, 4¾" tall, 4-footed, beaded handle, Inverted Fan and Feather pattern $750
Cruet with stopper, 6" tall, Inverted Fan and Feather pattern $1850
Lamp, 8¼" tall $850
Pitcher, 8" tall, Inverted Fan and Feather pattern $2350
Punch cup, Inverted Fan and Feather pattern $425
Saltshaker with metal top, Inverted Fan and Feather pattern $350
Sauce dish, 2½" tall, ball-shaped feet, Inverted Fan and Feather pattern $375
Spooner, Inverted Fan and Feather pattern $375
Sugar with cover, 4" tall, Inverted Fan and Feather pattern $850
Sugar with cover, 5½" tall, Inverted Fan and Feather pattern $900
Toothpick holder, Inverted Fan and Feather pattern $550
Tumbler, 3½" tall $375
Tumbler, 4" tall, Inverted Fan and Feather pattern $525
Tumbler, Grape and Vine design $225

QUEZAL ART GLASS AND DECORATING COMPANY
1901–1920s

Quezal was founded by Martin Bach and Thomas Johnson, who had worked for Tiffany. The company's products, therefore, are very similar to Tiffany's. Brilliant, iridescent forms of blue, gold, white, and green were much like "Favrile." "Quezal" was patented in 1902, and the name was often engraved in silver block letters on the underside; pieces not signed are confused with both Tiffany and Steuben.

Bowl, 6", ruffled, Iridescent gold $325
Bowl, 7", fluted, Iridescent gold $525
Compote, 6", pedestal base, signed, Iridescent gold $400
Compote, 7", thin stem, signed, Iridescent gold $425
Cup, scroll handle, signed, Iridescent gold $375
Lamp, 6" tall, bronze feet, signed, Iridescent gold $1250
Lamp, 28" tall, onyx and metal base and stand, ribbed opal shade with gold leaf and green bands, 5" shade that is signed twice $1000
Lamp, double, claw feet, pearlized base, calcite with gold interior $800
Perfume bottle with stopper, 8" tall, 4-sided cone shape, Iridescent gold . . . $375
Salt dip, 1¾", scalloped, ribbed, Iridescent gold $150
Salt dip, 2¾" tall, signed "Quezal," Gold $275
Saucer, 7", stretched, Iridescent gold $325
Sconce, double branched, gilded, 5" shades $525

Shade, 13¹/₂" tall, green pulled feathers with gold lining, signed "Quezal" . . . .
. . . . $1000
Shade, 4¹/₂" diameter, yellow with gold lining $325
Shade, 4³/₄" diameter, ribbed, iridescent gold with colored highlights $175
Shade, 6³/₄" tall, iridescent green with gold lining, King Tut pattern $1100
Shade, 6" tall, iridescent gold with blue and violet highlights $225
Shade, 7³/₄" tall, bullet-shaped, opal with green feathers and gold edging . . . $650
Shade, 7" tall, flared, ribbed sides, signed "Quezal," Yellow $300
Shade, 8³/₈" tall, opal with yellow feathers $750
Spittoon, 3¹/₂" tall, bulbous, latticed green and white with gold feathers, marked
"Quezal S 813" $575
Vase, 4¹/₂" tall, ruffled and stretched rim, signed $500
Vase, 4" tall, ivory with gold and green Feather design $1250
Vase, 5" tall, gold leaves, Iridescent dark blue $1400
Vase, 6" tall, Lightning design, Iridescent reddish gold $1500
Vase, 7³/₄" tall, gold rim, green with silver feathers, signed "Quezal 12" . . . $1250
Vase, 7" tall, footed, fluted, and crackle rim, amber with white leaves and green
edge, marked "Quezal 167" $1250
Vase, 7" tall, signed "Quezal," Iridescent blue $550
Vase, 8¹/₂" tall, Jack-in-the-Pulpit style, overhanging rim, footed, iridescent gold
with yellow leaves, inscribed "Quezal" $1250
Vase, 8³/₄" tall, ruffled, iridescent green with gold lining and gold feathers, signed .
. . . . $1250
Vase, 10" tall, iridescent gold with silver overlay $1100
Vase, 11" tall, trumpet, ribbed, white with gold lattice and gold interior, marked
"Quezal 6" $1000
Vase, 12" tall, 9" diameter, Banded Floral and Feather design, gold interior, marked
"Quezal #437" $6500
Vase, 13¹/₂" tall, Jack-in-the-Pulpit style, Amber $4500
Vase, 15" tall, Jack-in-the-Pulpit style, white with gold and green Feather design . .
. . . .$5500
Wine glass, 6" tall, signed, Iridescent gold $475

READING ARTISTIC GLASS WORKS   1884–1886

Although it went bankrupt after two years, Reading did manage to produce some
fine art glass. Amberina, opalescent, and decorated cut patterns were made. The
opalescent colors are particularly noteworthy and are found in beautiful blues,
greens, pinks, purples, and whites.

Bowl, 6", ruffled, Opalescent blue $200
Carafe, 10¹/₂" tall, red with crystal spout $275
Ewer, 13" tall, red with clear spout $275
Pitcher, water, 10¹/₂" tall, Thumbprint pattern, Pink $425
Pitcher, water, 11" tall, pink and white frosted Coin Dot design $450
Vase, 7³/₄" tall, overshot, blue opal $450
Vase, 9¹/₂" tall, pink with dark red opalescent neck $800

RUBENA OR RUBINA CRYSTAL VARIOUS COMPANIES, 1880s–1890s

"Rubena" is characterized by a gradual shading from crystal at the bottom to ruby red at the top. Some pieces have shading that is not gradual but have a distinct line of color separation. Pieces may also be accented with clear crystal (handles, lids, stoppers, feet, etc.). Many cut patterns were decorated with "Rubena" shading. George Duncan & Sons is credited with the introduction of this type of crystal.

Basket, 6″ tall, 4″ diameter $150
Bowl, 5½″, Inverted Thumbprint pattern $125
Bowl, 6½″, frosted $125
Bowl, 8″, Royal Ivy pattern $150
Bowl, 9″, frosted, Royal Ivy pattern $175
Bowl, oval, 9½″, overshot $225
Bowl, rose, 5½″, 4¾″ tall, Gold Floral design $175
Butter dish with cover, 7″ tall, gilded, signed "Northwood" $300
Butter dish with cover, frosted, Royal Ivy pattern $275
Candlestick, 9″ tall, cranberry to clear coloring $125
Carafe, water, 8″ tall, cranberry to clear coloring $225
Castor set, pickle dish with silver-plated holder and tongs (Northwood) $350
Castor set, pickle dish, silver-plated frame and cover, frosted insert $375
Cheese dish with cover, 6½″ tall, 10″ diameter $350
Compote, 8½″ tall, footed, Honeycomb pattern $225
Condiment set, 4-piece, 2 square bottles, rectangular salt dip, silver-plated holder $350
Cookie jar with cover, 9½″ tall, ribbed $375
Creamer, frosted, Royal Ivy pattern $250
Creamer, frosted, Royal Oak pattern $350
Creamer, Royal Oak pattern $175
Cruet with cut crystal stopper, 6″ tall, overshot $500
Cruet with stopper, 5½″ tall, Royal Oak pattern $600
Cruet with stopper, 5¼″ tall, frosted, Royal Ivy pattern $450
Cruet with stopper, 10″ tall $100
Decanter with stopper, 8″ tall, signed "Northwood" $400
Ice bucket, silver handle, enameled $175
Jam jar with cover, Swirl pattern $225
Jelly dish, triangular, crimped, silver-plated holder $250
Mug, 3¾″ tall, octagonal, gold and silver trim $100
Mustard jar with silver-plated cover, enameled floral design, Thumbprint pattern $225
Perfume bottle with faceted stopper, 5¾″ tall $200
Perfume bottle with silver-plated stopper, Diamond Quilted and Drape pattern $175
Pitcher, syrup with metal lid, 4¾″ tall $450
Pitcher, syrup with metal lid, 5¼″ tall, Inverted Thumbprint pattern $325
Pitcher, syrup with metal lid, 5¼″ tall, Royal Ivy pattern $425
Pitcher, water, 8½″ tall, Royal Ivy pattern $600
Pitcher, water, 8½″ tall, Royal Oak pattern $525
Punch cup, 4¼″ tall $75
Salt and pepper shakers, frosted, Royal Ivy pattern $175

Salt and pepper shakers, Royal Oak pattern $225
Salt dip, 2″ tall, hexagonal, silver-plated stand $150
Salt shaker, threaded (Northwood) $150
Sauce dish, several styles $60
Spooner, frosted, Royal Ivy pattern $125
Spooner, frosted, Royal Oak pattern $150
Sugar, frosted, Royal Ivy pattern $150
Sugar shaker, frosted, 5¼″ tall, Royal Ivy pattern $275
Sugar shaker, frosted, 5¼″ tall, Royal Oak pattern $275
Sugar with cover, frosted, Royal Oak pattern $425
Sugar with cover, Royal Oak pattern $225
Toothpick holder, several styles $175
Tumbler, 6″ tall, Royal Ivy pattern $135
Tumbler, enameled design, 6″ tall, inverted Thumbprint pattern $110
Tumbler, enameled floral design, 5½″ tall, Diamond Quilted pattern $100
Tumbler, frosted, 6″ tall, Royal Oak pattern $135
Vase, 8¾″ tall, trumpet-shaped, ruffled, gold floral decoration $250
Vase, 8″ tall, enameled floral decoration $175
Vase, 8″ tall, pedestal foot, ribbed, flared $125
Vase, 10″ tall, footed, applied crystal decoration $200
Vase, 13″ tall, trumpet-shaped, crystal pedestal foot, crystal applied threading ....
.... $250

RUBENA VERDE OR RUBINA VERDE   VARIOUS COMPANIES, 1880s–1890s

"Rubena Verde" is similar to many of the other shaded designs, such as "Amberina," and "Rubena Crystal." The colors in "Rubena Verde" vary from aqua green or greenish-yellow at the base, to ruby red at the top. Hobbs Brocunier is usually noted as the original maker.

Basket, bride's, 8″ diameter, Hobnail pattern $550
Basket, bride's, 8″ diameter, silver-plated holder $300
Bowl, 4¼″, ruffled, Hobnail pattern $125
Bowl, 4″, threaded design $110
Bowl, 7″, scalloped, enameled gold decorations $225
Bowl, 8″, 3-footed, Circle pattern (Hobbs Brocunier) $250
Bowl, rose, 5″, crimped, Hobnail pattern $150
Cheese dish, with yellow ball stopper and yellow matching underplate, Circle pattern (Hobbs Brocunier) $350
Creamer, 5″ tall, reeded handle, Inverted Thumbprint pattern $475
Cruet with stopper, 4″ tall, rounded design, Inverted Thumbprint pattern .. $525
Cruet with stopper, 6¾″ tall, triple-lipped top, Inverted Thumbprint pattern $575
Cruet with stopper, frosted, Hobnail pattern (Hobbs Brocunier) $500
Cup with yellow handle, Circle pattern (Hobbs Brocunier) $100
Epergne, 22″ tall, trumpet in center of bowl, hanging baskets $550
Perfume bottle with stopper, no handle, 5½″ tall, Inverted Thumbprint pattern (Hobbs Brocunier) $500
Pitcher, syrup with lid, Hobnail pattern $275
Pitcher, syrup with silver-plated lid, 5″ tall, Inverted Thumbprint pattern .. $250

Pitcher, water, 7¹/₂″ tall, enameled floral design $550
Pitcher, water, 8″ tall, clear handle, tricornered lip, enameled Daisy design . $500
Pitcher, water, 8″ tall, square top, greenish-yellow handle, Hobnail pattern . $475
Pitcher, water, 9″ tall, Inverted Thumbprint pattern $575
Salt and pepper shakers, 4¹/₂″ tall, pewter tops, enameled floral design $300
Sweetmeat dish, 5³/₄″ tall, octagonal, notched edge, greenish-yellow trim, silver-plated holder $200
Tumbler, 4″ tall, Diamond Quilted pattern $175
Tumbler, 4″ tall, Hobnail pattern $275
Vase, 6¹/₂″ tall, scalloped, Reverse Color pattern $200
Vase, 6³/₄″ tall, crimped, footed $150
Vase, 6″ tall, ruffled $175
Vase, 8″ tall, Jack-in-the-Pulpit style, applied greenish-yellow feet $200
Vase, 9¹/₄″ tall, pedestal feet, Drape pattern $225
Vase, 11″ tall, ruffled, green rim, Drape pattern $375
Wine glass, 4¹/₄″ tall, Inverted Thumbprint pattern $175
Witchball with chain, Hobnail pattern (Hobbs Brocunier) $125

SATIN GLASS VARIOUS COMPANIES, 1880s–EARLY 1900s

"Satin" is opaque milk, opal, or colored glass with a distinctive white lining. The satin texture or finish was created by a thin coating or washing with hydrofluoric acid.

Bell, 6″ tall, Blue $60
Biscuit jar with silver-plated cover and handle, 7″ tall, Pink Florette pattern $375
Biscuit jar with silver-plated cover and handle, 9″ tall, White Floral pattern $225
Bowl, 6¹/₂″ tall, 3-lobed rim, olive green with white interior, gold floral design $250
Bowl, 8″, ruffled, rainbow colors $300
Bowl, finger, 4¹/₂″ tall, Diamond Quilted pattern $60
Bowl, rose, 3¹/₂″, 3¹/₄″ tall, 8-crimped, blue overlay with embossed floral design $175
Cookie jar with silver-plated cover, 8″ tall, 5″ diameter, Shell and Seaweed overlay design $450
Creamer, marked "World's Fair—1893" (New England), Blue $400
Cruet with stopper, 7″ tall, multicolored $450
Epergne, 18″ tall, enameled bird and floral design $400
Ewer, 8¹/₂″ tall, swirled white with multicolored enameled stripes $500
Ewer, 9³/₄″ tall, blue with frosted handle, enameled flower design $275
Ewer, 12³/₄″ tall, pedestal foot, frosted handle, enameled flower design $425
Lamp, 8¹/₂″ tall, Gone with the Wind style, brass foot, red with 2 winged griffins on each globe $750
Lamp, miniature, 5″ tall, ruffled base and shade, swirled pink design $500
Lamp, miniature, 8¹/₂″ tall, globe shade, square base, red with crystal chimney, Drape pattern $475
Pitcher, milk, 6¹/₂″ tall, Diamond Quilted pattern, Blue $800
Pitcher, water, square top, reeded handle, white liner $375

Spittoon, white casing on light blue background $175
Sugar, marked "World's Fair—1893" (New England) $375
Sugar shaker, 4″ tall, blue with embossed leaf design $325
Toothpick holder, 3¼″ tall, blue and white enameled design $150
Vase, 6½″ tall, footed, ribbed, pink overlay with enameled floral design $125
Vase, 6″ tall, conical, ribbed, ruffled, Blue $150
Vase, 7½″ tall, acid cutback squares, pink overlay with enameled Floral design ...
.... $275
Vase, 7″ tall, gourd-shaped, light blue to turquoise coloring $275
Vase, 8″ tall, gourd-shaped, Blue $175
Vase, 8″ tall, ribbed, white with green lining $200
Vase, 9″ tall, blue overlay with gold scrolls and enameled floral design $200
Vase, 10½″ tall, peach overlay with enameled floral design $225
Vase, 11″ tall, ribbed, blue overlay with enameled floral and jewel design ... $225
Vase, 18″ tall, iris decoration, Blue $400
Vase, ruffled, pink and white swirls, white lining (Mt. Washington) $525

SINCLAIRE, H.P. COMPANY   1904–1930s

Sinclaire was primarily a producer of cut, engraved, and etched glassware. It obtained blanks early on from some of the best lead crystal makers (Corning, Dorflinger, Baccarat, etc.), but after 1920, the company produced its own blanks. In the 1920s, Sinclaire created many art glass pieces in various colors, using a style similar to that of Steuben.

Bowl, 10″, pedestal foot, black with white edge, signed $350
Bowl, 11½″, pink with etched floral design $225
Bowl, 11″, ruffled, blue with etched floral design $200
Candlestick, 7½″ tall, blue with etched scrolls $75
Candlestick, 8″ tall, dark amber etched design, signed $85
Candlestick, 9½″ tall, yellow with etched floral design $110
Candlestick, 10¼″ tall, swirl ribbed, light green, signed $85
Candlestick, 10″ tall, crystal, engraved Vintage pattern, signed $110
Cologne bottle with stopper, 5¼″ tall, etched floral design, signed $350
Compote, etched design, signed, Dark amber $200
Compote, rolled rim, pedestal foot, Light green $150
Pitcher, green with amber handle, etched Vintage pattern $325
Plate, 8½″ tall, Leaf design, Amber $55
Tumbler, green with amber base, etched Vintage pattern $85
Vase, 5½″ tall, 4″ diameter, interior ribbing, amethyst $85
Vase, 6″ tall, amethyst to crystal coloring, Lily pattern $250
Vase, 12″ tall, crystal, etched flower and foliage design $225
Vase, 13½″ tall, crystal, etched Tulip design $250
Wine glass, green to crystal coloring, Duchess pattern $85

SMITH BROTHERS   1870s–EARLY 1900s

The Smith Brothers (Harry and Alfred) were originally part of a decorating department at Mt. Washington. They formed their own decorating company but still used many blanks provided by their previous employer. Smith Brothers was noted for many cut, engraved, and enameled floral patterns. The company also produced decorated glass in a variety of popular designs.

Bowl, 4″, purple rim, floral design $250
Bowl, 5¹/₂″, beaded edge, blue and purple floral design $400
Bowl, 7¹/₂″, blue and white floral design, gold rim $475
Bowl, 8″, green and white floral design gilding $675
Box with cover, square, 3¹/₄″ × 3¹/₄″, pink and white floral design $375
Cookie jar with cover, 7¹/₄″ tall, pink and white floral design $850
Cookie jar with cover, 8¹/₂″ tall, multicolored floral design on cream background, signed $1250
Cracker jar, cube-shaped, silver-plated cover and handle, enameled Crab design $850
Cracker jar with cover, 7″ tall, silver-plated top, ridge, and handle, various enameled floral and foliage designs $750
Creamer, cream with enameled gold flowers $325
Creamer, cream with enameled lady's or soldier's head, silver-plated handle, various enameled floral designs $350
Humidor with cover, 6″ tall, 5″ diameter, Pansy design on body and cover . $275
Humidor with silver-plated cover, 7″ tall, cream, floral design, signed $675
Lamp shade, various enameled floral and foliage designs $150
Mustard dish, handled, Pansy design, signed $250
Mustard jar with silver-plated hinged cover, silver-plated handle, various enameled floral and foliage designs $225
Plate, 6³/₈″, ship design (Santa Maria) $650
Plate, 7″, Ship design $650
Salt bowl, various enameled floral designs $85
Salt shaker, egg-shaped, various enameled floral designs $150
Salt shaker, various enameled floral designs $125
Sugar shaker, 3″ tall, ribbed, silver-plated top, white with purple columbines $650
Sugar with silver-plated cover, cream with gold enameled flowers, silver-plated handle $375
Sugar with silver-plated cover, cream with gold enameled lady's or soldier's head, silver-plated handle $375
Sweetmeat dish, raised gold, enameled pansies, Rampant Lion mark $475
Toothpick holder, vertical ribbed (columns), white with enameled flowers . $175
Vase, 2¹/₂″ tall, ribbed, Daisy design, signed $375
Vase, 2¹/₂″ tall, ribbed, gold lettering "Season's Greetings," signed $375
Vase, 4¹/₂″ tall, pinched sides, Carnation design $475
Vase, 5″ tall, cream with enameled flowers, signed $350
Vase, 7³/₄″ tall, cream with birds and floral design, signed $625
Vase, 8¹/₂″ tall, flask-style, enameled ship (Santa Maria), signed $1350
Vase, 8¹/₂″ tall, Floral Mum design, signed $775
Vase, 9″ tall, cylindrical, enameled Bird design, signed $350
Vase, 10″ tall, banded glass at top and bottom, enameled Bird and Reed design, Pink $300

SPATTER GLASS   VARIOUS COMPANIES, 1880s–EARLY 1900s

"Spatter" refers to spotted or multicolored glass that has a white inner casing and crystal outer casing. At times, leftover colored glass was combined and blown into a mold to create a splotching or spattering effect. Many objects of a whimsical nature were produced in this fashion.

Basket, 8¼" tall, green spatter, white lining $250
Basket, bride's, 10" tall, crimped, rainbow spatter $200
Bowl, 6½", blue spatter, white interior $150
Bowl, 8", pink spatter $175
Bowl, 10", pleated top, blue spatter $175
Bowl, rose, 4½" tall, blue spatter $85
Candlestick, 8½" tall, pink spatter on white background $110
Candlestick, 8" tall, rainbow spatter on blue background $85
Candy jar with cover, 6¼" tall, 3½" diameter, yellow and blue spatter, enameled floral design $175
Cruet with stopper, 7½" tall, blue and yellow spatter $275
Cruet with stopper, 8" tall, crystal handle, blue and white spatter (Mt. Washington) $300
Decanter with crystal faceted stopper, 10" tall, pinched sides, red and white spatter $250
Pitcher, milk, 5½" tall, cranberry and frosted coloring with rainbow swirled spatter $300
Pitcher, water, 8¼" tall, blue and white spatter $250
Pitcher, water, 8" tall, rainbow spatter on blue background $250
Rolling pin, 15" long, 2" diameter, white with maroon and cobalt blue spatter $225
Salt dip, 1¾" tall, crystal footed, blue and white spatter $100
Toothpick holder, 2½" tall, rainbow spatter on red background $125
Tumbler, 5¾" tall, green and white spatter $85
Vase, 5¼" tall, blue and white spatter $125
Vase, 6" tall, speckled pink and white spatter $125
Vase, 6" tall, yellow casing with gold spatter $125
Vase, 8¾" tall, flared, pink, white, and red spatter $150
Vase, 8" tall, white lining, rainbow spatter $150
Vase, 9" tall, crystal thorn handles, rainbow spatter $175
Vase, 10½" tall, pink, white, and red spatter $175
Vase, 11" tall, ruffled, blue spatter $200
Vase, 12" tall, 3-petal top, yellow and white with enameled floral design ... $200

STEUBEN GLASS WORKS   1904–1933

Few names command attention in the art glass world as Frederick Carder and Thomas J. Hawkes, who formed Steuben. Hawkes was a maker of superb crystal, while Carder, like Tiffany, studied the art movement in Europe as well as various art styles from around the world. Carder became a world-class designer, and the bulk of Steuben's art glass creations is attributed to him. Most pieces were signed

"Steuben" or with Carder's signature. See "Aurene" for additional Steuben listings. See also Chapter 7 for Crystal Steuben listings since 1933.

Ashtray, topaz with blue leaf handle, signed $175
Bowl, 11″, Pomona green $175
Bowl, 4³/₄″ diameter, 11″ tall, air-trapped mica flecks, silverina design $1000
Bowl, 4″, blue to alabaster shading, acid cut back $2000
Bowl, 4-lobed, wavy rim, vertical ribbed, green to clear shading, stamped "Steuben" $375
Bowl, 6¹/₂″ diameter, 12″ tall, cranberry to clear shading $400
Bowl, 6″ tall, pedestal base, bubbled crystal $300
Bowl, 8″ tall, acid cutback, plum jade $2550
Bowl, footed, green pomona foot, Oriental Poppy design, signed "Steuben" ... $1100
Bowl, centerpiece, 13″ diameter, signed "Steuben," Selenium red $650
Bowl, centerpiece, acid cutback, etched York pattern, Jade $2750
Bowl, centerpiece, footed, Bristol yellow, signed $850
Bowl, centerpiece, topaz with floral design, signed $550
Candelabra, 14¹/₂″ tall, Silverina design $575
Candelabra, lamp-style, double, rib swirled flame center, Flemish blue design ...
.... $475
Candlestick, 6″ tall, acid cutback, jade green on alabaster background, Rose pattern $275
Candlestick, 10″ tall, double twist stem, Amber $250
Candlestick, 12″ tall, ribbed, dome foot, double ball stem, Amber $225
Candlestick, 14″ tall, swan stem, Venetian style, Green $200
Candlestick, airtraps, Silverina design, signed, Amethyst $250
Candlestick, alabaster foot, Roslaine designed cup, signed $200
Candy dish with cover, 6″ tall, pedestal base, Blue and topaz $250
Chalice, 12″ tall, griffin handles, snake stem, cobalt with gold foil and white streaks
.... $375
Champagne glass, 5³/₄″ tall, crystal twist stem, black rim, Cerise design $250
Champagne glass, 6¹/₄″ tall, Oriental Poppy design, signed $475

Steuben art glass. PHOTO BY ROBIN RAINWATER.

Compote, iridescent with stripes, Rose Cintra design, Venetian style, applied prunts, green rim $275
Compote with cover, 12″ tall, Venetian style, paperweight pear finial, signed "F. Carder—Steuben," Topaz $400
Cordial, 4³/₄″ tall, knobbed baluster stem, Selenium red $225
Goblet, 6″ tall, signed, Pomona green $100
Goblet, 6″ tall, Verre de Soie design $110
Goblet, 7¹/₈″ tall, Cintra design stem and border, opalescent, signed $350
Goblet, 7″ tall, threaded design, signed, Green $175
Goblet, 9″ tall, twisted amethyst stem, crystal bowl $200
Lamp, 17″ tall, calcite with gold and green feathers $2750
Lamp base, 14″ tall, acid cutback, Oriental design, Plum jade $1750
Lamp, marble base with 2 bronze nudes (kneeling), Moss Agate design ... $3500
Mug, 6″ tall, footed, crystal with green handle and decoration, Matsu-no-ke design $375
Nude, figural, black jade with knees in crystal circle $1500
Parfait, 6¹/₂″ tall, stemmed, Rosaline and Alabaster design $225
Pear, 5¹/₄″ tall, blown, jet black, marked "F. Carder—Steuben" $575
Perfume bottle with green stopper, 4″ tall, bulbous, Verre de Soie design $475
Perfume bottle with stopper, 12″ tall, Celeste blue $575
Perfume bottle with stopper, Bristol yellow with black threading, signed $275
Plaque, 5¹/₂″ square, mottled green and white with flesh-toned bare-breasted woman, Pâte de Verre design, signed "F. Carder 1915" $1750
Plaque, 8″ × 6¹/₂″, Thomas Edison $875
Plate, 8¹/₂″, Jade green $125
Plate, 8¹/₂″, crystal with amethyst rim, signed $175
Plate, 8¹/₄″, copper wheel–engraved rim, Marina blue design $175
Plate, 8″, crystal with black threading $100
Plate, 8″, intaglio border, crystal to amethyst coloring $150
Powder jar with cover, Rosa design, signed $175
Salt dip, Verre de Soie design $150
Shade, bell-shaped, Verre de Soie design $150
Shade, calcite with acid etched gold design $200
Shade, opal, yellow feathering outlined in green, gold lining $200
Sherbet with matching underplate, Jade green design $175
Sugar shaker, 8″ tall, Verre de Soie design $500
Tumbler, 5″ tall, amber with Flemish blue rim $125
Tumbler, 5″ tall, rainbow iridescence, Verre de Soie design $125
Urn, 13″ tall, banjo-shaped, footed, Venetian style, Topaz $250
Vase, 5″ tall, Selenium red design $275
Vase, 5″ tall, yellow to white Cluthra design $775
Vase, 6¹/₂″ tall, footed, opaque white swirls, Oriental Jade design $350
Vase, 6¹/₂″ tall, Jack-in-the-Pulpit, iridescent Ivrene design, signed $525
Vase, 6″ tall, acid cutback, black jade on alabaster, Pussy Willow design, signed $2250
Vase, 6″ tall, pedestal foot, ruffled, ribbed, iridescent, Ivrene design $425
Vase, 6″ tall, trumpet-shaped, alabaster pedestal foot, Rosaline design, signed $275
Vase, 6″ tall, trumpet-shaped, footed, Ivrene design, signed $425
Vase, 7¹/₂″ tall, crystal, acid finish, Diatreta Geometric design $17500
Vase, 7″ tall, thorned, 3-pronged, Emerald Green design $400

Vase, 8¼″ tall, trumpet-shaped, domed pedestal foot, ribbed, Celeste Blue design .
.... $350
Vase, 8″ tall, acid cutback, alabaster to jade shading $850
Vase, 8″ tall, acid cutback, alabaster, jade green rim $900
Vase, 8″ tall, white Cluthra design, signed $1500
Vase, 9¼″ tall, alabaster foot, engraved floral Rosaline design $950
Vase, 9¼″ tall, pedestal foot, engraved floral Rosaline design $850
Vase, 10¼″ tall, inverted lip, ribbed, Ivory design, signed $375
Vase, 10¾″ tall, footed, amber with variegated greens and blues, signed ... $1250
Vase, 10″ tall, flat oval-shaped, large bubbles, dark red to white shading, Cluthra design $1250
Vase, 11½″ tall, green to yellow jade shading, acid cutback $1750
Vase, 12″ tall, Floriform, ivory with black trim $1250
Vase, 13½″ tall, Tyrian design, signed $10500
Vase, 13″ tall, trumpet-shaped, fluted, green Florentia design, signed $2000
Vase, 14″ tall, blue jade, alabaster and black swirls, acid cutback, signed "F. Carder" $5750
Vase, 16″ tall, folded rim, optic ribs, Marina Blue design $500
Vase, fish attached to pedestal, signed "Steuben," Red $250
Wine glass, 4¾″ tall, ribbed, inverted baluster stem, Topaz $150
Wine glass, 7¼″ tall, twisted stem, jade and alabaster, signed $175
Wine glass, 8½″ tall, 2 knobs, circular foot, oval bowl with molded bubbles and threading, transparent green, marked "Steuben" $125
Wine glass, green swirled, signed $175

TIFFANY LAMPS   1870s–1920s

Some of the larger Tiffany Lamps are now commanding auction prices of $100,000 or more. Reproductions pose some problems, so fraudulent copies should be considered for. Most of the original lamps are signed "L.C.T.," Louis C. Tiffany," "Tiffany Studios," or other titles containing the word "Tiffany." See the "Favrile" section for additional lamp entries.

Candelabrum, 15″, 6-branched, green glass cabochons, snuffer in central handle, circular mark $4000
Ceiling fixture, 17″, iridescent gold shades inscribed "L.C.T." $3500
Chandelier, 22″ diameter, multicolored hanging Head Dragonfly design, impressed "Tiffany Studios New York" $35000
Chandelier, 24″ diameter, pink and blue Iris Blossom design, impressed "Tiffany Studios New York" $30000
Chandelier, 25″ diameter, multicolored Rose Bush design, impressed "Tiffany Studios New York" $30000
Chandelier, 25″ diameter, multicolored Wisteria design, impressed "Tiffany Studios New York" $37500
Chandelier, 27″ diameter, multicolored Fish design, impressed "Tiffany Studios New York" $32500
Chandelier, 30″ diameter, multicolored Grape Trellis design, impressed "Tiffany Studios New York" $47500
Lamp, 13½″ tall, bronze base and stem with iridescent green shade, Pine Needle design $2500

Tiffany art glass lamp. PHOTO BY ROBIN RAINWATER.

Tiffany art glass lamp. PHOTO BY MARK PICKVET, COURTESY OF THE CHICAGO ART INSTITUTE.

Lamp, 15″ tall, bronze base and stem, 9″ globe shade with carved butterflies and dragonflies $5250
Lamp, 14″ tall, Daffodil design, Iridescent gold $7500
Lamp, 16½″, leaded amethyst and green shade, white and yellow roses and butterflies $8500
Lamp, 16¾″, pony white wisteria with pink and green florals $25000
Lamp, 16″, leaded acorn, green and white shade, signed $4250
Lamp, 16″, red, amber, and green shaded Canterbury bells, signed $12500

Lamp, 18″, deep violet 16″ dragonfly shade, glass base enclosing fuel canister, 5 dragonflies and floral design in relief on base, impressed "Tiffany Studios New York" $95000

Lamp, 20″, 14″ blue and green dragonfly designed shade, impressed "Tiffany Studios New York" $60000

Lamp, 31½″, 10″ diameter globe shade, multicolored Autumn Leaf design $47500

Lamp, bronze desk, 11¼″ tall, Turtle-Back Tile design, top hook for hanging, impressed "Tiffany Studios New York" $10500

Lamp, bronze desk, 14½″ tall, adjustable oval shade, circular cast foot, green glass cabochons, green floral design, impressed "408 Tiffany Studios New York" $2750

Lamp, bronze desk, 29½″, twin green hemispherical shades, bronze base, gravity-feed fuel cansiter $3500

Lamp, bronze floor, 63″, leaded glass Turtle-Back Tile design 20″ shade, impressed "Tiffany Studios New York" $17500

Lamp, bronze floor, 64½″, leaded domical shade, 4-footed base, impressed "Tiffany Studios New York" $12500

Lamp, bronze floor, 68″, 27″ red and yellow salamander shade, impressed "Tiffany Studios New York" $47500

Lamp, bronze floor, 79″, gold patina base, 24″ shade with yellow flower clusters and green leaves on a blue ground, impressed "Tiffany Studios New York" $80000

Lamp, bronze table, 20½″, 16″ multicolored bamboo designed shade, impressed "Tiffany Studios New York" $37500

Lamp, bronze table, 21½″, seven lily-shaped gold globes, base marked "Tiffany Studios New York" $11500

Lamp, bronze table, 21¼″, leaded shade, 4 raised feet, orange acorns, green panels, marked "Tiffany Studios New York" $2750

Lamp, bronze table, 22″, multicolored 16″ fish design shade $26500

Lamp, bronze table, 23¼″, leaded shade, 5 ball-feet, multicolored dragonflies, stamped "Tiffany Studios New York" $12500

Lamp, bronze table, 26½″, leaded domical shade, 4-footed bronze base, pink and blue flowers, yellow centers, impressed "Tiffany Studios New York 1475–13" $27500

Lamp, bronze table, 27½″, leaded domical shade, bronze treeform base, blue flowers with bright green and yellow leaves, signed "Tiffany Studios New York" $55000

Lamp, bronze table, 26″, leaded hemispherical shade "558", bronze base "366," multicolored floral and leaf design, impressed "Tiffany Studios" $12500

Lamp, candle, 12″ tall, gold candlestick, green Acorn design, signed, Amber $7500

Lamp, candle, 13″ tall, gold shade, ruffled, gold candlestick, opal insert, green Feather design, signed $1750

Lamp, candle, 13″ tall, Turtle-Back Tile design, impressed "Tiffany Studios New York" $7750

Lamp, candle, 5″ tall, Turtle-Back Tile design, impressed "Tiffany Studios New York" $6500

Lamp, desk, 13″ tall, iridescent green and gold shade $4000

Lamp, electric candle, 15″ tall, gold shade, opal and green riser, signed on base and shade $2000

Lamp, Gone with the Wind style, 15″ tall, signed shade, signed bronze base, off-white satin background, orange feathers, signed "Tiffany Studios" $4000

Lamp, table, 13″ tall, globular shade, iridescent blue portrait style $2500

Lamp, table, 20¼" tall, feathered green and white shade, lily pad vase, marked "Tiffany Studios New York 381" $8500
Lamp, table, 22", leaded yellow daffodil shade, urn-shaped base, blue to green shading, green base, signed "Grueby" on base $17500
Lamp, table, 22", Spider Web, Apple Blossom design, signed $15000

TIFFANY, LOUIS COMFORT   1880s–1920s

Tiffany was leader of the Art Nouveau movement in the United States and one of the developers of art glass. His work was characterized by color effects, iridescent forms, expensive metallic designs, and original art styles. See "Favrile" and "Tiffany Lamps" for additional entries.

Bonbon dish, 4" diameter, iridescent yellow-orange with opalescent foot and stem, signed $375
Bowl, 5", ruffled, Blue $650
Bowl, 7", ruffled, intaglio cut, Iridescent gold $850
Bowl, 10", iridescent gold with green ivy, 2 flower frogs $800
Bowl, 12", footed, signed, Opal and yellow $1000
Bowl, 12", centerpiece, Opalescent pastel blue $1250
Bowl, finger, matching underplate, ruffled, ribbed, signed, Iridescent gold .. $150
Candelabrum, 2-light, 12", bronze with green glass inserts $1500
Candlestick, 8" tall, signed, Iridescent gold $325
Chalice, 11" tall, iridescent gold with green leaves $1500
Cologne bottle with double-lobed stopper, 10" tall, signed $1250
Compote, 12" diameter, stemmed, signed, Blue $1250
Cordial, 1½" tall, signed, Iridescent gold $325
Decanter with stopper, 8¾" tall, Merovingian pattern, Gold $1650
Decanter with stopper, 9" tall, brown Agate design with vertical white lines, signed $1500

Tiffany art glass. PHOTO BY MARK PICKVET.

Tiffany art glass. PHOTO BY ROBIN RAINWATER.

Inkwell, square (4″ × 4″), hinged lid, insert, bronze with green slag, Pine Needle design, signed $425

Inkwell, square, embossed brass frame, paneled, marked "Tiffany Studios, N.Y. 844" $575

Parfait, 5″ tall, footed, signed, Pastel lavender and opalescent $475

Plate, 11″, opalescent Starburst design, Light bluish-green $375

Plate, 6″, signed "LCT," Pastel blue $375

Punch bowl with stand, 15½″ diameter, Iridescent gold $2500

Punch goblet, 3½″ tall, hollow stem, signed, Gold $275

Salt dip, ruffled, signed "Tiffany," Iridescent blue and gold $250

Shade, 10″ diameter, domical, Gray, green, and iridescent amber $1250

Shade, 5″ tall, green King Tut pattern, Opal $775

Shade, 6¼″ tall, banded at base and rim, acid etched leaves and berries $325

Shade, iridescent orange with opal lining, King Tut pattern $475

Sherbet, 4¼″ diameter, yellow-orange with opalescent edge $375

Sherbet, 5″ tall, signed "L.C.T. T511," Blue $1000

Shot glass, iridescent gold with applied lily pads, signed $500

Stamp box, 3 glass inserts, signed "Tiffany Studios" $250

Stamp box, rectangular (4″ × 2¼″), bronze with green slag, 3 compartments, Pine Needle design $275

Toothpick holder, inverted dimple design, signed "L.C.T.—#R8844," Iridescent gold $450

Tumbler, 4″ tall, pinched sides, signed, Iridescent gold $400

Vase, 2″ tall, miniature, swirled green with berry clusters $1250

Vase, 4½″ tall, lava with cobalt overlay, gold trailings, signed $20000

Vase, 4½″ tall, tall collar, signed, Iridescent red $3750

Vase, 4¼″ tall, paperweight style, crystal with cream, mauve, and olive morning glories, signed "L.C.T. Y6889" $2000

Vase, 4¼″ tall, urn-shaped, iridescent gold with opalescent white flowers and green leaves, marked "L.C.T. USO99" $5250

Vase, 4″ tall, paperweight style, cameo floral and intaglio design, signed .. $6750

Vase, 5¹/₂″ tall, millefiori, iridescent gold with white flowers and green leaves $2100

Vase, 5¹/₄″ tall, cylindrical, cream neck, silver band below neck, translucent green glass edge, marked "L.C.T. Q4511" $850

Vase, 5¹/₄″ tall, ribbed, dimpled, Iridescent blue $850

Vase, 5″ tall, tan and brown Agate design, signed $1

Vase, 6¹/₂″ tall, iridescent lava, banded or beaded decoration, signed $7000

Vase, 6¹/₂″ tall, iridescent red and black paneled design, signed $4500

Vase, 6″ tall, crystal base, signed, Pastel yellow $650

Vase, 7¹/₂″ tall, iridescent shades of green, millefiori and gold leaves design, signed $2500

Vase, 7¹/₄″ tall, flask-shaped, lava, inscribed $5000

Vase, 7″ tall, paperweight style, Peacock Feather design, signed $5750

Vase, 8¹/₂″ tall, iridescent brown with double threading, signed $1250

Vase, 9¹/₂″ tall, Cypriote design, Iridescent brown $3500

Vase, 10″ tall, laminated tan and brown Agate Striped design, signed $3750

Vase, 11″ tall, iridescent red with gold overlay, signed $1350

Vase, 12″ tall, paperweight style, Gladiolus design, signed $5750

Vase, 13¹/₄″ tall, jack-in-the-pulpit style, signed "L.C.T. W8426" $2250

Vase, 13″ tall, pedestal base, ribbed, iridescent gold with blue highlights, signed $2000

Vase, 14¹/₂″ tall, trumpet-shaped, pedestal base with ball, iridescent gold foliage $2750

Vase, 15″ tall, bronze base, green striations, iridescent gold foliage $3000

Vase, 16¹/₂″ tall, paperweight style, bronze base, blue floral design $8500

Vase, 16″ tall, floriform, signed "L.C.T. 9708A," Iridescent gold $3250

Vase, 17¹/₄″ tall, curved gooseneck style, amber with gold feathers, signed "L.C.T. M4386" $3750

Vase, 18″ tall, bronze base, floriform, pink cameo decoration $3750

Vase, 19″ tall, jack-in-the-pulpit style, floriform, signed, Iridescent gold ... $1400

Vase, 19″ tall, stick-shaped, bronze support, signed, Iridescent blue $1250

Vase, bud, 6″ tall, signed, numbered, Iridescent gold $750

Vase, bud, 8¹/₄″ tall, green Triangle design, signed, Iridescent gold $750

Water goblet, 7″ tall, Vintage pattern, signed, Iridescent gold $650

Wine glass, 4″ tall, gold foot and bowl with amber stem, signed $275

Wine glass, 8¹/₂″ tall, gold with crystal stem, signed "L.C.T." $1350

VASA MURRHINA   VARIOUS COMPANIES, 1880s–1890s

The name "Vasa Murrhina" came from the Vasa Murrhina Art Glass Company of 1882–83. The glass produced by this company was ornamented with flecks of mica. Colored glass particles or tiny metallic sprinkles produced much the same effect. The company went out of business because of flaws in the basic formulas. These flaws were responsible for causing over two-thirds of the glass products to crack. Many other companies adopted this decorating technique and produced some glassware in this fashion.

Basket, 6″ tall, crystal twisted handle, pink with silver mica $275

Basket, 7″ tall, red to pink coloring $375

Bowl, 4³/₄″, ruffled, pink and red with gold mica $275

Vasa Murrhina art glass. PHOTO BY MARK PICKVET.

Bowl, finger, 4″, cranberry with silver mica $175
Bowl, rose, 5″, blue with yellow and silver mica $150
Creamer, 4½″ tall, crystal handle, pink and red with white lining and silver mica
.... $150
Creamer, ribbed, cobalt with gold mica $175
Cruet with crystal stopper, 6″ tall, crystal handle, pink with silver mica ... $325
Cruet with stopper, 6¼″ tall, blue with silver mica $300
Ewer, 9½″ tall, ruffled, pink, blue, and yellow with white lining and silver mica ...
.... $275
Mug, 4½″ tall, white with gold mica $150
Perfume bottle with silver threaded stopper, 5″ tall, Butterfly design, silver mica
.... $400
Pitcher, 7¾″ tall, blue with silver mica $275
Pitcher, syrup with metal lid, 5¾″ tall, blue with gold mica $350
Pitcher, water, 8½″ tall, bulbous, brown and red with gold mica $450
Sugar, ribbed, cobalt blue with gold mica $175
Toothpick holder, 2″ tall, yellow with red and silver mica $150
Tumbler, various designs with gold or silver mica $250
Vase, 6¼″ tall, fluted, footed, white with gold mica $175
Vase, 6″ tall, bulbous, white with amber and gold mica $175
Vase, 7¼″ tall, slender, cranberry with gold mica $225
Vase, 8½″ tall, yellow design on white background, silver mica, white lining $225
Vase, 8″ tall, trumpet-shaped, dark red with white and silver mica $200
Vase, 9¼″ tall, blue with white and lighter blue splotches, gold mica $225
Vase, 10″ tall, fluted top, multicolored mica flecks $225
Vase, 12¼″ tall, pink with silver mica $325

CHAPTER 5

CARNIVAL GLASS

The problem with art glass was that it was too expensive for the average person and catered to a very exclusive market. An inexpensive pressed glass substitute was Carnival glass, which was produced in the United States from about 1905 to the late 1920s. At first the new pressed glass was not called "Carnival," but borrowed its name from Tiffany's "Favrile" and Steuben's "Aurene." It soon added other exotic names such as "New Venetian Art," "Parisian Art," "Aurora," and "Art Iridescent."

The techniques for making this glass were borrowed from the Art Nouveau movement. Color is natural in glass, based on various oxides that are present in sand. Ordinarily, iron and common metals produce light green to brown glass. With the addition of various metallic oxides, variations in heat and length of time in the furnace, and minor formula changes, astounding color effects can be achieved. Carnival glass includes the color of the glass before any iridescence is fired on it. The base color can usually be found on the underside of an iridized glass object.

There were two major groups of colored Carnival glass. The bright Car-

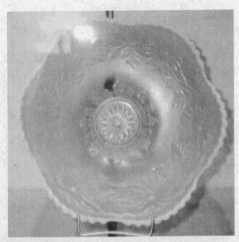

Westmoreland Daisy Wreath Carnival glass. PHOTO BY MARK PICKVET, COURTESY OF THE FENTON ART GLASS MUSEUM.

nival colors were red, blue, green, purple, amethyst, amber, and marigold. The pastel colors were a bit rarer and included clear, white, ice green, ice blue, clambroth, lavender, aqua opalescent, and smoke. Red was the rarest and was one of the most expensive to make since fair amounts of gold oxides were required to produce it. Naturally, red is the most valuable color today and commands very high prices. The pastel colors are also not as common and are quite valuable.

Marigold was the most popular Carnival color and is the one usually envisioned when one thinks of Carnival glass. This orange-brown flashing was applied to clear glass, which was then sprayed with iridescence. Pastels usually had clear bases with a very light coating of iridescence. Lavender had a purple tint, aqua a bluish-green tint, peach a yellowish-orange tint, smoke a light gray, and clambroth a pearly white or light yellow sheen. Other opaque and opalescent shadings were also made. Marigold, however, remains the most abundant and cheapest to acquire.

The glass itself was used to manufacture simple bowls and vases. As its popularity increased, water sets, table sets, punch bowls, berry and ice cream sets, dresser sets with matching cologne bottles, other bottles (wines, whiskey, soda), powder jars, trays, hatpin holders, lamps, paperweights, mugs, beads, advertising items, and souvenir pieces followed.

Unlike art glass, Carnival glass was sold in china shops and general stores, and by mail order, and was used as containers for food products such as pickles and mustard. It was the first to be used as prizes for promotional items for tea companies, candy companies, and furniture stores.

Carnival glass was exported to England and other parts of Europe. It even reached as far as Australia, and several foreign glassmakers began producing it, including companies in England, Australia, and Sweden. However, the fad would be short-lived.

By the late teens, the demand lessened, and by the early 1920s, the fad had pretty much ended. The new decor trends of the 1920s had no place for this odd, oily glassware. Manufacturers were left with huge inventories, and this remaining stock was sold at fairs, bazaars, and carnivals (hence the name) at below wholesale prices. Those who were stuck with it packed it away until the 1950s.

There were five major companies that produced Carnival glass: the Fenton Art Glass Company of Williamstown, West Virginia; the Imperial Glass Company of Bellaire, Ohio; the Millersburg Glass Company of Millersburg, Ohio; the Northwood Glass Company of Wheeling, West Virginia; and the Dugan Glass Company of Indiana, Pennsylvania.

Noted individuals were Frank and John Fenton, who founded Fenton. John also went on with another brother, Robert, to establish Millersburg. Jacob Rosenthal was employed by the Fentons and developed many Carnival glass formulas. Edward Muhleman founded Imperial, while Harry

Northwood (son of English glass artisan John Northwood) established Northwood. Harry Northwood's managers, Thomas E. Dugan (Harry Northwood's cousin) and W.G. Minnemeyer, went on to form the Dugan Glass Company.

Fenton and Imperial both made iridescent products in the modern era. Nearly all of Fenton's recent works are easily distinguished from the older versions, and the company continues in operation today. Imperial began reproducing Carnival glass in the early 1960s using some of the original molds; the new glass is marked "IG" on the base or bottom. Imperial survived several rough periods but finally shut down for good in 1982.

A few other companies that produced limited amounts of Carnival glass were Cambridge, Jenkins, Heisey, Indiana, Federal, Fostoria, McKee-Jeannette, Westmoreland, and U.S. Glass.

ACORN BURRS   NORTHWOOD GLASS COMPANY

This pattern is characterized by raised acorns and oak leaves. The opalescent varieties, including white, blue, green, and aqua, are quite rare, particularly the punch sets.

Bowl, berry, 5″
Amethyst $45
Blue $45
Green $45
Marigold $30
Purple $50
Ice blue $85
Ice green $85
Bowl, berry, 10″
Amethyst $175
Blue $150
Green $175
Marigold $90
Purple $175
Ice blue $400
Ice green $400
Butter dish with cover
Amethyst $400
Blue $400
Green $750
Marigold $300
Purple $400
Ice blue $700
Ice green $700
White $750
Creamer
Amethyst $250
Blue $250

Carnival glass. Left: "Acorn Burrs" pattern. DRAWING BY MARK PICKVET. Right: "Aztec" pattern. PHOTO BY ROBIN RAINWATER.

Green	$300
Marigold	$200
Purple	$250
Ice blue	$400
Ice green	$400
White	$400
Pitcher, water	
Amethyst	$650
Blue	$650
Green	$750
Marigold	$500
Purple	$675
Ice blue	$2000
Ice green	$2000
Punch bowl with base	
Amethyst	$750
Blue	$750
Green	$850
Marigold	$550
Purple	$800
Aqua opalescent	$35000
Ice blue	$4000
Ice green	$4500
White	$4000
Punch cup	
Amethyst	$90
Blue	$75
Green	$90
Marigold	$45

Purple $85
Aqua opalescent $2500
Ice blue $110
Ice green $150
White $105

Spooner
Amethyst $250
Blue $250
Green $300
Marigold $200
Purple $225
Ice blue $375
Ice green $375
White $375

Sugar dish with cover
Amethyst $300
Blue $300
Green $400
Marigold $225
Purple $300
Ice blue $450
Ice green $450
White $450

Tumbler
Amethyst $100
Blue $100
Green $110
Marigold $90
Purple $100
Ice blue $350
Ice green $350

Vase, whimsey
Amethyst $4000
Marigold $3000
Purple $4000

AZTEC   MCKEE BROTHERS

This is the same "Whirling Star" or "Aztec" pattern pressed by McKee in clear glass. Carnival colors were added later to a few of the surviving original molds. McKee produced only a limited amount of Carnival glass.

Bowl, rose, Clambroth $400
Creamer
Clambroth $300
Marigold $250
Pitcher, water, Marigold $2000

Sugar
Clambroth $325
Marigold $275
Tumbler, Marigold $500

BEADED SHELL DUGAN GLASS COMPANY

The scalloped shell of this pattern is large, and usually three or four of the shells circle each table item. The beading circles out in a radius from the bottom of each shell. The rims of many pieces are the tops of the shells, while the bases are ridged shells pointing downward.

Bowl, berry, 5″, footed
Amethyst $50
Marigold $35
Purple $50
Bowl, berry, 6½″, footed
Amethyst $60
Marigold $45
Purple $60
Bowl, berry, 9″, footed
Amethyst $100
Marigold $75
Purple $100
Butter dish with cover
Amethyst $275
Marigold $150
Purple $275
Creamer with cover
Amethyst $125
Marigold $90
Purple $110
Mug
Amethyst $100
Blue $125
Marigold $175
Purple $110
White $425
Mug, whimsey (irregular)
Amethyst $425
Purple $425
Pitcher, water
Amethyst $575
Blue $575
Marigold $450
Purple $575
Spooner
Amethyst $125
Marigold $75
Purple $125

Sugar with cover
Amethyst $135
Marigold $100
Purple $125
Tumbler
Amethyst $85
Blue $85
Marigold $60
Purple $85

BELLS AND BEADS   DUGAN GLASS COMPANY

This pattern is characterized by swirled, bell-shaped flowers with beaded stems.

Bowl, 6³/₄″
Blue $110
Green $110
Marigold $45
Peach opalescent $110
Purple $75
Bowl, 7¹/₂″
Blue $125
Green $125
Marigold $50
Peach opalescent $125
Purple $90
Compote
Amethyst $75
Marigold $50
Purple $75
Gravy boat, handled
Marigold $75
Peach opalescent $160
Purple $100
Hat
Marigold $50
Purple $75

Carnival glass, "Bells and Beads"
pattern. DRAWING BY MARK PICKVET.

Nappy
  Marigold $60
  Peach opalescent $125
  Purple $90
Plate, 6³/₄″
  Amethyst $100
  Purple $100
Plate, 8″
  Amethyst $150
  Purple $150

BIRDS AND CHERRIES   FENTON ART GLASS COMPANY

This pattern is characterized by five birds perched on cherry branches; the entire design is in relief. Plates and bowls are quite scarce. A few pieces have been discovered in pastel colors (increase the price for blue by 50%).

Bonbon dish
  Amethyst $65
  Blue $75
  Green $75
  Marigold $50
Bowl, 5″
  Amethyst $475
  Blue $550
  Marigold $500
Bowl, 9″
  Amethyst $750
  Blue $800
  Marigold $850
Compote
  Amethyst $90
  Blue $100
  Green $100
  Marigold $100
Plate, 10″
  Blue $1500
  Green $1750
  Marigold $1250

BLACKBERRY WREATH   MILLERSBURG GLASS COMPANY

This pattern is characterized by blackberry branches curved to form a wreath; within the wreath are fruit and foliage.

Bowl, 5″
  Green $75
  Marigold $50
  Purple $65

Bowl, 7″
  Blue $550
  Green $95
  Marigold $65
  Purple $80
Bowl, 9″
  Blue $575
  Green $125
  Marigold $75
  Purple $110
Bowl, 10″, ice cream
  Blue $875
  Green $400
  Marigold $150
  Purple $350
Plate, 6″
  Green $2750
  Marigold $1750
  Purple $2500
Plate, 8″, Green $4000
Plate, 10″
  Marigold $4500
  Purple $5000
Spittoon (whimsey), Green $4000

BUTTERFLY AND BERRY   FENTON ART GLASS COMPANY

This pattern is characterized by alternating panels of Monarch butterflies and triangular-shaped berries, along with a notched rim. Red pieces (as with most Carnival glass) are quite rare.

Bowl, berry, 5″
  Blue $125
  Green $125
  Marigold $40
  Purple $50
  Red $1250
  White $110
Bowl, berry, 10″, footed
  Amethyst $175
  Blue $200
  Green $225
  Marigold $85
  Purple $150
  White $450
Bowl, fernery
  Amethyst $1250
  Blue $1500
  Marigold $850
  Purple $1250

Carnival glass, "Butterfly and Berry" pattern. PHOTO BY MARK PICKVET, COURTESY
OF THE FENTON ART GLASS MUSEUM.

Butter dish with cover
  Amethyst $300
  Blue $325
  Green $350
  Marigold $150
  Purple $300
Creamer
  Amethyst $175
  Purple $175
Creamer with cover
  Blue $175
  Green $225
  Marigold $110
Cuspidor
  Amethyst $1100
  Blue $1250
  Purple $1100
Hatpin holder
  Blue $1000
  Marigold $850
Nut dish
  Amethyst $775
  Blue $850
  Purple $775
Pitcher, water
  Amethyst $500
  Blue $550
  Green $750
  Marigold $350

Purple	$500
White	$1200
Plate, footed, Blue	$1750
Spittoon, 2 styles	
Amethyst	$2600
Blue	$2750
Purple	$2600
Spooner	
Amethyst	$150
Blue	$175
Green	$200
Marigold	$110
Purple	$150
Sugar dish with cover	
Amethyst	$175
Blue	$175
Green	$225
Marigold	$110
Purple	$175
Tumbler	
Amethyst	$75
Blue	$75
Green	$90
Marigold	$50
Purple	$150
White	$150
Vase, 10″ tall	
Amethyst	$100
Blue	$75
Green	$225
Marigold	$75
Purple	$100
Red	$1000
White	$550

CAPTIVE ROSE FENTON ART GLASS COMPANY

This pattern is characterized by roses surrounded by diamonds, circles, and scales.

Bonbon dish	
Blue	$85
Green	$100
Marigold	$75
White	$175
Bowl, 8½″	
Amethyst	$75
Blue	$80
Green	$85
Marigold	$75
Purple	$75

White	$250

Bowl, 10″

Amethyst	$85
Blue	$90
Green	$95
Marigold	$85
Purple	$85
White	$275

Compote

Amethyst	$65
Blue	$75
Green	$85
Marigold	$55
Purple	$65
White	$125

Plate, 7″

Amethyst	$160
Blue	$175
Green	$200
Marigold	$125
Purple	$160
White	$500

Plate, 9″

Amethyst	$225
Blue	$250
Green	$300
Marigold	$175
Purple	$225
White	$600

CATTAILS AND WATER LILIES   FENTON ART GLASS COMPANY, NORTHWOOD GLASS COMPANY

Along with the Cattails and Water Lilies pattern, there is some molding at the bottom of the design (soil and grass).

Bonbon dish

Blue	$125
Marigold	$85
Purple	$110
Red	$750

Bowl, berry, 9″, Marigold $55

Bowl, oblong, banana, 4-footed

Amethyst	$160
Blue	$175
Green	$200
Marigold	$125
Purple	$160

Creamer, Marigold $100

Jelly dish, (resembles toothpick holder), Marigold $90

Pitcher, water, Marigold $225
Spooner, Marigold $75
Sugar dish with cover, Marigold $125
Tumbler, Marigold $55

CHECKERBOARD   WESTMORELAND GLASS COMPANY

"Checkerboard" is a diagonal crosscut pattern. All pieces with the possible exception of punch cups are quite rare. Note that this pattern has been reproduced. Reproductions have Westmoreland's newer mark (beginning in 1949), which consists of an intertwined W and G.

Cruet with stopper, Clambroth $750
Goblet
  Marigold $350
  Purple $400
Pitcher, water, Purple $3750
Punch cup
  Marigold $110
  Purple $150
Tumbler
  Marigold $700
  Purple $650
Vase, Purple $2500
Wine glass, Marigold $325

CHERRY AND CABLE   NORTHWOOD GLASS COMPANY

"Cherry and Cable" features a line or cable around each item; four leaves run through the cable and branch down into groupings of three cherries. Also, around the bottom are circular thumbprints (eight total). This pattern has been reproduced in miniature. Double the prices for blue Carnival made in this pattern.

Bowl, berry, 5″, Marigold $75
Bowl, berry, 9″, Marigold $125
Butter dish with cover, Marigold $400

Carnival glass, "Checkerboard" pattern. DRAWING BY MARK PICKVET.

Carnival glass. Left: "Cherry and Cable" pattern. Right: "Circle Scroll" pattern.
DRAWINGS BY MARK PICKVET.

Creamer, Marigold $200
Pitcher, water, Marigold $1500
Spooner, Marigold $225
Sugar with cover, Marigold $150
Tumbler, Marigold $400

CHERRY CIRCLES FENTON ART GLASS COMPANY

Fenton's "Cherry Circles" includes groups of three cherries in a wide band around the center of each object surrounded by foliage wreaths.

Bonbon dish
  Amethyst $65
  Blue $75
  Marigold $55
  Red $3000
Bowl, 8″
  Amethyst $65
  Blue $75
  Green $75
  Marigold $55
Compote
  Amethyst $125
  Blue $125
  Green $125
  Marigold $100
Plate, 9″
  Blue $225
  Marigold $400
  White $250
Plate, 10″, chop, Clambroth $275

CHERRY WREATH   DUGAN GLASS COMPANY

The cherries in this wreath design either are the color of the basic flashing or are flashed in red. For those in red, increase the listed prices by 50%.

Butter dish with cover
Amethyst $225
Blue $250
Green $225
Marigold $150
Purple $225
White $425
Creamer
Amethyst $150
Blue $150
Green $150
Marigold $100
Purple $150
White $325
Cuspidor, Marigold $1500
Lamp, cherub, White $500
Pitcher, water
Amethyst $425
Blue $450
Green $450
Marigold $275
Purple $425
White $850
Spooner
Amethyst $125
Blue $125
Green $125
Marigold $90
Purple $125
White $300
Sugar
Amethyst $150
Blue $150
Green $150
Marigold $100
Purple $150
White $325
Tumbler
Amethyst $95
Blue $100
Green $100
Marigold $65
Purple $95
White $200

CHERRY   DUGAN GLASS COMPANY, MILLERSBURG GLASS
COMPANY

The Dugan bowls, plate, and cruet are a separate pattern from the remaining Millersburg pieces. Dugan's "Cherry" is characterized by cherry branches, with the fruit in medallion form in the interior of the bowls. Millersburg's "Cherry" pattern consists of exterior panels of cherry foliage raised in relief. Some of Dugan's pieces in this pattern can be found in peach opalescent (double the amethyst prices for peach).

Banana dish

Amethyst	$3000
Blue	$3500
Purple	$3000

Bowl, 4″

Amethyst	$90
Blue	$850
Green	$100
Marigold	$60
Purple	$90

Bowl, 5½″

Amethyst	$90
Blue	$150
Green	$100
Marigold	$40
Purple	$90

Bowl, 5″, ruffled (Dugan)

Amethyst	$60
Blue	$150
Green	$75
Marigold	$40
Purple	$60

Bowl, 6″, ruffled, footed (Dugan)

Amethyst	$100
Blue	$150
Green	$125
Marigold	$45
Purple	$100

Bowl, 7″

Amethyst	$125
Green	$150
Marigold	$100
Purple	$125

Bowl, 8½″, ruffled, footed (Dugan)

Amethyst	$275
Blue	$300
Green	$300
Marigold	$200
Purple	$275

Bowl, 8″, ruffled (Dugan)

Amethyst	$110

Blue $175
Green $150
Marigold $60
Purple $110

Bowl, 9″ $125
Amethyst $275
Blue $150
Green $90
Marigold $125
Purple $125

Bowl, 10″, ice cream $325
Amethyst $950
Blue $325
Green $175
Marigold $325
Purple $325

Compote $850
Amethyst $2500
Blue $1000
Green $750
Marigold $850
Purple ....

Creamer $225
Amethyst $250
Green $100
Marigold $225
Purple ....

Cruet with stopper (Dugan) $250
Amethyst $650
Pastel $250
Purple ....

Pitcher, milk $475
Amethyst $475
Green $250
Marigold $475
Purple ....

Pitcher, water $1500
Amethyst $1500
Green $1000
Marigold $1500
Purple ....

Plate, 6″, (Dugan) $450
Amethyst $500
Green $950
Marigold $450
Purple ....

Plate, 7½″ $2500
Amethyst $3500
Green $750
Marigold $2500
Purple ....

Plate, 10″
   Green $5000
   Marigold $4500
Powder jar with cover, Green $1750
Spooner
   Amethyst $175
   Green $175
   Marigold $85
   Purple $175
Sugar dish with cover
   Amethyst $275
   Green $300
   Marigold $175
   Purple $275
Tumbler, 2 styles
   Amethyst $725
   Green $750
   Marigold $550
   Purple $725

CIRCLE SCROLL   DUGAN GLASS COMPANY

The scroll design of this pattern is inscribed in circles that band around each object. Above and below the circles are vertical panels with circular ends.

Bowl, 5″
   Amethyst $50
   Marigold $40
   Purple $50
Bowl, 10″
   Amethyst $75
   Marigold $60
   Purple $75
Butter dish with cover
   Amethyst $350
   Marigold $275
   Purple $350
Creamer
   Amethyst $200
   Marigold $150
   Purple $200
Pitcher, water
   Amethyst $2500
   Marigold $1750
   Purple $2500
Spooner
   Amethyst $175
   Marigold $125
   Purple $175

Sugar dish with cover
Amethyst $300
Marigold $225
Purple $300
Tumbler
Amethyst $600
Marigold $400
Purple $600
Vase
Amethyst $175
Marigold $150
Purple $175

COIN DOT   FENTON ART GLASS COMPANY, WESTMORELAND GLASS COMPANY

The original "Coin Dot" was produced by Fenton and is characterized by various sizes of pressed coins around each item. Westmoreland produced a slight variant, as noted in the pieces listed below.

Basket (Westmoreland pattern variant)
Blue $150
Marigold $100
Bowl (Westmoreland pattern variant)
Amethyst $100
Aqua opalescent $250
Blue $100
Green $100
Marigold $60
Peach opalescent $250
Bowl, 6″
Amethyst $50
Aquan opalescent $250
Blue $55
Green $50
Marigold $45
Purple $50
Red $1250
Bowl, 9″
Amethyst $55
Aqua opalescent $300
Blue $60
Green $55
Marigold $50
Purple $55
Bowl, 10″
Amethyst $60
Aqua opalescent $325
Blue $65

Green $60
Marigold $55
Purple $60
Red $1350
Bowl, rose
Amethyst $50
Aqua opalescent $250
Blue $50
Green $50
Marigold $40
Purple $50
Bowl, rose (Westmoreland pattern variant)
Amethyst $150
Marigold $100
Compote (Westmoreland pattern variant)
Amethyst $110
Aqua opalescent $200
Blue $125
Green $125
Marigold $75
Peach opalescent $200
Pitcher, water
Amethyst $500
Blue $550
Green $575
Marigold $350
Purple $500
Tumbler
Amethyst $175
Blue $225
Green $250
Marigold $175
Purple $175

COLONIAL   IMPERIAL GLASS COMPANY

This is a typical "Colonial" pattern featuring wide arched panels around each object.

Candlestick, Marigold $125
Creamer
Green $100
Marigold $55
Red $325
Goblet
Green $85
Marigold $50
Mug
Green $100
Marigold $55

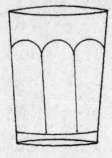

Carnival glass, "Colonial" pattern. DRAWING BY MARK
PICKVET.

Pitcher, water, Red $4500
Sugar
  Green $100
  Marigold $55
  Red $325
Tumbler, Red $375
Vase
  Green $75
  Marigold $60

COSMOS AND CANE   IMPERIAL GLASS COMPANY

This pattern is characterized by ferns and flowers that are placed from the bottom to
just below the rim; between the foliage is a diamond trellis design.

Bowl, berry, 5″
  Marigold $50
  White $150
Bowl, berry, 8″
  Marigold $65
  White $175
Bowl, berry, 10″
  Marigold $75
  White $200
Bowl, rose
  Amber $750
  Amethyst $500
  Marigold $325
  White $1000
Butter dish with cover
  Marigold $200
  White $275
Compote
  Marigold $200
  White $300

Creamer
Marigold $125
White $175
Pitcher, water
Marigold $750
White $1250
Plate, chop
Marigold $750
White $1000
Sherbet
Marigold $100
White $175
Spittoon
Marigold $4000
White $4500
Spooner
Marigold $100
White $150
Sugar dish with cover
Marigold $150
White $200
Tray
Marigold $200
White $300
Tumbler
Marigold $200
White $300
Tumbler with advertising
Marigold $275
White $450

COUNTRY KITCHEN   MILLERSBURG GLASS COMPANY

"Country Kitchen" includes flowers, triangular ridges, and wavy bands around each object. Cuspidors and spittoons are very rare and valuable.

Bowl, berry, 5″, Marigold $75
Bowl, berry, 9″, Marigold $275
Butter dish with cover
Amethyst $750
Marigold $500
Purple $750
Creamer
Amethyst $450
Green $600
Marigold $300
Purple $450
Cuspidor
Amethyst $4000
Purple $4000

Spittoon
Amethyst $4000
Purple $4000
Spooner
Amethyst $275
Marigold $200
Purple $275
Sugar
Amethyst $450
Green $600
Marigold $300
Purple $450
Vase, whimsey
Amethyst $600
Marigold $500
Purple $600

CRAB CLAW   IMPERIAL GLASS COMPANY

"Crab Claw" is an interlocking pattern that resembles cut glass. Within the design can be found curved files, hobstars, diamonds, and half flowers.

Bowl, 5″
Amethyst $50
Green $55
Marigold $40
Purple $50
Bowl, 10″
Amethyst $65
Green $75
Marigold $50
Purple $65
Bowl, fruit, footed
Amethyst $150
Green $175
Marigold $100
Purple $150
Cruet with stopper
Amethyst $1750
Green $2500
Marigold $1000
Purple $1750
Pitcher, water
Amethyst $1000
Green $1250
Marigold $750
Purple $1000
Tumbler
Amethyst $200
Green $250

Marigold $150
Purple $200

CRACKLE   VARIOUS COMPANIES

If common can be attributed to any Carnival glass, then "Crackle" is a prime candidate. It is true to the name "Carnival" in that many pieces were given away as prizes at fairs and exhibitions. Imperial was probably the largest maker of "Crackle" Carnival glass.

Bowl, berry, 5″
  Green $20
  Marigold $15
  Purple $20
Bowl, berry, 6″
  Green $25
  Marigold $20
  Purple $25
Bowl, berry, 8″
  Green $30
  Marigold $25
  Purple $30
Bowl, berry, 9″
  Green $35
  Marigold $30
  Purple $35
Bowl, berry, 10″
  Green $40
  Marigold $35
  Purple $40
Candlestick, 3¹/₂″ tall, Marigold $25
Candlestick, 7″ tall, Marigold $30
Candy jar with cover, Marigold $50
Creamer
  Green $35
  Marigold $30
  Purple $35

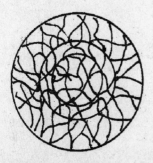

Carnival glass, "Crackle" pattern. DRAWING BY MARK PICKVET.

Pitcher, water, dome base
  Green $150
  Marigold $100
  Purple $150
Planter, window, Marigold $150
Plate, 6″
  Green $35
  Marigold $25
  Purple $35
Plate, 7″
  Green $40
  Marigold $30
  Purple $40
Plate, 8″
  Green $45
  Marigold $35
  Purple $45
Punch bowl with base
  Green $275
  Marigold $150
  Purple $275
Punch cup
  Green $30
  Marigold $25
  Purple $30
Spittoon, Marigold $75
Sugar
  Green $35
  Marigold $30
  Purple $35
Tumbler
  Green $30
  Marigold $25
  Purple $30
Vase, auto
  Green $35
  Marigold $30
  Purple $35
Vase, wall, Marigold $45

DAHLIA   DUGAN GLASS COMPANY

The large dahlias in this pattern are in relief and are spaced a little farther apart than typical pressed patterns. With the exception of the epergne, the pattern was made exclusively by Dugan.

Bowl, 5″, footed
  Amethyst $50
  Marigold $40

Purple $50
White $175
Bowl, 10″, footed
  Amethyst $150
  Marigold $90
  Purple $150
  White $350
Butter dish
  Amethyst $250
  Marigold $150
  Purple $250
  White $450
Creamer
  Amethyst $150
  Marigold $90
  Purple $150
  White $350
Epergne (Fenton)
  Marigold $300
  White $450
Pitcher, water
  Amethyst $1000
  Marigold $650
  Purple $1000
  White $1250
Spooner
  Amethyst $125
  Marigold $75
  Purple $125
  White $175
Sugar
  Amethyst $150
  Marigold $90
  Purple $150
  White $350
Tumbler
  Amethyst $150
  Marigold $90
  Purple $150
  White $175

DIAMOND LACE IMPERIAL GLASS COMPANY

This pattern is characterized by long, diagonal frames with central starbursts, beading, and stippling.

Bowl, berry, 5¹/₂″
  Marigold $30
  Purple $40

Carnival glass. Left: "Dahlia" pattern. Right: "Double Dolphin" pattern. DRAWINGS BY MARK PICKVET.

Bowl, berry, 8″
  Marigold $50
  Purple $80
Bowl, berry, 9″
  Marigold $55
  Purple $85
Bowl, fruit, 10½″
  Marigold $90
  Purple $115
Bowl, rose, whimsey, Marigold $1500
Pitcher, water
  Marigold $275
  Purple $350
  White $1000
Tumbler
  Marigold $55
  Purple $90
  White $200

DIAMOND POINT COLUMNS   FENTON ART GLASS COMPANY, IMPERIAL GLASS COMPANY

This pattern is characterized by alternating rows of panels with checkered diamonds.

Bowl, 4½″, Marigold $25
Butter dish, Marigold $85
Compote, Marigold $35
Creamer, Marigold $50
Pitcher, milk, Marigold $50
Plate, 7″, Marigold $40
Powder jar with cover, Marigold $75

Spooner, Marigold $45
Sugar, Marigold $50
Vase
  Green $75
  Marigold $45
  Purple $60
  White $75

DOUBLE DOLPHIN   FENTON ART GLASS COMPANY

Each object usually features a pair of scaled dolphins with flipped tails in relief. The colors are light iridescent pastels.

Bowl, 8″
  Ice blue $85
  Ice green $85
  Pink $85
Bowl, 9″, footed
  Ice blue $115
  Ice green $115
Bowl, 10″
  Ice blue $90
  Ice green $90
Bowl, 11″, footed
  Ice blue $125
  Ice green $125
Cake plate with center handle
  Ice blue $100
  Ice green $100
  Pink $100
Candlestick
  Ice blue $50
  Ice green $50
  Pink $50
  White $65
Candy dish with cover
  Ice blue $125
  Ice green $125
Compote
  Ice blue $95
  Ice green $95
  Tangerine $125
  Topaz $125
Vase, fan style
  Ice blue $100
  Ice green $100
  Pink $100
  Tangerine $125
  Topaz $125
  White $125

Carnival glass, "Elks" pattern.
PHOTO BY ROBIN RAINWATER,
COURTESY OF THE FENTON ART
GLASS MUSEUM.

ELKS   DUGAN GLASS COMPANY, FENTON ART GLASS COMPANY, MILLERSBURG GLASS COMPANY

This pattern is characterized by an elk head with a clock between the antlers (pointing to noon), the symbol for the Elks organization. Around the elk's head are floral and foliage designs. Dugan made only a nappy, and Millersburg produced a bowl and paperweight; the remaining advertising/souvenir pieces are Fenton.

Bell, 1911 Atlantic City, Blue $1750
Bell, 1914 Parkersburg, Blue $2250
Bell, 1917 Portland, Marigold $7500
Bowl, 8″, (Millersburg)
    Amethyst $1750
    Marigold $1750
    Purple $1750
Bowl, Atlantic City, Blue $1500
Bowl, Detroit
    Amethyst $1000
    Blue $650
    Green $750
    Marigold $1000
    Purple $1000
Nappy (Dugan)
    Amethyst $4000
    Purple $4000
Paperweight (Millersburg)
    Amethyst $1500
    Green $1750
    Purple $1500
Plate, 1914 Parkersburg
    Blue $1250
    Green $1500
Plate, Atlantic City
    Blue $1500
    Green $1750

Carnival glass, "Estate" pattern. DRAWING BY MARK PICKVET.

ESTATE   WESTMORELAND GLASS COMPANY

The "Estate" design resembles that of a maze of lines. Carnival pieces in this line are relatively small. For smoke-colored Carnival, double the prices for green.

Creamer
Aqua opalescent $200
Ice blue $175
Ice green $225
Marigold $65
Peach opalescent $175
Mug
Ice blue $250
Ice green $250
Marigold $100
Perfume bottle with stopper
Aqua opalescent $550
Ice green $500
Sugar
Aqua opalescent $200
Ice blue $175
Ice green $225
Marigold $65
Peach opalescent $175
Vase, 3″ tall, stippled
Ice blue $100
Ice green $115
Marigold $65
Vase, 6″ tall, bud
Ice blue $200
Ice green $225
Marigold $90

FASHION   IMPERIAL GLASS COMPANY

This pattern consists of diamonds, jewels, sunbursts, and beading over the entire surface.

Basket, bride's
Marigold $125
Smoke $175
Bowl, 9″
Green $100
Marigold $50
Smoke $125
Bowl, fruit, with base
Green $125
Marigold $75
Smoke $150
Bowl, rose
Amethyst $1250
Green $1000
Marigold $400
Butter dish
Amethyst $225
Marigold $85
Purple $225
Compote, Smoke $350
Creamer
Amethyst $150
Green $175
Marigold $50
Purple $150
Smoke $250
Pitcher, water
Amethyst $1500
Green $2000
Marigold $350
Purple $1250
Smoke $2500
Punch bowl with base
Amethyst $1000
Marigold $550
Purple $1000
Red $15000
Punch cup
Amethyst $75
Marigold $40
Purple $75
Red $1000
Sugar
Amethyst $150
Green $175
Marigold $50

Purple	$150
Smoke	$250
Tumbler	
Amethyst	$175
Green	$225
Marigold	$40
Purple	$175
Smoke	$275

FENTONIA FENTON ART GLASS COMPANY

"Fentonia" consists of scales and stitches within beaded frames. The pattern is set diagonally on each object and nearly covers the entire surface (except for a small area at the top). The pattern variant is known as the "Fentonia Fruit," which includes fruit within the diamonds of the pattern. The variant is rarer and more valuable than the original.

Bowl, 5″, footed	
Blue	$50
Green	$55
Marigold	$40
Purple	$55
Bowl, 6″, footed (Fentonia Fruit)	
Blue	$75
Marigold	$50
Purple	$55
Bowl, 7½″, footed	
Amethyst	$75
Blue	$75
Green	$85
Marigold	$50
Purple	$75
Bowl, 9½″, footed	
Amethyst	$100
Blue	$90
Green	$100
Marigold	$65
Purple	$100
Bowl, berry, 9″	
Amethyst	$80
Blue	$80
Green	$90
Marigold	$45
Purple	$80
Bowl, 10″, footed (Fentonia Fruit)	
Blue	$175
Marigold	$125
Bowl, fruit, 10″	
Blue	$100
Marigold	$80

Butter dish with cover
Blue $250
Marigold $175

Creamer, 2 styles
Amethyst $125
Blue $125
Marigold $100

Pitcher, water
Blue $750
Marigold $450

Pitcher, water, (Fentonia Fruit)
Blue $800
Marigold $600

Spooner
Amethyst $125
Blue $115
Green $150
Marigold $75
Purple $125

Sugar dish with cover, 2 styles
Amethyst $150
Blue $150
Marigold $125

Tumbler
Blue $200
Marigold $125

Tumbler (Fentonia Fruit)
Blue $225
Marigold $150

Vase (Fentonia Fruit)
Blue $250
Marigold $175

FERN   FENTON ART GLASS COMPANY, NORTHWOOD GLASS COMPANY

"Fern" consists of a series of ferns that alternate with branches emanating from the center. It is an interior pattern, but some ferns and foliage are also found on the exterior. The three Fenton bowls were made in blue, all other listed pieces are Northwood.

Bowl, 7″
Amethyst $65
Blue $100
Green $85
Marigold $45
Purple $65
Bowl, 7″ (Fenton), Blue $800

Bowl, 8¼″
Amethyst $75
Blue $110
Green $90
Ice blue $150
Ice green $150
Marigold $50
Purple $75
White $150
Bowl, 8″, (Fenton), Blue $900
Bowl, 9″, (Fenton), Blue $1000
Compote
Amethyst $75
Blue $110
Green $90
Ice blue $125
Ice green $125
Marigold $50
Purple $75
White $125
Hat
Amethyst $110
Blue $150
Green $125
Ice blue $150
Ice green $150
Marigold $75
Purple $110
White $150

FIELD THISTLE   U.S. GLASS COMPANY

This pattern consists of swirled foliage with daisies, as well as a central medallion with a clear glass daisy. The pattern covers the entire exterior.

Bowl, 6″, Marigold $45
Bowl, 10″, Marigold $55
Butter dish with cover
Ice Green $225
Marigold $125
Compote (large)
Ice Green $250
Marigold $175
Creamer
Ice Green $125
Marigold $75
Pitcher, water
Ice Green $450
Marigold $300

Plate, 6″
   Ice Green $250
   Marigold $175
Plate, 9″
   Ice Green $450
   Marigold $300
Spooner
   Ice Green $110
   Marigold $70
Sugar
   Ice Green $125
   Marigold $75
Tumbler
   Ice Green $100
   Marigold $65
Vase
   Ice Green $275
   Marigold $175

FILE   IMPERIAL GLASS COMPANY

"File" is characterized by a series of rounded panels with ridges (or files). A central band divides two rows of these file designs into pyramidlike shapes. The pattern was also produced in England. For pastel colors, increase the price by 50%.

Bowl, 5″
   Amethyst $45
   Marigold $30
   Purple $45
Bowl, 7″
   Amethyst $50
   Marigold $40
   Purple $50
Bowl, 9″
   Amethyst $55
   Marigold $45
   Purple $55
Bowl, 10″
   Amethyst $60
   Marigold $50
   Purple $60
Butter dish with cover, Marigold $250
Compote
   Amethyst $55
   Marigold $40
   Purple $55
Creamer, Marigold $125
Pitcher, water
   Amethyst $550

Marigold	$350
Purple	$550
Spooner, Marigold	$100
Sugar dish with cover, Marigold	$175
Tumbler, Marigold	$225
Vase, Marigold	$100

FINE RIB   DUGAN GLASS COMPANY, FENTON ART GLASS COMPANY, NORTHWOOD GLASS COMPANY

This is a simple pattern of vertical ribbing. The only Fenton piece made is the red vase, and the pattern is a slight variation of the Northwood design.

Banana dish, Peach Opalescent	$175
Bowl, 5″	
Amethyst	$45
Blue	$50
Green	$50
Marigold	$35
Purple	$45
Bowl, 9″	
Amethyst	$75
Blue	$80
Green	$80
Marigold	$60
Purple	$75
Bowl, 10″	
Amethyst	$80
Blue	$90
Green	$90
Marigold	$65
Purple	$80
Compote, Peach Opalescent	$175
Plate, 8″	
Amethyst	$75
Blue	$125
Green	$125
Marigold	$65
Purple	$75
Plate, 9″	
Amethyst	$100
Blue	$150
Green	$150
Marigold	$85
Purple	$100
Vase, 8″	
Amethyst	$100
Aqua Opalescent	$350
Blue	$125

Green $200
Ice Blue $150
Ice Green $150
Marigold $50
Peach Opalescent $350
Purple $100
Red $550
White $150
Vase, 12″
Amethyst $125
Aqua Opalescent $450
Blue $150
Green $250
Ice Blue $175
Ice Green $175
Marigold $65
Peach Opalescent $450
Purple $125
Red $750
White $175

FLUTE   IMPERIAL GLASS COMPANY, MILLERSBURG GLASS COMPANY, NORTHWOOD GLASS COMPANY

There are a number of "Flute" designs, but most are similar in style and price. Imperial's has wide paneled flutes, thick glass, and circular bases. Some Millersburg products have 16 thin flutes, while others were made with much wider flutes. Northwood's wide flutes are more arched or ridged than the others.

Bowl, 4″
Amethyst $65
Blue $75
Green $75
Marigold $45
Purple $65
Bowl, 5″
Amethyst $75
Blue $85
Green $85
Marigold $50
Purple $75
Bowl, 10″
Amethyst $250
Marigold $150
Purple $250
Bowl, 10″ (Northwood only)
Amethyst $75
Green $75
Marigold $65
Purple $75

Carnival glass, "Flute" pattern. PHOTO BY ROBIN RAINWATER.

Bowl, custard, 11″ (Imperial only)
Amethyst $300
Green $350
Purple $300
Butter dish
Amethyst $175
Green $200
Marigold $150
Purple $175
Butter dish with cover
Amethyst $300
Green $350
Marigold $225
Purple $300
Celery dish
Amethyst $400
Purple $400
Compote, 6″, clover-shaped base
Amethyst $550
Marigold $450
Purple $550
Creamer
Amethyst $125
Blue $150
Green $150
Marigold $100
Purple $125
Cruet (Imperial), Marigold $125
Pitcher, water
Amethyst $575
Blue $625
Green $625
Marigold $325
Purple $575

Punch bowl
Amethyst $500
Green $550
Marigold $325
Purple $500

Punch bowl with base
Amethyst $700
Green $750
Marigold $400
Purple $700

Punch cup
Amethyst $45
Blue $50
Green $50
Marigold $35
Purple $45

Ringtree (Northwood), Marigold $225

Salt dip, footed (Northwood)
Marigold $55
Vaseline $150

Sauce dish, 5″ diameter, Marigold $40

Sherbet (Northwood)
Amethyst $50
Blue $55
Green $55
Marigold $45
Purple $50

Spooner
Amethyst $105
Green $110
Marigold $65
Purple $105

Sugar
Amethyst $125
Blue $150
Green $150
Marigold $100
Purple $125

Sugar dish with cover
Amethyst $175
Blue $200
Green $200
Marigold $150
Purple $175

Toothpick holder
Amethyst $85
Aqua $200
Blue $100
Green $100
Marigold $75
Purple $85

Toothpick holder, handled
Marigold $100
Smoke $250
Tumbler, several styles
Amethyst $175
Blue $125
Green $200
Marigold $65
Purple $175
Vase, 6″
Amethyst $375
Blue $1500
Green $400
Marigold $275
Purple $375
Vase, 16″
Amethyst $375
Blue $1500
Green $400
Marigold $275
Purple $375
Vase, 19″
Amethyst $425
Blue $1750
Green $500
Marigold $300
Purple $425

FOUR SEVENTY-FOUR   IMPERIAL GLASS COMPANY

474 consists of a central four-petaled flower on a large stalk with thin leaves. The flower is framed by interlocking broken arches of sunbursts. The ridges are usually notched.

Bowl, 8″
Green $85
Marigold $60
Bowl, 9″
Green $95
Marigold $70
Butter dish with cover
Amethyst $250
Green $275
Marigold $150
Purple $250
Compote
Green $100
Marigold $75

Cordial
  Amethyst $175
  Marigold $100
  Purple $175
Creamer
  Amethyst $100
  Green $100
  Marigold $75
  Purple $100
Goblet
  Amethyst $100
  Green $75
  Marigold $55
  Purple $100
Pitcher, milk
  Amethyst $450
  Green $500
  Marigold $225
  Purple $450
Pitcher, water, 2 styles
  Amethyst $550
  Green $600
  Marigold $250
  Purple $550
Punch bowl with base
  Amethyst $650
  Green $750
  Marigold $350
  Purple $650
Punch cup
  Amethyst $45
  Green $50
  Marigold $35
  Purple $45
Sherbet
  Amethyst $90
  Green $90
  Marigold $65
  Purple $90
Sugar
  Amethyst $100
  Green $100
  Marigold $75
  Purple $100
Tumbler
  Amethyst $100
  Green $100
  Marigold $50
  Purple $100
Vase, 7″ tall
  Green $1250

Marigold $850
Red $3500
Vase, 8″ tall
   Green $1350
   Marigold $900
   Red $3750
Vase, 10″ tall
   Green $1400
   Marigold $950
Vase, 14″ tall
   Green $1500
   Marigold $1000
Wine glass, Marigold $100

FROSTED BLOCK   IMPERIAL GLASS COMPANY

This pattern is characterized by stippled glass in panels separated by beading. Some pieces are marked "Made in USA." Dealers in Carnival glass have indicated that they surcharge pieces by a quarter or a third if they are marked "Made in USA" on the underside.

Bowl, 5″
   Clambroth $40
   Marigold $25
   Smoke or White $50
Bowl, 6½″
   Clambroth $45
   Marigold $30
   Smoke or White $55
Bowl, 7½″
   Clambroth $50
   Marigold $35
   Smoke or White $60
Bowl, 8″
   Clambroth $55
   Marigold $40
   Smoke or White $65
Bowl, 9″
   Clambroth $60
   Marigold $45
   Smoke or White $75
Bowl, rose
   Clambroth $80
   Marigold $55
   Smoke or White $100
Bowl, square, 7″
   Clambroth $80
   Marigold $55
   Smoke or White $100

Bowl, square, 8″

   Clambroth $90

   Marigold $60

   Smoke or White $110

Butter dish with cover

   Clambroth $200

   Marigold $150

   Smoke or White $250

Compote

   Clambroth $125

   Marigold $80

   Smoke or White $175

Creamer

   Clambroth $75

   Marigold $50

   Smoke or White $100

Pickle dish, oval, handled

   Clambroth $100

   Marigold $75

   Smoke or White $125

Pitcher, milk

   Clambroth $275

   Marigold $175

   Smoke or White $350

Plate, 6½″

   Clambroth $50

   Marigold $35

   Smoke or White $65

Plate, 7½″

   Clambroth $65

   Marigold $40

   Smoke or White $85

Plate, 9″–9½″

   Clambroth $75

   Marigold $50

   Smoke or White $100

Spooner

   Clambroth $55

   Marigold $40

   Smoke or White $65

Sugar

   Clambroth $75

   Marigold $50

   Smoke or White $100

Tray, celery

   Clambroth $75

   Marigold $50

   Smoke or White $100

Vase, 6″ tall, pedestal feet
Clambroth $75
Marigold $50
Smoke or White $100

FRUIT AND FLOWERS   NORTHWOOD GLASS COMPANY

"Fruit and Flowers" consists of slight variations of apples, pears, and cherries, all with leaves, vines, and foliage.

Banana dish, 7″
Amethyst $350
Green $325
Purple $325
Bonbon dish, stemmed
Amethyst $100
Aqua Opalescent $550
Blue $150
Green $150
Ice Blue $500
Ice Green $500
Marigold $75
Purple $100
White $500
Bowl, berry, 5″
Amethyst $65
Blue $75
Green $75
Ice Blue $100
Ice Green $100
Marigold $45
Purple $65
White $100
Bowl, berry, 9″
Amethyst $100
Blue $150
Green $125
Ice Blue $200
Ice Green $200
Marigold $75
Purple $100
White $200
Bowl, 10″, footed
Amethyst $175
Aqua Opalescent $550
Blue $350
Green $250
Ice Blue $500
Ice Green $500

Marigold $100
Purple $175
White $500
Plate, 7″
Amethyst $125
Blue $150
Green $125
Marigold $75
Purple $125
White $250
Plate, 8″
Amethyst $175
Blue $200
Green $175
Ice Blue $350
Ice Green $350
Marigold $100
Purple $175
White $350
Plate, 9¹/₂″
Amethyst $300
Blue $325
Green $300
Ice Blue $500
Ice Green $500
Marigold $225
Purple $300
White $500

GOLDEN HONEYCOMB   IMPERIAL GLASS COMPANY

This pattern features a large central medallion or sunburst at the base, while the exterior surface has rows of thumbprints inscribed within squares (or honeycombs).

Bonbon dish, 5″ diameter
Amethyst, Purple, Green, or Amber $75
Marigold $50
Bowl, 5″, Marigold $35
Bowl, 7″, Marigold $50
Compote, Marigold $50
Creamer, Marigold $50
Plate, 7″, Marigold $55
Sugar, Marigold $50

GRAPE AND CABLE   FENTON ART GLASS COMPANY, NORTHWOOD GLASS COMPANY

Fenton produced fewer pieces than Northwood (only those noted in the parentheses below). The Fenton pattern features grape bunches alternating with large-veined leaves attached to a vine. The cable is a diagonal series of ridges curving up and down directly below the rim. Northwood's design has large bunches of grapes that are raised in relief from the center. The grapes alternate with the leaves. The cable is formed at the base with teardrops. This is one of the most common patterns of Carnival glass; assembling all varieties would be a monumental task.

Banana boat, 12″, footed
Amethyst	$300
Blue	$350
Green	$350
Ice Blue	$650
Ice Green	$650
Marigold	$225
Purple	$300
White	$650

Bonbon dish
Amethyst	$75
Aqua Opalescent	$800
Blue	$100
Green	$100
Ice Blue	$600
Ice Green	$600
Marigold	$50
Purple	$75
White	$600

Bowl, 4″, ice cream
Amethyst	$50
Blue	$50

Carnival glass, "Grape and Cable" pattern. PHOTO BY *ROBIN RAINWATER.*

Carnival glass, "Grape and Cable" pattern. PHOTO BY MARK PICKVET, COURTESY OF THE FENTON ART GLASS MUSEUM.

Green	$50
Ice Blue	$150
Ice Green	$150
Marigold	$40
Purple	$50
White	$150
Bowl, 5½″	
Amethyst	$45
Blue	$45
Green	$45
Ice Blue	$75
Ice Green	$75
Marigold	$35
Purple	$45
White	$75
Bowl, 5½″, scalloped	
Amethyst	$50
Aqua Opalescent	$750
Blue	$60
Green	$50
Ice Blue	$85
Ice Green	$85
Marigold	$40
Purple	$50
White	$85
Bowl, 7″, footed	
Amethyst	$95
Blue	$95
Green	$95
Ice Blue	$475
Ice Green	$475

Marigold $60
Purple $95
White $475

Bowl, 7″, scalloped
Amethyst $90
Blue $90
Green $90
Ice Blue $450
Ice Green $450
Marigold $55
Purple $90
White $450

Bowl, 7″, (Fenton)
Amethyst $125
Blue $150
Green $125
Marigold $100
Purple $55
Red $1250

Bowl, 8¼″, footed
Bowl, 9″, footed
Bowl, 11″, ice cream
Amethyst $300
Aqua Opalescent $2000
Blue $375
Green $150
Ice Blue $450
Ice Green $450
Marigold $225
Purple $300
White $450

Bowl, 11½″, scalloped
Amethyst $150
Aqua Opalescent $2250
Blue $150
Green $150
Ice Blue $500
Ice Green $500
Marigold $100
Purple 150
White $500

Bowl, berry, 5″
Amethyst $45
Blue $45
Green $45
Ice Blue $75
Ice Green $75
Marigold $35
Purple $45
White $75

Bowl, berry, 9″

Amethyst $125
Blue $125
Green $125
Marigold $100

Bowl, footed (Fenton)

Amethyst $225
Aqua Opalescent $900
Blue $425
Green $225
Red $1250
Marigold $175
Purple $225

Bowl, orange, footed

Amethyst $300
Aqua Opalescent $3000
Blue $350
Green $300
Ice Green $1750
Marigold $150
Purple $300

Butter dish

Amethyst $300
Blue $325
Green $300
Ice Blue $550
Ice Green $550
Marigold $225
Purple $300
White $550

Candlestick

Amethyst $200
Blue $225
Green $200
Marigold $150
Purple $200

Centerpiece, footed

Amethyst $650
Blue $650
Green $650
Ice Blue $850
Ice Green $850
Marigold $450
Purple $650
White $850

Cologne bottle with stopper

Amethyst $250
Green $275
Marigold $225
Purple $250

Compote

Amethyst	$750
Blue	$1250
Green	$1000
Ice Blue	$1000
Ice Green	$1000
Marigold	$525
Purple	$750
White	$1000

Compote with cover

Amethyst	$750
Ice Blue	$2500
Ice Green	$2500
Marigold	$2500
Purple	$750

Cookie jar with cover

Amethyst	$750
Aqua Opalescent	$7500
Blue	$1000
Green	$1000
Marigold	$350
Purple	$750
White	$2500

Creamer

Amethyst	$125
Blue	$150
Green	$150
Ice Blue	$275
Ice Green	$275
Marigold	$75
Purple	$125
White	$275

Cup

Amethyst	$75
Blue	$100
Green	$75
Ice Blue	$175
Ice Green	$175
Marigold	$35
Purple	$75
White	$175

Cuspidor

Amethyst	$7500
Blue	$7500
Green	$7500
Marigold	$7500
Purple	$7500

Decanter with stopper

Amethyst	$1500
Blue	$17500
Green	$1500

Marigold $1250
Purple $1500

Dresser tray
Amethyst $275
Blue $400
Green $300
Ice Blue $550
Ice Green $550
Marigold $175
Purple $275
White $550

Fernery
Amethyst $2000
Blue $2500
Green $2250
Ice Blue $5000
Ice Green $5000
Marigold $1750
Purple $5000
White $2000

Hat
Amethyst $60
Blue $75
Green $60
Ice Blue $100
Ice Green $100
Marigold $40
Purple $60
White $100

Hatpin holder
Amethyst $600
Aqua Opalescent $10000
Blue $1000
Green $750
Ice Blue $1750
Ice Green $1750
Marigold $250
Purple $600
White $1750

Lamp, candle
Amethyst $600
Blue $1000
Green $750
Marigold $500
Purple $600

Lamp shade
Amethyst $300
Blue $350
Green $325
Marigold $225
Purple $300

Nappy

Amethyst	$150
Blue	$200
Green	$175
Ice Blue	$350
Ice Green	$350
Marigold	$100
Purple	$150
White	$350

Pin tray

Amethyst	$250
Blue	$300
Green	$275
Ice Blue	$400
Ice Green	$400
Marigold	$175
Purple	$250
White	$400

Pitcher, tankard

Amethyst	$1250
Blue	$3000
Green	$2500
Ice Blue	$4000
Ice Green	$4000
Marigold	$1000
Purple	$1250
White	$4000

Pitcher, water

Amethyst	$500
Blue	$750
Green	$550
Ice Blue	$2500
Ice Green	$2500
Marigold	$350
Purple	$500
White	$2500

Plate, 6″

Amethyst	$400
Aqua Opalescent	$5000
Blue	$500
Green	$450
Ice Blue	$1000
Ice Green	$1000
Marigold	$125
Purple	$400
White	$1000

Plate, 7¹/₂″

Amethyst	$500
Aqua Opalescent	$6000
Blue	$600
Green	$550

Ice Blue $1250
Ice Green $1250
Marigold $150
Purple $500
White $1250

Plate, 9½″
Amethyst $600
Aqua Opalescent $7500
Blue $750
Green $650
Ice Blue $1500
Ice Green $1500
Marigold $175
Purple $600
White $1500

Plate with advertising
Green $750

Plate, footed
Amethyst $125
Blue $150
Green $125
Ice Blue $300
Ice Green $300
Marigold $100
Purple $125
White $300

Plate, footed, 9″, (Fenton)
Amethyst $300
Blue $200
Green $200
Marigold $155
Red $1750
Purple $300

Powder jar with cover
Amethyst $175
Aqua Opalescent $2000
Blue $250
Green $200
Ice Blue $500
Ice Green $500
Marigold $100
Purple $175
White $500

Punch bowl with base, 12″
Amethyst $650
Blue $1000
Green $750
Marigold $500
Purple $650

Punch bowl with base, 24″
Amethyst $3250

Aqua Opalescent $20000
Blue $4500
Green $3500
Ice Blue $7500
Ice Green $7500
Marigold $2500
Purple $3250
White $7500

Punch bowl, 16″
Amethyst $850
Blue $1250
Green $1000
Ice Blue $5000
Ice Green $5000
Marigold $600
Purple $850
White $5000

Punch cup
Amethyst $55
Aqua Opalescent $500
Blue $75
Green $60
Ice Blue $100
Ice Green $100
Marigold $35
Purple $55
White $100

Saucer
Amethyst $90
Ice Blue $175
Ice Green $175
Marigold $75
Purple $90
White $175

Sherbet
Amethyst $75
Green $75
Ice Blue $150
Ice Green $150
Marigold $45
Purple $75
White $150

Shot glass
Amethyst $300
Marigold $200
Purple $300

Spittoon
Amethyst $7500
Green $8000
Marigold $5000
Purple $7500

Spittoon (Fenton)
Marigold $2500
Spooner
Amethyst $175
Blue $175
Green $175
Ice Blue $350
Ice Green $350
Marigold $75
Purple $175
White $350
Sugar
Amethyst $100
Blue $100
Green $100
Ice Blue $200
Ice Green $200
Marigold $75
Purple $200
White $100
Sugar with cover
Amethyst $200
Blue $225
Green $150
Ice Blue $300
Ice Green $300
Marigold $100
Purple $200
White $300
Sweetmeat compote with cover
Amethyst $250
Blue $2500
Green $2000
Ice Blue $300
Ice Green $300
Marigold $1750
Purple $250
Sweetmeat dish
Amethyst $500
Blue $500
Green $500
Marigold $500
Purple $500
Tobacco jar with cover
Amethyst $750
Blue $1250
Green $1000
Marigold $425
Purple $750
Tray, dresser
Amethyst $250

Blue	$300
Green	$400
Ice Blue	$800
Ice Green	$800
Marigold	$175
Purple	$250
White	$800

Tumbler, 6 oz.

Amethyst	$100
Blue	$150
Green	$125
Ice Blue	$300
Ice Green	$300
Marigold	$75
Purple	$100
White	$300

Tumbler, 10 oz.

Ice Blue	$400
Ice Green	$400
Purple	$500
White	$150

Tumbler, 12 oz.

Amethyst	$125
Blue	$175
Green	$150
Marigold	$85

Tumbler, 16 oz.

Amethyst	$150
Blue	$225
Green	$175
Ice Blue	$500
Ice Green	$500
Purple	$150
White	$500

GRAPE AND GOTHIC ARCHES   NORTHWOOD GLASS COMPANY

This typical grape pattern includes leaves and large grape bunches connected by a vine. In the background are pointed arches that resemble a picket fence. Pearl is similar to clambroth in terms of pastel Carnival colors. The price for clambroth is the same as for pearl.

Bowl, 5″

Amethyst	$55
Blue	$50
Green	$55
Marigold	$35
Pearl	$75
Purple	$55

Carnival glass, "Grape and Gothic Arches" pattern.
DRAWING BY MARK PICKVET.

Bowl, berry, 10″
Amethyst $125
Blue $85
Green $95
Marigold $65
Pearl $200
Purple $125
Butter dish with cover
Amethyst $175
Blue $150
Green $175
Marigold $125
Pearl $450
Purple $175
Creamer
Amethyst $100
Blue $85
Green $95
Marigold $55
Pearl $225
Purple $100
Pitcher, water
Amethyst $425
Blue $400
Green $425
Marigold $250
Pearl $850
Purple $425
Spooner
Amethyst $90
Blue $75
Green $85
Marigold $50
Pearl $200
Purple $90
Sugar dish with cover
Amethyst $135
Blue $100

Green	$125
Marigold	$75
Pearl	$250
Purple	$135
Tumbler	
Amethyst	$85
Blue	$65
Green	$75
Marigold	$40
Pearl	$200
Purple	$85

GRAPE IMPERIAL GLASS COMPANY

Imperial's "Grape" is a fairly common pattern except for the larger items (cuspidors, pitchers, and punch bowls). Other Grape designs such as Fenton's and Northwood's are usually referred to as "Grape and Cable" (see entry). For vaseline pieces, use the same price as for smoke.

Basket	
Green	$100
Marigold	$75
Smoke	$200
Bottle, water	
Clambroth	$300
Green	$225
Marigold	$150
Purple	$200
Bowl, berry, 5″	
Green	$45
Marigold	$35
Purple	$45
Smoke	$75
Bowl, berry, 6″	
Green	$50
Marigold	$40
Purple	$50
Smoke	$80
Bowl, fruit, 8¾″	
Green	$55
Marigold	$45
Purple	$55
Red	$400
Smoke	$85
Bowl, rose	
Amethyst	$225
Green	$225
Marigold	$175
Purple	$225
Smoke	$325

Compote

Amethyst $60
Green $60
Marigold $45
Purple $60
Smoke $275

Cup

Amethyst $100
Green $50
Marigold $40
Purple $100
Smoke $50

Cuspidor

Green $2500
Marigold $1000

Decanter with stopper, wine

Amethyst $200
Green $175
Marigold $125
Purple $200
Smoke $500

Goblet

Amber $90
Amethyst $80
Green $80
Marigold $50
Purple $80
Smoke $150

Lamp shade, Marigold $100

Nappy

Green $45
Marigold $35
Smoke $75

Pitcher, milk

Amethyst $400
Green $350
Marigold $300
Purple $400
Smoke $750

Pitcher, water

Amethyst $350
Green $300
Marigold $150
Purple $350
Smoke $650

Plate, 6″

Amber $150
Amethyst $250
Green $150
Marigold $65

Purple $250
Smoke $325

Plate, 7″
Amber $175
Amethyst $300
Green $175
Marigold $75
Purple $300
Smoke $375

Plate, 8¹/₂″
Amethyst $100
Green $100
Marigold $75
Purple $100
Smoke $175

Plate, 8¹/₂″, ruffled
Amethyst $80
Green $80
Marigold $70
Purple $80
Smoke $90

Plate, 12″
Amber $325
Amethyst $375
Blue $1500
Green $325
Marigold $90
Purple $375
Smoke $675

Punch bowl with base
Amber $500
Amethyst $475
Green $400
Marigold $200
Purple $475
Smoke $750

Punch cup
Amber $50
Amethyst $45
Green $45
Marigold $35
Purple $45
Smoke $100

Saucer
Amethyst $50
Green $40
Marigold $30
Purple $50
Smoke $35

Spittoon
  Green $2500
  Marigold $1250
Tray, center handle
  Amber $100
  Marigold $75
Tumbler
  Amber $75
  Amethyst $60
  Green $55
  Marigold $35
  Purple $60
  Smoke $100
Wine glass
  Amethyst $55
  Green $50
  Marigold $40
  Purple $55

GREEK KEY   NORTHWOOD GLASS COMPANY

"Greek Key" is a common pattern that consists of a maze interlocking "e" designs. At the top are semicircles with tiny seven-petaled flowers. In the middle is the maze design, and at the bottom are stretched diamonds with circles at the top.

Bowl, 7″
  Blue $400
  Green $175
  Marigold $100
  Purple $150
Bowl, 8½″
  Blue $450
  Green $200
  Marigold $125
  Purple $175
Bowl, 8½″, dome, footed
  Green $100
  Marigold $75
  Purple $90
Hatpin (pattern variant), Purple $100
Pitcher, water
  Blue $2750
  Green $1750
  Marigold $750
  Purple $1250
Plate, 9″
  Aqua Opalescent $3000
  Blue $2750
  Green $1500

Marigold $750
Purple $1000
Plate, 11″
Aqua Opalescent $3250
Blue $3000
Green $1750
Marigold $850
Purple $1250
Tumbler
Blue $500
Green $400
Marigold $125
Purple $350

HEISEY CARNIVAL GLASS   A.H. HEISEY COMPANY

Although not a huge producer of Carnival glass, Heisey did make some iridized glass during this period.

Bottle, water (line #357), Marigold $275
Breakfast set, Pastel $550
Candy jar with cover, 11″ tall, stemmed, Floral Spray design, Ice Blue $325
Compote, Cartwheel style
Clambroth $525
Marigold $225
Creamer
Clambroth $450
Ice Blue $450
Marigold $150
Frog dish with cover
Ice Blue $1500
Marigold $750
White or Ice Green $1750
Punch cup (Flute design), Marigold $50
Sugar
Clambroth $450
Ice Blue $450
Marigold $150
Toothpick holder
Clambroth $425
Marigold $225
Tray
Clambroth $375
Ice Blue $375
Marigold $175
Tumbler (line #357), Marigold $85
Turtle dish with cover, Green or pink $750

HIGBEE CARNIVAL GLASS   HIGBEE GLASS COMPANY

Higbee did not produce much Carnival glass. Since the company was established in
1900, the beginning of the Carnival fad, it is easy to see that it would have produced
some iridized glassware. Note that much of Higbee's glass features the company's
raised bee trademark.

Bowl, 8″, Floral Oval pattern, Marigold $65
Creamer, Floral Oval pattern, Marigold $75
Creamer, Hawaiian Lei pattern, Marigold $85
Cruet with stopper, Diamond Fountain pattern, Marigold $1000
Mug, arched Fleur-de-Lys pattern, Marigold $250
Mug, Nell pattern, Marigold $100
Mug, ribbed ellipse design
    Amber $175
    Marigold $125
Pitcher, water, Heavy Heart pattern, Marigold $550
Pitcher, water, Paneled Thistle design, Marigold $750
Plate, 7″, Floral Oval pattern, Marigold $125
Sugar, Floral Oval pattern, Marigold $75
Sugar, Hawaiian Lei pattern, Marigold $85
Tumbler, Heavy Heart pattern, Marigold $150
Tumbler, Paneled Thistle design, Marigold $125

HOBNAIL   MILLERSBURG GLASS COMPANY

This pattern is quite common, especially in Westmoreland pieces; however, in Carnival glass it is quite rare. The knobs of the Millersburg pieces are very glossy and
refract quite well. There are fewer rows of hobs in the pattern variant.

Bowl (marigold has cherries in pattern)
    Amethyst $1250
    Blue $1500
    Green $1250
    Marigold $1000
    Purple $1250
Bowl, rose
    Amethyst $550
    Blue $750
    Green $600
    Marigold $200
    Purple $550
Bowl, rose (pattern variant), Marigold $1250
Butter dish
    Amethyst $750
    Blue $1000
    Green $800
    Marigold $550
    Purple $750

Carnival glass, "Hobnail"
pattern. PHOTO BY MARK PICKVET,
COURTESY OF THE FENTON ART
GLASS MUSEUM.

Creamer

Amethyst	$400
Blue	$500
Green	$450
Marigold	$275
Purple	$400

Hat vase

Amethyst	$1750
Blue	$2500
Green	$2000
Marigold	$1500
Purple	$1750

Jardiniere (pattern variant)

Amethyst	$1250
Blue	$1500

Pitcher, 6″ tall, miniature, Marigold $275

Pitcher, water

Amethyst	$2750
Blue	$3500
Green	$3000
Marigold	$2000
Purple	$2750

Spittoon

Amethyst	$1250
Blue	$1750
Green	$1500
Marigold	$750
Purple	$1250

Spooner

Amethyst	$350
Blue	$450
Green	$400
Marigold	$225
Purple	$350

Sugar dish with cover
Amethyst $550
Blue $650
Green $600
Marigold $350
Purple $550
Tumbler
Amethyst $750
Blue $1000
Green $900
Marigold $550
Purple $750
Tumbler, 2¹/₂″ tall, miniature, Marigold $60
Vase
Amethyst $300
Green $350
Vase (pattern variant)
Amethyst $1000
Green $1000
Marigold $900

HOBSTAR AND FEATHER   MILLERSBURG GLASS COMPANY

Feathers surround a finely molded hobstar in this pattern. Rims are usually scalloped, and the bottom has a horizontal band. A punch bowl with 12 matching cups
is especially impressive.

Bowl, 5″
Amethyst $500
Marigold $350
Purple $500
Bowl, 5″, diamond-shaped, Marigold $425
Bowl, 5″, heart-shaped, Marigold $400
Bowl, 10″, square, Purple $2250
Bowl, rose
Green $3000
Marigold $2500
Purple $3000
Butter dish with cover
Green $2000
Marigold $1500
Purple $2000
Compote
Amethyst $5500
Marigold $1750
Purple $5500
Creamer
Green $875
Marigold $775
Purple $875

Punch bowl with base
Amethyst $4000
Blue $5000
Green $4000
Marigold $2500
Purple $4000

Punch cup
Amethyst $325
Blue $350
Green $325
Marigold $250
Purple $325

Sherbet, Marigold $750

Spooner
Green $825
Marigold $725
Purple $825

Sugar dish with cover
Green $1250
Marigold $900
Purple $1250

Vase
Amethyst $3000
Green $3000
Marigold $2250
Purple $3000

HOBSTAR BAND   IMPERIAL GLASS COMPANY

The pattern has small hobstars within pointed ovals around the top. The lower part features vertical beading.

Bowl, Marigold $100
Celery dish, Marigold $100
Compote, Marigold $125
Pitcher, 2 styles, Marigold $325
Tumbler, 2 styles, Marigold $90

HOBSTAR   IMPERIAL GLASS COMPANY

This design is the same as that found on cut glass. The molding contains some fine faceting and is often confused with cut glass. The pattern variant features hobstars surrounded by beaded broken arches.

Basket, bride's, Marigold $100
Bowl, 5″
Marigold $35
Smoke $55

Bowl, 6″, ruffled
  Marigold $40
  Smoke $60
Bowl, 8″, ruffled
  Marigold $45
  Smoke $65
Bowl, 9″ **(pattern variant)**
  Amethyst $75
  Green $75
  Marigold $50
  Smoke $80
Bowl, 10″
  Marigold $50
  Smoke $75
Bowl, 12″, ruffled
  Marigold $65
  Smoke $85
Bowl, fruit, with base
  Amethyst $90
  Green $90
  Marigold $75
  Purple $90
Bowl, fruit, with base (pattern variant)
  Amethyst $125
  Green $125
  Marigold $100
  Smoke $175
Butter dish with cover
  Amethyst $225
  Green $225
  Marigold $100
  Purple $225
Cookie jar with cover
  Amethyst $175
  Green $175
  Marigold $125
  Purple $175
Creamer
  Amethyst $150
  Green $150
  Marigold $50
  Purple $150
  Smoke $200
Pickle castor, Marigold $750
Punch bowl with base
  Green $1000
  Marigold $750
Punch cup
  Green $85
  Marigold $50

Spooner

Amethyst	$125
Green	$125
Marigold	$40
Purple	$125

Sugar dish with cover

Amethyst	$200
Green	$200
Marigold	$75
Purple	$200
Smoke	$250

Vase, flared

Amethyst	$225
Green	$225
Marigold	$175
Purple	$225

HOLLY SPRIG   MILLERSBURG GLASS COMPANY

This pattern is often referred to as "Whirl" because of the whirling shape of the design. Within the design are holly leaves and berries in a circular style.

Bonbon dish

Green	$200
Marigold	$125
Purple	$175

Bowl, 7″

Clambroth	$150
Green	$85
Marigold	$65
Purple	$75

Bowl, 7″, tricornered

Green	$250
Marigold	$150
Purple	$200

Bowl, 10″, ruffled

Clambroth	$200
Green	$100
Marigold	$75
Purple	$90

Bowl, 10″, tricornered

Green	$325
Marigold	$200
Purple	$275

Bowl, rose

Green	$750
Marigold	$400
Purple	$600
Vaseline	$1250

Compote

Green $750
Marigold $400
Purple $600
Vaseline $1250

Nappy, tricornered

Green $150
Marigold $100
Purple $125

Sauce dish

Green $400
Marigold $200
Purple $350

Tray, handled

Green $200
Marigold $125
Purple $175

HOLLY   FENTON ART GLASS COMPANY

"Holly" is characterized by holly leaves and vines emanating from the center. The foliage also creates a raised circular pattern in relief.

Bowl, 7¼″

Amethyst $85
Blue $100
Green $125
Ice Blue $150
Ice Green $150
Marigold $65
Peach Opalescent $1000
Red $2000
Vaseline $175
White $150

Bowl, 8″

Amethyst $95
Blue $110
Green $150
Ice Blue $175
Ice Green $175
Marigold $75
Peach Opalescent $1000
Red $2250
Vaseline $200
White $175

Bowl, 10″

Amethyst $110
Blue $125
Green $175

Ice Blue $200
Ice Green $200
Marigold $85
Red $2500
Vaseline $225
White $200

Bowl, rose
Amethyst $600
Blue $750
Green $1000
Ice Blue $1000
Ice Green $1000
Marigold $500
Vaseline $1250
White $600

Compote, 5″ (small)
Amethyst $150
Blue $125
Green $175
Ice Blue $175
Ice Green $175
Marigold $55
Red $1750
Vaseline $200
White $175

Goblet
Amethyst $100
Blue $150
Green $175
Ice Blue $175
Ice Green $175
Marigold $40
Red $1500
Vaseline $200
White $100

Hat vase
Amethyst $100
Blue $150
Green $175
Ice Blue $175
Ice Green $175
Marigold $45
Red $1000
Vaseline $200
White $100

Plate
Amethyst $350
Blue $350
Green $450
Ice Blue $500
Ice Green $500

Marigold $175
Red $2750
Vaseline $500
White $350

INVERTED FEATHER   CAMBRIDGE GLASS COMPANY

Cambridge was not a major producer of iridized or Carnival glass; however, it did
manufacture a few inverted patterns. "Inverted Feather" covers the entire surface
with scrolls, hobstars, ridged frames, florals, and draped beading.

Butter dish with cover
Amethyst $550
Marigold $450
Compote
Amethyst $150
Marigold $85
Cracker jar with cover
Amethyst $450
Green $450
Marigold $275
Creamer
Amethyst $450
Marigold $350
Parfait dish
Amethyst $225
Marigold $125
Pitcher, milk
Amethyst $1750
Marigold $1000
Pitcher, water
Amethyst $5500
Green $5500
Marigold $4500
Punch bowl with base
Amethyst $4000
Green $4000
Marigold $3000
Punch cup
Amethyst $125
Green $125
Marigold $75
Spooner
Amethyst $375
Marigold $275
Sugar
Green $450
Marigold $350
Tumbler
Amethyst $750

Green $750
Marigold $600
Wine glass
Amethyst $300
Marigold $200

INVERTED STRAWBERRY   CAMBRIDGE GLASS COMPANY

The second of Cambridge's inverted patterns, this design is characterized by diamond-molded strawberries with branches and leaves.

Bowl, berry, 5″
Amethyst $85
Blue $100
Green $75
Marigold $50
Bowl, berry, 9″
Amethyst $325
Blue $350
Green $300
Marigold $125
Bowl, 10¹/₂″
Amethyst $375
Blue $400
Green $350
Marigold $150
Butter dish with cover
Amethyst $1000
Blue $1500
Green $1000
Marigold $750
Candlestick
Amethyst $250
Blue $400
Green $300
Marigold $150
Celery dish
Amethyst $700
Blue $750
Green $650
Marigold $350
Compote (large)
Amethyst $525
Blue $575
Green $500
Marigold $400
Compote (small)
Amethyst $475
Blue $500

Green $450
Marigold $350

Creamer
Amethyst $225
Blue $250
Green $200
Marigold $125
Purple $325

Cruet with stopper
Amethyst $2000
Blue $2250
Green $1750
Marigold $1000

Cuspidor
Amethyst $1750
Blue $1750
Green $1500
Marigold $1250

Honey dish, Marigold $150

Pitcher, milk
Amethyst $2250
Green $2000
Marigold $1250

Pitcher, water
Amethyst $3500
Green $3250
Marigold $2250

Powder jar
Green $325
Marigold $200

Spittoon
Amethyst $1250
Green $1000
Marigold $750

Spooner
Amethyst $200
Blue $200
Green $175
Marigold $100
Purple $225

Sugar
Amethyst $225
Blue $250
Green $200
Marigold $125
Purple $325

Sugar, stemmed, Purple $500

Tumbler
Amethyst $475
Blue $500

Green $450
Marigold $375

INVERTED THISTLE   CAMBRIDGE GLASS COMPANY

In this pattern, thistle replaces the strawberries in "Inverted Strawberry." The thistle branches and leaves are formed into scrolls.

Bowl, 5″
Amethyst $225
Green $225
Bowl, 9″
Amethyst $325
Green $325
Box with cover, Peach Opalescent $750
Butter dish with cover
Amethyst $650
Green $750
Marigold $450
Creamer
Amethyst $450
Green $500
Marigold $375
Pitcher, milk, Amethyst $3000
Pitcher, water
Amethyst $4000
Marigold $3500
Plate, chop
Amethyst $2500
Spittoon, Amethyst $3750
Spooner
Amethyst $425
Green $450
Marigold $350
Sugar
Amethyst $450
Green $500
Marigold $375

Carnival glass. Left: "Inverted Thistle" pattern. Right: "Luster and Clear" pattern (see page 358).
DRAWINGS BY MARK PICKVET.

Tumbler
Amethyst $450
Green $500
Marigold $400

KITTENS   FENTON ART GLASS COMPANY

This pattern consists of kittens scrambling over each other to drink from an oval bowl. A few pieces have been found in pastel colors such as aqua, smoke, and light lavender (increase the price for blue by 25%).

Bowl, 4"
Cobalt Blue $500
Marigold $200
Purple $450
Vaseline $475
Bowl, 6"
Cobalt Blue $550
Marigold $225
Bowl, flared straight sides
Cobalt Blue $500
Marigold $200
Purple $450
Cup
Cobalt Blue $750
Marigold $200
Plate, 4½"
Cobalt Blue $225
Marigold $150
Saucer
Cobalt Blue $450
Marigold $150
Spittoon
Cobalt Blue $4000
Marigold $3500
Spooner
Cobalt Blue $400
Marigold $150
Vaseline $400
Vase, 3"–3½" tall
Cobalt Blue $450
Marigold $200
Vaseline $425

LEAF TIERS   FENTON ART GLASS COMPANY

"Leaf Tiers" features rows of overlapping leaves. Purple is more common than blue or green, and all of the pieces are footed.

Banana dish, footed, Marigold $225
Bowl, berry, 5″, footed
   Blue $100
   Green $125
   Marigold $45
   Purple $85
Bowl, berry, 10″, footed
   Blue $125
   Green $150
   Marigold $75
   Purple $110
Butter dish, footed
   Blue $350
   Green $400
   Marigold $200
   Purple $300
Creamer, footed
   Blue $200
   Green $250
   Marigold $125
   Purple $175
Pitcher, water, footed
   Blue $850
   Green $950
   Marigold $550
   Purple $750
Spooner, footed
   Blue $175
   Green $200
   Marigold $100
   Purple $150
Sugar dish, footed
   Blue $200
   Green $250
   Marigold $125
   Purple $175
Tumbler, footed
   Blue $150
   Green $175
   Marigold $100
   Purple $125

LUSTER AND CLEAR   IMPERIAL GLASS COMPANY

This glass is transparent marigold and the design features pillars ending at the rim. There are also matching flutes. For colored pieces other than marigold, double the prices.

Bowl, 5″, Marigold $35
Bowl, 10″, Marigold $45
Bowl, rose, Marigold $100
Butter dish, Marigold $100
Compote, Marigold $55
Creamer, Marigold $65
Nappy, Marigold $55
Pitcher, water, Marigold $425
Salt and pepper shakers, Marigold $100
Sugar, Marigold $65
Tray, celery, 8″, Marigold $55
Tumbler, Marigold $65
Vase, 8″, footed, Marigold $125
Vase, wall, Marigold $55

LUSTER AND FLUTE   NORTHWOOD GLASS COMPANY

This pattern is characterized by vertical flutes or columns topped by a band of latticework.

Bonbon dish, 2-handled
  Amethyst $65
  Green $75
  Marigold $55
  Purple $65
Bowl, 5½″
  Amethyst $55
  Green $60
  Marigold $40
  Purple $55
Bowl, 8″
  Amethyst $75
  Green $85
  Marigold $50
  Purple $75
Compote
  Amethyst $55
  Green $60
  Marigold $45
  Purple $55
Creamer
  Amethyst $65
  Green $75

Carnival glass, "Luster and Flute" pattern. DRAWING BY MARK PICKVET.

Marigold $50
Purple $65
Hat
Amethyst $45
Green $50
Marigold $35
Purple $45
Nappy
Amethyst $65
Green $75
Marigold $45
Purple $65
Punch bowl with base
Amethyst $375
Green $400
Marigold $300
Purple $375
Punch cup
Amethyst $90
Green $100
Marigold $65
Purple $90
Sherbet
Amethyst $45
Green $50
Marigold $35
Purple $45
Sugar
Amethyst $65
Green $75
Marigold $50
Purple $65

LUSTER ROSE   IMPERIAL GLASS COMPANY

This early Imperial pattern consists of a band of roses within thorns and other foliage.

Bowl, 6″, ruffled
Amber $80
Clambroth $80
Green $55
Marigold $45
Purple $50
Smoke $80
Bowl, 7″
Amber $80
Clambroth $80
Green $55
Marigold $45
Purple $50
Smoke $80
Bowl, 8″
Amber $85
Clambroth $85
Green $60
Marigold $50
Purple $60
Smoke $85
Bowl, 9″
Amber $90
Clambroth $90
Green $65
Marigold $55
Purple $65
Smoke $90
Bowl, 11″
Amber $90
Clambroth $90
Green $70
Marigold $60
Purple $70
Smoke $90
Bowl, 12″, footed
Amber $95
Clambroth $95
Green $75
Marigold $65
Purple $75
Red $3750
Smoke $95
Bowl, berry, 5″
Amber $75
Clambroth $75
Green $50

Marigold $40
Purple $50
Smoke $75

Bowl, berry, 9″, footed
Amber $95
Clambroth $95
Green $70
Marigold $60
Purple $70
Red $3500
Smoke $95

Bowl, rose
Clambroth $175
Green $100
Marigold $75
Purple $100

Butter dish
Amber $125
Green $85
Marigold $75
Purple $85

Creamer
Amber $100
Green $65
Marigold $45
Purple $65

Fernery, footed
Amber $200
Clambroth $250
Green $85
Marigold $55
Purple $85
Smoke $225

Spooner
Amber $85
Green $60
Marigold $40
Purple $60

Sugar dish with cover
Amber $125
Green $75
Marigold $55
Purple $75

Tumbler
Amber $85
Clambroth $125
Green $75
Marigold $50
Purple $75
Smoke $100

MAPLE LEAF   DUGAN GLASS COMPANY

The maple leaves in this pattern are intertwined within ridging that gives a raised appearance. Above the design is a horizontal line of semicircles.

Bowl, 4½″, ice cream, stemmed (small)
  Amethyst $100
  Blue $85
  Marigold $65
  Purple $85
Bowl, 9″, ice cream, stemmed (large)
  Amethyst $125
  Blue $100
  Marigold $80
  Purple $100
Butter dish with cover
  Amethyst $175
  Blue $150
  Marigold $125
  Purple $150
Creamer
  Amethyst $85
  Blue $75
  Marigold $65
  Purple $75
Pitcher, water
  Amethyst $375
  Blue $350
  Marigold $175
  Purple $300
Spooner
  Amethyst $75
  Blue $70
  Marigold $60
  Purple $70
Sugar dish with cover
  Amethyst $115
  Blue $100
  Marigold $85
  Purple $100
Tumbler
  Amethyst $60
  Blue $50
  Marigold $45
  Purple $50

MELON RIB   IMPERIAL GLASS COMPANY

"Melon Rib" is a fairly simple pattern that consists of wide horizontal ribbing.

Bowl, 10″, Marigold $40
Candy jar with cover, Marigold $125
Decanter with stopper, Marigold $175
Pitcher, water, Marigold $150
Puff box with cover, Marigold $125
Salt and pepper shakers, Marigold $75
Tumbler, Marigold $40

MEMPHIS   NORTHWOOD GLASS COMPANY

Memphis is a cutlike geometric pattern with starred ovals and diamonds. For pastel colors such as ice blue and ice green, double the prices listed for blue. Pieces are available in plain crystal without Carnival flashing (half the price of marigold).

Bowl, 5″
   Amethyst $65
   Blue $100
   Green $75
   Marigold $50
Bowl, 10″
   Amethyst $175
   Blue $250
   Green $200
   Marigold $100
Bowl, fruit, with base
   Amethyst $650
   Blue $1250
   Green $750
   Marigold $400
Creamer
   Amethyst $100
   Blue $175
   Green $125
   Marigold $65
Punch bowl with base
   Amethyst $750
   Blue $1500
   Green $850
   Marigold $550
Punch cup
   Amethyst $75
   Blue $125
   Green $85
   Marigold $50

Sugar

Amethyst $100
Blue $175
Green $125
Marigold $65

OCTAGON   IMPERIAL GLASS COMPANY

"Octagon," as the name implies, consists of eight heavily mold-designed panels. The panels have a variety of stars, diamonds, beads, arches, and other geometrical designs.

Bowl, 4¹/₂″

Amethyst $45
Green $45
Marigold $30
Purple $45

Bowl, 8¹/₂″

Amethyst $55
Green $55
Marigold $45
Purple $55
White $100

Bowl, 10″

Amethyst $75
Green $75
Marigold $60
Purple $75

Bowl, 12″

Amethyst $100
Green $100
Marigold $75
Purple $100
White $150

Butter dish with cover

Amethyst $350
Green $350
Marigold $150
Purple $350

Compote (large)

Amethyst $350
Green $350
Marigold $125
Purple $350

Compote, 5″, (small)

Amethyst $300
Green $300
Marigold $100
Purple $300

Cordial
Marigold $125
White $200
Creamer
Amethyst $85
Green $85
Marigold $60
Purple $85
Cup
Amethyst $85
Green $85
Marigold $60
Purple $85
Decanter with stopper
Amethyst $400
Aqua $1000
Green $750
Marigold $175
Purple $400
White $850
Goblet
Amethyst $100
Green $100
Marigold $75
Purple $100
Nappy, handled
Amethyst $400
Green $400
Marigold $175
Purple $400
Pitcher, milk
Amethyst $250
Green $225
Marigold $175
Purple $250
Pitcher, water, 8″, small
Amethyst $325
Aqua $1500
Green $350
Marigold $200
Purple $325
White $450
Pitcher, water, large
Amethyst $450
Aqua $2500
Green $500
Marigold $300
Purple $450
White $950
Salt and pepper shakers
Amethyst $500

Marigold $300
Purple $500
Sherbet
Amethyst $100
Green $100
Marigold $75
Purple $100
Spooner
Amethyst $75
Green $75
Marigold $55
Purple $75
Sugar dish with cover
Amethyst $100
Green $100
Marigold $75
Purple $100
Toothpick holder
Amethyst $500
Green $500
Marigold $175
Purple $500
Tumbler, 2 styles
Amethyst $100
Aqua $325
Green $125
Marigold $45
Purple $100
Smoke $150
White $150
Vase, 8″ tall
Amethyst $175
Green $175
Marigold $100
Purple $175
Wine glass
Amethyst $75
Green $75
Marigold $50
Purple $75

OPTIC AND BUTTONS   IMPERIAL GLASS COMPANY

Vertical panels with a band of beads at the top make up this simple pattern by Imperial. It is believed that this pattern was produced only in marigold; however, there have been reports of pieces found in smoke and clambroth (double the listed prices).

Bowl, 5″, Marigold $30
Bowl, 6″, Marigold $35
Bowl, 8″, Marigold $40

Carnival glass, "Optic and Buttons" pattern.
DRAWING BY MARK PICKVET.

Bowl, 10″, Marigold $45
Bowl, 12″, 2-handled, Marigold $60
Bowl, rose, Marigold $80
Compote, Marigold $55
Cup, Marigold $75
Goblet, Marigold $75
Nut cup, 2-handled, Marigold $150
Pitcher, water, Marigold $225
Plate, 6″, Marigold $50
Plate, 7″, Marigold $60
Plate, 9¹/₂″, Marigold $75
Plate, 10¹/₂″, Marigold $85
Salt dish, open, 2-handled, Marigold $150
Saucer, Marigold $45
Tumbler, 2 styles, Marigold $100
Wine glass, Marigold $75

ORANGE TREE   FENTON ART GLASS COMPANY

This pattern is characterized by a thick tree trunk with three branches; the branches have orange blossoms with stippled centers.

Bowl, 8″
   Amethyst $65
   Blue $70
   Green $70
   Marigold $55
   Purple $65
   Red $2500
   White $125
Bowl, 10″
   Amethyst $75
   Blue $75
   Green $75
   Marigold $65
   Milk glass $450

Carnival glass, "Orange Tree" pattern. PHOTO BY MARK PICKVET, COURTESY OF THE FENTON ART GLASS MUSEUM.

Purple $75
Red $3000
White $175
Bowl, 11″, footed
Amethyst $150
Blue $175
Green $175
Marigold $100
Purple $150
Red $4000
White $250
Bowl, berry, 5¹/₂″, footed
Blue $65
Green $65
Marigold $50
White $125
Bowl, berry, 9″, footed
Blue $100
Green $100
Marigold $75
Red $3500
White $175
Bowl, orange, footed
Amethyst $150
Blue $175
Green $175
Marigold $100
Purple $150
White $250
Bowl, rose
Amethyst $70

Carnival glass, "Orange Tree" pattern. PHOTO BY MARK PICKVET, COURTESY OF THE FENTON ART GLASS MUSEUM.

Blue	$75
Green	$75
Marigold	$65
Purple	$70
Red	$3000
White	$275

Butter dish with cover

Blue	$350
Ice Blue	$500
Ice Green	$500
Marigold	$250
White	$400

Centerpiece, 12″ footed

Blue	$3000
Green	$1500
Marigold	$900

Compote

Aqua Opalescent	$500
Amethyst	$65
Blue	$75
Green	$90
Ice Blue	$175
Ice Green	$175
Marigold	$50
Purple	$65
White	$175

Creamer, 2 styles

Blue	$85
Ice Blue	$150

Ice Green $150
Marigold $60
White $150
Cruet, Blue $1500
Goblet
Aqua Opalescent $225
Blue $225
Marigold $90
Hatpin holder
Blue $350
Green $400
Marigold $225
Peach Opalescent $2750
White $475
Mug
Aqua Opalescent $200
Amber $275
Amethyst $125
Blue $150
Green $175
Marigold $90
Purple $125
Red $1000
Vaseline $500
White $1250
Mug, shaving
Amethyst $125
Blue $150
Green $175
Marigold $90
Purple $125
Pitcher, water, (pattern has scrolls)
Amethyst $650
Green $750
Marigold $375
Pitcher, water, footed
Blue $400
Ice Blue $5000
Ice Green $5000
Marigold $300
White $1000
Plate, 8″
Amethyst $350
Blue $375
Green $500
Marigold $175
Peach Opalescent $2250
Purple $350
White $650
Plate, 9¹/₂″
Amethyst $425

Blue $450
Green $650
Marigold $225
Peach Opalescent $2500
Purple $425
White $750

Powder jar with cover

Amethyst $175
Blue $175
Green $500
Marigold $150
Purple $175
White $250

Punch bowl with base

Amethyst $375
Blue $375
Green $500
Marigold $275
Peach Opalescent $2500
Purple $375
White $600

Punch cup

Amethyst $50
Blue $50
Green $60
Marigold $40
Peach Opalescent $275
Purple $50
White $75

Sherbet

Blue $50
Marigold $35

Spooner

Blue $85
Ice Blue $150
Ice Green $150
Marigold $60
White $150

Sugar

Blue $85
Ice Blue $150
Ice Green $150
Marigold $60
White $150

Sugar with cover

Blue $125
Ice Blue $200
Ice Green $200
Marigold $80
White $200

Tumbler (pattern has scrolls)
Blue $85
Marigold $65
White $100

Tumbler, footed
Blue $55
Ice Blue $175
Ice Green $175
Marigold $45
White $125

Wine glass
Aqua Opalescent $275
Blue $150
Green $300
Marigold $35
Peach Opalescent $275

PALM BEACH   U.S. GLASS COMPANY

Although U.S. Glass did not manufacture much iridized glass, it did produce a few odd pieces and patterns during the Carnival glass era.

Banana dish
Amber $200
Marigold $125
Purple $250
White $275

Bowl, 5″
Amber $100
Marigold $40
White $125

Bowl, 9″
Amber $125
Marigold $60
White $150

Bowl, rose
Marigold $125
White $300

Butter dish
Marigold $175
White $275

Creamer
Marigold $100
White $175

Pitcher, water
Marigold $525
White $850

Plate, 9″
Marigold $200

Purple	$300
White	$350

Spooner

Marigold	$85
White	$125

Sugar dish with cover

Marigold	$125
White	$200

Tumbler

Marigold	$150
White	$250

Vase

Marigold	$150
Purple	$175
White	$275

PANSY   IMPERIAL GLASS COMPANY

The pansies in this pattern are clustered with arches and other foliage on a stippled background.

Bowl, 8³/₄″

Amber	$200
Amethyst	$150
Aqua Opalescent	$300
Blue	$175
Green	$125
Marigold	$50
Purple	$150
Smoke	$225

Bowl, 9¹/₂″, ruffled

Amber	$225
Amethyst	$200
Blue	$225
Green	$175
Marigold	$60
Purple	$200
Smoke	$250

Creamer

Amber	$100
Amethyst	$60
Green	$55
Marigold	$40
Purple	$50
Smoke	$100

Dresser tray, oval

Amethyst	$110
Green	$100
Marigold	$70

Purple $110
Smoke $175

Nappy
Green $40
Marigold $30

Pickle dish, oval
Amethyst $55
Blue $150
Green $50
Marigold $35
Purple $55
Smoke $100

Plate, ruffled
Amethyst $150
Green $125
Marigold $85
Purple $150
Smoke $175

Relish dish
Amber $110
Amethyst $100
Aqua Opalescent $350
Green $100
Marigold $55
Purple $100
Smoke $125

Sugar
Amber $100
Amethyst $60
Green $55
Marigold $40
Purple $50
Smoke $100

Carnival glass, "Peach" pattern. DRAWING BY MARK PICKVET.

PEACH NORTHWOOD GLASS COMPANY

In this pattern, two peaches are bunched together with branches and vines and framed with horizontal beading. The design is set in relief and includes two outer horizontal bands (one near the top and one at the bottom).

Bowl, berry, 5″, White $85
Bowl, berry, 9″, White $250
Butter dish with cover, White $325
Creamer, White $175
Pitcher, water
  Cobalt Blue $750
  White $850
Spooner, White $150
Sugar dish with cover, White $250
Tumbler
  Cobalt Blue $125
  White $175

PEACOCK AND URN FENTON ART GLASS COMPANY, MILLERSBURG GLASS COMPANY, NORTHWOOD GLASS COMPANY

The patterns of the three companies are similar. The ridgework on the urn is more rigid in Millersburg than Fenton. Millersburg also includes a stylized bee within the bird's beak. The circle of leaves within the foliage wreath shows less detail and contains more plain glossy space in the Northwood design. One of the Millersburg variants includes wreaths that are sprays of foliage rather than an all-encompassing design. Some of the scrolling has no beading.

Bowl (Fenton only)
  Amethyst $300
  Blue $250

Carnival glass, "Peacock and Urn" pattern. PHOTO BY ROBIN RAINWATER.

Green $300
Marigold $125
Peach Opalescent $1750
Red $3500

Bowl, 5″
Amethyst $125
Aqua Opalescent $2500
Blue $150
Green $175
Ice Blue $1500
Ice Green $1500
Marigold $75
Purple $125

Bowl, 6″, (pattern variant, Millersburg)
Amethyst $225
Blue $750
Green $250
Marigold $200

Bowl, 6″ ice cream
Amethyst $175
Aqua Opalescent $2750
Blue $175
Green $200
Ice Blue $1750
Ice Green $1750
Marigold $125
Purple $175
White $300

Bowl, 8¹/₂″ (pattern variant, Millersburg)
Amethyst $450
Blue $3000
Green $500
Marigold $400

Bowl, 9¹/₂″ (pattern variant, Millersburg)
Amethyst $400
Blue $2500
Green $450
Marigold $350

Bowl, 9″
Amethyst $500
Green $550
Marigold $250
Purple $500

Bowl, 10″ (pattern variant, Millersburg)
Amethyst $1250
Blue $2500
Green $1750
Marigold $450

Bowl, 10″, ice cream
Amethyst $750
Aqua $5500

Aqua Opalescent $7500
Blue $1000
Green $1500
Ice Blue $1500
Ice Green $2000
Marigold $350
Purple $750
White $1250

Compote
Amethyst $100
Blue $125
Green $200
Marigold $55
Purple $100
Red $3000
Vaseline $750
White $175

Compote (large) (pattern variant, Millersburg)
Amethyst $1500
Green $1750
Marigold $1250
Red $5500

Compote (small) (pattern variant, Millersburg)
Amethyst $100
Blue $125
Green $200
Marigold $55

Goblet (Fenton only)
Amethyst $110
Blue $125
Marigold $85
Purple $110
Vaseline $175

Plate, 6″
Amethyst $600
Blue $750
Green $850
Marigold $350
Purple $600
White $850

Plate, 6″, stippled
Amethyst $750
Blue $850
Green $950
Marigold $400
Purple $750
White $950

Plate, 9″ (Fenton only)
Amethyst $1000
Blue $1750
Green $1750

Ice Blue $1750
Ice Green $1750
Marigold $400
Purple $1000

Plate, 10½″ (pattern variant, Millersburg)
Amethyst $7500
Marigold $3000

Plate, 11″
Amethyst $1250
Marigold $1000

Plate, chop, 12″
Amethyst $1250
Ice Green $2500
Marigold $1500

Spittoon
Amethyst $3500
Marigold $2750
Purple $3500

PEACOCK AT THE FOUNTAIN DUGAN GLASS COMPANY, NORTHWOOD GLASS COMPANY

Only two Dugan pieces are available, as noted below. The remaining pieces are Northwood. The peacock in this pattern is quite large and stands on a block pedestal with a daisy growing between the bricks. The fountain has lined ridges indicating water. This is a very popular design, and the aqua opalescent punch set is quite impressive.

Bowl, berry, 5″
Amethyst $65
Blue $75
Green $100
Ice Blue $250
Ice Green $300
Marigold $50
Purple $65
White $250

Bowl, berry, 9″
Amethyst $100
Blue $100
Green $150
Ice Blue $500
Ice Green $500
Marigold $75
Purple $100
White $450

Bowl, orange, footed
Amethyst $750
Aqua Opalescent $7500

Blue $1000
Green $1500
Ice Blue $1500
Ice Green $1750
Marigold $350
Purple $750
White $1500

Butter dish with cover
Amethyst $300
Blue $350
Green $450
Ice Blue $550
Ice Green $650
Marigold $250
Purple $300
White $550

Compote
Amethyst $550
Aqua Opalescent $3500
Blue $550
Green $750
Ice Blue $1250
Ice Green $1500
Marigold $450
Purple $550
White $1250

Creamer
Amethyst $175
Blue $250
Green $300
Ice Blue $750
Ice Green $850
Marigold $100
Purple $175
White $750

Pitcher, water
Blue $1000
Green $1500
Ice Blue $1500
Ice Green $2000
Marigold $400
Purple $750
White $1500

Pitcher, water (Dugan)
Blue $750
Marigold $450
Purple $650

Punch bowl with base
Amethyst $1000
Aqua Opalescent $25000
Blue $1250

Green $2500
Ice Blue $4500
Ice Green $5000
Marigold $550
Purple $1000
White $4500
Punch cup
Amethyst $50
Aqua Opalescent $1000
Blue $60
Green $75
Ice Blue $125
Ice Green $175
Marigold $35
Purple $50
White $125
Spittoon, Green $5000
Spooner
Amethyst $125
Blue $200
Green $250
Ice Blue $650
Ice Green $750
Marigold $85
Purple $125
White $650
Sugar with cover
Amethyst $250
Blue $300
Green $400
Ice Blue $850
Ice Green $1000
Marigold $175
Purple $250
White $850
Tumbler
Amethyst $60
Blue $75
Green $500
Ice Blue $325
Ice Green $425
Marigold $50
Purple $60
White $250
Tumbler (Dugan)
Blue $100
Marigold $55
Purple $85

PEACOCK TAIL   FENTON ART GLASS COMPANY

The pattern is characterized by a center circle of feathers with concentric circles that emanate out from each feather.

Bonbon dish with handle
Amethyst $85
Blue $85
Green $100
Marigold $75
Bowl, 4″
Amethyst $60
Blue $65
Green $250
Marigold $40
Red $2000
Bowl, 10″
Amethyst $70
Blue $75
Green $300
Marigold $50
Red $2250
Compote
Amethyst $60
Blue $65
Green $75
Marigold $40
White $125
Hat Vase
Amethyst $60
Blue $65
Green $75
Marigold $40
Plate, 6″
Amethyst $125
Blue $150
Green $350
Marigold $75
Plate, 9″
Amethyst $225
Blue $250
Green $425
Marigold $150

PEACOCK MILLERSBURG GLASS COMPANY

The feathers of the peacock in this pattern are set in relief, while the peacock itself is framed by a wreath of foliage. In the background are Greek columns and ferns at the bird's feet. Vaseline items are extremely rare and valuable.

Banana dish
    Amethyst $3250
    Purple $3250
Bowl, 5″
    Amethyst $125
    Blue $1000
    Green $175
    Marigold $75
    Purple $125
Bowl, 6″
    Amethyst $150
    Purple $150
Bowl, 7½″
    Amethyst $475
    Green $500
    Marigold $450
    Purple $475
Bowl, 9″
    Amethyst $425
    Green $450
    Marigold $250
    Purple $425
    Vaseline $5500
Bowl, 10″, ice cream
    Amethyst $700
    Green $750
    Marigold $500
    Purple $700
Bowl, rose
    Purple $3500
    Vaseline $6000
Plate, 6″
    Amethyst $850
    Marigold $750
    Purple $850
Plate, chop, Marigold $1500
Spittoon
    Amethyst $7500
    Marigold $5000
    Purple $7500

PERSIAN GARDEN   DUGAN GLASS COMPANY

"Persian Garden" is a geometric pattern with a center medallion; rows of arches with flowers and checkerboards flow outward, ending in a band of fountains with teardrops near the rim.

Bowl, berry, 5″
Blue $75
Green $65
Marigold $55
Purple $65
White $125
Bowl, berry, 10″
Marigold $175
Purple $225
White $325
Bowl, fruit with base
Marigold $125
Peach Opalescent $750
Purple $450
White $400
Bowl, ice cream, 6″
Blue $150
Green $150
Marigold $125
Purple $175
White $200
Bowl, ice cream, 11″
Blue $450
Green $500
Marigold $275
Peach Opalescent $1000
Purple $750
White $550
Plate, 6″
Blue $350
Green $375
Marigold $85
Peach Opalescent $750
Purple $450
White $400
Plate, chop, 13″
Peach Opalescent $6000
Purple $7500
White $2500

Carnival glass, "Persian Medallion" pattern. PHOTOS BY MARK PICKVET, COURTESY OF THE FENTON ART GLASS MUSEUM.

PERSIAN MEDALLION FENTON ART GLASS COMPANY

This pattern is characterized by varying shapes of floral medallions with bands of petaled circles and teardrops inscribed within the circles.

Bonbon dish, 5″
Amber	$250
Amethyst	$125
Blue	$150
Green	$175
Ice Blue	$750
Marigold	$75
Purple	$125
Red	$1500
Vaseline	$250
White	$250

Bowl, 5″
Amethyst	$55
Blue	$55
Green	$60
Marigold	$45
Purple	$55
Red	$1250

Bowl, 8³/₄″
Amethyst	$100
Blue	$125
Green	$150
Marigold	$55
Purple	$100
Red	$1500

Bowl, 10″, collar base
Amethyst	$150

Blue $175
Green $200
Marigold $75
Purple $150

Bowl, orange
Amethyst $250
Blue $300
Green $450
Marigold $100
Purple $250

Bowl, rose
Amber $125
Amethyst $85
Blue $90
Green $100
Marigold $75
Purple $85
White $150

Compote
Amethyst $200
Blue $150
Green $250
Marigold $100
Purple $200
Red $1250

Hair receiver
Amethyst $100
Blue $100
Green $125
Marigold $75
Purple $100

Plate, 7″
Amber $350
Amethyst $225
Blue $250
Green $350
Marigold $85
Purple $225
Vaseline $750
White $125

Plate, 9″
Amber $750
Amethyst $650
Blue $750
Green $850
Marigold $250
Purple $650
White $550

Plate, chop
Blue $850
Marigold $300

Purple $750
White $1000
Punch bowl with base
Amethyst $400
Blue $450
Green $550
Marigold $325
Purple $400
Punch cup
Amethyst $40
Blue $40
Green $50
Marigold $30
Purple $40

POPPY SHOW   IMPERIAL GLASS COMPANY, NORTHWOOD GLASS COMPANY

The patterns of both companies are similar. Both feature poppies, leaves, stems, and vines. Only Northwood produced the bowls and plate, as noted below; the remaining pieces are Imperial's. The pattern can be found in pastels such as white, clambroth, ice green, ice blue, smoke, and amber. Increase the amethyst prices by 50% for any pastels. Note that Imperial reproduced this pattern in the 1960s. Reproductions are marked "IG" on the underside.

Bowl, 8¹/₂″ (Northwood)
Amethyst $750
Blue $1000
Green $950
Marigold $500
Purple $850
Bowl, 9¹/₂″ (Northwood)
Amethyst $850
Blue $1250
Green $1100
Marigold $550
Purple $950
Lamp, hurricane
Amethyst $2500
Marigold $2000
Lamp, table
Amethyst $2500
Marigold $2000
Plate, 9″ (Northwood)
Amethyst $2250
Blue $3000
Green $2750
Marigold $1250
Purple $2500

Vase, 12″ tall
Amethyst $750
Blue $1000
Green $950
Marigold $500

RANGER   IMPERIAL GLASS COMPANY

"Ranger" is a fairly simple arched block pattern that is available only in marigold.

Bowl, 6″, Marigold $60
Bowl, 9″, Marigold $85
Bowl, 10″, Marigold $100
Butter dish with cover, Marigold $250
Creamer, Marigold $75
Nappy, Marigold $100
Perfume bottle with stopper, Marigold $250
Pitcher, milk, Marigold $250
Pitcher, water, Marigold $500
Sherbet, Marigold $75
Shot glass, Marigold $500
Sugar dish with cover, Marigold $150
Toothpick holder, Marigold $150
Tumbler, Marigold $125
Vase, 8″ tall, pedestal feet, Marigold $100

RASPBERRY   NORTHWOOD GLASS COMPANY

The raspberries of this pattern are shaped by beaded circles in low relief. Below the raspberries is a wide basket-weave panel.

Bowl, berry, 5″
Green $50
Marigold $40
Purple $45
Bowl, berry, 9″
Green $80
Marigold $60
Purple $75
Bowl, serving, footed
Blue $250
Green $85
Marigold $65
Purple $80
Compote
Green $70
Marigold $55
Purple $65

Pitcher, milk
Green $400
Ice Blue $2000
Ice Green $2500
Marigold $250
Purple $350
White $1750

Pitcher, water
Blue $750
Green $550
Ice Blue $2250
Ice Green $2750
Marigold $300
Purple $450
White $2000

Sauce boat, footed
Blue $175
Marigold $80
Purple $125

Tumbler
Blue $150
Green $75
Ice Blue $650
Ice Green $750
Marigold $50
Purple $65
White $550

SAILBOATS   FENTON ART GLASS COMPANY

As the name suggests, the basic design features sailboats within curved frames.
Each frame has a single sailboat on the water, with clouds in the background. The
main frames are separated by smaller frames that include a four-petaled star resembling the blades of a windmill.

Bowl, 6″
Amber $125
Blue $85
Green $100
Marigold $45
Red $3000

Compote
Amber $200
Blue $100
Green $150
Marigold $65

Goblet
Amber $300
Blue $250

Green	$275
Marigold	$200

Plate

Amber	$500
Blue	$400
Green	$450
Marigold	$250

Wine Glass

Amber	$200
Blue	$125
Green	$150
Marigold	$75

SEAWEED   MILLERSBURG GLASS COMPANY

This design consists of beads in bubble form, spiraling scrolls that twirl outward from the center, and a wavy background.

Bowl, 5″

Clambroth	$750
Green	$550
Marigold	$450

Bowl, 9″

Blue	$1750
Green	$425
Marigold	$300

Bowl, 10½″, ice cream

Clambroth	$750
Green	$550
Marigold	$450
Purple	$550

Bowl, 10½″, ruffled

Green	$350
Marigold	$325
Purple	$400

Bowl, 10″

Green	$1250
Marigold	$900
Purple	$1250

Lamp

Ice Blue	$550
Marigold	$350

Plate, 10″

Green	$1250
Marigold	$1000
Purple	$1250

Carnival glass, "Singing Birds" pattern. PHOTO BY ROBIN RAINWATER, COURTESY OF *THE FENTON ART GLASS MUSEUM.*

SINGING BIRDS   NORTHWOOD GLASS COMPANY

As the pattern name implies, the birds sitting on the branches have their beaks open as if they are engaged in singing.

Bowl, berry, 5"
Amethyst	$45
Blue	$100
Green	$50
Marigold	$35
Purple	$45

Bowl, berry, 10"
Amethyst	$85
Blue	$125
Green	$100
Marigold	$55
Purple	$85

Butter dish with cover
Amethyst	$350
Blue	$750
Green	$400
Marigold	$250
Purple	$350

Creamer
Amethyst	$150
Blue	$250
Green	$175
Marigold	$100
Purple	$150

Mug
Amethyst	$300

Aqua Opalescent $1500
Blue $400
Green $350
Ice Blue or Ice Green $1000
Marigold $250
Purple $300

Pitcher, water
Amethyst $400
Blue $750
Green $550
Marigold $325
Purple $400

Sherbet
Amethyst $350
Marigold $250
Purple $350

Spooner
Amethyst $125
Green $150
Marigold $85
Purple $125

Sugar
Amethyst $175
Blue $350
Green $225
Marigold $125
Purple $175

Tumbler
Amethyst $100
Blue $200
Green $150
Marigold $60
Purple $100

SKI STAR   DUGAN GLASS COMPANY

Dugan's "Ski Star" pattern is much like a kaleidoscope, featuring stars within circles and stars surrounding the circles. The star in the pattern is often compared to the eight points of a compass.

Banana dish
Amethyst $150
Blue $175
Marigold $100
Peach Opalescent $350
Purple $150

Basket, handled
Amethyst $200
Blue $225

Marigold $125
Peach Opalescent $500
Purple $200

Bowl, 5″
Amethyst $65
Blue $75
Green $100
Marigold $50
Peach Opalescent $150
Purple $65

Bowl, 8″
Amethyst $135
Blue $150
Marigold $75
Peach Opalescent $250
Purple $135

Bowl, 10″
Amethyst $150
Blue $175
Marigold $85
Peach Opalescent $275
Purple $150

Bowl, rose
Amethyst $250
Blue $275
Marigold $150
Peach Opalescent $750
Purple $250

Plate, 7½″
Amethyst $150
Blue $175
Marigold $85
Peach Opalescent $275
Purple $150

SPRINGTIME   NORTHWOOD GLASS COMPANY

"Springtime" features chained daisies within panels set in relief. Along the top and bottom of each piece are borders that resemble basket weave designs.

Bowl, berry, 5″
Amethyst $70
Green $85
Marigold $50

Bowl, berry, 9″
Amethyst $225
Green $250
Marigold $100

Butter dish with cover

Amethyst $450
Green $500
Marigold $300

Creamer

Amethyst $325
Green $350
Marigold $250

Pitcher, water

Amethyst $1000
Green $1250
Marigold $750

Spooner

Amethyst $300
Green $325
Marigold $225

Sugar

Amethyst $350
Green $400
Marigold $275

Tumbler

Amethyst $150
Green $200
Marigold $85

STAR AND FILE   IMPERIAL GLASS COMPANY

This is a simple geometric pattern consisting of a wide chain of hobstars separated by filed spears. Most pieces are in marigold; however, a few rare colors pop up now and then. For amber, clambroth, or ice green, triple the prices.

Bonbon dish, Marigold $45
Bowl, 7″, 2-handled, Marigold $45
Bowl, 7″, round or square, Marigold $40
Bowl, 8″, 2-handled, Marigold $50
Bowl, 8″, round or square, Marigold $45
Bowl, 9¹/₂″, Marigold $55

Bowl, rose

Marigold $85
Pastel Green or Blue $150

Celery vase, 2-handled

Marigold $55
Smoke $150

Champagne glass, Marigold $75
Compote, Marigold $50
Cordial, 1 oz., Marigold $275
Creamer, Marigold $40
Cup, custard, Marigold $35
Decanter with stopper, Marigold $175

Goblet, Marigold $125
Pickle dish, Marigold $50
Pitcher, water, Marigold $275
Plate, 6"–6¹/₂", Marigold $65
Relish dish, oval, 2-handled, Marigold $55
Sherbet, Marigold $40
Spooner, Marigold $35
Sugar, Marigold $40
Tumbler, Marigold $175
Vase, handled, Marigold $55
Wine glass, Marigold $65

STAR MEDALLION   IMPERIAL GLASS COMPANY

A wide band encompasses about three-quarters of the piece; in the center are sharp-edged, patterned stars. Surrounding the stars are hobstars extending out from small diamond patterning.

Bonbon dish, Marigold $50
Bowl, 6"
   Clambroth $55
   Marigold $35
   Smoke $65
Bowl, 6", square
   Clambroth $75
   Marigold $45
   Smoke $85
Bowl, 7"
   Clambroth $65
   Marigold $40
   Smoke $75
Bowl, 7", square
   Clambroth $85
   Marigold $50
   Smoke $100
Bowl, 9", square
   Clambroth $100
   Marigold $55
   Smoke $125
Butter dish with cover, Marigold $125
Celery vase, handled
   Clambroth $100
   Marigold $90
   Smoke $175
Compote
   Clambroth $75
   Marigold $50
Creamer, Marigold $65
Cup, custard, Marigold $30

Goblet
  Clambroth $100
  Marigold $60
  Smoke $125
Pickle dish, Marigold $45
Pitcher, milk
  Clambroth $200
  Green $125
  Marigold $85
  Smoke $150
Pitcher, water
  Green $200
  Marigold $150
Plate, 5″
  Clambroth $85
  Marigold $50
  Smoke $100
Plate, 6″
  Clambroth $95
  Marigold $55
  Smoke $110
Plate, 7¹/₂″
  Clambroth $110
  Marigold $60
  Smoke $125
Plate, 10″
  Clambroth $125
  Marigold $75
  Smoke $150
Punch bowl, Marigold $225
Punch cup, Marigold $40
Sherbet, Marigold $40
Spooner, Marigold $55
Sugar, Marigold $65
Tray, celery, Marigold $75
Tumbler
  Green $65
  Marigold $45
  Smoke $75
Vase, 6″ tall, Marigold $50

STIPPLED RAYS   FENTON ART GLASS COMPANY, IMPERIAL GLASS COMPANY, NORTHWOOD GLASS COMPANY

The Fenton version offers the most variety of pieces, except the footed creamer and sugar. This interior pattern is characterized by alternating stippled spears with clear portions that emanate from the center into a large star. The Imperial pattern is in low relief with scalloped edges. The only two pieces that were known to be made by Imperial are the footed creamer and sugar. Northwood produced a compote, as well, with the 8″ and 10″ bowls.

Bonbon dish
Amethyst	$55
Blue	$55
Green	$60
Marigold	$40
Red	$750

Bowl, 5″
Amethyst	$60
Blue	$55
Green	$65
Marigold	$40
Red	$750
Vaseline	$100
White	$100

Bowl, 8″, (Northwood)
Amethyst	$100
Green	$70
Marigold	$50

Bowl, 9″
Amethyst	$70
Blue	$65
Green	$75
Marigold	$50
Red	$850
White	$90

Bowl, 10″
Amethyst	$80
Blue	$75
Green	$85
Marigold	$55
Red	$1000

Compote
Amethyst	$80
Blue	$55
Green	$60
Marigold	$45

Creamer
Amethyst	$50
Blue	$50
Green	$55
Marigold	$40

Red $750

Creamer, footed (Imperial)

Green $65
Marigold $55
Red $850
Smoke $75

Plate, 7″

Amethyst $65
Blue $65
Green $75
Marigold $45
Red $750

Sugar

Amethyst $50
Blue $50
Green $55
Marigold $40
Red $750

Sugar, footed (Imperial)

Green $65
Marigold $55
Red $850
Smoke $75

STORK AND RUSHES   DUGAN GLASS COMPANY

The stork is a common image in Carnival pieces. Imperial also made several items such as vases and ABC plates with a stork pattern motif (see the entry for "Imperial Glass Company").

Bowl, berry, 4½″

Amethyst $50
Blue $100
Marigold $40
Purple $50

Bowl, berry, 10″

Amethyst $75
Blue $125
Marigold $60
Purple $75

Butter dish with cover

Amethyst $200
Blue $275
Marigold $150
Purple $200

Creamer

Amethyst $100
Blue $125
Marigold $75

Purple $100
Hat vase
Amethyst $75
Blue $55
Marigold $55
Purple $75
Mug
Amethyst $375
Aqua Opalescent $1500
Blue $450
Marigold $50
Purple $375
Pitcher, water
Amethyst $350
Blue $450
Marigold $275
Purple $350
Punch bowl with base
Amethyst $350
Blue $450
Marigold $275
Purple $350
Punch cup
Amethyst $40
Blue $50
Marigold $30
Purple $40
Spooner
Amethyst $90
Blue $100
Marigold $65
Purple $90
Sugar dish
Amethyst $100
Blue $125
Marigold $75
Purple $100
Tumbler
Amethyst $55
Blue $75
Marigold $45
Purple $55

**STRAWBERRY   DUGAN GLASS COMPANY, FENTON GLASS
COMPANY, MILLERSBURG GLASS COMPANY, NORTHWOOD GLASS
COMPANY**

For any other pastel colors, such as ice blue or ice green, the same price as vaseline
applies. Millersburg pieces feature strawberries and large or wide strawberry leaves

in a circular pattern. The leaves are much thinner in Northwood's pattern. To date, all that has been found by Fenton and Dugan are the bonbon dish and the epergne, respectively.

Banana boat
Blue	$2500
Green	$2250
Marigold	$1000
Purple	$2000
Vaseline	$3500

Bonbon dish
Blue	$150
Green	$85
Marigold	$65
Purple	$75
Red	$950
Vaseline	$200

Bowl, 5″
Blue	$100
Green	$85
Marigold	$65
Purple	$75
Vaseline	$750

Bowl, 6¹/₂″
Blue	$175
Green	$150
Marigold	$100
Purple	$150
Vaseline	$1000

Bowl, 8¹/₂″
Aqua Opalescent	$4500
Blue	$450
Green	$400
Marigold	$225
Purple	$375
Vaseline	$1750

Bowl, 8″
Blue	$350
Green	$300
Marigold	$175
Purple	$275
Vaseline	$1500

Bowl, 9¹/₂″, tricornered
Blue	$500
Green	$425
Marigold	$275
Purple	$400
Vaseline	$2000

Bowl, 10″
Blue	$400
Green	$350

  Marigold $225
  Purple $325
  Vaseline $1750

Compote
  Blue $400
  Green $350
  Marigold $225
  Purple $325
  Vaseline $1750

Epergne (Dugan)
  Marigold $1000
  Purple $1250

Gravy boat
  Blue $750
  Green $725
  Marigold $500
  Purple $700
  Vaseline $2250

Hatpin
  Blue $1500
  Green $1500
  Marigold $850

Plate, 7″
  Blue $500
  Green $475
  Marigold $350
  Purple $450
  Vaseline $2000

Plate, 9″
  Blue $2500
  Green $2250
  Marigold $1250
  Purple $2000
  Vaseline $3500

TEN MUMS   FENTON ART GLASS COMPANY

The basic design consists of 10 floral mounds or mums surrounding a common mum within a circle. Between the outer mums and the center circle are leaves, which also wind in a circular pattern.

Bowl, 8″
  Amethyst $225
  Blue $350
  Green $300
  Marigold $100

Bowl, 9″, footed
  Amethyst $400
  Blue $450

Green	$500
Marigold	$250
Bowl, 11″	
Amethyst	$250
Blue	$400
Green	$350
Marigold	$125
Pitcher, water	
Amethyst	$750
Blue	$1000
Green	$850
Marigold	$500
White	$1750
Plate, 10″	
Amethyst	$750
Blue	$1000
Green	$850
Marigold	$500
Tumbler	
Amethyst	$110
Blue	$150
Green	$125
Marigold	$85
White	$400

TREE BARK   IMPERIAL GLASS COMPANY, JEANNETTE GLASS COMPANY

"Tree Bark" is a very simple pattern. The exterior has haphazard vertical ridges that resemble the bark of trees. The pattern variant was produced by Jeannette and has straighter barklike designs than the original.

Bowl, 7¹/₂″, Marigold	$30
Candleholder with marble stand, pattern variant, Marigold	$100
Candlestick, 4¹/₂″, Marigold	$25
Candlestick, 7″, Marigold	$30
Candy jar with cover, Marigold	$50
Pickle jar, 7¹/₂″, Marigold	$45
Pitcher, water, Marigold	$85

Carnival glass, "Tree Bark" pattern. DRAWING BY MARK PICKVET.

Pitcher, water, pattern variant, Marigold $75
Pitcher, water, with lid, Marigold $100
Planter, pattern variant, Marigold $75
Plate 7″, Marigold $25
Plate 8″, Marigold $30
Sauce dish, 4″, Marigold $20
Tumbler, 2 styles, Marigold $30
Tumbler, pattern variant, Marigold $25
Vase, cone or ovoid shape
Clambroth $75
Marigold $50

TWINS   IMPERIAL GLASS COMPANY

This pattern features a sunburst in the center surrounded by a wreath of teardrop rosettes. The remaining portion consists of rounded arches and ridges in relief. It is much like an all-over pattern resembling that of cut glass.

Basket, bride's, Marigold $100
Bowl, 7″, footed
Marigold $45
Purple $55
Bowl, 8″
Marigold $45
Smoke $75
Bowl, 10″, footed, Marigold $55
Bowl, berry, 5″
Green $50
Marigold $35
Smoke $50
Bowl, berry, 9″
Green $60
Marigold $50
Smoke $80
Bowl, fruit with base, Marigold $85
Plate, 9½″, Marigold $350
Plate, 13″
Blue $750
Green $750
Marigold $550
Punch bowl with base, Marigold $225
Punch cup, Marigold $35
Vase, 7″
Marigold $65
Smoke $100
Vase, 8″
Marigold $75
Smoke $125

TWO FLOWERS   FENTON ART GLASS COMPANY

There are more than two flowers in the basic pattern, contrary to the pattern name. The name comes from the pair of flowers that encircle a common floral pattern within the center of each object.

Bowl, 5″, footed

Amethyst	$85
Blue	$75
Green	$100
Marigold	$60
Red	$4500

Bowl, 8″, footed

Amethyst	$100
Blue	$85
Green	$125
Marigold	$75
Red	$5000

Bowl, 10″, footed

Amethyst	$150
Aqua	$750
Blue	$100
Green	$175
Marigold	$85
Red	$6000

Bowl, rose

Amethyst	$275
Blue	$250
Green	$300
Marigold	$200

Plate, 9″, footed

Amethyst	$800
Blue	$750
Green	$850
Marigold	$500

Platter, 13″, round

Amethyst	$3750
Blue	$3500
Green	$4000
Marigold	$2500
Red	$7500

VINTAGE   DUGAN GLASS COMPANY, FENTON ART GLASS COMPANY, MILLERSBURG GLASS COMPANY, U.S. GLASS COMPANY

"Vintage" is another common grape and leaf pattern. The grapes and leaves are somewhat sparse and in low relief. There are three Dugan pieces referenced below. There are only two Millersburg pieces noted below; both feature hobnails, unlike the Fenton pieces. The wine glass is the only U.S. Glass piece listed.

Bowl, 5″, (Millersburg)
Blue $1750
Green $1000
Marigold $750
Bowl, 6¹/₂″
Amber $90
Amethyst $45
Blue $50
Green $50
Marigold $40
Purple $45
Red $7500
Bowl, 8″, flat
Amber $85
Amethyst $45
Blue $45
Green $45
Marigold $35
Purple $45
Red $4500
Bowl, 9″, (Millersburg)
Amethyst $1250
Blue $2500
Green $1250
Marigold $800
Purple $1250
Bowl, 10″, flat
Amethyst $75
Blue $100
Green $90
Marigold $55
Red $5250
Bowl, berry, 4¹/₂″
Amber $80
Amethyst $40
Blue $45
Green $45
Marigold $35
Purple $40
Bowl, berry, 8″
Amber $100
Amethyst $50
Blue $55
Green $55
Marigold $45
Purple $50
Red $5000
Bowl, fernery, footed
Amber $200
Amethyst $85
Blue $110

Green	$100
Marigold	$60
Purple	$85
Red	$5500

Bowl, orange, footed

Amber	$225
Amethyst	$100
Blue	$125
Green	$115
Marigold	$85
Purple	$100

Bowl, rose

Amber	$200
Amberina	$250
Amethyst	$90
Blue	$100
Green	$100
Marigold	$75
Purple	$90

Compote

Amethyst	$50
Blue	$55
Green	$55
Marigold	$45
Purple	$50

Cup

Amethyst	$35
Blue	$45
Green	$40
Marigold	$30
Purple	$35

Epergne, 2 styles

Amethyst	$150
Blue	$175
Green	$175
Marigold	$125
Purple	$150

Fernery, 2 styles

Amber	$200
Amethyst	$85
Blue	$110
Green	$100
Marigold	$60
Purple	$85
Red	$5500

Fernery, whimsey

| Amethyst | $225 |
| Purple | $225 |

Nut dish, 6-footed

| Amber | $100 |
| Amethyst | $85 |

Blue $85
Green $90
Marigold $55
Purple $85

Nut dish, trifooted
Amber $125
Amethyst $60
Blue $75
Green $65
Marigold $45
Purple $60

Perfume bottle with stopper (Dugan)
Amethyst $650
Blue $750
Green $700
Marigold $400
Purple $650

Plate, 7³/₄″
Amethyst $150
Blue $250
Green $225
Marigold $150
Purple $175

Plate, 7″
Amethyst $125
Blue $225
Green $200
Marigold $125
Purple $85

Plate, 9″
Blue $1000
Marigold $300

Plate, 11″, ruffled
Amethyst $250
Blue $300
Green $275
Marigold $200
Purple $250

Powder jar with cover (Dugan)
Amethyst $150
Blue $200
Green $175
Marigold $100
Purple $150

Punch bowl with base
Amber $750
Amethyst $450
Blue $550
Green $500
Marigold $300
Purple $450

Punch cup
Amber $75
Amethyst $40
Blue $50
Green $45
Marigold $35
Purple $40
Sandwich server
Amberina $250
Marigold $125
Spittoon, Marigold $5000
Tray, card, Marigold $75
Tray, dresser (Dugan), Marigold $100
Wine glass (U.S. Glass)
Amethyst $50
Marigold $40
Purple $50

WAFFLE BLOCK   IMPERIAL GLASS COMPANY

This is a simple all-over square pattern resembling waffles, as the name implies.
Teal is a bit darker than ice green.

Basket, 10″
Clambroth $200
Marigold $75
Teal $175
Bowl, 7″, Marigold $40
Bowl, 9″, Marigold $45
Bowl, fruit with base, Clambroth $250
Bowl, rose
Clambroth $350
Marigold $125
Creamer, Marigold $65
Nappy, Marigold $50
Parfait
Clambroth $100
Marigold $50

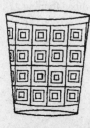

Carnival glass, "Waffle Block" pattern. DRAWING BY MARK PICKVET.

Pitcher, water
   Clambroth $275
   Marigold $175
Plate, 6″
   Clambroth $110
   Marigold $65
Plate, 10″
   Marigold $85
   Teal $175
Plate, 12″
   Marigold $100
   Teal $200
Punch bowl with base
   Clambroth $550
   Marigold $250
   Purple $350
   Teal $450
Punch cup
   Clambroth $75
   Marigold $25
   Purple $50
   Teal $65
Salt and pepper shakers, Marigold $100
Sherbet, Clambroth $75
Spittoon, Marigold $500
Sugar, Marigold $65
Tumbler, 2 styles
   Clambroth $250
   Marigold $225
Vase, 8″ tall
   Clambroth $125
   Marigold $65
Vase, 10″ tall
   Clambroth $150
   Marigold $90
Vase, 11″ tall
   Clambroth $175
   Marigold $100

WHIRLING STAR · IMPERIAL GLASS COMPANY

"Whirling Star" consists of rayed stars and hobstars within heavy lined framing.

Bowl, 9″
   Green $75
   Marigold $45
Bowl, 11″
   Green $85
   Marigold $55

Compote
  Green $90
  Marigold $60
Pitcher, water
  Green $750
  Marigold $350
Punch bowl with base
  Green $750
  Marigold $275
Punch cup
  Green $75
  Marigold $40
Tumbler
  Green $150
  Marigold $75

WIDE PANEL   FENTON ART GLASS COMPANY, IMPERIAL GLASS COMPANY, NORTHWOOD GLASS COMPANY, U.S. GLASS COMPANY, WESTMORELAND GLASS COMPANY

The panels extend about three-quarters of the way up the glass and end in three horizontal bands at the top for the most common items in this pattern. With so many companies producing this simple design, there are a number of variations, including varying degrees of width in the panels and pieces with only one or no top bands. The only U.S. Glass and Westmoreland pieces are noted below.

Bowl, 7¹/₂″, (Westmoreland), Teal $75
Bowl, 8¹/₄″, (Westmoreland), Amber or Teal $85
Bowl, 9″
  Marigold $45
  Purple $95
  Smoke $125
Bowl, 11″
  Marigold $85
  Purple $125
  Smoke $150
Bowl, 12″
  Marigold $95
  Purple $150
  Smoke $175
Cake plate, 12″
  Clambroth $350
  Marigold $125
  Pink $400
  Purple $250
  Red $1250
  Vaseline $400
  White $350
Cake plate, 15″
  Clambroth $450

Marigold $150
Pink $500
Purple $300
Red $1500
Vaseline $500
White $450

Candy dish with cover
Ice Blue $125
Ice Green $125
Marigold $55
Pink $175
Purple $65
Red $1250
White $125

Compote, Marigold $50
Compote, miniature, Marigold $45

Epergne
Aqua Opalescent $25000
Blue $2000
Green $2000
Marigold $750
Purple $1750
Red $10000
White $2500

Goblet (large)
Marigold $55
Red $1000

Goblet (small), Marigold $50
Pitcher, water or lemonade, Marigold $250
Plate, 8″
Clambroth $125
Ice Blue $125
Ice Green $125
Marigold $50
Purple $65
Red $300
Smoke $125

Plate, 10″
Clambroth $150
Ice Blue $150
Ice Green $150
Marigold $75
Purple $90
Red $350
Smoke $150

Plate, 11″
Clambroth $175
Ice Blue $175
Ice Green $175
Marigold $80
Purple $100

Red $400

Smoke $175

Platter, 14″, round

Clambroth $200

Ice Blue $200

Ice Green $200

Marigold $100

Purple $125

Smoke $200

Punch bowl

Marigold $175

Pink $250

Red $5000

White $1500

Punch cup

Marigold $40

Pink $50

Red $250

White $125

Salt dip (U.S. Glass Co.), Marigold $50

Spittoon, Marigold $550

Vase, 8″

Aqua Opalescent $750

Blue or Green $55

Marigold $40

Peach Opalescent $200

Purple $55

Red $1250

Teal $125

White $125

Vase, 12″

Aqua Opalescent $850

Blue or Green $60

Marigold $45

Peach Opalescent $250

Purple $60

Red $1500

Teal $150

White $150

Vase, 15″

Aqua Opalescent $1250

Green $250

Marigold $175

Purple $350

White $500

Vase, 21″

Aqua Opalescent $1500

Green $300

Marigold $225

Purple $400

White $600

WINDMILL   IMPERIAL GLASS COMPANY

The windmill in this pattern is raised in the center and is surrounded by trees within a ridged oval. Outside the oval frame are floral designs and paneled sides.

Bowl, berry, 4"
Green $40
Marigold $25
Purple $40
Smoke $75
Bowl, berry, 5"
Green $45
Marigold $30
Purple $45
Smoke $90
Bowl, berry, 8"
Green $50
Marigold $35
Purple $50
Smoke $100
Bowl, berry, 9"
Green $55
Marigold $40
Purple $55
Smoke $125
Bowl, fruit, 10½"
Amber $225
Green $60
Marigold $45
Purple $60
Smoke $150
Pickle dish, oval
Green $55
Marigold $30
Purple $55
Pitcher, milk
Green $175
Marigold $100
Purple $175
Pitcher, water
Green $300
Marigold $175
Purple $350
Smoke $750
Tray, dresser, oval
Green $125
Marigold $75
Purple $175
Smoke $350
Tumbler
Green $50

Marigold $30
Purple $125
Smoke $150

WISHBONE   NORTHWOOD GLASS COMPANY, IMPERIAL GLASS COMPANY

"Wishbone" features a small medallion surrounded by curving spears shaped like wishbones. Overlapping these wishbones are mothlike designs; a continuous line of scrolling is in the background. The only Imperial piece listed is the flower arranger.

Bowl, 8″
Blue $350
Green $175
Ice Blue $900
Ice Green $900
Marigold $150
Purple $175
White $900
Bowl, 9″, footed
Aqua Opalescent $5000
Blue $400
Green $225
Ice Blue $950
Ice Green $950
Marigold $175
Purple $200
Smoke $1250
White $950
Bowl, 10″
Blue $400
Green $225
Ice Blue $950
Ice Green $950
Marigold $175
Purple $200
White $950
Epergne
Blue $2250
Green $2000
Ice Blue $2000
Ice Green $2000
Marigold $500
Purple $1750
White $2000
Flower arranger (Imperial)
Ice Blue $175
Ice Green $175
Marigold $125

White $175
Pitcher, water
  Green $1250
  Marigold $1000
  Purple $1250
  White $2500
Plate, 9″ footed
  Green $1250
  Marigold $500
  Purple $1000
Plate, 10″
  Green $1750
  Marigold $750
  Purple $1500
Plate, chop, 11″
  Green $1500
  Marigold $600
  Purple $1250
Tumbler
  Green $250
  Marigold $125
  Purple $200
  White $450

WREATH OF ROSES   DUGAN GLASS COMPANY, FENTON ART GLASS COMPANY

Wreaths of vines and foliage surround this simple rose design. The only Dugan pieces are the rose bowl, nut dish, spittoon, and compote pattern variant.

Bonbon dish
  Amethyst $45
  Blue $50
  Green $45
  Marigold $35
  White $85
Bonbon dish, stemmed
  Amethyst $65
  Blue $65
  Green $65
  Marigold $45
  White $125
Bowl, rose (Dugan)
  Amethyst $75
  Marigold $55
Compote
  Amethyst $65
  Blue $65
  Green $65

Marigold $45
Compote (Dugan pattern variant)
   Amethyst $65
   Blue $65
   Green $65
   Marigold $55
Nut dish (Dugan), Marigold $75
Punch bowl with base
   Amethyst $400
   Blue $450
   Green $425
   Marigold $325
   Peach Opalescent $2500
Punch cup
   Amethyst $40
   Blue $50
   Green $45
   Marigold $30
   Peach Opalescent $350
Spittoon (Dugan), Marigold $150

WREATHED CHERRY   DUGAN GLASS COMPANY

The cherries in this pattern are of slightly darker color and are raised in relief. Surrounding the cherries is a wreath of draped, scalloped ridges that form a continuous band. Each wreath frames three cherries.

Bowl, berry, 5″, oval
   Amethyst $55
   Blue $100
   Marigold $40
   Purple $55
   White $75
Bowl, berry, 10½″, oval
   Amethyst $175
   Blue $325
   Marigold $100
   Purple $175
   White $400
Butter dish with cover
   Amethyst $225
   Marigold $150
   Purple $225
   White $300
Creamer
   Amethyst $150
   Marigold $85
   Purple $150
   White $200

Pitcher, water

Amethyst	$550
Marigold	$300
Purple	$550
White	$1000

Spooner

Amethyst	$125
Marigold	$75
Purple	$125
White	$175

Sugar

Amethyst	$200
Marigold	$100
Purple	$200
White	$350

Toothpick holder, Amethyst $225

Tumbler

Amethyst	$75
Marigold	$50
Purple	$75
White	$225

The remaining entries in this chapter are miscellaneous patterns by the five major American Carnival glass producers: Dugan, Fenton, Imperial, Millersburg, and Northwood. Fewer than five pieces in each pattern exist in the following listings.

DUGAN GLASS COMPANY   MISCELLANEOUS PATTERNED CARNIVAL GLASS

In the past, much of Dugan's work was attributed to Northwood, since the company leased a factory from Harry Northwood. However, Dugan has now been recognized as a distinct maker of Carnival glass, with many of its own patterns. During the Carnival glass period, glassmaking companies continued to copy patterns, although to a lesser degree than during the pressed glass era. By the Depression of the 1930s the practice had ended, as companies became more careful about applying for and obtaining patents. Thomas Dugan, who was Harry Northwood's cousin, began producing Carnival glass in 1908 after Northwood left Indiana, Pennsylvania, for Wheeling, West Virginia. Many of Northwood's molds were left behind, which adds a little to the confusion. The Dugan/Diamond plant burned in 1931, and the company stopped producing glass. In the 1970s, the L.G. Wright Glass Company, which had purchased what was left of the business, reproduced some of Dugan's Carnival Glass from the original surviving molds. The new glass contains a trademark with a slanted W underlined within a circle. Refer to the appendix on manufacturer's marks.

Ashtray, Polo Pony pattern

Clear	$100
Marigold	$75
Pastels	$250

Carnival Glass by Dugan Glass Company. Left: "Question Marks" pattern. Right: "Fanciful" pattern. PHOTOS BY MARK PICKVET, COURTESY OF THE FENTON ART GLASS MUSEUM.

Banana Bowl, Corinth pattern
  Clear $100
  Pastels $300
Banana bowl, Dogwood Sprays pattern
  Clear $200
  Peach Opalescent $350
Banana bowl, Petals pattern
  Clear $150
  Marigold $100
  Pastels $250
Banana bowl, Single Flower pattern, Peach Opalescent only $400
Basket, Beaded Basket pattern
  Clear $250
  Marigold $100
  Smoke $300
Basket, Big Basketweave pattern $75
Bonbon dish, 2-handled, Puzzle pattern
  Clear $100
  Marigold $60
  Pastels $150
Bonbon dish, Question marks pattern
  Clear $85
  Marigold $55
  Pastels $125
Bowl, 4^{1}/$_{2}$″, Soda Gold Spears pattern, Marigold only $45
Bowl, 5″, Cobblestones pattern $75
Bowl, 5″, Flowers and Spades pattern
  Clear $75
  Marigold $45
  Pastels $225

Bowl, 5″, Heavy Grape pattern
　Clear $85
　Marigold $55
Bowl, 5″, Jeweled Heart pattern
　Clear $75
　Peach Opalescent $250
Bowl, 5″, Petal and Fan pattern
　Clear $75
　Marigold $55
　Pastels $175
Bowl, 6¼″, Four Flowers pattern
　Clear $65
　Blue or Peach Opalescent $150
Bowl, 7½″, Grape Vine Lattice pattern
　Clear $75
　Marigold $45
　White $150
Bowl, 7″, Golden Grape pattern
　Clear $75
　Marigold $45
Bowl, 8½″, Petals pattern
　Clear $90
　Marigold $65
　Pastels $200
Bowl, 8½″, Soda Gold Spears pattern, Marigold only $60
Bowl, 8″, Corinth pattern $85
Bowl, 9″, Apple Blossoms pattern
　Clear $75
　Pastels $175
Bowl, 9″, Cobblestones pattern $100
Bowl, 9″, footed, Dogwood Sprays pattern
　Clear $250
　Pastels $400
Bowl, 9″, Lattice and Daisy pattern, Marigold only $90
Bowl, 9″, Malaga pattern
　Clear $175
　Marigold $100
Bowl, 9″, Raindrops pattern
　Clear $175
　Pastels $350
Bowl, 9″, Single Flower Framed pattern
　Clear $125
　Marigold $75
　Pastels $350
Bowl, 10″, Flowers and Spades pattern
　Clear $90
　Marigold $60
　Pastels $275
Bowl, 10″, Four Flowers pattern
　Clear $100
　Blue or Peach Opalescent $200

Bowl, 10″, Heavy Grape pattern
Clear $100
Marigold $90
Peach Opalescent $950
Bowl, 10″, Jeweled Heart pattern
Clear $125
Peach Opalescent $350
Bowl, 10″, Petal and Fan pattern
Clear $100
Marigold $65
Pastels $225
Bowl, Double Stem Rose pattern
Clear $175
Marigold $100
Peach Opalescent $350
Bowl, Fish on Lily Pad pattern
Clear $50
Pastels $250
Bowl, Flowers and Frames pattern
Clear $125
Marigold $75
Pastels $350
Bowl, footed, Five Hearts pattern
Clear $150
Marigold $100
Bowl, Holly and Berry pattern
Clear $75
Marigold $50
Peach Opalescent $150
Bowl, Lattice pattern
Clear $100
Marigold $75
Bowl, Long Leaf pattern, Peach Opalescent only $175
Bowl, Long Thumbprint pattern
Clear $75
Marigold $50
Bowl, Polo Pony pattern
Clear $225
Marigold $100
Pastels $750
Bowl, Round-Up pattern
Clear $125
Marigold $90
Bowl, Single Flower pattern
Clear $75
Marigold $45
Pastels $175
Bowl, Six Petals pattern
Clear $75
Marigold $55
Pastels $325

Bowl, Stippled Flower pattern, Peach Opalescent only $175
Bowl, Stippled Petals pattern $125
Bowl, Victorian pattern
  Clear $550
  Peach Opalescent $1750
Bowl, Vining Twigs pattern
  Clear $65
  Marigold $45
  White $175
Bowl, Wind Flower pattern
  Clear $85
  Marigold $60
Bowl, with or without dome base, Weeping Cherry pattern
  Clear $125
  Marigold $85
  Pastels $325
  Peach Opalescent $400
Bowl, rose, Fluted Scroll pattern, Amethyst only $1750
Bowl, rose, Golden Grape pattern
  Clear $85
  Marigold $60
Bowl, rose, Grape Delight pattern
  Clear $90
  Marigold $65
  White $175
Bowl, rose, Honeycomb pattern
  Clear $250
  Peach Opalescent $550
Bowl, round or square, Butterfly and Tulip pattern
  Clear $1500
  Marigold $750
Bowl, with or without foot, Border Plants pattern
  Clear $125
  Pastels $225
Candlestick, Adam's Rib pattern
  Clear $75
  Pastels $275
Coaster, Concave Diamond pattern $40
Compote, Coin Spot pattern
  Clear $75
  Marigold $45
  Pastels $175
Compote, Constellation pattern
  Clear $150
  Marigold $85
  Pastels $250
Compote, Dogwood Sprays pattern
  Clear $85
  Marigold $45
Compote, Floral and Wheat pattern
  Clear $50

Marigold $35
Pastels $150
Peach Opalescent $250
Compote, Georgia Belle pattern
Clear $75
Marigold $60
Peach Opalescent $200
Compote, Long Thumbprint pattern
Clear $75
Marigold $55
Compote, Petals pattern
Clear $100
Marigold $75
Pastels $225
Compote, Puzzle pattern
Clear $85
Marigold $60
Pastels $200
Compote, Question Mark pattern
Clear $85
Marigold $65
Pastels $200
Compote, Starfish pattern
Clear $85
Marigold $65
Peach Opalescent $225
Creamer, S-Repeat pattern $100
Hat Vase, Daisy Web pattern
Clear $100
Marigold $75
Peach Opalescent $225
Hatpin holder, Formal pattern $350
Mug, Fish on Lily Pad pattern
Clear $225
Pastels $1500
Mug, Heron pattern
Clear $225
Marigold $125
Mug, Vintage Banded pattern
Clear $85
Marigold $60
Smoke $150
Nappy, Leaf Rays pattern
Clear $55
Marigold $40
Pastels $175
Nappy, Wind Flower pattern
Clear $100
Marigold $75
Nappy, handled, Holly and Berry pattern
Clear $100

Marigold $75
Peach Opalescent $250
Nut Dish, Grape Delight pattern
Clear $100
Marigold $75
White $225
Pitcher, Adam's Rib pattern
Clear $375
Pastels $750
Pitcher, water, Concave Diamond pattern
Clear $750
Green $1000
Pitcher, water, Floral and Grape pattern
Clear $450
Marigold $225
White $750
Pitcher, water, God and Home pattern, Blue only $2500
Pitcher, water, Heavy Iris pattern
Clear $1250
Marigold $750
Peach Opalescent $3500
Pitcher, water, Jeweled Heart pattern, Marigold only $1250
Pitcher, water, Quill pattern
Clear $3750
Marigold $2250
Pitcher, water, Rambler Rose pattern
Clear $425
Marigold $275
Pitcher, water, tankard-style, Lattice and Daisy pattern
Clear $425
Marigold $250
Pitcher, water, Vineyard pattern
Clear $475
Marigold $225
Pitcher, water, Vintage Banded pattern, Marigold only $350
Plate, 6$^1/2''$, Four Flowers pattern
Clear $150
Pastels $325
Plate, 6'', ruffled, Petal and Fan pattern
Clear $175
Marigold $100
Pastels $275
Plate, 7$^1/2''$, Grape Vine Lattice pattern
Clear $100
Marigold $75
White $225
Plate, 7'', Fish on Lily Pad pattern
Clear $100
Marigold $60
Pastels $250
Plate, 8$^1/2''$, Apple Blossoms pattern $275

Plate, 9½″, 1″ dome footed, Vintage pattern
Clear $750
Marigold $550
Plate, 10½″, Four Flowers pattern, Green only $1250
Plate, Polo Pony pattern
Clear $450
Marigold $300
Plate, Round-up pattern
Clear $350
Peach Opalescent $850
White $550
Plate, Soda Gold Spears pattern, Marigold only $100
Plate, Wind Flower pattern
Clear $400
Marigold $250
Plate, dome foot, Double Stem Rose pattern, Peach Opalescent only $250
Plate, grill, Four Flowers pattern
Clear $550
Peach Opalescent $1500
Purple $1250
Powder jar with cover, Vintage pattern
Clear $350
Marigold $175
White $550
Punch bowl, S-Repeat pattern $3500
Punch Bowl with base, Many Fruits pattern
Clear $750
Marigold $450
White $1750
Punch cup, Many Fruits pattern
Clear $45
Marigold $35
White $75
Punch cup, S-Repeat pattern $75
Sauce dish, Fan pattern
Clear $50
Marigold $35
Sugar, Long Thumbprint pattern
Clear $125
Marigold $75
Swan figurine
Marigold $125
Pastels $175
Peach Opalescent $375
Toothpick holder, S-Repeat pattern $450
Tray, dresser, Vintage pattern, Marigold only $225
Tumbler, Adam's Rib pattern
Clear $65
Pastels $125
Tumbler, Concave Diamond pattern
Clear $75

Green $750

Tumbler, Floral and Grape pattern
Clear $55
Marigold $35
White $175

Tumbler, Heavy Iris pattern
Clear $100
Marigold $65
White $225

Tumbler, Jeweled Heart pattern
Clear $250
White $1000

Tumbler, Quill pattern
Clear $750
Marigold $550

Tumbler, Ramber Rose pattern
Clear $75
Marigold $45

Tumbler, Vineyard pattern
Clear $75
Marigold $45

Tumbler, Vintage Banded pattern, Marigold only $750
Vase, 3-handled, Mary Ann pattern, Marigold only $750

Vase, 6″ tall, Three Diamonds pattern
Clear $100
Marigold $85
Peach Opalescent $325
White $75

Vase, 7″ tall, Corinth pattern
Clear $75
Marigold $45
Pastels $225

Vase, 7″ tall, Paneled Tree Trunk pattern
Clear $250
Marigold $150
Pastels $450

Vase, Adam's Rib pattern
Clear $85
Pastels $175

Vase, Beauty Bud pattern
Clear $125
With feet $250

Vase, Big Basketweave pattern
Clear $125
Marigold $100
Pastels $250

Vase, jack-in-the-pulpit style, Formal pattern
Clear $175
White $450

Vase, Lattice and Points pattern
Clear $100

Marigold $75
White $225
Vase, Lined Lattice pattern
Clear $100
Marigold $75
Pastels $225
Vase, Paneled Hobnail pattern
Clear $150
Marigold $100
Pastels $325
Vase, Pulled Loop pattern
Clear $125
Marigold $85
Peach Opalescent $300
Vase, Spider Web and Tree Bark pattern, White only $275
Vase, Summer Days pattern
Clear $150
Marigold $85
Vase, Wide Rib pattern
Clear $100
Marigold $75
Pastels $225

FENTON ART GLASS COMPANY   MISCELLANEOUS
PATTERNED CARNIVAL GLASS

Many Carnival companies were interrelated. Fenton, was no exception; Frank L. Fenton had previously worked as an apprentice, then foreman, at one of the Northwood factories. Fenton produced much Carnival glass from its founding in 1907 to about 1920. Production continued on a much more limited basis throughout the 1920s. There are more Fenton red Carnival examples and water sets (pitchers and tumblers) available than for other makers. The most noteworthy of Fenton's colors was a bright iridescent blue or cobalt blue. Fenton is the only original Carnival glassmaker still in operation today. The company has recently revived many iridescent forms. In the 1970s, Fenton reproduced and created a few new novelty Carnival items, such as bells, butterflies, birds, cats, covered animal dishes, and souvenir plates. Reproductions include a Butterfly and Berry tumbler, an Orange Tree candle bowl, a Persian Medallion compote and plate, a Fenton Flowers nut bowl, a large oval Hearts and Flowers flared bowl, and a Butterfly and Berry bowl with a Peacock Tail interior.

Banana boat, Cherry and Daisies pattern
Clear $1250
Marigold $1000
Basket, Pearl and Jewels pattern, White only $225
Bonbon dish, Butterflies pattern
Clear $100
Marigold $75

Carnival glass, "Lily of the Valley" pattern, by Fenton. PHOTO BY MARK PICKVET, COURTESY OF THE FENTON ART GLASS MUSEUM.

Bonbon dish, Daisy pattern
   Clear $350
   Marigold $250
Bonbon dish, Honeycomb and Clover pattern
   Clear $75
   Amber $100
   Marigold $50
Bonbon dish, Illusion pattern
   Clear $95
   Marigold $65
Bonbon dish, Leaf Chain pattern
   Clear $85
   Marigold $65
Bonbon dish, Lotus and Grape pattern
   Clear $200
   Marigold $150
   Red $1250
   Vaseline or Aqua Opalescent $250
Bonbon dish, Pond Lily pattern
   Clear $85
   Marigold $55
   White $125
Bonbon dish, Prayer Rug pattern, Milk White or Peach Opalescent only $850
Bowl, 5½″, Little Fishes pattern
   Clear $175
   Marigold $75
   Purple or Amethyst $250
Bowl, 5″, Fan-Tails pattern
   Clear $75
   Marigold $45
Bowl, 5″, footed, Panther pattern
   Clear $225
   Marigold $75

Carnival glass, "Paneled Dandelion" pattern, by Fenton. PHOTO BY MARK PICKVET, COURTESY OF THE FENTON ART GLASS MUSEUM.

Red	$2750
White	$500

Bowl, 5″, Little Flowers pattern

Clear	$75
Amber	$175
Marigold	$40
Vaseline	$125

Bowl, 7¹/₂″, Lion pattern

Clear	$550
Marigold	$400

Bowl, 7″, Acorn pattern

Clear	$100
Aqua Opalescent	$1000
Marigold	$75
Red	$1250

Bowl, 7″, Lion pattern

Clear	$350
Marigold	$150

Bowl, 7″, with or without foot, Horse's Head pattern

Clear	$100
Marigold	$80
Vaseline	$450

Bowl, 8¹/₂″, Feather Stitch pattern

Clear	$150
Marigold	$100

Bowl, 8³/₄″, Coral pattern

Clear	$140
Marigold	$75

Bowl, 8″, Concord pattern

Clear	$150
Marigold	$85

Carnival glass, "Plaid" pattern, by Fenton. PHOTO BY MARK PICKVET, COURTESY OF THE FENTON ART GLASS MUSEUM.

Bowl, 8″ or 9″, Little Daisies pattern
   Clear $1500
   Marigold $1500
Bowl, 8″, Hearts and Trees pattern
   Clear $250
   Marigold $175
Bowl, 9¹/₂″, Stream of Hearts pattern
   Clear $150
   Marigold $100
Bowl, 9″, Fan-Tails pattern
   Clear $100
   Marigold $75
Bowl, 9″, Heart and Horseshoe pattern
   Clear $85
   Marigold $65
Bowl, 9″, Heart and Vine pattern
   Clear $175
   Marigold $125
Bowl, 9″, Little Flowers pattern
   Clear $175
   Marigold $100
   Red $7500
Bowl, 9″ or 10¹/₂″, Feathered Serpent pattern
   Clear $100
   Marigold $75
Bowl, 9″, with or without feet, Dragon and Strawberry pattern
   Clear $1000
   Marigold $500
Bowl, 9″, footed, Panther design
   Clear $500
   Marigold $150
   White $1250

Carnival glass, "Milady" pattern, by Fenton. PHOTO BY MARK PICKVET, COURTESY OF THE FENTON ART GLASS MUSEUM.

Bowl, 9″, Peacock and Dahlia pattern
  Blue $150
  Clear $100
  Marigold $75
  Pastels $250
Bowl, 10″, Chrysanthemum pattern
  Clear $85
  Pastels $225
  Red $2750
Bowl, 10″, footed, Chrysanthemum pattern
  Clear $100
  Pastels $350
  Red $3000
Bowl, 10″, Rose Tree pattern
  Clear $1500
  Marigold $1000
Bowl, 10″, Little Fishes pattern
  Clear $350
  Marigold $250
  White $1250
Bowl, 11″, footed, Dragon's Tongue pattern, Marigold only $1000
Bowl, 11″, Panels and Balls pattern
  Clear $125
  Marigold $75
Bowl, Age Herald pattern, Amethyst only $1500
Bowl, Autumn Acorns pattern $75
Bowl, Blackberry pattern $65
Bowl, Cut Arcs pattern $50
Bowl, footed, Stag and Holly pattern
  Clear $400
  Marigold $150
  Red $3500

Carnival glass, "Peacock and Grapes" pattern, by Fenton. PHOTO BY MARK PICKVET, COURTESY OF THE FENTON ART GLASS MUSEUM.

Bowl, Goddess of Harvest pattern
  Clear $7500
  Marigold $6000
Bowl, Heavy Pineapple pattern $1000
Bowl, Illusion pattern
  Clear $125
  Marigold $90
Bowl, Leaf Chain pattern
  Clear $75
  Marigold $60
Bowl, Lotus and Grape pattern
  Clear $76
  Marigold $60
Bowl, Northern Star pattern, Marigold only $55
Bowl, Peacock and Grapes pattern
  Clear $65
  Marigold $50
  Peach Opalescent $425
  Red $2750
Bowl, Peter Rabbit pattern
  Clear $1750
  Marigold $1250
Bowl, Pinecone pattern
  Clear $65
  Marigold $50
Bowl, Plaid pattern
  Clear $125
  Marigold $75
  Pastels $1000
  Red $5500
Bowl, Ragged Robin pattern
  Clear $100
  Marigold $75
  White $325

Bowl, Ribbon Tie pattern
Clear $100
Marigold $75
Red $5500

Bowl, Scale Band pattern
Clear $75
Marigold $55

Bowl, Two Fruits pattern
Clear $175
Marigold $90
White $350

Bowl, Wild Blackberry pattern
Clear $125
Marigold $75

Bowl, with or without foot, Dragon and Lotus pattern
Clear $100
Marigold $75
Peach Opalescent $550
Red $3500

Bowl, rose, Garland pattern
Clear $100
Marigold $65

Bowl, rose, Horse's Head pattern
Clear $225
Marigold $150
Vaseline $750

Bowl, rose, Small Rib pattern
Clear $85
Marigold $65

Bowl, rose, Stag and Holly pattern
Clear $750
Marigold $400

Bowl, rose, Two Flowers pattern
Clear $85
Marigold $65
Vaseline $225

Carnival glass, "Dragon and Lotus" pattern, by Fenton. PHOTO BY MARK PICKVET, COURTESY OF THE FENTON ART GLASS MUSEUM.

Candlestick, Cut Ovals pattern
   Clear $55
   Marigold $35
Candlestick, Florentine pattern
   Clear $200
   Marigold $75
   Red $1500
Candy dish, Basketweave pattern
   Clear $125
   Pastels $275
Compote, Blackberry Bramble pattern $100
Compote, Cut Arcs pattern $75
Compote, Fan-Tails pattern
   Clear $75
   Marigold $55
Compote, Mikado pattern
   Clear $550
   Marigold $300
   Red $7500
   White or Green $1250
Compote, Scotch Thistle pattern $75
Compote, Small Rib pattern
   Clear $75
   Marigold $60
Compote, Sunray pattern, Marigold only $85
Compote, Coral pattern
   Clear $125
   Marigold $75
   Pastels $350
Compote, Iris pattern
   Clear $125
   Marigold $75
   White $550
Compote, Stream of Hearts pattern
   Clear $150
   Marigold $100
Epergne, Dahlia Twist pattern
   Clear $750
   Marigold $450
Goblet, Iris pattern
   Clear $125
   Marigold $75
Hat Vase, Basketweave pattern
   Clear $100
   Red $2500
Hat vase, Blackberry Banded pattern $75
Hat Vase, Blackberry pattern
   Clear $125
   Pastels $250
   Red $2500

Hat vase, Fern Panels pattern
   Clear $75
   Marigold $55
   Red $2500
Jardiniere, Diamond and Rib pattern
   Clear $1250
   Marigold $750
Pitcher, cider, Wine and Roses pattern, Marigold only $750
Pitcher, water, Apple Tree pattern
   Clear $500
   Marigold $300
   White $1000
Pitcher, water, applied decoration, Prism Band pattern
   Clear $650
   Marigold $375
Pitcher, water, Banded Drape pattern
   Clear $550
   Marigold $275
   White $950
Pitcher, water, Blackberry Block pattern
   Clear $750
   Pastels $2500
Pitcher, water, Blueberry pattern $750
Pitcher, water, Bouquet pattern
   Clear $750
   Marigold $425
Pitcher, water, Butterfly and Fern pattern
   Clear $750
   Marigold $375
Pitcher, water, Cherry Blossoms pattern, Blue only $350
Pitcher, water, Fluffy Peacock pattern
   Clear $1000
   Blue $2250
   Marigold $750
Pitcher, water, Inverted Coin Dot pattern
   Clear $600
   Marigold $350
Pitcher, water, Lily of the Valley pattern
   Marigold $3500
   Cobalt Blue $7500
Pitcher, water, Milady pattern
   Clear $1250
   Marigold $750
Pitcher, water, Orange Tree Orchards pattern
   Clear $550
   Marigold $350
   White $950
Pitcher, water, Paneled Dandelion pattern
   Clear $750
   Marigold $550

Pitcher, water, Scale Band pattern
   Clear $500
   Marigold $350
Pitcher, water, Silver Queen pattern, Marigold only $425
Pitcher, water, Strawberry Scroll pattern
   Clear $4000
   Marigold $3000
Pitcher, water, tankard-style, Lattice and Grape pattern
   Clear $550
   Marigold $375
   White $1500
Pitcher, water, Zig Zag pattern
   Clear $550
   Green $750
   Marigold $375
Plate, Plaid pattern
   Clear $275
   Marigold $200
Plate, 6½", Horse's Head pattern
   Clear $250
   Marigold $150
Plate, 6", Pinecone pattern
   Clear $125
   Marigold $75
Plate, 7½", Autumn Acorns pattern $90
Plate, 7", Leaf Chain pattern
   Clear $225
   Marigold $175
Plate, 7", Little Flowers pattern, Marigold only $125
Plate, 8½", Peacock and Dahlia pattern
   Clear $450
   Marigold $300
Plate, 8¼", Coral pattern
   Clear $450
   Marigold $275
Plate, 8", Heart and Vine pattern
   Clear $250
   Marigold $150
Plate, 8", Pinecone pattern
   Clear $150
   Marigold $100
Plate, 9½", Dragon and Lotus pattern
   Clear $1250
   Marigold $1000
   Red $7500
Plate, 9½", Lotus and Grape pattern
   Clear $1500
   Marigold $250
Plate, 9", Acorn pattern $600
Plate, 9", Concord pattern
   Clear $650

Marigold $450
Plate, 9″, footed, Stag and Holly pattern
 Clear $2500
 Marigold $750
Plate, 9″, Heart and Horseshoe pattern
 Clear $250
 Marigold $150
Plate, 9″, Leaf Chain pattern
 Clear $275
 Marigold $225
 Red or Aqua Opalescent $5500
Plate, 10″, Little Flowers pattern, Marigold only $275
Plate, 13″, footed, Stag and Holly pattern
 Clear $3000
 Marigold $1000
Plate, Age Herald pattern, Amethyst only $2500
Plate, footed, Scale Band pattern
 Clear $125
 Marigold $75
Plate, Northern Star pattern, Marigold only $100
Plate, Peacock and Grapes pattern
 Clear $450
 Marigold $250
Plate, Peter Rabbit pattern
 Clear $2750
 Marigold $2250
Plate, Ribbon Tie pattern
 Clear $350
 Marigold $250
Plate, Soldiers and Sailors pattern
 Clear $2500
 Marigold $1500
Shot glass, Arched Flute pattern
 Clear $250
 Marigold $175
Spittoon, Blackberry pattern $4000
Spittoon, Rib and Panel pattern, Marigold only $550
Toothpick holder, Arched Flute pattern
 Clear $175
 Marigold $100
 Pastels $350
Tumbler, Apple Tree pattern
 Clear $100
 Marigold $65
 White $250
Tumbler, applied decoration, Prism Band pattern
 Clear $125
 Marigold $70
Tumbler, Banded Drape pattern
 Clear $75
 Marigold $45

White $225
Tumbler, Blackberry Block pattern
  Clear $175
  Pastels $325
Tumbler, Blueberry pattern $125
Tumbler, Bouquet pattern $150
Tumbler, Butterfly and Fern pattern
  Clear $95
  Marigold $75
Tumbler, Cherry Blossoms pattern, Blue only $75
Tumbler, Fluffy Peacock pattern
  Clear $75
  Blue $175
  Marigold $55
Tumbler, Inverted Coin Dot pattern
  Clear $200
  Marigold $125
Tumbler, Lattice and Grape pattern
  Clear $85
  Marigold $60
  White $350
Tumbler, Lily of the Valley pattern
  Marigold $750
  Cobalt Blue $1250
Tumbler, Milady pattern
  Clear $250
  Marigold $150
Tumbler, Orange Tree Orchards pattern
  Clear $85
  Marigold $65
  White $225
Tumbler, Paneled Dandelion pattern
  Clear $100
  Marigold $75
Tumbler, Scale Band pattern
  Clear $65
  Green $325
  Marigold $45
Tumbler, Silver Queen pattern, Marigold only $85
Tumbler, Strawberry Scroll pattern
  Clear $450
  Marigold $400
Tumbler, Zig Zag pattern
  Clear $85
  Blue $125
  Marigold $65
Vase, 7″ diameter, Target pattern
  Clear $75
  Marigold $55
  Peach Opalescent $350
Vase, April Showers pattern $75

Vase, Cut Arcs pattern $85
Vase, Diamond and Rib pattern
  Clear $75
  Marigold $50
  Smoke $250
Vase, Heavy Hobnail pattern $750
Vase, Knotted Beads pattern
  Clear $75
  Amber or Vaseline $125
  Marigold $60
Vase, Leaf Swirl and Flower pattern
  Clear $100
  Marigold $75
Vase, Paneled Diamond and Bows pattern
  Clear $75
  Marigold $55
  Pastels $225
Vase, Plume Panels pattern
  Clear $100
  Marigold $75
  Pastels $350
  Red $3500
Vase, Pulled Loop pattern
  Clear $75
  Marigold $55
  Pastels $275
  Red $3000
Vase, Rib and Panel pattern, Marigold only $85
Vase, Rustic pattern
  Clear $75
  Marigold $55
  Pastels $275
  Red $3750
Vase, Swirled Flute pattern
  Clear $75
  Marigold $55
  Red $3500
  White $250
Wine glass, Wine and Roses pattern
  Clear $150
  Marigold $85
  Pastels $350

IMPERIAL GLASS COMPANY   MISCELLANEOUS PATTERNED CARNIVAL GLASS

Edward Muhleman, Imperial's founder, was related to the Fentons. He established his own company in 1901, four years before the Fenton brothers. The factory was not completed until early 1904, when glass production officially began. Imperial's Carnival glass production started about 1910 and lasted until about 1930. Imperial stopped making Carnival glass when the market turned sour. Beginning in 1962 and continuing into the 1970s, the company reproduced a good deal of iridescent glass using many of the original molds. All reissues are marked "IG" (overlapping letters) for easy identification. In 1972 Imperial was purchased by Lenox, Inc., and the name of the company was changed to the IGC Liquidating Corporation. The corporation was sold to Arthur Lorch in 1981 and once again to Robert Strahl in 1982. Strahl declared bankruptcy in 1985, and all the molds were sold.

Basket, Plain Jane pattern, Marigold only $100
Basket, Spring Basket pattern
    Clear $125
    Marigold $75
Bonbon dish, Cobblestone pattern
    Clear $75
    Marigold $55
Bonbon dish, Honeycomb pattern $60
Bowl, 5″, Heavy Grape pattern
    Clear $55
    Amber $125
    Marigold $40
Bowl, 5″ or 9″, Cobblestone pattern
    Clear $75
    Marigold $55
Bowl, 5″, Optic Flute pattern
    Clear $45
    Smoke $175
Bowl, 6″, handled, Honeycomb pattern, Marigold only $55
Bowl, 7½″ or 10″ oval, Cane pattern $55
Bowl, 7″, Star Spray pattern
    Clear $70
    Marigold $50
Bowl, 8″, Broken Arches pattern $85
Bowl, 8″, Acanthus pattern $100
Bowl, 8″, Long Hobstar pattern, Marigold only $65
Bowl, 9½″, Acanthus pattern $125
Bowl, 9″, Hat-Tie pattern
    Clear $85
    Marigold $65
    Smoke $175
Bowl, 9″, Heavy Grape pattern
    Clear $110
    Amber $175
    Marigold $75
Bowl, 9″, Wheels pattern, Marigold only $75
Bowl, 9″, footed, Double Dutch pattern
    Clear $75
    Marigold $50
Bowl, 10″, A Dozen Roses pattern $750
Bowl, 10″, Long Hobstar pattern, Marigold only $85

Bowl, 10″, Optic Flute pattern
Clear $75
Smoke $225
Bowl, Arcs pattern
Clear $60
Marigold $40
Smoke $175
Bowl, Blossoms and Band pattern, Marigold only $45
Bowl, Diamond and Sunburst pattern
Clear $85
Marigold $55
Bowl, Diamond Ring pattern
Clear $70
Marigold $50
Bowl, dome foot or oval, Double Scroll pattern
Clear $75
Marigold $50
Red $1275
Bowl, Heavy Diamond pattern, Marigold only $40
Bowl, Mayflower pattern
Clear $75
Marigold $50
Peach Opalescent $275
Bowl, Premium pattern
Clear $175
Marigold $75
Bowl, Rococo pattern
Clear $65
Marigold $45
Bowl, Scroll Embossed pattern
Clear $75
Marigold $55
Bowl, Shell pattern
Clear $75
Marigold $50
Smoke $225
Bowl, Soda Gold pattern
Clear $100
Marigold $75
Bowl, Star Center pattern
Clear $65
Marigold $45
Smoke $175
Bowl, Star of David pattern
Clear $150
Marigold $100
Smoke $250
Bowl, fruit, with base, Royalty pattern
Clear $75
Marigold $55
Bowl, rose, Hat-Tie pattern, Marigold only $125

Cake plate with center handle, Balloons pattern
Clear $250
Smoke $350
Candlestick, Premium pattern
Clear $100
Marigold $45
Candlestick, Soda Gold pattern
Clear $75
Marigold $55
Candy dish, Propeller pattern
Clear $70
Marigold $55
Compote, Arcs pattern
Clear $65
Marigold $40
Smoke $150
Compote, Balloons pattern
Clear $125
Smoke $200
Compote, Columbia pattern $40
Compote, Honeycomb and Clover pattern
Clear $125
Marigold $75
Compote, Long Hobstar pattern, Marigold only $85
Compote, Mayflower pattern
Clear $85
Marigold $60
Smoke $175
Compote, Optic Flute pattern, Marigold only $55
Compote, Propeller pattern
Clear $75
Marigold $55
Creamer, Heavy Diamond pattern, Marigold only $40
Decanter with stopper, Diamond and Sunburst pattern
Clear $350
Marigold $250
Decanter with stopper, Forty-niner pattern, Marigold only ... $350
Goblet, Flute and Cane pattern, Marigold only $65
Goblet, Tulip and Cane pattern
Clear $125
Marigold $85
Hat Vase, Florentine pattern, Pastels only $175
Hat Vase, Mayflower pattern
Clear $100
Marigold $75
Smoke $225
Lamp shade, Mayflower pattern
Clear $85
Marigold $60
Smoke $175

Lamp, Zipper Loop pattern
Marigold $750
Smoke $1000
Mug, Robin pattern, Marigold only $100
Paperweight, Plain Jane pattern, Marigold only $225
Pitcher, milk, Beaded Acanthus pattern
Clear $175
Green $350
Pitcher, milk, Field Flower pattern
Clear $350
Marigold $175
Pitcher, milk, Flute and Cane pattern, Marigold only $250
Pitcher, milk, Poinsettia pattern
Clear $375
Marigold $225
Smoke $550
Pitcher, water, Chatelaine pattern, Purple only $3750
Pitcher, water, Field Flower pattern
Clear $450
Marigold $275
Pitcher, water, Forty-niner pattern, Marigold only $350
Pitcher, water, Oklahoma pattern, Marigold only $750
Pitcher, water, Robin pattern, Marigold only $400
Pitcher, water, Soda Gold pattern
Clear $450
Marigold $350
Pitcher, water, Studs pattern, Marigold only $175
Pitcher, water, Tiger Lily pattern
Clear $450
Marigold $275
Plate, 7¹/₂″, Star Spray pattern
Clear $150
Milk White $100
Plate, 7″, Heavy Grape pattern
Clear $150
Amber $225
Marigold $75
Plate, 7″, Stork ABC pattern, Marigold only $150
Plate, 9¹/₂″–10″, Acanthus pattern
Clear $200
Smoke $325
Plate, Laurel Leaves pattern
Clear $150
Marigold $85
Plate, Scroll Embossed pattern
Clear $175
Marigold $100
Purple $225
Plate, Shell pattern
Clear $350

Marigold $200
Smoke $500
Plate, Star Center pattern
    Clear $125
    Marigold $85
    Smoke $250
Plate, grill, 12″, Heavy Grape pattern
    Clear $550
    Amber $850
    Marigold $375
Punch bowl with base, Broken Arches pattern $750
Punch cup, Royalty pattern
    Clear $55
    Marigold $40
Punch cup, Broken Arches pattern $50
Spooner, Honeycomb and Clover pattern, Marigold only $125
Sugar dish with cover, Hexagon and Cane pattern, Marigold only $125
Sugar, Heavy Diamond pattern, Marigold only $35
Toothpick holder, Square Daisy and Button pattern, Smoke only $250
Tray, Studs pattern, Marigold only $150
Tray, center handle, Three Flowers pattern
    Clear $150
    Marigold $100
Tumbler, Oklahoma pattern, Marigold only $275
Tumbler, Chatelaine pattern, Purple only $500
Tumbler, Field Flower pattern
    Clear $75
    Marigold $55
Tumbler, Forty-Niner pattern, Marigold only $110
Tumbler, Soda Gold pattern
    Clear $125
    Marigold $75
Tumbler, Studs pattern, Marigold only $55
Tumbler, Tiger Lily pattern
    Clear $100
    Marigold $65
Vase, 4″ tall, Columbia pattern $55
Vase, 14″ tall, Ripple pattern
    Clear $125
    Marigold $75
    Pastels $250
    Red $1500
Vase, Beaded Bull's-Eye pattern $75
Vase, Colonial Lady pattern $125
Vase, Loganberry pattern
    Clear $400
    Marigold $200
    Amber or Smoke $750
Vase, Mitered Ovals pattern
    Clear $8000
    Marigold $7000

Vase, Parlor Panels pattern
  Clear $125
  Marigold $75
Vase, Poppy and Fish Net pattern, Red only $1000
Vase, Poppy Show pattern
  Clear $750
  Marigold $450
  Pastels $2500
Vase, Rococo pattern
  Clear $125
  Marigold $75
Vase, Scroll and Flowers Panels pattern
  Clear $350
  Marigold $200
Vase, Star and Fan pattern $375
Vase, Stork pattern, Marigold only $125
Vase, Thumbprint and Oval pattern
  Clear $750
  Marigold $500
Wine glass, Cane pattern $55
Wine glass, Diamond and Sunburst pattern
  Clear $85
  Marigold $45
Wine glass, Flute and Cane pattern, Marigold only $55
Wine Glass, Forty-Niner pattern, Marigold only $85

MILLERSBURG GLASS COMPANY   MISCELLANEOUS PATTERNED CARNIVAL GLASS

Established by another member of the Fenton family (John W. Fenton), Millersburg has the distinction of being the scarcest name to find out of the big five in the Carnival glass world. The company operated only a few short years, and an archeological dig of the site of the original factory was necessary for some pattern identification. As many prices indicate, there are several rare and valuable Millersburg items. The company began operation in Millersburg, Ohio, in 1908. It declared bankruptcy in 1911 after producing a good deal of glassware. After filing for bankruptcy, Millersburg glass continued to be produced under the Radium Glass Company name until 1913. The company was then sold to the Jefferson Glass Company, which produced lighting glassware until 1916, when it closed the plant. Note that Millersburg glass is often referred to as "rhodium ware" or "Radium" because of the traces of radiation measurable in the glass.

Bonbon dish, Night Stars pattern
  Clear $500
  Amethyst or Green $750
Bonbon dish, Tracery pattern $850
Bowl, 8¹/₄" or 9¹/₂", Cactus pattern
  Clear $65
  Marigold $50

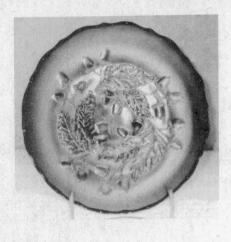

Carnival glass, "Acorn" pattern, by Millersburg. PHOTO BY MARK PICKVET, COURTESY OF THE FENTON ART GLASS MUSEUM.

Bowl, 9″ or 9³/₄″, Big Fish pattern $750
Bowl, 9″, fluted edge, Many Stars pattern
   Clear $450
   Blue $1000
Bowl, 9″, Whirling Leaves pattern
   Clear $175
   Marigold $100
   Vaseline $750
Bowl, 10″, Nesting Swan pattern
   Clear $2500
   Blue or Vaseline $3500
   Marigold $1500
Bowl, 11″, Whirling Leaves pattern
   Clear $225
   Marigold $125
   Vaseline $950
Bowl, Fleur-de-Lys pattern
   Clear $100
   Marigold $75
Bowl, Grape Leaves pattern
   Clear $750
   Marigold $500
   Vaseline $1250
Bowl, Grape Wreath pattern
   Clear $90
   Marigold $75
Bowl, Greengard Furniture pattern, Amethyst only $1000
Bowl, Mayan pattern $2500
Bowl, Primrose pattern
   Clear $225
   Blue $3250
   Marigold $175

Carnival glass, "Trout and Fly" pattern, by Millersburg. PHOTO BY ROBIN RAINWATER, COURTESY OF THE FENTON ART GLASS MUSEUM.

Bowl, Rays and Ribbon pattern
Clear $100
Marigold $75
Bowl, Trout and Fly pattern $750
Lavender $1250
Marigold $600
Bowl, Zig Zag pattern
Clear $550
Marigold $375
Bowl, advertising (Bernheimer), Blue only $1500
Bowl, footed, Fleur-de-Lys pattern
Clear $500
Marigold $250
Bowl, rose, Big Fish pattern, Vaseline only $8500
Bowl, rose, Daisy Squares pattern
Clear $500
Gold $750
Bowl, rose, Nesting Swan pattern, Marigold only $3250
Bowl, rose, Swirl Hobnail pattern
Clear $450
Green $650
Marigold $350
Bowl, round, Many Stars pattern
Clear $750
Marigold $500
Vaseline $1750
Card tray, Night Stars pattern
Clear $500
Amethyst only $750
Card tray, Zig Zag pattern, Green only $1250
Compote, 1 handle, Fruit Basket pattern, Amethyst only $2000

Compote, 9″, Tulip pattern
  Clear $1250
  Marigold $750
Compote, Acorn pattern
  Clear $1500
  Vaseline $4000
Compote, Boutonniere patttern $75
Compote, Deep Grape (Relief) pattern
  Clear $2250
  Marigold $1500
  Vaseline $4000
Compote, Dolphins design, pedestal feet, scalloped
  Clear $2000
  Blue $5000
Compote, Flowering Vine pattern $1500
Compote, Olympic pattern $4000
Compote, Peacock Tail pattern
  Clear $150
  Marigold $100
Compote, Poppy pattern $1500
Compote, Wild Flower pattern
  Clear $1750
  Green $2250
  Marigold $1500
Compote, miniature, Leaf and Little Flowers pattern
  Clear $500
  Marigold $400
Pin tray, Sea Coast pattern $550
Pin tray, Sunflower pattern $550
Pitcher, milk, Potpourri pattern, Marigold only $2500
Pitcher, water, Diamonds pattern
  Clear $1000
  Marigold $500
Pitcher, water, Feather and Heart pattern
  Clear $1000
  Marigold $750
Pitcher, water, Fruits and Flowers pattern
  Clear $10000
  Marigold $8500
Pitcher, water, Gay '90s pattern $9000
Pitcher, water, Marilyn pattern
  Clear $1250
  Green $1750
  Marigold $750
Pitcher, water, Morning Glory pattern
  Clear $10000
  Marigold $8000
Pitcher, water, Perfection pattern $5000
Plate, 9″, Cosmos pattern, Green only $175
Plate, Mayan pattern $750

Plate, Rays and Ribbons pattern
    Clear $275
    Marigold $200
Plate, Spring Opening pattern, Amethyst only $375
Plate, Trout and Fly pattern, Purple only $8000
Punch bowl, Fruits and Flowers pattern
    Clear $1750
    Blue $4000
    Marigold $1500
Punch bowl with base, Big Thistle pattern $10000
Punch bowl with base, Diamonds pattern $3000
Punch cup, Fruits and Flowers pattern
    Clear $75
    Blue $150
    Marigold $65
Sherbet, Fruits and Flowers pattern $900
Spittoon, Grape Wreath pattern, Marigold only $850
Spittoon, Nestling Swan pattern, Green only $5000
Spittoon, Swirl Hobnail pattern
    Clear $1000
    Marigold $750
Tumbler, Diamonds pattern $65
Tumbler, Feather and Heart pattern
    Clear $250
    Marigold $175
Tumbler, Gay '90s pattern $1250
Tumbler, Marilyn pattern
    Clear $275
    Green $550
    Marigold $200
Tumbler, Morning Glory pattern
    Clear $1500
    Marigold $1000
Tumbler, Perfection pattern $750

Carnival glass, "Basket" pattern, by Northwood. PHOTO BY ROBIN RAINWATER..

Vase, Bull's-Eye and Loop pattern $500
Vase, Honeycomb and Hobstar pattern $7500
Vase, People's Vase pattern, elaborate design of an adult watching
children inscribed within a circle $10000
Vase, Rose Columns pattern
   Clear $2500
   Blue $10000
Vase, Tulip Scroll pattern
   Clear $350
   Marigold $275

NORTHWOOD GLASS COMPANY   MISCELLANEOUS
PATTERNED CARNIVAL GLASS

Northwood was one of the largest producers of Carnival glass. Its owner, Harry
Northwood, had gained glassmaking experience by working for several firms, including Hobbs, Brocunier. He later would purchase the Wheeling, West Virginia,
company. Northwood Glass company experimented with and produced more original colors than other firms, particularly pastel examples. Only red seems to be lacking in Northwood's Carnival glass. When Harry Northwood passed away in 1919,
much of Northwood's output ended, although Carnival items had already severely
declined by the late teens. Northwood's factory completely stopped production in
December 1925. Unlike other companies such as Imperial, Northwood products
have not been reproduced in large quantities; however, some reproductions do
exist. The original Northwood trademark, an N with a line under it in a circle, is
owned by the American Carnival Glass Society and cannot be reproduced. A similar mark was used by the L.G. Wright Glass Company after purchasing what was
left of the Dugan/Diamond firm in 1931. The N includes an extra squiggle.
W. Wright's pieces are reproductions of Dugan items only. The Mosser Glass
Company also used a similar trademark in the early 1980s. This mark is like Northwood's original except that the circle is not complete around the N. Refer to
Appendix 4 for more information on manufacturers' marks. Note that iridescent
glass has been made in Taiwan over the past decade. Taiwan glass includes paper
labels only, not molded trademarks. These paper labels are easily removed, which
adds to the confusion.

Basket, Basket pattern
   Clear $250
   Pastels $750
Basket, bride's, Grape Leaves pattern $275
Bonbon dish, Butterfly pattern $55
Bonbon dish, Rose Wreath pattern, Amethyst only $350
Bonbon dish, Three Fruits pattern
   Clear $85
   Aqua Opalescent $750
   Marigold $65
   Pastels $200
Bowl, 3-footed, Blackberry pattern $85

Carnival glass, "Stippled Rays" pattern, by Northwood. PHOTO BY MARK PICKVET, COURTESY OF THE FENTON ART GLASS MUSEUM.

Bowl, 5″, Three Fruits pattern
  Clear $65
  Aqua Opalescent $750
  Marigold $50
  Pastels $175
Bowl, 5″, Strawberry Intaglio pattern, Marigold only $55
Bowl, 5″, Valentine pattern
  Clear $200
  Marigold $125
Bowl, 6″, fluted, Wild Rose pattern
  Clear $70
  Marigold $55
Bowl, 6″, Smooth Rays pattern
  Clear $80
  Marigold $65
  Pastels $175
Bowl, 7½″, Grape Leaves pattern
  Clear $100
  Ice Blue $250
  Marigold $65
Bowl, 8½″, Bull's-Eye and Leaves pattern $75
Bowl, 8½″, Sunflower pattern
  Clear $100
  Blue $450
  Marigold $75
  Pastels $225
Bowl, 8½″, Wild Strawberry pattern, Purple and Green only $100
Bowl, 8″ or 9″, Beaded pattern $55
Bowl, 8″, Rose Show pattern
  Clear $1000
  Aqua Opalescent $2500
  Marigold $500

Bowl, 8″, Wild Rose pattern
Clear $65
Ice Blue $750
Marigold $55
Bowl, 9″, Embroidered Mums pattern
Clear $75
Aqua Opalescent $550
Pastels $175
Bowl, 9″, Good Luck pattern
Clear $500
Marigold $250
Pastels $1750
Bowl, 9″, Hearts and Flowers pattern
Clear $90
Marigold $65
Pastels $175
Bowl, 9″, Nippon pattern
Clear $300
Aqua Opalescent $1750
Marigold $200
Pastels $1000
Bowl, 9″, Strawberry Intaglio pattern, Marigold only $75
Bowl, 10″, Apple and Pear pattern, Marigold only $125
Bowl, 10″, Three Fruits pattern
Clear $75
Aqua Opalescent $2500
Marigold $350
Pastels $3500
Bowl, 10″, Valentine pattern
Clear $275
Marigold $200
Bowl, Paneled Holly pattern $75
Bowl, Poinsettia pattern
Clear $550
Aqua Opalescent $2500
Marigold $350
Pastels $3500
Bowl, Poppy pattern
Clear $55
Marigold $45
Bowl, Rosette pattern
Clear $110
Marigold $65
Bowl, Soutache Pattern, Marigold only $85
Bowl, Star of David and Bows pattern
Clear $100
Marigold $75
Bowl with cover, Wheat pattern, Amethyst only $7500
Bowl, footed, Lovely pattern
Clear $750
Marigold $500

Bowl, footed, Rosette pattern
Clear $125
Marigold $75
Bowl, rose, Beaded Cable pattern
Clear $150
Pastels $950
Bowl, rose, Daisy and Plume pattern
Clear $85
Aqua Opalescent $3500
Marigold $55
Pastels $225
Bowl, rose, Drapery pattern
Clear $75
Aqua Opalescent $750
Marigold $65
Pastels $175
Bowl, rose, Fine Cut and Roses pattern
Clear $100
Aqua Opalescent $1000
Marigold $80
Pastels $225
Bowl, rose, footed, Leaf and Beads pattern
Clear $100
Aqua or Peach Opalescent $950
Marigold $75
Pastels $275
Bowl, rose, Smooth Rays pattern
Clear $75
Marigold $60
Bowl, ruffled, Rib pattern
Clear $85
Marigold $65
Bowl, ruffled, Rings and Daisy Band pattern, Amethyst only $150
Candy dish, Beaded Cable pattern $75
Candy dish, Daisy and Plume pattern
Clear $55
Marigold $40
Pastels $175
Candy dish, footed, Fine Cut and Roses pattern
Clear $100
Marigold $65
Pastels $225
Candy dish, Leaf and Beads pattern
Clear $85
Aqua Opalescent $750
Marigold $65
Pastels $300
Compote, Amaryllis pattern
Clear $100
Marigold $75

Compote, Blackberry pattern $65
Compote, Blossomtime pattern
    Clear $85
    Pastels $225
Compote, Daisy and Plume pattern
    Clear $100
    Marigold $75
    Pastels $275
Compote, Hearts and Flowers pattern
    Clear $125
    Marigold $85
    Pastels $450
Compote, Hobstar Flower pattern
    Clear $125
    Marigold $85
Compote, Small Blackberry pattern
    Clear $85
    Marigold $65
Compote, Smooth Rays pattern, Marigold only $55
Creamer, Double Loop pattern
    Clear $75
    Aqua Opalescent $750
    Marigold $55
Jardiniere, Tree Trunk pattern
    Clear $5000
    Marigold $2000
Lamp shade, Leaf Column pattern, White only $175
Lamp shade, Pearl Lady pattern, White only $175
Mug, Dandelion pattern
    Clear $150
    Aqua Opalescent $750
    Marigold $100
Pitcher, water, Paneled Holly pattern, Amethyst only $5000
Pitcher, water, Pretty Panels pattern
    Clear $550
    Marigold $250
Pitcher, water, Swirl Rib pattern, Marigold only $250
Pitcher, water, tankard-style, Dandelion pattern
    Clear $550
    Marigold $350
    Pastels $1000
Pitcher, water, tankard-style, Grape Arbor pattern
    Clear $750
    Ice Blue or Green $3750
    Marigold $450
    White $1250
Pitcher, water, tankard-style, Oriental Poppy pattern
    Clear $750
    Blue $3500
    Marigold $550
    Pastels $2000

Plate, 7″, Smooth Rays pattern, Marigold only $85
Plate, 7″, Wild Strawberry pattern, Purple and Green only $100
Plate, 8″, Wild Strawberry pattern, Purple and Green only $150
Plate, 9½″, Hearts and Flowers pattern
    Clear $350
    Aqua Opalescent $1750
    Marigold $200
    Pastels $550
Plate, 9″, Good Luck pattern
    Clear $300
    Marigold $175
    Pastels $550
Plate, 9″, Nippon pattern
    Clear $550
    Marigold $450
    White $1000
Plate, Embroidered Mums pattern
    Clear $125
    Marigold $85
    Pastels $175
Plate, Rose Show pattern
    Clear $2000
    Lime Green Opalescent $7500
    Marigold $1500
    Milk $10000
Plate, Soutache pattern, Peach Opalescent only $550
Plate, Three Fruits pattern
    Clear $175
    Aqua Opalescent $1750
    Marigold $100
    Pastels $1000
Plate, footed, Sunflower pattern
    Clear $500
    Marigold $250
Relish dish, Poppy pattern
    Clear $85
    Marigold $75
    Pastels $200
Spooner, Two Fruits pattern, Blue only $600
Sugar, Double Loop pattern
    Clear $75
    Aqua Opalescent $500
    Marigold $55
Sugar, Two Fruits pattern, Blue only $600
Tray, 11″ round, Holiday pattern, Marigold only $275
Tumbler, Interior Poinsettia pattern, Marigold only $550
Tumbler, Dandelion pattern
    Clear $100
    Marigold $75
    Pastels $225

Tumbler, Grape Arbor pattern
Clear $85
Marigold $55
Pastels $325
Tumbler, Oriental Poppy pattern
Clear $85
Blue $350
Marigold $65
Pastels $250
Tumbler, Poinsettia pattern, Marigold only $400
Tumbler, Pretty Panels pattern $85
Tumbler, Swirled Rib pattern $85
Vase, 7″ tall, Feathers pattern
Clear $75
Marigold $45
Pastels $150
Vase, 11″ tall, Diamond Point pattern
Clear $125
Pastels $450
Vase, Daisy and Drape pattern
Clear $275
Marigold $175
Pastels $1500
Vase, Drapery pattern
Clear $85
Marigold $55
Pastels $175
Vase, Ear of Corn style
Clear $450
Pastels $750
Vase, Graceful pattern
Clear $125
Marigold $85
Vase, Leaf Column pattern
Clear $75
Marigold $55
White $125
Vase, Pulled Corn Husk pattern, Purple or Green only $10000
Vase, Superb Drape pattern, Aqua Opalescent only $3500
Vase, Tornado pattern
Clear $550
Blue $1250
Marigold $400
White $1250
Vase, Tree Trunk pattern
Clear $200
Aqua or Peach Opalescent $1750
Marigold $150
Pastels $325
Vase with husk base, Ear of Corn style $3500

Vase, ribbed, Tornado pattern
Clear $600
Blue or Ice Blue $1750
Marigold $450

CHAPTER 6

DEPRESSION GLASS

It had been nearly forty years since the United States had experienced a serious economic downswing. Many people had either forgotten or had not lived through the hard times of the 1890s. A major shock was on its way: the Great Depression of the late 1920s and 1930s.

Several factors were responsible for this decline. The Agricultural Marketing Act of 1929 and the Hawley-Smoot Tariff enacted in 1930 increased rates on both farm and manufacturing goods. President Herbert Hoover signed the bill despite widespread opposition by most leading economists. The tariff alone raised the cost of living, encouraged inefficient production, and hampered exports. Foreign retaliation against expensive exports followed.

Through September 1929, the stock market continued an upward trend, but the increase was due to speculation and manipulation of existing securities. Banks gambled heavily on this speculation, businesses overstocked inventories, consumer spending suddenly decreased by a factor of four, commodity prices rapidly declined, and interest rates soared. Despite these poor economic indicators, the stock market boomed, but it all came to a grinding halt on October 23, 1929. Security prices unexpectedly fell following panic selling. The following day nearly 13 million shares were

Depression glass, dresser pieces. PHOTO BY ROBIN RAINWATAR.

dumped on the market, a new record. Five days later, the record was broken again as the volume reached 16 million shares.

The dumping of so many shares crashed the market and spawned the Great Depression. Thousands of banks closed, robbing nearly $3 billion from depositors; over 100,000 businesses went bankrupt; the gross national product was cut nearly in half; and millions of Americans were suddenly out of work. Even agricultural output suffered from poor weather conditions and incredibly low prices. As a result, massive foreclosures followed.

Despite the nation's severe problems, more glass was manufactured during these years than any other time in American history, an amazing feat considering the state of the nation's economy. A great battle ensued in the glass industry between handmade glass and machineware. Hand-cut crystal was far superior in quality, but it was very expensive and lost out to mass-produced machine-made glass on price alone.

The new manufactured glass was flawed, but the price was several times lower than handmade glass. Flaws included noticeable air bubbles, inconsistent coloring, and tiny trails of excess glass. These minor flaws do not detract from the value, but chips and cracks render glass virtually worthless. The glass companies that folded during the Depression were those that did not convert to automation. Competing with "Two for a nickel" tumblers and complete sets of tableware that sold for as little as $2.00 was impossible.

Machine-made glassware first appeared on the market in significant quantities following the end of World War I. It sold well, but intense competition and price cutting followed. The profit margin on such products was very low and higher sales volume was required to sustain such profits, not an easy objective to achieve during an upcoming depression. Cheap handmade imported glass also nearly tripled in volume during the 1920s, providing even more competition for U.S. glass manufacturers.

Despite these difficulties, the Depression era was a banner time for glass production in the United States. More patterns, shapes, and colors were produced then than in any other period in American glass history. Depression glass includes nearly all glass made in the United States from the 1920s and 1930s. The affordable glass was marketed to middle- and working-class Americans and could be purchased by the piece or in complete sets. It was available from general or department stores and factory outlets, by mail order, and wherever household furnishings and kitchenware were sold. Table sets usually included soup and serving bowls, tumblers, plates, and saucers. Added to this could be creamers and sugars, punch sets, vases, candy and cracker jars, water pitchers, butter dishes, dessert dishes, serving platters, salt and pepper shakers, measuring cups, and nearly everything imaginable for the table. Some sets number over 100 distinct pieces in the same pattern.

The gaudy art and oily Carnival glass colors went out of style quickly and were replaced by the simple non-opaque colors of the new Depression glass. Color was added to many items in the Roaring 20s, including such things as automobiles and appliances. Colored glass was used as cheap prizes at fairs and exhibitions; complete sets were given away as promotional items with furniture and appliance purchases; and smaller pieces served as bonuses in oatmeal cans, cereal boxes, and household supply containers. With the coming of the Depression, glass was so inexpensive that it was no longer a luxury for the well-to-do only. Middle- and working-class Americans purchased it in large quantities.

Colored glass had been in existence for centuries, but it was only during the Depression that it reached its peak in popularity. Nearly every U.S. glassmaking company perfected color and further experimented with new combinations. Pink was by far the most common, which is evidenced by the slightly lower value of pink Depression glass. In terms of quantity, green was a close second to pink, followed by amber. Other colors, though somewhat rarer, can also be found in glass of this period.

To produce color, metallic as well as nonmetallic elements are necessary. Metals produce the most vibrant and distinct colors, while the nonmetallic agents of phosphorus, selenium, sulphur, and tellurium serve to heighten or intensify specific colors. Manganese produces an amethyst color and is the oldest known glass additive, being traced to Egypt around 1400 B.C. Copper imparts a light blue and was also used by the ancient Egyptians. Cobalt is responsible for the richest, deepest, and most powerful blue coloring. Cobalt blue has long been a staple in glassmaking. Examples of this beautiful blue glass were found in King Tut's tomb, in stained glass windows of 12th-century Europe, and in pottery glazes for both the Tang and Ming dynasties of China.

Lead produces the most outstanding clear crystal. Generally, the higher the concentration of lead, the better the clarity and quality of the crystal. Silver is used to produce crystal, although the pieces are not as fine. Chromium produces a dark green color that can be heightened by other elements. Iron can be mixed with chromium for a darker green or with sulphur and carbon to produce amber-colored glass. Manufacturers usually avoid sand containing high concentrations of iron since it tends to make glass a murky green or dull brown. Gold, one of the more expensive coloring agents, imparts a brilliant ruby red color. Andread Cassius in 1685 is usually credited with this discovery. Luxurious ruby red glass generally has a higher value than most colors because of the addition of gold. Rarer colors exist too, such as a prominent bright yellow produced from uranium and smoky gray-colored glass from nickel.

Besides improvements in coloring, decorating techniques flourished during the Depression years. Some hand etching and copper wheel engraving survived, but technological advances made it possible for machines to do these more quickly and efficiently. The quality suffered to some extent, but the labor savings alone more than made up for it. Crackle glass was made by dipping hot glass fresh from a machine mold into cold water to induce numerous cracks over the entire surface of the glass. The cracked glass was then reheated and reformed within the mold. Frosted glass gained in popularity and consisted of a complete light acid etching over the entire exterior surface of the glass object. The result was a murky light gray coloring.

Machines applied enameling in exactly the right position, which was much quicker than application by hand. Enameled glass was then refired to fuse the paintlike substance permanently. Silk screens were also used to apply patterns, monograms, crests, and so on. Even decals were fired on some cheaper glassware. The most permanent trademark decorating technique applied to Depression glass was simple patented patterns pressed into molds by machine.

The popularity of Depression glass faltered in the late 1930s as Americans tired of the colored glass. A return to crystal, as well as new technological advances in ceramics and plastics, ended the era of one of the most notable periods in American glass history. Depression glass was packed away for years until collectors of the 1960s began reassembling sets. A major resurgence in Depression glass popularity ever since has produced a multitude of collectors; skyrocketing prices; numerous clubs, books, and newsletters; and simply the most popular glass collecting medium in America.

ADAM JEANNETTE GLASS COMPANY, 1932–1934

A few odd pieces were made in yellow and opaque blue (or delphite), triple the prices below. With most patterns, green is slightly more valuable than pink but the "Adam" pattern is an exception. A good deal of green is available, along with the pink. The pattern contains a large central flower with vertical ribbing. There are a few rare pieces, including two versions of the original butter dish. Be careful that the "Adam Sierra" butter dish bottom or top is not mixed up with the plain "Adam" or plain "Sierra" pattern (see the "Sierra" listings). Also note that the butter dish has been reproduced, but the color of the new version is lighter than the original. The candy lid and sugar lid are identical, which is common with Jeannette glassware.

Ashtray, 4¹/₂″ $25
Bowl, 4³/₄ $15
Bowl, 5³/₄″ $35
Bowl, 7³/₄″ $25
Bowl, 9″, with cover $75
Bowl, 10" oval $30
Butter dish with cover, (green is rare $500) $100
Butter dish with cover, (Sierra pattern) $850
Cake plate, 10″, footed $30
Candlestick, 4″ tall $45

Candy jar with cover	$100
Coaster, 3¼"	$25
Creamer	$25
Cup	$25
Lamp	$275
Pitcher, milk, 1 qt.	$50
Plate, 6"	$10
Plate, 7¾" square	$15
Plate, 7¾" round	$65
Plate, 9" grill, 3 divisions	$25
Plate, 9" square	$30
Platter, 11¾"	$30
Relish dish	$25
Salt and pepper shakers	$100
Saucer, 6" square	$10
Saucer, 6" round	$65
Sherbet	$35
Sugar with cover	$40
Tumbler, 4½"	$30
Tumbler, 7½"	$55
Vase, 7½", (pink is rare $200)	$65

AMERICAN PIONEER   LIBERTY WORKS, 1931–1934

Color and size variances are often found in nearly all Depression patterns. Different shades of green are quite common in the "American Pioneer" pattern. Piece sizes often vary because of mold or manufacturing changes. Primary colors include pink, green, and crystal. For crystal, reduce the prices by about 25%. A few pieces have also been discovered in amber, double the listed prices. "American Pioneer" is a round hobnail pattern.

Bowl, 5", 2 handled	$25
Bowl, 9", 2-handled	$30
Bowl, 10¾"	$65
Bowl with cover, 8¾"	$125
Bowl with cover, 9¼"	$125
Candlestick, 6½"	$45
Candy jar with cover, 2 varieties (narrow and wide)	$125
Cheese and cracker set, 2-piece, plate with indentation and matching compote ...	$75
Coaster, 3½"	$30
Cocktail glass	$45
Creamer, 2 styles	$25
Cup	$15
Dresser set, 2 cologne bottles with stoppers, powder jar, and matching tray	$400
Goblet	$45
Ice bucket or pail	$75
Lamp, 8½" tall	$125
Lamp with metal pole	$60

Lamp, globe shaped $75
Mayonnaise dish $85
Pitcher with cover, 5″ tall $175
Pitcher with cover, 7″ tall $250
Plate, 6 .... $15
Plate, 6″, 2-handled $17
Plate, 8″ $15
Plate, 11½″, 2-handled $20
Saucer $6
Sherbet, 2 styles $25
Sugar, 2-handled, 2 styles $25
Tumbler, 5 oz. $35
Tumbler, 8 oz. $45
Tumbler, 12 oz. $55
Vase, 7″ tall, several styles $100
Vase, 9″ tall $250
Whiskey tumbler, 2¼″ tall, 2 oz. $55
Wine glass $45

AMERICAN SWEETHEART   MACBETH–EVANS GLASS COMPANY, 1930–1936

"American Sweetheart" comes in a variety of opaque or nearly opaque colors. A light, nearly transparent milk white, a deep cobalt blue, ruby red, beige, and some trimmed pieces in gold can all be found. Blue and red are beautiful but rare (double the listed prices). For gold trim and opaque versions, increase the prices by 25%. The pattern contains a slightly irregular edge caused by sets of three vertical ribs. For the flatter pieces, the ribbing is only on the edges.

Bowl, 3¾″ or 4½″ $50
Bowl, 6″ $15
Bowl, 9″ or 9½″ $55
Bowl, 10,″ oval $60
Bowl, 11″ oval $75
Bowl, 18″ console $400
Creamer $15
Cup $20
Lamp shade $500
Pitcher, 2½ qt. $750
Pitcher, 2 qt. $600
Plate, 6″ or 6½″ $5
Plate, 8″ $10
Plate, 9¾″ or 10¼″ $25
Plate, 9″ $12
Plate, 11″, chop $20
Plate, 12″ $20
Platter, 13″ oval $50
Platter, 15½″ round $225
Salt and pepper shakers $400

Saucer	$4
Sherbet, 2 styles	$20
Sugar dish	$15
Tidbit, 2-tier	$100
Tidbit, 3-tier	$250
Tumbler, 5 oz.	$75
Tumbler, 9 oz.	$85
Tumbler, 10 oz.	$95

AUNT POLLY   U.S. GLASS COMPANY, LATE 1920s

"Aunt Polly" patterned glass is difficult to find in perfect condition. Minor flaws are evident in much Depression glass, but the seams and mold lines are especially heavy and uneven in this pattern. The pattern is diamond on the bottom half and paneled on the top (plates are just the opposite). Blue is the most popular color; there are varying shades of green and a few iridescent pieces available (decrease the price by half for colors other than blue).

Bowl, 4³/₄", 2 styles	$25
Bowl, 5¹/₂", 1 handle tab	$30
Bowl, 7¹/₄" oval, 2-handled	$40
Bowl, 8¹/₂" oval	$85
Bowl, 8"	$40
Butter dish with cover	$275
Candy jar with cover, 2-handled	$500
Compote, 5¹/₄", footed, 2-handled	$75
Creamer	$45
Pitcher, 1¹/₂ qt.	$200
Plate, 6"	$15
Plate, 8"	$20
Salt and pepper shakers	$250
Sherbet	$15
Sugar dish with cover	$175
Tumbler, 3¹/₂" tall, 8 oz.	$40
Tumbler, 6¹/₂" tall, footed	$75
Vase, 6¹/₂" tall	$50

AURORA   HAZEL ATLAS GLASS COMPANY, LATE 1930s

The prices are primarily for cobalt blue, which is the desirable color. Pieces were also made in pink and green (same price).

Bowl, 4¹/₂"	$35
Bowl, 5¹/₂"	$20
Cup	$15
Pitcher, milk, 4¹/₂" tall	$30
Plate, 6¹/₂"	$15

Depression glass, "Aurora" pattern. DRAWING BY MARK PICKVET.

Saucer $7
Tumbler, 4³/₄″ tall $25

AVOCADO (No. 601)   INDIANA GLASS COMPANY, 1923–1933

The primary colors in this pattern are pink and green with a bit of crystal. Note that green prices command a slightly higher premium than pink in most patterns, even more so with "Avocado." Increase the prices by 25% for green; cut by half for plain crystal. Reproductions abound in this pattern, as is typical with the Indiana Glass Company. The "Avocado" pattern was remade in the 1970s under the Tiara Product line in pink, frosted pink, yellow, blue, red, amber, amethyst, and dark green.

Bowl, 5¹/₄″, 2-handled $30
Bowl, 7¹/₂″ $40
Bowl, 7″, 1 handle $25
Bowl, 8″ oval, 2-handled $45
Bowl, 9¹/₂″ $125
Cake plate, 10 ¹/₄″, 2-handled $50
Creamer $35
Cup, 2 styles $35
Pitcher, 2 qt. $750
Plate, 6¹/₂″ $15
Plate, 8¹/₄″ $20
Relish, 6″, footed $25
Saucer $25
Sherbet $50
Sugar $35
Tumbler $150

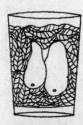

Depression glass, "Avocado" pattern. DRAWING BY MARK PICKVET.

BEADED BLOCK IMPERIAL GLASS COMPANY, 1927-1930s

"Beaded Block" comes in a variety of colors, especially green, pink, and amber. For crystal, cut the prices by 25% to 35%. Other colors include a medium blue, vaseline, iridescent, red, opalescent, and milk white (double the prices). The pattern includes squares separated by vertical and horizontal beaded rows. Imperial reproduced a few pieces, but all of Imperial's reproductions are marked "IG" on the bottom. Note that there are many bowls in "Beaded Block."

Bowl, 4½"-5½", with or without handles $10
Bowl, 6¾", flared $15
Bowl, 6"-6½", with or without handles $12
Bowl, 7"-7½", plain, fluted, or flared edges $20
Bowl, 8¼" $20
Celery dish $20
Compote $20
Creamer $20
Marmalade dish, stemmed, 2 styles $15
Pickle dish, 2-handled $20
Pitcher, 1 pt. $110
Plate, 7¾" square $10
Plate, 8¾" $20
Sugar $20
Vase, 6", footed $20

BLOCK OR BLOCK OPTIC HOCKING GLASS COMPANY, 1929-1933

The basic colors are green, pink, and yellow. A few frosted and crystal pieces exist but are not highly desired (reduce the prices by 50%). Pieces have also been found in amber (same price) and the covered butter dish comes in a few rare colors such as cobalt blue ($500.00) and opalescent green ($225.00). The pattern consists of ridged horizontal ribbing intersecting with vertical ribbing to create the block effect.

Bowl, 4½" $25
Bowl, 4¼" $10
Bowl, 5¼" $20
Bowl, 7"-7¼" $35
Bowl, 8½" $30
Bowl, 11¾", console $75
Butter dish with cover $65
Candlestick $50
Candy jar with cover, 2 styles $75
Cocktail glass, 4¼" tall $35
Compote $45
Creamer, several styles $15
Cup, several styles $10
Goblet, several styles $35

Depression glass, "Block" pattern. DRAWING BY MARK PICKVET.

Ice Bucket	$55
Mug	$35
Pitcher, water, 1½ qt., several styles	$75
Pitcher, water, 2½ qt.	$100
Plate, 6″	$5
Plate, 8″	$6
Plate, 9″	$25
Plate, 9″ grill, divided	$30
Plate, 10¼″	$20
Reamer	$25
Salt and pepper shakers	$85
Sandwich server with handle	$65
Saucer, 2 styles	$10
Sherbet, 3¼″ tall	$10
Sherbet, 4¾″ tall	$15
Sugar, several styles	$15
Tumble-up, bottle with matching tumbler	$75
Tumbler, 3 oz.	$20
Tumbler, 5 oz.	$25
Tumbler, 9-9½ oz., with or without feet	$20
Tumbler, 10-11 oz.	$25
Tumbler, 10-11 oz., footed	$30
Tumbler, 12 oz.	$30
Tumbler, 15 oz.	$35
Vase, 5¾″ tall	$300
Whiskey tumbler, 1 oz.	$40
Whiskey tumbler, 2 oz.	$35
Wine glass	$35

BOW KNOT   UNKNOWN MANUFACTURER, DEPRESSION YEARS

In her classic books on Depression glass, Hazel Marie Weatherman listed this pattern as unknown, and no one has yet identified it. The only color is green, and the center consists of a hexagonal flower surrounded by scrolling, bowlike designs,

Bowl, 4½″, Green	$15
Bowl, 5½″, Green	$20

Cup, Green $10
Plate, 7″, Green $15
Sherbet, Green $15
Tumbler, 5″ tall, with or without foot, Green $20

CAMEO or BALLERINA or DANCING GIRL, HOCKING GLASS COMPANY, 1930–1934

"Cameo" is the queen of the Depression glass patterns. It is very beautiful, highly collectible, and easily recognizable with the cameo dancing girl design. Pink, green, and yellow are the primary colors. A few pieces were made in crystal with a platinum rim (reduce the prices by 25%); a few others appear in frosted green (reduce the prices by 50%). Reproductions of the salt and pepper shakers are found in pink, green, and cobalt blue (1970s), but the colors are weaker and easily distinguished from the originals. Miniature sets that include about 40 pieces have been reproduced in pink, green, and yellow and are easily distinguished by their size (see Chapter 7 for pricing information).

Bowl, 4¼″ $10
Bowl, 4¾″ $100
Bowl, 5½″ $35
Bowl, 7¼″ $55
Bowl, 8¼″ $45
Bowl, 9″ $60
Bowl, 10″ oval $35
Bowl, 11″, 3-footed $100
Butter dish with cover $250
Cake plate, 10½″ $100
Cake plate, 10″, 3-footed $25
Candlestick $50

Depression glass, "Cameo" pattern. PHOTO BY ROBIN RAINWATER.

Candy jar with cover, 4″ tall $75
Candy jar with cover, 6¹/₂″ tall $150
Compote $35
Cookie jar with cover $60
Creamer, 2 styles $30
Cup, 2 styles $15
Decanter with stopper, 10″ tall $200
Domino tray $175
Goblet, 6″ tall $55
Ice bucket, 2 tab handles $225
Jam jar with cover, 2″ tall $175
Pitcher, 1 qt. $75
Pitcher, milk, 1 qt. $250
Pitcher, water, 2 qt. $85
Plate, 6″ or 7″
Plate, 8″ $12
Plate, 8¹/₂″ square $50
Plate, 9¹/₂″ or 10″ $20
Plate, 10¹/₂″, grill, 2 handled $50
Plate, 10¹/₂″, grill, no handles $15
Plate, 10¹/₂″, with or without handles $20
Platter, 12″, 2 tab handles $35
Relish, footed, 3 divisions $35
Salt and pepper shakers $100
Sandwich server with center handle (rare) $5000
Saucer, 6″ $5
Saucer with ring $175
Sherbet, 3″ tall $15
Sherbet, 5″ tall $20
Sugar, 2 styles $30
Tumbler, 5 oz. $30
Tumbler, 9 oz., with or without feet $30
Tumbler, 11 oz. $40
Tumbler, 10 oz., with or without feet $35
Tumbler, 11 oz., footed $65
Tumbler, 15 oz. $75
Tumbler, 15 oz., footed $500
Vase, 5³/₄″ $200
Vase, 8″ tall $50
Water bottle $40
Wine glass, 4″ tall $65

CHERRY BLOSSOM　　JEANNETTE GLASS COMPANY, 1930–1939

The primary colors are pink and green. A few pieces were made in a light opaque blue, sometimes referred to as delphite blue (same prices). A few others were made in yellow, amber, red, and opaque green; quadruple the prices. A few reproductions have been made in "Cherry Blossom," including water sets (pitchers and tumblers), bowls, cups and saucers, butter dishes, salt and pepper shakers, the two-handled tray, and the cake plate (cut the prices in half). The colors differ in the reproductions and include brighter versions of pink and green, yellow, cobalt blue, ruby red, iridized colors, and transparent blue.

* The pieces marked with an asterisk were part of a children's miniature set produced in pink and delphite blue.

Bowl, 4³/₄″	$20
Bowl, 5³/₄″	$40
Bowl, 7³/₄″	$60
Bowl, 8¹/₂″	$50
Bowl, 9″ oval	$40
Bowl, 9″, 2-handled	$65
Bowl, 10¹/₂″, 3-footed	$85
Butter dish with cover	$100
Cake plate, 10¹/₄″, 3-footed	$35
Coaster	$15
Creamer	$20
Cup	$20
Mug	$250
Pitcher, 1¹/₂″ qt.	$75
Pitcher, milk, 1 qt.	$60
Plate, 6″	$10
Plate, 7″	$20
Plate, 9″	$25
Plate, 9″, grill, 3 divisions	$30
Plate, 10″, grill	$100
Platter, 9″ oval	$1000
Platter, 11″ oval	$50
Platter, 13″ oval	$65
Platter, 13″ oval, 3 divisions	$75
Salt and pepper shakers	$1250
Saucer	$7
Sherbet	$20
Sugar with cover	$35
Tray, 10 ¹/₂″	$25
Tumbler, 4 oz.	$20
Tumbler, 8-9 oz.	$35
Tumbler, 12 oz.	$65
***14 piece set**	*$350
***Creamer**	$50
***Cup**	$40
***Plate,** 6″	$15
***Saucer**	$10
***Sugar**	$50

CHERRYBERRY U.S. GLASS COMPANY, EARLY 1930s

The basic colors are pink and green; however, most pieces can be found in crystal and a light iridized marigold color (reduce the prices by 25% for crystal or marigold). Iridized pieces are often confused with earlier Carnival glass because of the

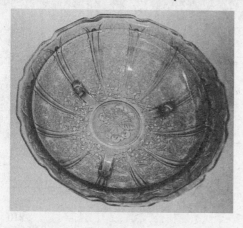

Depression glass, "Cherryberry" pattern. PHOTO BY ROBIN RAINWATER.

marigold color. "Cherryberry" is very similar to "Strawberry" except for the difference in the berry pattern.

Bowl, 4″	$10
Bowl, 6¹/₂″	$25
Bowl, 6¹/₄″	$50
Bowl, 7¹/₂″	$25
Butter dish with cover	$175
Compote	$25
Creamer (large), 4¹/₂″ tall	$45
Creamer (small)	$20
Olive dish, 5″, 1 tab handle	$20
Pickle dish, 8¹/₄″ oval	$20
Pitcher	$175
Plate, 6″	$10
Plate, 7¹/₂″	$15
Sherbet	$10
Sugar (large), with cover	$100
Sugar (small), open	$20
Tumbler, 3¹/₂″ tall	$25

CIRCLE   HOCKING GLASS COMPANY, 1930s

Pink and green are the two primary colors. For any crystal pieces, reduce the prices by 25% to 35%. Many goblets have green stems with crystal bowls (same price). As with a good deal of Depression glass, color variations from one batch to the next often vary, and many pieces of "Circle" have a yellowish-green tone. Many pieces have a star on the bottom, but all feature horizontal circular ribbing.

Bowl, 4¹/₂″	$10
Bowl, 5″-5¹/₂″	$12
Bowl, 8″	$20

Bowl, 9¹/₂″ $25
Creamer $12
Cup, 2 styles $7
Decanter $55
Goblet $15
Pitcher, 2 or 2¹/₂ qt. $40
Plate, 6″ $3
Plate, 8¹/₄″ $6
Plate, 9¹/₂″ $15
Platter, 10″ $20
Reamer, (fits the 2¹/₂ qt. pitcher) $15
Saucer $3
Sherbet, 3¹/₈″ tall $5
Sherbet, 4³/₄″ tall $7
Sugar $12
Tumbler, 4 oz. $10
Tumbler, 8 oz. $12
Tumbler, 10 oz. $20
Tumbler, 15 oz. $25
Wine glass $15

CLOVERLEAF   HAZEL ATLAS GLASS COMPANY, 1930–1936

The primary colors are pink, green, and yellow. The pattern was also produced in black (double the prices) and crystal (reduce by 25% to 35%). The clover leaves are between two circular bands near the top or outer rim of each piece.

Ashtray $20
Bowl, 4″ $25
Bowl, 5″ $30
Bowl, 7″ $40
Bowl, 8″ $50
Candy dish with cover $75
Creamer $20
Cup $10
Plate, 6″ $7
Plate, 8″ $10
Plate, 10¹/₄″ grill, 3 divisions $25

Depression glass, "Cloverleaf" pattern. DRAWING BY MARK PICKVET.

Salt and pepper shakers	$45
Saucer	$5
Sherbet	$7
Sugar, 2-handled	$20
Tumbler, 9 oz.	$50
Tumbler, 10 oz, with or without feet	$35

COLONIAL BLOCK   HAZEL ATLAS GLASS COMPANY, EARLY 1930s

The prices below are for green and pink. For crystal, frosted, and reproduction milk glass, reduce the prices by 50%. For any black, increase the prices by 50%. Most pieces in this pattern are marked with the Hazel-Atlas "H" and "A" overlapping symbol. This symbol is sometimes confused with both Atlas-Mason (overlapping "A" and "M") and Anchor-Hocking because of the "A" and "H." Refer to Appendix 4 for manufacturers' marks. This block pattern is similar to "Block Optic" except that "Colonial Block" has a star at the bottom or center of each piece.

Bowl, 4″	$10
Bowl, 7″	$20
Butter dish with cover	$65
Butter tub with cover	$55
Candy jar with cover	$45
Creamer	$15
Goblet	$15
Pitcher	$50
Powder jar with cover	$20
Sherbet	$10
Sugar dish with cover, 2-handled	$25

COLONIAL FLUTED or ROPE   FEDERAL GLASS COMPANY, 1928–1933

The basic color is green. Some pieces are marked with the Federal trademark ("F" inscribed in a shield on the underside). The pattern includes vertical ribbing with a roping on the outer or top edge.

Bowl, 4″	$7
Bowl, 6½″	$20
Bowl, 6″	$10
Bowl, 7½″	$20
Creamer	$10
Cup	$7
Plate, 6″	$4
Plate, 8″	$6
Saucer	$3
Sherbet	$7
Sugar with cover, 2-handled	$25

Depression glass. Left: "Colonial Block" pattern. Right: "Colonial Rope" pattern. DRAWINGS BY MARK PICKVET.

COLONIAL KNIFE AND FORK   HOCKING GLASS COMPANY, 1934–1938

The basic colors are pink, green, and crystal. For crystal, reduce the prices by 50%. A few pieces were produced in milk white (same prices) as well as darker royal ruby (quadruple the prices). The pattern consists of wide arched flutes with extra vertical ribbing between the flutes.

Bowl, 3³/₄″	$50
Bowl, 4¹/₂″	$75
Bowl, 5¹/₂″	$75
Bowl, 7″	$65
Bowl, 9″	$35
Bowl, 10″ oval	$35
Butter dish with cover, (pink is rare $750)	$75
Celery dish	$150
Cheese dish with cover	$250
Claret glass, 5¹/₄″ tall	$25
Cocktail glass, 4″ tall	$25
Cordial glass, 3³/₄″ tall	$30
Creamer	$30
Cup	$15
Goblet, 5³/₄″ tall	$35
Mug, 4¹/₂″ tall	$500
Pitcher, 7″ or 8″ tall, with or without ice lip	$100
Plate, 6″	$7
Plate, 8¹/₂″	$10
Plate, 10″	$55
Plate, 10″ grill, 3 divisions	$30
Platter, 12″ oval	$35
Salt and pepper shakers	$150
Saucer	$7
Sherbet, 2 styles	$15
Sugar with cover, 2-handled	$55
Tumbler, 3 oz., with or without feet	$20
Tumbler, 5 oz.	$20
Tumbler, 5 oz., footed	$35
Tumbler, 9 oz.	$25
Tumbler, 10 oz., footed	$50

Tumbler, 11 oz. $40
Tumbler, 12 oz. $50
Tumbler, 15 oz. $75
Whiskey tumbler, 2½″ tall, 1½ oz. $15
Wine glass, 4½″ tall $25

CORONATION or BANDED RIB or SAXON HOCKING GLASS COMPANY, 1936–1940

The listed prices are for pink and green. Saucers were made in crystal ($1.00), and several pieces were also made in Hocking's dark red royal ruby (double the prices). The wide vertical ribbing ends about halfway up into very thin banded rims spaced closely together.

Bowl, 4¼″ $20
Bowl, 4¼″, 2 tab handles $7
Bowl, 6½″ $7
Bowl, 8″ $50
Bowl, 8″, 2 tab handles $12
Cup $7
Pitcher, 2 qt. $550
Plate, 6″ $2
Plate, 8½″ $7
Saucer $2
Sherbet $5
Tumbler, 5″ tall, footed $25

CRACKLE GLASS VARIOUS COMPANIES, 1920s–1930s

"Crackle" glass was made by plunging a hot object into lukewarm or cold water to induce cracks; the object was then refired. The pattern was produced by many companies but not in huge quantities. There are still good buys out there in Depression-styled "Crackle" glass. The colors are usually amber, green, and pink. For crystal, reduce the listed prices by half.

Candlestick, By Cracky pattern (L.E. Smith) $15
Candy jar with cover, By Cracky pattern (L.E. Smith) $40

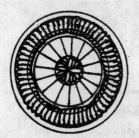

Depression glass, "Coronation" pattern. DRAWING BY MARK PICKVET.

Frog, By Cracky pattern (L.E. Smith) $30
Pitcher, iced tea with cover, Craquel pattern (U.S. Glass) $125
Pitcher, iced tea with cover, Jack Frost design (Federal) $100
Pitcher, lemonade, Jack Frost design (Federal) $85
Pitcher, water, Jack Frost design, Depression colors (Federal) $85
Plate, 7″, By Cracky pattern, (L.E. Smith) $10
Plate, 8″ octagonal, By Cracky pattern (L.E. Smith) $25

Depression glass, "Crackle" pattern. PHOTO BY ROBIN RAINWATER.

L. E. SMITH GLASS CO.
MOUNT PLEASANT, PA.

1. *No. 33 Candle Holder*
2. *3 inch Flower Block*
3. *8 inch Octagon Plate*
4. *Luncheon Set with Sherbet*

MADE IN CRYSTAL, CANARY AND AMBER

Depression glass, "Crackle" pattern. Reproduced from a 1928 advertisement.

Sherbet, By Cracky pattern (L.E. Smith) $12
Tumbler, iced tea, Jack Frost design (Federal) $15
Tumbler, iced tea, footed, Craquel pattern (U.S. Glass) $10
Tumbler, lemonade, Jack Frost design (Federal) $15
Tumbler, water, Jack Frost design (Federal) $15

CUBE or CUBIST   JEANNETTE GLASS COMPANY, 1929–1933

The basic colors are pink and green, but quite a few other colors are available. For crystal, amber, or milk white, reduce the prices by half. For yellow, blue, or ultramarine, double them. "Cube" is often confused with many similar pressed crystal patterns, such as Fostoria's "American" pattern.

Bowl, 4½″ $10
Bowl, 6½″ $15
Butter dish with cover $85
Candy jar with cover $40
Coaster $10
Creamer, 2½″ $5
Creamer, 3½″ $10
Cup $10
Pitcher $225
Plate, 6″ $5
Plate, 8″ $7
Powder jar with cover, 3-footed $30
Salt and pepper shakers $40
Saucer $4
Sherbet $7
Sugar, 2½″ $5
Sugar with cover, 3″ $20
Tray, for the large creamer and sugar, 7½″, Crystal only $7
Tumbler, 4″ tall, 9 oz. $60

Depression glass, "Cube" pattern. Reproduced from a 1930 advertisement.

Depression glass, "Cube" pattern. PHOTOS BY ROBIN RAINWATER.

CUPID   PADEN CITY GLASS COMPANY, 1930s

The primary colors are pink, green, and blue, but pieces have been found in amber, black, and yellow (increase the prices by 50%). For crystal, reduce them by 50%. The samovar, a Russian design, is an urn with a spigot at its base. In this pattern, two winged Cupids face each other between a cameolike bell. Paden City Depression products are rare, making them quite valuable.

Bowl, 8½″ oval, footed $225
Bowl, 9¼″, footed $200
Bowl, 10¼″-10½″ $175
Bowl, 11″ $150
Bowl with center handle, 9¼″ $175
Cake plate, 11¾″ $175
Cake stand, footed $175
Candlestick $75
Candy jar with cover, with or without foot $250
Compote $100
Compote with cover, 3-part $225
Creamer, 4½″-5″ $100
Ice bucket or tub $225
Lamp with silver trimming $425
Mayonnaise dish $150
Plate, 10½″ $125
Samovar $850
Sugar, 4¼″-5″, 2-handled $100
Tray, 11″ oval, footed $175
Tray with center handle, 10¾″ $150
Vase, 8¼″ $500
Vase, fan-shaped $275

Depression glass, "Cupid" pattern. Reproduced from a 1929 Paden City patent submission.

DIAMOND QUILTED or FLAT DIAMOND   IMPERIAL GLASS COMPANY, LATE 1920s–EARLY 1930s

The prices listed are for pink and green. For the rarer colors, such as light blue, black, red, and amber, double the prices; for crystal, reduce them by 50%. Be careful not to confuse this pattern with a similar diamond pattern by Hazel Atlas. The quilting on Hazel Atlas pieces ends in a straight line at the top, while that on Imperial pieces ends unevenly in points at the top.

Bowl, 4¾"	$12
Bowl, 5½", 1 tab handle	$10
Bowl, 5"	$10
Bowl, 7"	$12
Bowl, 10½"	$25
Cake saver, 10"	$65
Candlestick	$15
Candy jar with cover, footed	$85
Compote, 6" tall	$50
Compote with cover, 11½"	$85
Cordial, 1 oz.	$15
Creamer	$10
Cup	$12
Goblet, 6" tall, 9 oz.	$15
Ice bucket	$60
Mayonnaise set with ladle, plate, and compote	$60
Pitcher, 2 qt.	$65
Plate, 6"	$5
Plate, 7"	$7
Plate, 8"	$8
Platter, 14"	$15
Punch bowl with stand	$500
Sandwich server with center handle	$40
Saucer	$4
Sherbet	$6
Sugar, 2 handled	$10
Tumbler, 6 oz., footed	$10
Tumbler, 9 oz.	$10
Tumbler, 9 oz., footed	$10
Tumbler, 12 oz.	$12
Tumbler, 12 oz., footed	$17

Vase, fan-shaped, double dolphin handles $75
Whiskey, 1½ oz. $10
Wine glass, 2 or 3 oz. $15

DIANA FEDERAL GLASS COMPANY, 1937–1941

Basic colors consist of pink and amber. For crystal, crystal trimmed in colors, or frosted pieces, reduce the prices by 50%. "Diana" is sometimes confused with spirals, swirls, and twisted patterns; however, the centers of "Diana" pieces are swirled, whereas the others are plain. The shading also seems to be a little duller on the "Diana" pieces.

Ashtray, 3½" $4
Bowl, 5"-5½" $12
Bowl, 9" $25
Bowl, 11" $45
Bowl, 12" $35
Candy jar with cover $40
Coaster $10
Creamer $15
Cup $15
Cup, 2 oz., demitasse $35
Junior set, 6 cups, 7 saucers with a round metal rack (rack contains grooves for saucers and hooks for hanging cups) $125
Plate, 6" $5
Plate, 9½" $20
Plate, 11¾" $30
Platter, 12" oval $35
Salt and pepper shakers $100
Saucer $5
Saucer, demitasse, 4½" $10
Sherbet $15
Sugar, 2-handled $15
Tumbler, 9 oz. $40

Depression glass, "Diana" pattern. DRAWING BY MARK PICKVET.

DOGWOOD or APPLE BLOSSOM or WILD ROSE
MACBETH-EVANS GLASS COMPANY, 1928-1932

The primary pieces include pink and green. For yellow, double the prices; for the opaque cremax, monax, and crystal pieces, reduce the prices by 50%. Beware of undecorated glass made by Macbeth-Evans in the same shape as "Dogwood" patterned glass; sometimes it is passed off as this pattern but is worth much less.

Bowl, 5½"	$30
Bowl, 8½"	$65
Bowl, 10¼"	$350
Cake plate, 11", footed	$750
Cake plate, 13", footed	$150
Coaster	$500
Creamer, 2 styles	$25
Cup, 2 styles	$20
Pitcher	$500
Plate, 6"	$10
Plate, 8"	$12
Plate, 9¼"	$35
Plate, 10½" grill, 3 divisions	$25
Platter, 12" oval	$500
Platter, 12" salver	$35
Saucer	$10
Sherbet, footed	$50
Sugar, 2-handled, 2 styles	$25
Tidbit set, 2-tiered (8"and 12" plates with metal handle)	$150
Tumbler, 5 oz.	$275
Tumbler, 10 oz.	$75
Tumbler, 11 oz.	$100
Tumbler, 12 oz.	$125

DORIC AND PANSY JEANNETTE GLASS COMPANY, 1937-1938

Colors consist of pink, green, and ultramarine. For crystal, reduce the listed prices by 50%. Color variations exist in ultramarine from a bluelike tint to almost green. This pattern is a derivative of "Doric" in that it has flowers (pansies) inserted where the original "Doric" has blank or clear glass.

Bowl, 4½"	$15
Bowl, 8"	$75
Bowl, 9", 2-handled	$30
Butter dish with cover	$500
Creamer	$100
Cup	$17
Plate, 6"	$10
Plate, 7"	$35
Plate, 9"	$30
Salt and pepper shakers	$425

Saucer $5
Sugar, 2-handled $100
Tray, 10″, 2-handled $35
Tumbler $75

DORIC AND PANSY   "PRETTY POLLY PARTY DISHES"
(CHILDREN'S SET)

14-piece Tea set $325
Creamer $40
Cup $40
Plate $10
Saucer $10
Sugar $40

DORIC   JEANNETTE GLASS COMPANY, 1935–1938

The primary colors are pink and green. For the rare opaque delphite blue, quadruple
the prices. A reproduction iridescent three-part candy dish was produced in the
1970s in the "Doric" pattern with the original molds and is priced at about $10.00.
The candy and sugar lids are not interchangeable, as in most Jeannette patterns,
since the candy lid is a little wider and taller than the sugar. Note that the complete
relish set in the "Doric" consists of the 8″ × 8″ bottom tray, two 4″ × 4″ top trays,
and one 4″ × 8″ top tray.

Bowl, 4½″ $10
Bowl, 5½″ $75
Bowl, 5″ $400
Bowl, 8¼″ $20
Bowl, 9″, 2-handled $20
Bowl, 9″, oval $35
Butter dish with cover $100
Cake plate, 10″, 3-footed $25
Candy dish, 3-part $10
Candy dish, 3-part in metal holder $50
Candy dish with cover $45
Coaster $20
Creamer $15
Cup $12
Pitcher, 1½ qt. $500
Pitcher, 1 qt. $75
Plate, 6″ $5
Plate, 7″ $20
Plate, 9″ $20
Plate, 9″ grill, 3 divisions $35
Platter, 12″ oval $35
Relish, 4″ square $15
Salt and pepper shakers $45

Depression glass, "Doric" pattern. DRAWING BY
MARK PICKVET.

Saucer	$5
Sherbet	$15
Sugar with cover, 2-handled	$45
Tray, 8″ square	$20
Tray, 10″, 2-handled	$20
Tumbler, 9-10 oz., with or without foot	$75
Tumbler, 12 oz., footed	$100

EARLY AMERICAN SANDWICH   DUNCAN & MILLER GLASS COMPANY, 1925–1930s

The primary colors are pink, green, and amber. For crystal, reduce the prices by 50%. Duncan & Miller was the first company to re-create the old "Sandwich" designs in the new automatic machine-pressed process of the Depression. Ruby red and a yellow-green were added in the 1940s (same price). The Indiana Glass Company later acquired a few of the molds and reproduced some items, but the colors are different. Indiana also developed a "Sandwich" pattern that does not include as many spirals as the original Duncan & Miller design. The prices tend to stay down because of the different varieties of "Sandwich" that are available.

Ashtray, 2³/₄″ square	$7
Basket, 6″ tall	$75
Basket, 10″ tall	$65
Basket, 10″ tall, ruffled	$85
Bonbon dish with handle	$20
Bonbon with cover, 7¹/₂″ tall	$75
Bowl, 4″	$7
Bowl, 4″ (fits 6¹/₂″ plate)	$10
Bowl, 5″	$12
Bowl, 5″, footed	$14
Bowl, 6″, 3 styles	$15
Bowl, 6″, footed	$17
Bowl, 10″, 3 divisions	$25
Bowl, 11¹/₂″, crimped	$15
Bowl, 11¹/₂″, 1¹/₂″ tall, shallow	$15
Bowl, 11″, 2″ tall, serrated	$35
Bowl, 12″, flared	$35
Bowl, 12″, 3³/₄″ tall, oblong	$30

Butter dish with cover	$225
Candelabrum, 3-light, 16″	$100
Candelabrum, 1-light	$50
Candelabrum, 3-light, 10″	$85
Candlestick, 4″	$12
Candlestick, 2-branch, 5″	$20
Candlestick, 3-branch, 5″	$25
Candy jar with cover, 5″ tall	$75
Candy jar with cover, 8½″ tall	$100
Cheese and cracker set, 2-piece, 13″ plate, 5½″ cheese stand	$75
Cigarette box with cover	$50
Cigarette holder, 3″, footed	$35
Compote, 5½″, inner liner	$30
Compote, 6″, 2 styles	$35
Compote, 7½″, flared	$50
Creamer, 3″ tall	$20
Creamer, 4″ tall	$25
Cruet with stopper, 5¾″ tall, 3 oz.	$40
Cup, 6 oz.	$7
Deviled egg platter, 12″, (holds 1 dozen eggs)	$175
Fruit cup, 2½″, 6 oz.	$12
Jelly dish, 3″ diameter	$10
Ladle	$25
Lamp, hurricane, 15″	$175
Mayonnaise, 2¾″ tall, 5″ diameter	$10
Parfait, 5¼″, 4 oz.	$15
Pickle dish, oval (7″ × 3¾″)	$15
Pitcher, 1 qt.	$125
Pitcher, syrup, 1 qt.	$100
Plate, 5″	$5
Plate, 6½″, indentation for 4″ finger bowl	$7
Plate, 6″	$6
Plate, 7″	$8
Plate, 8″	$10
Plate, 9½″	$15
Plate, 12″	$17
Plate, 12″ grill, 3 divisions	$20
Plate, 13″	$20
Relish, oval (7″ × 3¾″), 3 divisions	$15
Relish, oval (10″ × 4½″), 3 divisions	$20
Relish, rectangular, (10½″ × 6¾″), 3 divisions	$20
Salt and pepper shakers with glass tops	$65
Salver, cake, 12″	$30
Salver, cake, 13″	$35
Saucer	$5
Sherbet, 4¼″, 5 oz.	$10
Stemware, 2¾″, 5 oz., low foot	$10
Stemware, 4¼″ or 4½″, 3 oz.	$12
Stemware, 5¼″, 5 oz.	$14
Stemware, 6″, 9 oz.	$15
Sugar, 2¾″ tall, low footed, 2-handled	$20

Sugar, 3¹/₄″ tall, low footed, 2-handled $25
Sugar shaker, 13 oz. $25
Sundae, 3¹/₂″, 5 oz., flared $20
Tray, 6″ round, 1 handle $10
Tray, 8″ oval, 2 handles $15
Tray, 10″ oval $20
Tray, rectangular, (10 ¹/₂″ × 6³/₄″) $20
Tumbler, 3¹/₄″ tall, 5 oz., footed $15
Tumbler, 4³/₄″ tall, 9 oz., footed $17
Tumbler, 5 ¹/₄″ or 5¹/₂″ tall $20
Urn with cover, 12″ $150
Vase, 3″ tall, footed $15
Vase, 4¹/₂″ tall $20
Vase, 5″ tall, footed $25
Vase, 10″ tall, footed $50

ENGLISH HOBNAIL   WESTMORELAND GLASS COMPANY, 1920s–1970s

The colors covered in the pricing include pink, green, amber, and a light copper blue. For cobalt blue or ruby red, double the prices; for crystal, reduce them by 50%. In the earliest of Westmoreland's advertisements, "English Hobnail" was referred to as a "Sandwich Reproduction." It is also Westmoreland's #555 pattern.

Ashtray, many styles $25
Bonbon dish, 1-handle $30
Bottle, toilet, 5 oz. $30
Bowl, 3″ $20
Bowl, 4¹/₂″-5″, several styles $20
Bowl, 4″ $50
Bowl, 6″-6¹/₂″ $22
Bowl, 7″ $25
Bowl, 8″, footed, 2-handled $75
Bowl, 8″, several styles $30
Bowl, 9″, oval $35
Bowl, 10″ $40
Bowl, 11″ $45
Bowl, 12″ $50
Bowl, 12″, oval $50
Butter dish with cover, 6¹/₂″ diameter $50
Candlestick, 3¹/₂″ tall $20
Candlestick, 8¹/₂″-9″ tall $35
Candy dish, 3-footed $50
Candy jar with cover (large), 15″ tall $225
Candy jar with cover (small) $65
Celery dish, 9″ tall $25
Celery dish, 12″ tall $35
Cigarette box with cover $35
Cigarette jar with cover $50

Depression glass, "English Hobnail" pattern. Reproduced from a 1926 Westmoreland catalog.

Claret glass, 5 oz.	$25
Cocktail glass, 3 oz.	$25
Cologne bottle with stopper	$40
Compote, 5″, footed	$30
Compote, 6″, footed	$35
Compote, 8″, footed	$60
Cordial, 1 oz.	$30
Creamer, square footed	$45
Creamer, hexagonal	$25
Cup	$20
Cup, demitasse	$35
Decanter with stopper	$150
Egg cup	$75
Goblet, 5 oz.	$25
Goblet, 6¼ oz.	$30
Goblet, 8 oz.	$35
Ice tub, 4″	$55
Ice tub, 5 ½″	$75
Jam jar with cover	$65
Lamp, 6¼″	$75
Lamp, 9¼″ tall	$125
Marmalade dish with cover	$50
Mayonnaise dish, 6″	$25

Nut dish, footed	$15
Pitcher, 1¹/₂ pt.	$175
Pitcher, 1 qt.	$200
Pitcher, 2 qt.	$300
Plate, 5¹/₂″	$10
Plate, 6″-6¹/₂″	$12
Plate, 8″-8¹/₂″	$15
Plate, 10″	$35
Platter, 14″	$55
Salt and pepper shakers	$100
Salt dip, 2″, footed	$75
Saucer	$4
Saucer, demitasse	$15
Sherbet, several styles	$20
Sugar, 2-handled, hexagonal	$25
Sugar, square footed	$45
Tidbit, 2-tier	$50
Tumbler, 5 oz.	$20
Tumbler, 8 oz.	$25
Tumbler, 10 oz.	$30
Tumbler, 12 oz.	$35
Urn with cover	$350
Vase, 7¹/₂″ tall	$100
Vase, 8¹/₂″ tall	$125
Vase, 10″ tall	$100
Whiskey, 1¹/₂ oz.	$20
Wine glass, 2 oz.	$30

FLORAL AND DIAMOND BAND   U.S. GLASS COMPANY, 1920s

Colors include pink and shades of green ranging from light green to aqua green. For marigold or black pieces, double the prices; for crystal, reduce them by 50%. Some green is nearly opaque and appears frosted or satinized. The mold lines also tend to be rough. The pattern consists of a six-petaled flower with diamond bands near the top or outer rim. The diamond banding is cut off by smaller six-petal flowers.

Bowl, 4¹/₂″	$10
Bowl, 5³/₄″, 2-handled	$12
Bowl, 8″	$15
Butter dish with cover	$150
Compote	$15
Creamer (large), 4³/₄″	$20
Creamer (small)	$12
Pitcher	$110
Plate, 8″	$40
Sherbet	$8
Sugar (small)	$12
Sugar with cover, 5¹/₄″ (large), 2-handled	$100

Tumbler, 4" tall $25
Tumbler, 5" tall $40

FLORAL POINSETTIA   JEANNETTE GLASS COMPANY, 1931–1935

The primary colors are pink and green, but there are other variations. For opaque blue (delphite), opaque green (jadeite), yellow, or red, triple the prices; for crystal, reduce them by 50%; for amber, use the same prices as listed. The salt and pepper shakers have been reproduced in pink, dark green, and cobalt blue. "Floral Poinsettia" is an all-over pattern of large poinsettia blossoms with vertical ribbing.

Bowl, 4" $20
Bowl, 5^1/$_2$" $750
Bowl, 7^1/$_2$" $25
Bowl, 9" oval $30
Bowl with cover, 8" $50
Bowl, rose $500
Butter dish with cover $125
Candlestick $45
Candy jar with cover $50
Canister, 5^1/$_4$" tall (coffee, tea, cereal, or sugar) $20
Coaster $15
Compote, 9" $800
Creamer $15
Cup $15
Frog, flower $650
Ice tub, 3^1/$_2$" oval, 2 tab handles $850
Lamp $275
Pitcher, 1^1/$_2$ qt. $250
Pitcher, 1 qt. $50
Pitcher, milk, 1^1/$_2$ pt. $550
Plate, 6" $7
Plate, 8" $12
Plate, 9" $15
Plate, 9" grill, 3 divisions $200
Platter, 10^3/$_4$" oval $30
Platter, 12", oval $100
Refrigerator dish with cover, 5" square $75
Relish dish, oval, 2-part, 2 tab handles $20
Salt and pepper shakers, 2 styles $75
Saucer $10
Sherbet $20
Sugar with cover, 2-handled $30
Tray, 6" square, 2-handled $20
Tray, 9^1/$_4$", oval $200
Tumbler, 3 oz., footed $175
Tumbler, 5 oz., footed $20
Tumbler, 7 oz., footed $25

Tumbler, 9 oz. $200
Tumbler, 9 oz., footed $50
Vase, 3-footed $500
Vase, 7″ tall, hexagonal $500

FLORENTINE NO. 1 or OLD FLORENTINE or POPPY NO. 1
HAZEL ATLAS GLASS COMPANY, 1932–1935

The colors included in the prices are pink, green, and yellow. For cobalt blue, double the prices; for crystal, reduce them by 50%. "Florentine No. 1" can be distinguished from "Florentine No. 2" (see next entry) by shape: most No. 1 pieces are hexagonal, while all No. 2 pieces are round. Note that in both "Florentine" designs, the butter and oval bowl covers are interchangeable. Also, the salt and pepper shakers have been reproduced in pink and cobalt blue.

Ashtray $30
Bowl, 5″ $15
Bowl, 5″, ruffled $20
Bowl, 6″ $25
Bowl, 8½″ $30
Bowl with cover, 9½″, oval $60
Butter dish with cover $175
Coaster $25
Compote $25
Creamer $20
Creamer, ruffled $40
Cup $12
Pitcher, 1½ qt., with or without ice lip $125
Pitcher, 1 qt. $55
Plate, 6″ $7
Plate, 8½″ $15
Plate, 10″ $25
Plate, 10″ grill, 3 divisions $20
Platter, 11½″ oval $25
Salt and pepper shakers $65
Saucer $5
Sherbet $12
Sugar dish, ruffled, (no cover) $40
Sugar with cover $40
Tumbler, 4 oz. $15
Tumbler, 5 oz. $20
Tumbler, 9 oz. $25
Tumbler, 10 oz. $25
Tumbler, 12 oz. $30

FLORENTINE NO. 2 or POPPY NO. 2   HAZEL ATLAS GLASS COMPANY, MID TO LATE 1930s

As with "Florentine No. 1," the prices cover pink, green, and yellow. For colors such as amber, cobalt blue, light blue, and fired-on versions, double the prices; for crystal, reduce them by 50%.

Ashtray	$20
Bowl, 4¹/₂″	$20
Bowl, 4³/₄″	$22
Bowl, 5¹/₂″	$35
Bowl, 6″	$40
Bowl, 7¹/₂″	$75
Bowl, 8″	$35
Bowl, 9″	$35
Bowl with cover, 9″ oval	$65
Butter dish with cover	$175
Candlestick	$30
Candy dish with cover	$150
Coaster	$20
Compote	$25
Creamer	$12
Cup	$10
Custard cup	$75
Gravy boat	$85
Parfait, 6″ tall	$35
Pickle dish, 10″ oval	$35
Pitcher, milk	$50
Pitcher, water, 1¹/₂ qt.	$125
Pitcher, water, 2¹/₂ qt.	$225
Plate, 6¹/₄″, with indentation	$20
Plate, 6″	$5
Plate, 8¹/₂″	$10
Plate, 10¹/₄″ grill, 3 divisions	$20
Plate, 10¹/₄″, with indentation for 4³/₄″ bowl	$35
Plate, 10″	$15
Platter, 11¹/₂″, matches gravy boat	$50
Platter, 11″, oval	$20
Relish dish, 10″, 3 divisions	$30
Salt and pepper shakers	$60
Saucer	$5
Sherbet	$10
Sugar with cover, 2-handled	$27
Tray, condiment	$50
Tumbler, 5 oz.	$15
Tumbler, 5 oz., footed	$17
Tumbler, 6 oz.	$20
Tumbler, 9 oz.	$20
Tumbler, 9 oz., footed	$25
Tumbler, 12 oz.	$30

FLOWER GARDEN WITH BUTTERFLIES or BUTTERFLIES AND ROSES   U.S. GLASS COMPANY, LATE 1920s

The colors included in the prices are pink, green, aqua, and amber. For light blue or yellow, increase the prices by 50%; for crystal, decrease them by 50%; for black, quadruple the prices. The black pieces are rare and particularly valuable. Note that some of the pieces have gold banding or rings near the top or around the edging, but the prices do not vary for these. This is a very dense all-over pattern of leaves, butterflies, and five-petal flowers.

Ashtray $200
Bonbon dish with cover $75
Bowl, 8½″ $50
Bowl, 9″ $55
Bowl, 11″ $60
Bowl, 12″ $65
Bowl with cover, 7¼″ $125
Candlestick, 4″ $35
Candlestick, 8″ $75
Candy jar with cover, 6″ $175
Candy jar with cover, 7½″ $175
Cheese and cracker dish, footed $100
Cigarette box with cover $50
Cologne bottle with stopper $200
Compote, various styles, 5″ tall and under $40
Compote, various styles, 6″ tall and over $85
Creamer $75
Cup $65
Heart-shaped jar with cover $1250
Mayonnaise set, dish, plate, and ladle $100
Plate, 7″ $25
Plate, 8″, 2 styles $25
Plate, 10″, with or without indentation $45
Powder jar with cover $125
Sandwich server with center handle $75
Saucer $25
Sugar, 2-handled $65
Tray, 10″, oval $55
Tray, 11¾″, rectangular $65
Tumbler, various styles $175
Vase, 6¼″ tall $125
Vase, 8″ tall $125
Vase, 9″ tall $150
Vase, 10″-10½″ tall $175

GLASSWARE

Depression glass, "Fortune" pattern. DRAWING BY MARK PICKVET.

FORTUNE HOCKING GLASS COMPANY, 1937–1938

The only colored glass in this pattern is pink. For crystal, reduce the price by 50%. The pattern contains angled vertical flutes for somewhat of an optic effect. This angling produces a notched edge except in the drinking vessels, which are cut off by a horizontal line and have a smooth outer edge.

Bowl, 4½″ $6
Bowl, 4½″, with 2 tab handles $7
Bowl, 4″ $5
Bowl, 5¼″ $6
Bowl, 7¾″ $15
Candy dish with cover $25
Cup $5
Plate, 6″ $4
Plate, 8″ $15
Saucer $3
Tumbler, 3½″ tall, 5 oz. $10
Tumbler, 4″ tall, 9 oz. $12

FRUITS HAZEL ATLAS GLASS COMPANY, 1931–1933

The primary colors in this pattern are pink and green. For crystal, reduce the price by 50%; for iridized pieces, use the same prices as for pink and green. In this vertically paneled pattern, two fruits with leaves are shown on the top or outer edge of each piece.

Bowl, 5″ $25
Bowl, 8″ $40
Cup $7
Pitcher $100
Plate, 7″ $75
Plate, 8″ $10
Saucer $5
Sherbet $10
Tumbler, 3½″ tall $25
Tumbler, 4″ tall $30
Tumbler, 5″ tall, 12 oz. $100

Depression glass, "Georgian Lovebirds" pattern. PHOTO BY ROBIN RAINWATER.

GEORGIAN LOVEBIRDS   FEDERAL GLASS COMPANY, 1931–1936

This pattern was made only in green. For crystal, reduce the prices by 50%. The pattern features lovebirds sitting side by side except on tumblers, hot plates, and some plates. Also, on some pieces, the design is only in the center, while other pieces include it on the edges.

Bowl, 4½"	$10
Bowl, 5¾"	$25
Bowl, 6½"	$65
Bowl, 7½"	$70
Bowl, 9" oval	$65
Butter dish with cover	$110
Coaster	$15
Creamer, 3"	$15
Creamer, 4"	$20
Cup	$10
Hot plate, 5"	$50
Pitcher	$500
Plate, 6"	$7
Plate, 8"	$10
Plate, 9¼"	$25
Platter, 11½", 2 tab handles	$65
Saucer	$5
Sherbet	$15
Sugar with cover, 2-handled, 3"	$50
Sugar with cover, 2-handled, 4"	$150
Tumbler, 4" tall, 9 oz.	$55
Tumbler, 5¼" tall, 12 oz.	$110

HERITAGE FEDERAL GLASS COMPANY, 1930s–1970s

The basic colors are pink and green. For light blue, increase the prices by 50%; for crystal, decrease them by 50%. This pattern was reproduced in the 1960s and the 1970s in green, amber, and crystal. Most are marked "MC" (for McCrory's), and the patterns are weaker for the new pieces. The new green is also darker than the original, and some of the crystal was trimmed in gold. "Heritage" is similar to "Sandwich" patterns in that it includes an all-over pressed design.

Bowl, 5" $30
Bowl, 8½" $75
Bowl, 10½" $20
Creamer $35
Cup $5
Plate, 8" or 9¼" $7
Plate, 12" $10
Saucer $2
Sugar, 2-handled $35

HEX OPTIC or HONEYCOMB JEANNETTE GLASS COMPANY, 1928–1932

The primary Depression colors are pink and green. Iridescent or light marigold pieces were reproduced in the 1950s (reduce the prices by 25%). This is a rather simple pressed hexagonal pattern.

Bowl, 4¼" $7
Bowl, 7½" $10
Bowl, 7¼" $15
Bowl, 8¼" $20
Bowl, 9" $25
Bowl, 10" $30
Butter dish with cover $100
Creamer, 2 styles $7
Cup, 2 styles $6
Ice bucket with metal handle $25
Pitcher, milk, 1 qt. $35
Pitcher, water, 1½ qt. $55
Pitcher, water, 3qt. $250
Plate, 6" $4
Plate, 8" $6
Platter, 11" $15
Reamer (fits ice bucket) $50
Refrigerator dish with cover, 4" square $15
Salt and pepper shakers $30
Saucer $4
Sherbet $5
Sugar, 2-handled, 2 styles $7
Sugar shaker $175

Depression glass, "Hex Optic" or "Honeycomb" pattern. Reproduced from a 1930 advertisement.

Tumbler, 7 oz., footed $10
Tumbler, 9 oz. $8
Tumbler, 12 oz. $10
Tumbler, 16 oz., footed $15
Whiskey, 2″ tall, 1 oz. $10

HORSESHOE or NO. 612   INDIANA GLASS COMPANY, 1930–1933

Basic colors are green and yellow. Pink pieces are rare; quadruple the prices. For crystal, reduce them by 50%. Indiana did not patent a name for this pattern except the designation "No. 612." "Horseshoe" pieces vary in thickness.

Bowl, 4$\frac{1}{2}$″ $25
Bowl, 6$\frac{1}{2}$″ $30
Bowl, 7$\frac{1}{2}$″ $25
Bowl, 8$\frac{1}{2}$″ $35
Bowl, 9$\frac{1}{2}$″ $40
Bowl, 10$\frac{1}{2}$″, oval $35
Butter dish with cover $750
Candy dish with cover, metal holder $200
Creamer $20

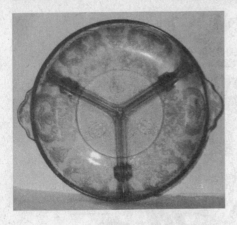

*Depression glass, "Horseshoe"
or "No. 612" pattern. PHOTO BY
ROBIN RAINWATER.*

Cup	$15
Pitcher, 2 qt.	$300
Plate, 6″	$10
Plate, 8½″	$12
Plate, 9½″	$15
Plate, 10½″	$15
Plate, 10½″ grill, 3 divisions	$75
Platter, 10¾″ oval	$40
Platter, 11½″	$40
Relish, 3-part, footed	$30
Saucer	$5
Sherbet	$17
Sugar, 2-handled	$15
Tumbler, 4¼″–4¾″ tall	$150
Tumbler, 5½″ tall, footed	$35
Tumbler, 6¼″ tall, footed	$150

IRIS or IRIS AND HERRINGBONE   JEANNETTE GLASS
COMPANY, 1928–1932, 1950s–1970s

The items priced are for crystal and the reproduction marigold, blue, and amethyst
(1950s–1970s). For the rarer green and pink, quadruple the prices. The pattern consists of irises with vertical ribbing.

Bowl, 4½″	$40
Bowl, 5″, cereal bowl	$125
Bowl, 5″, ruffled, sauce dish	$25
Bowl, 7½″	$150
Bowl, 8″	$75
Bowl, 9½″	$25
Bowl, 11½″	$35

Bowl, 11″ $65
Butter dish with cover $75
Candlestick $25
Candy jar with cover $175
Claret glass $25
Coaster $100
Cocktail glass, 4 oz., 4½″ tall $35
Creamer $15
Cup $15
Cup, demitasse $75
Goblet, 4 oz., 5½″ tall $35
Goblet, 8 oz., 5½″ tall $45
Lamp shade, 11½″ $100
Nut set (metal base and holder for nut crackers and picks) $75
Pitcher $50
Plate, 5½″ $15
Plate, 8″ $100
Plate, 9″ $75
Platter, 11¾″ $55
Saucer $15
Saucer, demitasse $150
Sherbet, 2 styles $25
Sugar with cover, 2-handled $30
Tumbler, 4″ tall $125
Tumbler, 6½″ tall, footed $35
Tumbler, 6″ tall, footed $25
Vase, 9″ $35
Wine glass, 4″-4½″ tall $35

JUBILEE   LANCASTER GLASS COMPANY, EARLY 1930s

The only colors are pink and yellow. "Jubilee" is a difficult pattern to obtain for there are few common pieces. Be careful of other less valuable Lancaster patterns. "Jubilee" has a center flower with 12-petal flowers surrounding it. Other patterns have 12- or 16-petal flowers with a smaller petal between each large one.

Bowl, 8″, 3-footed $250
Bowl, 9″, 2-handled $125
Bowl, 11½″ $200
Bowl, 11″, 3-footed $250
Bowl, 13″, 3-footed $275
Cake plate, 11″, 2-handled $75
Candlestick $100
Candy jar with cover, 3-footed $350
Champagne glass, 7 oz. $100
Cheese and cracker set $250
Cordial, 1 oz. $250
Creamer $50
Cup $40

Depression glass, "Jubilee" pattern.
DRAWING BY MARK PICKVET.

Goblet, water, 11 oz. $150
Mayonnaise set (plate, bowl, and ladle) $325
Plate, 7″ $25
Plate, 8³/₄″ $30
Platter, 13¹/₂″ $100
Platter, 14″, 3-footed $250
Saucer, 2 styles $15
Sherbet $75
Sugar, 2-handled $50
Tray, 11″, with center handle $225
Tumbler, 5″ tall, footed $100
Tumbler, 6″ tall $125
Vase, 12″ tall $400
Wine glass, 3 oz. $125

KITCHENWARE   VARIOUS COMPANIES, 1920s–1930s

The basic colors are pink, green, amber, yellow, and light blue. For opaque versions
and crystal, reduce the prices by 50%. For cobalt blue, ruby red, amethyst, or ultramarine, double the prices. For black, quadruple them. Some of the largest makers of
kitchen products during the Depression era were Hocking/Anchor-Hocking (many
canister sets, Vitrock, Fire-King, and nearly every type of piece made), Jeannette
(Jennyware products—in ultramarine and other colors), Hazel Atlas (famous for the
"Crisscross" pattern), and McKee (many opaque and milk white patterns, some with
colored dots and red or black ships). Kitchenware can be difficult to identify at times
because of the many plain and unmarked styles. These products were also made in
every color, including delphite blue, jadeite green, custard yellow or beige, and milk
white. Many were decorated by embossing and enameling, as well as fired on decals
or transfers. Cookie jars generally are larger than patterned cracker jars. Canisters
come in a variety of shapes and markings—flour, sugar, coffee, tea, cereal, spices,
salt, oatmeal, cocoa, etc. Glass silverware, primarily knives, serving spoons, and la-
dles, are becoming more difficult to find. Cups may have up to three spouts. Range
bowls or sets are often marked "drips" or "drippings" and have matching canisters.
The only known cobalt blue water cooler was made by L.E. Smith. Reamers are

probably the most common pieces—increase the price by 50% if there is a matching collecting bowl or cup. Mechanical items such as extractors and grinders should include a glass collecting device.

Bottle, water, (usually with metal screw-on lid) $35
Bowl, mixing, 7¹/₈″ to 9″ $20
Bowl, mixing, 7″ $15
Bowl, mixing, over 9″ $25
Butter dish with cover, 1 lb. block size $50
Butter dish with cover, ¹/₄ lb. stick size $35
Cake preserver with cover $100
Cake tub $50
Canister, covered, up to 16 oz. $35
Canister, covered, 17-28 oz. $40
Canister, covered, 29-48 oz. $45
Canister, covered, over 48 oz. $65
Cocktail shaker, covered $25
Cookie jar with cover $35
Cruet with stopper $50
Dispenser, liquid (usually glass with metal spigot) $125
Dispenser, liquid, 2-part, (usually with glass top and bottom, may have metal handles, spigot, and base) $300
Egg beater jar $35
Egg cup $15
Funnel $55
Ice bucket or pail, over 24 oz. $35
Ice bucket or pail, up to 24 oz. $25
Iron (very rare) $750
Juice dispenser $125
Knife $35
Ladle (large) $30
Ladle (small) $20
Marmalade jar with cover and matching spoon $85
Measuring cup, 1 cup $17
Measuring cup, ¹/₂ cup $15
Measuring cup, ¹/₃ cup $12
Measuring cup, ¹/₄ cup $10
Measuring cup, 2 cups $20
Measuring cup, over 2 cups $25
Mechanical attachments $45
Mustard dish with matching cover and spoon $85
Pie dish $45
Pitcher, 17-28 oz. $65
Pitcher, over 48 oz., (add $25 to pitchers with lids) $95
Pitcher, syrup, up to 16 oz. $60
Pitcher, 29-48 .... $80
Punch ladle $40
Range bowl, covered $35
Range bowl, uncovered $20
Reamer, lemon (small), over 3″ tall $15
Reamer, lemon (small), under 3″ tall $10

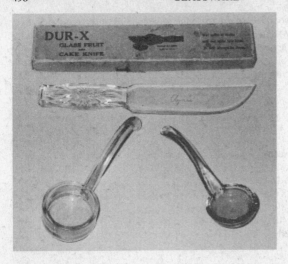

Depression glass, kitchenware. PHOTO BY ROBIN RAINWATER.

Reamer, orange (large), over 3″ tall $17
Reamer, orange (large), under 3″ tall $15
Refrigerator bowl with cover, round, over 8″ diameter $30
Refrigerator bowl with cover, round, up to 6″ diameter $20
Refrigerator dish with cover, over 32 square inches, square or rectangular .. $40
Refrigerator dish with cover, up to 32 square inches, square or rectangular . $30
Rolling pin $150
Salt and pepper shakers $55
Salt box $85
Scoop $55
Soap dish $25
Straw dispenser (usually with metal cover) $150
Sugar shaker $35
Teapot (very rare in colors) $350
Tray, oval or rectangular
   Clear $30
   Opaque $25
Tumblers, over 8 oz. $15
Tumblers, up to 8 oz. $12
Water cooler with spout $125

LACE EDGE or OPEN LACE   HOCKING GLASS COMPANY, 1935-1938

The primary color is transparent pink. For satinized or frosted pink and crystal, reduce the prices by 50%. "Lace" patterns are notorious for chipping and cracking because of the delicate edging. Be sure to scrutinize pieces very carefully before purchasing. Chipped, cracked, or damaged glass has little value except for historical purposes. Several companies produced "Lace" glassware, but Hocking's pink is a bit duller.

Aquarium, 1 gal., Crystal only $35
Bowl, 6½″ $25
Bowl, 7¾″ $45
Bowl, 8¼″ $35
Bowl, 9½″ $35
Bowl, 10 ½″, 3-footed $200
Butter dish with cover $100
Candlestick $125
Candy jar with cover $75
Compote, 9″, no cover $800
Compote with cover, 7″ $75
Cookie jar with cover $85
Creamer $35
Cup $25
Flower bowl with crystal frog $55
Plate, 7¼″ $25
Plate, 8¼″ $20
Plate, 8¾″ $25
Plate, 10½″ $35
Plate, 10½″ grill, 3 divisions $45
Plate, 10½″ relish, 3-part (parallel divisions) $45
Platter, 12¾″ or 13″, with or without divisions $55
Relish bowl, 7½″, 3-part $65
Saucer $12
Sherbet $100
Sugar, 2-handled $35
Tumbler, 3½″ $75
Tumbler, 4½″ $30
Tumbler, 5″ tall $50
Vase, 7″ tall $400

LACED EDGE or KATY BLUE   IMPERIAL GLASS COMPANY, EARLY 1930s

The prices are for light blue and green with opalescent edging. The opalescent coloring was referred to as "sea foam." As with Hocking's "Lace Edge" pattern beware of damaged edges.

Bowl, 4½″ $35
Bowl, 5½″ $45
Bowl, 5″ $40
Bowl, 7″ $85
Bowl, 9″ $100
Bowl, 11″ oval, with or without divisions $125
Candlestick $80
Creamer $45
Cup $35
Mayonnaise, 3-piece (bowl, plate, and ladle) $150
Plate, 6½″ $20

Depression glass, "Lace Edge" pattern. DRAWING BY MARK PICKVET.

Plate, 8″	$35
Plate, 10″	$100
Platter, 12″	$100
Platter, 13″	$150
Saucer	$15
Sugar, 2-handled	$45
Tidbit, 2-tiered, includes 8″ and 10″ plates	$125
Tumbler, various styles	$75
Vase	$100

LINCOLN INN   FENTON GLASS COMPANY, LATE 1928–1939

This pattern comes in more colors than most. Basic prices cover pink or rose, green, light blue, amethyst, amber, and opaque shades of green (i.e., jade green). For cobalt blue, ruby red, and black, double the prices; for crystal, reduce them by half. This is a fairly simple pattern characterized by vertical ribbing that does not quite make it to the top of each piece. Fenton did not produce much Depression glass. The company continues to operate today in Williamstown, West Virginia.

Ashtray	$12
Bonbon, square or oval, 2-handled	$15
Bowl, 4″	$12
Bowl, 5″	$12
Bowl, 6″	$15
Bowl, 9″	$20
Bowl, 9¹/₄″, footed	$25
Bowl, 10¹/₂″ footed	$35
Candy dish, oval, footed	$17
Compote	$17
Creamer	$17
Cup	$12
Goblet	$25
Nut dish, footed	$15
Olive dish, handled	$15
Pitcher, 1¹/₂ qt.	$800
Plate, 6″	$6

Plate, 8″ $10
Plate, 9¼″ $12
Platter, 12″ $20
Salt and pepper shakers $175
Sandwich server with center handle $125
Saucer $5
Sherbet, 2 styles $15
Sugar, 2-handled $17
Tumbler, 5¼″ tall, footed $17
Tumbler, 6″ tall, footed $22
Vase, 9¾″ tall, footed $100
Vase, 12″ tall, footed $125
Wine glass $25

LORAIN BASKET   INDIANA GLASS COMPANY, 1929–1932

The primary colors are green and yellow. For crystal, reduce the prices by 50%. Edges tend to be rough because of poor molding, especially the inner rims of bowls. Note that sherbets were reproduced in milk white and opaque green in the 1950s and 1960s. This pattern is also referred to as Indiana's "No. 615" and features heavy scrolling around the edges and corners and a large center design.

Bowl, 6″ $45
Bowl, 7¼″ $50
Bowl, 8″ $100
Bowl, 9¾″ oval $55
Creamer $25
Cup $15
Plate, 5½″ $10
Plate, 7¾″ $12
Plate, 8½″ $20
Plate, 10¼″ $50
Platter, 11½″ $45
Relish, 8″ square, 4-part, 2-handled $25
Saucer $5
Sherbet $25
Sugar, 2-handled $25
Tray, 2-handled $35
Tumbler, 9 oz., footed $25

MADRID   FEDERAL GLASS COMPANY, 1932–1938

The basic colors are pink, green, and amber. Light blue is rare; double the prices. For crystal, reduce them by 50%. The blue color was referred to as "Madonna Blue." "Madrid" is characterized by a large center diamond surrounded by scrolling. Scrolling is also on the edges. Reproductions are a problem with "Madrid." In 1976 Federal reproduced "Madrid" under the name "Recollection" for the U.S. Bicentennial. It was issued only in amber and dated "1976." When Federal went out of business, the Indiana Glass Company purchased the molds and removed the "1976" date. Indiana has also reproduced many pieces in a lighter pink and brighter blue.

Ashtray, 6″, square	$150
Bowl, 4³/₄″	$15
Bowl, 5″	$10
Bowl, 7″	$20
Bowl, 8″	$20
Bowl, 9¹/₂″	$25
Bowl, 10″, oval	$25
Bowl, 11″	$20
Butter dish with cover	$85
Cake plate, 11¹/₄″	$20
Candlestick	$15
Coaster	$40
Cookie jar with cover	$55
Creamer	$12
Cup	$10
Gravy boat with platter	$1250
Jello mold	$15
Lazy susan (wood with glass coasters)	$1000
Marmalade	$25
Pitcher, 2¹/₂ qt., with or without ice lip	$75
Pitcher, 2 qt.	$65
Pitcher, milk, 1 qt.	$50
Plate, 6″	$5
Plate, 7¹/₂″	$10
Plate, 9″	$12
Plate, 10¹/₂″	$35
Plate, 10¹/₂″ grill, 3 divisions	$20
Platter, 11¹/₂″, oval	$25
Platter, 11¹/₄″	$20
Relish dish, 10¹/₄″	$20
Salt and pepper shakers	$100
Saucer	$5
Sherbet, 2 styles	$12
Sugar with cover	$50
Tumbler, 4¹/₄″ tall, 9 oz.	$25
Tumbler, 4″ tall, 5 oz.	$20
Tumbler, 4″ tall, 5 oz., footed	$25
Tumbler, 5¹/₂″ tall, 10 oz.	$30
Tumbler, 5¹/₂″ tall, 12 oz.	$35

MANHATTAN or HORIZONTAL RIBBED   ANCHOR HOCKING GLASS COMPANY, 1938–1943

The basic color is pink. For crystal, reduce the prices by 50%. For ruby red, double the prices. The pattern is a simple vertically ribbed design. Anchor Hocking produced a similar pattern in 1987 called "Park Avenue," but the pieces have different dimensions.

Depression glass, "Manhattan" pattern. DRAWING BY MARK PICKVET.

Ashtray, 4¹/₂", square $20
Ashtray, 4", round $15
Bowl, 4¹/₂" $12
Bowl, 4¹/₂", handled $15
Bowl, 5¹/₂", handled $20
Bowl, 5¹/₄" $25
Bowl, 7¹/₂" $20
Bowl, 8", tab handles $25
Bowl, 9¹/₂", 1 handle $35
Bowl, 9" $25
Candlestick $10
Candy dish with cover, 3-footed $50
Coaster $15
Compote $35
Creamer $12
Cup $75
Pitcher, 2¹/₂ qt. $75
Pitcher, milk $50
Plate, 6" $25
Plate, 8¹/₂" $30
Plate, 10¹/₄" $50
Platter, 14", 3 divisions $75
Relish tray with 5 glass inserts and center bowl $75
Salt and pepper shakers $55
Saucer $25
Sherbet $15
Sugar, 2-handled $12
Tumbler, various styles $20
Vase, 8" tall $25
Wine glass $15

MAYFAIR OPEN ROSE   HOCKING GLASS COMPANY, 1931–1937

The prices are for pink and ice blue. Green and yellow are much rarer; double the prices. For crystal, reduce them by 50%. Some pieces are satinized or frosted with enameling (reduce the prices by 25%). As indicated below, there are a few extremely rare and valuable pieces in this pattern. "Mayfair Open Rose" is probably the most popular and recognized Depression glass pattern with its stemmed rose and vertical ribbing. "Cameo" is probably the only serious competition for the number of different pieces made and value of those pieces. Many reproductions of this have been made since the 1970s. The colors and dimensions of the new pieces are different. Salt and pepper shakers, cookie jars, small pitchers, and whiskey tumblers have all been reproduced.

Bowl, 5½″ $40
Bowl, 5″ $50
Bowl, 7″ $45
Bowl, 9½″, oval $75
Bowl, 9″, 3-footed (extremely rare) $5000
Bowl, 11¾″ or 12″ $75
Bowl with cover, 10″ $125
Butter dish with cover $175
Cake plate, 10″, footed $75
Cake plate, 12″, 2-handled $85
Candy dish with cover $100
Celery dish, 9″ or 10″, with or without divisions $75
Celery dish with cover $75
Claret glass, 5¼″ tall $750
Cocktail glass, 4″ tall $100
Cookie jar with cover $75
Cordial, 1 oz. (extremely rare) $1000
Creamer $55
Cup $35
Decanter with stopper, 1 qt. $200
Goblet, 5¾″ tall, 9 oz. $125
Goblet, 7¼″ tall, 9 oz. $200
Pitcher, 8½″ tall, 2½ qt. $200
Pitcher, 8″ tall, 2 qt. $175
Pitcher, milk, 1 qt. $150
Plate, 5¾″ $20
Plate, 6½″ $20
Plate, 8½″ $35
Plate, 9½″ $55
Plate, 9½″ grill, 3 divisions $60
Plate, 11½″ grill, 2-handled $75
Platter, 12″ oval, 2-handled, with or without divisions $85
Relish, 8½″, 4 divisions $75
Relish, 8½″, no divisions $300
Salt and pepper shakers $100
Sandwich server with center handle $85
Saucer $35
Sherbet, 2¼″ tall $125
Sherbet, 3″ tall $25
Sherbet, 4¾″ tall $100
Sugar dish $55
Sugar dish with cover (cover is extremely rare) $1500
Tumbler, 3½″ tall, 5 oz. $50
Tumbler, 3¼″ tall, 3 oz., footed $85

Tumbler, 4¼″ tall, 9 oz. $65
Tumbler, 4¾″ tall, 11 oz. $150
Tumbler, 5¼″ tall, 10 oz., footed $175
Tumbler, 5¼″ tall, 14 oz. $150
Tumbler, 6½″ tall, 15 oz., footed $200
Vase $150
Whiskey tumbler, 2¼″ tall, 1½ oz. $75
Wine glass, 4½″ tall $100

MAYFAIR   FEDERAL GLASS COMPANY, 1934

Prices are for green and amber; for crystal, reduce them by 50%. The green pieces differ somewhat from the amber and crystal. Hocking obtained a patent on "Mayfair" before Federal; as a result, Federal redesigned the molds twice in order to produce the "Rosemary" pattern (see separate listing). The green pieces are part "Mayfair" and part "Rosemary" since they were a result of Federal's design before the final conversion. Most experts consider the green glassware examples of "Mayfair." The pieces caught between the switch feature arching in the bottom but no waffling or grid design between the top arches, as in the original "Mayfair." The glass under the arches of "Rosemary" is plain.

Bowl, 5″, shallow $12
Bowl, 5″, deep $20
Bowl, 6″ $25
Bowl, 10″ oval $35
Creamer $20
Cup $10
Plate, 6¾″ $10
Plate, 9½″ $15
Plate, 9½″ grill, 3 divisions $17
Platter, 12″ oval $35
Saucer $5
Sugar $20
Tumbler, 4½″ tall, 9 oz. $30

MISS AMERICA or DIAMOND   HOCKING GLASS COMPANY, 1933–1938

The basic colors are pink and green. For ruby red, quadruple the prices; for crystal or flashed on crystal, reduce them by 50%. "Miss America" is a pressed diamond pattern with rays in the center of equal length. Reproductions cause problems with this pattern. Butter dishes, shakers, tumblers, and pitchers were all remade; however, as with most reproductions, the colors vary significantly from the original Depression glass (the new colors usually are lighter and the pattern not as heavy).

Bowl, 4½″ $12
Bowl, 6½″ $20
Bowl, 8¾″ $65

Bowl, 8″ $75
Bowl, 10″ oval $35
Bowl, 11″ $100
Butter dish with cover $600
Cake plate, 12″, footed $45
Candy jar with cover $150
Celery dish, 10½″ long $35
Coaster $25
Cocktail glass, 4¾″ tall, 5 oz. $85
Compote $30
Creamer $25
Cup $20
Goblet, water, 5½″ tall, 10 oz. $55
Pitcher, with or without ice lip $150
Plate, 5¾″ $10
Plate, 6¾″ $15
Plate, 8½″ $25
Plate, 10¼″ $35
Plate, 10¼″ grill, 3 divisions $35
Platter, 12¼″ oval $45
Relish dish, 8¾″, 4 divisions $25
Relish dish, 11¾″, 4 divisions $1000
Salt and pepper shakers $75
Saucer $7
Sherbet $15
Sugar $20
Tumbler, 4½″ tall, 10 oz. $60
Tumbler, 4″ tall, 5 oz. $50
Tumbler, 5¾″ tall, 14 oz. $75
Wine glass, 3¾″ tall, 3 oz. $75

MODERNTONE   HAZEL ATLAS GLASS COMPANY, 1934–1942 (GLASS COLORS), 1940s–1950s (PLATONITE COLORS)

The basic colors are cobalt blue and amethyst, although a few pink and green examples are available (same price). Note that the cobalt is slightly lighter than ordinary cobalt blue but still fairly valuable. The amethyst is a dark, almost burgundy, color. Platonite colors are fired on like porcelain and include shades of turquoise, orange, yellow, pink, gray, red, green, burgundy, and gold. There are also a few opaque white pieces with red or blue trims, as well as white pieces with an Oriental river scene. Those with the scenery are priced the same; cut the prices by half for regular platonite colors or for plain crystal. The children's sets come in basically the same platonite colors as the full-scale pieces; however, the nonpastel colors are more desirable.

Ashtray, 7¾″, with match holder in center $175
Bowl, 4¾″ $25
Bowl, 5″, berry with rim $30
Bowl, 5″, berry without rim $35

Bowl, 5″ cereal, deep $40
Bowl, 5″ soup, ruffled $50
Bowl, 6½″ $75
Bowl, 7½″ $125
Bowl, 8¾″ $50
Bowl, 8″ with rim $100
Bowl, 8″ without rim $110
Butter dish with metal cover $125
Cheese dish, 7″ **with metal cover** $500
Creamer $15
Cup $12.50
Cup without handle $20
Plate, 5⅞″ $7.50
Plate, 6¾″ $12.50
Plate, 7¾″ $15
Plate, 9″ $20
Plate, 10½″ $60
Platter, 11″, oval $65
Platter, 12″, oval $75
Salt and pepper shakers $50
Saucer $5
Sherbet $15
Sugar dish with metal cover $50
Tumbler, 5 oz. $40
Tumbler, 9 oz. $35
Tumbler, 12 oz. $100
Whiskey tumbler, 1½ oz. $25

CHILDREN'S MODERNTONE LITTLE HOSTESS PARTY SET

14-piece set
  Dark $200
  Pastel $75
Creamer, 1¾″
  Dark $10
  Pastel $7
Cup, ¾″
  Dark $7
  Pastel $5
Plate, 5¼″
  Dark $10
  Pastel $6
Saucer, 3⅞″
  Dark $4
  Pastel $2
Sugar, 1¾″
  Dark $10
  Pastel $7
Teapot with cover, 3½″, Dark $75

MT. PLEASANT DOUBLE SHIELD   L.E. SMITH COMPANY, 1920s–1934

The basic colors are pink and green. For cobalt blue, milk white, and dark amethyst (almost black), double the prices. Many pieces were trimmed in platinum; if the band is completely intact, the pieces are worth a little more. For crystal, reduce the listed prices by 50%. If the band is scattered or only partial, the remaining part can be removed with a pencil eraser. The pattern is plain with elegant banding, arcs, and rounded triangles around the edges. Some of the dark amethyst pieces have enameled roosters or baskets of fruit, while the milk pieces feature black bands (double the listed prices as for plain dark amethyst or milk white).

Bonbon, 7″, with handle	$20
Bowl, 4″	$20
Bowl, 5″	$15
Bowl, 6″, square, 2-handled	$15
Bowl, 7″, 3-footed	$17
Bowl, 8″, 2-handled, square or scalloped	$25
Bowl, 9¼″, square, footed	$25
Bowl, 9″, footed	$25
Bowl, 10″	$30
Bowl, 10″, 2-handled	$30
Cake plate, 10½″, footed	$35
Candlestick, double	$20
Candlestick, single	$15
Creamer	$20
Cup	$10
Leaf-shaped dish, 8″ long	$15
Leaf-shaped dish, 11¾″ long	$20
Mayonnaise dish, footed	$20
Mint dish, 6″, center handle	$20
Plate, 7″, 2-handled	$12
Plate, 8¼″, indentation for matching cup	$17
Plate, 8″, square or scalloped	$15
Plate, 9″, grill, 3 divisions	$15
Plate, 10½″, 2-handled	$25
Platter, 12″, 2-handled	$30
Salt and pepper shakers, 2 styles	$40
Sandwich server with center handle	$25

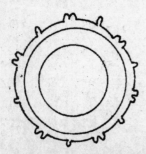

Depression glass, "Mt. Pleasant" pattern. DRAWING BY MARK PICKVET.

Saucer $4
Sherbet $12
Sugar, 2-handled $20
Tumbler, footed $12
Vase, 7¼″ tall $25

NEW CENTURY   HAZEL ATLAS GLASS COMPANY, 1930-1935

The basic colors are pink and green. Double the prices for cobalt blue or amethyst; reduce them by 50% for crystal. This pattern is sometimes referred to as "Lydia Ray," which was a temporary name used by Hazel Atlas but was not patented. It is characterized by vertical ribbing cut off near the top by three horizontal bands. Round pieces usually have rays that are equidistant from the center.

Bowl, 4½″ $20
Bowl, 4¾″ $25
Bowl, 8″ $30
Bowl with cover, 9″ $75
Butter dish with cover $85
Coaster $30
Cocktail glass, 3½″ oz. $25
Cordial, 1 oz. $50
Creamer $10
Cup $7
Decanter with stopper $75
Pitcher, 7¾″ tall, 2 qt., with or without ice lip $50
Pitcher, 8″ tall, 2½ qt., with or without ice lip $65
Plate, 6″ $4
Plate, 7″ $10
Plate, 8½″ $12
Plate, 10″ $20
Plate, 10″ grill, 3 divisions $15
Platter, 11″ oval $25
Salt and pepper shakers $55

Depression glass, "New Century" pattern. Reproduced from a 1930 trade catalog.

Saucer $4
Sherbet $10
Sugar with cover $35
Tumbler, 3¹/₂" tall, 5 oz. $15
Tumbler, 3¹/₂" tall, 8 oz. $20
Tumbler, 4¹/₄" tall, 9 oz. $17
Tumbler, 4" tall, 5 oz., footed $20
Tumbler, 5¹/₄" tall, 12 oz. $30
Tumbler, 5" tall, 10 oz. $20
Tumbler, 5" tall, 9 oz., footed $25
Whiskey, 2¹/₂" tall, 1¹/₂ oz. $15
Wine glass, 3 oz. $25

NEWPORT HAIRPIN   HAZEL ATLAS GLASS COMPANY, LATE 1930s

The prices are for pink. For cobalt blue and dark amethyst, double the prices. Platonite colors were made in the 1940s and 1950s and can be found in Chapter 7. This pattern was made near the end of the Depression and is characterized by intersecting vertical waves.

Bowl, 4¹/₄" $10
Bowl, 4³/₄" $10
Bowl, 5¹/₄" $15
Bowl, 8¹/₄" $20
Creamer $10
Cup $7
Plate, 6" $4
Plate, 8¹/₂"-8³/₄" $10
Platter, 11¹/₂" $20
Platter, 11³/₄", oval $25
Salt and pepper shakers $45
Saucer $3
Sherbet $8
Sugar, 2-handled $10
Tumbler, 4¹/₂" tall, 9 oz. $15

NORA BIRD   PADEN CITY GLASS COMPANY, 1929-1930s

The primary colors are pink and green. There are a few crystal pieces in this pheasantlike etched pattern (reduce the prices by half). For any rare amber examples, double the prices. The bird on each piece is etched in two poses, one in flight and the other about to take off.

Candlestick $50
Candy dish with cover, 6¹/₂", 3 divisions $150
Candy jar with cover, 5¹/₄" tall, footed $150
Creamer, 2 styles $50

*Depression glass, "Nora Bird"
pattern. Reproduced from a 1929
Paden City patent design.*

Cup $50
Ice tub, 6″ $125
Mayonnaise dish with inner liner $100
Plate, 8″ $30
Saucer $20
Sugar, 2-handled, 2 styles $50
Tumbler, 2¼″ tall $40
Tumbler, 3″ tall $45
Tumbler, 4¾″ tall, footed $60
Tumbler, 4″ tall $50
Tumbler, 5¼″ tall $65

NORMANDIE BOUQUET AND LATTICE   FEDERAL GLASS
COMPANY, 1933–1940

The basic colors are pink and amber. For iridescent marigold, reduce the prices by 25%. As a rule, iridescent Depression glass is cheaper than true Carnival glass and does not cause too many problems for experienced collectors.

Bowl, 5″ $7
Bowl, 6½″ $30
Bowl, 8½″ $25
Bowl, 10″, oval $35
Creamer $12
Cup $10
Pitcher, water, 2½ qt. $150
Plate, 6″ $5
Plate, 7¾″ $12
Plate, 9¼″ $15
Plate, 11″ $50
Plate, 11″, grill, 3 divisions $25
Platter, 11¾″ $30
Salt and pepper shakers $85
Saucer $4
Sherbet $10

Sugar with cover $200
Tumbler, 4$^1/_4$" tall, 9 oz. $55
Tumbler, 4" tall, 5 oz. $50
Tumbler, 5" tall, 12 oz. $75

OLD CAFE   HOCKING GLASS COMPANY, 1936–1940

The primary color is pink. For crystal, reduce the prices by 50%. Royal ruby red was produced for one year only, 1940 (double the prices). "Old Cafe" was produced near the end of the Depression glass era.

Bowl, 3$^3/_4$" $4
Bowl, 4$^1/_2$", tab handle $5
Bowl, 5$^1/_2$" $7
Bowl, 5" $6
Bowl, 9", 2 tab handles $15
Candy dish $12
Candy jar with cover $25
Cup $5
Lamp $25
Olive dish $7
Pitcher, 2$^1/_2$ qt. $125
Pitcher, milk, 1 qt. $100
Plate, 6" $3
Plate, 10" $30
Saucer $3
Sherbet $7
Tumbler, 3" tall $12
Tumbler, 4" tall $15
Vase, 7$^1/_4$" tall $20

OLD ENGLISH THREADING   INDIANA GLASS COMPANY, LATE 1920s–EARLY 1930s

The basic colors are pink, green, and amber. For crystal or dark forest green, reduce the prices by 50%. The pattern features concentric ribs spaced closely together.

Bowl, 4" $20
Bowl, 9$^1/_2$" $35
Bowl, 9", footed $30
Candlestick $20
Candy dish with cover $65
Candy jar with cover $75
Compote $25
Compote, 2-handled $25
Creamer $20
Egg cup $20
Fruit stand, 11", footed $55

Depression glass, "Old English Threading" pattern.
DRAWING BY MARK PICKVET.

Goblet	$35
Pitcher with cover	$150
Plate	$20
Sandwich server with center handle	$65
Sherbet, 2 styles	$25
Sugar with cover, 2-handled	$55
Tumbler, 4½" tall, footed	$25
Tumbler, 5½" tall, footed	$35
Vase, 5½" tall	$55
Vase, 8" tall, footed	$60
Vase, 12" tall, footed	$65

ORCHID   PADEN CITY GLASS COMPANY, 1930s

The prices are for pink, green, yellow, and amber. For the more desirable cobalt blue and ruby red, double the prices; for the rare black, triple them. As the name indicates, this pattern is characterized by etched orchids. Leaves and stems are also included in the design. Many of the pieces are square in shape or have square bases.

Bowl, 5"	$25
Bowl, 8½", 2-handled	$60
Bowl, 8¾", square	$55
Bowl, 10", footed	$60
Bowl, 11", square	$65
Candlestick	$40
Candy dish with cover, 3 divisions	$100
Compote, 3¼" tall	$30
Compote, 6½" tall	$45
Creamer	$35
Ice bucket	$100
Mayonnaise set (bowl, plate, and ladle)	$90
Plate, 8½"	$30
Sandwich server with center handle	$50
Sugar, 2-handled	$35
Vase, 8" tall	$75
Vase, 10" tall	$100

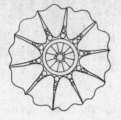

Depression glass, "Oyster and Pearl" pattern.
DRAWING BY MARK PICKVET.

OYSTER AND PEARL ANCHOR HOCKING GLASS CORPORATION, 1938–1940

The pieces listed include crystal, pink, and fired on versions of pink, green, and white. For ruby red, double the prices. "Oyster and Pearl" was made toward the end of the Depression after the merger of the two companies. It represents a transition period from the colored glass of the Depression to the more ceramic, porcelainlike colors of the 1940s. The pattern consists of a starlike outcropping from a circular center. On the arms of the star are three progressively smaller circles.

Bowl, 5½", 1 handle	$10
Bowl, 6½", 2-handled	$12
Bowl, 10½"	$25
Candleholder	$12
Heart-shaped bowl, 1 handle	$10
Platter, 13½"	$25
Relish dish, 2 divisions	$12

PANELED ASTER U.S. GLASS COMPANY, EARLY 1930s

The basic colors are pink, green, yellow, and light amber. As the name indicates, the pattern consists of asters separated into vertical sections. Watch for rough mold seams. "Primo" is the official U.S. Glass name for this pattern; however, "Paneled Aster" is the more common label.

Bowl, 4½"	$15
Bowl, 5½"	$20
Bowl, 8"	$25
Bowl, 9"	$30
Cake plate, 10", 3-footed	$30
Coaster	$10
Creamer	$15
Cup	$12
Pitcher	$250
Plate, 7½"	$12
Plate, 10"	$25
Plate, 10", grill, 3 divisions	$20

Saucer $4
Sherbet $15
Sugar $15
Tumbler, various styles $25

PARROT   FEDERAL GLASS COMPANY, 1931–1932

The basic colors are green and amber. For light blue, double the prices; for crystal, reduce them by 50%. Many "Parrot" pieces are becoming quite rare and valuable. "Parrot" is an easily recognized pattern and consists of two parrots sitting together on one branch and a lone parrot on another branch. The branches are palmlike.

Bowl, 5″ $25
Bowl, 7″ $45
Bowl, 8″ $100
Bowl, 10″, oval $75
Butter dish with cover (rare in amber $1500) $500
Creamer $75
Cup $50
Hot plate, 2 styles $1000
Marmalade dish $50
Pitcher, 2½ qt. $3000
Plate, 5¾″ $40
Plate, 7½″ $45
Plate, 9″ $55
Plate, 10½″, grill, round or square, 3 divisions $50
Platter, 11¼″, oblong $75
Salt and pepper shakers $325
Saucer $20
Sherbet $35
Sugar with cover, 2-handled $200
Tumbler, 4¼″, 10 oz. $150
Tumbler, 5½″ tall, 12 oz. $200
Tumbler, 5½″ tall, 10 oz., footed $175
Tumbler, 5¾″ tall, footed $175

Depression glass, "Parrot" pattern. DRAWING BY MARK PICKVET.

PATRICIAN or SPOKE   FEDERAL GLASS COMPANY, 1933–1937

The basic colors are pink, green, and amber. For crystal, reduce the prices by 50%. The inner circle of each piece resembles a wheel with spokes; hence the nickname. The pattern also develops into a star, contains zigzag designs near the outer edges or tops of each piece, and has an additional edging made of semicircles.

Bowl, 4³/₄″ $20
Bowl, 5″ $15
Bowl, 6″ $25
Bowl, 8¹/₂″ $35
Bowl, 10″, oval $40
Butter dish with cover $225
Cookie jar with cover $175
Creamer $15
Cup $12
Marmalade dish $35
Pitcher $150
Plate, 6″ $10
Plate, 7¹/₂″ $15
Plate, 9″ $17
Plate, 10¹/₂″ $40
Plate, 10¹/₂″, grill, 3 divisions $25
Platter, 11¹/₂″, oval $35
Salt and pepper shakers $85
Saucer $10
Sherbet $15
Sugar with cover, 2-handled $75
Tumbler, 4¹/₄″ tall, 9 oz. $30
Tumbler, 4″ tall, 5 oz. $30
Tumbler, 5¹/₂″ tall, 14 oz. $50
Tumbler, 5¹/₄″ tall, 8 oz., footed $50

PATRICK   LANCASTER GLASS COMPANY, 1930s

"Patrick" was made in two colors, pink and yellow. The pattern consists of etched floral and scrolled designs. Pieces in this pattern have risen sharply in value and are quite scarce.

Bowl, 5³/₄″ $75
Bowl, 9″, 2-handled $150
Bowl, 11″ $150
Candlestick $75
Candy dish, 3-footed $150
Cheese and cracker set $175
Cocktail glass, 4″ tall $100
Creamer $65
Cup $50
Goblet, 4³/₄″ tall $100
Goblet, 6″ tall $125

Mayonnaise set (bowl, plate, and ladle)	$200
Plate, 7½″	$30
Plate, 7″	$25
Plate, 8″	$45
Sandwich server with center handle	$150
Saucer	$20
Sherbet	$65
Sugar, 2-handled	$20
Tray, 11″, 2-handled	$65
Tumbler, several styles	$75
Wine glass	$100

PEACOCK AND WILD ROSE   PADEN CITY GLASS COMPANY, 1930s

Prices are for pink, green, or blue-green, amber, light blue, and yellow. For ruby red and cobalt blue, double the prices; for black, triple them; for crystal, reduce them by 50%. If any of Paden City's glassware could be considered common, this pattern would be at the top of the list; however, it is still rare compared to other Depression glass patterns. Black is about the only Depression glass color that outprices ruby red and cobalt blue. This holds true for this pattern. The green is very pale, like ultramarine. The pattern is similar to "Peacock Reverse" except that the peacock faces forward.

Bowl, 5″	$50
Bowl, 8½″, oval, footed	$100

Depression glass, "Peacock and Wild Rose" pattern. Reproduced from a 1928 Paden City patent design.

Bowl, 8¾", footed $100
Bowl, 9½", center handle $100
Bowl, 9½", footed $100
Bowl, 10½" $125
Bowl, 10½", center handle $125
Bowl, 11" $125
Bowl, 14" $150
Cake plate, footed $110
Candlestick $75
Candy dish with cover $175
Cheese and cracker set $150
Compote $75
Ice bucket or tub $175
Pitcher, milk, 1 qt. $250
Pitcher, water, 2 qt. $350
Plate, 7½" $75
Relish, 3 divisions $100
Tumbler, several styles $125
Vase, 10" tall, 2 styles $150
Vase, 12" tall $200

PEACOCK REVERSE   PADEN CITY GLASS COMPANY, 1930s

The prices are for pink, green, yellow, and amber. For ruby red and cobalt blue, double the prices; for black, triple them; for crystal, reduce them by 50%. This pattern was supposedly made in pink, green, yellow, amber, blue, red, black, and crystal. Advertisements and catalogs list all of the above colors including crystal, but not all have been rediscovered. As with Paden City's other glassware, there are only a few pieces still available. The peacock in the pattern is referred to as "Reverse" because the head of the peacock is turned to face its tail section, while the body remains straight.

Bowl, 5", square $50
Bowl, 8¾" square $100

Depression glass, "Peacock Reverse" pattern. Reproduced from a 1929 Paden City patent design.

Bowl, 8³/₄" square, 2-handled $125
Bowl, 11³/₄" $125
Candlestick $75
Candy dish, square $175
Compote, 3¹/₄" tall $75
Compote, 4¹/₄" tall $100
Creamer $100
Cup $100
Plate, 6" $35
Plate, 7¹/₂" $45
Plate, 8¹/₂" $55
Plate, 10 ¹/₂", 2-handled $75
Sandwich server with center handle $100
Saucer $25
Sherbet $75
Sugar, 2-handled $100
Tumbler, 4" tall, 10 oz. $85
Vase, several styles $150

PHILBE FIRE-KING DINNERWARE   HOCKING GLASS
COMPANY, 1937–1938

The primary colors include pink, green, and a light copper blue. For crystal, reduce the prices by 50%. The original "Fire-King Dinnerware" was introduced by Hocking near the end of the Depression glass era. Many pieces are trimmed in platinum. After the Depression and the merger with Anchor, numerous Fire-King pieces were produced in a variety of styles (see Chapter 7).

Bowl, 5¹/₂" $50
Bowl, 7¹/₄" $65
Bowl, 10" oval $100
Candy jar with cover $750
Cookie jar with cover $1000
Creamer $125

Depression glass, "Peacock and Wild Rose" pattern. Reproduced from a 1928 advertisement.

Depression glass, Philbe Fire-King dinnerware. Reproduced from a 1937 patent design.

Cup	$125
Goblet	$175
Pitcher, 1 qt.	$750
Pitcher, 2 qt.	$1000
Plate, 6″	$55
Plate, 8″	$50
Plate, 10½″ grill, 3 divisions	$55
Plate, 10″ or 10 ½″	$60
Platter, 11½″	$65
Platter, 12″, 2 tab handled	$125
Saucer, 6″	$50
Sugar, 2-handled	$125
Tumbler, 4 oz., footed	$150
Tumbler, 9 oz.	$125
Tumbler, 10 oz., footed	$85
Tumbler, 15 oz., footed	$100
Tumbler, several styles	$75

PRETZEL INDIANA GLASS COMPANY, 1930s

The prices are for crystal and embossed crystal pieces; for ultramarine, double the prices. As with many of Indiana's numbered patterns, "Pretzel" is the adopted name because of its wavy, pretzel-like design. It was patented simply as "No. 622." As with so much of Indiana's glass, "Pretzel" has been reproduced. The celery dish was re-issued in the 1970s in amber, avocado green, and blue, and is still being made today.

Bowl, 4½″	$10
Bowl, 7½″	$15
Bowl, 9½″	$20
Celery tray, 10¼″	$20
Creamer	$10
Cup	$7

Pattern No. 622
MACHINE MADE
Design Patent Number D-104618—D-104619

Handled Cream
4 doz. ctn. 31 lbs.

Cup
6 doz. ctn. 31 lbs.
Saucer
6 doz. ctn. 33 lbs.

Handled Sugar
4 doz. ctn. 33 lbs.

7½" Coupe Soup
4 doz. ctn. 47 lbs.

9¾" Berry
2 doz. ctn. 42 lbs.

9¾" Berry with 11½" Plate makes 2-piece Salad Set

11½" Sandwich or Cake Plate
2 doz. ctn. 43 lbs.

9¾" Dinner Plate
4 doz. ctn. 47 lbs.

8¾" Salad Plate
4 doz. ctn. 37 lbs.

6" Plate
6 doz. ctn. 25 lbs.

Depression glass, "Pretzel" pattern. Reproduced from a 1935 trade catalog.

Depression glass, "Pretzel" pattern.
PHOTO BY ROBIN RAINWATER.

Leaf-shaped dish $10
Pickle dish, 2-handled $10
Pitcher, 1 qt. $175
Plate, 6″ $7
Plate, 6″, 1 handle $8
Plate, 7¼″ square $10
Plate, 8½″ $12
Plate, 9½″ $15

Platter, 11¹/₂″ $20
Saucer $12
Sugar, 2-handled $10
Tumbler, various styles $20

PRINCESS   HOCKING GLASS COMPANY, 1931–1935

The prices are for pink, green, and light amber. For bright yellow (named "Topaz" by Hocking) and light blue, double the prices. "Princess" is a popular pattern characterized by a somewhat paneled curtain design. Note that many pieces are octagonal in shape.

Ashtray $75
Bowl, 4¹/₂″ $30
Bowl, 5″ $35
Bowl, 9¹/₂″ $45
Bowl, 9″ $40
Bowl, 10″ oval $40
Butter dish with cover $125
Cake plate, 10″ $35
Candy dish with cover $75
Coaster $55
Cookie jar with cover $65
Creamer $20
Cup $15
Pitcher, 2 qt. $100
Pitcher, milk, 1 qt, 6″ tall $75
Pitcher, milk, 24 oz., 7³/₈″ tall, footed (rare) $550
Plate, 5¹/₂″ $12
Plate, 8″ $15
Plate, 9¹/₂″ $30
Plate, 9¹/₂″ grill, 3 divisions $20
Plate, 10¹/₂″ grill, 3 divisions, 2-handled $20
Platter, 12″, 2 tab handles $35
Relish dish, divided $35
Relish dish, no divisions $125
Salt and pepper shakers $75
Sandwich server with center handle $35
Saucer $12
Sherbet $25
Sugar shaker $40
Sugar with cover $45
Tumbler, 3″ tall, 5 oz. $30
Tumbler, 4³/₄″ tall, 9 oz., footed $75
Tumbler, 4″ tall, 9 oz. $30
Tumbler, 5¹/₄″ tall, 10 oz., footed $40
Tumbler, 5¹/₄″ tall, 13 oz. $45
Tumbler, 6¹/₂″ tall, 13 oz., footed $100
Vase, 8″ tall $50

Depression glass, "Princess" pattern.
PHOTO BY ROBIN RAINWATER.

PYRAMID or NO. 610   INDIANA GLASS COMPANY, 1926–1932

The prices are for pink, green, and yellow. For crystal or milk glass, reduce the prices by 50%. Like other Indiana numbered patterns, "Pyramid" was unpatented but nicknamed by dealers and collectors because of the pattern's shape. Under the "Tiara" label, "Pyramid" pieces were reproduced in blue and black in the 1970s (same price as crystal).

Bowl, 5″	$20
Bowl, 6″	$25
Bowl, 8½″	$30
Bowl, 9½″, oval	$35
Creamer	$25
Ice tub	$85
Ice tub with cover	$750
Pitcher, milk, 1 qt.	$350
Pitcher, water, 2 qt.	$450
Relish tray, 4 divisions, 2-handled	$65
Sugar	$25
Tray, for creamer and sugar	$30
Tumbler, 8 oz., footed, 2styles	$55
Tumbler, 11 oz., footed	$75

QUEEN MARY   HOCKING GLASS COMPANY, 1936–EARLY 1950s

The original color for this pattern was pink and was produced in the late 1930s. Reduce the prices by 50% for crystal. For royal ruby and forest green, which were produced in the 1950s, use the same prices as the pink. This pattern is sometimes referred to as "Vertical Ribbed" because of the vertical ribbing.

Ashtray, 2 styles	$5

Depression glass, "Pyramid" or "No. 610" pattern. Reproduced from a 1930 trade catalog.

Bowl, 4½″ $7
Bowl, 4″ $5
Bowl, 4″, 1 handle $6
Bowl, 5½″, 2-handled $12
Bowl, 5″ $10
Bowl, 6″ $15
Bowl, 7″ $15
Bowl, 8¾″ $20
Butter dish with cover $150
Candlestick, double $15
Candy dish with cover $40
Cigarette jar, oval $10
Coaster, round $5
Coaster, square $6
Compote $15
Creamer, footed $25

Creamer, oval $10
Cup, 2 styles $7
Pickle dish, 10″ long $20
Pitcher $150
Plate, 6½″ $6
Plate, 6″ $5
Plate, 8¾″ $25
Plate, 9¾″ $50
Platter, 12″ $25
Platter, 14″ $35
Salt and pepper shakers $100
Saucer $5
Sherbet $10
Sugar, footed $25
Sugar, oval $10
Tray, relish, 12″, 3 divisions $20
Tray, relish, 14″, 4 divisions $25
Tumbler, 3½″, 5 oz. $10
Tumbler, 4″ tall, 9 oz. $12
Tumbler, 5″ tall, 1″ oz., footed $50

RAINDROPS or OPTIC DESIGN   FEDERAL GLASS COMPANY, 1929–1933

"Raindrops" is a simple pattern that features small pressed circles. The prices are for green; for crystal, reduce the prices by 50%. As with most Federal products, the underside of the pieces show the company mark (F in a shield).

Bowl, 4½″ $7
Bowl, 6″ $10
Bowl, 7½″ $25
Creamer $10
Cup $7

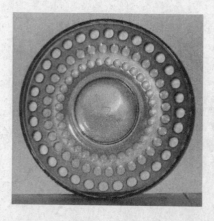

Depression glass, "Raindrops" or "Optic" pattern. PHOTO BY ROBIN RAINWATER.

Plate, 6″ $4
Plate, 8″ $7
Salt and pepper shakers $300
Saucer $3
Sherbet $7
Sugar with cover $50
Tumbler, 3″ tall, 4 oz. $5
Tumbler, 4″ tall, 5 oz. $7
Tumbler, 4″ tall, 9 oz. $10
Tumbler, 5¹/₂″ tall, 14 oz. $15
Tumbler, 5″ tall, 10 oz. $12
Whiskey tumbler, 1³/₄″, 1 oz. $7
Whiskey tumbler, 2 ¹/₄″ tall, 2 oz. $7

RIBBON   HOCKING GLASS COMPANY, LATE 1920s–EARLY 1930s

The basic colors are pink and green. For black, double the prices; for crystal, reduce them by 50%. This is another simple Depression pattern of vertical panels that nearly reach the top of each item.

Bowl, 4″ $20
Bowl, 5″ $25
Bowl, 7″ $30
Bowl, 8″ $35
Candy jar with cover $55
Creamer $15
Cup $7
Plate, 6¹/₄″ $5
Plate, 8″ $7
Salt and pepper shakers $55
Saucer $3
Sherbet $7
Sugar, 2-handled $15
Tumbler, 5¹/₂″ or 6″ tall $30

Depression glass, "Ribbon" pattern.
PHOTO BY ROBIN RAINWATER.

RINGS or BANDED RINGS   HOCKING GLASS COMPANY, 1927–1933

Hocking produced many banded ring combinations. Colors include blue, green, orange, pink, red, and yellow. The company also trimmed or ringed pieces in gold, silver, and platinum. For plain crystal, reduce the prices by 50%. The biggest problem with these fired-on enameled rings is that they are difficult to find completely intact. Nicks, scratches, incomplete bands, fading, and other problems plague banding. Damaged pieces are worth less than completely intact pieces (the prices reflect complete, undamaged banding).

Bowl, 5¼", 2 divisions $15
Bowl, 5" $7
Bowl, 7" $15
Bowl, 8" $15
Cocktail glass, 3¾" tall, 3 oz. $20
Cocktail shaker with metal top $30
Creamer $8
Cup $7
Decanter with stopper $50
Goblet, water, 7¼" tall, 9 oz. $20
Ice bucket or tub $40
Pitcher, 2 qt. $35
Pitcher, 2½ qt. $45
Plate, 6½", with off-center ring for sherbet $7
Plate, 6¼" $5
Plate, 8" $7
Platter, 11¾" $15
Salt and pepper shakers $50
Sandwich server with center handle $30
Saucer $3
Sherbet $15
Sugar $8
Tumbler, 3½" tall, footed $12
Tumbler, 3½" tall, 5 oz. $7
Tumbler, 3" tall, 4 oz. $7
Tumbler, 4¼" tall, 9 oz. $12
Tumbler, 4¾" tall, 10 oz. $15
Tumbler, 4" tall, 8 oz. $20
Tumbler, 5½" tall, footed $12
Tumbler, 5" tall, 12 oz. $17
Tumbler, 6½" tall, footed $17
Vase, 8" tall $40
Whiskey, 2" tall, 1½ oz. $12
Wine glass, 4½" tall, 3½ oz. $25

ROCK CRYSTAL or EARLY AMERICAN ROCK CRYSTAL
MCKEE GLASS COMPANY, 1920s–1930s

"Rock Crystal" is one of the most common Depression glass patterns and comes in a variety of colors and designs including shades of amber, amethyst, aquamarine, light blue, green, milk, pink, vaseline, yellow, frosted colors, frosted or decorated crystal, and marbleized or slag designs. The prices vary for ruby red and cobalt blue (double the prices) and plain crystal (reduce them by 50%). The pattern is characterized by scrolling and vining around five-petal flowers.

Bonbon dish	$35
Bowl, 4½"	$25
Bowl, 4"	$25
Bowl, 5"	$30
Bowl, 7"	$40
Bowl, 8½", center handle	$75
Bowl, 8"	$40
Bowl, 9"	$55
Bowl, 10½"	$60
Bowl, 11½", 2 divisions	$60
Bowl, 12½", 5 divisions	$100
Bowl, 12½", footed	$125
Bowl, 13"	$75
Bowl, 14", 6 divisions	$110
Butter dish with cover	$350
Cake stand, 11", footed	$55
Candelabra, double-light	$100
Candelabra, triple-light	$125
Candlestick, 5½" tall	$40
Candlestick, 8" tall	$75
Candy jar with cover	$100
Celery dish, 12" long	$50
Champagne glass, 6 oz.	$25
Claret glass, 2 oz.	$35
Cocktail glass, 3½ oz.	$25
Compote, 7"	$55
Compote with cover, footed	$100
Cordial, 1 oz.	$40
Creamer	$35
Cruet with stopper	$150
Cup	$30
Goblet, 8 oz.	$35
Goblet, 11 oz.	$40
Ice dish, various styles	$55
Lamp, electric	$300
Marmalade dish	$35
Parfait, 3½ oz.	$40
Parfait, 6 oz.	$30
Pitcher, tankard-style	$550
Pitcher with cover, 3 qt.	$550
Pitcher, milk, 1 qt.	$325

Pitcher, syrup with lid $200
Pitcher, water, 2 qt. $425
Plate, 6″ $10
Plate, 7½″ $12
Plate, 8½″ $15
Plate, 9″ $25
Plate, 10 ½″ $30
Platter, 11½″ $35
Punch bowl with stand $750
Punch cup $35
Salt and pepper shakers $150
Salt dip $50
Sandwich server with center handle $50
Saucer $10
Sherbet $30
Spooner $50
Sugar with cover, 2-handled $75
Tray, oval $75
Tumbler, 5 oz. $25
Tumbler, 9 oz. $30
Tumbler, 12 oz. $40
Vase, 11″ tall $125
Vase, cornucopia style $125
Whiskey tumbler, 2½ oz. $25
Wine glass, 3 oz. $30
Wine glass, 7 oz. $35

ROSE CAMEO   BELMONT TUMBLER COMPANY, 1931

This pattern was made only in green. The Belmont Tumbler Company filed a patent for it in 1931. Do not confuse this pattern with Hocking's "Ballerina." In "Rose Cameo," a rose is in the cameo. In Hocking's version, a dancing girl or ballerina is in the cameo.

Bowl, 4½″ $12
Bowl, 5″ $15
Bowl, 6″ $20

Depression glass, "Rosemary" pattern. DRAWING BY MARK PICKVET.

Plate, 7″ $15
Sherbet $15
Tumbler, 5″ tall, footed, rim design varies $25

ROSEMARY or DUTCH ROSE   FEDERAL GLASS COMPANY, 1935–1936

The prices are for green and amber. Pink is much rarer (increase the prices by 50%). "Rosemary" is a derivative of Federal's "Mayfair" pattern and includes rose blossoms in the center and within the arches.

Bowl, 5″, berry, (shallow) $10
Bowl, 5″, soup (deep) $20
Bowl, 6″ $30
Bowl, 10″, oval $35
Creamer $15
Cup $10
Plate, 6¾″ $10
Plate, 9½″ $15
Plate, 9½″ grill, 3 divisions $15
Platter, 12″, oval $25
Saucer $5
Sugar, 2-handled $15
Tumbler, 4¼″ tall, 9 oz. $35

ROULETTE   HOCKING GLASS COMPANY, 1935–1939

The primary colors are pink and green; for crystal, reduce the prices by 50%. "Roulette" is sometimes called "Many Windows" because of the two horizontal rows of miniature rectangles.

Bowl, 8″ $12
Bowl, 9″ $15
Cup $7
Pitcher, 1 qt. $45
Plate, 6″ $5

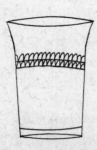

Depression glass, "Roulette" pattern. DRAWING BY MARK PICKVET.

Plate, 8½" $7
Platter, 12" $17
Saucer $4
Sherbet $6
Tumbler, 3¼" tall, 5 oz. $25
Tumbler, 3¼" tall, 7½ oz. $45
Tumbler, 4¼" tall, 9 oz. $30
Tumbler, 5½" tall, 10 oz., footed $35
Tumbler, 5" tall, 12 oz. $35
Whiskey tumbler, 2½" tall, 1½ oz. $20

ROUND ROBIN   UNKNOWN MANUFACTURER, 1920s–1930s

The colors include green and light marigold. For crystal, reduce the prices by 50%. This is another simple vertically ribbed pattern but with no sure patents. The domino tray is a unique piece in this pattern; it consists of a center ring for a creamer and the remaining surrounding area for sugar cubes.

Bowl, 4" $7
Creamer $10
Cup $7
Domino tray $50
Plate, 6" $4
Plate, 8" $5
Platter, 12" $12
Saucer $3
Sherbet $6
Sugar, 2-handled $10
Tumbler $25

Depression glass, "Round Robin" pattern. DRAWING
BY MARK PICKVET.

ROYAL LACE   HAZEL ATLAS GLASS COMPANY, 1934–EARLY 1940s

The prices are for pink and green. For amethyst and cobalt blue, double the prices; for crystal, reduce them by 50%. Production of this paneled lace pattern by Hazel Atlas continued into the 1940s, but the majority of the colored glass was made in the 1930s. The story behind "Royal Lace" is that General Mills had commissioned Hazel Atlas to manufacture Shirley Temple pieces (cobalt blue glass with pictures of Shirley Temple applied as decals). When General Mills discontinued the order, Hazel Atlas was left with several tanks of molten blue glass. The "Royal Lace" molds, which were nearby, promptly were filled with the blue glass.

Bowl, 4³/₄″	$25
Bowl, 5″	$30
Bowl, 10″	$35
Bowl, 10″, 3-footed, ruffled or rolled edge	$65
Bowl, 10″, 3-footed, straight edge	$50
Bowl, 11″ oval	$40
Butter dish with cover	$175
Candlestick, various styles	$35
Cookie jar with cover	$75
Creamer	$25
Cup	$20
Nut bowl	$400
Pitcher, 1¹/₂ qt.	$100
Pitcher, 2 qt., with ice lip	$100
Pitcher, 2 qt., without ice lip	$85
Pitcher, 3 qt.	$150
Plate, 6″	$10
Plate, 8¹/₂″	$15
Plate, 9″ grill, 3 divisions	$25
Plate, 10″	$25
Plate, 10″ grill, 3 divisions	$30
Platter, 13″, oval	$40
Salt and pepper shakers	$100
Saucer	$10
Sherbet	$25
Sugar with cover, 2-handled	$75
Tumbler, 3¹/₂″ tall, 5 oz.	$30
Tumbler, 4¹/₄″ tall, 9 oz.	$35
Tumbler, 5¹/₂″ tall, 12 oz.	$65
Tumbler, 5″ tall, 10 oz.	$65

SANDWICH   INDIANA GLASS COMPANY, 1920s–1930s

Indiana's "Sandwich" causes more problems than any other pattern. All of the colors were made during the Depression era; however, all except pink have been reproduced since. Prices for crystal and amber cover new as well as old pieces; they're quite a bit lower than what the originals would be on their own. The problem that

Depression glass, "Sandwich" pattern. PHOTO BY ROBIN RAINWATER.

arises is that the majority of the original molds were put back into service to make virtually identical pieces. Pink is the only original color that is easily distinguished since all pieces are old. The original green is yellowish, while the new version is paler. The original also glows under a dark or black light (a common test for older Depression glass because of the ores utilized in the ingredients); the new version does not glow. Other colors were produced after the Depression and appear in Chapter 7. These include teal blue, smoky blue, milk white, and red. A few red original pieces were made in the 1930s but are nearly impossible to tell from reproductions.

Ashtray set, 4-piece card suits

Amber	$10
Crystal	$5
Green	$25
Pink	$20

Basket, 10″ tall

Amber	$40
Crystal	$35

Bowl, 4¼″ tall

Amber	$5
Crystal	$4
Green	$10
Pink	$7

Bowl, 6″

Amber	$4
Crystal	$4
Green	$10
Pink	$7

Bowl, 6″, hexagonal

Amber	$6
Crystal	$5
Green	$12
Pink	$10

Bowl, 8½″

Amber	$12
Crystal	$10
Green	$17
Pink	$15

INDIANA GLASS COMPANY
DUNKIRK, INDIANA

MANUFACTURERS OF

PRESSED AND BLOWN GLASSWARE
CRYSTAL, COLORED AND DECORATED

SANDWICH PATTERN
No. 170—8¼" SALAD PLATE

Depression glass,
"Sandwich" pattern.
Reproduced from a
1925 advertisement.

Bowl, 9″
Clear $25
Amber $15
Crystal $13
Pink $20
Bowl, 11½″
Amber $20
Crystal $17
Green $30
Pink $25
Butter dish with cover
Amber $35
Crystal $25
Green $250
Pink $200
Candlestick, 3½″
Amber $12
Crystal $10
Green $25
Pink $20
Candlestick, 7″
Amber $15
Crystal $12
Green $30
Pink $25
Celery, 10½″
Amber $15
Crystal $12

Green $30
Pink $25

Creamer
Amber $12
Crystal $10
Green $25
Pink $20
Red $50

Creamer and sugar set on diamond-shaped tray
Amber $30
Crystal $25
Green $50
Pink $40

Cruet with stopper
Amber $35
Crystal $30
Green $175
Pink $150

Cup
Amber $5
Crystal $3
Green $7
Pink $6
Red $35

Decanter with stopper
Amber $30
Crystal $25
Green $150
Pink $125
Red $100

Goblet, 9 oz.
Amber $15
Crystal $12
Green $25
Pink $20
Red $50

Mayonnaise
Amber $15
Crystal $12
Green $25
Pink $20

Pitcher, 68 oz.
Amber $40
Crystal $30
Green $175
Pink $150
Red $150

Plate, 6″
Amber $4
Crystal $3
Green $7

Pink $6

Plate, 7″
Amber $5
Crystal $4
Green $9
Pink $7

Plate, 8³/₄″
Amber $5
Crystal $4
Green $9
Pink $7
Red $25

Plate, 8″, oval with indentation for the sherbet
Amber $6
Crystal $5
Green $12
Pink $10

Plate, 10¹/₂″
Amber $12
Crystal $10
Green $25
Pink $20

Plate, 13″
Amber $15
Crystal $12
Green $35
Pink $30
Red $40

Puff box
Amber $20
Crystal $15

Punch bowl, 13″, Green $250
Punch cup, Green $20
Salt and pepper shakers
Amber $20
Crystal $17

Sandwich server with center handle
Amber $25
Crystal $20
Green $40
Pink $35
Red $50

Saucer
Amber $3
Crystal $2
Green $6
Pink $5
Red $10

Sherbet, 3¹/₄″
Amber $7
Crystal $6

Green $12
Pink $10
Sugar with cover
Amber $30
Crystal $25
Green $50
Pink $40
Red $75
Tumbler, 3 oz., footed
Amber $12
Crystal $10
Green $25
Pink $20
Tumbler, 8 oz., footed
Amber $15
Crystal $12
Green $30
Pink $25
Tumbler, 12 oz., footed
Amber $17.5
Crystal $14
Green $35
Pink $30
Wine glass, 3″ tall, 4 oz.
Amber $10
Crystal $7
Green $30
Pink $25
Red $15

SHARON CABBAGE ROSE   FEDERAL GLASS COMPANY, 1935–1939

The Depression colors priced include pink, green, and amber; for crystal, reduce prices by 50%. Note that there are a few rare colored items priced separately. This pattern gets its name from the roses that resemble cabbage heads. There are several reproductions to be aware of in this pattern. Butter dishes were produced in 1976 in pink, dark pink, green, dark or forest green, light or cobalt blue, red, and amber. Only the regular pink and green reproductions cause confusion since they resemble the originals. Creamer and sugar sets, as well as salt and pepper shakers in very light pink, were reissued in the late 1970s and the 1980s, but the color is much fainter than the original. Candy jars were also reproduced in both pink and green.

Bowl, 5″, berry (shallow) $15
Bowl, 5″, soup (deep) $45
Bowl, 6″ $25
Bowl, 7³/₄″ $50
Bowl, 8¹/₂″ $35
Bowl, 9¹/₂″ $35
Bowl, 10¹/₂″ $40

Depression glass, "Sharon Cabbage Rose" pattern. PHOTO BY ROBIN RAINWATER.

Butter dish with cover $85
Cake plate, 11½″, footed $50
Candy jar with cover (rare in green $200.00) $75
Cheese dish with cover (rare in pink or green $1000.00) $225
Creamer $25
Cup $20
Marmalade dish (rare in pink $250.00) $45
Pitcher, 2½ qt., with or without ice lip (rare in green $500.00) $200
Plate, 6″ $10
Plate, 7½″ $25
Plate, 9½″ $25
Platter, 12½″ oval $35
Salt and pepper shakers $65
Saucer $12
Sherbet $20
Sugar with cover, 2-handled $50
Tumbler, 4″ tall, 9 oz. $45
Tumbler, 5¼″ tall, 12 oz. $50
Tumbler, 6½″ tall, 15 oz. (rare in amber $150.00) $75
Vase $125

SIERRA PINWHEEL   JEANNETTE GLASS COMPANY, 1931–1933

The primary colors are pink and green, but there were a few pieces made in ultra-marine (same price). The pattern consists of vertical ribbing that extends out to an irregular edge that is prone to chipping, so examine pieces carefully. Jeannette did make a butter dish and cover with a combination of the "Adam" (see separate entry) and "Sierra" patterns. This dish, along with the cover, is valued at about $850.00.

Bowl, 5½″ $15
Bowl, 8½″ $30

Depression glass, "Sierra Pinwheel" pattern. PHOTO BY ROBIN RAINWATER.

Depression glass. Left: "Sierra Pinwheel" pattern creamer; right: "Ribbon" pattern double-handle sugar. PHOTO BY ROBIN RAINWATER.

Bowl, 9¼″, oval (rare in green $125.00) $45
Butter dish with cover $75
Creamer $25
Cup $15
Pitcher, milk, 1 qt. $100
Plate, 9″ $25
Platter, 11″ oval $50
Salt and pepper shakers $55
Saucer $7
Sugar with cover, 2-handled $50
Tray, 10¼″, 2-handled $25
Tumbler, 4½″ tall, footed $65

SPIRAL   HOCKING GLASS COMPANY, 1928–1930

The prices are for pink and green. For crystal, reduce the prices by 50%. This pattern is sometimes confused with "Swirl" and "Twisted Optic." "Swirl" is easy to recognize because the arcs or curves are straighter and not as sharply angled. Like "Twisted Optic," "Swirl" curves go counterclockwise; "Spiral" curves move clockwise. The important thing to remember is to look at the piece from the correct angle.

Depression glass, "Spiral" pattern. PHOTO BY ROBIN RAINWATER.

Bowl, 4³/₄″ $7
Bowl, 7″ $12
Bowl, 8″ $15
Bowl, 9″ $20
Creamer $10
Creamer, footed $12
Cup $7
Ice tub $30
Marmalade with cover $35
Pitcher, 2 qt. $45
Plate, 6″ $3
Plate, 8″ $5
Platter, 12″ $30
Salt and pepper shakers $55
Sandwich server with center handle $45
Saucer $3
Sherbet $6
Sugar, 2-handled $10
Sugar, 2-handled, footed $12
Tumbler, 3″ tall $7
Tumbler, 5″ tall $10
Tumbler, 6″ tall $20

STRAWBERRY   U.S. GLASS COMPANY, EARLY 1930s

The basic colors are pink and green; however, most pieces can be found in crystal and a light iridized marigold (reduce the prices by 25% for crystal and marigold). This is the sister pattern of "Cherryberry," also produced by U.S. Glass. The dimensions of the pieces are identical, but the fruits on the pattern are obviously different.

Bowl, 4″ $10
Bowl, 6¹/₂″ $25

Bowl, 6¹/₄″ $50
Bowl, 7¹/₂″ $25
Butter dish with cover $175
Compote $25
Creamer (large), 4¹/₂″ tall $45
Creamer (small) $20
Olive dish, 5″, 1 tab handle $20
Pickle dish, 8¹/₄″ oval $20
Pitcher $175
Plate, 6″ $10
Plate, 7¹/₂″ $15
Sherbet $10
Sugar, (large) with cover $100
Sugar, (small) open $20
Tumbler, 3¹/₂″ tall $25

SUNFLOWER   JEANNETTE GLASS COMPANY, 1930s

The basic colors are pink and green. For odd colors like ultramarine, delphite blue, and other opaque colors, triple the prices. The pattern consists of sunflower blossoms connected by long stalks or vines along with one large sunflower blossom in the center. The cake plate was once given away free in flour bags and remains one of the most commonly found Depression glass items.

Ashtray, 5″ $15
Cake plate, 10″, with 3 legs $15
Creamer $20
Cup $15
Plate, 9″ $20
Saucer $10
Sugar, 2-handled $20
Trivet, 7″, with 3 legs. $325
Tumbler, 4³/₄″ tall, footed $35

SWIRL or PETAL SWIRL   JEANNETTE GLASS COMPANY, 1937–1938

"Swirl" pieces come with two different edge designs: plain or ruffled. The values are the same for both. The colors priced include pink, ultramarine, amber, light blue, and an opaque or delphite blue. "Swirl" is fairly easy to distinguish from spiral and twisted optic patterns since the curves or arcs are not as wide as in the other designs.

Bowl, 5¹/₄″ $15
Bowl, 9″ $25
Bowl, 10¹/₂″, footed $30
Bowl, 10″, 2 tab handles, footed $35
Butter dish with cover $250

Depression glass, "Swirl" pattern. DRAWING BY MARK PICKVET.

Candleholder, double branch $25
Candleholder, single branch $35
Candy dish with 3 legs $20
Candy dish with cover $150
Coaster $15
Creamer $15
Cup $12
Pitcher, 1½ qt., footed (rare) $1750
Plate, 6½″ $10
Plate, 7¼″ $12
Plate, 8″ $15
Plate, 9¼″ $20
Plate, 10½″ $35
Platter, 12½″ $45
Platter, 12″ oval $40
Salt and pepper shakers $75
Saucer $7
Sherbet $20
Sugar, 2-handled $15
Tray, 10½″, 2-handled $35
Tumbler, 4⅝″ tall, 9 oz. $30
Tumbler, 4″ tall, 9 oz. $30
Tumbler, 5¼″ tall, 13 oz. $55
Tumbler, 9 oz., footed $35
Vase, 6½″ tall $30
Vase, 8½″ tall $35

TEA ROOM   INDIANA GLASS COMPANY, 1926–1931

Colors include pink, green, and amber; for crystal, reduce the prices by 50%. "Tea Room" is a fairly popular but expensive pattern. There are many fountain items that were specifically made for ice cream stores (banana boats or splits, parfait glasses, footed tumblers, etc.); for tea rooms, as its name implies (several creamer and sugars, mustards, marmalades, etc.); and for restaurants.

Banana dish, 7½″ long $85
Banana dish, 7½″ long, footed $75
Bowl, 4″ $50

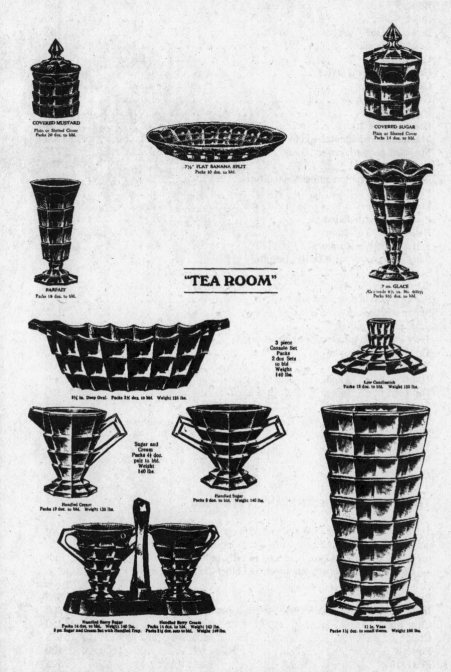

COVERED MUSTARD
Plain or Slotted Cover
Packs 20 doz. to bbl.

7½" FLAT BANANA SPLIT
Packs 10 doz. to bbl.

COVERED SUGAR
Plain or Slotted Cover
Packs 14 doz. to bbl.

PARFAIT
Packs 18 doz. to bbl.

"TEA ROOM"

7 oz. GLACE
Also made 6½ oz. No. 6009½
Packs 8½ doz. to bbl.

9½ in. Deep Oval. Packs 3½ doz. to bbl. Weight 125 lbs.

3 piece
Console Set
Packs
2 doz Sets
to bbl
Weight
140 lbs.

Low Candlestick
Packs 18 doz. to bbl. Weight 130 lbs.

Sugar and
Cream
Packs 4½ doz.
pair to bbl.
Weight
140 lbs.

Handled Cream
Packs 10 doz. to bbl. Weight 130 lbs.

Handled Sugar
Packs 8 doz. to bbl. Weight 140 lbs.

Handled Berry Sugar
Packs 14 doz. to bbl. Weight 140 lbs.
9 pc. Sugar and Cream Set with Handled Tray.

Handled Berry Cream
Packs 14 doz. to bbl. Weight 140 lbs.
Packs 3½ doz. sets to bbl. Weight 140 lbs.

11 in. Vase
Packs 1½ doz. to small tierce. Weight 180 lbs.

Depression glass, "Tea Room" pattern. Reproduced from a 1930 trade catalog.

Bowl, 5″ $50
Bowl, 8¼″ $60
Bowl, 8¾″ tall $85
Bowl, 9½″ oval $65
Candlestick $30
Creamer, several styles $25
Cup $50
Goblet $75
Ice bucket $60
Lamp, 9″, electric $100
Marmalade with notched cover $200
Mustard jar with cover $175
Parfait $75
Pitcher, 2 qt. (rare in amber $500.00) $175
Plate, 6½″ $35
Plate, 8¼″ $40
Plate, 10½″, 2-handled $50
Relish dish, 3 divisions $30
Salt and pepper shakers $75
Sandwich server with center handle $200
Saucer $30
Sherbet, several styles $35
Sugar, 2-handled, several styles $25
Sugar with cover, several styles $125
Sundae dish, ruffled $100
Tray for rectangular creamer and sugar $50
Tumbler, 6 oz., footed $40
Tumbler, 8 oz. $100
Tumbler, 8 oz., footed $40
Tumbler, 11 oz., footed $50
Tumbler, 12 oz., footed $65
Vase, 6½″ tall $125
Vase, 9½″ tall $100
Vase, 11″ tall $125
Vase, 11″ tall, ruffled $200

THISTLE   MACBETH–EVANS, 1929–1930

The primary colors are pink and green; for crystal, reduce prices by 50%. There are only seven pieces listed here, with a couple that are rare. The Mosser Glass Company of Cambridge, Ohio, produced heavily molded pieces in this pattern, including butter dishes, pitchers, tumblers, and others, beginning in the 1980s.

Bowl, 5½″ $25
Bowl, 10¼″ (rare in pink $350) $200
Cake plate, 13″ $150
Cup $25
Plate, 8″ $20
Plate, 10¼″ $25
Saucer $12

THUMBPRINT or PEAR OPTIC   FEDERAL GLASS COMPANY, 1929-1930

"Pear Optic" is Federal's official name for this pattern, but it is more commonly referred to as "Thumbprint." It is green and features an elongated pressed thumbprint design. Note that the design is oval in shape and a little bigger than "Raindrops," a similar Federal pattern. Also note that the pieces are marked with Federal's F within a shield.

Bowl, 4¾"	$5
Bowl, 5"	$7
Bowl, 7"	$10
Bowl, 8"	$12
Creamer	$15
Cup	$7
Plate, 6"	$5
Plate, 8"	$7
Plate, 9¼"	$10
Salt and pepper shakers	$75
Saucer	$3
Sherbet	$7
Sugar	$15
Tumbler, 4" tall, 5 oz.	$7
Tumbler, 5½" tall, 12 oz.	$12
Tumbler, 5" tall, 10 oz.	$10
Whiskey tumbler, 2¼" tall, 1¼" oz.	$10

TWISTED OPTIC   IMPERIAL GLASS COMPANY, 1927-1930

The prices are for pink, green, and amber. For yellow (canary or yellow with a green tint) or light copper blue, double the prices. "Twisted Optic" is commonly confused with Hocking's "Spiral" pattern and less often with some "Swirl" patterns. The curving spirals of "Twisted Optic" turn counterclockwise, while "Spiral" curves move in a clockwise direction. "Spiral" was made only in pink and green, while "Twisted Optic" includes light blue, amber, and yellow pieces.

Basket, 10" tall	$50
Bowl, 4¾" tall	$25
Bowl, 5"	$10
Bowl, 7"	$12
Bowl, 8"	$15
Bowl, 9"	$20
Bowl, 10½"	$25
Bowl, 11½"	$25
Candlestick, 3" tall	$12
Candlestick, 8" tall	$15
Candy jar with cover, with or without feet (several styles)	$40
Cologne bottle with stopper	$50
Creamer	$10

Depression glass, "Twisted Optic" pattern. PHOTO BY ROBIN RAINWATER.

Cup	$6
Marmalade dish with cover	$40
Mayonnaise	$25
Pitcher, 2 qt.	$50
Plate, 6″	$5
Plate, 7″	$6
Plate, 8″	$7
Plate, 9″, oval with indentation	$10
Plate, 10″	$12
Powder jar with cover	$40
Sandwich server with center handle	$30
Saucer	$3
Sherbet	$7
Sugar, 2-handled	$10
Tray, 2-handled	$20
Tumbler, 4¹/₂″ tall, 9 oz.	$7
Tumbler, 5¹/₄″ tall, 12 oz.	$10
Vase, 7¹/₄″ tall, 2-handled	$25
Vase, 8″ tall, 2-handled	$30
Vase, 8″ tall, fan-style, 2-handled	$35

U.S. SWIRL   U.S. GLASS COMPANY, LATE 1920s

The basic colors are pink and green; for crystal, reduce the prices by 50%. A few iridized pieces have been found (same prices as listed). Most of the "U.S. Swirl" pieces have a star in the bottom, which helps in differentiating it from other swirls, spirals, and twisted patterns.

Bowl, 4¹/₂″	$7
Bowl, 5¹/₂″, 1 handle	$12
Bowl, 8¹/₂″ oval	$55
Bowl, 8¹/₄″ oval	$45
Bowl, 8″	$20
Bowl, 10″, octagonal, footed	$75
Butter dish with cover	$125

Candy jar with cover, 2-handled	$40
Creamer	$20
Pitcher, 1½ qt.	$75
Plate, 6″	$3
Plate, 8″	$7
Salt and pepper shakers	$55
Sherbet	$7
Sugar with cover 2-handled	$50
Tumbler, 3½″ tall, 8 oz.	$15
Tumbler, 4¾″ tall, 12 oz.	$20
Vase	$25

VERNON or NO. 616   INDIANA GLASS COMPANY, 1930–1932

This is the last of Indiana's numbered patterns in this chapter. Basic colors are yellow and green. For crystal, reduce the prices by 50%. The yellow is a little more abundant than the green, but both colors are not common. Demand is not great since there are only seven pieces altogether. Some of the crystal pieces were trimmed in platinum. With the platinum completely intact, the crystal pieces are worth a few dollars more than the prices listed. Once again, sparse or incomplete banding can easily be removed, but do not use abrasives that will damage the glass.

Creamer, footed	$30
Cup	$20
Plate, 8″	$12
Plate, 11½″	$35
Saucer	$7
Sugar, footed	$30
Tumbler, 5″, footed	$40

VICTORY   DIAMOND GLASS-WARE COMPANY, 1929–1932

The prices are for amber, pink, and green. For cobalt blue, double the prices; for black, triple them. Cobalt blue and opaque black glass are highly desirable and collectible. Some of the black pieces are trimmed in gold and decorated with flower patterns or other designs (the value is the same as the usual black). The pattern consists of vertical panels (much like a spoke design on the flat rounded pieces). Gravy boats and platters are not commonly found in Depression sets, and the boat here is quite rare.

Bonbon dish	$15
Bowl, 6½″	$15
Bowl, 8½″	$25
Bowl, 9″, oval	$35
Bowl, 11″	$35
Bowl, 12½″	$40
Bowl, 12″	$40

Candlestick $17
Cheese and cracker set (indented plate with compote) $55
Compote $20
Creamer $20
Cup $12
Goblet, 5" tall $25
Gravy boat with matching platter $200
Mayonnaise set (dish, underplate, and ladle) $75
Pitcher, 2 qt. $200
Plate, 6" $7
Plate, 7" $10
Plate, 8" $12
Plate, 9" $20
Platter, 12" $35
Sandwich server with center handle $40

DIAMOND GLASS-WARE CO.
INDIANA, PA.

VICTORY LUNCHEON SET

It is featured in pink or green in many stores. Ask about
it and other items in our extensive line of colored glassware and specialties.

—REPRESENTATIVES—

New York—Fred Skelton, 200 Fifth Avenue.
Chicago—George Turner, 17 North Wabash Avenue.
San Francisco—Himmelstern Bros., 718 Mission Street.
Los Angeles—Himmelstern Bros., 643 S. Olive Street.
Seattle, Wash.—Joseph Brunner.
Boston, Mass.—G. J. Rosenfield.

*Depression glass,
"Victory" pattern.
Reproduced from a
1929 advertisement.*

Saucer	$5
Sherbet	$15
Sugar, 2-handled	$20
Tumbler, various styles	$35

WATERFORD or WAFFLE HOCKING GLASS COMPANY, 1938–1944

The basic color is pink; for crystal, reduce the prices by 50%. Pieces can also be found in milk white, yellow, and reproduction forest green; reduce the prices by 25%. This pattern is similar to Hocking's "Miss America." Both feature a diamond design, although the diamonds are much larger in "Waterford." Some pieces also have the exact same mold design. Note that "Waffle" is a nickname only. This pattern was made after "Miss America" toward the end of the Depression era.

Ashtray, 4″	$12
Ashtray, 4″, with advertising	$20
Bowl, 5½″	$35
Bowl, 5″	$20
Bowl, 8¼″	$30
Butter dish with cover	$225
Coaster	$10
Creamer	$17
Cup	$15
Goblet	$25
Lamp, miniature, 4″	$50
Pitcher, milk, 1 qt.	$100
Pitcher, water, 2½ qt.	$150
Plate, 6″	$7
Plate, 7″	$10
Plate, 9½″	$25
Plate, 10¼″, 2-handled	$25
Platter, 13¾″	$35
Relish, 5 divisions	$30
Salt and pepper shakers	$100
Saucer	$7
Sherbet	$15
Sugar with cover	$40
Tumbler, several styles	$25
Wine glass	$25

WINDSOR or WINDSOR DIAMOND JEANNETTE GLASS COMPANY, 1936–1940s

The basic colors are pink and green. For odd-colored pieces, including light blue, delphite blue, and yellow, double the prices. For the rare red amberina, quadruple them. As with most Depression glass, colored glass production of this pattern ended by 1940; however, pieces were made in crystal through the 1940s (reduce the prices by 50%). The pressed diamond pattern covers most pieces from top to bottom.

Ashtray $40
Boat dish, 11³/₄" oval $50
Bowl, 4³/₄" $15
Bowl, 5" $25
Bowl, 5¹/₂" $25
Bowl, 7", 3-footed $35
Bowl, 8¹/₂" $40
Bowl, 8" $40
Bowl, 9¹/₂" oval $40
Bowl, 8", 2-handled $40
Bowl, 10¹/₂" $40
Bowl, 10¹/₂", pointed edge $100
Bowl, 10¹/₂", pointed edge $100
Bowl, 12¹/₂" $100
Butter dish with cover $100
Cake plate, 10³/₄", footed $25
Candlestick, 3" tall $45
Candy jar with cover $60
Coaster $20
Compote $15
Creamer, 2 styles $15
Cup $12
Pitcher, 1¹/₂ qt. $85
Pitcher, 1 pt. $125
Plate, 6" $10
Plate, 7" $20
Plate, 9" $25
Plate, 10¹/₄", 2-handled $25
Plate, 10", 2-handled $25
Platter, 11¹/₂", oval $30
Platter, 13¹/₃" $50
Powder jar $75
Relish, 3 divisions (common in crystal $15.00) $200
Salt and pepper shakers $55
Saucer $7
Sherbet $35
Sugar with cover, 2 styles $27

Depression glass, "Windsor Diamond" pattern. DRAWING BY MARK PICKVET.

Tray, 4″, square $50
Tray, 4″, square, 2-handled $25
Tray, 9³/₄″ oval $75
Tray, 9³/₄″ oval, 2-handled $35
Tray, 9″, oval, 2-handled $25
Tray, 9″ oval $55
Tumbler, 3¹/₄″ tall, 5 oz. $35
Tumbler, 4¹/₂″ tall, 11 oz. $35
Tumbler, 4″ tall, footed $35
Tumbler, 4″ tall, 9 oz. $35
Tumbler, 5″ tall, 11 oz., footed $40
Tumbler, 5″ tall, 12 oz. $50
Tumbler, 7¹/₄″ tall, footed $60

CHAPTER 7

MODERN AND
MISCELLANEOUS
AMERICAN GLASS

At the turn of the century, the United States was on a wave of growth fueled by invention, technology, industrialization, and the rise of powerful corporations. The glass industry was no exception. After the Depression, smaller companies were overtaken by larger, machine-production-oriented corporations.

Colored glass production of the Depression era was drastically reduced for two primary reasons. One is that many of the elemental metals necessary for coloring were needed for World War II weapons' manufacture. The other is that the Depression colors simply went out of style. Many glass manufacturers qualified as industry essentials and produced glass for the war effort. These included radar, x-ray, and electronic tubes, as well as heat-treated tumblers manufactured specifically for extra strength.

After the war, corporations such as Libbey (a division of Owens-Corning) and Anchor-Hocking emerged as industrial giants, boasting high-speed machinery and high-volume capacity. Handmade, hand-cut, hand-etched, and nearly all other hand operations that had squeaked through the Depression folded by the late 1950s. Such firms as Pairpoint, Heisey, and Cambridge shut down permanently.

A few others, such as Fostoria and Westmoreland, survived into the 1980s, but many more were purchased and swallowed up by larger firms; some continued operation as divisions of these larger companies (Hazel-Ware under Continental Can, for instance). Finally, there were a rare few exceptions, such as Fenton and Steuben, that survived the economic downswings and hard times of the marketplace. They have operated continuously since the turn of the century and continue to etch their mark in glassmaking history.

Despite the difficulties, a variety of collectible glassware has been produced in the United States since the Depression era. Colors were still popular, especially with Jeannette, which made several Depression look-alike patterns such as "Anniversary." Darker colors, like forest green and royal ruby (Anchor-Hocking), and Moroccan amethyst (Hazel-Ware), were used for table sets.

Animal figures and covered animal dishes have been popular since the 19th century, and modern examples have been made by numerous companies (Heisey, New Martinsville, Fenton, Steuben, etc.). The Boyd Art Glass Company has been in existence only since 1978 and already is well established, producing miniature animals and other colorful figurines. Decorated enameled wares include not only animals but also a host of other character figures. "Swanky Swigs" (a product of Kraft Foods), tumblers, pitchers, and other items with machine-applied enameling or transfers have flourished over the past 50 years.

As the Depression colors were phased out, a good deal of crystal, milk, and porcelainlike items were produced. Heisey, Cambridge, and Fostoria all made quality crystal table sets in the 1940s and 1950s. Westmoreland's "Paneled Grape" and Fenton's "Crest" patterns were the largest sets ever produced in milk glass. Chinex, Fire-King, and a host of others produced both oven and tableware that resemble porcelain.

Modern collectible glass includes many reproduction forms, such as Imperial's "New Carnival," other iridescent forms, Carnival-like punch bowl and water sets, popular Depression patterns, Jeannette's miniature "Cameo Ballerina," and others that can be quite confusing when compared to the originals. One firm that has been quite controversial in making reproductions is the Indiana Glass Company. Over the past two decades the company has reproduced a variety of items in the "Sandwich" pattern that originally dates to the early Depression years.

Naturally, the people most upset with reproductions are those who have invested or collected the original. Yet, a company has a legal right to do what it wishes with its own patented lines and machinery. Reproductions give new collectors a chance to acquire beautiful and appealing patterns. Hundreds of years from now, it will probably matter very little if a particular pattern was produced in the 1930s or the 1970s.

On the side of the collector, no one really wishes to see his or her collection devalued because of remakes. Some companies have responded and made their new pieces with slightly different dimensions in new molds or even with different colors. Exact reproductions with original molds can be confusing to buyers and sellers alike, especially if new pieces are advertised or sold unknowingly as antiques. It is still up in the air whether or not reproductions help or hamper the collector's market, but some companies have had mixed results remaking certain styles and patterns of old.

A resurgence in glass and glass collecting has occurred in the United

States over the past 20 years. Several new art glass companies have surfaced, as well as revitalized older ones, resulting in a good deal of quality new glassware. Fenton continues to pour out fancy colored baskets; Steuben, the finest crystal; and Pilgrim, cameo engraving. Such items as spun glass Christmas ornaments are now available.

There are also companies that continue to commission glass lines and new products from various makers. Avon, for example, commissioned Fostoria to make its own Coin Glass items.

Along with modern glassware, this chapter contains some miscellaneous older collectible glass items that do not fit into the other categories. These items include fruit or canning jars, marbles, and animal figurines.

AKRO AGATE   AKRO AGATE COMPANY, 1914–1951

Akro Agate began as a marble manufacturer and quickly became America's leading maker of marbles. The company expanded into novelties, children's miniature dishes, and other generally small items. Akro Agate made glass in solid, opaque, and transparent colors, but its most famous designs were the swirled or spiraled marblelike colors such as red and blue onyx. The most common trademark used was a crow in flight clutching marbles within its claws.

Ashtray, 4½" hexagonal, marbleized colors $25
Ashtray, 4⅛" across, leaf-shaped, marbleized colors $15
Ashtray, 4", round, 1931 Firemen's Convention, solid opaque colors $100
Ashtray, 4", round, Hotel Edison or Hotel Lincoln, solid opaque colors $55
Ashtray, 5¼" oval, Heinz 57 Varieties $55
Ashtray, 5" square, marbleized colors
   Clear $75
   Black $150

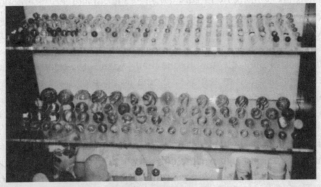

Akro Agate Marbles. PHOTO BY MARK PICKVET.

Ashtray, scallop shell shape, marbleized colors $15

Basket, 4″ tall, 2-handled, marbleized colors $35

Basket, 5″ tall, 1-handled, marbleized colors $250

Bell, 5¹/₄″ tall, marbleized colors $50

Bell, 5¹/₄″ tall, solid or transparent colors $35

Bowl, 5¹/₄″, 3-footed, marbleized colors $25

Bowl, 5¹/₄″, 3-footed, solid colors $15

Bowl, 7¹/₄″, 2 tab handles, marbleized colors $30

Bowl, 7¹/₄″, 2 tab handles, solid colors $20

Bowl, 8″, stemmed, marbleized colors $250

Bowl, 8″, stemmed, solid colors $150

Candlestick, 1³/₄″ tall, marbleized colors $150

Candlestick, 1³/₄″ tall, solid colors $100

Candlestick, 4¹/₄″ tall, marbleized colors $200

Candlestick, 4¹/₄″ tall, solid colors $150

Children's play set, 16-piece concentric ring style (teapot and cover, creamer and sugar, 4 cups and 4 saucers, 4 plates), solid colors

Clear $250

Transparent Cobalt Blue $450

Children's play set, 16-piece concentric ring style (teapot and cover, creamer and sugar, 4 cups and 4 saucers, 4 plates), marbleized colors $375

Children's play set, 21-piece concentric ring style (teapot and cover, creamer and covered sugar, 4 cups and 4 saucers, 4 cereal bowls, 4 plates), marbleized colors $500

Children's play set, 21-piece concentric ring style (teapot and cover, creamer and covered sugar, 4 cups and 4 saucers, 4 cereal bowls, 4 plates), solid colors

Clear $400

Transparent Cobalt Blue $550

Children's play set, 21-piece octagonal style, dark green, blue, or white (4 plates, 4 cups, 4 saucers, pitcher, 4 tumblers, teapot with cover, creamer, and sugar) . . $175

Children's play set, 21-piece octagonal style, lemonade or Ox blood (4 plates, 4 cups, 4 saucers, pitcher, 4 tumblers, teapot with cover, creamer, and sugar) . . $550

Children's play set, 21-piece stacked disk and interior panel design (teapot with cover, creamer and sugar, 4 cups and 4 saucers, 4 plates, pitcher and 4 tumblers (solid opaque colors) $400

Children's play set, 21-piece stacked disk and interior panel design (teapot with cover, creamer and sugar, 4 cups and 4 saucers, 4 plates, pitcher, and 4 tumblers), transparent cobalt blue or transparent green $500

Children's play set, 21-piece stacked disk style (teapot with cover, creamer and sugar, 4 cups and 4 saucers, 4 plates, pitcher and 4 tumblers), solid colors other than green or white $175

Children's play set, 21-piece stacked disk style (teapot with cover, creamer and sugar, 4 cups and 4 saucers, 4 plates, pitcher and 4 tumblers), solid green or white $125

Children's play set, 8-piece concentric ring style (tea pot and cover, sugar and creamer, 4 saucers), solid colors

Clear $175

Transparent Cobalt Blue $200

Children's play set, 8-piece concentric ring style (teapot and cover, sugar and creamer, 4 saucers), marbleized colors $275

Children's play set, 8-piece stacked disk and interior panel design (teapot with cover, creamer and sugar, 2 cups, 2 saucers, 2 plates), solid opaque colors .. $150

Children's play set, 8-piece stacked disk and interior panel design (teapot with cover, 2 cups, 2 saucers, and 2 plates), transparent cobalt blue $225

Children's play set, 8-piece stacked disk style (pitcher with cover, 2 cups, 2 saucers, and 2 plates) solid green or white $55

Children's play set, 8-piece stacked disk style (teapot with cover, 2 cups, 2 saucers, and 2 plates), solid colors other than green or white $75

Cup and saucer, demitasse, 2⅛″ tall, 4 ¼″ diameter, marbleized colors $30

Cup and saucer, demitasse, 2⅛″ tall, 4 ¼″ diameter, solid colors

   Clear $20

   Solid orange or black $125

   Transparent colors $200

Flower pot, 3″ tall, smooth or scalloped top, solid colors $20

Flower pot, 3″ tall, smooth or scalloped top, marbleized colors $30

Jardiniere, 5″ tall, scalloped or rectangular top, with or without tab handles, marbleized colors $45

Jardiniere, 5″ tall, scalloped or rectangular top, with or without tab handles, solid colors $30

Marble, glass, 1 marble in 1⅛″ square single box $800

Marble, glass, 10-piece set with original box $40

Marble, glass, 35-piece set with original box, large opaque slags $750

Marble, glass, 5-piece set with original box $25

Marbles, glass, 10-piece set with Popeye pouch $850

Marbles, glass, 100-piece set with original box, striped onyx marbles $750

Marbles, glass, 25-piece set with original box $75

Marbles, glass, 50-piece set with original box $150

Marbles, glass, 70-piece set in tin with pouch $550

Marbles, glass, Chinese checker set, 36-piece $75

Marbles, glass, solitary checker set, 25-piece $75

Marbles, glass, 100-piece set with original box $300

Puff box, Apple style (includes cover) solid colors $250

   Crystal only $75

Puff box with colonial lady cover, solid covers $75

Puff box with colonial lady cover, transparent colors $1000

Puff box with Scottish terrier cover, solid colors $75

Puff box with Scottish terrier cover, transparent colors $250

Smoker's set, 4 small ashtrays and cigarette holder (holder resembles a tumbler), marbleized colors $75

Urn, 3¼″ tall, square foot, marbleized colors $25

Vase, 3¼″ tall, cornucopia, marbleized holder $25

Vase, 6¼″ tall, scalloped or smooth tip, with or without tab handles, solid colors $35

Vase, 6¼″ tall, scalloped or smooth top, with or without tab handles, marbleized colors $50

ANNIVERSARY   JEANNETTE GLASS COMPANY, 1947–1949,1970s

Pink and crystal "Anniversary" patterned glass is easily confused with Depression glass, while the newer iridized pieces are confused with Carnival glass; however, both were produced years later than the older periods. Iridized pieces sell for slightly less than pink or about double the crystal prices. A few pieces were trimmed in gold (increase prices by 25%).

Bowl, 7¹/₂″
Crystal $6
Pink $15

Bowl, 9″
Crystal $10
Pink $18

Bowl, berry, 4³/₄″
Crystal $2
Pink $6

Butter dish with cover
Crystal $25
Pink $55

Cake plate, 12¹/₂″
Crystal $7.5
Pink $15

Cake plate with metal cover
Crystal $8
Pink $17

Candlestick
Crystal $5
Pink $10

Candy jar and cover
Crystal $17
Pink $35

Compote, 3-footed
Crystal $3
Pink $10

Creamer
Crystal $3
Pink $10

Cup
Crystal $2
Pink $8

Pickle dish
Crystal $3
Pink $8

Plate, 6¹/₄″
Crystal $1
Pink $3

Plate, 9″
Crystal $2
Pink $9

Platter, 12$\frac{1}{2}$"
    Crystal $4
    Pink $12
Relish dish
    Crystal $3
    Pink $10
Saucer
    Crystal $2
    Pink $4
Sherbet
    Crystal $3
    Pink $8
Sugar with cover
    Crystal $7
    Pink $20
Vase, 6$\frac{1}{2}$" tall
    Crystal $12
    Pink $27
Wine glass, 2$\frac{1}{2}$ oz.
    Crystal $6
    Pink $16

AVON GLASS COLLECTIBLES   1920s–PRESENT

Although not a maker of glass products, Avon has commissioned hundreds of products since the late 1920s. Popular modern sets that are issued a piece at a time (two or three annually) include the ruby red "Cape Cod" pattern, the "Hummingbird" crystal pattern (made in France), and even some coin glass and other glass products made by Fostoria.

Basket, candle, crystal with gold handle, Diamond pattern, Fostoria $17
Bell, 4$\frac{3}{4}$" tall, crystal with red heart handle $17
Bell, 5$\frac{3}{4}$" tall, Etched Frosted Hummingbird pattern $17
Bell, 5" tall, crystal heart handle $17
Bell, 6$\frac{1}{2}$" tall, red, Cape Cod pattern $15
Bowl, 5$\frac{1}{4}$", etched Frosted Hummingbird pattern $15
Bowl, finger (small), (held bath cubes), Cape Cod pattern, Red $10
Butter dish with cover, 7" long, $\frac{1}{4}$ lb. size, Cape Cod pattern, Red $22
Cake plate, 12" diameter, footed, Etched Frosted Hummingbird pattern $40
Candleholder, 2$\frac{5}{8}$" tall, Etched Frosted Hummingbird pattern $15
Candleholder, 3$\frac{3}{4}$" diameter, Cape Cod pattern, Red $10
Candleholder, hurricane, Cape Cod pattern, Red $15
Candlestick, 3" tall, crystal with holly decoration $7
Candlestick, 7" tall, Crystal Heart pattern, Fostoria $17
Candlestick cologne bottle with stopper, 5 oz., Cape Cod pattern, Red $12
Candlette, turtle figure (shell holds candle), 4$\frac{1}{2}$" long, Crystal Diamond pattern .
.... $12
Candy dish, 3$\frac{1}{2}$" tall, 6" diameter, Cape Cod pattern, Red $15
Candy dish with cover, 6" tall, Etched Frosted Hummingbird pattern $37

Avon, Fostoria Coin glass. PHOTO BY ROBIN RAINWATER.

Canning jar replica, blue glass with glass lid and wire bail, Pressed Sunburst (Aztec) pattern $8
Champagne glass, 9″ tall, Etched Frosted Hummingbird pattern $17
Chess set, 16 dark amber and 16 light amber 3 oz. bottles with silverplated chess piece tops (complete 32 piece set). $450
Chess set, 3 oz., amber bottles, 6-piece set (king, queen, rook, bishop, knight, and pawn) $100
Christmas ornament, 3¹/₂″ tall, Etched Frosted Hummingbird pattern $10
Christmas ornament, 3¹/₄″ across, hexagon, red with plaid cloth bow, Cape Cod pattern $10
Cold cream box with silver color, Rose brand, early 1930s, Milk White $55
Compote, 4″ tall, crystal with holly decoration $15
Condiment tray (small), Cape Cod pattern, Red $15
Creamer, 3¹/₂″ tall, Cape Cod pattern, Red $12
Cruet with stopper, 5 oz., Cape Cod pattern, Red $12
Cup, 3¹/₂″ tall, Cape Cod pattern, Red $10
Cup, loving, no handle, 6⁷/₈″ tall, Crystal Heart pattern, Fostoria $20
Decanter, miniature with stopper, 5 oz., bath oil, Hobnail design, 1972, Milk White $10
Decanter, wine with stopper, 16 oz., (held bubble bath) Cape Cod pattern, Red $22
Goblet, 8¹/₄″ tall, Etched Frosted Hummingbird pattern $17
Goblet, 8¹/₈″ tall, blue with frosted George Washington medallion, Fostoria Coin Glass $22
Goblet, 8¹/₈″ tall, blue with frosted Martha Washington medallion, Fostoria Coin Glass $22
Goblet, water, with candle, Cape Cod pattern, Red $12
Harvester, 1973, Amber $7
Heart box with cover, 4″ across, Cape Cod pattern, Red $18
Mug, 5″ tall, footed, Cape Cod pattern, Red $6
Napkin ring, 1¹/₂″ long, Cape Cod pattern, Red $6
Pitcher, milk, 8″ tall, Etched Frosted Hummingbird pattern $32
Pitcher, miniature Grecian, 5 oz., bath oil, 1972, Milk White $7

Pitcher, sauce, 5¹/₂″ tall, blue with frosted Mount Vernon medallion, Fostoria Coin Glass $27
Pitcher, water, 8¹/₄″ tall, Cape Cod pattern, Red $27
Plate, 7¹/₂″, Etched Frosted Hummingbird pattern $15
Plate, dessert, Cape Cod pattern, Red $15
Plate, dinner, Cape Cod pattern, Red $18
Platter, round, 11″, crystal with holly and berry design $17
Platter, round, 12¹/₂″, Etched Frosted Hummingbird pattern $45
Powder box, 3 oz., "Nearness Body," satin with blue speckled lid, 1956 ..... $17
Powder sachet, 1¹/₂ oz., cranberry with silver cover, 1969 .... $12
Salt and pepper shakers with stainless steel tops, 3″ tall, Etched Frosted Hummingbird pattern $25
Salt cellar, 4 feet, crystal with matching silver spoon, Fostoria $12
Saltshaker, Cape Cod pattern, Red $8
Sauce boat, 8″ long, 1 handle, pouring lip, Cape Cod pattern, Red $30
Saucer, 5³/₄″, Cape Cod pattern, Red $10
Tumbler, 3³/₄″ tall, footed, Cape Cod pattern, Red $10
Tumbler, 5¹/₂″ tall, Cape Cod pattern, Red $10
Vase, 5″ tall, heart-shaped, Fostoria, Crystal $12
Vase, 7¹/₂″ tall, thick, Etched Frosted Hummingbird pattern $40
Vase, 8″ tall, Cape Cod pattern, Red $20
Vase, bud, 9¹/₂″ tall, Etched Frosted Hummingbird pattern $27
Vase, grape bud, 6 oz., bath oil, 1973, Amethyst $7
Wine glass, 6³/₄″ tall, Etched Frosted Hummingbird pattern $17
Wine glass with candle, Cape Cod pattern, Red $12

BEADED EDGE   WESTMORELAND GLASS COMPANY, LATE 1930s–1950s

The original name of this pattern is Westmoreland's "Pattern #22 Milk Glass." "Beaded Edge" is a nickname given to it by collectors. The coral red color was named by Westmoreland and is simply milk glass with a fired-on red edge. Decorated patterns include eight different fruits as well as eight different flowers (total of 16 decorated patterns). Westmoreland also made a few pieces in a similar pattern referred to as "#108." For coral red or decorated patterns, double the prices.

Bowl, 5″ $7
Bowl, 6″ oval $10
Creamer $12
Cup $20
Plate, 6″ $7
Plate, 7″ or 8¹/₂″ $10
Plate, 10¹/₂″ $20
Plate, 15″, cake $35
Platter, 12″ oval, with 2 handle tabs $35
Relish dish, 3-part $32
Salt and pepper shakers $35
Saucer $3
Sherbet $9

Sugar $12
Tumbler $12

BICENTENNIAL/PATRIOTIC GLASS   VARIOUS COMPANIES, 20TH CENTURY

Many glass companies like Fenton produced souvenir items for the U.S. Bicentennial. "Stars and Stripes" was a patriotic pattern much like souvenir glass created by Anchor Hocking during World War II. The pattern was adapted from the old Hocking Glass Company "Queen Mary" molds.

Bell, Patriot Cameo Embossed design, 1974-1976, chocolate, Patriot red, or Independence blue Carnival colors (Fenton) $50
Compote with cover, bald eagle finial, Jefferson Memorial design, 1974-1976, chocolate color, limited edition of 3600 (Fenton) $225
Compote with cover, bald eagle finial, Jefferson Memorial design, 1974–1976, Independence blue Carnival color, limited edition of 7600 (Fenton) $175
Compote with cover, bald eagle finial, Jefferson Memorial design, 1974–1976, Patriot red color, limited edition of 3600 (Fenton) $225
Fruit jar, Ball Ideal, 1 pt., clear with various Bicentennial scenes on reverse $3
Fruit jar, Ball Ideal, 1 qt., clear with various Bicentennial scenes on reverse $5
Paperweight, bald eagle design with circle base, chocolate, Patriot red, or Independence blue Carnival colors, 1974–1976 (Fenton) $50
Planter, Patriot Cameo Embossed design, 1974–1976, Valley Forge milk white or Independence blue Carnival colors (Fenton) $50
Plate, 8″, Stars and Stripes pattern, 1942 (Anchor-Hocking), Crystal $20
Plate, bald eagle design, chocolate or Patriot red colors, 1974–1976 (Fenton) ... $75
Platter, 15″, milk glass with multicolored enameled American eagle $50
Sherbet, Stars and Stripes pattern, 1942 (Anchor-Hocking) $25
Stein, no lid, Valley Forge design, chocolate or Patriot red colors, 1974–1976 (Fenton) $75
Swanky Swig tumbler, Bicentennial issue, 3³/₄″ tall, 1975–1976, green, red, and yellow $7
Tumbler, 5″, 10 oz., Stars and Stripes pattern, 1942 (Anchor-Hocking), Crystal $20

BLENKO GLASS COMPANY   1922–PRESENT

This company was founded by English immigrant William J. Blenko in 1922. The company began as a producer of stained glass windows but later switched to more contemporary art glass forms. Characterisitc of the pieces are bright, vibrant colors and art styles such as crackling and bubbling.

Apple, 2¹/₂″ tall, ruby red with applied crystal stem $20
Ashtray, 6¹/₂″ diameter, bubble effect, Blue $12
Ashtray, 7″ diameter, Hinged Clam Shell design, Green $12
Ball, hollow, 5″ diameter, Ruby Red $35
Basket, 8³/₄″ tall, Cobalt Blue $25

Blenko glass. PHOTOS BY ROBIN RAINWATER.

Bowl, rose, 5½″ tall, Cobalt Blue $15
Bowl, rose, 7¾″ tall, Pale Emerald Green $17
Candlestick, green with crystal twist stem $40

Champagne Bucket, 11³/₄″, top handle, Opaline Yellow $25
Compote, 7¹/₂″ tall, 9³/₄″ diameter, Opaline Yellow or Cobalt Blue $20
Decanter with stopper, 13″ tall, Ruby Red $75
Decanter, ship's, 10″ tall, green with crystal stopper $35
Fish, 10″ tall, globe-shaped, fin feet, large mouth opening, Crystal $35
Fish, 16″ long, fin feet, large mouth opening, Opaline Yellow $40
Fish, 22″ long, fin feet, large mouth opening, Cobalt Blue $55
Goblet, flattened knob on stem, Cobalt Blue $30
Hat vase, 7¹/₂″ tall, 16″ diameter, crystal with yellow band $40
Highball glass, crystal with green foot $20
Penguin, 9¹/₂″ tall, sapphire blue cased in crystal $35
Penguin, 14″ tall, sapphire blue cased in crystal $45
Pitcher, milk, 5¹/₂″ tall, 32 oz., Green Crackle design $20
Pitcher, water, 14″ tall, Ruby Red $75
Pitcher, water, deep blue, Bubble Effect design $35
Plate, 9″, Ruby Red $17
Plate, 12″, crimped, Blue $25
Platter, 13¹/₂″, circular, circles, X's, and squares $17
Punch bowl, 11″ tall, aquamarine on crystal stand $175
Punch cup, crystal with ruby red handle $12
Sherbet, 6″ tall, ruby with crystal twist stem $30
Tumbler, 7″ tall, ruby red crackle glass $10
Tumbler, iced tea, footed, Dark Amethyst $17
Vase, 7¹/₂″ tall, flared, Amber $17
Vase, 7¹/₂″ tall, 7″ diameter, Opaline Yellow $30
Vase, 11¹/₂″ tall, flared, footed, amber with optic ribbing $60
Vase, 11″ tall, ruffled, crystal with circular blue lines $35
Vase, 14¹/₂″ tall, cylindrical, Pale Emerald Green $25
Vase, 22″ tall, 11¹/₂″ diameter top, Crystal $45
Vase, 24″ tall, tapered neck at top, Cobalt Blue $50

BOYD ART GLASS   1978–PRESENT

Boyd began production in 1978. All pieces are marked with a "B" in a diamond; some have a single line under the diamond (1983–1988) or an additional line above the diamond (1988–present). The pieces are all miniatures, and colors come in satins, slags, swirls, etc. Colors are named by the company.

Airplane, black Carnival $20
Basket, 4¹/₂″ tall, Olde Lyme (Forest Green) $12
Bear, fuzzy, Cambridge blue $10
Bear, Patrick balloon, Carmel $10
Bear, Patrick balloon, Enchantment $27
Bear, Patrick balloon, Spinnaker blue $10
Bell, owl head finial, Translucent white opal $12
Bunny salt dip, Blue $22
Bunny salt dip, Sunburst $16
Bunny, Brian, Vaseline $12
Bunny, Brian, Oxford gray $11

Boyd art glass miniatures.
PHOTOS BY ROBIN RAINWATER.

Bunny, Brian, Ruby red $22
Butterfly, Katie, Light Windsor blue $9
Candy dish with cover, Persimmon $12
Car slipper, Platinum carnival $17
Car, Tucker model, Buckeye $12
Cat, kitten, Miss Cotton, Light Windsor blue $9
Chick, Bermuda, 1″ $16
Chick, Enchantment, 1″ $8
Chick, John's Surprise, 1″ $27
Chick, Royalty, 1″ $80
Clown, Freddie Hobo, Cobalt Blue Carnival $12
Deer, Bingo, Heliotrope (very dark brown) $12
Dog, Bull Dog's Head, Golden Delight (amber) $8
Dog, Parlour Pup #1, Mulberry Mist (light lilac) $8
Dog, Parlour Pup #2, Milk White Opal $8
Dog, Parlour Pup #3, Carmel $8
Dog, Parlour Pup #4, Bermuda slag (reddish-brown) $8
Doll, Elizabeth, Black satin $11
Doll, Elizabeth, Lime Carnival $35
Duck salt dip, Dove Blue $12
Duck salt dip, Light Peach $8
Duck, Debbie, Shasta White (light tan) $8
Duckling, Shasta White (light tan) $6
Elephant, Zack, Cobalt blue $45
Elephant, Zack, Flame $45
Elephant, Zack, Furr green $27

Hen, 3″, Carmine $70
Hen, 3″, Pink Champagne $35
Hen, 5″, Ruby-gold $60
Hen covered dish, Shasta White (light tan) $15
Honey jar with cover, Lemonade (vaseline) $16
Horse, Joey, Chocolate $40
Horse, Joey, Zack Boyd slag $12
Jewel box, Cornsilk $12
Jewel box, Sam Jones slag $42
Kitten with pillow, Apricot $22
Kitten with pillow, Royalty $25
Lamb covered dish, 5″ long, Golden Delight (amber) $12
Lamp salt dip, Lime Carnival $10
Mouse, Willie, Lime Carnival $10
Owl, Mulberry Mist (light lilac) $10
Penguin, Artie, Black Carnival $12
Pig, Suee, Shasta White (light tan) $8
Robin covered dish, Golden Delight (amber) $12
Skate boot, Heather $15
Slipper, Cat, Orange Calico $12
Squirrel, Sammie, Shasta White (light tan) $8
Swan, 3″ long, Azure Blue $8
Tomahawk, Milk White $13
Toothpick holder, forget-me-not, Carmine $40
Toothpick holder, forget-me-not, Teal Swirl $12
Toothpick holder, heart, Mint Green $25
Train, 6-piece, Teal $75
Train, 6-piece, (yellow engine, baby blue coal car, dark cobalt blue box car, Candyland coal hopper, bamboo tank car, and ruby red caboose) $60
Tucker car, Cobalt Blue $12
Tugboat, Teddy, Peridot Green $10
Turkey covered dish, 5″ long, Shasta White (light tan) $12
Turtle, Alexandrite $8
Unicorn, Lucky, Mulberry Carnival $10
Vase, Candy Swirl $16
Vase, Dark Tangerine slag $20
Vase, 6″ tall, beaded, Lilac $17
Woodchuck, Touch of Pink $8

BUBBLE or BULL'S-EYE or PROVINCIAL ANCHOR–HOCKING GLASS COMPANY, 1934–1965

The basic colors are forest green, royal ruby, jadeite, and a very light ice blue. For crystal, reduce the prices by 50%.

Bowl, 4″ $17
Bowl, 5¹⁄₂″ $12
Bowl, 5″ $10
Bowl, 7³⁄₄″ $12

Bowl, 8¹/₂″ $15
Candlestick $10
Creamer $25
Cup $6
Lamp, Crystal only $60
Pitcher, water $75
Plate, 6³/₄″ $4
Plate, 9¹/₂″ $7
Plate, 9¹/₂″ grill (divided) $20
Platter, 12″ oval $17
Saucer $2
Sugar $25
Tidbit, 2-tier $35
Tumbler, 4¹/₂″ tall, 12 oz. $10
Tumbler, 5⁷/₈″ tall, 16 oz. $15
Tumbler, 5⁷/₈″ tall, 16 oz., footed $17
Tumbler, 6 oz. $7

CAMBRIDGE ANIMALS   1920s–1958

Cambridge was a large producer of crystal dinnerware and stemware. The quality of the crystal was quite good, and the company survived the Depression by making colored glass products. After some profitable years following World War II, Cambridge eventually had trouble competing with cheaper products that assailed the market. The wildlife re-creations here are just some of Cambridge's collectible glassware. Note that some of the Cambridge animal molds were purchased by the Summit Art Glass Company in the 1980s. Some have been reproduced.

Blue jay flower holder $225
Buffalo Hunt console, Mystic Blue $350
Dog (Bridge Hound), 1¹/₂″, variety of colors $40
Eagle bookend $125
Heron, 9″, flower frog (small) $100
Heron, 12″, flower frog (large) $150
Heron and Cattails cocktail shaker, 10″ tall, cobalt blue with sterling silver cover
.... $100
Lion bookend $150
Pigeon, Pouter, bookend $100
Scottish terrier bookend $125
Scottish terrier, Frosted $100
Sea Gull flower frog $75
Swan, 3¹/₂″ long, Carmen $150
Swan, 3¹/₂″ long, Crown Tuscan $65
Swan, 3¹/₂″ long, Pink $65
Swan, 3¹/₂″ long, Smoke or Transparent gray $400
Swan, 3¹/₂″ long, Yellow $65
Swan, 3¹/₂″ long, Ebony $85
Swan, 3¹/₂″ long, Emerald green $50
Swan, 3¹/₂″ long, Milk White $125
Swan, 3¹/₂″ long, Milk White with gold trim $150
Swan, 3¹/₂″ long, Peach $65

Swan, 4¹/₂″ long, Milk White $150
Swan, 4¹/₂″ long, signed, Ebony $125
Swan, 6¹/₂″ long, Carmen $325
Swan, 6¹/₂″ long, Yellow (Mandarin Gold) $150
Swan, 6¹/₂″ long, Crystal $75
Swan, 6¹/₂″ long, Ebony $150
Swan, 6¹/₂″ long, Emerald green $100
Swan, 6¹/₂″ long, Milk White $175
Swan, 8¹/₂″ long, Milk White $300
Swan, 8¹/₂″ long, Amber $500
Swan, 8¹/₂″ long, Blue (rare) $1250
Swan, 8¹/₂″ long, Carmen $350
Swan, 8¹/₂″ long, Crystal $85
Swan, 8¹/₂″ long, Ebony $175
Swan, 8¹/₂″ long, Emerald green $150
Swan, 8¹/₂″ long, variety of colors, Crown Tuscan $175
Swan, 8¹/₂″ long, with enameled floral design, Crown Tuscan, Opalescent White . .
.... $750
Swan, 10¹/₂″ long, Ebony $275
Swan, 10¹/₂″ long, Pink $375
Swan, 12¹/₂″ long, Amber $100
Swan, 12¹/₂″ long, Ebony $350
Swan, 13″, with amber shading, Ruby Red $175
Swan candlestick, 4¹/₂″ tall, Milk White $225
Turkey dish with cover, Green $500
Turkey dish with cover, Blue $550
Turkey dish with cover, Pink $450
Turtle-shaped flower frog, Opaque Pink $350

CAMEO MINIATURES   MOSSER GLASS, INC., 1980s–PRESENT

The original "Cameo" was made in full scale during the Depression (see Chapter 6). Those pieces listed here are miniature reproductions made in yellow, pink, and green (the prices are the same for all colors). The pattern is a little weaker on the small versions but is still very pretty, especially when an entire set is acquired. Thanks to their size, there is no problem distinguishing them from the originals. This version of "Cameo" is also referred to as "Ballerina" or "Dancing Girl," in reference to the image in the medallion.

Bowl, cereal, 2¹¹/₁₆″ $5
Bowl, fruit, 5¹/₂″, 1¹/₂″ tall, 3-footed $12
Bowl, salad, 4³/₁₆″, 1″ tall $8
Bowl, serving, 5″ oval, ⁷/₈″ tall, (including 2 tab handles) $11
Bowl, soup, 4¹/₂″ $6
Butter dish with cover, 2¹/₄″ tall, 3¹/₂″ underplate diameter, 2⁵/₈″ dome diameter . . .
.... $12
Cake plate, 5″ diameter, 3 feet, ⁵/₈″ tall $12
Candlestick, 2″ tall $7
Cracker jar with cover, 3³/₄″ tall $17
Creamer, 1¹¹/₁₆″ tall $7

Creamer, 2¹/₄″ tall $7
Cup, 1¹/₈″ tall $3
Goblet, 3″ tall $6
Ice cream bucket, 1¹/₂″ tall, 2⁵/₈″ diameter, 2 tab handles $11
Jam jar with cover, 2¹/₂″ tall, 3″ bottom diameter $12
Mayonnaise dish, 1⁵/₈″ tall, stemmed, 2³/₄″ top diameter $8
Mayonnaise jar with cover, 2¹/₂″ tall, 3″ bottom diameter $12
Parfait, 2³/₈″ tall, round foot $5
Pitcher, milk, 3″ tall, slim $8
Pitcher, water, 3″ tall, wide $12
Plate, 4³/₄″ $6
Plate, dessert, 3¹/₁₆″ $3
Plate, grill, 5¹/₄″ $6
Plate, octagonal, 4³/₁₆″ across $5
Relish dish, 3¹¹/₁₆″ diameter, 2 tab handles, ⁷/₈″ tall $8
Saucer, 3″ $3
Sherbet, 1⁵/₈″ tall $4
Sugar, 2-handled $7
Sugar dish, 1⁹/₁₆″ tall, 2-handled $6
Tray, 5⁷/₈″ oval, (including 2 tab handles) $11
Tumbler, water, 11³/₁₆″ tall $3
Vase, 4¹/₈″ tall $15

CANDLEWICK   IMPERIAL GLASS COMPANY, 1936–1982

This is another popular set that was made continuously from the 1930s until Imperial closed in 1982. Candlewick is unmarked except for paper labels; however, it is easily identified by beaded crystal stems, handles, and rims. The name of the pattern is derived from tufted needlework.

Ashtray, 2³/₄″ $5
Ashtray, 4¹/₄″ × 3″ rectangular $5
Ashtray, 6¹/₂″, Eagle design $60
Ashtray, 6¹/₂″, Heart design $25
Basket, 5″ tall, Beaded handle $200
Bell, 4″ tall $40
Bowl, 5″, Blue $55
Bowl, 5″ across, heart-shaped $17
Bowl, 5″ square $60
Bowl, 6″, 3-footed $45
Bowl, 7″ square $80
Bowl, 7″, 2 handles $20
Bowl, 8¹/₂″, divided, 2 handles $65
Bowl, 9″ across, Heart-shaped $85
Bowl, 10″, Blue $125
Bowl, 10″, 2 handles $60
Bowl, 10″, flared, fluted, footed $200
Bowl, 11″, flared $75
Bowl, 14″ oval, flared $175
Bowl, rose, 7¹/₂″, footed $150

IMPERIAL GLASS CORPORATION, BELLAIRE, OHIO

"Candlewick" pattern. Reproduced from a 1940s advertisement.

Brandy glass	$30
Bunny on nest dish, Blue satin	$55
Butter dish with cover, ¼ lb. size	$30
Butter dish with cover, 5½″ round	$35
Cake stand, 10″, low foot	$55
Cake stand, 11″	$65
Calender desk, 1947 edition	$125
Candleholder, 2-light	$25
Candleholder, 3½″ tall	$27
Candleholder, 5″ tall, Heart design	$40
Candleholder, 6″ tall, urn-shaped	$65

Candy box with cover, 7″ tall $175
Celery dish, 11″ oval $60
Cigarette box with cover $40
Claret glass $40
Clock, 4″, circular $175
Coaster, 4″ $7
Compote, 5½″, plain stem $20
Compote, 5″, 2-beaded stem $30
Cordial $75
Creamer, domed feet $75
Creamer, footed $12
Creamer, individual (small) $10
Cruet with stopper, etched "Vinegar" $60
Cup $10
Decanter with stopper, 11½″ tall $50
Egg cup $45
Egg plate, 12″, center handle $125
Fork (large), serving $25
Goblet, 10 oz., footed $22
Goblet, 9 oz., footed $20
Gravy boat $200
Ice tub, 5½″ × 8″, 2 handles $100
Knife, butter $175
Ladle, mayonnaise $10
Mirror, standing, 4½″ diameter $100
Mustard jar with cover $50
Nut cup $12
Perfume bottle with stopper $50
Pickle dish, 7½″ oval $25
Pitcher, 40 oz. $250
Pitcher, 64 oz. $75
Pitcher, 80 oz. $250
Pitcher, low foot (small), 16 oz. $250
Plate, 4½″ $6
Plate, 8½″ $15
Plate, 8″ $12
Plate, 9″ oval $30
Plate, 10″, 2 tab handles $25
Plate, 12 ½″ torte, cupped edge $45
Plate, 14″, Birthday Cake design, holes for 72 candles $350
Platter, 13″ oval $80
Platter, 14″ round $75
Punch bowl with matching underplate $275
Punch cup $15
Punch ladle $35
Relish dish, 6″, 2 divisions $25
Relish dish, 6 divisions $55
Relish dish, 8½″, 4 divisions $35
Relish dish, 10½″, 3 divisions, 3-footed $100
Relish dish, 13 ½″, 5 divisions $75
Salt and pepper shakers, chrome tops, beaded foot $22

Salt dip, 2¼″ $10
Sandwich server, 11¾″, center handle (run red $750). $45
Sandwich server with heart center handle, 8½″ $35
Saucer $5
Sherbet, 5 oz. $20
Sherbet, 6 oz. $25
Spoon (large), serving $25
Sugar dish, footed $25
Sugar, individual (small) $10
Tidbit, 3-piece $110
Tray, 4½″ (for salt and pepper shakers) $17
Tray, 5½″, 2 upturned handles $25
Tray, 6½″ $20
Tray, 8½″, 2 handles $30
Tray, 9″ oval, beaded foot $30
Tumbler, 5 oz. $20
Tumbler, 9 oz., footed $22
Tumbler, 10 oz. $25
Tumbler, 12 oz. $50
Tumbler, 16 oz. $75
Vase, 10″ tall, footed $150
Vase, 8½″ tall, flared, beaded foot $100
Vase, 8″ tall, crimped $50
Vase, 8″ tall, fan style, beaded handles $35
Vase, bud, 4″ tall $55
Vase, bud, 7″ tall $175
Wine glass, 4 oz. $25

CANNING JARS   1850s–PRESENT

Canning or fruit jars have been made in the millions for well over a century. There are off brands and rare colors from the 19th and early 20th centuries, however, that are quite valuable today. Nearly all jars feature embossed writing and/or designs. Where a color is not designated below, the jar is clear glass. Also, assume that the top is threaded for a zinc or brass screw-on cap unless glass cover or glass lid is indicated.

A.G. Smalley & Co., Boston and New York, ½ pt. $17
Acme LG Co., 1893, ½ gal. $300
Acme, ground lip glass, 1 qt., Emerald Green $300
AD & H Chambers Union fruit jar, 1 qt., wax sealer, Blue $165
Agee or Agee Victory, 1 qt., Light green or Amber $35
Amazon Swift Seal, 1 qt., Blue $12
Anchor-Hocking, embossed Anchor logo, 1 qt. $2
Atlas, E-Z Seal, glass cover, 1 pt., Aqua $35
Atlas Good Luck, 1 qt., Clover design, Clear $4
Atlas Strong Shoulder Mason, 1 pt., Aqua $5
Atlas Strong Shoulder Mason, glass cover, Light blue or Olive green $20
Atlas, E-Z Seal, 1 qt., Apple green $25

American glass, canning jars. PHOTO BY ROBIN RAINWATER.

Atlas, E-Z Seal, glass cover, 1 qt., Amber $50
Automatic Sealer, 1 qt., Aqua $150
Ball Eclipse, 1 pt., Clear $6
Ball Ideal, 1 pt., clear with various Bicentennial scenes on reverse $3
Ball Ideal, 1 qt., clear with various Bicentennial scenes on reverse $5
Ball Ideal, 1/2 pt., Blue $35
Ball Mason, 1 pt., Olive Green $35
Ball Perfect Mason, 1 qt., zinc cover, Blue $15
Ball Perfect Mason, 1 pt., Dark Olive green $65
Ball Perfect Mason, 2 qt., Amber $65
Ball Perfect Mason, 2 qt., Emerald Green $75
Ball Sanitary Sure Seal, 1 qt., Blue $8
Banner, 1 qt., Blue $10
Banner, Widemouth, 1/2 pt., Blue $75
Banner, Widemouth, 1/2 pt. $50
Beaver, Embossed Name and Animal, 1 qt., Aqua or blue $85
Beaver, Embossed Name and Animal, 1 qt. $25
Beaver, Embossed Name and Animal, 1/2 gal., Olive Green or amber $750
Boyd's, 1 qt., Light Green or aqua $5
Brockway Sur-Grip Mason, 1 qt., Clear $5
Burlington, 1 qt. $60
C.F. Spencer's Patent, Rochester, N.Y., 1 qt., Aqua $150
Canton, 2 qt., 1870–1890, Cobalt Blue $5000
Canton Domestic, 1 pt. $175
Carter's Butter and Fruit Preserving, glass lid, 1897 .... $150
Clark's Peerless, 1 pt., Cornflower Blue or Emerald Green $35
Coronet with embossed crown, 1 qt. $150
Dandy, glass lid, 1 qt., Aqua $15
Dolittle, 1 pt., Clear or Aqua $50
Double Safety, 1/2 pt., Clear $10
Double Safety, 2 qt., Clear $5
Drey Square Mason, 1 qt., Clear $10
Eagle, 1 qt., Aqua $150

Eclipse, 1 qt., (rare in amber $1000.00), Light Green $125
Electric, embossed world globe, 1 qt., Aqua $150
Empire, wing nut screw glass lid, 1 qt., (without original lid $250.00), Aqua ....
.... $1000
Erie Lightning, 1 qt., Amethyst $75
Eureka, glass lid, ¹/₂ pt., Aqua $35
Excelsior, 1 qt., Aqua $55
Fearman's Mincemeat, 1 qt., Amber $65
Flaccus Brothers, embosssed steer, 1 pt. $75
Forrest City, 1 qt., Amber $100
Forster, 1 qt., Clear $20
Franklin Dexter, 2 qt., Aqua $65
Gem, 1 qt., Aqua $10
Gem, 2 qt., Aqua $15
Globe, wire closure, 1 pt., (rare in black amethyst $3000.00), Amber $60
Green Mountain CA Co., 1 pt., Aqua $15
Haines Patent March 1st 1870, 1 qt., Aqua $175
Hamilton Glass Works 1 Quart, 1 qt., Aqua $250
Hazel Atlas E-Z Seal, 1 pt., Aqua $12
Hazel Preserve Jar, ¹/₂ pt., Clear $50
Hero, glass cover, 1 pt., Aqua $50
Ideal Imperial, 1 pt., Aqua $75
Ideal Imperial, 1 qt., Aqua $30
Improved Jam, 2 qt. $125
J.M. Clark & Co., round shoulder, 1 qt., Green $100
Kerr Self Sealing, Mason, ¹/₂ pt., Clear $2
King, 1 pt., Banner and Crow design, Clear $17
L & W, 1 qt., Aqua $55
Lafayette, embossed portrait, 1 pt., Aqua $200
Lafayette, embossed portrait, ¹/₂ gal., Aqua $150
Lighting, 2 qt., Aqua $50
Lightning, glass cover, 2 qt., Amber or blue $75
Lightning, glass cover, 2 qt., Aqua $75
Magic Fruit Jar, 1 qt., Star design, Amber $1000
Mason, 3 gal. $550
Mason, 1858 trademark, 2 qt., Aqua $150
Mason, Pat. Nov. 30th, 1858, Dark aqua $35
Mason, Pat. Nov. 30th, 1858, 1 pt. $12
Mason, Pat. Nov. 30th, 1858, 2 qt., reverse cross, Amber $100
McDonald's New Perfect Seal, 1 pt., Blue $10
Millville Atmospheric, glass lid, 1 qt., Aqua $50
National, Pat. June 27 1876, 1 pt. $12
Premium, glass lid, 1 pt. $25
Queen Wide Mouth, square-shaped, glass lid, 1 pt. $17
Queen, glass lid, 1 pt. $15
Quick Seal, 1 qt., Blue $3
Royal, 1 qt., Clear $7
Safety with glass cover, 2 qt., Aqua $45
Schram Automatic Sealer, 1 pt., flag $15
Sealfast, glass cover, 1 qt. $125
Smalley, glass cover, 1pt. or 1 qt. $10

Star Glass Co., 1 qt.
Aqua $40
Cobalt Blue $500
Swayzee's Improved Mason, 2 qt., Dark Olive $55
TM Lightning Reg. U.S. Patent Office, 1 qt., Aqua $4
Victory, 1 qt., Aqua $55
Whitney Mason, Pat. 1858, 1 pt., Aqua $15
Winslow Jar, 1 qt., Aqua $65
Worcester, 1 qt., Aqua $175

CHARACTER GLASS   VARIOUS PRODUCERS, 1930s–PRESENT

The term "character glass" refers to cartoon, comic book, movie stars, and other figures etched, enameled, or transferred on glass. Fired-on decals are also used. In
1937, Libbey won a contract with Walt Disney to produce tumblers for the movie
Snow White and the Seven Dwarfs. The movie was a smash hit, and eight separate
tumblers with a picture of each character enameled on the surface were designed.
The tumblers were shipped by the thousands across the country and used for pack-
aging cottage cheese. This was the first use of "character" tumblers. Other food
items include cheese (see listings under "Swanky Swigs"), jams, and jellies. Since
the 1970s, fast-food restaurants, often with the backing of the soft drink industry,
promote decorated tumblers far more than any other medium. See the section "Disney Glass Collectibles" for additional listings.

Actors' Series tumblers, (Abbot and Costello, Charlie Chaplin, Laurel and Hardy,
Little Rascals, Mae West, and W.C. Fields), Arby's, 1979 .... $6
Actors' Series tumblers, (Jack Albertson, Monty Hall, Teddy Kollack, Jan Murray,
Mary Tyler Moore, and Don Rickles), Coca-Cola, 1970s $12
B.C. Comic Tumblers, (Anteater, B.C., Broad, Grog, Thor, and Wiley), Arby's,
1981 .... $7
Bald Eagle tumbler, endangered species, Burger Chef $7
Bullwinkle tumblers, Ward Collector Series (over 20 styles), Pepsi, 1960s–1970s
.... $17
California Raisins tumbler, 12 oz., 1989 .... $4
Care Bears mug, days of the week, American Greetings $5
Care Bears tumblers, (Cheer Bear, Friends Bear, Funshine Bear, Good Luck Bear,
Grumpy Bear, and Tenderheart Bear), Pizza Hut, 1983 .... $5
Chipmunks tumblers, (Alvin, Chipettes, Simon, and Theodore), Hardee's, 1985
.... $6
Clara Peller Tumbler, Where's the beef?, Wendy's $6
Dr. Seuss jelly tumblers, several styles, Welch's, 1997 .... $2
Endangered Species Series jelly tumblers, (12 styles, including panda, cheetah,
elephant), Welch's, 1990s $2
Flintstone Kids tumblers, (Barney, Betty, Fred, and Wilma), Pizza Hut, 1986 . $4
Garfield mugs, 4 styles, McDonald's, 1987 .... $4
Garfield tumblers, 4 styles, McDonald's, 1987 .... $4
Great Muppet Caper tumblers, (4 styles), McDonald's, 1981 .... $3
Hanna Barbera Collector Series tumblers, (Dynomutt, The Flintstones, Huckle-
berry Hound and Yogi Bear, Josie and the Pussycats, Mumbly, and Scooby Doo),
Pepsi, 1977 .... $15

Character glass. PHOTOS BY ROBIN RAINWATER.

Happy Days tumbler, (Fonzie, Richie, Joanie, Ralph, Potsie, and the Cunninghams), Pizza Hut/Dr. Pepper $7
Kelloggs Cartoon tumblers, (7 styles, Dig Um, Tony the Tiger, Tony Jr., Toucan Sam, and Snap! Crackle! Pop!), 1977 .... $8
King King tumbler, Burger Chef/Coca-Cola, 1976 .... $6
McDonald Action Series tumblers, (12 styles), 1977 .... $6
Muppets tumblers, The Great Muppet Caper, 4 styles, 1981 .... $4
Noid tumblers, 5 styles, Domino's Pizza, 1988 .... $4
Pac Man Series tumblers, (11 styles), Bally, 1980 .... $6
Peanuts Tumblers, 6 styles, McDonald's, 1983 .... $4
Peanuts tumblers, 8 styles, Dolly Madison, 1980s $5
Popeye Kollect-a-Set tumblers, (6 styles), Burger King/Coca-Cola, 1975 .... $7
Popeye tumblers, 8 styles, original 1936 series $65
Shirley Temple bowl, cobalt blue with white figure, 1930s $45
Shirley Temple Creamer, cobalt blue with white figure, 1930s $40
Shirley Temple Mug, cobalt blue with white figure, 1930s $45
Shirley Temple pitcher, 9 oz., cobalt blue with white figure, 1930s $65
Shirley Temple plate, cobalt blue with white figure, 1930s (rare) $300
Shirley Temple sugar, cobalt blue with white figure, 1930s $50
Sloth and Goonies tumbler, Godfather's Pizza, 1985 .... $5
Smurfs tumblers, 14 styles, Hardee's, 1982-1983 .... $6
Star Trek III: The Search for Spock tumblers, (4 styles), Taco Bell, 1984 .... $15
Star Trek tumblers, cartoon series characters (4 styles), Dr. Pepper, 1976 ... $50
Star Trek tumblers, 4 styles, Dr. Pepper, 1978 .... $65
Star Trek: The Motion Picture tumblers, (3 styles), Coca-Cola, 1980 ..... $35
Star Wars tumblers, (4 styles), Burger King/Coca-Cola, 1977 .... $25
Star Wars: Return of the Jedi tumblers, (4 styles), Burger King/Coca-Cola, 1983 .... $15
Star Wars: The Empire Strikes Back tumblers, (4 styles) Burger King/Coca-Cola, 1980 .... $15
Superheroes Cartoon Series tumblers, (over 30 styles), Pepsi, 1976-1979 .. $17
Superman: The Movie tumblers, (6 styles), Pepsi, 1978 .... $7
Tom and Jerry jelly tumblers, several styles, Welch's, 1992 .... $2
Tom and Jerry tumblers, several styles, Pepsi, 1975 .... $12
Under Dog Series tumblers, (Under Dog, Sweet Polly, and Simon Bar Sinister), Pepsi, 1970s $17

Universal Studios' Monster tumblers, (Creature from the Black Lagoon, Dracula, Frankenstein, Mummy, Mutant, and Wolfman), 1980 .... $15

Urchins tumblers, (6 styles), Coca-Cola, 1976 .... $8

Walter Lantz Cartoon Collector Series tumblers, (16 styles including Andy Panda, Chilly Willy, Woody Woodpecker), Pepsi, 1977 .... $17

Warner Brothers Collector Series tumblers, (Over 30 styles including Bugs Bunny, Porky Pig, Elmer Fudd, Daffy Duck, Coyote, Roadrunner), Pepsi, 1973 ...
.... $12

Warner Brothers tumblers, (16 styles), Welch's, 1974, 1976 .... $7

Warner Brothers' Interaction Series tumblers, (over 25 styles, all major characters), Pepsi, 1976 (Special Run Characters $20.00) $12

Warner Brothers' Looney Tunes Collector Series tumblers (13 styles), Pepsi, 1979, 1980 .... $10

Wizard of Oz Land of Oz tumblers, (4 styles), Kentucky Fried Chicken, 1984 ..
.... $15

Wizard of Oz tumblers, (18 styles), Swift's Peanut Butter, 1950 .... $17

Ziggy tumblers, (4 styles), 7-Up, 1977 .... $5

Ziggy tumblers, (4 styles), Hardee's and Pizza Inn, 1979 .... $6

CHINTZ   FOSTORIA GLASS COMPANY, 1940s–1950s

This is one of the most beautiful etched crystal patterns of the post-Depression period. Several pieces are already quite rare and desirable. "Chintz" was also known as Fostoria's #338 line, and a variety of numbered blanks were cut for this pattern (Nos. 869, 2083, 2375, 2419, 2496, 2496½, 2586, 4108, 4128, 4143, 5000, 6023, 6026, and possibly others).

Bell, Crystal $90

Bonbon dish, 7³/₈″, footed, Crystal $30

Bowl, #6023 line (large), Crystal $75

Bowl, 4½″, Crystal $45

Bowl, 4½″, with 3 corners, Crystal $30

Bowl, 5″, Crystal $35

Bowl, 5″ with handle, Crystal $30

Bowl, 7½″, Crystal $40

Bowl, 8½″, with handles, Crystal $60

Bowl, 9½″, Crystal $75

Bowl, 10½″, with handles, Crystal $80

Bowl, 10″, with handles, Crystal $70

Bowl, 11½″, flared, Crystal $75

Candlestick, 3½″ tall, double, Crystal $35

Candlestick, 4″ tall, Crystal $25

Candlestick, 5″ tall, Crystal $30

Candlestick, 6″ tall, triple, Crystal $50

Candlestick, double, #6023 line (large), Crystal $40

Candy dish with cover, 3-part, Crystal $125

Celery dish, 11″ oval, Crystal $40

Champagne glass, 5½″ tall, 6 oz., Crystal $25

Claret glass, 5½″ tall, 4½ oz., Crystal $45

Cocktail glass, 3¹/₂″ tall, 4 oz., Crystal $30
Cocktail glass, 5″ tall, 4 oz., Crystal $30
Compote, 3¹/₄″, Crystal $30
Compote, 4³/₄″, Crystal $35
Compote, 5¹/₂″, Crystal $40
Cordial, 4″ tall, 1 oz., Crystal $50
Creamer, 3³/₄″, footed (large), Crystal $30
Creamer, individual, 3¹/₈″ tall, 4 oz., (small), Crystal $25
Cruet with stopper, 5¹/₂″ tall, 3¹/₂ oz., Crystal $125
Cup, footed, Crystal $25
Goblet, 6¹/₄″ tall, 9 oz., Crystal $35
Goblet, 7¹/₂″ tall, 9 oz., Crystal $40
Ice bucket with metal handle, Crystal $150
Jelly dish with cover, 7¹/₂″, Crystal $100
Mayonnaise set, 3-piece, 3¹/₂″ holder, with matching underplate and ladle, Crystal
.... $75
Pickle dish, 8″ oval, Crystal $40
Pitcher, 9³/₄″ tall, 1¹/₂ qt., footed, Crystal $375
Plate, 6″, Crystal $15
Plate, 7¹/₂″, Crystal $20
Plate, 8¹/₂″, Crystal $30
Plate, 9¹/₂″, Crystal $50
Plate, 10¹/₂″, cake with handles, Crystal $60
Plate, 11″, Crystal $55
Plate, 14″, with upturned edge, Crystal $65
Plate, cake, 16″, Crystal $125
Platter, 12″ oval, Crystal $110
Relish, 6″, square, 2-part, Crystal $45
Relish, 10″, oval, 3-part, Crystal $55
Relish, 5-part, Crystal $65
Salad dressing bottle with stopper, 6¹/₂″ tall, 7oz., Crystal $300
Salt and pepper shakers, 2³/₄″ tall, Crystal $110
Sauce boat liner, 8″, oblong, Crystal $35
Sauce boat, oval, divided, Crystal $80
Sauce boat, oval, Crystal $85
Saucer, Crystal $10
Sherbet, 4¹/₂″ tall, Crystal $25
Sugar, 3¹/₂″, footed, 2 handles (large), Crystal $30
Sugar, individual, 2⁷/₈″ tall, 2 handles (small), Crystal $25
Syrup, Sani-cut, (with metal tab on pouring spout), Crystal $325
Tidbit, 8¹/₄″, with upturned edge, 3-footed, Crystal $45
Tray, 6¹/₂″, for individual creamer and sugar set, 2 tab handles, Crystal $35
Tray, 11″, with center handle, Crystal $55
Tumbler, 5 oz., 4³/₄″ tall, footed, Crystal $30
Tumbler, 9 oz., Crystal $30
Tumbler, 13 oz., 6″ tall, footed, Crystal $35
Vase, 5″, (2 styles), Crystal $85
Vase, 6″, footed, Crystal $100
Vase, 7¹/₂″, footed, Crystal $125

CHRISTMAS CANDY   INDIANA GLASS COMPANY, 1950s

"Christmas Candy" is sometimes referred to as the "No. 624" pattern in Indiana's advertisements. The terrace green color was also referred to as seafoam by Indiana. Other companies call it teal.

Bowl, 7³/₈″
  Crystal $7
  Terrace Green $25
Creamer
  Crystal $10
  Terrace Green $25
Cup
  Crystal $7
  Terrace Green $20
Mayonnaise or gravy bowl with glass ladle
  Crystal $25
  Terrace Green $175
Plate, 6″
  Crystal $5
  Terrace Green $10
Plate, 8¹/₄″
  Crystal $7
  Terrace Green $15
Plate, 9¹/₂″
  Crystal $10
  Terrace Green $20
Plate, 11¹/₄″
  Crystal $15
  Terrace Green $40
Saucer
  Crystal $3
  Terrace Green $5
Sugar
  Crystal $10
  Terrace Green $25

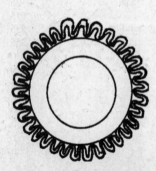

"Christmas Candy" pattern. DRAWING BY MARK PICKVET.

CHRISTMAS ORNAMENTS VARIOUS COMPANIES (BLOWN AND SPUN GLASS), 1970s–PRESENT

Christmas ornaments have been made by some small glass novelty companies; others have been made in Taiwan for distribution in the United States.

Acorn on branch, 3″ tall $10
Angel, 9″ tall, gold glitter on wings $20
Angel playing flute, 2″ tall $8
Angel with hands clasped, 2⁵/₈″ tall $8
Angel with hands clasped, 3¹/₄″ tall $12
Balloon, flying, 3¹/₂″ tall $15
Balloon, flying with detachable basket, 3³/₄″ tall $25
Basket, 2¹/₂″ tall, green and red holly and bow, brass bell at top $10
Basket, 2″ tall, red bow at top $8
Bell, 1³/₄″ tall $5
Bell, 2″ tall, ringer connected to inner side $6
Bell, 2¹/₄″ tall, 10 flutes, Pressed Diamond pattern at top, crystal ringer $15
Bench, park, 2³/₈″ tall, 2¹/₄″ across $10
Boot, 1¹/₂″ tall $5
Buggy, baby, 2¹/₄″ tall, 2³/₄″ across, 4 wheels $12
Candelabra, 3¹/₄″ tall, double—2 sets of 4 candles $12
Candle, 2¹/₄″ tall, green and red holly and bow, brass bell near bottom $8
Candy cane, 2³/₄″ tall $6
Carousel horse with pole, 3³/₄″ tall $15
Carousel with 3 horses, 3¹/₈″ tall, 2¹/₄″ diameter $30
Cello, 4″ long, 3 strings $20
Elephant standing on crystal ball, 3″ tall $10
Ewe, 2¹/₂″ long $8
Fire engine with ladder, 2³/₄″ across, 4 wheels $20
Gazebo with dancing couple, 4″ tall $25
Harp, 3¹/₂″ tall $12
Heart, 2″ tall, 2″ wide $5
Horse, winged rocking (Pegasus), 3¹/₄″ tall $15
Hummingbird, 2¹/₂″ tall $8
Key, 3¹/₂″ long $8
Lamp, 3⁷/₈″ tall, Tiffany style $15
Lighthouse, 3¹/₂″ tall $15
Mushrooms, 2¹/₂″ tall, 1 small and 1 large blown together $8
Peacock, 2¹/₂″ tall, tail open, 2³/₄″ diameter $12
Peacock, 3″ tall, tail down $10
Piano, baby grand, 2¹/₂″ tall $10
Reindeer, 3¹/₈″ tall, green and red holly and bow $10
Rocking chair, 3¹/₂″ tall, songbird on seat $10
Sewing machine with table, 2¹/₂″ tall $20
Ship, 3¹/₈″ tall, Nina, Pinta, and Santa Maria $15
Ship, sailing, 3³/₄″ tall, red flag at top $15
Sled, 2¹/₂″ across $6
Snowman with rake, 2¹/₄″ tall $10
Star, 2″ across, (5-pointed) $5
Swan, 2³/₄″ tall $10

Swans, 2″ tall, 3″ across, 2 swans blown together $12
Teapot, 2/8″ tall $10
Teardrop, 2¼″ tall, solid crystal $10
Telephone, 1¾″ tall, 1¾″ across, rotary dial $10
Tree, Christmas, 2⅜″ tall, solid glass, ½″ thick $10
Tree, Christmas, 3¼″ tall $10
Tugboat, 3¼″ long $15
Umbrella, 3½″ tall, clear bow on top and frosted bow on handle $15
Unicorn with green and red bow, 3⅛″ tall $10
Vase, 2⅝″ tall, pitcher-style with handle and lip, top half frosted with bow ... $12
Watering can, 3½″ across $10
Wine glass, 2¾″ tall $10
Wishing well with detachable bucket, 4″ tall $25

COCA-COLA GLASS COLLECTIBLES VARIOUS COMPANIES, 1886–PRESENT

Coca-Cola was first produced in Atlanta in 1886 and since then has become a major American icon. Just having the patented "Coca-Cola" or "Coke" trademarks will often double or triple the price of ordinary collectible items. The most popular Coca-Cola glass items are bottles. Over the past 50 years, over 1000 commemorative Coca-Cola bottles have been issued. These include such things as music legends, U.S. presidents, sports stars and coaches, and commemorative events such as centennials. A few, like the Ty Cobb 1983 Georgia Peach bottle and the Jimmy Carter 1976 bottle, already are valued at over $100. Both 19th and early 20th century colored bottles are rare and sell for over $100. Newer bottles should be full and sealed; if not, their value is reduced by as much as 50%.

Ashtray, 4″ × 2″, elongated octagon shape, 2 tab handles, yellow glass, embossed Coca-Cola, Akro Agate, 1930s $950
Ashtray, 4″ × 2″, elongated octagon shape, no handles, pink glass, embossed Coca-Cola, Akro Agate, 1930s $950
Ashtray, crystal with red enameled Coca-Cola $25
Bottle, 20″ tall, light green glass with white Coca-Cola, plastic bottle cap (decoration) $60
Bottle, Christmas, 1923, Green $25
Bottle, North Carolina Tarheels National Basketball Champions, 1982 ...... $10
Bottle, 75th Anniversary, 1961, Amber $15
Bottle, Clemson, 1981 National Football Champion $7
Bottle, Cleveland, Ohio, Amber $50
Bottle, Crimson Tide, 9½″ tall, Bear Bryant $10
Bottle, Jimmy Carter, 39th President $125
Bottle, Johnny Lee Steakhouse, 1986 .... $50
Bottle, Macon, Georgia, 1918 .... $30
Bottle, Ty Cobb, The Gerogia Peach, 1983 .... $300
Bottle, Wal-Mart 25th Anniversary, 1962-1987 .... $20
Pitcher, syrup, metal lid, clear with white Coca-Cola $200
Pitcher, water, Dallas Cowboys Football, Green $50
Plate, 13″, clear with embossed Coca-Cola $65

Coca-Cola bottle. PHOTO BY ROBIN RAINWATER.

Shot glass, 2¼″ tall, 1½ oz., enameled green 1969 Christmas $12
Shot glass, 2¼″ tall, 1½ oz., enameled red and green designs, annual issue from 1977 to 1988 (price is for each glass) $15
Straw dispenser, 11″ tall, chrome base and top, enameled Coca-Cola design $30
Sugar shaker with enameled red metal twist off lid, 6″ tall, enameled Coca-Cola $12
Tumbler, 12 oz. to 16 oz., wide variety of styles, enameled multicolored designs $8
Tumbler, over 16 oz., wide variety of styles, enameled multicolored designs $10
Tumbler, various Disney characters, several styles $12
Tumbler, wide variety of styles, enameled multicolored designs, less than 12 oz. $7
Tumbler, wide variety of styles, enameled white writing only $5

COIN GLASS   FOSTORIA GLASS COMPANY, 1958–1982

Some crystal pieces feature gold decorated coins. As long as the gilding is completely intact, the value for these pieces is the same as emerald green. Blue is a light coppery shade while ruby red is slightly dark and not as brilliant as some of the typical older ruby reds. There are four basic coin designs: Liberty Bell, colonial soldier cameo, torch, and eagle. Fostoria's "Coin Glass" is a very popular pattern and prices continue to rise while availability, especially in emerald green and blue, is quite scarce. The original Fostoria glass has frosted coins; however, Dalzell-Viking (a division of the Lancaster Colony Corporation, which purchased Fostoria) continues to reproduce many of the items without frosted coins. Reproductions without frosted coins generally sell for about half the original Fostoria frosted versions. There are other "Coin" patterns available; Avon, for example, has issued some commissioned Fostoria pieces.

Ashtray, 10″
  Amber $45
  Crystal $40
  Emerald Green $65

Coin glass. PHOTO BY ROBIN RAINWATER.

Light Blue	$60
Olive Green	$50
Ruby Red	$55

Ashtray, 4″ oblong

Amber	$22
Crystal	$15
Emerald Green	$30
Light Blue	$25
Olive Green	$18
Ruby Red	$24

Ashtray, 5″

Amber	$25
Crystal	$16
Emerald Green	$35
Light Blue	$30
Olive Green	$20
Ruby Red	$28

Ashtray, 7$^1/_2$″ round

Amber	$40
Crystal	$30
Emerald Green	$50
Light Blue	$45
Olive Green	$35
Ruby Red	$42

Ashtray, 7$^1/_2$″, with center coin

Amber	$35
Crystal	$25
Emerald Green	$45
Light Blue	$40
Olive Green	$30
Ruby Red	$32

Ashtray with cover
Amber $25
Crystal $16
Emerald Green $35
Light Blue $30
Olive Green $20
Ruby Red $28

Bowl, 8¹/₂″, footed
Amber $110
Crystal $65
Emerald Green $150
Light Blue $125
Olive Green $100
Ruby Red $120

Bowl, 8¹/₂″, footed, with cover
Amber $175
Crystal $125
Emerald Green $250
Light Blue $225
Olive Green $150
Ruby Red $200

Bowl, 8″
Amber $70
Crystal $45
Emerald Green $100
Light Blue $90
Olive Green $60
Ruby Red $85

Bowl, 9″ oval
Amber $95
Crystal $65
Emerald Green $125
Light Blue $110
Olive Green $85
Ruby Red $100

Bowl, wedding, with cover
Amber $125
Crystal $85
Emerald Green $150
Light Blue $140
Olive Green $90
Ruby Red $130

Candleholder, 4¹/₂″
Amber $35
Crystal $25
Emerald Green $45
Light Blue $40
Olive Green $30
Ruby Red $37

Candlestick, 8″
Amber $60

Crystal $45
Emerald Green $85
Light Blue $75
Olive Green $50
Ruby Red $70

Candy box with cover
Amber $70
Crystal $45
Emerald Green $100
Light Blue $90
Olive Green $60
Ruby Red $85

Candy jar with cover
Amber $70
Crystal $45
Emerald Green $100
Light Blue $90
Olive Green $60
Ruby Red $85

Cigarette box with cover
Amber $70
Crystal $45
Emerald Green $100
Light Blue $90
Olive Green $60
Ruby Red $85

Cigarette holder with cover
Amber $70
Crystal $45
Emerald Green $100
Light Blue $90
Olive Green $60
Ruby Red $85

Cigarette urn, $3^3/_8''$, footed
Amber $35
Crystal $30
Emerald Green $55
Light Blue $50
Olive Green $40
Ruby Red $45

Condiment set, 4-piece, (cruet, 2 shakers, and tray)
Amber $275
Crystal $200
Emerald Green $400
Light Blue $350
Olive Green $250
Ruby Red $300

Condiment tray
Amber $70
Crystal $45

Emerald Green $100
Light Blue $90
Olive Green $60
Ruby Red $85

Creamer
Amber $27
Crystal $17
Emerald Green $35
Light Blue $30
Olive Green $22
Ruby Red $28

Cruet, 7oz., with stopper
Amber $110
Crystal $85
Emerald Green $150
Light Blue $130
Olive Green $100
Ruby Red $120

Decanter, 16 oz., with stopper
Amber $275
Crystal $175
Emerald Green $400
Light Blue $350
Olive Green $250
Ruby Red $300

Goblet, 10½ oz.
Amber $70
Crystal $45
Emerald Green $100
Light Blue $90
Olive Green $60
Ruby Red $85

Jelly dish
Amber $37
Crystal $27
Emerald Green $45
Light Blue $40
Olive Green $35
Ruby Red $38

Lamp chimney, coach
Amber $70
Crystal $45
Emerald Green $100
Light Blue $90
Olive Green $60
Ruby Red $85

Lamp chimney, handled
Amber $70
Crystal $45
Emerald Green $100

Light Blue $90
Olive Green $60
Ruby Red $85

Lamp, electric, 10¹/₈″, handled
Amber $225
Crystal $125
Emerald Green $300
Light Blue $275
Olive Green $200
Ruby Red $250

Lamp, electric, 13¹/₂″
Amber $275
Crystal $150
Emerald Green $350
Light Blue $325
Olive Green $250
Ruby Red $300

Lamp, electric, 16⁵/₈″
Amber $325
Crystal $175
Emerald Green $400
Light Blue $375
Olive Green $300
Ruby Red $350

Lamp, oil, 13¹/₂″
Amber $275
Crystal $150
Emerald Green $350
Light Blue $325
Olive Green $250
Ruby Red $300

Lamp, oil, 16⁵/₈″
Amber $325
Crystal $175
Emerald Green $400
Light Blue $375
Olive Green $300
Ruby Red $350

Lamp, oil, 9³/₄″, handled
Amber $200
Crystal $100
Emerald Green $275
Light Blue $250
Olive Green $175
Ruby Red $225

Nappy, 4¹/₂″
Amber $25
Crystal $16
Emerald Green $35
Light Blue $30
Olive Green $20

Ruby Red $28

Nappy, 5³/₈″, with handle

Amber $35
Crystal $25
Emerald Green $45
Light Blue $40
Olive Green $30
Ruby Red $37

Pitcher, 32 oz., 6¹/₄″

Amber $125
Crystal $85
Emerald Green $150
Light Blue $140
Olive Green $90
Ruby Red $130

Plate, 8″

Amber $35
Crystal $25
Emerald Green $60
Light Blue $50
Olive Green $30
Ruby Red $45

Punch bowl, 14″

Amber $600
Crystal $250
Emerald Green $750
Light Blue $650
Olive Green $550
Ruby Red $625

Punch bowl base

Amber $125
Crystal $100
Emerald Green $250
Light Blue $175
Olive Green $100
Ruby Red $150

Punch cup

Amber $22
Crystal $15
Emerald Green $30
Light Blue $25
Olive Green $18
Ruby Red $24

Salt and pepper shakers with chrome tops

Amber $110
Crystal $85
Emerald Green $150
Light Blue $130
Olive Green $100
Ruby Red $120

Salver, footed
Amber $125
Crystal $100
Emerald Green $250
Light Blue $175
Olive Green $100
Ruby Red $150

Sherbet, 5¹/₄″, 9 oz.
Amber $45
Crystal $30
Emerald Green $70
Light Blue $60
Olive Green $35
Ruby Red $55

Sugar with cover
Amber $50
Crystal $35
Emerald Green $75
Light Blue $65
Olive Green $40
Ruby Red $60

Tumbler, 3⁵/₈″, 9 oz.
Amber $50
Crystal $35
Emerald Green $75
Light Blue $65
Olive Green $40
Ruby Red $60

Tumbler, 4¹/₄″, 9 oz.
Amber $60
Crystal $45
Emerald Green $85
Light Blue $75
Olive Green $50
Ruby Red $70

Tumbler, 5¹/₈″, 12 oz.
Amber $70
Crystal $45
Emerald Green $100
Light Blue $90
Olive Green $60
Ruby Red $85

Tumbler, 5³/₁₆″, 14 oz.
Amber $70
Crystal $45
Emerald Green $100
Light Blue $90
Olive Green $60
Ruby Red $85

Tumbler, 5³/₈″, 10 oz.
Amber $35

Crystal $25
Emerald Green $60
Light Blue $50
Olive Green $30
Ruby Red $45
Urn with cover, 12³/₄″ tall, footed
Amber $125
Crystal $100
Emerald Green $250
Light Blue $175
Olive Green $100
Ruby Red $150
Vase, 10″, footed
Amber $70
Crystal $45
Emerald Green $100
Light Blue $90
Olive Green $60
Ruby Red $85
Vase, 8″
Amber $50
Crystal $35
Emerald Green $75
Light Blue $65
Olive Green $40
Ruby Red $60
Wine glass, 4″, 5oz.
Amber $60
Crystal $45
Emerald Green $85
Light Blue $75
Olive Green $50
Ruby Red $70

COLUMBIA   FEDERAL GLASS COMPANY, 1938–1942

"Columbia" is borderline Depression Glass since it was first made in the late 1930s, although most pieces were released in the early 1940s. A few pieces were made in pink. Although, it is a bit paler than the average Depression pink, it still commands prices 4 or 5 times that of the crystal. The butter dishes (bottoms and tops) are also available in a variety of flashed designs as well as with decals. Complete flashed butter dishes are priced at about $30.00, except for the ruby red flashed version, which is valued at $35.00.

Bowl, 10¹/₂″, Crystal $25
Bowl, 5″, Crystal $15
Bowl, 8¹/₂″, Crystal $20
Bowl, 8″, Crystal $20
Butter dish with cover, Crystal $25
Cup, Crystal $10

Plate, 11″, chop, Crystal $12
Plate, 6″, Crystal $4
Plate, 9½″, Crystal $10
Saucer, Crystal $4
Snack plate, Crystal $40
Tumbler (large), 9 oz., Crystal $30
Tumbler (small), 4 oz., Crystal $25

CORREIA ART GLASS   1973–PRESENT

In operation only since 1973, Correia has already achieved an excellent reputation for contemporary art glass. As proof of their achievements, works by Correia can be found in the permanent collections of the Corning Museum of Glass, the Chrysler Museum of Art, the Metropolitan Museum of Art, and the Smithsonian Institution, to name a few. Everything produced by Correia is completely handmade without utilizing any molds; freehand blowing by superb artists is the company's trademark.

Apple, Opaque black or transparent red $125
Bowl, wide rim, with gold swirls, Iridescent ruby $375
Bowl, rose, with gold swirls, Iridescent aqua $200
Globe paperweight, 2½″, violet with gold waves and crescent moon $125
Globe paperweight, 2¼″, dark opaque green with transparent blue ring, Saturn design $125
Globe paperweight, 2¼″, luster gold with violet miniature hearts $125
Globe paperweight, 2¼″, world globe, with gold continents, Iridescent blue .. $125
Globe paperweight, 3″, black or light iridescent gold with snake in relief .. $150
Globe paperweight, 3″, opalescent white with black and white zebras $125
Globe paperweight, 4″ tall, 4¼″ diameter, Curious cat design, black cat at top of fishbowl, muticolored fish and seaweed encased in crystal $325
Lamp, gold luster, etched design, Iridescent blue $900
Perfume bottle with black stopper, 3″ tall, black and aqua striped design $250
Perfume bottle with crystal stopper, 3″ tall, crystal and aqua swirls $150
Perfume bottle with crystal stopper, 7″ tall, Cobalt Blue and aqua $275
Vase, 6½″ tall, with gold swirls, Iridescent ruby red $250
Vase, black with silver swirls $200
Vase, cylinder-form, black with silver and red swirls $275
Vase, jack-in-the-pulpit style, black with silver swirls $350

CREST   FENTON ART GLASS COMPANY, EARLY 1940s–PRESENT

For the most part, most of Fenton's Crest pieces are milk glass, excluding edging and in some pieces the handles and stoppers. "Aqua Crest" features a greenish-blue or aqua trim, while "Blue Crest" has a darker blue trim. "Emerald Crest" has an emerald green trim; "Silver Crest" a crystal trim. "Peach Crest" features a clear glass trim with a milk glass exterior and pink interior. "Snow Crest" is forest green, rose, ruby red, or amber with a milk white trim. "Rose Crest" has a pink trim, while "Silver Rose" is opaque pink with a clear glass trim. "Ruby Crest" has a ruby red trim. "Ivory Crest" is custard glass with a clear glass trim. "Gold Crest" has an amber trim.

"Silver Jamestown" features a milk glass exterior, transparent light blue interior, and crystal trim. "Silver Turquoise" is light blue opaque glass with crystal trim; "Black Crest" has a black trim and "Flame Crest" an orange-red trim. "Aqua Crest" was the original pattern first issued in 1940. "Silver Crest" followed in 1943 and remains the most popular pattern; it is still in production. "Emerald Crest" was made from 1949 to 1955. "Peach Crest" was popular and was produced from 1940 to 1969. "Snow Crest" was made from 1950 to 1954. "Rose Crest" was made from 1944 to 1947. "Ivory Crest" was made in 1940 and 1941. "Gold Crest" was produced from 1943 to 1945 and was reissued 1963 to 1964. "Silver Rose" was only produced in 1956 and 1957. "Silver Turquoise" was only made from 1956 to 1958. "Silver Jamestown" was made from 1957 to 1959. "Flame Crest" and "Blue Crest" were produced in 1963. "Ruby Crest" was made in 1979. "Black Crest" was produced in 1970. Certain Crest patterns, such as Emerald, Snow, Black, Rose, Blue, Peach, Gold, Ivory, Flame, Silver Rose, Silver Jamestown, and Silver Turquoise, are becoming difficult to find, and some are quite rare due to limited production years. Silver and Aqua Crest are fairly common since some pieces are still being made. Rarely do glass sets contain so many pieces and varieties. In general, with the "Crest" lines, the bigger the piece, the more valuable it is. This is particularly true with plates and bowls; notice how the price climbs as the pieces increase in dimension. Beginning in the late 1960s, some Silver Crest items feature hand-painted floral designs (increase the below listed Silver Crest prices by 25%). There were over 100 designated "lines" used for the "Crest" patterns, but some are older than others. In dating pieces, the formula for the base milk color was changed in 1958; the originals have a very light opalescence to them when held up to a light. The "Fenton" signature also appears on all products made after 1973. Note that Fenton combined similarly colored trims on many of its products, such as the cranberry, hobnail, and swirled designs; however, they were not referred to as "Crest" and are not included in the list.

Ashtray

Aqua Crest	$35
Emerald Crest	$50
Peach Crest	$45
Rose Crest	$55
Silver Crest	$20

Basket, 10″

Aqua Crest	$65
Emerald Crest	$100
Ivory Crest	$175
Peach Crest	$90
Silver Crest	$55

Basket, 12″

Aqua Crest	$75
Emerald Crest	$125
Peach Crest	$100
Silver Crest	$60

Basket, 13″

Aqua Crest	$85
Emerald Crest	$150
Ivory Crest	$200
Peach Crest	$110
Silver Crest	$65

Left and below: Fenton's "Crest" pattern. PHOTOS BY MARK PICKVET.

Basket, 2½″ to 4½″
Aqua Crest $45
Emerald Crest $70
Peach Crest $65
Silver Crest $35
Snow Crest $75
Basket, 5″-5½″, several styles
Aqua Crest $45
Emerald Crest $75
Peach Crest $70
Rose Crest $85
Silver Crest $40
Basket, 6½″
Aqua Crest $55
Emerald Crest $85
Peach Crest $80
Silver Crest $45
Basket, 7″
Aqua Crest $65

Black Crest $150
Emerald Crest $90
Ivory Crest, Silver Turquoise $85
Peach Crest $85
Silver Crest $55
Silver Jamestown, Silver Rose $85

Bonbon, 5¹/₂″

Aqua Crest $15
Black Crest $65
Emerald Crest $35
Peach Crest $25
Silver Crest $12
Silver Rose or Silver Jamestown $35

Bonbon, 8″

Aqua Crest $20
Emerald Crest $45
Peach Crest $35
Silver Crest $15

Bowl, 10″

Aqua Crest $55
Emerald Crest $85
Peach Crest $80
Silver Crest $50
Snow Crest or Ivory Crest $95

Bowl, 11¹/₂″

Aqua Crest $70
Emerald Crest $100
Flame, Gold, or Blue Crest $125
Peach Crest $90
Silver Crest $65

Bowl, 11″

Aqua Crest $60
Emerald Crest $90
Peach Crest $85
Silver Crest $55

Bowl, 13″

Aqua Crest $75
Emerald Crest $125
Peach Crest $100
Silver Crest $70

Bowl, 14″

Aqua Crest $80
Emerald Crest $135
Peach Crest $110
Silver Crest $75

Bowl, 5¹/₂″

Aqua Crest $35
Emerald Crest $45
Peach Crest $40
Silver Crest $30

Bowl, 5″
Aqua Crest $25
Emerald Crest $40
Peach Crest $35
Silver Crest $20

Bowl, 6¹/₂″
Aqua Crest $40
Emerald Crest $60
Gold Crest $75
Peach Crest $55
Silver Crest $35

Bowl, 7″
Aqua Crest $45
Emerald Crest $70
Peach Crest $60
Silver Crest $40
Silver Rose or Silver Jamestown $85

Bowl, 8¹/₂″, flared
Aqua Crest $45
Emerald Crest $75
Peach Crest $65
Silver Crest $40

Bowl, 9¹/₂″
Aqua Crest $50
Emerald Crest $80
Peach Crest $70
Silver Crest $45

Bowl, square, tall, footed
Aqua Crest $70
Emerald Crest $100
Peach Crest $85
Silver Crest $65

Bowl, tall, footed $75

Bowl, tall, footed
Aqua Crest $65
Emerald Crest $85
Peach Crest $75
Silver Crest $60

Bowl, banana, high, footed
Aqua Crest $50
Emerald Crest $80
Peach Crest $70
Silver Crest $45

Bowl, banana, low, footed
Aqua Crest $45
Emerald Crest $75
Peach Crest $65
Silver Crest $40

Bowl, deep dessert
Aqua Crest $40
Emerald Crest $60

Peach Crest $55
Silver Crest $35
Bowl, dessert, low or shallow
Aqua Crest $35
Emerald Crest $50
Peach Crest $45
Silver Crest $30
Bowl, finger
Aqua Crest $25
Emerald Crest $40
Peach Crest $35
Silver Crest $20
Bowl, rose
Aqua Crest $40
Emerald Crest $60
Ivory or Snow Crest $75
Peach Crest $55
Silver Crest $35
Bowl, square, tall, footed $100
Bowl, 8½″
Aqua Crest $45
Emerald Crest $75
Peach Crest $65
Silver Crest $40
Cake plate, 13″, footed
Aqua Crest $65
Emerald Crest $95
Peach Crest $85
Silver Crest $55
Cake plate, low, footed
Aqua Crest $55
Blue or Gold Crest $100
Emerald Crest $85
Peach Crest $75
Silver Crest $45
Silver Rose Flame $100
Candleholder, 6″ with crest on the bottom
Aqua Crest $30
Emerald Crest $45
Flame, Blue, or Gold Crest $75
Peach Crest $40
Silver Crest $25
Candleholder, cornucopia-shaped
Aqua Crest $55
Emerald Crest $75
Ivory Crest $75
Peach Crest $65
Silver Crest $45
Candleholder with flat saucer-shaped base
Aqua Crest $25
Emerald Crest $45

Peach Crest $35
Silver Crest $20

Candleholder, globe holder
Aqua Crest $15
Emerald Crest $30
Peach Crest $25
Silver Crest $12

Candleholder, high, ruffled
Aqua Crest $25
Emerald Crest $45
Peach Crest $35
Silver Crest $20

Candleholder, low, ruffled
Aqua Crest $15
Emerald Crest $25
Peach Crest $20
Silver Crest $12
Silver Turquoise $30

Candy box
Aqua Crest $70
Emerald Crest $100
Peach Crest $85
Silver Crest $60

Candy box, tall stem, footed
Aqua Crest $125
Emerald Crest $175
Peach Crest $150
Silver Crest $100

Candy jar with cover
Aqua Crest $150
Emerald Crest $200
Peach Crest $175
Silver Crest $125

Chip and dip set, 2-piece, (low bowl with mayonnaise bowl in the center)
Aqua Crest $75
Emerald Crest $100
Peach Crest $85
Silver Crest $60

Comport, 6″, flared, footed
Aqua Crest $25
Emerald Crest $45
Peach Crest $35
Silver Crest $20

Comport, 6″, flared, footed
Comport, footed, crimped
Aqua Crest $30
Blue or Gold Crest $75
Emerald Crest $50
Peach Crest $40
Silver Crest $22

Silver Turquoise or Flame Crest $75
Comport, footed, low
   Aqua Crest $30
   Emerald Crest $50
   Gold or Rose Crest $75
   Peach Crest $40
   Silver Crest $22
   Silver Turquoise Crest $75
Comport, high, footed
   Aqua Crest $25
   Emerald Crest $45
   Peach Crest $35
   Silver Crest $17
Creamer, reeded with 1 handle
   Aqua Crest $22
   Emerald Crest $45
   Peach Crest $35
   Silver Crest $17
Creamer, reeded with 2 handles
   Aqua Crest $27
   Emerald Crest $50
   Peach Crest $40
   Silver Crest $22
Creamer, straight sides
   Emerald Crest $55
   Aqua Crest $35
   Peach Crest $45
   Silver Crest $30
Creamer, threaded handle
   Aqua Crest $22
   Emerald Crest $40
   Peach Crest $30
   Silver Crest $17
Creamer, ruffled
   Aqua Crest $45
   Emerald Crest $65
   Peach Crest $55
   Silver Crest $40
Cruet, 9″ tall, (no stopper)
   Aqua Crest $65
   Emerald Crest $100
   Peach Crest $85
   Silver Crest $60
Cup, reeded handle
   Aqua Crest $25
   Emerald Crest $45
   Peach Crest $35
   Silver Crest $20
Cup, threaded handle
   Aqua Crest $25
   Emerald Crest $45

Peach Crest $35
Silver Crest $20

Dessert cup or dish, (no handle)
Aqua Crest $25
Emerald Crest $40
Peach Crest $30
Silver Crest $20

Epergne set, 2-piece, vase in bowl
Aqua Crest $65
Emerald Crest $90
Peach Crest $75
Silver Crest $55
Ivory Crest $150

Epergne set, 3-piece, 2 vases in bowl
Aqua Crest $100
Emerald Crest $150
Peach Crest $125
Silver Crest $90

Epergne set, 4-piece, 3 vases in bowl
Aqua Crest $110
Emerald Crest $175
Peach Crest $150
Silver Crest $95
Rose Crest $150

Epergne set, 5-piece, 4 vases in bowl
Aqua Crest $125
Emerald Crest $200
Peach Crest $175
Silver Crest $100

Epergne set, 6-piece
Aqua Crest $150
Emerald Crest $250
Peach Crest $200
Silver Crest $110

Flower pot with attached saucer
Aqua Crest $70
Emerald Crest $85
Peach Crest $75
Silver Crest $65
Snow Crest $95

Lamp, hurricane
Aqua Crest $80
Emerald Crest $125
Peach Crest $100
Silver Crest $70
Silver Turquoise $125

Mayonnaise bowl
Aqua Crest $25
Emerald Crest $45
Peach Crest $35
Silver Crest $17

Mayonnaise ladle

Aqua Crest $25
Emerald Crest $45
Peach Crest $35
Silver Crest $17
Plain crystal $10

Mayonnaise liner

Aqua Crest $17
Emerald Crest $35
Peach Crest $25
Silver Crest $12

Mayonnaise set, 3-piece

Aqua Crest $70
Emerald Crest $125
Peach Crest $100
Silver Crest $50

Mustard with cover and spoon

Aqua Crest $75
Emerald Crest $100
Peach Crest $85
Silver Crest $65

Nut dish, footed

Aqua Crest $17
Emerald Crest $35
Peach Crest $25
Silver Crest $12

Oil bottle with stopper

Aqua Crest $75
Emerald Crest $95
Peach Crest $85
Silver Crest $70

Pitcher (large), 70 oz.

Aqua Crest $200
Emerald Crest $300
Peach Crest $250
Silver Crest $150

Pitcher (small)

Aqua Crest $50
Emerald Crest $75
Peach Crest $60
Silver Crest $40

Plate, 5¹/₂″, (2 styles)

Aqua Crest $10
Emerald Crest $15
Peach Crest $12
Silver Crest $7

Plate, 6¹/₂″

Aqua Crest $15
Emerald Crest $22
Peach Crest $17
Silver Crest $12

Plate, 6″
Aqua Crest $12
Emerald Crest $20
Peach Crest $15
Silver Crest $10

Plate, 8¹/₂″
Aqua Crest $17
Emerald Crest $27
Peach Crest $22
Silver Crest $15

Plate, 10″
Aqua Crest $22
Emerald Crest $35
Peach Crest $27
Silver Crest $17

Plate, 10¹/₂″
Aqua Crest $25
Emerald Crest $40
Peach Crest $35
Silver Crest $20

Plate, 11¹/₂″
Aqua Crest $30
Emerald Crest $45
Peach Crest $40
Silver Crest $25
Ivory Crest $50

Plate, 12″
Aqua Crest $35
Emerald Crest $55
Peach Crest $45
Silver Crest $30

Plate, 12¹/₂″
Aqua Crest $35
Emerald Crest $55
Peach Crest $45
Silver Crest $35

Plate, 16″, cake or torte
Aqua Crest $55
Emerald Crest $75
Peach Crest $65
Silver Crest $50

Punch bowl
Aqua Crest $275
Emerald Crest $400
Peach Crest $350
Silver Crest $225

Punch bowl base
Aqua Crest $65
Emerald Crest $100
Peach Crest $85
Silver Crest $55

Punch cup
Aqua Crest $12
Emerald Crest $25
Peach Crest $17
Silver Crest $10

Punch ladle, (plain crystal only)
Aqua Crest $25
Emerald Crest $25
Peach Crest $25
Silver Crest $25

Relish, divided
Aqua Crest $40
Emerald Crest $60
Peach Crest $50
Silver Crest $30

Relish, heart-shaped, with handle
Aqua Crest $40
Emerald Crest $60
Peach Crest $50
Silver Crest $30
Silver Rose $75
Ruby Red or Snow $85

Salt and pepper shakers
Aqua Crest $75
Emerald Crest $100
Peach Crest $85
Silver Crest $65

Saucer
Aqua Crest $10
Emerald Crest $15
Peach Crest $12
Silver Crest $7

Sherbet, footed
Aqua Crest $17
Emerald Crest $35
Peach Crest $25
Silver Crest $12

Sugar, with reeded handles
Aqua Crest $27
Emerald Crest $50
Peach Crest $40
Silver Crest $22

Sugar, with ruffled top
Aqua Crest $45
Emerald Crest $65
Peach Crest $55
Silver Crest $40

Tidbit, 2-tier plates $75
Aqua Crest $50
Emerald Crest $70
Peach Crest $60

Silver Crest $45
Flame Blue or Gold Crest $75

Tidbit, 2-tier, (plate and ruffled bowl)
Aqua Crest $50
Emerald Crest $70
Peach Crest $60
Silver Crest $45

Tidbit, 3-tier, (2 plates and ruffled bowl)
Aqua Crest $75
Emerald Crest $90
Peach Crest $85
Silver Crest $65

Tidbit, 3-tier plates
Aqua Crest $65
Emerald Crest $85
Peach Crest $75
Silver Crest $55

Toothpick holder
Aqua Crest $45
Emerald Crest $65
Peach Crest $55
Silver Crest $40

Top hat, 5″ vase
Aqua Crest $50
Emerald Crest $70
Peach Crest $60
Silver Crest $45
Gold Crest $85

Top hat, 7″ vase
Aqua Crest $80
Emerald Crest $125
Peach Crest $100
Silver Crest $70
Snow Crest $200

Tray, sandwich
Aqua Crest $40
Emerald Crest $60
Peach Crest $50
Silver Crest $30

Tumbler, footed
Aqua Crest $50
Emerald Crest $70
Peach Crest $60
Silver Crest $45

Vase, 10″
Aqua Crest $110
Emerald Crest $175
Ivory or Snow Crest $200
Peach Crest $150
Silver Crest $100

Vase, 12″
   Aqua Crest $125
   Emerald Crest $200
   Peach Crest $175
   Silver Crest $110
Vase, 4¹/₂″-5″, several styles
   Aqua Crest $22
   Emerald Crest $40
   Peach Crest $30
   Silver Crest $15
   Snow or Ivory Crest $50
Vase, 6¹/₂″
   Aqua Crest $30
   Emerald Crest $50
   Pastels $40
   Rose, Snow, or Ivory Crest $75
   Silver Crest $25
   Silver Jamestown $85
Vase, 6¹/₄″, crimped
   Aqua Crest $25
   Emerald Crest $45
   Peach Crest $35
   Silver Crest $20
Vase, 6¹/₄″, fan-shaped
   Aqua Crest $30
   Black Crest $90
   Emerald Crest $50
   Peach Crest $40
   Silver Crest $25
Vase, 6″
   Aqua Crest $25
   Emerald Crest $45
   Ivory Crest $55
   Peach Crest $35
   Silver Crest $20
Vase, 6″, crimped
   Aqua Crest $25
   Black Crest $85
   Emerald Crest $45
   Peach Crest $35
   Silver Crest $20
Vase, 7″-7¹/₂″
   Aqua Crest $30
   Emerald Crest $50
   Ivory or Snow Crest $75
   Peach Crest $40
   Silver Crest $25
Vase, 8¹/₂″, crimped
   Aqua Crest $45
   Emerald Crest $65

Peach Crest $55
Rose, Snow, or Ivory Crest $85
Silver Crest $37

Vase, 8″
Aqua Crest $35
Emerald Crest $55
Ivory or Snow Crest $80
Peach Crest $45
Silver Crest $27

Vase, 8″, crimped
Aqua Crest $35
Emerald Crest $55
Peach Crest $45
Rose or Snow Crest $85
Silver Crest $27
Silver Jamestown $100

Vase, 8″, globe holder
Aqua Crest $45
Emerald Crest $65
Peach Crest $55
Silver Crest $40

Vase, 8″, wheat
Aqua Crest $40
Emerald Crest $60
Peach Crest $50
Silver Crest $35

Vase, 9″
Aqua Crest $50
Emerald Crest $75
Peach Crest $60
Silver Crest $40

Vase, cornucopia-shaped
Aqua Crest $70
Emerald Crest $100
Ivory Crest $125
Peach Crest $85
Silver Crest $60

DAISY   INDIANA GLASS COMPANY, 1933–1970s

"Daisy" is sometimes referred to as Indiana's "No. 620" pattern run. The prices are for the original amber produced in the 1940s. Prior to that the pattern was produced in crystal (reduce the prices in half) and a fired-on red (double the price). A darker forest green was added in the 1960s (reduce the prices by half).

Bowl, 10″ oval $20
Bowl, 4¹/₂″ $7
Bowl, 6″ $17
Bowl, 7¹/₂″ $15

Bowl, 9³/₈" $22
Creamer, footed $10
Cup $6
Plate, 10³/₈", with indentation for 4¹/₂" bowl $22
Plate, 6" $3
Plate, 7¹/₂" $7
Plate, 8¹/₂" $8
Plate, 9³/₈" $10
Plate, cake, 11¹/₂" $15
Platter, 10³/₄" $15
Relish dish, 3 divisions $22
Saucer $2
Sherbet $7
Sugar, 2-handled $10
Tumbler, 12 oz., footed $27
Tumbler, 9 oz., footed $17

DEWDROP   JEANNETTE GLASS COMPANY, 1953–1956

"Dewdrop" is a typical 1950s crystal pattern. The pattern features alternating panels of clear glass and tiny horizontal rows of miniature hobs.

Bowl, 10³/₈", Crystal $15
Bowl, 4³/₄", Crystal $5
Bowl, 8¹/₂", Crystal $10
Butter dish with cover, Crystal $25
Candy dish with cover, 7", Crystal $25
Creamer, Crystal $7
Cup, Crystal $4
Leaf-shaped dish, Crystal $10
Pitcher, 1 qt., Crystal $25
Plate, 11¹/₂", Crystal $15
Punch bowl, 1¹/₂ gal., Crystal $35
Punch bowl base, Crystal $10
Sugar with cover, Crystal $15
Tray, lazy susan, 13", Crystal $20
Tumbler, various styles, Crystal $8

"Dewdrop" pattern. DRAWING BY MARK PICKVET.

Disney tumblers. PHOTO BY ROBIN RAINWATER.

DISNEY GLASS COLLECTIBLES   1930–PRESENT

Disney Collectibles range from decorated tumblers to limited edition hand-sculptured crystal items. All feature Disney characters. Those released in limited editions are usually sold out very quickly.

Alice in Wonderland tumbler, 1950 (8 styles) $22
Bell, 4¹/₂″ tall, crystal with gold-plated Mickey Mouse ringer $20
Cinderella tumbler, 1950 (8 styles) $12
Cinderella's coach, 5³/₄″ tall, 5″ long, 7⁷/₈″ wide, crystal ball with gold frame and finial $100
Cinderella's slipper on pillow base, 2³/₈″ tall, 3″ long, 3″ wide, limited edition (4000), made in Germany $150
Coca-Cola tumblers with Disney characters, several styles $12
Dalmations, 101, tumbler, Wonderful World of Disney $15
Donald Duck tumbler, 1942, several styles $22
Dopey crystal figurine, 4¹/₂″ tall, limited edition (1800) $135
Dumbo crystal figurine, 4¹/₂″ tall, limited edition (1000), made in Val St. Lambert, Belgium $200
Dumbo tumbler, 1941, two-color (5 styles) $45
Eeyore crystal figurine, 4¹/₄″ tall, limited edition (2000), made in Germany ... $175
Ferdinand the Bull tumbler, 4³/₄″ tall, All-Star Parade, 1939 .... $45
Goofy frosted crystal figurine, 2⁷/₈″, Goebel $35
Jiminy Cricket crystal figurine, 4¹/₂″ tall, limited edition (1800) $135
Jiminy Cricket crystal sculpture, 14″ tall, on wood lit base, engraved glass figure, limited edition (1000), made by Arnold Ruiz $450
Jungle Book Pepsi tumblers $40
Lady and the Tramp tumbler, 1955 (8 styles) $22
Little Mermaid crystal figurine, 4⁵/₈″ tall, limited edition (1800) $150
McDonald's Disneyland tumbler, (4 styles) $7
Mickey Mouse crystal figurine, 4¹/₂″ tall, limited edition (1800) $135
Mickey Mouse frosted crystal figurine, 2⁷/₈″, Goebel $35
Mickey Mouse Sorcerer's Apprentice crystal figurine, 4¹/₂″ tall, limited edition (1800) $135

Mickey Mouse Through the Years mug, 1940 Fantasia, pepsi, Milk White $17
Mickey Mouse tumbler, limited edition, 1971 .... $12
Pinocchio tumbler, 4⅝" tall, 1940s $17
Pluto frosted crystal figurine, 2⅞" tall, Goebel $35
Robin the Boy Wonder tumbler, 5" tall $17
Simba the Lion, crystal figurine, 5¼" tall, limited edition (2000), made in Germany $275
Sleeping Beauty crystal castle, 4⅝" tall, limited edition (1800) $225
Sleeping Beauty crystal castle, 5¼" tall, 4¾" wide, made in Germany $200
Sleeping Beauty tumbler, several styles, 1958 .... $20
Snow White and the Seven Dwarfs tumblers, (8 styles) originally held cottage cheese, Libbey, late 1930s, complete set $135
Snow White crystal figurine, 5¼" tall, limited edition (4000), made in Germany .
.... $175
Sorcerer's Apprentice crystal hat sculpture, 3" tall, includes hat on open book, limited edition (2000), made in Germany $100
Sorcerer's Apprentice sculpture, 6¼" tall, crystal wave with miniature pewter Mickey Mouse finial, Franklin Mint $175
The Rescuers Pepsi tumblers, 1977 (8 styles) $12
Tigger cut crystal miniature, 3" tall, limited edition (2500), made in Austria ....
.... $150
Tinker Bell crystal figurine, 4½" tall, limited edition (1800) $135
Tumbler, 25th Anniversary (1997), 5" tall, 3¼" diameter, McDonald's issue (4 styles), Disney characters $2
Winnie the Pooh crystal figurine, 4½" tall, limited edition (1800) $150
Winnie the Pooh cut crystal miniature, 1¹⁵⁄₁₆" tall, limited edition (2500), Made in Austria $150
Winnie the Pooh tumbler, several styles, 1950s–1960s $12

DUNCAN & MILLER ANIMALS 1920s-1955

Duncan & Miller created animal figurines starting in the Depression until it closed. Most of the creations are water birds, such as swans and ducks. A few were made into practical items such as ashtrays and cigarette boxes.

Bird of paradise $550
Donkey with cart and peon $550
Duck, ashtray, 4" $20
Duck, ashtray, 8" $30
Duck, mallard, cigarette box with cover, 4½" × 3½" $65
Goose, 6" tall $300
Grouse, ruffled $2000
Heron, 7" tall $125
Swan, 10½" tall, with crystal neck, Ruby Red $250
Swan, 10½" tall, with red neck, Milk White $550
Swan, 10" tall, Crystal $55
Swan, 10" tall, 12½" wingspan, Green Opalescent $275
Swan, 10" tall, 12½" wingspan, Blue Opalescent $300
Swan, 12" tall, Milk White with green or ruby red $275

Swan, 13½″ tall, with crystal neck, Ruby Red $250
Swan, 3″ tall, Crystal $35
Swan, 5½″ tall, with crystal neck, Ruby Red $100
Swan, 5″ tall, Crystal $40
Swan, 6″ tall, Ruby Red $55
Swan, 7″ tall, Chartreuse $65
Swan, 7″ tall, Crystal $55
Swan, 7″ tall, Red $65
Swan, 8″ tall, Crystal $75
Swan, 8″ tall, Red $75
Swan, 8″ tall, Ruby Red $65
Swan, 8″ tall, with floral design, Ruby Red $75
Swan, ashtray, 4″, blue neck on crystal swan $55
Swordfish, Blue Opalescent $575
Swordfish, Crystal $225

FENTON ART GLASS   1930s–PRESENT

The listings here are for glassware produced beginning in the 1930s because Fenton primarily manufactured Carnival glass before this time (see Chapter 5 for extensive listings on Fenton). See additional Fenton Listings under Chocolate in Chapter 4, under Lincoln Inn in Chapter 6, and under Bicentennial, Crest, and Ruby Red in this chapter. Fenton has a distinguished career in the glassmaking industry and survived the upheavals and downswings in the glass market for most of this century. Much of its work could easily be labeled art glass, but since the pieces are newer, I have listed the company here. Fenton is noted for fancy art baskets made in a variety of styles—opalescent, satin, iridescent, etc.

Basket, 10 ½″ diameter, mulberry blue with clear handle $375
Basket, 11″ diameter, Hobnail pattern, Milk glass $75

Fenton glass baskets. PHOTO BY ROBIN RAINWATER.

Basket, 4½″ diameter, crystal handle, Hobnail pattern, Opalescent Cranberry ... $100

Basket, 5″, black with crystal handle, enameled floral design $55

Basket, 5″ diameter, (light blue and milk colored), Peking blue $100

Basket, 5″ diameter, 3-footed, pressed Daisy and Star pattern, Iridescent amethyst $50

Basket, 5″ diameter, opaque rose pastel with transparent pink handle $90

Basket, 5″ diameter, with wicker handle, Opaque cobalt blue $175

Basket, 7½″ diameter, crystal handle, Hobnail pattern, Blue Opalescent $110

Basket, 7″ diameter, milk base, pink interior, black trim and handle $200

Basket, 7″ diameter, with clear handle, Coin Dot pattern, Opalescent cranberry $150

Basket, 4½″ diameter, with rose trim and handle, Milk $85

Bowl, 13½″ diameter, 2-handled (17″ long), Jade green $175

Bowl, 6″, cupped, "Fenton Ebony," Black $85

Candleholder, 4½″ tall, cornucopia style, Crystal with silvertone $55

Candlestick, 3½″ tall, Double Dolphin design, Jade Green $55

Candlestick, 6″ tall, Hobnail pattern, Milk glass $20

Candlestick, 8″ tall, with ebony base, Milk glass $125

Candy jar with cover, 10½″ tall, orange "Flame" $175

Candy jar with cover, Double Dolphin handles, Ebony $250

Compote, 7″ tall, 10″ diameter, Mikado pattern, Black $375

Cookie jar with cover and wicker, 70 tall, Big Cookies or Circle pattern, Ebony $275

Cruet with crystal stopper and handle, 6″ tall, Hobnail pattern, Lime Opalescent $125

Pitcher, water, crimped, Hobnail pattern, Lime Opalescent $200

Sandwich server with center dolphin handle, 10″ diameter, Emerald Green $150

Tray, dresser, 10¾″ across, fan-shaped, Diamond Optic pattern, Amethyst or amber $75

Vase, 12″ tall, cobalt blue with engraved floral design $150

Vase, 6½″ tall, crimped, Periwinkle Blue $85

Vase, 7½″ tall, large thumbprints, satin finish, Opalescent cranberry $125

Vase, 7⅝″ tall, cobalt blue base with multicolored design and black threading, paper label "Fenton Art Glass" $600

Vase, 9″ tall, cobalt blue base with multicolored design and black threading $500

Vase, 9″ tall, Dancing Ladies pattern, Blue $275

Fenton milk glass, "Hobnail" pattern. PHOTO BY ROBIN RAINWATER.

American glass, Fire-King, "Alice" pattern. Reproduced from a patent design.

Vase, 9″ tall, Dancing Ladies pattern, Green $325
Vase, footed, Hearts and Vines design, Karnak red $600
Vase, Hanging Hearts design, Ivory $275
Vase with cover, 12″ tall, Dancing Ladies pattern, Blue $650

FIRE-KING DINNERWARE "ALICE"   1940s

The cups and saucers were given away in boxes of oats, while the dinner plates had to be purchased separately. The trim colors of "Alice" are either light blue or red.

Cup
  Jadeite $2
  White with Trim $6
Plate, 9¹⁄₂″
Saucer
  Jadeite $1
  White with Trim $2

FIRE-KING DINNERWARE "CHARM"   1950s

Azurite is a very light opaque blue. The dishes are all square-shaped, identical to Anchor-Hocking's square pieces found in the "Forest Green" and Ruby Red" patterns listed later in this chapter.

Bowl, 4³⁄₄″
  Azurite $7
  Jadeite $5
Bowl, 7³⁄₈″
  Azurite $12
  Jadeite $9
Creamer
  Azurite $11
  Jadeite $7
Cup
  Azurite $5
  Jadeite $3
Plate, 6⁵⁄₈″
  Azurite $6
  Jadeite $4
Plate, 8³⁄₈″
  Azurite $9

Jadeite	$6

Platter, oval

Azurite	$16
Jadeite	$12

Saucer

Azurite	$2
Jadeite	$1

Sugar

Azurite	$11
Ivory	$7

FIRE-KING DINNERWARE "FLEURETTE"   1950s–1960s

"Fleurette" is the sister pattern of "Honeysuckle." The pieces are identical in size and shape.

Bowl, 4⅝", White with flower decals	$2
Bowl, 6⅝", White with flower decals	$3
Bowl, 8¼", White with flower decals	$5
Creamer, White with flower decals	$3
Cup, White with flower decals	$2
Plate, 6¼", White with flower decals	$1
Plate, 7⅜", White with flower decals	$2
Plate, 9⅛", White with flower decals	$3
Platter, oval, White with flower decals	$7
Saucer, White with flower decals	$1
Sugar with cover, White with flower decals	$5

FIRE-KING DINNERWARE "GAME BIRD"   1950s–1960s

Ducks, geese, grouse, and pheasants can be found on this glassware in many combinations. Some pieces feature pairs of one breed, while others have all four on the same object.

Ashtray, 5¼", White with Bird decals	$6
Bowl, 4⅝", White with Bird decals	$5
Bowl, 5", White with Bird decals	$6
Bowl, 8¼", White with Bird decals	$9
Creamer, White with Bird decals	$6
Mug, 8 oz., White with Bird decals	$7
Plate, 7⅜", White with Bird decals	$4
Plate, 9⅛", White with Bird decals	$6
Sugar with cover, White with Bird decals	$9
Tumbler, 11oz., White with Bird decals	$6

FIRE-KING DINNERWARE "GRAY LAUREL" 1950s

"Gray Laurel" is the sister pattern of "Peach Lustre." The pieces are identical except for color, although "Gray Laurel" had a shorter production run.

Bowl, 4⅞", Light Opaque Gray $3
Bowl, 7⅝", Light Opaque Gray $5
Bowl, 8¼", Light Opaque Gray $7
Creamer, footed, Light Opaque Gray $4
Cup, 8 oz., Light Opaque Gray $3
Plate, 11", Light Opaque Gray $10
Plate, 7⅜", Light Opaque Gray $4
Plate, 9⅛", Light Opaque Gray $7
Saucer, Light Opaque Gray $1
Sugar, footed, Light Opaque Gray $4

FIRE-KING DINNERWARE "HONEYSUCKLE" 1950s–1960s

"Honeysuckle" is the sister pattern of "Fleurette." Both were made in the late 1950s and early 1960s. Nearly everything is identical except the decal work. For some reason, "Honeysuckle" has tumblers and "Fleurette" does not.

Bowl, 4⅝", White with flower decals $2
Bowl, 6⅝", White with flower decals $4
Bowl, 8¼", White with flower decals $6
Creamer, White with flower decals $3
Cup, 8 oz., White with flower decals $4
Plate, 6¼", White with flower decals $1
Plate, 7⅜", White with flower decals $2
Plate, 9⅛", White with flower decals $4
Platter, oval, White with flower decals $10
Saucer, White with flower decals $1
Sugar with cover, White with flower decals $6
Tumbler, 12 oz., White with flower decals $6
Tumbler, 5 oz., White with flower decals $3
Tumbler, 9 oz., White with flower decals $4

FIRE-KING DINNERWARE "JANE-RAY" 1940s–1960s

"Jane-Ray" is a simple pattern with little in the way of decoration except for the light opaque jade color and the lined edges.

Bowl, 4⅞", Jadeite $2
Bowl, 5⅞", Jadeite $3
Bowl, 7⅝", Jadeite $5
Bowl, 8¼", Jadeite $7
Creamer, Jadeite $5
Cup, Jadeite $3

Demitasse cup and saucer, Jadeite $17
Plate, 7³/₄″, Jadeite $4
Plate, 9¹/₈″, Jadeite $5
Platter, 12″, Jadeite $12
Saucer, Jadeite $1
Sugar with cover, Jadeite $7

FIRE-KING DINNERWARE "PEACH LUSTRE"   1950s–1960s

"Peach Lustre" is the sister pattern of "Gray Laurel." The pieces are identical except for the color. "Peach Lustre" was made for over a decade, while "Gray Laurel" was produced only in the early 1950s. The color of "Peach Lustre" is much like a light marigold Carnival iridescent. It is more abundant and a little cheaper than "Gray Laurel."

Bowl, 4⁷/₈″, Opaque Peach or Iridescent $3
Bowl, 7⁵/₈″, Opaque Peach or Iridescent $4
Bowl, 8¹/₄″, Opaque Peach or Iridescent $5
Creamer, footed, Opaque Peach or Iridescent $3
Cup, 8 oz., Opaque Peach or Iridescent $2
Plate, 11″, Opaque Peach or Iridescent $6
Plate, 7³/₈″, Opaque Peach or Iridescent $1
Plate, 9¹/₈″, Opaque Peach or Iridescent $2
Saucer, Opaque Peach or Iridescent $1
Sugar, footed, Opaque Peach or Iridescent $3

FIRE-KING DINNERWARE "RESTAURANT WARE"
EARLY 1950s

Anchor-Hocking's Fire-King "Restaurant Ware" was designed for restaurants, or "mass feeding establishments," as the company advertised. The most interesting piece is the five-compartment serving plate, which has 4 identical compartments and a small circle (the fifth compartment) in the middle. The pieces were also advertised as being "inexpensive," "heat-resistant," "rugged," "stain-resistant," "sanitary," and "colorful." Unfortunately, the pieces were not a huge seller and had a short production run.

Bowl, 10 oz., Jadeite $7
Bowl, 15 oz., Jadeite $10
Bowl, 4³/₄″, Jadeite $5
Bowl, 8 oz., with flanged rim, Jadeite $6
Cup, 6 oz., (straight), Jadeite $5
Cup, 7 oz., (heavy), Jadeite $6
Cup, 7 oz., with narrow rim, Jadeite $6
Mug, 7 oz., Jadeite $6
Plate, 5¹/₂″, Jadeite $1
Plate, 6³/₄″, Jadeite $2
Plate, 8⁷/₈″, oval with partitions, Jadeite $8

Plate, 8″, Jadeite $3
Plate, 9³/₄″, Jadeite $6
Plate, 9⁵/₈″, 5-compartment, Jadeite $12
Plate, 9⁵/₈″, 3-compartment, Jadeite $7
Plate, 9″, Jadeite $5
Platter, 11¹/₂″, oval, Jadeite $12
Platter, 9¹/₂″, oval, Jadeite $10
Saucer, Jadeite $1

FIRE-KING DINNERWARE AND OVEN GLASS
ANCHOR–HOCKING GLASS CORPORATION, 1940s–1960s

Anchor-Hocking's "Fire-King" line was made in several patterns as well as the rare "Philbe" pattern in Chapter 6. All "Fire-King" is heat resistant for use in the oven, an advance over Depression glass.

FIRE-KING DINNERWARE and OVEN WARE "PRIMROSE"
EARLY 1960s

"Primrose" is interesting in that the pieces doubled for use in the oven as well as on the table. That naturally was the object for the baking dishes, but the common table settings, such as cups, plates, and bowls were marked as being "heat-proof." The various covers on the casserole dishes are clear crystal.

Bowl, 4⁵/₈″, White with flower decals $2
Bowl, 6⁵/₈″, White with flower decals $3
Bowl, 8¹/₄″, White with flower decals $5
Cake pan, 8″ round, White with flower decals $6
Cake pan, 8″ square, White with flower decals $7
Casserole, 1¹/₂ qt., with knob cover, White with flower decals $12
Casserole, 1 pt., with knob cover, White with flower decals $6
Casserole, 1 qt., with knob cover, White with flower decals $10
Casserole, ¹/₂ qt., oval with au gratin cover, White with flower decals $12
Casserole, 2 qt., with knob cover, White with flower decals $15
Creamer, White with flower decals $3
Cup, 5 oz., (small), White with flower decals $2
Cup, 8 oz., White with flower decals $3
Custard, 6 oz., (low), White with flower decals $2
Pan, 5″ × 9″, loaf, deep, White with flower decals $8
Pan, 5″ × 9″, with cover, White with flower decals $12
Pan, 6¹/₂″ × 10¹/₂″, White with flower decals $10
Pan, 8″ × 12¹/₂″, White with flower decals $12
Plate, 6¹/₄″, White with flower decals $1
Plate, 7³/₈″, White with flower decals $2
Plate, 9¹/₈″, White with flower decals $3
Platter, oval, White with flower decals $8
Saucer, White with flower decals $1
Sugar with cover, White with flower decals $6

Tray, rectangular, 11″ × 6″, White with flower decals $5
Tumbler, 13 oz., White with flower decals $6
Tumbler, 5 oz., White with flower decals $3
Tumbler, 9 oz., White with flower decals $4

FIRE-KING OVEN GLASS ANCHOR–HOCKING GLASS CORPORATION, 1941–1950s

This pale blue ovenware was popular and durable. It was a top seller for Anchor-Hocking, and some of it is still being used today. It was not designed for microwave use. Some pieces are available in crystal, ivory, and jadeite. Jadeite is a pale opaque green (the color of light jade green) and shows up in several of the Fire-King lines.

Baker, 1½ qt.
  Blue $11
  Ivory $7
Baker, 1 pt., round, Blue $5
Baker, 1 pt., square
  Blue $5
  Ivory $4
Baker, 1 qt.
  Blue $6
  Ivory $5
Baker, 2 qt.
  Blue $12
  Ivory $9
Baker, 6 oz., individual
  Blue $3
  Ivory $2
Bowl, 16 oz., measuring, Blue $20
Bowl, 4⅜″, pie plate, Blue $11
Bowl, 5⅜″, deep-dish pie plate
  Blue $12
  Ivory $9
Cake pan, 8¾″, deep, Blue $17
Cake pan, 9″
  Blue $17
  Ivory $12
Casserole, 1½ qt., with cover (knob handle)
  Blue $20
  Ivory $15
Casserole, 1½ qt., with cover (pie plate cover), Blue $20
Casserole, 1 pt., with cover (knob handle)
  Blue $12
  Ivory $10
Casserole, 1 qt., with cover (knob handle)
  Blue $15
  Ivory $12
Casserole, 1 qt., with cover (pie plate cover), Blue $17

Casserole, 10 oz., individual, Blue $12
Casserole, 2 qt., with cover (knob handle)
    Blue $22
    Ivory $17
Casserole, 2 qt., with cover (pie plate cover), Blue $25
Coffee mug, 7 oz., 2 styles
    Blue $25
    Ivory $22
Cup, 8 oz., dry measure without spout, Blue $125
Cup, 8 oz., measuring with 1 spout, Blue $15
Cup, 8 oz., measuring with 3 spouts, Blue $20
Custard cup, 5 oz.
    Blue $3
    Ivory $2
Custard cup, 6 oz., 2 styles
    Blue $4
    Ivory $3
Loaf pan, $9^1/_8''$, deep
    Blue $22
    Ivory $17
Nipple cover, Blue $110
Nurser, 4 oz., Blue $15
Nurser, 8 oz., Blue $20
Percolator top, $2^1/_8''$, Blue $6
Percolator top, $2/_8''$, Blue $5
Pie plate, $10^3/_8''$, juice saver
    Blue $65
    Ivory $55
    Jadeite $75
Pie plate, $8^3/_8''$, Blue $10
Pie plate, $9^5/_8''$, Blue $12
Pie plate, $9''$
    Blue $11
    Ivory $7
Refrigerator jar with cover, $4^1/_2'' \times 5''$
    Blue $12
    Ivory $7
    Jadeite $15
Refrigerator jar with cover, $5^1/_8'' \times 9^1/_8''$
    Blue $30
    Ivory $25
    Jadeite $35
Roaster, $10^3/_8''$, Blue $55
Roaster, $8^3/_4''$, Blue $40
Table server with handles, (also used as hot plate)
    Blue $15
    Ivory $12
Utility bowl, $1^{m}/_8''$, Blue $15
Utility bowl, $6^7/_8''$, Blue $12
Utility bowl, $8^3/_8''$, Blue $14

Utility pan, 10 ¹/₂″
  Blue $20
  Ivory $15
Utility pan, 8¹/₈ × 12¹/₂″, Blue $16

FIRE-KING OVEN WARE "SWIRL"   1950s–1970s

Jadeite is very common. The white and ivory pieces are usually trimmed in gold or
dark yellow. Some of the pink pieces are trimmed in a darker shade of pink or red
near the top. "Swirl" is confusing because of the numerous color variations made
throughout its production.

Bowl, 4³/₄″
  Blue $4
  Ivory $2
  Jadeite $2
  Pink $5
  Trimmed $4
  White $1
Bowl, 4⁷/₈″
  Blue $4
  Ivory $3
  Jadeite $3
  Pink $5
  Trimmed $4
  White $2
Bowl, 6³/₈″
  Blue $5
  Ivory $4
  Jadeite $4
  Pink $6
  Trimmed $5
  White $3
Bowl, 7¹/₄″
  Blue $7
  Ivory $5
  Jadeite $6
  Pink $9
  Trimmed $7
  White $4
Bowl, 7⁵/₈″
  Blue $8
  Ivory $5
  Jadeite $6
  Pink $10
  Trimmed $8
  White $4
Bowl, 8¹/₄″
  Blue $9

Ivory $6
Jadeite $7
Pink $12
Trimmed $9
White $5

Creamer
Blue $5
Ivory $4
Jadeite $5
Pink $7
Trimmed $5
White $3

Creamer, footed
Blue $5
Ivory $4
Jadeite $5
Pink $7
Trimmed $4
White $3

Cup
Blue $4
Ivory $3
Jadeite $4
Pink $5
Trimmed $3
White $2

Demitasse cup and saucer
Blue $12
Ivory $9
Jadeite $10
Pink $20
Trimmed $15
White $7

Plate, 10″
Blue $7
Ivory $5
Jadeite $6
Pink $11
Trimmed $8
White $3

Plate, 11″
Blue $8
Ivory $5
Jadeite $6
Pink $12
Trimmed $9
White $4

Plate, 6⅞″
Blue $4
Ivory $1
Jadeite $2

Pink	$6
Trimmed	$5
White	$1

Plate 7¼″

Clear	
Blue	$4
Ivory	$1
Jadeite	$2
Pink	$6
Trimmed	$5
White	$1

Plate, 7⅜″

Blue	$4
Ivory	$2
Jadeite	$3
Pastels	$6
Trimmed	$5
White	$1

Plate, 9⅛″

Blue	$6
Ivory	$4
Jadeite	$5
Pink	$10
Trimmed	$7
White	$3

Platter, 12″, oval

Blue	$9
Ivory	$6
Jadeite	$8
Pink	$13
Trimmed	$10
White	$5

Platter, 13″, oval

Blue	$10
Ivory	$8
Jadeite	$10
Pink	$15
Trimmed	$12
White	$6

Saucer

Blue	$1
Ivory	$1
Jadeite	$1
Pink	$2
Trimmed	$2
White	$1

Sugar with cover

Blue	$6
Ivory	$4
Jadeite	$6
Pink	$10

Trimmed $7
White $3
Sugar, footed, with cover
Blue $5
Ivory $3
Jadeite $4
Pink $9
Trimmed $6
White $2
Tumbler, 12 oz.
Blue $6
Ivory $5
Jadeite $6
Pink $9
Trimmed $7
White $4
Tumbler, 5 oz.
Blue $4
Ivory $2
Jadeite $4
Pink $6
Trimmed $5
White $1
Tumbler, 9 oz.
Blue $5
Ivory $3
Jadeite $5
Pink $7
Trimmed $6
White $2

FIRE-KING OVEN WARE "TURQUOISE BLUE"   LATE 1950s

This is a fairly common opaque pattern except for the batter bowl with the spout and the 10″ plate. The relish and egg plates are usually trimmed in gold, which increases their value. Pieces are not recommended for microwave use.

Ashtray, 3½″, Blue $7
Ashtray, 4⅝″, Blue $10
Ashtray, 5¾″, Blue $12
Bowl, 4½″, Blue $5
Bowl, 5″, Blue $7
Bowl, 6⅝″, Blue $12
Bowl, 8″, Blue $15
Bowl, batter with spout, Blue $50
Bowl, round, 1 qt., Blue $12
Bowl, round, 3 qt., Blue $20
Bowl, round, 4 qt., Blue $25
Bowl, round, 2 qt., Blue $17
Bowl, tear, 1 pt., Blue $10

Bowl, tear, 1 qt., Blue $15
Bowl, tear, 2 qt., Blue $17
Bowl, tear, 3 qt., Blue $22
Creamer, Blue $5
Cup, Blue $3
Egg plate, Blue $15
Mug, 8 oz., Blue $10
Plate, 10″, Blue $22
Plate, 6⅛″, Blue $7
Plate, 7″, Blue $8
Plate, 9″, Blue $9
Plate, 9″, with indentation for cup, Blue $10
Relish dish, 3-part, Blue $12
Saucer, Blue $1
Sugar, Blue $5

FIRE-KING OVEN WARE "WHEAT"   1960s

The "Wheat" Fire-King pattern was fairly popular and lasted through the 1960s. It is the older sister pattern of "Blue Mosaic." The pieces for the two are identical in dimensions and differ only in color and decal; however, the blue did not sell as well and had a much more limited production run. As a consequence, there are few varieties of the pieces available in blue.

Bowl, 4⅝″, White with wheat decal $3
Bowl, 6⅝″, White with wheat decal $4
Bowl, 8¼″, White with wheat decal $6
Cake pan, 8″ round, White with wheat decal $8
Cake pan, 8″ square, White with wheat decal $8
Casserole, 1½ qt., oval, with au gratin cover, White with wheat decal $15
Casserole, 1½ qt., with knob cover, White with wheat decal $12
Casserole, 1 pt., with knob cover, White with wheat decal $7
Casserole, 1 qt., with knob cover, White with wheat decal $10
Casserole, 2 qt., round, with au gratin cover, White with wheat decal $20
Casserole, 2 qt., with knob cover, White with wheat decal $17
Creamer, White with wheat decal $4
Cup, 5 oz., (small), White with wheat decal $2
Cup, 8 oz., White with wheat decal $3
Custard, 6 oz., White with wheat decal $2
Pan, baking, 5″ × 9″, with cover, White with wheat decal $10
Pan, baking, 6½″ × 10½″, White with wheat decal $12
Pan, baking, 8″ × 12½″, White with wheat decal $15
Pan, loaf, 5″ × 9″, White with wheat decal $10
Plate, 10″, White with wheat decal $5
Plate, 7⅜″, White with wheat decal $3
Platter, oval, White with wheat decal $10
Saucer, White with wheat decal $1
Sugar with cover, White with wheat decal $6
Tray, rectangular, 11″ × 6″, White with wheat decal $8

FIRE-KING OVENWARE "BLUE MOSAIC"   1960s

Bowl, 4⅝", Cream with Blue Decoration $5
Bowl, 6⅝", Cream with Blue Decoration $7
Bowl, 8¼", Cream with Blue Decoration $12
Creamer, Cream with Blue Decoration $6
Cup, Cream with Blue Decoration $3
Plate, 10", Cream with Blue Decoration $5
Plate, 7⅜", Cream with Blue Decoration $3
Platter, oval, Cream with Blue Decoration $12
Saucer, Cream with Blue Decoration $1
Sugar with cover, Cream with Blue Decoration $10

FLORAGOLD LOUISA   JEANNETTE GLASS COMPANY, 1950s

This pattern is often confused with the "Louisa" design of the Carnival glass era. A few crystal pieces exist that were not iridized (reduce the above prices by about a third). A few candy dishes were reproduced in the 1960s and the 1970s in light blue, reddish-yellow, pink, and light iridized marigold. The original salt and pepper shaker tops were brown or white plastic, but they broke easily; metal tops are a common replacement and do not lower the value of the shakers.

Ashtray, 4", Iridescent $5
Bowl, 12" ruffled, Iridescent $15
Bowl, 4½" square, Iridescent $6
Bowl, 5½" round, Iridescent $25
Bowl, 5½" ruffled, Iridescent $30
Bowl, 8½" square, Iridescent $20
Bowl, 9½" deep, Iridescent $35
Bowl, 9½" ruffled, Iridescent $35
Butter dish with cover, oblong, (for ¼ lb stick), Iridescent ..,....... $30
Butter dish with cover, round, (6¼" square base), Iridescent $35
Candlestick, Iridescent $35
Candy dish, 1 handle, Iridescent $10
Candy dish, 5¼" long, 4-footed, Iridescent $7
Candy jar with cover, 6¾", Iridescent $55
Coaster, 4", Iridescent $6
Creamer, Iridescent $7
Cup, Iridescent $5
Pitcher, 1 qt., Iridescent $25
Pitcher, 2 qt., Iridescent $35
Plate, 5¼", Iridescent $10
Plate, 8½", Iridescent $25
Platter, 11¼", Iridescent $20
Salt and pepper shakers with plastic tops, Iridescent $45
Saucer, 5¼", (no cup ring), Iridescent $10
Sherbet, footed, Iridescent $7
Sugar with cover, 2-handled, Iridescent $17
Tidbit tray with a white wooden post, Iridescent $35

Tray, 13½" oval, Iridescent	$30
Tumbler, footed, 10 oz., Iridescent	$20
Tumbler, footed, 15 oz., Iridescent	$25
Vase, Iridescent	$200

FOREST GREEN   ANCHOR-HOCKING GLASS CORPORATION, 1950-1957

The original "Forest Green" by Anchor-Hocking spawned a new color era for glass. The dark green color was copied by others and sold well for the Christmas season, along with the "Royal Ruby" pattern. Depression glass collectors have an easy time distinguishing this color from the lighter Depression green colors; this makes dating quite easy. Anchor-Hocking was the only producer with a pattern named "Forest Green."

Ashtray, several styles, Green	$6
Bowl, 4¾" or 5¼", Green	$7
Bowl, 6", Green	$12
Bowl, 7½", Green	$15
Bowl, 8½" oval, Green	$25
Bowl with pouring spout, Green	$12
Creamer, Green	$7
Cup, square, Green	$5
Goblet, various styles, Green	$12
Mixing bowl set, 3 pieces, Green	$25
Pitcher, 1½ pt., Green	$25
Pitcher, 1 qt., Green	$30
Pitcher, 3 qt., Green	$35
Plate, 10", Green	$17
Plate, 6½" or 6¾", Green	$3
Plate, 8½", Green	$5
Platter, rectangular, Green	$22
Punch bowl, Green	$30

"Forest Green" vase. PHOTO BY ROBIN RAINWATER.

Punch bowl stand, Green $22
Punch cup, round, Green $3
Saucer, Green $1
Sherbet, Green $6
Sugar, Green $7
Tumbler, 3″-5″ tall, Green $4
Tumbler, over 5″ tall, Green $6
Vase, various styles, Green $7
Wine glass, various styles, Green $12

GIBSON GLASS   1983–PRESENT

Gibson opened a small shop and factory in Milton, West Virginia, in 1983. The company offers a fine line of paperweights, marbles, Christmas ornaments and figurines, vases, baskets, animals, and other novelty items.

Angel figure, 6½″ tall, cased in crystal, Light Blue $50
Basket, 4½″ tall, various molded pattern designs, Cobalt Blue carnival $20
Basket, 4½″ tall, various molded pattern designs, Cobalt Blue $15
Basket, 5″ tall, Pressed Diamond pattern, Crystal with light iridescence $20
Basket, 8½″ tall, crimped, cased, Light Blue and crystal $60
Bird, 1¾″ tall, 1¾″ long, Light Blue with crystal overlay $12
Bird, 1¾″ tall, 1¾″ long, Cobalt Blue $8
Candy, glass, multicolored with crystal wrapper, various designs $6
Compote, 8″ diameter, crimped, crystal base and stem, Iridescent Pink $50

Gibson glass. PHOTO BY ROBIN RAINWATER.

Gibson paperweights. PHOTO BY ROBIN RAINWATER.

Cruet with stopper, 7³/₄″ tall, Cobalt Blue with iridescent spatter $32
Dolphin, 5″ long, Cobalt Blue $15
Duck, 3¹/₄″ tall, 4″ long, Cobalt Blue $15
Duck, 3¹/₄″ tall, 4″ long, Crystal $12
Egg, Cranberry or Light Blue spatter $10
Marble, 1¹/₂″, multicolored swirls $20
Marble, 1¹/₄″, multicolored swirls $17
Marble, 1³/₄″, multicolored swirls $25
Marble, 2″, multicolored swirls, Sulphide $27
Paperweight, 2″ spherical, tan 7 gray seal encased in crystal, Sulphide $25
Paperweight, pastel pink and yellow rabbit in egg, limited edition, Sulphide . $85
Penguin, 3″ tall, Cobalt Blue $10
Vase, 7″ tall, crimped, Cranberry with crystal base $50
Whale, 4″ long, Cobalt Blue $15

HEISEY ANIMALS   A.H. HEISEY AND COMPANY, 1920s–1957

Originally, the famous Heisey animals were relatively inexpensive and were purchased for children and adults alike. They were rather durable and well constructed, but beware of some that might be damaged or scratched from excessive play. Heisey animals continue to increase sharply in value and are difficult to find. Prices below are for crystal.

Airedale, 5³/₄″ tall $550
Airedale, 6″ tall $600

Chick, 1″ tall, head down	$100
Chick, 1″ tall, head up	$100
Clydesdale, 7 1/4″ tall	$550
Clydesdale, 8″ tall	$650
Dog head bookends, 5″ tall, Scottie, pair	$300
Dog head bookends, 6 1/4″ tall, pair	$600
Dog, Scottie, 3 1/2″ tall	$175
Donkey, 6 1/2″ tall	$250
Duck, 2 1/4″ tall, floating	$150
Duck, 2 5/8″ tall, floating	$175
Duck, mallard, 4 1/2″ tall, wings half up	$550
Duck, mallard, 5″ tall, wings half up	$250
Duck, mallard, 6 3/4″ tall, wings up	$275
Duck, wood, 4 1/2″ tall	$550
Duck, wood, 5 1/2″ tall	$750
Elephant, 4″ tall, trunk down	$300
Elephant, 4 1/2″ tall, trunk up, Amber	$375
Elephant, 4 1/2″ tall, trunk up, Crystal	$325
Elephant, 5 7/8″ tall	$375
Fish bookends, 6″ tall, pair	$250
Fish, candlestick, 5″ tall	$250
Fish, centerpiece, 12″ tall, tropical fish with coral	$1500
Fish, match holder, 3″ tall	$175
Fishbowl, 9″ tall	$900
Gazelle, 11″ tall	$1500
Giraffe, 11″ tall, head turned to rear	$225
Giraffe, 11″ tall, head turned to side	$225
Goose, 2 3/4″ tall, wings down	$225
Goose, 4 1/2″ wings half up	$175
Goose, 5 3/4″ tall, wings down	$275
Goose, 6 1/2″ tall, wings half up	$175
Goose, 6 1/2″ tall, wings up	$175
Hen, 4 1/4″ tall	$450
Hen, 5 1/2″ tall	$525
Horse, 7 3/8″ tall, show	$600
Horse, 8 1/4″ tall, filly, head backward	$750
Horse, 8 1/4″ tall, filly, head forward	$750
Horse, 8 7/8″ tall, flying mare	$1500
Horse, 8 7/8″ tall, flying mare, Sahara yellow	$2500
Horse head bookends, 6 7/8″ tall, pair	$250
Horse, plug, 4″ tall	$150
Horse, plug, 4 1/4″ tall, Sparky, Cobalt Blue	$1250
Horse, pony, 3 3/4″ tall, rearing	$150
Horse, pony, 4 1/8″ tall, kicking	$175
Horse, pony, 5″ tall, standing	$225
Horse, rearing, bookends, 7 7/8″ tall, pair	$350
Pheasant, Asiatic, 10 1/2″ tall	$650
Pheasant, ring-necked, 4 3/4″ tall	$225
Pig, 7/8″ tall, standing, piglet	$125
Pig, 1″ tall, sitting, piglet	$150
Pig, 3 1/8″ tall, sow	$550

Pigeon, pouter, 6½" tall $775
Rabbit, 2⅜" tall, head down $225
Rabbit, 2⅜" tall, head up $225
Rabbit, 4⅝" tall.. $550
Rabbit head bookends, 6¼" tall, pair $1500
Rabbit, paperweight, 2¾" tall $225
Ram's head decanter stopper $450
Rooster, 5⅝" tall $400
Rooster, 8" tall, fighting, Crystal $550
Rooster cocktail glass, 4¼" tall, Crystal $55
Rooster cocktail shaker, 14" tall $175
Rooster head decanter stopper $100
Rooster vase, 6½" tall, Crystal $175
Sparrow, 2¼" tall, Crystal $150
Swan, 2⅛" tall, cygnet, Crystal $125
Swan, 7" tall $1000
Tiger paperweight, 2⅜" tall $1250

HOMESPUN   Children's Tea Set

Complete set of 12 pieces (crystal only) $175
Complete set of 14 pieces (pink only) $350
Cup
  Crystal $25
  Pink $35
Plate
  Crystal $10
  Pink $12
Saucer
  Crystal $25
  Pink $35
Teapot with cover
  Crystal $12
  Pink $15

HOMESPUN or FINE RIB   JEANNETTE GLASS COMPANY, 1939–1949

This "Fine Rib" pattern is not unlike the pressed glass of old, with a fairly simple vertical ribbing on each piece. The complete children's tea sets are particularly valuable.

Bowl, 4½"
  Crystal $10
  Pink $12
Bowl, 5"
  Crystal $25
  Pink $30

Bowl, 8¼″
  Crystal $25
  Pink $30

Butter dish with cover
  Crystal $55
  Pink $75

Coaster
  Crystal $7
  Pink $10

Creamer
  Crystal $10
  Pink $12

Cup
  Crystal $10
  Pink $12

Plate, 6″
  Crystal $6
  Pink $7

Plate, 9¼″
  Crystal $15
  Pink $20

Platter, 13″, 2-handled
  Crystal $20
  Pink $25

Saucer
  Crystal $4
  Pink $5

Sherbet
  Crystal $15
  Pink $20

Sugar
  Crystal $10
  Pink $12

Tumbler, 13 oz.
  Crystal $30
  Pink $35

Tumbler, 15 oz., footed
  Crystal $35
  Pink $40

Tumbler, 5 oz.
  Crystal $7
  Pink $10

Tumbler, 6 oz.
  Crystal $15
  Pink $20

Tumbler, 9 oz.
  Crystal $15
  Pink $20

IMPERIAL'S ANIMALS   1920s–1982

Imperial made its first animal figurines when the Carnival glass era ended. It acquired the molds of several other companies after they had gone out of business (Central in 1940, Heisey in 1958, and Cambridge in 1960), all makers of animal figurines. Imperial was considerate enough to mark all of its new products, including reproductions, with "IG."

Airedale, Caramel slag $125
Airedale, Ultra blue $100
Chick, head down or up, Milk White $15
Clydesdale, 5¼″ tall, Verde green $200
Clydesdale, 5¼″ tall, Amber or salmon $325
Colt, Aqua or amber $75
Cygnet, 4″ tall, Black $65
Cygnet, 4″ tall, Light Blue $30
Donkey, 6″ tall, Caramel slag or ultra blue $75
Donkey, 6″ tall, Green carnival $125
Elephant, 1″ tall, Caramel slag $65
Elephant, 1″ tall, Green carnival $110
Elephant, 4″ tall, Pink satin or light blue $175
Filly, head backward, Verde green $175
Filly, head forward, Satin $85
Fish candleholder, Sunshine yellow $55
Fish match holder, Sunshine yellow satin $30
Gazelle, 11″, Ultra blue $125
Giraffe, 10¼″ tall, Etched crystal $200
Hen, 4½″ tall, Sunshine yellow $100
Hen covered dish, on nest, 4½″, Beaded brown $35
Horse head bookends, Pink $550
Mallard duck, wings down, Light Blue satin $30
Mallard duck, wings down, Caramel slag or amber $200
Mallard duck, wings half up, Caramel slag $45
Mallard duck, wings half up, Light Blue satin $30
Mallard duck, wings up, Caramel slag $45
Mallard duck, wings up, Light Blue satin $30
Owl, Milk White $55
Pheasant, Asiatic, Amber $375
Piglet, sitting, 1″ tall $55
Piglet, standing, Ruby Red $110
Piglet, standing, Ultra blue $55
Rabbit, 4⅜″ tall, Ultra blue $175
Rabbit, paperweight, Milk White $45
Rooster, Amber $475
Rooster, fighting, Pink $225
Sow, 3⅛″ tall, Amber $450
Swan, Caramel slag or iridescent green $40
Swan, Milk White $35
Swan nut dish, footed $45
Terrier, Caramel slag $110
Tiger, paperweight, Black $85

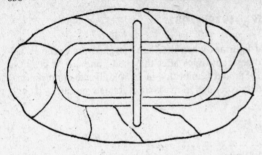

"Jamestown" pattern.
DRAWING BY MARK PICKVET.

Tiger, paperweight, Jade green $110
Wood duck, caramel slag, ultra blue satin, amber, or sunshine yellow satin .. $55
Wood duckling, floating or standing, sunshine yellow or sunshine yellow satin
....$25
Woodchuck, 4¹/₂″ tall, Amber $55

JAMESTOWN FOSTORIA GLASS COMPANY, 1958–1985

Several lines were used for Fostoria's "Jamestown" pattern, and many pieces below
are similar but differ slightly in dimensions. Stemware had a much longer production run and is therefore more easily found than some of the tableware items.
Brown and amber are not desirable. Fostoria usually made a fairly good grade of
crystal, and the crystal "Jamestown" pieces are most in demand, followed closely
by ruby red. Other colors include amethyst, green, light blue, smoke, and pink.

Bowl, 10″
    Amber or brown $40
    Crystal $30
    Other Colors $55
    Ruby Red $35
Bowl, 10″, with 2 handles
    Amber or brown $35
    Crystal $45
    Other Colors $40
    Ruby Red $60
Bowl, 4¹/₂″
    Amber or brown $25
    Crystal $25
    Other Colors $20
    Ruby Red $35
Butter dish with cover, ¹/₄ lb., rectangular
    Amber or brown $40
    Crystal $50
    Other Colors $45
    Ruby Red $65
Cake plate, 9¹/₂″, with 2 handles
    Amber or brown $25

Crystal $35
Other Colors $30
Ruby Red $50

Celery, 9¼″
Amber or brown $20
Crystal $30
Other Colors $25
Ruby Red $45

Creamer, 3½″
Amber or brown $17
Crystal $25
Other Colors $20
Ruby Red $35

Goblet, various styles
Amber or brown $17
Crystal $25
Other Colors $20
Ruby Red $35

Marmalade dish with cover
Amber or brown $45
Crystal $65
Other Colors $55
Ruby Red $85

Pickle, 7½″
Amber or brown $25
Crystal $35
Other Colors $30
Ruby Red $50

Pitcher, 1½ qt.
Amber or brown $75
Crystal $100
Other Colors $90
Ruby Red $150

Plate, 8″
Amber or brown $16
Crystal $10
Other Colors $25
Ruby Red $14

Plate, cake, 14″
Amber or brown $35
Crystal $45
Other Colors $40
Ruby Red $65

Relish, 9″, 2-part
Amber or brown $30
Crystal $20
Other Colors $45
Ruby Red $25

Salad set, 4-piece, (10″ bowl, 14″ plate, wooden fork and spoon)
Amber or brown $100
Crystal $75

Other Colors $150
Ruby Red $90

Salt and pepper shakers with chrome tops
Amber or brown $40
Crystal $30
Other Colors $55
Ruby Red $35

Salver, 10″
Amber or brown $45
Crystal $65
Other Colors $55
Ruby Red $90

Sauce dish with cover
Amber or brown $35
Crystal $45
Other Colors $40
Ruby Red $65

Sugar, 3½″
Amber or brown $17
Crystal $25
Other Colors $20
Ruby Red $35

Tray, 9½″, 2-handled
Amber or brown $45
Crystal $50
Other Colors $45
Ruby Red $75

Tumbler, over 5″ tall
Amber or brown $17
Crystal $30
Other Colors $25
Ruby Red $45

Tumbler, under 5″ tall
Amber or brown $15
Crystal $25
Other Colors $20
Ruby Red $35

Wine glass, various styles
Amber or brown $15
Crystal $25
Other Colors $20
Ruby Red $35

MILK GLASS   VARIOUS COMPANIES, LATE 19TH CENTURY–PRESENT

Milk glass is an opaque or semi-opaque opalescent glass colored originally by a compound of arsenic or calcined bone or tin. The result is a white color resembling milk. Modern milk glass usually contains aluminum and fluorine as additives to produce the desired effect. Milk glass is often trimmed, hand-painted, or machine enameled, since most colors go with white. There are many covered animal dishes in milk glass, without a mark or signature; most are not easily identified, while some are impossible. Common covered dishes (e.g., roosters and hens) are priced in the $20.00 to $25,00 range, while uncommon pieces sell for more (e.g., horses and lions). Known makers, marked pieces, older rare pieces, and even colored animal dishes sell for much more. Refer to entries on Fenton's "Crest" and Westmoreland's "Beaded Edge" and "Panel Grape" in this chapter for additional milk glass listings.

Apple-shaped dish, 9½″ across, 2 divisions (Imperial), 1950s $30
Basket, 8¾″ long, laced edge (Imperial), 1950s $40
Battleship shape (Maine from Spanish-American War), 7½″ long $100
Battleship shape (The Newark) $85
Boar's head covered dish, 1888 (rare) $2000
Bowl, fruit, 10⅝″, laced edge, Monroe pattern (Fostoria), 1960s $35
Cake stand, 10⅜″ square, 6¾″ tall, hole in center (Indiana), 1960s $15
Candleholder, double, 5¼″ tall, circular base (Imperial), 1930s $35
Candlestick, 7½″ tall, Vinelf design (Imperial), 1950s $40
Candy jar with cover, 6½″ diameter, enameled floral design $1250
Cat covered dish, various styles $25
Compote, 7″ diameter, 4⅛″ tall, circular base with bird stem $50
Compote, octagon base, Grape design (Anchor-Hocking), 1960s $15
Covered wagon shape, 6″-6½″ long, (Conestoga) $175
Creamer, 4¾″, Chrysanthemum Sprig design (Northwood) $200
Cruet with stopper, 7″ tall, hobnail (Fenton) $40
Dog covered dish, various styles $40
Dog, Pekingese covered dish, late 19th century $750
Donkey and cart, 9⅜″ long, 4⅛″ tall $35
Dove covered candle dish, (Avon), 1970 .... $15
Duck covered dish, various styles $25
Eagle covered dish, (American Eagle style) $75
Easter egg shape, 6″ long, 2-piece (includes cover), gold trim and enameled floral design $40
Egg shape, 2¾″ long, 2-piece (includes cover) $10
Gas globe, Sinclair or Texaco $400
Hat shape, 3¾″ tall, gold ruffled rim, enameled floral design (Fenton) $30
Hen covered dish, various styles $25
Horse covered dish, various styles $50
Iron covered dish, 7″ long $75
Lamb covered dish, various styles $25
Lamp shade, 7¼″, globe-shaped, embossed foliage design $150
Lamp, owl-shaped, 7½″ tall $1000
Liberty bell, 3½″ tall, metal clapper $20
Mug, Anchor-Hocking or Hazel Atlas advertising, 1940s $7
Perfume bottle with stopper, 7″ tall, Pansy design outlined in gold trim $50
Pitcher, milk, 7″ tall, (Cambridge), 1940s $75
Powder jar with cover, 5½″ diameter, 4½″ tall, enameled 3 kittens design with gold trim (Westmoreland) $60
Punch bowl, Pineapple pattern (Westmoreland) $150
Punch cup, Pineapple pattern (Westmoreland) $20
Rabbit covered dish, various styles $25
Rooster covered dish, 4½″ long, 3¾″ tall, Hazel Atlas mark $35

Rooster covered dish, various styles $25
Salt and pepper shakers, 3″ tall, embossed Diamond Quilted design $25
Salt and pepper shakers, 6″ tall, John and Mary Bull, aluminum tops (Imperial), 1950s (marked IG) $50
Sugar with cover, 4³/₄″, Chrysanthemum Sprig design (Northwood) $250
Swan covered dish, various styles $25
Vase, 3³/₄″ tall, Double Horse Head design $15
Vase, 6″ tall, cornucopia-style (Westmoreland), 1930s $40
Vase, 9³/₄″ tall, 11¹/₂″ wide, embossed Geese design (Consolidated) $150
Vase, 9″ tall, embossed Grape design (L.E. Smith), 1970s $25
Vase, 9″ tall, embossed Loganberry design (Imperial), 1950s $30

MISCELLANEOUS MODERN GLASS COLLECTIBLES
VARIOUS COMPANIES

There are numerous one-of-a-kind items that have been produced in the United States over the past two or three decades. Some of the more interesting include chess sets, museum reproductions, items made with Mt. St. Helen's volcanic ash, and pieces by new artists or companies that do not yet have large offerings.

Apple, 4³/₄″ tall, (Lenox), Crystal $75
Bell, 3″ tall, crystal with Beatrix Potter pewter finials, several styles (Mrs. Rabbit, Flopsy, Mopsy, Cottontail, and Peter), price is for each $25
Biscuit jar, 9¹/₄″ tall, with 3-faced frosted finial on cover, reproduction of the museum of Fine Arts, Boston, Crystal $60
Bottle, milk with plastic cover, 8″ tall, enameled brown and white Oreo cookies $25
Bowl, 5″, Cape Cod pattern reproduction, Smithsonian, Cobalt Blue $65
Bowl, 7″, Cape Cod pattern reproduction, Smithsonian, Cobalt Blue $80
Bowl, 8″ diameter, 4″ tall, 48 oz., reproduction of Dorflinger's Cut Crystal Prism design, Smithsonian $90
Cake plate, 11″ diameter, 4″ tall, crystal with ringed stem, Modern Tiffany commission $75
Candleholder, 3″ tall, 4¹/₂″ long, sparrow-shaped, Crystal $8
Candlestick, 11″ tall, square base, dolphin-shape reproductions, Museum of Fine Arts, Boston, Crystal or Azure blue $50
Candlestick, 4″ tall, hexagonal shape, Frank Lloyd Wright Foundation, Crystal $50
Candlestick, 8³/₄″ tall, with 3-faced frosted design on stem, reproduction of the Museum of Fine Arts, Boston, Crystal $45
Candy jar with cover, 5″ tall, 6″ long, 4″ wide, old-fashioned angled style, 1 qt., enameled brown Hershey's Chocolate design $25
Candy jar with cover, 10″ tall, 7″ diameter, enameled red and yellow design of Life Savers $40
Candy jar with cover, 10″ tall, 7″ diameter, enameled red, white, and yellow design of Hershey's Chocolate $50
Candy, glass, old-fashioned clear plastic wrapped design, multicolored glass candy (several styles) $7
Car, 1956 Thunderbird, 7¹/₈″ long, crystal sculpture with 24 kt. gold top, bumpers and steering wheel, Franklin Mint $175

Mt. St. Helen's ash glass. PHOTO BY ROBIN RAINWATER.

Chess set, 15″ square glass board, 3″ kings, 2 styles, 32 pieces (16 clear and 16 black or frosted) $80
Coach, Cindarella's, crystal with gold frame, wheels border, and top finial, Franklin Mint $175
Dragon, 6½″ long, 3¾″ tall, handblown crystal with gold and black accents $60
Egg, 1¾″ tall, faceted crystal, gold stand, gold and amethyst applied ornamentation $75
Egg, 3½″ tall, clear square base, frosted lavender with 3 prancing clear unicorns $30
Egg, 3½″ tall, crystal with iridescent purple, white, and blue floral design, from Mt. St. Helen's Volcanic ash $35
Globe, world, 4″ diameter, frosted crystal with clear continents $40
Goblet, 10″ tall, 8 oz., crystal with frosted stem, applied pink and frosted Lalique style heart at top of stem $50
Grandfather clock, 7½″ tall, spun crystal with gold ringer, string sides, and top piece $40
Honey pot with cover and serving spoon, 4½″ tall, 12 oz., crystal Horizontal Cut design, Monticello commission $40
Jaguar porcelain figure on crystal tree sculpture, 8″ tall, Franklin Mint $200
Lamp, desk, 11″ tall, bronze base and stem, Tiffany style multicolored Grape Cluster patterned shade $125
Lamp, desk, 19″ tall, bronze base and stem, Tiffany style multicolored Grape Cluster patterned shade $200
Lamp, desk, 23″ tall, bronze base and stem, Tiffany style multicolored Grape Cluster patterned shade $275
Lamp, desk, 25½″ tall, Lily pad bronze base and bronze stem, Tiffany style multicolored Hummingbird shade $300
Lamp, oil, 2½″ tall, 4⅜″ wide, 8 oz., from Mt. St. Helen's volcanic ash, Iridescent purple or aqua $30
Paperweight, 3″ diameter, violet opaline with enameled moon, stars, and waves (Lundberg Studios) $100

New York Metropolitan Museum of Art reproduction 3-face jar. PHOTO BY ROBIN RAINWATER.

Penguin figurine, 4¹/₄″ tall, (Dansk), Crystal $50
Perfume bottle with stopper, 6″ tall, frosted stopper with applied crystal clear hummingbird finial, Pastel Pink $30
Pineapple shape paperweight, 4¹/₂″ tall, solid crystal, Diamond pattern $20
Pitcher, 7¹/₂″ tall, double lip carafe style, 36 oz., Forest Green or Amethyst ... $20
Pitcher, water, 9″ tall, 60 oz., tinted pale green, applied emerald green handle and cactus decoration $30
Pitcher, water, 64 oz., crystal with engraved Lily of the Valley Floral pattern, Modern Tiffany commission $75
Pitcher, water, 8³/₄″ tall, 64 oz. $20
Plate, Christmas, 10″, bubble textured crystal with fused green and white and red and white candy canes, limited edition (500) $45
Platter, 12″ hexagonal, crystal with concentric line triangle lines (Reidel) .. $100
Platter, 13″ round, crystal with 5 pressed cats $15
Pumpkin figure, 7¹/₄″ tall, 6¹/₂″ diameter, hand-blown orange pumpkin with applied Dark green stem $50
Ram figurine, 3¹/₂″ tall, Dansk, Crystal $50
Rocking horse, 5¹/₂″ tall, crystal with 22 kt. gold saddle, feet, and rocker legs ... $45
Star Trek Enterprise (NCC 1701), 2¹/₂″ tall, crystal miniature on round crystal base $225
Star Trek: The Next Generation crystal paperweight, 3″ diameter (circular), etched design of the Starship Enterprise (NCC 1701D) $75
Swizzle stick, various colors (green, blue, white, etc.), twist designs $17
Tumbler, 12 oz., old-fashioned style, crystal with etched evergreen (Canadian Hemlock, blue spruce, Scotch pine, White pine, Balsam fir, or Eastern red cedar), National Wildlife Federation commission $8
Tumbler, 9 oz., enameled brown and white Oreo cookies $5
Vase, 10″ tall, classic 2-handled design, Smithsonian reproduction, Cobalt Blue or crystal $60
Vase, 6″ tall, made from Mt. St. Helen's volcanic ash, Iridescent aqua $40
Whale with Jonah figure within, 4¹/₄″ long, handblown crystal $25

MOONSTONE ANCHOR–HOCKING GLASS CORPORATION, 1941–1946

The large, round "Moonstones" on the glass articles resemble the hobs in hobnail patterns. The color is white opalescent, which serves as an edging on most pieces. The base is crystal, and the opalescent coating does not render the glass opaque. There are a few light green and pink opalescent pieces, but most were experimental and are kept in storage at Anchor-Hocking. The Fenton Glass Company has made a few pieces that are similar to "Moonstone" including salt and pepper shakers and cologne bottles. The hobs on Fenton's pieces are more pointed than the round ones on "Moonstone."

Bowl, 5¹/₂", Light Opalescent $12
Bowl, 6¹/₂", 2-handled, Light Opalescent $15
Bowl, 7³/₄", Light Opalescent $15
Bowl, 9¹/₂", crimped, Light Opalescent $20
Candleholder, Light Opalescent $10
Candy jar with cover, Light Opalescent $35
Cigarette jar with cover, Light Opalescent $20
Cloverleaf-shaped dish, 3 divisions, Light Opalescent $15
Creamer, Light Opalescent $7
Cup, Light Opalescent $7
Goblet, 5¹/₂" tall, 10 oz., Light Opalescent $20
Heart-shaped dish, 1 handle, Light Opalescent $15
Plate, 10", Light Opalescent $20
Plate, 6¹/₄", Light Opalescent $5
Plate, 8", Light Opalescent $12
Puff box with cover, 4³/₄", round, Light Opalescent $20
Relish dish, Light Opalescent $10
Saucer, Light Opalescent $5
Sherbet, Light Opalescent $10
Sugar, 2-handled, Light Opalescent $7
Vase, 5" tall, Light Opalescent $15

"Moonstone" pattern. PHOTO BY
ROBIN RAINWATER.

NAVARRE   FOSTORIA GLASS COMPANY, LATE 1930s–1985

"Navarre" is Fostoria's Plate Etching #327 and is a very elegant etched pattern. Nearly all of the stemware and one tumbler are available in light pink or light blue with the same etching (increase the price by 25% for pink and blue items). There are quite a few pieces here, and the pitchers and cruets are already rare.

Bell, Crystal	$40
Bonbon dish, 7³/₈″ diameter, 3-footed, Crystal	$30
Bowl, 10¹/₂″, with or without handles or feet, Crystal	$55
Bowl, 10″ oval, Crystal	$45
Bowl, 12¹/₂″ oval, Crystal	$70
Bowl, 12″, Crystal	$65
Bowl, 4″ or 4¹/₂″, 1 handle, Crystal	$15
Bowl, 5″, with or without handle, Crystal	$17
Bowl, 6¹/₄″, 3-footed, Crystal	$25
Bowl, 6″, Crystal	$20
Bowl, 7¹/₂″ oval, 2 tab handles, Crystal	$35
Candlestick, 4¹/₂″ or 5″ tall, double, Crystal	$40
Candlestick, 4″ tall, Crystal	$22
Candlestick, 5¹/₂″ tall, Crystal	$30
Candlestick, 6³/₄″ tall, double or triple, Crystal	$65
Candlestick, 6″ tall, triple, Crystal	$65
Candy dish with cover, Crystal	$110
Celery, 11″, Crystal	$40
Celery, 9″, Crystal	$30
Cheese dish, 3¹/₄″ tall, 5¹/₄″ diameter, stemmed, Crystal	$35
Compote, various styles, Crystal	$110
Cordial, Crystal	$30
Cracker dish, 11″, flat, Crystal	$40
Creamer, 4¹/₄″ tall, 6³/₄ oz., Crystal	$25
Creamer, individual, 3¹/₈″ tall, 4 oz., Crystal	$17
Cruet with stopper, 6¹/₂″ tall, Crystal	$275
Cup, CR	$17
Goblet, various styles, Crystal	$40
Ice bucket, 4¹/₂″ tall, Crystal	$85
Ice bucket, 6″ tall, Crystal	$110
Mayonnaise set, 3-piece (2 styles), Crystal	$85
Pickle, 8″ or 8¹/₂″, Crystal	$30
Pitcher, 1 ¹/₂ qt., Crystal	$350
Pitcher, syrup, Crystal	$250
Plate, 10¹/₂″, oval, Crystal	$55
Plate, 6″, Crystal	$12
Plate, 7¹/₂″, Crystal	$15
Plate, 8¹/₂″, Crystal	$20
Plate, 9¹/₂″, Crystal	$30
Plate, cake, 10″, 2 handles, Crystal	$50
Plate, cake, 16″, Crystal	$100
Plate, cake, 14″, Crystal	$75
Relish, 10″, 4 divisions, Crystal	$60
Relish, 10″ oval, 3 divisions, Crystal	$50

Relish, 13¹/₄″, 5 divisions, Crystal $85
Relish, 6″, square, 2 divisions, Crystal $40
Salt and pepper shakers, Crystal $85
Sauce dish, 6¹/₂″, divided, Crystal $50
Sauce dish, 6¹/₂″ × 5¹/₄″ oval, Crystal $110
Sauce dish liner, 8″, oval, Crystal $30
Saucer, Crystal $10
Sugar, 3⁵/₈″ tall, 2-handled, Crystal $25
Sugar, individual, 2 ⁷/₈″ tall, Crystal $17
Syrup, 5¹/₂″, Sani-Cut, Crystal $250
Tidbit, 8¹/₄″, 3-footed, Crystal $35
Tray, 6¹/₂″, (for individual creamer and sugar set), Crystal $30
Tumbler, 10 oz., Crystal $35
Tumbler, 13 oz., Crystal $40
Tumbler, 5 oz., footed, Crystal $25
Vase, 10″, footed, Crystal $150
Vase, under 10″ tall, various styles, Crystal $85
Wine glass, various styles, Crystal $40

NEW ENGLAND CRYSTAL COMPANY   1989–PRESENT

One of the newest art glass companies in the United States, New England Crystal has already established itself as a producer of high-quality new products. Fine cut lead crystal, pate de verre, and copper wheel engraving are only just the beginning for this operation. Of particular note are the pate de verre animals and the unique "Crystal Scrimshaw" collections.

Bowl, 3¹/₄″ long, irregular shape, frosted Oyster Shell with Pearl design $75
Bowl, 8″, cut antelope, Bird or Fish design $100
Cross crystal sculpture, 3¹/₂″ tall, (crucifix-shaped) $35
Cross crystal sculpture, 3¹/₂″ tall, (crucifix-shaped), Diamond Cut design ... $45
Cross crystal sculpture, 3¹/₂″ tall, (crucifix-shaped), engraved design $55
Fish, 2″ tall, 3³/₄″ tall, Pate de Verre design, Pink or blue $100
Fish, 4″ tall, 3³/₄″ long, Pate de Verre on crystal base, Pink or blue $175
Frog, 1⁵/₈″ tall, 2¹/₂″ wide, Pate de Verre design $100
Frog, 2³/₈″ tall, 2³/₄″ wide, Pate de Verre on crystal base, Pink or blue $175
Masquerade crystal prism sculptures, 4″ tall, copper wheel-engraved Moon and Star, Theater Masks, and Sun and Moon designs $125
Paperweight, 2¹/₄″, copper wheel-engraved Federal and Primrose patterns ... $50
Paperweight, 2³/₄″, copper wheel-engraved Arbor Floral pattern $100
Paperweight, 2³/₄″, copper wheel-engraved Jefferson Foliage pattern $75
Paperweight, 3″, cut Hobstar pattern $50
Paperweight, cut Triple Diamond pattern $50
Perfume bottle with atomizer, 4¹/₂″ tall, copper wheel-engraved Federal and Primrose patterns $125
Perfume bottle with atomizer, 4¹/₂″ tall, cut Triple Diamond pattern $125
Perfume bottle with stopper, 5″ tall, copper wheel-engraved Federal and Primrose patterns $100
Perfume bottle with stopper, 5″ tall, cut Triple Diamond pattern $100

*"Pate de Verre frog" by New England
Crystal Company. Reproduced from a
1993 company catalog.*

Scrimshaw crystal sculpture, 4³/₄″ tall, copper wheel-engraved ship and ocean
scene ("The Chase") $400
Scrimshaw crystal sculpture, 5″ long, copper wheel-engraved ship and ocean
scene ("Going Home") $400
Scrimshaw crystal sculpture, 9¹/₂″ long, copper wheel-engraved ship, whale, and
boat scene ("The Capture") $450
Shot glass, 2¹/₄″ tall, 1 oz., copper wheel-engraved Fly Caster's pattern $80
Shot glass, 2⁵/₈″ tall, copper wheel-engraved Federal and Primrose patterns .. $75
Shot glass, 2⁵/₈″ tall, cut Triple Diamond pattern $75
Tumbler, 11.5 oz., old-fashioned glass, copper wheel-engraved Fly Caster's pattern
(2 styles) $40

NEW MARTINSVILLE ANIMALS   1920s–1950s

New Martinsville's line of animals was continued by Viking, which purchased the
company in 1944. Viking continued using the New Martinsville molds but marked
the products "Rainbow Art" or with the Viking name. In 1991, Viking was purchased by Kenneth Dalzell (former president of Fostoria), and some of the old
molds are still being used.

Bear, baby, 3″ tall, 4¹/₂″ long, Crystal $75
Bear, black, with wheelbarrow, (2-piece set), Crystal $275
Bear, Mama, 4″ tall, 6″ long, Crystal $300
Bear, Papa, 4³/₄″ tall, 6¹/₂″ long, Crystal $350
Chick, 10 tall, Crystal $75
Dog bookends, German Shepherd, pair, Crystal $175
Dog bookends, Russian Wolfhound, 7¹/₄″ tall, pair, Crystal $200
Dove bookends, 6″ tall, frosted, pair, Crystal $85
Duck, fighting, head up or head down (Viking), Crystal $40
Eagle, Crystal $75
Elephant bookends, pair, Crystal $150
Gazelle bookends, 8¹/₂″ tall, pair, Crystal $125
Hen, 5″ tall, Crystal $75
Horse, 12″ tall, pony, oval base, Crystal $110
Pelican, 8″ tall, lavender tint, Crystal $70
Pig, 3³/₄″ tall, sow, Crystal $275
Piglet, 1¹/₄″ tall, Crystal $75
Police dog on rectangular base, 5″ tall, 5″ long, Crystal $110
Porpoise, Crystal $525
Rabbit, 1″ tall, ears back, Crystal $75

Rabbit, 1″ tall, ears down, Crystal $75
Rabbit, 1″ tall, ears up, Crystal $75
Rabbit, 3″ tall, Crystal $100
Rooster, 8″ tall, Crystal $110
Seal candlestick, 4³/₄″ tall, baby seal, Crystal $75
Seal light, 7¹/₄″ tall, with bulb, Crystal $85
Seal with ball bookends, pair, Crystal $150
Squirrel bookends, 5¹/₄″ tall, on base, pair, Crystal $150
Starfish bookends, 7³/₄″ tall, pair, Crystal $150
Swan bonbon dish, 6″, Cobalt Blue $60
Swan bowl, 10¹/₂″, Amber $50
Tiger bookends, 6³/₄″ tall, on base, pair, Crystal $325

PANEL GRAPE   WESTMORELAND GLASS COMPANY, 1950–1970s

The color is an opaque milk white; some pieces (mostly plates) are available with birds, flowers, and fruits for color decoration applied on the white. "Panel Grape" is also known as Westmoreland's "Pattern #1881" and was highly successful. In the Modern or even Post-Modern era of glassware, there are few patterns that can boast so many pieces (excluding different color combinations). Milk glass collectors seem to always have a few pieces of "Panel Grape," and some argue that no milk glass collection is complete without one.

Appetizer set, 3-piece, (relish dish, round fruit cocktail, and small ladle),
White $75
Basket, 6¹/₂″, oval, White $55
Basket, 8″, White $125
Bottle, water, 5 oz., White $85
Bowl, 10¹/₂″, round or oval, White $95
Bowl, 10″, White $85
Bowl, 11¹/₂″, round or oval, White $110
Bowl, 11″, round or oval, White $100
Bowl, 12¹/₂″, oval or bell-shaped, White $150
Bowl, 12″, White $125
Bowl, 14″, shallow, White $175
Bowl, 6¹/₂″, oval, White $50
Bowl, 8″, White $60
Bowl, 9¹/₂″, White $75
Bowl, 9″, White $70
Bowl, 9″, with cover, round or square, White $100
Bowl, 9″, bell-footed, White $100
Bowl, rose, White $35
Butter dish with cover, rectangular (¹/₄ lb.), White $45
Cake salver, 10 ¹/₂″, White $55
Cake salver, 11″, footed, White $85
Canape set, 3-piece (3¹/₂″ fruit cocktail with ladle and 12¹/₂″ tray), White ... $175
Candelabra, triple, White $250
Candleholder, 4″ tall, octagonal, White $17
Candleholder, 5″ tall, White $22

Candleholder, 8″ tall, double, White $35
Candy box with cover, 6½″, White $25
Candy jar with cover, with or without feet, White $35
Canister with cover, 11″, White $25
Canister with cover, 7″, White $85
Canister with cover, 9½″, White $150
Celery, 6″ tall, White $17
Cheese dish with cover, White $25
Compote, 4½″, crimped, White $35
Compote, 9″, White $175
Compote with cover, 7″, White $15
Condiment set, 5-piece, (2 oil bottles, puff box, and a 13½″ oval tray),
White $250
Egg plate, 12″, White $75
Egg tray, 10″, with a metal center handle, White $45
Epergne set, 2-piece, (12″ lipped bowl and 8½″ vase), White $175
Epergne set, 2-piece, (14″ flared bowl and 8½″ vase), White $250
Epergne set, 2-piece, (9″ lipped bowl and 8½″ vase), White $100
Epergne set, 3-piece, (12″ lipped bowl, 5″ bowl base, and 8½″ vase), White .....
.... $300
Epergne set, 3-piece, (14″ flared bowl, 5″ bowl base, and 8½″ vase), White ......
.... $400
Flower pot, White $65
Fruit cocktail, round or bell-shaped, with 6″ plate, White $35
Goblet, various styles, White $25
Jardiniere, 5″ tall, White $35
Jardiniere, 6½″ tall, White $40
Jelly dish with cover, 4½″ tall, White $35
Marmalade dish with ladle, White $75
Mayonnaise, 4″, footed, White $30
Mayonnaise set, 3-piece, (round fruit cocktail, 6″ plate, and ladle), White ... $65
Napkin ring, White $20
Nappy, 10″, bell-shaped, White $80
Nappy, 4½″, White $17
Nappy, 5″, handled or bell-shaped, White $25
Nappy, 7″, White $35
Nappy, 8½″, White $60
Nappy, 9″, White $75
Parfait, White $30
Pickle, White $30
Pitcher, 1 pt., White $50
Pitcher, 1 qt., White $65
Planter, free-standing, various styles, White $55
Planter, wall, various styles, White $100
Plate, 10½″, White $60
Plate, 6″, White $25
Plate, 7″, White $35
Plate, 8½″, White $45
Platter, 14½″, White $125
Platter, 18″, White $225

Puff box with cover, White $55
Punch bowl, 13″, White $275
Punch bowl base, White $200
Punch cup, White $15
Punch ladle, White $75
Relish, 9″, 3-part, White $45
Salt and pepper shakers, various styles, White $45
Sauce boat and tray, White $75
Saucer, White $15
Sherbet, various styles, White $20
Soap dish, White $75
Sugar, White $25
Sugar with cover, White $35
Sugar, individual (small), White $17
Tidbit tray with metal handle on the 10½″plate, White $65
Tidbit, 2-tier, (8½″ and 10½″ plates), White $100
Toothpick holder, White $35
Tray, 10″ oval, White $125
Tray, 13½″ oval, White $150
Tray, 9″ oval, White $100
Tumbler, various styles, White $35
Vase, over 9″ tall, several styles, White $50
Vase, up to 9″ tall, various styles, White $40
Water bottle, 5 oz., White $75
Wine glass, various styles, White $25

PILGRIM GLASS COMPANY   1949–PRESENT

Pilgrim was established in 1949, by Alfred E. Knobler in Ceredo, West Virginia. The company is well known in the contemporary art glass field. Its most impressive designs are superbly crafted cameo products. Along with cameo engraving, Pilgrim has revived other older styles including cranberry, crackle, and iridescent designs.

Bottle, 21″ tall, red with crystal stopper, Gurgle design $50
Canister with cover, Crackle design, Amber $45
Cruet with crystal stopper, 7″ tall, cranberry with applied crystal handle ... $35
Decanter with crystal ball stopper, 13″ tall, Blue glass $50
Egg, 2½″ tall, cranberry and crystal rose on white cameo $225
Egg, 3″ tall, various transparent colors (green, amethyst, blue, etc.) with cameo cut floral and wildlife designs $35
Egg, 3″ tall, white on red cameo, Snowman and Evergreens design $250
Lamp, 10″ tall, brass base, white on blue cameo, Evergreens and covered bridge scene $1250
Lamp, 24″ tall, all glass (base, stem, and shade), cranberry with cameo floral design $950
Owl paperweight, Crystal $20
Paperweight, 4½″, crystal with blue flower and wine swirls $50
Perfume bottle with stopper, 6″ tall, Cranberry $80

Pilgrim Glass. PHOTOS BY ROBIN RAINWATER.

Pitcher, milk, 6″ tall, opaque tangerine with frosted handle $20
Pitcher, miniature, 3¹/₂″ tall, Green crackle $15
Pitcher, miniature, 4¹/₂″ tall, Diamond and Swirl design, applied crystal handle, Amethyst $20
Pitcher, miniature, 5″ tall, Thumbprint pattern, Transparent Milk glass $25
Pitcher, water, 7¹/₂″ tall, Ruby red crackle design $35
Plate, 12″, Christmas issue, Della Robbia design, Crystal $25
Powder jar with white cover, 1¹/₂″ tall, white "Summer Meadow" on pink cameo, Foliage and Clover design $325
Vase, 10″ tall, bud, Cranberry $75
Vase, 11″, 5-color cameo, dark brown, tan, and black Night Hawk landing design, white stars, shaded light gray ground $1300
Vase, 12″ tall, jack-in-the-pulpit style, Cranberry $110
Vase, 12″ tall, jack-in-the-pulpit style, Iridescent $100
Vase, 12″ tall, light blue on aqua cameo, Ladies in the Aviary design $400
Vase, 12″ tall, red and white rhododendron and blue leaves on white cameo . . . $900
Vase, 13″ tall, dark and light blue on tan cameo, Parrots design $425
Vase, 5″ tall, fluted top, crystal base, white with cranberry streaking $20
Vase, 7″ tall, black bears (with white eyes and red mouths) on green cameo, Appalachia Folk Art design $1100
Vase, 7″ tall, light blue and white daisies on green cameo $550
Vase, 8″ tall, Classic Ming style, plum cast with milk white interior $40
Vase, 8″, bud, crystal globe base, Ruby Red $25
Vase, 9″ tall, 4-color cameo, brown and tan koala bears on dark gray ground . . . $925

PLANTER'S PEANUTS 1906–PRESENT

The Planters Nut and Chocolate Company was founded in 1906 in Wilkes-Barre, Pennsylvania. The trademark Mr. Peanut figurine was adopted in 1916. The company was sold to Standard Brands, Inc. in 1961, which later merged with Nabisco in 1981. There are many barrel-shaped jars with peanut finial covers. Early jars were commissioned by Planters from Tiffin in the 1930s. Mr. Peanut jars can be difficult to date since many are being reproduced. Be careful, since the older emerald green Depression style jars sell for about 10 times the price of the new darker forest green jars.

Aquarium or fishbowl, embossed clear glass, rectangular Planter's logo, 1930s–1940s $150
Jar with knobbed cover, round, embossed clear glass Planter's logo, 1930s–1940s . . . .
Jar with knobbed cover, round, enameled red and white, Planter's logo, 1960s $50
Jar with knobbed cover, round, Mr. Peanut 75th Anniversary $50
Jar with knobbed cover, round, Planter's logo, 1980s–1990s, Dark or Forest Green $35
Jar with peanut finial cover, barrel-shaped, 1930s, Emerald Green $300
Jar with peanut finial cover, barrel-shaped, 1980s–1990s, Dark or Forest Green $35
Jar with peanut finial cover, barrel-shaped, clear glass with enameled Mr. Peanut, 1960s–1980s $35

Planter's Peanuts jar. Reproduced from a 1930 Tiffin Co. catalog.

Jar with peanut finial cover, barrel-shaped, reproduction, Cobalt Blue $75
Jar with peanut finial cover, square-shaped, embossed clear glass Planter's design, 1930s $150
Jar with peanut finial cover, octagonal, 1930s, Emerald Green $300
Marble, Mr. Peanut, 1960 .... $20
Mug, yellow glass, Mr. Peanut $65
Paperweight, Mr. Peanut, Tennis Player, 1938 .... $75
Pilsner glass, Mr. Peanut 75th Anniversary $35
Pitcher, water, 60 oz., enameled black and yellow Mr. Peanut design, 1990s ... $25
Tumbler, 16 oz., enameled black and yellow Mr. Peanut design, 1990s $5
Tumbler, enameled black and tan Mr. Peanut $25
Tumbler, yellow glass, Mr. Peanut $45

PYREX   CORNING GLASS WORKS, 1915–PRESENT

The items below are all original crystal Corning Pyrex products. We plan to cover some of the milk glass and enamel transferred items in the next edition. Note that none of the measuring items carry metric system measurements (introduced in the late 1960s). Corning began as the Bay State Glass Company in East Cambridge, Massachusetts in 1851. A few years later, the company was moved to Somerville, Massachusetts, and renamed the Union Glass Company. Amory Houghton was one of the early directors. In 1864 Houghton, along with his two sons, purchased the Brooklyn Flint Glass Works and moved the operations to New York. In 1868 the factory's equipment in Brooklyn was transferred to Corning, New York, and renamed the Corning Flint Glass Works. The company was further incorporated in 1875 as the Corning Glass Works. In 1989 the name was changed to Corning, Inc. In the late 19th century, Corning produced specialty glass products such as light bulbs for Edison's new lamps, pharmaceutical and laboratory glass, and railroad signal lenses. Research continued on developing a glass that could withstand extreme temperature changes since flamed railroad lanterns had a habit of shattering when exposed to rain or snow. In 1912, Dr. Otto Schott perfected a borosilicate formula that withstood cold and hot temperature extremes. The formula worked well for lanterns as well as for battery jars. The glass was adapted to ovenware and kitchenware in 1915.

Baking dish, 13″ × 9″ rectangular, 2 tab handles $10
Baking dish, 9½ oz., square $4
Bowl, mixing, 1½ pt., 2 tab handles $3
Bowl, mixing, 1½ qt., 2 tab handles $5
Bowl, mixing, 1qt., 2 tab handles $4
Bowl, mixing, 2 qt., 2 tab handles $6
Bowl, mixing, 3 qt., 2 tab handles $7
Bread pan, 8½″ rectangular, 2 tab handles $7
Cake dish, 9″ square $8
Cake dish, 8½″ square $7
Cake dish, 8½″ square, 2 tab handles $8
Cake dish, 9″ square, 2 tab handles $9
Casserole, 1½ qt., with cover, oval, knob handle $10
Casserole, 1½ qt., with cover, round, knob handle $12
Casserole, 1½ qt., with cover, square, knob center handle and 2 tab side handles ..
.... $16
Casserole, 1½ qt., with cover, square, knob handle $15

NEW Number 2000 PYREX Roaster

No. 2000

PYREX SALES DIVISION
CORNING GLASS WORKS
CORNING, N. Y.
ORIGINATORS AND PATENTEES OF OVEN GLASSWARE

Pyrex roaster. Reproduced from a 1926 Corning advertisement.

Casserole, 1 pt., with cover, oval, knob handle $7
Casserole, 1 pt., with cover, round, knob handle $8
Casserole, 1 qt., with cover, oval, knob handle $8
Casserole, 1 qt., with cover, round, knob handle $10
Casserole, 3 qt., with pie plate cover, round $17
Casserole, 2 qt., with cover, round, knob handle $15
Custard cup, 3 horizontal bands $2
Measuring cup, 1 cup $3
Measuring cup 1 pt. $5
Measuring Cup, 1 qt. $7
Mushroom dish with dome cover, 2 tab handles on dish $75
Pie plate, 10″ $6
Pie plate, 11″ $7
Pie plate, 5″ $2
Pie plate, 6″ $2
Pie plate, 7″ $3
Pie plate, 8½″, 2 tab handles $7
Pie plate, 8″ $4
Pie plate, 9″ $5
Platter, 13⅔″ oval $20
Platter, 15¾″ $25
Refrigerator dish with cover, 1½ cup $5
Refrigerator dish with cover, 1½ pt. $10
Refrigerator dish with cover, 1 pt. $7
Refrigerator dish with cover, 1 qt. $12
Refrigerator dish with cover, 1½ qt. $15
Roaster with glass bowl cover, 3 qt., 10¼″ diameter, 2 tab handles on top and bottom $65
Teapot with cover, 4 cup, short, squat style $60
Teapot with cover, 6 cup, engraved floral design, short, squat style $110
Teapot with cover, 6 cup, engraved floral design, tall style $150
Teapot with cover, 6 cup, short, squat style $75
Teapot with cover, 6 cup, tall style $110
Teapot with cover, 4 cup, tall style $95

ROYAL RUBY   ANCHOR–HOCKING GLASS COMPANY, 1938–1970s

"Royal Ruby" is the older sister pattern of "Forest Green." It was first made in the late 1930s but is usually considered as later than the Depression era. The pattern is named for the color, which is a little darker than ruby red. Note that many pieces from Depression patterns were made in this color. These include "Coronation," "Old Cafe," "Oyster and Pearl," "Queen Mary," and "Sandwich." Anchor-Hocking has a patent on the "Royal Ruby" name. Both "Royal Ruby" and "Forest Green" were made in great quantities, and pieces are usually not too difficult to find. Assembling a complete set in both colors might still be a challenge, however. Some pieces contain a combination of crystal ruby red. See the "Ruby Red Glass" entry for ruby glass made by other companies.

Ashtray, 4½″ or 5″, leaf-shaped, Red $7
Beer bottle, 12 oz., Red $25

Beer bottle, 16 oz., Red $30
Beer bottle, 32 oz., Red $45
Beer bottle, 7oz., Red $20
Bonbon dish, 6¹/₂″, Red $10
Bonbon dish, 9″, Red $15
Bowl, 10¹/₂″, Red $35
Bowl, 11¹/₂″, Red $40
Bowl, 3³/₄″, Red $7
Bowl, 4¹/₂″, 1 handle, Red $8
Bowl, 4¹/₄″, Red $7
Bowl, 4³/₄″, round or square, Red $8
Bowl, 4″, ivy (similar to a rose bowl only narrower), Red $10
Bowl, 5¹/₂″, Red $10
Bowl, 5¹/₄″, Red $10
Bowl, 5″, round or square, Red $10
Bowl, 6¹/₂″, Red $15
Bowl, 6¹/₂″, 1 handle, Red $15
Bowl, 7¹/₂″, round or square, Red $17
Bowl, 8¹/₂″, Red $25
Bowl, 8″, 2-handled, Red $20
Bowl, 8″, oval, Red $35
Bowl, 9″, 2 tab handles, Red $25
Bowl, 10″, Red $30
Candleholder, 3¹/₂″ tall, Red $25
Candleholder, 4¹/₂″ tall, Red $30
Candy jar with cover, Red $25
Celery dish, 9″ long, Red $20
Cigarette box or card holder, Red $65
Cordial, Red $10
Creamer, Red $10
Creamer, footed, Red $12
Cup, round, Red $6
Cup, square, Red $7
Goblet, Various styles, Red $12
Heart-shaped dish, 5¹/₄″ long, 1 handle, Red $15
Lamp, Red $35
Lazy susan, crystal tray with 5 ruby red inserts and crystal center bowl $90
Leaf-shaped dish, 6¹/₂″ across, Red $12
Mint dish Red $15
Mustard jar, crystal with notched ruby cover and ruby spoon, ... $25
Pickle dish, 6″ long, Red $15
Pitcher, 1¹/₂ qt., Hobnail pattern, Red $65
Pitcher, 1 qt., Red $45
Pitcher, 2 qt., Bubble or Provincial pattern, Red $75
Pitcher, 22 oz., tilted, Red $35
Pitcher, 3qt., Red $85
Plate, 6¹/₂″, Red $5
Plate, 7″, Red $6
Plate, 7³/₄″, round or square, Red $7
Plate, 8¹/₂″, round or square, Red $10
Plate, 9″, round or square, Red $11

Plate, 9¼", round or square, Red $12
Plate, 9⅜", Bubble or Provincial pattern, Red $15
Platter, 13½"-13¾", Red $45
Platter, 14", Red $50
Puff box with cover, Red $15
Punch bowl, Red $55
Punch bowl base, Red $35
Punch cup, Red $6
Relish tray, crystal with 5 ruby red inserts and crystal center bowl with cover .. $100
Saucer, round or square, Red $3
Sherbet, Red $10
Sugar dish, Red $10
Sugar with cover, footed, Red $25
Tidbit tray, center handle, Red $25
Tumbler, 3½" tall $12
Tumbler, 3" tall, crystal foot, Red $10
Tumbler, 4½" tall, Hobnail pattern, Red $15
Tumbler, 4" tall, Red $15
Tumbler, 4" tall, crystal foot, Red $15
Tumbler, 5" tall, Red $20
Tumbler, 6" tall, Red $20
Tumbler, 6" tall, Bubble or Provincial pattern, Red $20
Tumbler, 8½" tall, crystal foot, Red $22
Vase, 6⅜" tall, Banded Ring design, Red $10
Vase, 4" tall, Red $12
Vase, 6½" tall, Red $15
Vase, 7¼" tall, Red $17
Vase, 9", Red $20
Wine glass, various styles, Red $12

RUBY RED GLASS　　VARIOUS COMPANIES, 1890s–PRESENT

Ruby red glass is named for the deep rich red color made originally by the addition of gold. Since the late 1930s, the element selenium has replaced gold as the primary coloring agent. Ruby red glass has been made throughout the 20th century by many companies, including Cambridge, Duncan & Miller, Fenton, Fostoria, Imperial, New Martinsville, and Viking. For additional ruby red examples, refer to other patterns in this chapter as well as Chapter 6. These include "Royal Ruby," "Crest," "Coin Glass," "Jamestown," references in many Depression patterns, and companies with separate listings, such as Blenko, Viking, and Westmoreland.

Banana boat, 11½" long, 1930s (New Martinsville), Ruby Red $45
Basket, 10 ½" diameter, wicker handle, embossed circles, 1933 (Fenton), Ruby Red $175
Bonbon dish, 7" diameter, Basketweave pattern, 1930s (Fenton), Ruby Red .. $75
Bowl, 10", cupped, 3 dolphin feet, 1930 (Fenton), Ruby Red $125
Bowl, 11", crimped, 3-footed, Pineapple pattern, 1937 (Fenton), Ruby Red $175
Bowl, 6", shallow, 1921 (Fenton), Ruby Red $75
Bowl, 8", cupped with base, 1929 (Fenton), Ruby Red $85

Bowl, orange, 10″, crimped, 1921 (Fenton), Ruby Red $400
Bowl, rose, Reeded design, 1930s (Imperial), Ruby Red $30
Candelabrum, 3-light, 5¼″ tall, 1930s, (New Martinsville), Ruby Red $65
Candelabrum, 3-light, 1930s, (Imperial), Ruby Red $150
Candleholder, 1-light, 5¼″ tall, 1930s (New Martinsville), Ruby Red $50
Candlestick, 3½″ tall, Double Dolphin design, 1930 (Fenton), Ruby Red $75
Candlestick, 5″ tall, horizontally ribbed, 1930s (Cambridge), Ruby Red $50
Candlestick, 8½″ tall, cut ovals, 1922 (Fenton), Ruby Red $275
Candy jar with cover, 7″ across, Clover Leaf design, 1930s (Paden City), Ruby Red $100
Candy jar with cover, 6″, marbleized or slag color, 1970s (Imperial, IG on bottom), Ruby Red $50
Chalice with cover, 9½″ tall, Hapsburg Crown design, 1960s (Fostoria), Ruby Red $100
Compote, 10″ diameter, double dolphin handles, 1933 (Fenton), Ruby Red $175
Creamer, 4″ tall, clear base, 1930 (Fenton), Ruby Red $40
Creamer, Colony pattern, 1980s (Fostoria), Ruby Red $25
Cup, 3¼″ diameter, Georgian pattern, 1930s (Fenton), Ruby Red $30
Decanter, 21 oz., Georgian patttern, 1930s (Fenton), Ruby Red $125
Decanter with crystal ball stopper, Radiance design, 1940s (New Martinsville), Ruby Red $150
Epergne, 3-piece (stand, bowl, and single vase), 1930s, (Paden City), Ruby Red $300
Fish, 7¼″ tall, 1960s (Fostoria), Ruby Red $75
Goblet, 7″ tall, Diamond Optic pattern, 1928 (Fenton), Ruby Red $75
Jug, ball-shaped, 80 oz., applied crystal handle, 1930s (Cambridge), Ruby Red $175
Lamp, electric, 9½″ tall, Diamond Optic pattern, 1931 (Fenton), Ruby Red $75
Nappy, 7¾″, laced edge, Diamond design, 1930s (Imperial), Ruby Red $35
Nappy, 8″ diameter, 3-footed, crimped, 1934 (Fenton), Ruby Red $75
Pickle dish, 7″ long, Diamond design, 1930s (New Martinsville), Ruby Red $25
Piggy bank, 7″ long, 4″ tall, mouth blown (James Joyce), Ruby Red $45
Pitcher, 8″ oz., Reeded design, 1930s (Imperial), Ruby Red $125
Plate, 10″, Sheffield pattern, 1936 (Fenton), Ruby Red $75
Plate, 7″, Cape Cod pattern (Imperial), Ruby Red $25
Plate, 8″ square, Mount Vernon design (Imperial), Ruby Red $25
Plate, torte, 14″, Radiance design, 1930s (New Martinsville), Ruby Red $75
Platter, 12″, 2-handled, 1980s (New Martinsville), Ruby Red $50
Punch bowl with underliner plate, globe-shaped, Radiance design, 1930s (New Martinsville), Ruby Red $500
Punch bowl, footed, 13″ diameter, 1930s (Cambridge), Ruby Red $300
Punch cup, (matches bowl above) 1930s (Cambridge), Ruby Red $40
Punch cup, (matches bowl above), Radiance design, 1930s (New Martinsville), Ruby Red $30
Punch ladle, (matches bowl above), Radiance design, 1930s (New Martinsville), Ruby Red $100
Relish dish, 8½″ diameter, 3 divisions, 3-footed, 1930s (Paden City), Ruby Red $35
Relish dish, 8″ diameter, 2-handled, 1931-1956 (Cambridge), Ruby Red $35
Salt and pepper shakers with chrome tops, 4½″ tall, Georgian pattern, 1930s (Fenton), Ruby Red $125

Sandwich server with center handle, 10¹/₂″, Threaded design, 1930s (Paden City), Ruby Red $75
Sherbet, footed with clear base, 1930 (Fenton), Ruby Red $50
Sugar, 3¹/₂″ tall, clear base, 1930 (Fenton), Ruby Red $40
Sugar, Colony pattern, 1980s (Fostoria), Ruby Red $25
Tray, 12″ rectangular, 2-handled, 1932 (Fenton), Ruby Red $100
Tray, 8¹/₂″ long, leaf-shaped, Leaf Vein design, 1936 (Fenton), Ruby Red ... $100
Tumbler, 12 oz., Reeded design, 1930s (Imperial), Ruby flashed $20
Tumbler, 4¹/₄″ tall, large round flutes, 1933 (Fenton), Ruby Red $35
Tumbler, 6″ tall, Plymouth pattern, 1930s (Fenton), Ruby Red $40
Vase, 12″ tall, engraved floral design, 1931 (Fenton), Ruby Red $200
Vase, 14″ tall, cornucopia-shaped, 1940s (Duncan & Miller), Ruby Red $175
Vase, 6¹/₂″ tall, 1926 (Tiffin), Ruby Red $100
Vase, 6¹/₂″ tall, jack-in-the-pulpit style, 1933 (Fenton), Ruby Red $75
Vase, 6³/₄″ tall, Sheffield pattern, 1936 (Fenton), Ruby Red $50
Vase, 8¹/₂″ tall, fan-style, Diamond Optic pattern, 1928 (Fenton), Ruby Red .. $65
Vase, 9″ tall, embossed dancers, 1933 (Fenton), Ruby Red $300

SANDWICH   ANCHOR–HOCKING GLASS COMPANY, 1939–1970s

There are several odd-colored pieces: darker royal ruby, forest green, amber (which Anchor-Hocking refers to as "desert gold"), pink, and milk white. Green is the rarest (triple the prices below). Milk white is not as desirable (reduce the prices by 25%). For all other colors, double the prices below. Pink and royal ruby are the oldest colors and were made for only two short years (1939–1940); the rest were made in the 1950s and 1960s. A cookie jar was reproduced in the 1970s in crystal but is an inch taller and noticeably wider by a few inches than the original (priced at $15.00). This pattern is sometimes confused with Indiana's "Sandwich," but there are more leaves surrounding each symmetrical flower pattern in Hocking's design (four leaves off the main stem as opposed to Indiana's two). One other prolific "Sandwich" pattern was Duncan & Miller's; there are more spiral curves in Duncan & Miller's design than either Hocking's or Indiana's.

Bowl, 4³/₈″, Crystal $5
Bowl, 4⁷/₈″, Crystal $6
Bowl, 5¹/₄″, Crystal $7
Bowl, 5″, ruffled, Crystal $12
Bowl, 6¹/₂″, Crystal $8
Bowl, 7″-7¹/₄″, Crystal $9
Bowl, 8″-8¹/₄″, Crystal $10
Bowl, 9″, Crystal $25
Butter dish with cover, Crystal $50
Cookie jar with cover, Crystal $50
Creamer, Crystal $7
Cup, Crystal $3
Custard Cup, Crystal $7
Custard Cup, 5 oz., ruffled, Crystal $12
Custard cup liner, Crystal $12
Pitcher, 2 qt., Crystal $100

Pitcher, milk, 1pt, Crystal $75
Plate, 12″, Crystal $15
Plate, 7″, Crystal $12
Plate, 8″, Crystal $5
Plate, 9″, Crystal $17
Plate, 9″, with indentation for punch cup, Crystal $5
Punch bowl, 9³/₄″, Crystal $30
Punch bowl stand, Crystal $25
Punch cup, Crystal $3
Saucer, Crystal $1
Sherbet, Crystal $10
Sugar with cover, Crystal $25
Tumbler, 3 oz., Crystal $12
Tumbler, 5 oz., Crystal $15
Tumbler, 9 oz., footed, Crystal $30

SANDWICH   INDIANA GLASS COMPANY, 1920s–PRESENT

The colors below are all reproductions of Indiana's "Sandwich" pattern, which was first made in the 1920s. Teal blue was made from the 1950s to the 1970s, particularly for Tiara home products. Other colors were added for Tiara (amber, crystal, light green, milk white, red, and smoky blue). Teal blue is blue aquamarine, while smoky blue is a darker midnight blue but much duller than cobalt blue. There are a few odd milk white pieces that are priced like smoky blue. The teal blue piece that causes the most trouble is the butter dish. The $150.00 price is for the original made in the 1950s; the reproduction is priced at $20.00. Refer to Chapter 6 for pricing on the original as well as the newer colors.

Ashtrays, set of 4 (card suits)
  New Crystal $5
Basket, 10″
  New Crystal $35
Basket, 10¹/₂″, with handles
  Light Green $10
  New Crystal $7
Bowl, 4″
  Light Green $5
  New Crystal $4
Bowl, 4¹/₄″
  Light Green $5
  New Crystal $4
Bowl, 6″
  Light Green $4
  New Crystal $3
Bowl, 6″, hexagonal
  Light Green $6
  Teal Blue $15
  Smoky Blue $12
  New Crystal $5

Bowl, 8″
  Light Green $5
  Teal Blue $12
  Smoky Blue $10
  New Crystal $4
Bowl, 8½″
  Light Green $12
  New Crystal $10
Bowl, 9″
  Light Green $17
  New Crystal $15
Bowl, 11½″
  Light Green $20
  New Crystal $17
Butter dish bottom
  Light Green $10
  Teal Blue $50
  New Crystal $9
Butter dish top
  Light Green $20
  Teal Blue $125
  New Crystal $17
Butter dish with cover
  Light Green $35
  Teal Blue $125
  New Crystal $30
  Teal Blue Reproduction $25
Candlestick, 3½″
  Light Green $12
  Teal Blue $17
  Smoky Blue $15
  New Crystal $10
Candlestick, 7″
  Light Green $16
  Teal Blue $20
  Smoky Blue $17
  Orange-Red $25
  New Crystal $15
Candlestick, 8½″
  Light Green $10
  Teal Blue $7
Celery, 10½″
  Light Green $17
  Teal Blue $15
Creamer
  Light Green $17
  Teal Blue $25
  Smoky Blue $20
  New Crystal $15
Creamer and sugar with diamond-shaped tray
  Light Green $25

Teal Blue $35
Smoky Blue $30
New Crystal $22

Cruet, 6½″, with stopper
Teal Blue $150

Cup, 9 oz.
Light Green $4
Teal Blue $10
Smoky Blue $7
Orange-Red $30
New Crystal $3

Cup for indented plate
Light Green $3
Teal Blue $8
Smoky Blue $6
New Crystal $1

Decanter with stopper
Light Green $35
Smoky Blue $45
New Crystal $27

Goblet, 8 oz.
Light Green $15
Smoky Blue $20
New Crystal $12

Goblet, 9 oz.
Light Green $17
Smoky Blue $22
Orange-Red $45
New Crystal $15

Mayonnaise, footed
Light Green $17
New Crystal $15

Pitcher, 68 oz.
Orange-Red $175
New Crystal $45

Pitcher, 8″ tall, 68 oz., with fluted rim
Light Green $50
New Crystal $40

Plate, 6″
Light Green $4
Teal Blue $7
New Crystal $3

Plate, 7″
Light Green $5
New Crystal $4

Plate, 8″
Light Green $6
New Crystal $5

Plate, 8,″ oval, with indentation for sherbet
Teal Blue $12
Orange-Red $25

Plate, 8³/₈″
Light Green $6
Orange-Red $25
New Crystal $5

Plate, 8¹/₂″, oval
Light Green $6
New Crystal $5

Plate, 10¹/₂″
Light Green $7
New Crystal $6

Plate, 13″
Light Green $20
Teal Blue $35
Smoky Blue $30
Orange-Red $45
New Crystal $15

Puff box
Light Green $25
New Crystal $20

Salt and Pepper shakers
Light Green $25
New Crystal $20

Sandwich server with center handle
Light Green $35
Orange-Red $65
New Crystal $25

Saucer, 6″
Light Green $4
Teal Blue $7
Smoky Blue $5
Orange-Red $10
New Crystal $3

Sherbet
Light Green $7
Teal Blue $15
Smoky Blue $12
New Crystal $6

Sugar
Light Green $17
Teal Blue $25
Smoky Blue $20
New Crystal $15

Sugar cover
Light Green $17
Teal Blue $25
Smoky Blue $20
New Crystal $15

Tray, 10″ (for wine decanter and goblets)
Light Green $15
Smoky Blue $20
New Crystal $10

Tumbler, 3 oz., footed
Light Green $12
Smoky Blue $15
New Crystal $10
Tumbler, 8 oz., footed
Light Green $15
Smoky Blue $17
New Crystal $12
Tumbler, 12 oz., footed
Light Green $17
Smoky Blue $20
New Crystal $15
Wine Glass, 3″, 4 oz.
Light Green $12
Smoky Blue $15
New Crystal $10

SHELL PINK MILK GLASS   JEANNETTE GLASS COMPANY, LATE 1950s

The color is very light opaque pink, nearly milk glass. There are several pattern variations, but all were produced under the "Shell Pink" pattern name. There are eagles, pheasants, feathers, fruits, thumbprints, and even insects. The pieces referred to as "Napco" are marked "Napco, Cleveland," on the bottom and were made specifically for Napco Ceramics of Cleveland, Ohio.

Ashtray, butterfly-shaped, Pink $22
Base with ball bearings (for lazy susan), Pink $40
Bowl, 10½″, footed, Pink $40
Bowl, 10″, footed, Pink $35
Bowl, 11″, 4-footed, Pink $50
Bowl, 17½″, Pink $55
Bowl, 6½″, with cover, Pink $30
Bowl, 8″, footed, Pink $40
Bowl, 8″, with cover, Pink $45
Bowl, 9″, footed, Pink $30
Cake stand, 10″, Pink $40
Candleholder, 3-footed, Pink $30
Candleholder, double, Pink $25
Candy dish, 5½″, 4-footed, Pink $35

Candy dish with cover, 6¹/₂″ tall, square, Pink $50
Candy jar with cover, 5¹/₂″, 4-footed, Pink $55
Celery, 12¹/₂″, 3-part, Pink $55
Cigarette box, Pink $100
Compote, 6″, Pink $30
Cookie jar with cover, 6¹/₂″ tall, Pink $100
Creamer, Pink $25
Goblet, Pink $25
Honey jar with notched cover for spoon, bee hive-shaped, Pink $55
Napco, berry bowl, footed, Pink $25
Napco, Bowl with sawtooth top, Pink $30
Napco, Compote, square, Pink $25
Napco, cross-hatched design pot, Pink $25
National candy dish, Pink $20
Pitcher, 1¹/₂ pt., Pink $55
Powder jar with cover, 4³/₄″, Pink $55
Punch base, 3¹/₂″ tall, Pink $50
Punch bowl, 7¹/₂ qt., Pink $100
Punch cup, 5 oz., Pink $15
Punch ladle (plastic), Pink $12
Relish, 12″, 4-part, octagonal, Pink $55
Sugar with cover, Pink $45
Tray, 10″ × 7³/₄″, oval with indentation for cup (punch cup fits the indentation), Pink $25
Tray, 12¹/₂″ × 9³/₄″, oval with 2 handles, Pink $65
Tray, 13¹/₂″, lazy susan, 5-part, Pink $75
Tray, 15³/₄″, 5-part with 2 handles, Pink $75
Tray, 16¹/₂″, 6-part, Pink $85
Tray set, (lazy susan with base), Pink $85
Tumbler, various styles, Pink $20
Vase, 5″ tall, cornucopia-shaped, Pink $35
Vase, 7″ tall, Pink $45
Vase, 9″ tall, Pink $65
Wine glass, Pink $25

SHOT GLASSES   VARIOUS COMPANIES, 1830s–PRESENT

Shot glasses generally hold 1 or 2 ounces of liquid and are no more than 3″ tall. They have been around since the 1830s and cover nearly every category of glass. The most desirable by collectors are the pre-prohibition era whiskey sample or advertising glasses. Most feature etched white writing of a distiller, company, proprietor, or other alcohol-related advertising. These glasses sell for around $35.00 to $50.00, but recently some rare examples have been auctioned off for more than $100.00. Shot glass collectors are usually quantity collectors, often boasting of hundreds of glasses. See the "Souvenir Glass" entry for a few ruby red examples.

19th-Century cut patterns $125
Barrel-shaped $7
Black porcelain replica $4

Nineteenth-century pillar fluted shot glass. PHOTO BY MARK PICKVET.

Carnival colors with patterns	$200
Carnival colors, plain or fluted	$75
Culver 22 kt. gold	$7
Depression colors	$10
Depression colors, patterns or etchings	$25
Depression tall, general designs	$12
Frosted with gold designs	$8
General advertising	$4
General etched designs	$7
General frosted designs	$4
General porcelain	$6
General tourist	$3
General with an enameled design	$3
General with gold designs	$8
Glasses with inside eyes	$7
Mary Gregory/Anchor-Hocking ships	$175
Nude shot glasses	$25
Plain shot glass with or without flutes	$1
Pop or soda advertising (i.e., Coca-Cola and Pepsi)	$15
Porcelain tourist	$4
Rounded European designs with gold rims	$5
Ruby flashed glasses	$45
Square glass with etching	$10
Square glasses with 2-tone bronze/pewter	$17
Square glasses with pewter	$15
Square shot glasses, general	$7
Standard glasses with pewter	$10
Taiwan tourist	$2
Tiffany/Galle/Fancy Art	$750
Turquoise and gold tourist	$7
Whiskey or beer advertising, modern	$5
Whiskey sample glasses	$75

Whiskey sample shot glass. PHOTO BY ROBIN RAINWATER.

SOUVENIR GLASS   VARIOUS PRODUCERS, LATE 19TH CENTURY-PRESENT

Some of the earliest souvenirs were made in 1876 for the U.S. centennial celebration; the most popular were glass Liberty Bells. In the 1880s through the Depression years, ruby flashed or ruby stained over crystal were quite popular and showed up most often in small tumblers and toothpick holders. Today, souvenirs abound with fired-on decals or machine-applied enamels; these include tumblers, mugs, shot glasses, and a wide variety of other items.

Ashtray, 5″ × 3″, black glass, 1962 World's Fair, Seattle $25
Butter dish, Button Arches pattern, Atlantic City, 1919, Ruby stained $85
Creamer, miniature, arched flutes, 1908, Ruby stained $35
Liberty Bell covered dish, globe finial, crystal with embossed "1776" and various phrases $125
Mug, 1³/₄″ tall, 1901 Pan American Exposition, Ruby flashed $30
Mug, arched flutes, Boston, Ruby stained $35
Mug, small corona, St. Joseph, MO, Ruby stained $35
Paperweight, 2¹/₂″, etched bird and rose, 1904 St. Louis Fair, Ruby flashed .. $85
Paperweight, 3¹/₄″, seashells, 1904 St. Louis Fair, Crystal $30
Paperweight, 4″, 1893 Columbian Exposition Agricultural Building, Crystal .. $100
Paperweight, 4″, 1901 Pan American Exposition, Temple of Music, Crystal $85
Plate, 10″, hobnail border, Cleveland reform $45
Plate, 10″, U.S. Capitol Building (Imperial), 1969, Red Carnival $40
Shot glass, 2³/₈″ tall, ruby stained with etched "State Fair 1908" $30
Shot glass, 2³/₈″ tall, ruby stained with etched "Souvenir Bellevue, Mich." ... $30
Shot glass, 2³/₈″ tall, ruby stained with etched "State Fair 1908" $30
Toothpick holder, 2¹/₈″ tall, ruby-stained Co-Op's Royal, Charleston, 1903 .. $40
Toothpick holder, 4″ tall, ruby stained with etched "Souvenir of Grand Rapids, Mich." $35
Tumbler, 3¹/₂″ tall, custard, Rangley Lakes Maine (Heisey) $55

American souvenir glass. PHOTO BY ROBERT DARNOLD.

Tumbler, 3½″ tall, etched crystal, 1893 Columbian Exposition, Mines and Mining Building $45
Tumbler, 3½″ tall, Lacy Medallion pattern, Atlantic City, 1901 .... $65
Tumbler, 3¾″ tall, Admiral George Dewey Commemorative $45
Tumbler, 5″ tall, 1904 St. Louis Fair, embossed Cascade Gardens, Crystal ... $35
Tumbler, 6″ tall, enameled Eastern Airlines, various designs, 1950s $7

SPORTSMAN SERIES or SAILBOAT AND WINDMILLS or SHIPS AND WINDMILLS   HAZEL-ATLAS GLASS COMPANY, LATE 1930s

White designs on this glass include sailboats and windmills, as well as sports. Fishing, golfing, horseback riding, and skiing are also part of the "Sportsman Series." Be sure that the design is fully intact. Damaged, worn, or missing designs are worth only a fraction of completely intact decorations. Some pale yellow decorations due to factory discolorations exist in this pattern, but as long as the complete decoration is there, the value is the same as listed below. Although there are a lot of tumblers in this design, the 2-ounce whiskey tumbler price is not a fluke. Take it from a long-time shot glass collector; there are a lot of collectors who would gladly pay the price to obtain this glass. There are few shot glasses worth this amount except for a few rare fancy cut crystal pieces, art glass such as Tiffany, and some rare 19th century advertising examples.

Cocktail mixer with stirrer (metal lid), Cobalt Blue with white designs $30
Cocktail shaker (metal lid), Cobalt Blue with white designs $35
Cup, Cobalt Blue with white designs $12
Ice bowl, Cobalt Blue with white designs $40
Pitcher, 2½ qt., Cobalt Blue with white designs $65
Pitcher, 2½ qt., with ice lip, Cobalt Blue with white designs $55
Plate, 5⅞″, Cobalt Blue with white designs $25

Plate, 8″, Cobalt Blue with white designs $25
Plate, 9″, Cobalt Blue with white designs $30
Saucer, Cobalt Blue with white designs $20
Tumbler, 8 oz., Cobalt Blue with white designs $17
Tumbler, 10½ oz., Cobalt Blue with white designs $20
Tumbler, 12 oz., Cobalt Blue with white designs $25
Tumbler, 4 oz., Cobalt Blue with white designs $30
Tumbler, 5 oz., Cobalt Blue with white designs $15
Tumbler, 6 oz., Cobalt Blue with white designs $15
Tumbler, 9 oz., Cobalt Blue with white designs $17
Whiskey tumbler, 2¼″ tall, 2 oz., Cobalt Blue with white designs $175

SQUARE   CAMBRIDGE GLASS COMPANY, 1950s

This was one of Cambridge's last patterns and was issued before the company went out of business. The Imperial Glass Company acquired many of Cambridge's molds and reproduced several "Square" pieces in color, such as red and black. Colored pieces sell for about 1½ times the crystal prices listed below.

Ashtray, 3½″ $10
Ashtray, 6½″ $12
Bonbon, 7″ $20
Bonbon, 8″ $25
Bowl, 10″, round or oval $35
Bowl, 11″ $40
Bowl, 12″, round or oval $45
Bowl, 4½″ $15
Bowl, 6½″ $20
Bowl, 9″ $30
Buffet set, 4-piece (plate, divided bowl, and 2 ladies) $65
Candleholder, 1¾″ tall $12
Candleholder, 2¾″ tall $15
Candleholder, 3¾″ tall $17
Candy box with cover $45
Celery, 11″ $30
Cocktail glass $20
Compote, 6″ $25
Cordial glass, 1½ oz. $20
Creamer $15
Creamer, indivdual (small) $12
Cruet with stopper, 4½ oz. $30
Cup $12
Cup, tea (small) $10
Decanter, 1qt. $100
Goblet, various styles $25
Ice tub, 7½″ $45
Iced tea goblet, 12 oz. $25
Icer, cocktail with liner $40
Juice glass, 4½ oz., footed $12

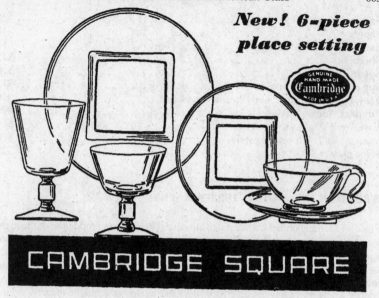

"Square" pattern. Reproduced from a 1952 trade catalog.

Lamp, hurricane, 2-piece	$75
Mayonnaise set, 3-piece (bowl, plate, and ladle)	$50
Plate, 11½″	$35
Plate, 13½″	$40
Plate, 6″	$12
Plate, 7″	$15
Plate, 9½″	$25
Plate, 9½″, tidbit	$30
Relish, 10″, 3-part	$45
Relish, 6½″, 2-part	$25
Relish, 8″, 3-part	$35

Salt and pepper shakers	$35
Saucer	$10
Saucer (small for tea cup)	$7
Sherbet	$15
Sugar	$15
Sugar, individual (small)	$12
Tray, 8″, oval (for individual creamer and sugar)	$20
Tumbler, various styles	$20
Vase, over 7″ tall, various styles	$50
Vase, under 7″ tall, various styles	$35
Wine glass, various styles	$25

STEUBEN CRYSTAL   1933–PRESENT

Since 1933, Steuben has concentrated almost exclusively on production of the highest grade of crystal. A few deviations, such as silver or gold accents, have been added, but no complete colored pieces have been produced. Some pieces are one-of-a-kind in that they were given as awards, presentations to heads of state, gifts to museums, and so on. Steuben's grade of crystal rivals any made in the world today; copper wheel engraving, prism effects, outstanding designs, and the industry's most gifted artists are all evident in Steuben's glass products. All modern crystal items feature the "Steuben" signature in fine diamond point script.

Apple, 4″ tall, paperweight, Crystal	$375
Ashtray with single rest, 5″ across, Crystal	$100
Balloon sculpture, 10¼″ tall, 5⅛″ width, triangular, 6 engraved hot air balloon, Crystal	$13750
Bear, 2½″ tall, hand cooler, Crystal	$175
Bear, teddy, 2½″ tall, hand cooler, Crystal	$175
Beaver, 4½″ long, Crystal	$525
Beaver, 5½″ long, Crystal	$525
Beaver, 6¼″ long, Crystal	$1100
Beaver, 9″ long, Crystal	$1100
Bird, shore, 8¼″ long, slender design, Crystal	$500
Bird, water, 10″ tall, 9¾″ long, in flight, Crystal	$1200
Bookend, 3½″ cube, air bubbles, Crystal	$775
Bowl, 10″, sunflower center/base, Crystal	$475
Bowl, 11½″, Archaic Etruscan design, Crystal	$1725
Bowl, 11¾″, magnolia, Crystal	$500
Bowl, 13½″, twist base, Crystal	$925
Bowl, 15½″, sunflower center/base, Crystal	$1025
Bowl, 16¼″, engraved Dragonfly design, Crystal	$15500
Bowl, 16″, 3⅞″ tall, sterling frame, Crystal	$17600
Bowl, 6″, blocks of cut lines, 1936	$400
Bowl, 7¼″ oval, folded, Crystal	$225
Bowl, 7¾″, floret, 4 feet, Crystal	$475
Bowl, 7″, spiral base	$400
Bowl, 8¼″, bubbled spherical center/base, Crystal	$475
Bowl, 8¼″, twist base, Crystal	$450

Steuben crystal.
PHOTO BY ROBIN
RAINWATER.

Bowl, 9³/₄″, draped design, Crystal $575
Bowl, 9³/₄″, Trillium design, Crystal $650
Bowl, 9″ oval, folded, Crystal $325
Bowl, 9″, ribbed, Crystal $325
Bull, 2¹/₂″ tall, hand cooler, Crystal $175
Candlestick, 10¹/₄″ tall, Baluster, Crystal $750
Candlestick, 10³/₄″ tall, Starlight Bubble design, Crystal $525
Candlestick, 4¹/₂″ tall, teardrop in stem, Crystal $550
Candlestick, 4³/₄″ tall, Scroll design, Crystal $275
Candlestick, 4″ tall, Teardrop design, Crystal $150
Candlestick, 6″ tall, ruffled, Athena design, Crystal $250
Candlestick, 6″, twist stems, Crystal $650
Candlestick, 8³/₄″ tall, Teardrop design, Crystal $675
Candlestick, 9³/₄″ tall, Starlight Bubble design, Crystal $500
Candy dish with cover, 5″ tall, 2¹/₄″ diameter, ram's head finial on cover, Crystal
.... $675
Carousel, 7¹/₂″ tall, 4¹/₂″ diameter, engraved horses with sterling pennant, Crystal .
.... $4350
Castle sculpture, 6¹/₈″ tall, 10 ⁵/₈″ width, black leather base, Crystal $2700
Cat, 2¹/₂″ width, hand cooler, Crystal $175
Cat, 8³/₄″ tall, sitting upright, Crystal $825
Cat, Roman, 5¹/₄″ long, crouched, sitting position, Crystal $475
Cathedral, 15³/₄″ tall, prismatic form, engraved cathedral with apostles, Crystal ..
.... $15750
Christmas tree, 6¹/₄″ tall, cone-shaped, air bubbles, Crystal $625
Circle, 9³/₄″ diameter, Stardust Bubble design, Crystal $2750
Circle sculpture, 6¹/₂″ tall, cut hemispheres, black leather base, Crystal ... $6875
Columbus circular sculpture on walnut base, 4⁵/₈″ diameter, crystal circle with 3
ships, Crystal $425
Compote, 10″ diameter, Cloud Bowl design, Crystal $700
Crystal ball, 4¹/₂″ diameter, black slate base, Crystal $1400
Cube, 2″, engraved "Love and Hope," Crystal $350
Decanter with circular stopper, 10″ tall, 32 oz., Ship's Flask design, Crystal ....
.... $1450
Decanter with Eagle finial on ball stopper, 10¹/₂″ tall, 32 oz., Crystal $1150
Decanter with mushroom stopper, 9¹/₂″ tall, 24 oz., Stardust Bubble design,
Crystal $1375
Deer, engraved buck prism sculpture, 7¹/₄″ tall, walnut base, Crystal $8225

Steuben crystal. PHOTO BY MARK PICKVET, COURTESY OF THE CHICAGO ART INSTITUTE.

Dog, 5″ tall, ears down, head and flowing neck, Crystal $500
Dog, puppy, 2³/₄″ width, Crystal $200
Domes, flower, 5¹/₂″ diameter, various engraved state flowers, Crystal $750
Dragon, 2″ long, hand cooler, Crystal $175
Dragon, 7¹/₂″ long, Crystal $800
Eagle, 2³/₄″ long, hand cooler, Crystal $175
Eagle, 3¹/₈″ tall, 4¹/₄″ width, standing with wings open, Crystal $375
Eagle, 4³/₄″ tall, 5¹/₂″ long, wings closed, Crystal $775
Eagle, 6¹/₄″ tall, 12″ wingspan, crystal ball base, Crystal $725
Eagle, 9¹/₂″ tall, In Flight design, Crystal $3500
Eagle bowl, 9¹/₂″ tall, 4 copper wheel-engraved eagles, feathers form the top rim, Crystal $27500
Eagle's crag, 10³/₄″ tall, crystal ice sculpture with miniature sterling eagle at top, limited edition, Crystal $14300
Earth globe on walnut and slate base, copper wheel-engraved continents, Crystal $6050
Elephant, 5¹/₂″ tall, trunk above head, Crystal $550
Elephant, 7¹/₂″ tall, trunk above head, Crystal $900
Equestrians crystal sculpture, 2¹/₄″ tall, 3″ width, Crystal $425
Excalibur, 4¹/₂″ width, crystal rock with 8″ sterling sword (18 kt. gold handle), Crystal $3425
Fawn, woodland, 4³/₄″ width, semicircle, Crystal $325
Fig, 3¹/₄″ tall, paperweight, Crystal $225
Fish, trigger, 10″ tall, pair together, Crystal $1500
Fisherman, Arctic, 6¹/₂″ tall, crystal ice sculpture with engraved fish and sterling fisherman, Crystal $4250

Flag, American Star-Spangled Banner on walnut base, 6″ long, engraved stars and stripes, Crystal $1750
Fossil sculpture, 14¼″ tall, 14″ width, Crystal $6500
Fox, 3¼″ tall, cub, Crystal $200
Fox, 4¼″ tall, Crystal $350
Frog, 2½″ long, hand cooler, Crystal $175
Galaxy, 3½″ sphere, Stardust Galaxy Bubble design, Crystal $850
Gander, 5¼″ tall, (matches Goose), Crystal $400
Gazelle bookends, 6¾″ tall, pair, Crystal $750
Gazelle bowl, 6½″ diameter, 6¾″ tall, copper wheel-engraved gazelles, Crystal ...
.... $25250
Gmelin shell, 2¾″ width, Spiral design, Crystal $225
Golf green sculpture with 18 kt. gold flag, 7¾″ tall, Crystal $5000
Golf prism sculpture, 3½″ tall, 3″ width, Crystal $475
Goose, 4″ tall, (matches gander), Crystal $400
Heart paperweight, 1½″ tall, 2⅝″ long, small heart within a large heart, Crystal ..
.... $200
Heart paperweight, 2⅞″ width, heart formed by 2 turtle doves, Crystal $350
Heart pillar, 3½″ tall, Crystal $450
Heart pillar, 4″ tall, Crystal $450
Heart sculpture, 3¼″ tall, Crystal $400
Hippopotamus, 6¼″ long, Crystal $850
Horse head, 5″ tall, Crystal $350
House, 3½″ trapezoidal, 3 engraveable lines, Crystal $525
Hunter, 6¼″ tall, ice sculpture, frosted arch, sterling hunter in boat, Crystal .. $4575
Ice bear (sterling silver) on crystal iceberg, 6″ width, miniature bear at top, Crystal $4175
Jar with cover, 15″ tall, engraved design from each state in the union (50 in all), Crystal $3250
Leopard in tree sculpture, 7½″ tall, 8″ width, engraved leopard sitting in tree, Crystal $13750
Lion, 9½″ width, walnut base, Crystal $2650
Menorah, 9½″ width, semicircle with 9 silver-plated candle cups, Crystal $3925
Moby Dick sculpture, 8″ tall, 11¼″ long, frosted whale curved over boat with harpooner and rowers, Crystal $25750
Monkey, 2¾″ tall, hand cooler, Crystal $175
Moravian star, 2½″ tall, 2½″ width, engraved stars, cube effect, Crystal ... $425
Moth to flame bowl sculpture, 10″ tall, 8¾″ diameter, air trap, engraved moths, Crystal $21500
Mouse, 3½″ long, Crystal $350
Mouse, woodland, 2⅝″ width, semicircle, Crystal $150
New York Sculpture, 17″ tall, 3¾″ width, engraved skyscrapers (Woolworth, Chrysler, World Trade Center, and Empire State), Crystal $31500
Nut bowl, 6″ width, lip on side, Crystal $275
Olive dish, 5½″ diameter, single spiral handle, Crystal $375
Owl, 2½″ tall, hand cooler, Crystal $175
Owl on base, 5⅛″ tall, Crystal $825
Paperweight, 2¾″ tall, pyramidal, Old Glory flag, Crystal $375
Paperweight, 3¼″ tall, 3″ diameter, pyramidal with inner teardrop, Crystal ... $1425
Paperweight, 3″ tall, 3″ width, triangular prism effect ("Cubique"), Crystal $625
Peach, 3″ tall, paperweight, Crystal $300

Peacock, 10″ tall, 14¹/₂″ width, semicircle tail, Crystal $1650
Pear, 5³/₄″ tall, 18 kt., gold partridge in a pear tree inside pear, Crystal $4225
Pear Christmas ornament, 3³/₄″ tall, Crystal $100
Penguin, 3¹/₂″ tall, Crystal $225
Peony jar, 6¹/₄″ tall, 6¹/₂″ width, copper wheel-engraved Peony design, Crystal ....
.... $3850
Pig, 3¹/₈″ long, hand cooler, Crystal $175
Pisces Zodiac sculpture, 2³/₄″ tall, 2 fish, Crystal $200
Plate, 10″, copper wheel-engraved Aquarius Star design, Aluminum stand, Crystal
$3850
Plate, 10″, various engraved signs of the Zodiac (12 plates in all), Crystal .. $750
Plate, 10″, various engraved American birds (12 Audubon plates in all), Crystal ...
.... $750
Plate with center handle, 13¹/₄″, droplet style, Crystal $625
Plates, 10″, various engraved seashell designs (12 plates in all), Crystal $750
Polar bear, 5″ tall, 7¹/₂″ long, Crystal $700
Polo players sculpture, 2 ¹/₄″ tall, 3″ width, Crystal $425
Porpoise, 12¹/₈″ long, (bottlenosed dolphin), Crystal $1200
Porpoise, 6¹/₈″ long, (bottlenosed dolphin), Crystal $450
Porpoise, 9¹/₄″ long, (bottlenosed dolphin), Crystal $650
Prism sculpture, 7″ tall, 6¹/₄″ width, quartz design, Crystal $3575
Pronghorn, 7″ tall, 14″ width, semicircle with 5 copper wheel-engraved pronghorn,
Crystal $24500
Quail, 5¹/₂″ tall, Crystal $475
Rabbit, 2³/₄″ long, hand cooler, Crystal $175
Sailboat, 6¹/₂″ width, Crystal $575
Sailboat, 12³/₄″ tall, cut sails with engraved lines, Crystal $5200
Salmon bowl, 7¹/₂″ tall, 10¹/₄″ width, 7 copper wheel-engraved salmon, 7 flies,
bubbles, Crystal $19500
Saturn with bubbled ring, 5¹/₂″ diameter, Crystal $525
Scallop shell, 3¹/₂″ width, Crystal $225
Seal sculpture, 8³/₄″ tall, 2 engraved seals pursuing 3 tiny fish, Crystal ....: $3500
Seashell, 3¹/₂″ width, Irregular Spiral design, Crystal $350
Skiers prism sculpture, 3¹/₂″ tall, 3″ width, Crystal $475
Snail, 3¹/₄″ tall, Crystal $250
Snow crystal, 2³/₄″ triangular, engraved snowflake, Crystal $300
Snow pine, 4¹/₄″ width, pentagram, Crystal $500
Star of David, 2¹/₂″ tall, 2¹/₂″ width, engraved Stars of David, cube effect, Crystal .
.... $12000
Star paperweight, 4¹/₄″ width, pentagram, Crystal $875
Star prism sculpture, 5″ tall, slate base, Crystal $1475
Star scream, 5¹/₄″ tall, pentagram swirl sculpture, Crystal $475
Starfish, 4³/₄″ width, Crystal $225
Stork, 14″ tall, slender legs, circular base, Crystal $625
Swan, 6¹/₂″ long, straight neck, Crystal $575
Swan, 7¹/₂″ long, curved neck, Crystal $575
Swan bowl, 9″ diameter, 8″ tall, bowl formed by 3 copper wheel-engraved swans,
Crystal $38500
Swordfish rising from crystal sculpture, 7¹/₂″ tall, Crystal $12000
Tennis prism sculpture, 3¹/₂″ tall, 3″ width, 3 engraved tennis players, Crystal ...
.... $475

Terebra shell, 4⅝″ long, spiraled, Crystal $225
Trout, 8″ tall, with 18 kt. gold fly, Crystal $2375
Tumbler, 4⅛″ tall, Stardust Bubble base design, Crystal $350
Tumbler, highball, 4½″ tall, Crystal $275
Tumbler, old-fashioned, 3½″ tall, 9 oz., Crystal $225
Turtle, 2½″ long, hand cooler, Crystal $175
Urn, 6½″ tall, copper wheel-engraved Grecian figures, Crystal $38500
Urn, 9½″ tall, 2 scroll handles, Crystal $1025
Vase, 10″ tall, Swirled design, Crystal $650
Vase, 11½″ tall, rose, clasps on stem, Crystal $775
Vase, 11″ tall, globe-shaped, bubbled, Crystal $800
Vase, 12½″ tall, Calypso, Crystal $850
Vase, 12½″ tall, silhouette, Crystal $375
Vase, 12¼″ tall, Seawave design, Crystal $825
Vase, 13″ tall, Calypso, Crystal $1000
Vase, 13″ width, Archaic Etruscan design, Crystal $2625
Vase, 16½″ tall, 6½″ diameter, sterling frame, Crystal $14300
Vase, 17½″ tall, sculptural, Crystal $1000
Vase, 5¼″ tall, classic Juliet style, Crystal $225
Vase, 6½″ tall, cinched waist, Crystal $350
Vase, 6½″ tall, spiral base, Crystal $400
Vase, 6¼″ tall, pirouette, Crystal $275
Vase, 6¾″ tall, 3½″ width, engraved angel with trumpet, Crystal $625
Vase, 7⅛″ tall, circular base, engraved gazelle, Crystal $2750
Vase, 7¾″ tall, ancient Lyre design, Crystal $450
Vase, 7¾″ tall, concentric "Momentum" design, Crystal $1275
Vase, 7″ tall, handkerchief, Crystal $250
Vase, 8½″ tall, classic Palace design, Crystal $550
Vase, 8¼″ tall, 8½″ diameter, 24 cut facets, Crystal $11550
Vase, 8⅛″, Twist Stem design, Crystal $650
Vase, 8″ tall, engraved by Waugh, 1935, Crystal $1250
Vase, 8″ tall, Seawave design, Crystal $600
Vase, 8″ tall, Twist Bud design $325
Vase, 8″ tall, 8½″ diameter, sterling frame $12100
Vase, 9½″ tall, handkerchief, Crystal $675
Vase, 9½″ tall, Mondo, Slender Cylindrical design, Crystal $900
Vase, 9¾″ width, Archaic Etruscan design, Crystal $1875
Walrus with sterling silver tusks, 7″ long, Crystal $3250
Whale, Nantucket, limited edition, Crystal $5500
Wreath, Christmas, 3½″ diameter, engraved snowflakes and evergreen bows,
Crystal $250
Wren, 3″ width, sitting, Crystal $200
Zodiac sphere sculpture, engraved constellations, Crystal $13500

SWANKY SWIGS DECORATED JARS FROM KRAFT CHEESE SPREADS, 1933–1970s

Swanky Swigs were small jars issued by Kraft Foods. Cheese spreads included American Spread, Limburger Spread, Old English, Olive-Pimento, Pimento, Pimento-

American, Pineapple, Relish, and Zestful Roka. Even the original lids to these jars are selling for a dollar or two. Note that the original production runs were 1933–1940 and 1947–1958. They were discontinued from 1941–1946 and then reissued in the 1970s.

Animal patterns (large), over 4″, Color combinations include black duck and horse, blue bear and pig, brown squirrel and deer, green cat and rabbit, orange dog and rooster, and red bird and elephant $10
Animal patterns (small), under 4″ $7
Antique patterns (large), over 4″, Color combinations include black coffee pot and trivet, blue kettle and lamp, brown clock and coal scuttle, green coffee grinder and plate, orange churn and cradle, and red spinning wheel and bellows $10
Antique patterns (small), under 4″ $7
Band patterns (large), over 4″ (1-4 bands), Color combinations include black, blue, red, black and red, blue and red, blue and white, and red and green. $7
Band patterns (small), under 4″ (1-4 bands) $5
Bicentennial issue (1975-1976), 3³/₄″, in green, red, and yellow (small) $7
Centennial Celebration Issues (various states), Large, over 4″, enameled colors .
.... $10
Centennial Celebration Issues (various states), Small, under 4″, enameled colors
.... $7
Centennial Celebration Issues, 4³/₄″, with enameled colors, Cobalt Blue glasses
.... $35
Flower patterns (large), over 4″, all enameled colors for cornflowers, daisies, forget-me-nots, posies, starbursts, tulips, and miscellaneous flower designs .. $15
Flower patterns (small), under 4″ $10
Multiple or miscellaneous designs (large), over 4″, Enameled designs include blocks, dots, and bursts in several colors. $10
Multiple or miscellaneous designs (small), under 4″ $7
People patterns (large), over 4″, All enameled colors include elderly woman, woman in plaid dress, and man in pinstripe suit $10

American glass, Swanky Swig "Sailboat" pattern. DRAWING BY MARK PICKVET.

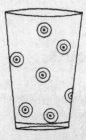

American glass, Swanky Swig "Circles and Dots" pattern. DRAWING BY MARK PICKVET.

People patterns (small), under 4″ $7
Sailboat patterns (large), over 4″, All enameled colors include blue, green, red, and yellow (may or may not have enameled designs) $20
Sailboat patterns (small), under 4″ $15
Solid opaque colors (large), over 4″, Opaque colors include blue, green, red, and yellow (may or may not have enameled designs) $15
Solid opaque colors (small), under 4″ $10

THIMBLES　　VARIOUS COMPANIES, 1940s–PRESENT

Thimbles come in a variety of styles and materials. Those featured here are by American companies. All of those listed here are of standard size, except for those with a decorative finial. There are a few other thimbles listed in Chapter 1, most notably from Germany.

Thimble, 1½″ tall, spun crystal with green and blue turtle finial $12
Thimble, 1½″ tall, spun crystal with multicolored parrot finial $12
Thimble, 1½″ tall, teapot-shaped with handle, spout, and ball top, crystal with blue applied porcelain rose $12
Thimble, 1¼″ tall, spun crystal with multicolored glass gem finial (several styles) $10
Thimble, 1¾″ tall, crystal, birdbath with 2 birds finial $15
Thimble, 1¾″ tall, spun crystal with lavender dragon finial $12
Thimble, 1¾″ tall, spun crystal with multicolored clown finial $10
Thimble, 1¾″ tall, spun crystal with multicolored mushroom finial $10
Thimble, 1″ tall, crystal Diamond pattern with ruby red insert in top $25
Thimble, 1″ tall, crystal with enameled red and yellow roses with green leaves $7
Thimble, 1″ tall, ruffled edge, shank rim near bottom (to hold rings), crystal with gold trim $10
Thimble, 1″ tall, ruffled, crystal with enameled blue and white cornflower $7
Thimble, 1″ tall, ruffled, crystal with enameled yellow roses $7
Thimble, 1″ tall, scalloped, etched white floral design $9
Thimble, 1″ tall, with multicolored miniature paperweight in top, Ruby Red $40
Thimble, 1″ tall, with multicolored miniature paperweight in top, Cobalt Blue ... $40
Thimble, 2½″ tall, spun crystal, hummingbird and blossom finial, gold trim and accents $35
Thimble, 2¼″ tall, spun crystal with light blue and clear sailing ship finial ... $12
Thimble, 2⅛″ tall, spun crystal with green hummingbird finial $10
Thimble, 2⅛″ tall, spun crystal with light blue dolphin finial $10
Thimble, 2⅛″ tall, spun crystal with yellow saxophone finial $10
Thimble, 2″ tall, bell-shaped, crystal, octagonal shape $12
Thimble, 2″ tall, spun crystal with amethyst elephant finial $10

VIKING GLASS COMPANY　　1940s–PRESENT

Viking is noted for its ruby red novelties and figurines. The company purchased New Martinsville in 1944 and continued using some of New Martinsville's original molds; new issues are marked "Rainbow Art" or with the Viking name. In 1991,

Viking was purchased by Kenneth Dalzell (former president of Fostoria) to become Dalzell-Viking. The company is still in operation today in West Virginia, manufacturing some novelties and colored glass tableware.

Apple shape, 3¾″ tall, with green stem, Ruby Red $20
Apple shape, 5″ tall, with green stem, Ruby Red $30
Bell, 3½″-3¾″ tall, Leaf design, Ruby Red $20
Bell, 4¾″ tall, Mount Vernon pattern, Ruby Red $20
Bell, 6″ tall, Georgian pattern, Ruby Red $25
Bell, Liberty Bell shape, 3¾″ tall, Ruby Red $25
Bird, 2¾″ long, Cobalt Blue $10
Bonbon dish, 7″, Ruby Red $20
Bowl, 10″ diameter, crystal with enameled floral transfer $7
Bowl, 10″ diameter, light opaque swirled amethyst, irregular edge $20
Bowl, 7¾″ diameter, crystal with enameled floral transfer $5
Candy dish, 10″ long, 7″ diameter, including two finger hole applied handles, pressed Hobstar and Buzzstar design on underside, notched edge, Cobalt Blue ....
.... $20
Candy jar, 7″ tall, with 3-faced frosted finial on frosted cover, similar to the reproduction of the Museum of Fine Arts, Boston, Crystal $25
Compote, 5½″ diameter, 2½″ tall, with candlewick edging, Purple $10
Cube-shaped box, 3″ dimensions, clear glass with various molded designs $5
Duck, baby, 5″ tall, Ruby Red $25
Duck, mother, 9″ tall, Ruby Red $45
Lamp, oil, 9″ tall, Ruby Red $75
Mushroom shape, 2″ tall, Ruby Red $15
Owl, 2⅜″ tall, winking, black glass miniature $6
Owl, 2⅜″ tall, winking, clear glass miniature $5
Owl glimmer, 7″ tall, Ruby Red $30
Paperweight, 3½″ diameter, 1″ thick, circular, clear glass with large etched letters of the alphabet (26 total, price is for each) $5
Paperweights, 3½″ diameter, 1″ thick, circular, clear glass with large etched letters of the alphabet, set of 26 .... $150
Pear shape, 8½″ tall, with green stem, Ruby Red $50
Plate, 8½″ diameter, light opaque swirled amethyst, candlewick edging $10

Viking candy dishes. PHOTO BY ROBIN RAINWATER.

Viking owl. PHOTO BY ROBIN RAINWATER.

Salt and pepper shakers, Diamond and Thumbprint pattern, Ruby Red $35
Snowman glimmer, 9″ tall, Ruby Red $30
Stove glimmer, pot-bellied stove shape, Ruby Red $30
Strawberry paperweight, with green stem, Ruby Red $20
Swan candleholder, 6¼″, with crystal neck, Ruby Red $50
Swan dish, 6½″ long, Ruby Red $25
Swan dish, 6¼″, with crystal neck, Ruby Red $50
Vase, 16″ tall, with crystal lip, Ruby Red $20

WESTMORELAND GLASS 1889-1985

The operation began as the Westmoreland Specialty Company in 1889 in Grapeville, Pennsylvania. Into the early part of the 20th century, the company processed such foods as vinegar, mustard, and baking powder to fill the glass containers they made. In 1924 the name was officially changed to the Westmoreland Glass Company to emphasize its glassmaking. Westmoreland produced a variety of items, adapting readily to changing fads. Production included cut glass, some Carnival and Depression glass, a few art styles, and modern examples, as given below. See separate listings for Westmoreland products under "Beaded Edge" and "Panel Grape" in this chapter. Also refer to cut glass examples in Chapter 3, "English Hobnail" in Chapter 6, and a few Carnival examples in Chapter 5. Note that Mary Gregory glass, which originated with the Boston & Sandwich Glass Company (see Chapter 4), features Victorian scenes of children. Laced edge pieces are fragile and crack easily along the edges, so take extra precautions when purchasing.

Basket, 14″, Maple Leaf design, Ruby Red $125
Basket, 5″ tall, Mary Gregory (Victorian scene of girl), with enameled white designs, Ruby Red $35
Bell, 6½″ tall, with enameled white floral design, Ruby Red $30
Bowl, 10½″, Maple Leaf design $45
Bowl, 13″, octagonal shape, crystal with enameled floral design $55
Bowl, 8½″, octagonal shape, crimped, Pink $45
Bowl, rose, 5¾″, laced edge, Ruby Red $35
Butter dish with cover, 8½″ long ¼ lb., Pressed Cube design, Ruby Red $35
Cake stand, 10″ diameter, 4″ tall, reproduction Cherry and Cable pattern, Opalescent Green $75

Westmoreland "Cherry" pattern candy jar. PHOTO BY ROBIN RAINWATER.

Candlestick, 4^1/$_2$" tall, laced edge, Ruby Red $20
Candlestick, 9" tall, dolphin stem, Pink or green $65
Candy dish with cover, 3-footed, Shell design and shell finial, Ruby Red ... $55
Candy jar with cover, 8" tall, fluted, reproduction Cherry and Cable pattern, 2-handled, Opalescent Green $75
Candy jar with cover, octagonal shape, Pink $55
Candy jar with silver cover, 7^1/$_2$" tall, Colonial Fluted design, light amethyst with silver cover, enameled floral design $100
Cat dish with cover, 5^1/$_2$" long, light blue and milk opaque glass $125
Cheese and cracker set (bowl with underplate), 10" diameter, black with white enameled floral design $85
Chest with lid, 4^1/$_4$" rectangular, Mary Gregory (Victorian scene of girl and boy), with enameled white designs, Ruby Red $35
Cracker jar with cover, 8^1/$_2$" tall, reproduction Cherry pattern
   Opalescent Green $75
   Ruby Red $150
Creamer, crystal with etched fruit design $35
Creamer, octagonal shape, black with enameled Bleeding Heart Floral design ... $30
Creamer, Strutting Peacock pattern, Ruby Red $45
Creamer, pouring spout, notched top (fits tray below), Light Blue, green, or pink
   .... $20
Cruet with stopper, 5^1/$_4$" tall, Diamond Quilted design, Ruby Red $65
Dog dish with cover, 5^1/$_2$" long, Light blue and milk opaque glass $150
Duck dish with cover, 5^1/$_2$" long, Milk and custard opaque glass $150
Flower bowl stand, 4" or 5" diameter, 3-footed, yellow with continuous etched leaf design (black glass, no etching $50.00) $40
Goblet, 8 oz., crystal with etched fruit design $30
Jewel box with lid, 4^1/$_2$" square, footed, Mary Gregory (Victorian scene of boy), with enameled white designs, Ruby Red $30
Lamb dish with cover, 5^1/$_2$" long, Opaque cobalt blue and milk glass $175
Lamp, 10" tall, Lotus line, Blue or green $75

Leaf-shaped dish, 9″ long, Green with veining $25

Pitcher, milk, 1 pt., Pressed Cube design, Ruby Red $45

Plate, 3″, Butterfly and Heart design, Ruby Red $15

Plate, 8½″, Mary Gregory (various Victorian scenes), laced edge, ruby red with enameled white designs $75

Plate, 9″, crystal with etched Fruit design $35

Plate, heart-shaped, 7¼″ across, Mary Gregory (Victorian Scene of girl), laced edge, with enameled white designs, Ruby Red $50

Platter, 14″, crystal with etched Fruit design $50

Revolver, toy, 5″ long, crystal with black stock $125

Rooster dish with cover, 5½″ long, Opaque cobalt blue and milk glass $250

Sandwich server with center handle, milk glass with crystal handle and enameled Floral and Bird design $60

Slipper, 5″ long, with enameled white shoelace, Ruby Red $25

Sugar, 2-handled, crystal with etched Fruit design $25

Sugar, 2 angled handles, notched top (fits tray below), Light Blue, Green, or Pink $20

Sugar, 2-handled, octagonal shape, black with enameled Bleeding Heart Floral design $30

Sugar with cover, Strutting Peacock pattern, Ruby Red $55

Tray with center handle (for creamer and sugar), 8″, Light Blue, Green, or Pink $25

Tumbler, 1½″ tall, 1 oz., embossed "Just A Thimbleful," originally issued in crystal, reissued in emerald green and cobalt blue (same price) $7

Vase, 8½″ tall, Diamond, Circle, and Fan pressed design, circular footed, Ruby Red $30

Vase, 8¾″ tall, Pressed Buzz Star design, Ruby Red $30

Vase, 9½″ tall, fan shape, green with etched floral design $50

PERIODICALS AND CLUBS

Air Capital Carnival Glass Club
C/O Don Kime
1202 W. 4th St.
Haysville, KS 67060

Akro Agate
10 Bailey St.
Clarksville, WV 26301

The Akro Agate Gem
Joseph Bourque
P.O. Box 758
Salem, NH 03079

Aladdin Knights
C/O J.W. Courter
Route 1
Simpson, IL 62985

American Carnival Glass
   Glass Association
P.O. Box 235
Littlestown, PA 17340

American Cut Glass Association
3228 S. Boulevard, Ste. 221
P.O. Box 1775
Edmond, OK 73083-1775

Art Glass Salt
   Shaker Collectors Society
2832 Rapidan Trail
Maitland, FL 32751

The Antiques Trader
P.O. Box 1050
Dubuque, IA 52004-1050

The Antique Press
12403 N. Florida Ave.
Tampa, FL 33612

Antique Review
P.O. Box 538
Worthington, OH 43085-9928

Antique Week
27 N. Jefferson
P.O. Box 90
Knightstown, IN 46148

Arts and Crafts Quarterly
P.O. Box 3592, Station E
Trenton, NJ 08629

Avon Times
P.O. Box 9868, Dept. P
Kansas City, MO 64134

Boyd Art Glass
   Collectors Guild
P.O. Box 52
Hatboro, PA 19040

Cambridge Collectors Inc.
P.O. Box 416
Cambridge, OH 43725

Canadian Carnival Glass
Association
Gladys Lawson
532 Chiddington Ave.
London, Ont., Canada N6C 2W3

Candlewick Club
C/O Virginia R. Scott
275 Milledge Terrace
Athens, GA 30606

Collector Glass News
P.O. Box 308
Slippery Rock, PA 16057

Collectible Carnival Glass
Association
C/O Wilma Thurston
2360 N. Old S.R. 9
Columbus, IN 47203

Collectors of Findlay Glass
P.O. Box 256
Findlay, OH 45839-0256

Czechoslovakian Collectors
Guild International
P.O. Box 901395
Kansas City, MO 64190

Depression Glass Daze
P.O. Box 57
Otisville, MI 48463

Early American Pattern
Glass Society
P.O. Box 340023
Columbus, OH 43234

Fenton Art Glass Collectors
of America, Inc.
P.O. Box 384
Williamstown, WV 26187

Fostoria Glass Collectors
21901 Lassen St., #112
Chatsworth, CA 91311

The Fostoria Glass Society
of America, Inc.
P.O. Box 826
Moundsville, WV 26041

Fostoria OH Glass Association
109 N. Main St.
Fostoria, OH 44830

Fruit Jar Newsletter
364 Gregory Ave.
West Orange, NJ 07052-3743

H.C. Fry Glass Society
P.O. Box 41
Beaver, PA 15009

Gateway Carnival Glass Club
C/O Karen E. Skinner
108 Riverwoods Cove
East Alton, IL 62024

The Glass Art Society
C/O Tom McGlauchlin
Toledo Museum of Art
Toledo, OH 43609

Glass Collectors
Club of Toledo
2727 Middlesex Dr.
Toledo, OH 43606

Glass Collector's Digest
P.O. Box 553
Marietta, OH 45750-9979

Glass Knife Collector's Club
C/O Adrienne Escoe
P.O. Box 342
Los Alamitos, CA 90720

Glass Research Society
of New Jersey
Wheaton Village
Millville, NJ 08332

Great Lakes Carnival Glass
C/O Maxine Burkhardt
12875 Chippewa Dr.
Grand Ledge, MI 48837

Heart of America Carnival
Glass Association
C/O Lucille Britt
3048 Tamarek Dr.
Manhattan, KS 66502

Heisey Collectors of
America, Inc.
169 W. Church St.
Newark, OH 43055

Heisey Publications
P.O. Box 102
Plymouth, OH 44865

Hoosier Carnival Glass Club
C/O Eunice Booker
944 W. Pine St.
Griffith, IN 46391

International Carnival Glass
Association
C/O Lee Markley
R.R. #1, P.O. Box 14
Mentone, IN 46539

Keystone Carnival Glass Club
C/O Mary Sharp
719 W. Brubaker Valley Rd.
Lititz, PA 17543

Kovel's Newsletter
P.O. Box 22200
Beachwood, OH 44122

R. Lalique
11028 Raleigh Ct.
Rockford, IL 61111

Lincoln-Land Carnival Glass Club
C/O Ellen Hem
N. 951 Hwy. 27
Conrath, WI 54731

Maine Antique Digest
P.O. Box 1429
Waldoboro, ME 04572

Marble Collector's Society
P.O. Box 222
Trumbull, CT 06611

Michiana Association of
Candlewick Collectors
17370 Battles Rd.
South Bend, IN 46614

Morgantown Collectors
of America
420 1st Avenue N.W.
Plainview, MN 55964

Mt. Washington
Art Glass Society
P.O. Box 24094
Fort Worth, TX 76124

National Association of
Avon Collectors
6100 Walnut, Dept. P
Kansas City, MO 64113

National Depression
  Glass Association
P.O. Box 69843
Odessa, TX 79769

The National Duncan
  Glass Society
P.O. Box 965
Washington, PA 15301

The National Early American
  Glass Club
P.O. Box 8489
Silver Spring, MD 20907

The National Fenton
  Glass Society
P.O. Box 4008
Marietta, OH 45750

The National Greentown
  Glass Association
1807 W. Madison St.
Kokomo, IN 46901

The National Imperial
  Glass Collectors Society
P.O. Box 534
Bellaire, OH 43906

The National Insulator Association
3557 Nicklaus Dr.
Titusville, FL 32780

The National Milk Glass
  Collectors Society
1113 Birchwood Dr.
Garland, TX 75043

The National Reamer Association
C/O Larry Branstad
R.R. 3, Box 67
Frederic, WI 54837

The National Westmoreland
  Glass Collectors Club
P.O. Box 372
Export, PA 15632

New England Antiques Journal
4 Church St.
Ware, MA 01082

New England Carnival
  Glass Association
Marie M. Heath
HCR 31, Box 15
St. Johnsbury, VT 05819

Northern California Carnival
  Glass Club
C/O June McCarter
1205 Clifton Dr.
Modesto, CA 95355

Ohio Candlewick
  Collectors' Club
613 S. Patterson St.
Gibsonburg, OH 43431

Old Morgantown Glass
  Collectors' Guild
420 First Ave. NW
Plainview, MN 55964

Pacific Northwest Carnival Club
C/O Pat Dolezal
3515 N.E. Hancock
Portland, OR 97212

Pairpoint Cup Plate Glass
  Collectors of America, Inc.
P.O. Box 52 D
East Weymouth, MA 02189

Paperweight Collectors
P.O. Box 1059
Easthampton, MA 49125

Perfume and Scent Bottles
  Collectors
2022 E. Charleston Blvd.
Las Vegas, NV 89104

Perfume Bottle Association
P.O. Box 529
Vienna, VA 22183

Phoenix and Consolidated
  Collectors Association
P.O. Box 81974
Chicago, IL 60681

Rose Bowl Collectors
5214 Route 309
Center Valley, PA 18034

San Diego Carnival Glass Club
C/O Kathy Harris
5860 Torca St.
San Diego, CA 92124

San Joaquin Carnival Glass Club
C/O Marie McGee
3906 E. Acacia Ave.
Fresno, CA 93726

The Shot Glass Club of America
5071 Watson Dr.
Flint, MI 48506

Southern California Carnival
  Glass Collectors
C/O Judy Maxwell
31091 Bedford Dr.
Redlands, CA 92373

The Stretch Glass Society
P.O. Box 770643
Lakewood, OH 44107

Tampa Bay Carnival Glass Club
C/O Barbara Hobbs
5501 101 Ave. N.
Pinellas Park, FL 34666

Texas Carnival Glass Club
C/O Kim Smith
902 S. Blackwell St.
Tyler, TX 75023

Thimble Collectors
  International
6411 Montego Rd.
Louisville, KY 40228

Three Rivers Depression Era
  Glass Society
4038 Willett Rd.
Pittsburgh, PA 15227

Tiffin Glass Collectors Club
P.O. Box 554
Tiffin, OH 44883

Toothpick Holder Collector's Club
Red Arrow Hwy., P.O. Box 246
Sawyer, MI 49125

Westmoreland Glass Society, Inc.
C/O Harold Mayes
2712 Glenwood Street
Independence, MO 64052

Westmoreland Glass
  Collector's Newsletter
P.O. Box 143
North Liberty, IA 52317

Whimsey Glass Club
4544 Cairo Dr.
Whitehall, PA 18052

World's Fair Collectors
   Society, Inc.
P.O. Box 20806
Sarasota, FL 34238

INTERNET/WEB SITES

The Internet offers a wealth of information for glassware collectors. If you type in "Glass," "Glass Collecting," "Antiques," or similar key words into any of the popular search engines, you can easily access hundreds of thousands of World Wide Web sites. I tried "Glass" under Netscape Navigator and came up with over 300,000 sites. All of the on-line services provide some sort of search functions for key words such as "Glass."

Much of what you find is dedicated to business and industry, but there are some noteworthy sites. The Corning Museum of Glass site, for example, offers a lot of history, a calendar of museum events, a glossary, and pictures of glass. The Fenton Glass Company maintains a similar site.

Most of the sites, however, seem geared to advertising and selling items. I have seen everything from fancy art glass products to marbles for sale on-line. It's a good idea to check out these sources as you would any mail order company, particularly for more expensive items like art, cut, or Carnival glass. I personally prefer to inspect things up close before purchasing, with the exception of new items. Once you have established a good relationship with a dealer, hopefully you can trust him or her on future purchases.

As most Internet service providers warn, be careful about giving out personal information on-line such as your name, address, social security number, and credit card numbers. Who knows who or what is lurking in cyberspace?

Right now, it seems to be safer dealing through direct mail, but that doesn't mean you can't get some good contacts on the Net. Here are a few sites with some interesting stuff:

ANTIQUE GLASS
http://www.tias.com/amdir/specglass.html

CELIA'S ART GLASS
http://www.dmsv.umich.edu/dros/glass

CORNING
http://www.pennynet.org/glmuseum

FENTON
http://www.web.com/www/fenton-glass/profile.html

BARBARA FLOURNOY'S ANTIQUES
http://www.tias.com/stores/barbaraf/c10-1.html

GLASS LINE NEWSLETTER
http://www.hotglass.com

REYNE HOGAN ANTIQUES
http://www.tias.com/stores/RHA/html

SEVERN'S ART GLASS
http://home.earthlink.net/~bsevern/zs01

MUSEUMS

Allen Art Museum
Oberlin College
Oberlin, OH 44074

Art Institute of Chicago
Michigan Ave. & Adams St.
Chicago, IL 60603

The Bennington Museum
W. Main St.
Bennington, VT 05201

Bergstrom Art Center
  and Museum
165 N. Park Ave.
Neenah, WI 54956

The Cambridge Glass Museum
506 S. 9th St.
Cambridge, OH 43725

Carnegie Institute
Museum of Art
4400 Forbes Ave.
Pittsburgh, PA 15213

Chrysler Museum at Norfolk
Olney Rd. and Mowbray Arch
Norfolk, VA 23510

Corning Museum of Glass
  and Glass Center
One Museum Way
Corning, NY 14830

Currier Gallery of Art
192 Orange St.
Manchester, NH 03104

Degenhart Paperweight
  and Glass Museum, Inc.
P.O. Box 186
Cambridge, OH 43725

Fenton Art Glass Co.
700-T Elizabeth St.
Williamstown, WV 26187

Greentown Glass Museum, Inc.
624 W. Main St.
Greentown, IN 46936

Henry Ford Museum
P.O. Box 1970
Dearborn, MI 48121

Lightner Museum
75 King St.
St. Augustine, FL 32084

Metropolitan Museum of Art
1000 5th Ave.
New York, NY 10028

Minneapolis Institute of Arts
2400 Third Ave. S.
Minneapolis, MN 55404

Milan Historical Museum
10 Edison Dr.
Milan, OH 44846

Museum of Beverage
  Containers and Advertising
1055 Ridgecrest Dr.
Goodlettsville, TN 37072

Museum of Modern Art
11 W. 53rd St.
New York, NY 10019

National Bottle Museum
76 Milton Ave.
Ballston Spa, NY 12020

National Heisey Glass Museum
1609 W. Church St.
Newark, OH 43055

Oglebay Institute-Mansion
  Museum
Oglebay Park
Wheeling, WV 26003

Old Sturbridge Village
1 Old Sturbridge Village Rd.
Sturbridge, MA 01566

Philadelphia Museum of Art
P.O. Box 7646
Philadelphia, PA 19101

Portland Art Museum
Seven Congress Square
Portland, ME 04101

Sandwich Glass Museum
P.O. Box 103
Sandwich, MA 02563

Seneca County Museum
28 Clay St.
Tiffin, OH 44883

Smithsonian Museum of History
Smithsonian Institution
Washington, DC 29560

Toledo Museum of Art
P.O. Box 1013
Toledo, OH 43697

Wadsworth Athenum
600 Main St.
Hartford, CT 06103

Westmoreland Glass Museum
1815 Trimble Ave.
Port Vue, PA 15133

GLOSSARY

Abrasion The technique of grinding shallow decorations in a glass object with the use of a wheel. The decorated areas are usually left unpolished.

Acid cut back The process of dipping an object into acid for a controlled amount of time in order to achieve a desired cutting depth.

Acid etching The process of covering glass with an acid-resistant protective layer, scratching on a design, then applying hydrofluoric acid to etch the pattern into the glass.

Acid polishing The technique of giving cut glass a polished surface by dipping it into a hydrofluoric acid bath.

Acid stamping The process of etching a trademark or signature in glass with acid after it has been annealed. Acid stamps are similar to rubber stamps.

Adams & Co. Founded in 1856 by John Adams in Pittsburgh, Pennsylvania; Adams was a major producer of pressed pattern glass. The firm became part of U.S. Glass in 1891.

Advertising glass A glass vessel displaying information about a manufacturer, company, proprietor, brand, person, establishment, event, and so on.

Agata glass Art glass characterized by mottled purple or brown finishes produced by alcohol added on top of the color. Agata glass was produced by the New England Glass Company in the late 19th century.

Air twist An 18th-century English decorating technique in which air bubbles were purposefully injected in the base of an object; the object was then pulled down and twisted into a stem.

Akro Agate Glass Co. Established in 1911 in Akron, Ohio; the company was noted for opaque marble but added other opaque glass novelty items after operations were moved to West Virginia. The company closed in 1951.

Alabaster glass A translucent ornamental glass first developed by Frederick Carder at Steuben. Alabaster resembles the white mineral alabaster and is produced by spraying stannous chloride on a piece before it is reheated.

Alaskan A name given to a Carnival glass color produced by the Northwood Glass Company. Alaskan consists of glass with a green base color that is iridized with the common Carnival marigold color.

Albany Glass Co. Albany Glass was founded in the 1780s in Albany, New York, and continued production until about 1820. The company made windows, bottles, and a few other items.

Albertine glass Albertine was produced by the Mt. Washington Glass Company in the late 19th century. It is characterized by opaque glass and ornate decoration and was applied primarily to show items such as vases. It is sometimes referred to as "Crown Milano."

Ale glass An early-17th-century English glass with a capacity of 3 to 5 ounces, short-stemmed, and used for drinking ale or beer.

Alexandrite glass Art glass produced by Thomas Webb in England in the late 19th century. It is characterized by various shadings of blue, pink, red, and yellow achieved through several stages of refiring.

C.G. Alford & Co. Founded in 1872 in New York City, Alford operated as a watch and jewelry store as well as a cut glass operation. It closed in 1918.

Alkali A soluble salt mixture consisting primarily of potassium carbonate and sodium carbonate. An essential ingredient in glass, it helps reduce the melting point of silica.

Almy & Thomas Founded in 1903 by Charles H. Almy and G. Edwin Thomas. The pair purchased the Knickerbocker Cut Glass Company and continued cutting glass until 1918. The Corning Glass Works supplied the company with blanks.

Aluminosilicate glass A type of heat-resistant glass developed by Corning for its "Flameware" brand of Pyrex kitchenware. This formula is more heat resistant than the original borosilicate formula.

Amber A yellowish-brown glass produced by the addition of iron, carbon, and sulphur. The color resembles fossilized tree sap of the same name.

Amberette Pressed glassware that was frosted or stained with dark yellow or yellowish-brown colors to resemble art glass.

Amberina Art glass produced in the United States in the late 19th century. It is characterized by transparent glass that is lightly shaded with light amber at the base and gradually shaded darker to ruby red at the top. Joseph Locke received a patent for amberina in 1883.

Amelung glass High-quality glass made in the United States in the late 18th century by German immigrant John Frederick Amelung.

American Flint Glass Works Established at Wheeling, Virginia, in the 1840s (before West Virginia became a state). The company produced pressed, mold-blown, and handblown glass in crystal (using flint and lead) and colored glass.

American Glass Co. Established in 1899 in Indiana, Pennsylvania; the firm purchased the Dugan/Northwood factory and made some pressed wares. It was bought by the Diamond Glass Company in 1913.

Amethyst A light purple-colored glass produced by the addition of manganese. Some amethyst glass is made so dark that it is referred to as "black amethyst."

Anchor Cap and Closure Corp. A U.S. manufacturer established in Long Island City, New York, in the early 1900s; it was a major manufacturer of containers and merged with Hocking in 1937 to form the Anchor-Hocking Glass Corporation.

Anchor-Hocking Glass Corp. A huge U.S. glass manufacturer of containers, tableware, and other items established in 1937 when the Anchor Cap and Closure Corp. merged with the Hocking Glass Company.

Animal dishes Covered glass dishes or glass objects made in the shapes of various animals (roosters, horses, cats, dogs, elephants, etc.). Animal dishes were very popular from about 1890 to 1910, during the Depression era, and from the 1970s on.

Annealing A process that toughens glass and eliminates stress by heating and gradually cooling in an annealing oven or lehr.

Annealing crack A crack or fissure that develops in glass from improper cooling or annealing.

AOP An abbreviation for "all-over pattern." All-over patterns generally cover the entire glass object but may be limited to the outside only.

Application Attaching molten glass rods to blanks in order to form handles, foots, pedestals, and so on.

Apricot A deep yellow or dark ambered colored glass.

Aqua or Aquamarine A light greenish-blue color in glass like the color of seawater.

Aqua opalescent Aqua or aquamarine colored glass with an opalescent edge.

Aqua regia A mixture of two strong acids that serve to dissolve gold dust in the making of red or ruby red glassware. In more recent times, selenium has replaced gold in producing the color red.

Arissing The process of removing sharp edges from glass.

Art or Art Nouveau glass Expensive handblown glass with unusual effects of color, shape, and design. Art glass is primarily ornamental and was most popular from the 1880s to 1920.

Ashtray A shallow bowl-like glass receptacle used for cigarette butts and tobacco ashes.

Atomizer See **Cologne bottle** and **Perfume bottle**.

Aurene Iridescent ornamental art glass created by Frederick Carder at the Steuben Glass Works in 1905.

Aventurine An ancient Egyptian technique of applying small flakes of metal such as gold and copper in colored glass. This technique was popular during the Art Nouveau period.

Averbeck Cut Glass Co. Established in New York City in 1892; Averbeck ran a jewelry store and a mail order business featuring cut glass products. The company ceased operation in 1923.

Baccarat Fine glass first made in France and Belgium in the late 18th century. Baccarat Glass was particularly noted for paperweights but also produced tableware and other decorative glass. Today, Baccarat Crystal produces some of the finest made pieces. The original company was founded in 1764 in Baccarat, France.

Backstamp An identification mark that is printed or molded on a piece of glass. The mark may include a company name, logo, and item number.

Bakewell, Pears, and Co. Established in Pittsburgh, Pennsylvania, in 1807; the company began producing glass furniture knobs and handles and then added tableware and barware. The business closed in 1882.

Ball stopper A spherical glass object that rests at the top of glass bottles, jugs, decanters, etc. Its diameter is larger than the mouth of the vessel.

Baluster A type of English drinking glass or goblet created in the late 17th century. The stem is in the shape of a short vertical support with a circular section (baluster-shaped).

Banana boat or dish A long, flat or shallow dish, with sides that are possibly curved upward, with or without a separate base, and used for serving bananas or banana splits.

Bar tumbler A glass tumbler with or without flutes produced in the United States in various shapes and sizes beginning in the mid 19th century primarily for hotels and saloons.

Barbini Glassworks Established by Alfredo Barbini in Murano, Italy, in 1950. The company operates today creating Venetian novelties and knicknacks.

Bartlett-Collins Co. Established in Sapulpa, Oklahoma, in 1914; the company is noted for tableware, lamps, and glass decorated with Western themes.

Base color The color of glass before any coating is applied, usually the color of Carnival glass before it is iridized.

Basket A glass receptacle with semicircular handle used for foods, decoration, or for displaying flowers.

Batch The mixture of raw materials fused together before heating.

Beading The process by which chips or small relief beads are fused to a glass object in the form of a continuous row.

Beaumont Glass Company Established in Martins Ferry, Ohio, in 1895 as a maker of pressed glass; the company was sold to the Hocking Glass Company in 1905.

Bell or Dinner bell A hollow device with ringer and single top handle used for summoning or signaling when rung (e.g., to announce dinnertime).

Belmont Tumbler Co. Established in the early 1900s in Bellaire, Ohio; the company produced tumblers and some Depression items. The factory burned in 1952 and was never rebuilt.

Bergen, J.D. Co. Founded in Meriden, Connecticut, by James D. Bergen and Thomas Niland; Bergen bought out Niland in 1885 and continued operating as a cut glass operation until 1922.

Best metal The highest-quality batch of glass made by a company using the purest ingredients and highest lead content.

Berry bowl A concave glass vessel used for serving fruits and other foods. Note that a berry set is a large bowl with one or more matching smaller bowls.

Bevel Slanted or angled cuts usually beginning at the bottom or sides of a glass object (sometimes referred to as flutes at the bottom).

Biscuit jar A tall, wide-mouthed canister-shaped glass receptacle with cover used for holding biscuits, crackers, or cookies (the predecessor of the cookie jar).

Bitters bottle Small bottle used for containing bitters or tonics made in the United States in the mid-19th and later 19th century.

Black amethyst An extremely dense, nearly opaque shade of purple made by the addition of manganese. Black amethyst glass is so dark that it cannot be seen when held to light.

Black bottle A dark opaque green English invention in the mid 17th century used for transporting and storing various beverages such as water, beer, wine, and rum.

Black glass Dark opaque ebony glass created by the combination of oxide of manganese, cobalt, and oxide of iron added to a batch of glass.

Blackmer Cut Glass Co. Established by Arthur L. Blackmer in New Bedford, Massachusetts, in 1894 and incorporated as A.L. Blackmer in 1902. The company produced cut glass products until 1916.

Blank An uncut piece of glass, ordinarily a bowl or vase, that has been specifically made of heavy, high-quality lead glassware.

Blenko Glass Co. Originally founded by English immigrant William J. Blenko in 1922 in Milton, West Virginia; the company started out as a maker of stained glass windows and later switched to contemporary art glass forms.

Blobbing The process by which chips of colored glass are embedded in the thickness of blown glass to form an irregular scattering of contrasting colors.

Blowing The process of blowing air through a metal tube or blowpipe in order to shape the molten glass blob attached to its end.

Blowpipe A hollow metal tube used to gather molten glass from the pot and then to blow air through it in order to shape glass.

Bluerina Art glass made in America in the late 19th century. Similar to Amberina, the colors gradually meld from blue at the base to amberina at the top.

Boda Glassworks Founded in 1864 in southern Sweden, Boda merged with Kosta in 1946 to form Kosta-Boda.

Bohemian glass German-made glass of the 17th century characterized by ornate decoration, heavy cutting, and bright colors.

Bonbon or Bon bon dish A small, usually flat or shallow circular dish, with or without handles (center handle possible), used for serving small finger foods such as nuts, bonbons, or tiny fruits.

Boot glass A small glass vessel shaped like a boot with a capacity of about 3 ounces.

Booze bottle A flask made in the United States in the 1860s in the form of a two-story house by the Whitney Glass Works for Edmund G. Booze.

Borosilicate glass The original or first heat-resistant formula for glassware that contains boric oxide. It was developed by the Corning Glass Works for railroad lantern lenses and for battery cases. It was adapted to Pyrex kitchenware in 1915.

Boston & Sandwich Glass Co. Established in Boston, Massachusetts, by Deming Jarves in 1826; the company produced pressed and cut glassware before closing in 1888.

Boston Silver Glass Co. Established in 1857 by A. Young in Cambridge, Massachusetts; the company produced some pressed glassware and silverplating before closing in 1871.

Bottle A glass container with a narrow neck and mouth; may or may not have a handle. Bottles come in all shapes and sizes and can be made of other materials.

Bowl A concave glass vessel, hemispherical in shape, used for holding liquids and other foods (e.g., soup, salad, cereal, berries, and vegetables). The bowl of a wine or stemmed beverage glass is the portion that holds the liquid.

Boyd Art Glass Co. Established in Cambridge, Ohio, in 1978; Boyd is noted for highly collectible miniature art glass figurines created in a variety of colors and styles.

Brandy glass A short, rounded glass with a foot and very tiny stem; shorter but wider as compared to a rounded wine glass.

Bread and butter plate A round, flat plate that is usually 6″ in diameter.

Bride's basket A fancy bowl held within a silver or silver-plated frame. It was a popular wedding gift during the Brilliant period after the product debuted at the World's Columbian Exposition in Chicago, 1893.

Brilliant Glass Works Established by Joseph Beatty, Sr., in Brilliant, Ohio, in 1880; it remained in operation until 1893 and produced some pressed glassware.

Brilliant period The era of U.S. handmade glassware from 1880 to 1915 characterized by fine cutting, engraving, polishing, and fancy patterns.

Bristol glass Crystal, colored, and milk glass items produced in several factories in Bristol, England, in the 17th and 18th centuries.

Bristol-type glass 19th-century American and English-made Victorian opaque glassware characterized by hand enameling.

Bryce Brothers Formed in the mid 19th century in Mt. Pleasant, Pennsylvania. The company specialized in handblown stemware and barware and became part of the U.S. Glass Company in 1891.

Bubble An air- or gas-filled cavity within glass. Intentional bubbles are often created for decorative effects, while unintentional ones result from improper fusing of the ingredients. Tiny bubbles are also known as seeds.

Bullicante A technique originated in Venice that places air bubbles in a regular pattern within glass (popular in modern paperweights).

Bumper Another term for a firing glass.

Burmese glass Glass objects characterized by various light opaque shadings in pastel colors of pink, yellow, and white produced with the addition of uranium. It was first created by the Mt. Washington Glass Company in the late 19th century and then produced by others.

Butter dish A glass dish that is ordinarily flat or footed, with or without a glass dome or rectangular cover, used for serving butter, margarine, or other spreads.

Butter plate A miniature glass plate used for serving individual portions of butter, margarine, or other spreads.

Butter tub A glass vessel shaped like a small bucket or pail (usually smaller than an ice bucket), with or without semicircular handle, used for serving butter balls.

Cable A pattern in glass that resembles the twisted strands of rope or cable.

Caddy A small glass container with a cover used for holding tea or tea bags.

Cake plate A large flat or footed glass plate, usually round in shape, used for holding cakes.

Calcite glass A brightly colored cream-white colored glass that resembles the mineral calcite (calcite is not used in its manufacture). Calcite glass was first produced by Frederick Carder at the Steuben Glass Works in the early 20th century.

Cambridge Glass Co. Established in Cambridge, Ohio, in 1901; the Cambridge Glass Company was a major producer of colored glassware and cut crystal until 1958, when the factory closed.

Cameo engraving An engraving process in which the background is carved away to leave the design in relief (see **Relief cutting**).

Campbell, Jones and Co. Established in 1865 in Pittsburgh, Pennsylvania, by James Campbell and Jenkins Jones; the company operated until 1895 and made mostly pressed glassware.

Camphor glass A nearly opaque white pressed glass produced in America in the 19th century.

Canary yellow A bright yellow colored glass similar to amber colored glass (also made with various amounts of iron, carbon, and sulphur).

Candelabra or Candelabrum A branched candlestick with several sockets for holding candles.

Candleholder A small glass tumbler-like vessel designed to hold candles of 2″ in diameter or smaller.

Candlestick A raised glass object with one socket for holding a single candle.

Candlette A small bowl-like glass object with one socket for holding a single candle.

Candy dish An open, shallow bowl-like glass receptacle used for serving candy; may or may not be footed.

Candy jar A tall, wide-mouthed glass receptacle with cover used for serving candy; may or may not be footed.

Cane A cylindrical piece or stick of glass used for stems of drinking glasses or cut up into small slices for producing millefiori paperweights.

Canton Glass Co. Established in Canton, Ohio, in 1883; the company produced pressed and novelty items before becoming part of the National Glass Company in 1900.

Cape Cod Glass Works Established in 1858 by Deming Jarves in Boston, Massachusetts. The firm produced pressed wares and art glass designs such as gold-ruby, peachblow, and "Sandwich Alabaster" until 1869.

Carafe A large glass bottle with stopper used for serving beverages (usually water or wine).

Caramel slag See **Chocolate glass**.

Card tray A flat glass object, usually rectangular in shape, with possibly a center handle and two separate sections; used for holding standard-size playing cards.

Carder, Frederick A famous glassmaker, designer, and producer. Carder founded the Steuben Glass Company in 1903 and was responsible for most of the factory's production into the early 1930s.

Carnival glass Pressed glassware with a fired-on iridescent finish made in the United States from 1905–1925 (reproductions were made beginning in the 1960s).

Carpet A condensely arranged set of glass canes used in making millefiori paperweights.

Carving The removal of glass from the surface of an object usually by means of handheld tools.

Cased glass 19th-century glass that was blown in multiple layers of separate colors. The glass was then decorated by cutting away all or part of these layers.

Casserole dish A deep round, oblong, or square dish, with or without cover, with or without handles or tabs, and used to bake as well as serve food.

Cast glass Glass made in simple molds and then surface-ground with polishing wheels fed by abrasives.

Castor set A set of glass serving objects held on glass or metal trays. These objects might include small pitchers, cruets, small jars, salt and pepper shakers, and other small dishes.

Celery dish A long flat or shallow narrow glass dish, usually oval in design, and used for serving celery. A few odd celery dishes have been produced in tall cylindrical shapes (celery vases).

Centerpiece A large circular or oval fancy glass bowl used as an adornment in the center of a table.

Central Glass Works Established in 1866 in Wheeling, West Virginia; Central was noted for pressed patterns and art "Coin Glass" and was one of the first to develop popular colors of the Depression era. The company closed in 1939.

Chain Glass threads that are formed or applied to objects in interconnected links or rings.

Chalk glass A colorless glass containing powdered chalk. It was developed in Bohemia in the late 17th century for making thick vessels. The vessels were then engraved or enameled.

Champagne glass A tall glass with foot and stem and a large round but shallow bowl.

Chalice A fancy drinking vessel with a large, rounded bowl (may or may not be stemmed).

Challinor & Taylor Ltd. Founded in 1866 by David Challinor and Taylor in Pittsburgh, Pennsylvania. The company moved to Tarentum in 1884 and produced pressed glass, lamps, and novelties before becoming part of the U.S. Glass Company in 1891.

Chandelier An ornate branched glass lighting fixture suspended from a ceiling.

Chartreuse Yellowish-green colored opaque glass.

Checkered Diamond A cut design pattern with several small diamonds inscribed within one large one.

Cheaters Small whiskey tumblers with extremely thick glass bottoms and walls that were made to look as if they held more capacity than in actuality.

Cheese and cracker dish A serving dish with two levels (two-tiered), one for holding cheese or a cheese ball (usually the upper part), and the other for crackers.

Cheese dish A glass dish that is ordinarily flat or footed with a separate glass cover (usually dome-shaped) and used for serving cheese. Note that cheese dishes are a little larger than butter dishes.

Cherry jar A small, wide-mouthed glass receptacle with cover used for holding cherries. Most pieces are wider at the bottom and taper off near the top.

Chigger bite A small chip or nick in a piece of glass.

Chimney A cylindrically shaped glass tube that is open at both ends, used to shield the flame of an oil lamp and to trap soot and increase the draft.

Chintz A style of glass patented by A. Douglas Nash. It was characterized by colored ribbed, striped, or swirled glass marvered into opaque, opalescent, and transparent glass. The process was expensive and difficult since the separate colors often ran together.

Chocolate glass A variegated opaque glass that shades from dark brown to light tan. It was first developed by Jacob Rosenthal, who worked at the Indiana Tumbler & Goblet Company. It is sometimes referred to as caramel slag.

Chop plate A large, flat glass object, usually round or oval in shape, used for serving food. A chop plate serves the same function as a platter, tray, or salver.

Chunked Glass that has been heavily damaged, usually cracked, seriously chipped, or considerably worn.

Cigar jar A large, wide-mouthed glass canister with cover used for holding and storing cigars and tobacco.

Cigarette box A small covered glass receptacle designed to hold a single standard pack of cigarettes.

Cigarette holder A flat glass dish or ashtray containing notches that are used for holding cigarettes (may or may not have a cover).

Cigarette jar or urn A small, wide-mouthed glass canister with cover used for holding and storing cigarettes.

Clambroth or Clam broth Grayish-colored, semitransparent glass. In Carnival glass, clambroth is an iridized pastel color often compared to ginger ale.

Clamp A tool used in place of a pontil to hold a blown glass vessel at its closed end while the open end is being shaped (usually avoids leaving a pontil mark).

Claret glass A tall glass with foot and stem with a large round, deep bowl specifically designed for serving claret wine.

Clark, T.B. & Co. Established in Honesdale, Pennsylvania, in 1884 by Thomas Byron Clark; the company cut blanks provided by Dorflinger and became one of the most successful cut glass operations. It closed in 1930.

Clichy A famous French glassmaking town that was noted for paperweight production beginning in the 1840s. The factories closed in the 1880s as the popularity for paperweights declined.

Cluster A collection or gathering of similar canes used in making millefiori paperweights.

Cluthra An art glass form developed by Steuben in 1920. It is characterized by a cloudy opaque design permeated by bubbles. Offshoots of the basic design were produced by other companies, such as Kimble.

Coaster A very shallow or flat container used to protect surfaces.

Cobalt blue Metallic coloring agent producing the most powerful deep blue color within glass.

Cocktail glass A tall glass with foot, stem, and angled or straight-edged bowl.

Cocktail shaker A tall, tumbler-like glass vessel with cover used for mixing alcoholic drinks.

Coin glass Originally in the 18th and 19th centuries, a tumbler or tankard with a real coin visibly placed in the foot or stem. Later 20th-century versions contain glass coin replicas inscribed within the glass.

Cologne bottle A small glass receptacle with narrow neck and stopper used for holding colognes or perfumes.

Combing A decorating technique in which bands of molten or soft colored glass are dragged along the surface of an object at right angles to form a repetitive pattern.

Compote or Comport A glass serving bowl that may have a base, stem, or foot, used for serving candy, fruits, or nuts. Comports are most commonly referred to as raised candy dishes.

Condiment set See **Castor set**.

Console bowl A large concave glass vessel, hemispherical in shape, and used as a centerpiece or for serving large items. Console bowls are sometimes accompanied by a pair of matching candlesticks.

Consolidated Lamp & Glass Co. Established in 1894 in Coraopolis, Pennsylvania; the company was noted most for art glass lamps and its Martele line of art glass. It closed in 1967.

Cookie jar A tall, wide-mouthed, canister-shaped, glass receptacle (larger than a candy jar) with cover, without foot or stem, and used for holding cookies.

Co-Operative Flint Glass Company A pressed glass manufacturer established in Beaver Falls, Pennsylvania, in 1879. The company ceased operations in 1934.

Copper wheel engraving Process of hand engraving by holding a glass to a revolving copper wheel, which instantly cuts through the surface. Some of the best glass ever produced was done by highly skilled copper wheel engravers who kept the cutting pattern in their minds.

Coral Various shadings of yellow to red layers applied to glass objects with opaque-colored bases.

Coralene glass Art glass that was first made in 19th century Europe and then in the United States. It is characterized by enamel and colored or opaque glass drops applied to raised branches that resembled coral.

Cordial glass A miniature wine glass with foot, stem, and small bowl.

Core forming Process of glassmaking by spinning glass around a core.

Corning Glass Works Established in Corning, New York, in 1868 as the Corning Flint Glass Works. The name was changed permanently in 1875 and the company's most notable purchase was that of Steuben in the 1930s. The company continues to operate today as Corning, Inc. (final name change in 1989).

Correia Art Glass Founded in 1973 by Steven V. Correia in Santa Monica, California; the company's contemporary art glass products can already be found in major art museums (e.g., Smithsonian Institution, Corning Museum of Glass, and Metropolitan Museum of Art).

Cosmos Pressed milk glass made in America in the early 1900s.

Cracker jar A tall, wide-mouthed, canister-shaped glass receptacle with cover used for holding crackers.

Cracking off The process of removing an object from the pontil. Cooled by scoring, the pipe is then gently tapped, and the object falls into a sand tray or V-shaped holder held by an assistant.

Crackling A decorating technique applied to glassware by plunging a hot object into cold water to induce cracks, then reforming the piece within a mold.

Cranberry glass First developed in England in the 19th century, cranberry glass is characterized by a light red tint (the color of cranberries) produced by the addition of gold dust that is dissolved in two acids (aqua regia). Originally it was a cheaper substitute for ruby red, but now the name is applied to any cranberry-colored glass.

Cream soup bowl A concave glass vessel, hemispherical in shape, usually with two handles, and used for serving soup or other foods.

Creamer A small cuplike vessel ordinarily with a handle and used for serving cream (with coffee and tea, usually paired with a sugar dish).

Cremax An opaque, lightly beige-colored glass first produced and named by the MacBeth-Evans Glass Company.

Crest A name given to several Fenton Glass products that contain a base color (most often milk glass) and a colored or crystal trim.

Cristallo A nearly colorless, highly esteemed soda glass invented by Venetian glassmakers in the 16th century.

Crizzling A deteriorated condition that results from alkaline elements in the glass that react to moisture. The consequence is the formation of droplets or tears of alkaline moisture on the surface. Crizzling is also known as weeping, sweating, or sick glass (also spelled "Crisseling").

Crown Milano See **Albertine glass**.

Cruet A small glass bottle or decanter with top used to hold a condiment such as oil, vinegar, or salad dressing, for use at the table.

Crystal Colorless glass containing a high lead content.

Crystal Glass Works An Australian company founded in Sydney in the early 1900s; it was noted for Carnival and other glass production.

Cullets Shards or scraps of glass that are remelted and added to a new batch of glass to aid in the fusion process.

Cup An open, somewhat bowl-shaped or cylindrical vessel, usually with a handle, and used for drinking liquids such as coffee, tea, and punch.

Cuspidor A fancy glass vessel or receptacle used for containing saliva (see **Spittoon**).

Custard cup A smaller than ordinary cup, with or without a handle, used for serving desserts in small portions, such as pudding and custard.

Custard glass A yellowish-colored or yellow cream-colored opaque glass (the color of custard) first developed in the early 1900s.

Cut glass Heavy flint glass cut with geometric patterns into the glass with grinding wheels and abrasives. The design is then further smoothed and polished. Cutting originated in Germany and was introduced in the United States in the late 18th century.

Cut velvet Colored art glass consisting of two fused, mold-blown layers that leaves the outer surface design raised in relief.

Daisy in Hexagon A cut design pattern featuring a flower inscribed within a hexagon.

Darner A glass needle with large eye for use in darning. Glass darners are sometimes whimsical creations.

Daum A French glass company established in 1875 in the town of Nancy, France. "Daum" or "Nancy Daum" or "Cristalleries de Nancy" are all names associated with glass produced by this company. The company began as a producer of many styles of Art Nouveau glass and continues to operate today.

De Vilbiss Co. A decorating firm established around 1900 in Toledo, Ohio; the firm primarily decorated perfume bottles and atomizers in many art glass styles until the late 1930s.

Decal A picture, design, or label from specially prepared paper that is transferred to glass usually by heating.

Decanter An ornamental or fancy glass bottle with cover or stopper, with or without handles, used for serving wine or other alcoholic beverages.

Delphite A pale blue opaque glass; it is sometimes referred to as "blue milk glass."

Demitasse Matching cups and saucers that are much smaller (1/2 size or less) than their ordinary counterparts. Note that demitasse cups and saucers are still slightly larger than those found in children's miniature tea sets.

Dennis Glassworks A glass operation founded near Stourbridge, England, by the Webb family in 1855. The company produced art glass and continues to operate today.

Depression glass Mass-produced, inexpensive, and primarily machine-made glass dinner sets and giftware in clear and many colors produced in the United States between 1920 and 1940.

Devitrification A deteriorated condition of glass in which crystals have formed within the glass due to technical faults in the manufacturing process.

Diamond-Daisy A cut glass design pattern featuring daisies inscribed within diamonds or squares.

Diamond Glass Co., Ltd. A Canadian company that operated in Montreal from 1890 to 1902. It was noted for many pressed glass designs, tableware, and lamps.

Diamond Glass-Ware Co. Established in Indiana, Pennsylvania, in 1891; the company was noted for high-quality handmade colored glassware. It closed in 1931 when the factory was destroyed by fire.

Diamond Point A cut glass design pattern featuring faceted diamonds that intersect at a common point.

Diamond point engraving Hand cutting or machine cutting of glass with a diamond point tool (note that hardened metal by heat treating to a sharp point has since replaced the more expensive diamonds for machine cutting).

Diatreta glass Art glass made by applying tiny pieces of ornamental glass in patterns to other larger glass objects. This process was first developed by Frederick Carder in the early 1900s.

Dinner plate A flat glass object, usually round in shape, about 8″ to 11″ in diameter, and used for serving food.

Dip mold A one-piece mold with an open top used for embossing or imprinting decorations and lettering.

Dispenser A large glass container or bottle with a spigot originally used for obtaining cold water from the refrigerator.

Dithridge & Company Founded by Edward Dithridge, Sr. Dithridge purchased the Fort Pitt Glass Works, for which he worked, in the 1860s. He died in 1873. His son, Edward Dithridge, Jr., continued operations until reorganizing and moving the company to a new location in 1881.

Dithridge Flint Glass Co. Founded by Edward D. Dithridge, Jr., in 1881 in Martins Ferry, Ohio. The business moved to New Brighton, Pennsylvania, in 1887 and continued to produce cut and engraved glass, as well as blanks for others. Dithridge ceased operations in 1891.

Dominion Glass Co. A Canadian company that operated from 1886 to 1898 (separate from the modern company of the same name) in Montreal. It was noted for pressed wares and lamps.

Domino tray A serving dish with a built-in container for cream and a surrounding area specifically designed for holding sugar cubes.

Dorflinger Glass Works The original factory was established in White Mills, Pennsylvania, in the 1840s by German immigrant Christian Dorflinger. Dorflinger was noted for making high-quality cut glass tableware and was a major supplier of lead crystal blanks. The company remained in operation as C. Dorflinger & Sons until 1921.

Double cruet Two glass bottles (cruets) that are fused together into one larger capacity bottle used for serving condiments.

Dram glass Small English or Irish glass made of metal used for drinking a single measure of strong liquor (most were made between 1750 and 1850 and exported to the United States).

Dresser set A set of glass bath or bedroom objects held on a matching tray. These objects might include perfume or cologne bottles; jars; and tiny boxes for gloves, hair or hat pins, jewelry, and so on.

Dugan Glass Co. Established in Indiana, Pennsylvania, in 1892 by Harry White, Thomas E. Dugan, and W.G. Minnemyer; the company produced a good deal of Carnival glass. The firm became the Diamond Glass Co. in 1913 and operated until a fire destroyed it in 1931.

Duncan, George & Sons See **Ripley & Co.**

Duncan Miller Glass Co. Established in 1892 by James and George Duncan, Jr., along with John Ernest Miller, in Washington, Pennsylvania; the company produced pressed wares and novelty items through the Depression era.

Durand Art Glass Co. Established in Vineland, New Jersey, by French immigrant Victor Durand, Sr., in 1924; the company produced several art glass styles until Durand's death in 1931.

Edinburgh Crystal Glass Co. Established in the late 19th century in Edinburgh, Scotland; the company produced hand-cut crystal wares and exported some of these products to the United States.

Ebony glass Another name for black-colored or very dark black opaque glass.

Egg cup or holder A small, cuplike vessel without handle used to hold a single egg. Occasionally, double egg holders have been made.

Egg plate A flat, thick plate with oval indentations for serving boiled or deviled eggs.

Eggington, O.F. Co. Established in Corning, New York, in 1899 by Oliver Eggington; the company purchased blanks from the Corning Glass Works and operated as a cut glass operation until it closed in 1920.

Electric An effect attributed to some Carnival glass. The iridescence applied is so bright that it resembles neon or electric light.

Embossing Mold-blown or pressed glassware in which the design is applied directly on the object from the mold. Embossed patterns are usually in relief.

Emerald green A deep, powerful green color usually made with chromium and iron (the color of the gemstone emerald).

Empire Cut Glass Co. Established in New York City in 1896 by Harry Hollis; Hollis sold the company to his employees, who operated it briefly as a cooperative. They in turn sold it to H.C. Fry in 1904, who moved operations to Flemington, New Jersey (Flemington Cut Glass Co.).

Enameling A liquid medium similar to paint applied to glassware and then permanently fused on the object by heating.

Encased overlay A single or double overlay design further encased in clear glass.

Engraving The decoration of glass applied by holding the piece against the edge of revolving wheels made of stone, copper, or other materials.

Enterprise Cut Glass Co. Founded by George E. Gaylord in Elmira Heights, New York; the company produced cut glass products until it ceased operation in 1917.

Epergne A large table centerpiece that includes a large bowl surrounded by several matching smaller dishes.

Erickson Glassworks Established in Bremen, Ohio, by Swedish immigrants Carl and Steven Erickson in 1943. The brothers produced mold-blown glass products distinguished by heavy casing, controlled bubbles, and a heavy ball for a base. The company ceased operation in 1961.

Etching See **Acid etching**.

Ewer A round glass juglike object, with or without a foot, that usually has a long handle and spout.

Favrile An American Art Nouveau style of glass created by Louis Comfort Tiffany in the late 19th century. The original pieces are often referred to as "Tiffany Favrile."

Federal Glass Co. Established in Colombia, Ohio, in 1900. The company began as a cut glass operation, switched to automation during the Depression era, and continues to operate today as a subsidiary of the Federal Paper Board Company.

Fenton Art Glass Co. Established in Martins Ferry, Ohio, in 1905, the company moved to Williamstown, West Virginia, in 1906. Fenton was a major producer of carnival, opalescent, and other pressed and molded glassware. Fenton still operates today in Williamstown, producing hand-decorated glassware, including lamps and novelty items.

Fern bowl or Fernery A glass container with a liner, with or without a foot, designed for holding ferns or other plants.

Fern glass Glass objects decorated with etched or engraved fern or similar leaf patterns.

Figurine A small individual etched or molded statue (or figure).

Filigree A technique developed in Venice that uses glass threads or fine canes twisted around a clear cane to produce finely threaded patterns. See **Latticino**.

Findlay glass Art glass characterized by various shades of brown.

Finger bowl A small concave glass vessel, usually circular and shallow in shape, used for rinsing fingers at the table.

Filigrana A general term for blown glass made with white or sometimes colored canes.

Finial A crowning ornament or decorative knob found most often in stemware and at the top of glass covers.

Fire polishing Reheating a finished piece of glass at the glory hole in order to remove tool marks (more commonly replaced with acid polishing).

Fired on Finishing colors that are baked on or fused by heating to the outer surface of glass objects.

Fired-on iridescence A finish applied to glass by adding metallic salts, after which the glass is refired.

Firing glass A small glass vessel with thick base, waisted sides, and possibly a stem or base that could withstand considerable abuse. The resulting noise of several glasses being slammed at once was comparable to that of a musket "firing." Some were made of metal and most were produced in the 18th and early 19th centuries in both Europe and the United States.

Flameworking The technique of shaping objects when they are hot (heated by a gas-fueled torch) from rods or tubes of glass.

Flashed-on iridescence A finish applied to glass by dipping hot glass into a solution of metallic salts.

Flashing A very thin coating of a different color from that of the base color (thinner than a casing or an overlay).

Flask A glass container with narrow neck and mouth, with stopper or cover, and used for carrying alcoholic beverages.

Flint glass A term for fine glassware made in the 19th century. A name for lead glass, although original experimenters used powdered flints as substitutes for lead oxides.

Floret or Florette A slice from a large cane of several colored rods arranged to form a floral pattern.

Floriform A tall glass vase with narrow stem and top that is in the shape of a flower bloom.

Flower bowl A large shallow hemispherical container used for holding or floating flowers with relatively short stems.

Fluting Vertically cut decoration in long, narrow or parallel sections such as bevels (usually wheel-cut but sometimes molded).

Flux A substance such as soda, wood ash, potash, or lead oxide added to the basic ingredients in order to stabilize and lower the melting point of a batch of glass.

Folded foot The turned-over edge of the foot of a wine glass or similar glass object to give added strength to the vessel.

Foot The part of a glass other than the base on which it rests.

Footmaker An assistant to a glassmaker who forms the foot of the glass in the glassblowing process.

Forest green A dark green color not as deep or rich as emerald green. It was first made in the late 1930s and early 1940s by the Hazel-Atlas

Glass Company, which patented the name. The term has been applied to glassware made by other companies in the same color.

Fostoria Glass Co. Established in Fostoria, Ohio, in 1887; the company produced cut crystal items early on, several Depression tableware patterns, and continued in operation until 1986.

Founding The making of glass by melting and fusing the ingredients together in a furnace.

Fractional shot A small glass tumbler with a capacity of less than 1 ounce.

Frances ware Mold-blown tableware characterized by amber color, fluted rims, and hobnail patterns; it was produced by Hobbs, Brocunier Co. in the 1880s.

Free-blown glass An ancient technique of handblowing glass without the use of molds.

Frog A small but thick and heavy glass object, usually round or domed, that contains perforations, holes, or spikes for holding flowers in place within a vase.

Frosted glass A light opalescence or cloudy coloring of a batch of glass using tin, zinc, or an all-over acid etching, as in Depression glass. A frosted coating can also be applied on the surface of clear or crystal glass by spraying on white acid (a solution of ammonium bifluoride).

Fruit or nut dish A small, flat or shallow circular container, with or without handles, used for serving small fruits, nuts, candies, etc.

Fry, H.C. An American glassmaker who founded the Rochester Tumbler Company in 1872 and the H.C. Fry Glass Company in 1901, both in Rochester, Pennsylvania. The glass that was produced in his later factory is sometimes referred to as "Fry Glass" and included some art glass as well as tableware. The company closed in 1934.

Full lead crystal Colorless glass with a minimum of 30% lead content.

Furnace An enclosed structure for the production and application of heat. Furnaces today are usually heated by natural gas for clean burning. In glassmaking, furnaces are used for melting a batch of glass, maintaining pots of glass in a molten state, and reheating partially formed objects at the glory hole.

Fusion The process of liquefying or when the melting point is reached for a batch of glass. Temperatures can range from 2,000° to 3,000° Fahrenheit, depending on the ingredients used.

Gadget A special rod developed to replace the pontil to avoid leaving a mark on the foot. A spring clip at the end of the gadget grips the foot of a just-finished piece of glass while the worker trims the rim and applies the finishing touches on the glass.

Gadrooning A decorative band derived from a silver form made of molded, applied, or deep-cut sections of reeding. Gadrooning is sometimes referred to as "knurling."

Gaffer A term of respect for an experienced master or head glassmaker dating back to the 16th century.

Gall A layer of scum that forms at the surface of a batch of glass during the heating process (it is skimmed off).

Gallé, Emile A French glassmaker and pioneer of the 19th-century Art Nouveau style. He is noted for Art Cameo and floral designs created in several color effects and styles.

Gather A blob of molten glass attached to the end of a blowpipe, pontil, or gathering iron.

Gibson Glass Established in Milton, West Virginia, by Charles Gibson in 1983. Gibson is noted for animals, figurines, paperweights, and other novelty items produced in a variety of colors and styles.

Gilding An applied decorating technique with gold enamels or paints to finished glass objects.

Gillinder & Sons Founded by English immigrant William T. Gillinder, who once was superintendent of The New England Glass Co. Gillinder, along with his sons James and Frederick, established their own cutting and art glass business in 1867 in Philadelphia. The firm later became part of the U.S. Glass Company in 1892.

Glass A hard, brittle, artificial substance made by fusing silicates (sand) with an alkali (soda or potash) and sometimes with metallic oxides (lead oxide or lime).

Glassboro Glassworks Established in Glassboro, New Jersey, by Jacob Stanger in 1781; the company produced windows, bottles, and tableware into the 20th century.

Glasshouse The building that contains the glass-melting furnaces and in which the actual handling and shaping of molten glass takes place.

Glass picture A design that is ordinarily etched on flat sheets or flat pieces of glass.

Glove box A rectangular glass object, with or without cover, used specifically on dressing tables or vanities for holding gloves.

Glory hole A small-sized opening in the side of the furnace used for inserting cool glass objects in order to reheat them without melting or destroying the shape (sometimes called the reheating furnace).

Goblet A drinking vessel with a large bowl of various sizes and shapes that rests on a stemmed foot.

Gone with the Wind lamp A kerosene or electric table lamp that features a glass base with a round, globe-shaped glass shade.

Graal A technique developed by Orrefors of Sweden. Graal is created by cutting a pattern within the core of colored glass that is encased in clear glass and then blown into its final shape (much like the reverse of cameo glass, since the cutaway portion forms the design instead of the background).

Grapefruit bowl A concave glass vessel, usually circular in shape, ordinarily with a wide foot, and used for serving half of a grapefruit.

Gravy boat An oblong, bowl-like object with a handle and a spout used for pouring gravy (may or may not be accompanied by a matching platter or pedestal).

Green glass The natural color of ordinary alkaline or lime-based glassware usually produced by iron present in the sand. Additional iron and chromium are added to make a clear green.

Greensburg Glass Co. Established in Greensburg, Pennsylvania, in 1889; the company produced pressed glass until becoming part of the National Glass Company in 1900.

Grill plate A large individual or serving plate with divisions (similar to relish dishes, only larger).

Ground The background or base glass object on which decorations are applied.

Gunderson Glass Works Robert Gunderson, along with Thomas Tripp and Isaac Babbitt, purchased the silverware and glass departments of Pairpoint in 1939 and continued production until Gunderson's death in 1952. Glass made by Gunderson is often referred to as "Gunderson's Pairpoint."

Hairpin box A small square, rectangular, or circular glass container, with or without cover, used specifically on a dressing table or vanity for holding hairpins.

Hair receiver A circular glass object, usually with a cover that has a large hole in the middle, used on tables, dressers, and vanities to hold hair that accumulates in a hairbrush.

Half lead crystal Colorless glass containing a minimum of 24% lead content (lower quality than full lead crystal).

Hammonton Glassworks Established in Hammonton, New Jersey, by William Coffin and Jonathan Haines in 1817; the company produced windows, bottles, and some tableware before going out of business.

Handblown glass Glass formed and shaped with a blowpipe and other hand-manipulated tools without the use of molds.

Hand cooler A solid ovoid or small glass object originally developed in ancient Rome for ladies to cool their hands. Later, hand coolers were also used by ladies when being wooed or for darning.

Handpressed glass Glass that is made in hand-operated mechanical presses.

Handel, Philip J. An American glassmaker who founded the Handel Company in Meriden, Connecticut, in 1885. He was noted for producing Art Nouveau acid cut-back cameo vases and Art Nouveau lamps similar to but less expensive than Tiffany lamps.

Handkerchief box A rectangular glass receptacle with cover used for storing handkerchiefs.

Hat pin holder A tall glass object in the shape of a cylinder used on tables, dressers, and vanities for holding hat pins.

Hat or Hat vase A whimsical glass object in the shape of an upside-down head covering or top hat. The space where one's head would usually rest is often used for holding flowers or tiny objects.

Hawkes, T.G. & Co. Established in Corning, New York, in the late 19th century by Thomas Gibbon Hawkes; the company produced high-quality cut crystal tableware and blanks for others. In 1903 T.G. Hawkes and Frederick Carder merged to form the Steuben Glass Works.

Hazel-Atlas Glass Co. Established in Washington, Pennsylvania, in 1902; the company produced machine-pressed glassware, especially during the Depression period. Factories were added throughout Ohio, Pennsylvania, and West Virginia until the company sold out in 1956.

Heisey, A. H., Glass Co. Established in Newark, Ohio, in the 1860s; Heisey was noted for cut patterns and finely etched glass. The company produced pressed wares during the Depression era, as well as collectible glass animals. The factory closed in 1956.

Helios A name given to a style of Carnival glass by the Imperial Glass Company. Helios is characterized by a silver or gold iridescent sheen over green glass.

Higbee Glass Co. Established by John B. Higbee in 1900 in Bridgeville, Pennsylvania; Higbee once worked with John Bryce in 1879 before opening his own business. The company operated for only a short time, but the glass is easily identified by its famous raised bee trademark.

Highball glass A tall, narrow tumbler of at least 4-ounce capacity used for mixed drinks.

Hoare, J. & Co. Established in Corning, New York, in 1868 by John Hoare. Hoare formed many partnerships beginning in 1853 (Hoare & Burns, Gould & Hoare, Hoare and Dailey, etc.) before forming his own cut glass department under the Corning Flint Glass Co.

Hobbs, Brocunier, & Co. Established in Wheeling, West Virginia, in 1863 by John Hobbs. Hobbs formed many partnerships beginning as early as 1820 (Hobbs and Barnes) before teaming up with Brocunier. The company was noted for a cheap lime glass formula used as a substitute for lead glass. It became part of the U.S. Glass Company in 1891.

Hobnail A pressed or cut pattern in glassware resembling small raised knobs referred to as "hobs" or "prunts." The name originated in England and referred to the large heads of hobnail fasteners.

Hocking Glass Co. Established in Lancaster, Ohio, by I.J. Collins in 1905; it began as a hand operation but converted fully to automation during the Depression era. The company was one of the largest manufacturers of machine-pressed tableware and merged with the Anchor Cap and Closure Corporation in 1937 to form Anchor-Hocking.

Holly amber A type of art glass made in 1903 by the Indiana Tumbler and Goblet Company; it is a pressed design characterized by creamy opalescent to brown amber shading (golden agate) with pressed holly leaves.

Honesdale Decorating Co. Established by Christian Dorflinger and his sons in Honesdale, Pennsylvania, in 1901; the company produced hand-cut quality crystal wares with some gold decoration until the business closed in 1932.

Honey dish A tiny flat or shallow dish used for serving honey.

Hope Glass Works Established in Providence, Rhode Island, in 1872 by Martin L. Kern; the company was noted primarily for cut glass. In 1891 Kern's son resumed the business; in 1899 it was sold to the Goey family, who continued to operate under the "Hope" name until 1951.

Horehound A Northwood iridized Carnival glass color named for horehound Candy. The color is often compared to root beer.

Horseradish jar A small to medium-sized covered glass receptacle used for serving horseradish.

Hot plate A usually thick, sturdy flat glass object used to protect a surface from hot items.

Humidor A glass jar or case used for holding cigars in which the air is kept properly humidified.

Hunt Glass Co. Established in Corning, New York, in 1895 by Thomas Hunt. The company used blanks from the Corning Glass Works as well as pressed blanks from the Union Glass Co. It operated as a cut glass firm until the early 1910s.

Hydrofluoric acid An acid similar to hydrochloric acid that attacks silica. It is used to finish as well as etch glass.

Ice blue A very light shade or tint of transparent blue-colored glass (the color of ice) usually applied as an iridescence on Carnival glass.

Ice bucket or tub A glass vessel shaped as a medium-sized bucket or pail, with or without semicircular handle, used for holding ice.

Ice cream plate A small, flat glass plate, usually round in shape, used for serving a single scoop of ice cream.

Ice cream tray A large shallow or flat glass container used for serving ice cream.

Ice glass A type of art glass characterized by a rough surface that resembles cracked ice.

Ice green A very light shade or tint of transparent green-colored glass (the color of ice) usually applied as an iridescence on Carnival glass.

Ice lip A rim at the top of a pitcher that prevents ice from spilling out of the spout when the pitcher is tilted.

Ideal Cut Glass Co. Founded by Charles E. Rose in 1904 in Corning, New

York; the company moved its cut glass business to Syracuse, New York, in 1909 and operated until 1934.

IGC Liquidating Corporation A subsidiary of Lenox, Inc. of New Jersey; Lenox purchased the Imperial Glass Company in 1972 and continued to produce glass under the IGC name until it was sold to Arthur Lorch in 1981. Lorch sold the company to Robert Strahl in 1982, and the company closed in 1985.

Imperial Glass Co. Established by Edward Muhleman in Bellaire, Ohio, in 1901; it was a major producer of Carnival glass in the early 20th century and was responsible for many reproductions of it later. The company was sold to Lenox in 1972, which continued producing glass under the IGC Liquidating Corporation name until 1982.

Incising The technique of cutting or engraving designs into the surface of glass.

Incrustation A sulphide design within crystal or clear glass paperweights.

Indiana Glass Co. Established in 1907; it was noted for many machine-pressed Depression patterns and more recent reproductions of them. The company continues to operate today as a subsidiary of the Lancaster Colony Corporation.

Indiana Tumbler & Goblet Co. Established in 1896 in Greentown, Indiana; it is noted for inexpensive experimental colored tableware, including caramel slag glass. The company closed when the factory burned down in 1903.

Inkwell A small but heavy glass container used for holding ink (originally for quill pens).

Inlay An object that is embedded into the surface of another.

Intaglio An engraving or cutting made below the surface of glass so that the impression left from the design leaves an image in relief (Italian for "engraving").

Intarsia The name given to a type of glass produced by Steuben in the 1920s. It is characterized by a core of colored glass blown between layers of clear glass, then decorated by etching into mosaic patterns.

Iridescence A sparkling, rainbow-colored finish applied to the exterior of glass objects that is produced by adding metallic salts.

Iridized Glass that has been coated with iridescence.

Irving Cut Glass Co., Inc. Established in Honesdale, Pennsylvania, in 1900 by William Hawken and five partners. The company purchased blanks from H.C. Fry and was noted for cutting flowers and figures. Many of its products were shipped to Asia, South Africa, and Spain. The company closed in 1930.

Ivory A cream or off-white opaque glass (the color of ivory).

Ivrene A white opaque glass with a light pearl-like iridescent coating; originally made by Steuben.

Jadeite A pale, lime-colored opaque green glass (the color of jade).

Jack-in-the-pulpit A style of vase made to resemble the woodland flower. It usually features a circular base, thin stem, and large, open ruffled bloom at the top.

Jam jar A small covered glass receptacle used for serving jams and jellies. The cover usually has an opening for a spoon handle.

Jardiniere An ornamental glass stand or vaselike vessel used for holding plants or flowers.

Jarves, Deming An early pioneer in glassmaking in America. He founded the New England Glass Company in 1818, the Boston & Sandwich Glass Company in 1825, as well as several other firms.

Jelly dish or tray A small, flat or shallow dish used for serving jelly, jam, marmalade, and other preserves.

Jeannette Glass Co. Established in Jeannette, Pennsylvania, in 1902; the company was noted for several color patterns during the Depression era and continues to make glassware today.

Jenkins, D.C. Glass Co. Once employed by the Indiana Tumbler & Goblet Co. and the Kokomo Glass Co., David C. Jenkins built his own factory in Kokomo, Indiana, in 1905. His new company produced some pressed wares until the early 1930s.

Jennyware The nickname for kitchenware glass made by the Jeannette Glass Company.

Jersey Glass Co. Established by George Drummer in Jersey City, New Jersey, in 1824; the company produced cut and pressed glass tableware.

Jewel box A glass receptacle usually rectangular in shape, with or without cover, used for storing jewelry.

Jewel Cut Glass Co. Established by C.H. Taylor in Newark, New Jersey, in 1906; the company began as the C. H. Taylor Glass Co. and made cut glass products.

Jug A large, deep glass vessel, usually with a wide mouth, pouring spout, and handle, used for storing liquids.

Juice glass A short, narrow glass tumbler, with or without foot, with a capacity of 3 to 6 ounces, used for drinking fruit and vegetable juices.

Kanawa Glass Co. Established in 1955 in Dunbar, West Virginia; Kanawa was noted for glass novelty items, pitchers, and vases. The company was purchased by the Raymond Dereume Glass Company in 1987.

Kew Blas A name given to a type of opaque art glass produced by the Union Glass Company in the 1890s. The primary color is brown, with shadings of brown and green.

Keystone Cut Glass Co. Established in Hawley, Pennsylvania, in 1902; the company produced cut glass until 1918.

Kick A small indentation in the bottom of a glass object.

Kiln An oven used for firing or refiring glass objects. Kilns are also used for fusing enamels on glass objects.

Kimble Glass Co. Evan F. Kimble purchased Durand's factory in Vineland, New Jersey, in 1931; Kimble operated for a short time and was noted for the art glass "Cluthra."

King, Son, and Co. Established in 1859 as the Cascade Glass Works near Pittsburgh, Pennsylvania. The company was primarily a manufacturer of tableware and became part of the U.S. Glass Company in 1891.

Knife rest A small, thick, barbell-shaped glass object used to balance knife blades off the table when eating.

Knop An ornamental ball-shaped swelling on the stem of a glass, such as a wine glass.

Kosta Glassworks Established in 1742 in Sweden; it is one of the oldest glassmakers still in operation today. The factory originally produced windows, then later added chandeliers and tableware. In 1946 it merged with the Boda Glassworks to form Kosta-Boda.

LaBelle Glass Company Established in Bridgeport, Ohio; the company operated from the mid-1870s to the 1880s and made pressed and some limited engraved glassware.

Lace glass A mid-16th-century Venetian-styled glass characterized by transparent threaded designs layered on the sides of various glass objects.

Lacy pressed glass A mid-19th-century American style of pressed glass characterized by an overall angular and round braiding pattern.

Ladle A handled (long or short) spoon used for dipping jam, gravy, punch, or other foods and liquids from jars or bowls.

Lalique, René A French glassmaker and leader of the 19th-century Art Nouveau style. He is noted for multiple-faced or figured crystal and colored art glass items, and his success continued well into the 20th century. Glass is still made today with the etched "Lalique" signature in France.

Lamp shade Glass coverings that shelter lights in order to reduce glare. At times, large glass bowls are converted to lamp shades by drilling holes in their centers to attach them above the light.

Lampwork The process of forming delicate glass objects out of thin rods or canes while working at a small flame (the flame is referred to as the "lamp"; hence "lampwork").

Lancaster Glass Co. Established in Lancaster, Ohio, in 1908, the company was sold to the Hocking Glass Co. in 1924, which continued to use the Lancaster name through 1937.

Latticino A 16th-century Venetian-styled glass characterized by white opaque glass threads applied to clear glass objects.

Laurel Cut Glass Co. Founded in 1903 as the German Cut Glass Co. in Jermyn, Pennsylvania; the name was changed to Laurel soon after. In 1906 the company changed its name briefly to the Kohinur Cut Glass Co. but switched back to Laurel in 1907. The company produced limited cut glass and merged with the Quaker City Cut Glass Co. after World War I. The two split soon after, and Laurel disbanded in 1920.

Lava glass A style of art glass invented by Louis Comfort Tiffany characterized by dark blue and gray opaque hues (the color of cooled lava) and sometimes coated with gold or silver decorations.

Lavender A light pastel shade of purple-colored glass produced by the addition of manganese. See also **Amethyst** and **Purple**.

Layered glass Glass objects with overlapping levels or layers of glass.

Lazy Susan A large revolving tray used for serving condiments, relishes, or other foods.

Lead crystal Crystal or colorless glass made with a high lead content (see **Half lead crystal** and **Full lead crystal**).

Lehr An annealing oven with a moving base that travels slowly through a controlled loss of heat until the objects can be taken out at the opposite end. The rate of speed is adjustable as needed.

Libbey Glass Co. Established as the New England Glass Company in 1818 and purchased by William L. Libbey in the 1870s. Libbey produced high-quality cut and pressed glass and continues to operate today as one of the nation's largest glass producers.

Liberty Works Established in Egg Harbor, New Jersey, in 1903; the company produced some cut and pressed glass tableware before going out of business in 1934.

Lily pad A name given to a decoration applied to glass objects characterized by a superimposed layer of glass. Several styles of leaves (including lily pads), flowers, and stems were then designed on this layer.

Lime glass A glass formula developed by William Leighton as a substitute for lead glass. Calcined limestone was substituted for lead, which made glass cheaper to produce. Lime glass also cools faster than lead glassware but is lighter and less resonant.

Lime ice green A light shade or tint of transparent yellowish-green colored glass (the color of ice) usually applied as an iridescence on Carnival glass. Note that lime is slightly darker than ice green Carnival glass.

Locke, Joseph An English pioneer in the art glass field who moved to the United States. He is noted for designing and creating several varieties of art glass, including Agata.

Lotz or Loetz glass Art Nouveau glass produced by Johann Lotz of Austria in the late 19th and early 20th centuries.

Loving cup A glass drinking vessel, with or without a foot, and usually with 2 handles.

Low relief An engraving process in which the background is cut away to a very low degree (see **Relief cutting**).

Luncheon plate A flat glass object, usually round in shape, about 8″ in diameter (an inch or two smaller than a dinner plate but larger than a salad plate), used for serving lunch.

Lustered An iridescent form or finish applied to glass by use of a brush to apply metallic salt solutions to glass that has already been cooled to room temperature. The glass is then placed in a lehr to produce the lustrous iridescent finish.

Lutz glass A thin, clear glass striped with colored twists first created by Nicholas Lutz of the Boston & Sandwich Glass Company. It is sometimes referred to as "candy stripe glass."

Luzerne Cut Glass Co. Established in the early 1900s in Pittston, Pennsylvania; the company made some cut glass products before going out of business in the late 1920s.

MacBeth-Evans Glass Co. Established in Indiana in 1899; the company began as a hand operation and switched to machine-pressed patterns. It was acquired by Corning in 1936 and continues to operate today.

Mallorytown Glass Works Established in 1825 in Mallorytown, Ontario; it was Canada's first glassmaker, producing blown vessels and containers. The company closed in 1840.

Maple City Glass Co. Established in 1910 in Honesdale, Pennsylvania; the company produced some limited cut glassware into the early 1920s.

Marbled glass Glass objects with single or multiple color swirls made to resemble marble.

Marigold The most common iridized form of Carnival glass. Marigold consists of a flashed-on iridescent orange color.

Marmalade dish See **Jelly dish**.

Marmalade jar See **Jam jar**.

Marquetry A decorating technique whereby hot glass pieces are applied to molten glass, then marvered onto the surface creating an inlaid effect.

Marver A marble, metal, or stone plate or base on which blown glass is shaped. Marvers are also used to pick surface embellishments, such as mica or gold leaf.

Mary Gregory Clear and colored glassware (commonly pastel pink) decorated with white enamel designs of one or more boys and/or girls playing in Victorian scenes. Mary Gregory worked as a decorator for the Boston & Sandwich Glass Co. from 1870 to 1880, but it is not known if she ever painted the glass of her namesake.

Mayonnaise dish A small, flat or shallow indented dish used specifically for serving mayonnaise.

McKee Brothers Established in Pittsburgh, Pennsylvania, by Samuel and James McKee in 1834. The company began as a hand operation and continued producing a variety of glass until 1961, when it was purchased by the Jeannette Glass Company.

Mercury glass Glass objects characterized by two outer layers of clear glass with an inner layer of mercury or silver nitrate between them.

Merese An ornamental notch or knob between the stem and bowl of stemware.

Meriden Cut Glass Co. Established in 1895 in Meriden, Connecticut; this cut glass operation operated as a subsidiary of the Meriden Silver Plate Co., which in turn became part of the International Silver Co. Cut glass was produced until 1923.

Metal A term used by chemists for a batch of glass (see **Best metal**).

Milk glass A semiopaque opalescent glass colored originally by a compound of arsenic or calcined bones or tin. The result is a white color resembling milk. Modern milk glass usually contains aluminum and fluorine as additives.

Millefiori An 18th-century European-style paperweight made with several different colored glass rods in a pattern, then covered with an extremely thick outer layer of glass. Multicolored canes are embedded in clear glass to create the "thousand flower" design.

Millersburg Glass Co. Established by John and Robert Fenton in Millersburg, Ohio, in 1908; the company was a major producer of Carnival glass, but the business lasted only until 1911. After filing for bankruptcy, Millersburg Glass continued to be produced under the Radium Glass Company name until 1913, when it was sold to the Jefferson Glass Company, which produced lighting glassware until 1916, when it too closed. Note that Millersburg glass is often referred to as "rhodium ware" or "radium" because of the minor traces of radiation measurable in the glass.

Mint dish See **Bonbon dish** and **Fruit or nut dish**.

Miter cut engraving Glass cut with a sharp groove on a V-edged wheel.

Moil Waste glass left on the blowpipe or pontil.

Mold A wooden or iron form used to shape glass. Pattern or half-molds are used before glass has totally expanded. Full or three-part molds are used to give identical or same-size shapes to glassware.

Molded glass Blown or melted glass that is given its final shape by the use of molds.

Monart glass An art glass of Spain characterized by opaque and clear marble swirls.

Monax A partially opaque or nearly transparent cream-colored or off-white glass first produced and named by the MacBeth Evans Glass Company.

Monroe, C.F. Co. Established in Meriden, Connecticut, in 1880; it was noted for some art glass designs, particularly "Kelva," "Nakara," and "Wave Crest." The company also made some cut glass and novelty items before ceasing operation in 1916.

Morgantown Glass Works Established in Morgantown, West Virginia, in the 1880s; the company produced pressed wares as well as some colored glass. The business closed permanently in 1972.

Mosaic A surface of a glass object that is decorated by many small adjoining pieces of varicolored materials, such as stone or glass to form a picture.

Moser, Ludwig A famous Austrian glassmaker who opened an art glass studio in 1857 in Karlsbad, Czechoslovakia; he is noted for deeply carved and enameled wildlife scenes.

Moss agate An art glass first created by Steuben characterized by red, brown, and other swirled or marblelike colors.

Mosser Glass Company Established by Tom Mosser in Cambridge, Ohio, in 1964; the company is noted for glass miniatures and novelty items and continues to operate today.

Mother-of-pearl An art glass technique produced by trapping air between layers of glass.

Mount Vernon Glass Co. An American art glass company founded in the late 19th century and noted for fancy glass vases and glass novelty items.

Mt. Washington Glass Works Established by Deming Jarves in South Boston, Massachusetts, in 1837; the company was noted for high-quality art glass designs, such as Burmese glass, Crown Milano, and cameo-engraved designs. The company was sold to the Pairpoint Manufacturing Company in 1894.

Muffle kiln A low temperature oven used for refiring glass to fix or fire on enameling.

Mug A cylindrical drinking vessel with one handle; larger mugs with hinged metal lids are usually referred to as "steins."

Murrhine or Murrina A Venetian technique in which colored cane sections are embedded within hot glass before a piece is blown into its final shape. The result is a colorful mosaic design.

Mustard dish or jar A small flat or shallow dish, with or without cover, used specifically for serving mustard. A lid may or may not have an opening for a matching spoon.

Nailsea Glass House A glass factory established in Somerset, England, in the late 18th century. The company was noted for producing many unusual glass items, such as rolling pins and walking canes.

Napkin ring A small, circular glass band used for holding napkins.

Napoli Glass objects that are completely covered with gold or gold enamels, both inside and out. Additional decorations may be applied to the gold covering.

Nappy An open shallow serving bowl without a rim that may contain one or two handles.

Nash A wealthy American family of English heritage that included several glass designers and manufacturers. They are noted for expensive high-quality art glass similar to Tiffany designs and styles.

Near cut Pressed glass patterns similar to designs of hand-decorated cut glass.

Neck The part of a glass vessel such as a bottle or jug between the body and mouth.

Needle etching A process of etching glass by machine. Fine lines are cut in glass by a machine through a wax coating, then hydrofluoric acid is applied to etch the pattern into the glass.

New Bremen Glass Manufactory Established by Johann F. Amelung in New Bremen, Maryland, 1784; it was one of the first glassmakers of useful tableware. Many of the products were signed and dated (rare for that period).

New Carnival Reproduction iridescent glass made since 1962, sometimes with the original Carnival glass molds.

New England Crystal Company Established in 1990 by Philip E. Hopfe in Lincoln, Rhode Island; the company is noted for hand-cut and copper wheel engraved art forms, as well as pâte de verre styles.

New England Glass Co. Established in 1818 by Deming Jarves and associates in Cambridge, Massachusetts. One of the first highly successful American glass companies, it produced pressed, cut, and a variety of art glass patterns, such as Agata, Amberina, Pomona, and Wild Rose Peachblow. The company was bought by Libbey in the 1870s.

New Geneva Glass Works Established in 1797 by Albert Gallatin in Fayette County, Pennsylvania; the company made some tableware and windows before closing.

New Martinsville Glass Co. Established in 1901 in New Martinsville, West Virginia; it began as an art glass company and later produced pressed pattern glass, some novelty items, and Depression glass. It was sold to the Viking Glass Company in 1944.

Nipt Diamond Waves A pattern applied to glass objects produced by compressing thick vertical threads into diamondlike shapes.

Northwood Glass Co. Established in Wheeling, West Virginia, in 1887. It was noted for decorated glass with gold and opalescent edges, as well as Carnival glass. It closed in 1925.

Northwood, Harry Born in 1860 in Stourbridge, England, Northwood came to the United States in 1881 and served as a glass etcher for Hobbs, Brocunier. He founded the Northwood Glass Co. in 1887. The company operated until Northwood's death in 1919.

Nut dish A small, flat or shallow dish used for serving nuts.

Obsidian A dark mineral formed by volcanic action. Black glass is sometimes referred to as "obsidian glass." Obsidian is considered to be the first form of glass ever used by humans and has been found in arrow-heads, spears, knives, and other simple tools.

Off-hand glass Glass objects such as whimseys, art pieces, and other novelty items created by glassmakers from leftover or scrap glass.

Ogival-Venetian Diamond A pattern applied to glass objects produced by pressing or cutting. The shape is of large or wide diamonds and is sometimes referred to as "Reticulated Diamond" or "Expanded Diamond."

Oil bottle A glass receptacle with top used for serving vinegar or other salad oils (see **Cruet**).

Old gold A deep amber stain or amber applied to glass made to resemble gold.

Olive dish A small flat or shallow glass object, oblong or rectangular, that may or may not be divided; used specifically for serving olives.

Olive green A green color similar to Army olive drab. Olive green can be found in regular transparent glass as well as some flashed-on Carnival glass items.

Olive jar A small to medium-sized glass container with wide mouth and cover used for serving olives.

Onyx glass A dark-colored glass characterized by streaking of white or other colors and made by mixing molten glass with various color mediums.

Opal glass An opalescent opaquelike white milk glass usually produced by tin or aluminum and fluorine (see **Milk glass**).

Opalescence A milky or cloudy coloring of glass. Opalescent coating is usually made by adding tin or zinc and phosphate. Opalescent glass was first made by Frederick Carder at Steuben in the early 20th century.

Opaline glass An opaque art glass, pressed or blown, that was developed by Baccarat in the early 19th century.

Opaque glass Glass that is so dark in color that it does not transmit light (milk glass, for example).

Optic mold An open mold with a patterned interior in which a parison of glass is inserted, then inflated to decorate the surface.

Orange glass Glass that is colored by the addition of selenium and cadmium sulfide. Orange flashed glass is referred to as marigold in Carnival glass.

Ormolu A decorative object usually made of brass, bronze, or gold applied to glass objects (such as a knob on stemware).

Orrefors Glasbruck Established in 1898 in Smaaland, Sweden; the company continues to operate today. It is noted for contemporary art glass forms, including engraving (see also **Graal**).

Overlay glass The technique of placing one colored glass on top or over another, with designs cut through the outermost layer only.

Overshot glass A type of glass with a very rough or jagged finish produced by rolling molten glass objects into crushed glass.

Owens, Michael J. A glassblower who began his career at Libbey in 1888. Owens invented the automatic bottle blowing machine in 1903, which produced bottles quickly and efficiently at a much lower cost. He went on to form Owens-Illinois Inc.

Owens-Illinois Inc. Established in 1929 in Toledo, Ohio, when the Owens Bottle Machine Company under Michael Owens merged with the Illinois Glass Company. In 1936 it acquired the Libbey Glass Company and continues producing glass under the Libbey name today.

Paden City Glass Co. Established in Paden City, West Virginia, in 1916; it was noted for many elegant Depression glass patterns and closed in 1951.

Pairpoint Manufacturing Co. Established in New Bedford, Massachusetts, in 1865. Pairpoint acquired the Mt. Washington Glass Company in 1894 and continued producing glass until 1958. A new Pairpoint opened in 1967 in Sagamore, Massachusetts, producing handmade glassware.

Pane A large piece of flat sheet glass used for glazing windows.

Paperweight A small, heavy glass object with an inner design used as a weight to hold down loose papers. Paperweights are often oval or rounded and are made of extremely thick glass.

Parison A blob of molten glass that is gathered at the end of the blowpipe, pontil, or gathering iron (see also **Gather**).

Parfait A tall, narrow glass with short stem and foot used for serving ice cream.

Pâte de verre French for "paste of glass"; it is an ancient material made from powdered glass or glasslike substances that is formed into a paste by heating and then hardened. The resulting form is carved, painted, or applied with other decorations.

Pattern glass Glass produced by mechanically pressing it into molds. The design is cut directly in the mold.

Pattern-molded glass Glass that is first impressed into small molds, then removed and blown to a larger size (blown-molded).

Peachblow glass An American art glass produced by several companies in the late 19th century. It is characterized by multicolored opaque shades such as cream, white, pink, orange, and red.

Peach opalescent Peach-colored glass with a white opalescent edge or background (usually found in iridized Carnival glass).

Pearl or Pearlized glass Custard glass with a delicate, pastel iridescence.

Pearl ornaments A molded glass pattern consisting of diamonds, squares, and other diagonal bandings.

Pearline glass A late-19th-century art glass style characterized by color variance of pale to deep dark opaque blues.

Pegging The technique of poking a tiny hole in a molten glass object in order to trap a small quantity of air. The hole is then covered with other molten glass, which expands the air bubble into a tear shape or teardrop.

Peking Cameo Cameo engraved glass first made in China in the late 17th century in the city of Peking. It was made to resemble more expensive Chinese porcelain.

Peloton glass A style of art glass first made by Wilhelm Kralik in Bohemia in 1880. It was produced by rolling colored threads into colored glass directly after it was removed from the furnace.

Perfume bottle A tiny glass receptacle with narrow neck and stopper used for holding perfume.

Perthshire Paperweights, Ltd. Established in 1970 by Stuart Drysdale in Crieff, Scotland. Perthshire is noted for high-quality paperweights; many are produced in limited editions.

Phoenix glass A term applied to cased milk glass, also known as "mother-of-pearl," that was made by the Phoenix Glassworks Company in Pittsburgh, Pennsylvania, in the late 19th century.

Phoenix Glass Co. Established in Monaca, Pennsylvania, in 1880; the company later moved to Pittsburgh and was noted for cut glass gas and electric lighting fixtures, general glass items, and some figured art glass. Phoenix became a division of Anchor-Hocking in 1970 and was later sold to the Newell Group in 1987.

Photochromic glass A glass developed by the Corning Glass Works in Corning, New York, in 1964. When the glass is exposed to ultraviolet radiation such as sunlight, it darkens; when the radiation is removed, the glass clears.

Pickle castor A glass jar in a silver or silver-plated metal frame, usually with a handle and matching spoon, that was used for serving pickles. Pieces were especially popular during the Victorian era.

Pickle dish A flat or shallow dish, usually oblong or rectangular, used specifically for serving pickles (smaller than a celery dish).

Pie plate A large, shallow, round glass dish used for baking and serving pies.

Pigeon blood A color of glass characterized by brown highlighting over ruby red.

Pilgrim Glass Co. A contemporary art glass company founded in 1949 by Alfred E. Knobler in Ceredo, West Virginia; Pilgrim is noted for paperweights and modern cameo glass.

Pillar cutting A decorative pattern of cut glass in the form of parallel vertical ribs in symmetrical pillar shapes (similar to flute cutting).

Pilsner or Pilsener glass A tall, slender, footed glass vessel used for drinking beer.

Pin tray A flat or shallow glass dish used for holding hairpins.

Pink glass Glass that is colored by the addition of neodymium and selenium. Pink-colored glass was most popular during the Depression era.

Pitcher A wide-mouthed glass vessel usually with a spout and a handle, with or without a lip, used for pouring or serving liquids.

Pitkin & Brooks Established as a cut glass operation and distributor of crocks and glassware in Chicago, Illinois, in 1872. Edward Hand Pitkin and Jonathan William Brooks operated as a partnership until closing in 1920.

Pittsburgh Flint Glass Works The early name for Benjamin Bakewell's first glass company established in 1808 (see **Bakewell, Pears, and Co.**).

Pittsburgh glass High-quality pressed glass made by several companies in and around Pittsburgh, Pennsylvania, in the late 18th and 19th centuries.

Plate A flat glass object usually round in shape (occasionally square or oval) used for serving food.

Plated glass Glass that is covered by more than one layer; usually clear glass that is dipped or completely covered with colored glass.

Platinum band A metallic silver-colored trim applied to rims or by banding around glass objects (made of genuine platinum).

Platonite A heat-resistant, opaque, white-colored glass first produced and named by Hazel-Atlas in the 1930s and 1940s.

Platter A large, flat glass object, usually round or oval in shape (larger than dinner plates), used for serving food.

Plunger The device that presses molten glass against a mold to create the interior or primary pattern of an object (the mold produces the pattern on the outside surface).

Pokal A Bohemian-style goblet with stemmed foot and cover (cover may or may not contain a finial).

Polychromic glass Glass characterized by two or more colors.

Pomona glass An art glass created by applying or dipping the object into acid to produce a mottled, frosted appearance. It was first developed by Joseph Locke at the New England Glass Co. in the late 19th century.

Pontil A solid iron rod used for fashioning hot glass. The glassblower uses the pontil to remove the object from the blowing iron, allowing the top to be finished. Prior to the 19th century, the pontil on the glass left a mark, but since then the glass has been grounded flat. Also referred to as "pontie," "ponty," and "puntee."

Pot A vessel made of fired clay in which a batch of glass ingredients is heated before being transferred to the furnace. Most pots last only three to six weeks before breaking up. Modern pots hold 1100 to 1650 pounds of glass.

Pot arch A furnace in which a pot is fired before being transferred to the main furnace for melting.

Potash Potassium carbonate that is used as a substitute for soda as an alkali source in a glass mixture.

Powder jar A small glass receptacle, usually with a cover, used for holding various body powders. Powder jars are ordinarily part of dresser sets.

Preserve dish A small, flat or shallow dish, with or without a foot, used for serving jelly, jam, and other fruit preserves.

Pressed glass Molten glass mechanically forced into molds under pressure (an important invention of the 1820s was the handpress).

Pressing The process begins with molten glass poured into a mold, which forms the outer surface of an object. A plunger lowered into the mass leaves a smooth center with a patterned exterior. Flat plates and dishes are formed in a base mold, and an upper section folds down to mold the top (like a waffle iron).

Prism cutting Cut glass made with long, horizontal grooves or lines that usually meet at a common point.

Proof A term often used in Carnival glass to describe a trial impression from a plunger and mold combination. Often in a proof, certain areas have incomplete patterns (if noticed by glassworkers in the factory, proofs were usually pressed back into the mold to complete the pattern).

Prunts A German decoration or ornamentation characterized by small glass knobs or drops attached to drinking vessels; also hobs on hobnail patterned glass.

Pucellas A glassmaker's tool shaped like tongs used for gripping or holding glass objects while being worked.

Puff box A small square, rectangular, or circular glass container with cover used on dressing tables or vanities for holding powders.

Pumice Volcanic rock that is ground into powder and used for polishing glass objects.

Punch bowl A concave glass vessel, usually hemispherical in shape, used for serving beverages.

Punch cup An open, somewhat bowl-shaped or cylindrical vessel, usually with a single handle, used for drinking punch as dipped from a punch bowl.

Punch stand A matching support base on which a punch bowl rests.

Purled glass Glass characterized by a ribbing applied around the base of the object.

Purple A violet-colored glass produced by the addition of manganese. See also **Amethyst**.

Pyrex A type of glass created by Corning Glass in 1912. It contains oxide of boron, which makes the glass extremely heat resistant (sometimes referred to as "borosilicate glass"; see separate entry).

Quaker City Cut Glass Co. Established in Philadelphia, Pennsylvania, in 1902; the company produced cut glass until 1927.

Quartz glass An art glass characterized by a variety of colors and shades created by Steuben (designed to imitate the appearance of quartz).

Quatrefoil A form based on four leaves or four-petaled flowers originally applied to stained glass windows in medieval Europe. It was later applied to glass objects.

Quezel Art Glass & Decoration Co. Established in Brooklyn, New York, in 1901; the company was noted for opalescent art glass known as "Quezal glass"; see separate entry.

Quezal glass An iridescent, semiopaque imitation of Tiffany's "Favrile" art glass made by the Quezal Art Glass & Decoration Co. in the early 20th century.

Quilling A wavy pattern applied to glass by repeated workings with pincers.

Radium A brilliant transparent iridescence applied to Carnival glass (most by Millersburg). The base color can usually be observed without holding the iridized piece up to a light.

Radium Glass Co. Established by Samuel Fair, John W. Fenton, C.J. Fisher, and M.V. Leguillon. Radium assumed control of the Millersburg Glass Company after it filed for bankruptcy in 1911. The company continued to produce glass until 1913, when it was sold to the Jefferson Glass Company.

Range sets Kitchenware glass sets developed during the Depression era. Items might include canisters, flour jars, sugar jars, and shakers.

Ratafia glass A cordial glass used to serve the liqueur ratafia.

Ravenscroft, George The first commercially successful glassmaker in England, Ravenscroft developed a high-quality durable lead crystal formula in 1632.

Rayed A sunburst cut design usually applied to the bottom of glass objects.

Reading Artistic Glass Works Established in 1884 by French immigrant Lewis Kremp in Reading, Pennsylvania; the factory produced several styles of high-quality art glass but closed in 1886.

Reamer A juice extractor with a ridge and pointed center rising in a shallow dish, usually circular in shape.

Red Carnival glass An iridized coating produced by a gold metallic coloring agent that in turn produces a brilliant cherry red finish. Red Carnival glass is rare and very valuable.

Reeding A decorating technique applied with very fine threads or tiny rope-like strings of glass. The strings are usually colored and applied in a variety of patterns.

Refrigerator dishes Stackable square or rectangular covered glass containers of various sizes used for storing foods in the refrigerator.

Relief cutting A difficult and expensive method of cutting glass by designing the outline on the surface, then cutting away the background. The design is raised in relief, similar to that of cameo engraving.

Reliquary A glass vessel used for storing sacred religious relics.

Relish dish A small to medium-sized shallow glass serving tray with divisions, usually rectangular or oval in shape, and with one or two handles.

Renninger blue A medium iridized blue color named by the Northwood

Glass Co. for some of its Carnival glass products. The color is darker than sapphire but lighter than cobalt.

Resonance The sound that results when a glass object is struck; sometimes used as a test for crystal, although other types of glass produce similar sounds.

Reverse painting Designs painted on the back side of glass that appear in proper perspective when viewed from the front.

Rib mold A pattern mold for bowls, bottles, tumblers, and so on that is marked with heavy vertical lines or ribbing.

Richards & Hartley Established in 1869 by Joseph Richards and William T. Hartley in Pittsburgh, Pennsylvania. The company moved to Tarentum in 1881 and manufactured pressed wares before becoming part of the U.S. Glass Co. in 1891.

Rigaree A narrow vertical band decoration applied to glass in various colors.

Ringtree A glass object in the shape of a miniature tree with knobs that taper upward (the knobs are used to hold finger rings).

Ripley & Co. Established in 1866 by Daniel Ripley and George Duncan in Pittsburgh, Pennsylvania; the company produced pressed glass items until the partners split in 1874. Both continued on their own (Ripley & Co. and George Duncan & Sons) until becoming part of the U.S. Glass Company in 1891.

Riverside Glass Company Established in Wellsburg, West Virginia, in 1879; the company produced pressed glass until it joined the National Glass Company in 1900.

Roaster A deep round, oblong, or angled dish, with or without cover, with or without handles, used to bake or cook foods.

Rod A thin, solid cylinder or small stick of glass. Rods are joined together to form a cane.

Rolled edge A curved lip or circular base.

Rope edge A twirled, threadlike design usually applied around the edge of a glass object.

Rose A deep red, cranberry-colored glass applied by staining or flashing (not as dark as ruby red).

Rose bowl A small, round, concave glass vessel usually with three feet (trifooted) and a small opening in the center for holding a single or a few flowers.

Rousseau, Eugene A French glassmaker and pioneer of the 19th-century Art Nouveau style. He is noted for floral and Oriental designs created in several color effects and styles.

Royal Flemish glass An art glass made by the Mt. Washington Glass Works characterized by a raised gilding decoration and light staining.

Rubigold A name given to a marigold-colored Carnival glass by the Imperial Glass Company. Rubigold was advertised as a dark red iridescence with tints of other colors but it is truly marigold only and not Red Carnival glass.

Rubina glass Glass that is characterized by a crystal color at the bottom and a cranberry or rose color at the top.

Rubina verde Glass that is characterized by a light yellow-green at the bottom and a cranberry or rose color at the top.

Ruby red A gold metallic coloring agent that produces the most powerful red color in glass. Since the mid 20th century, ruby red glass has been produced using the chemical selenium instead of gold.

Sabino, Marius-Ernest A French art glass designer noted for opalescent gold figurines produced in the 1920s–1930s and 1960s–1970s.

Sachet jar A small glass receptacle, with or without a cover, used for holding perfumed powders for scenting clothes and linens.

Saint Louis A famous French glassmaking town that was producing glass as far back as the 16th century. In the 1840s, the factories there were noted for paperweight production, but most closed when the popularity of paperweights severely declined. The art form was revived in the 1950s and continues today.

Salad plate A flat glass object, usually round in shape and ordinarily about 7″ to 7¹/₂″ in diameter (slightly smaller than a lunch plate), used for serving salads.

Salt cellar A small open bowl, with or without a foot, used for sprinkling salt on food (may or may not have a matching spoon).

Salts bottle A small glass bottle with a silver or silver-plated top used for holding smelling salts. Pieces were especially popular during the Victorian era.

Salve box A small jar with a cover used on dressing tables and vanities for holding salves, ointments, or cold creams.

Salver A large platter or tray used for serving food or beverages. Most have a pedestal foot.

Samovar An urn-shaped lamp usually containing a metal spigot and metal hardware (base, top, and handle). Samovars originated in Russia.

Sand The most common form of silica used in making glass. The best sands are found along inland beds near streams and have a low iron content and low amounts of other impurities.

Sandblasting A process in which the design on a piece of glass is coated with a protective layer. The exposed surfaces that remain are then sandblasted with a pressurized gun to create the design.

Sandwich glass A pressed glass produced in the Eastern United States in the 19th century. It was a substitute for more expensive hand-cut crystal glass.

Sandwich server A large platter or serving tray with an open or closed center handle.

Sapphire blue The color of sapphire or sky blue, darker than ice blue but lighter than cobalt blue.

Sardine dish A small, oblong or oval, flat or shallow dish, used for serving sardines.

Satin glass An American art glass form characterized by a smooth, lustrous appearance obtained by giving layers of colored glass an all-over acid vapor bath.

Sauce boat An oblong, bowl-shaped vessel usually with a handle on each end used for serving sauces or gravy.

Sauce dish A small, usually flat or shallow dish, with or without handles, possibly footed, used for serving condiments or sauces.

Saucer A small flat or shallow plate usually with an indentation for a matching cup.

Scent bottle See **Cologne bottle** and **Perfume bottle**.

Sconce A glass candlestick bracket with one or more sockets for holding candles.

Screen printing A decorating technique that involves the passage of a printing medium through a stenciled specialized fabric.

Seeds Tiny air bubbles in glass indicating an underheated furnace or impurities caused by flecks of dirt or dust.

Selenium A chemical element that produces red or ruby red coloring in glass. Selenium serves as a gold substitute in red glassware.

Seneca Glass Co. Established in 1891 in Fostoria, Ohio; the company later moved to Morgantown, West Virginia, where it continues to make pressed tableware and novelty items.

Shaker A small upright container, usually cylindrical or angular in shape, with metal or plastic covers with holes; used for sprinkling salt, pepper, and other spices.

Sham A very thin, fragile glass tumbler.

Shaving mug A cylindrical glass vessel, with or without handles, usually larger than a drinking mug, and used for rinsing shaving cream from a razor.

Sherbet A small footed dish, with or without a small stem, used for serving desserts such as pudding and ice cream.

Sherry glass A tall glass with a foot and stem and a shallow angled or straight-edged bowl.

Shot glass A small whiskey tumbler with a capacity of at least 1 ounce but not more than 2. Height ranges from $1^3/4''$ to $3''$.

Sickness Glass that is not properly tempered or annealed. It ordinarily shows random cracks and flaking and eventually breaks or disintegrates.

Signature The mark of the maker or manufacturer usually applied near the bottom or the underside of glass objects.

Silica An essential ingredient in making glass. The most common form is sand, which is an impure silica. Sand is usually taken from the seashore or along inland beds near water. The Venetians historically used ground white pebbles from rivers. Powdered flints were once used as silica (see **Flint glass**).

Silveria glass The technique of rolling an extremely thin layer of silver over glass, then blowing it, which shatters the silver into decorative flecks.

Silverina A type of art glass created by Steuben in the early 20th century using particles of silver and mica applied to the glass object.

Sinclaire, H.P. & Co. Established in 1904 by H.P. Sinclaire in Corning, New York; the company used blanks from Dorflinger for cutting and engraving. It closed in 1929.

Skittle A small clay pot used for melting a specialized small batch of colored glass or enamel.

Slag glass A type of glass made with various scrap metals, including lead, that was first produced in England in the mid 19th century. Slag is characterized by swirling or marbleized designs.

Smith, L.E. Co. Established in 1907 by Lewis E. Smith in Mt. Pleasant, Pennsylvania. Smith left in 1911, but the company continued producing unique novelty items as well as colored glass during the Depression era. The firm is still in operation today.

Smith Brothers Harry A. and Alfred E. Smith worked in the art glass decorating department of Mt. Washington in 1871. They opened their own shop in 1874 in New Bedford, Massachusetts, and produced cut, engraved, and other art glass products.

Smoke A smoky or light to medium gray charcoal color. Smoke is most often found in iridized Carnival glass.

South Jersey glass Tableware made in New Jersey in the 18th century; it was fairly crude but bold, and the style spread to Europe.

Soda Sodium carbonate, which is used as an alkali in a glass mixture. Soda serves as a flux to reduce the melting point of glass.

Souvenir glass Decorated glass objects depicting cities, states, countries, tourist attractions, and so on.

Sowerby & Co. Established in 1763 in Gateshead-on-Tyne, England (originally called the New Stourbridge Glass Works) by John Sowerby. The name was officially changed by John's son, John George Sowerby. After John George's death, the name was changed again by his son-in-law to Sowerby's Ellison Glassworks, Ltd. Sowerby was a large producer of pressed glass, including Carnival glass.

Spangled glass A late-19th-century American art glass characterized by flakes of mica in the clear glass inner layer and overlaid by transparent colored glass. Most items produced in this style were glass baskets with decorated handles and rims.

Spatter glass An opaque white or colored glass produced in both England and America in the late 19th century. The exterior is sometimes mottled with large spots of colored glass.

Spittoon A fancy glass vessel or receptacle used for containing saliva (or spit; hence the name). Also referred to as a cuspidor.

Spoon dish A flat or shallow glass object, rectangular or oval in shape, used for holding dessert spoons horizontally.

Spooner or Spoon holder A tall, cylindrical glass vessel, with or without handles, used for holding dessert spoons vertically.

Spout A tubular protuberance through which the contents of a vessel are poured.

Sprayed-on iridescence Iridescence added to glass by spraying it with particles of metallic salts.

Spun glass Glass threading that was originally spun by hand on a revolving wheel. Glass fibers are spun by machine today.

Stained glass An imitation colored glass created by painting clear glass with metallic stains or transparent paints.

Star Holly A milk glass design created by the Imperial Glass Co. in the early 1900s. It was made to duplicate pressed English Wedgwood and was characterized by intertwined holly leaves raised in relief with background color mattes of blue, green, or coral.

Stave A basketlike enclosure used in millefiori paperweights.

Stein A cylindrical or square drinking vessel used for serving beer. It has a single handle and may have a hinged lid (the lid as well as the handles may be metal). The original capacity was 1 pint.

Stem The cylindrical support connecting the foot and bowl of a glass vessel (goblets, wine glasses, compotes, etc.).

Sterling Cut Glass Co. Established in 1904 in Cincinnati, Ohio, by Joseph Phillips and Joseph Landenwitsch. The company, noted for cut glass, closed in 1950.

Steuben Glass Co. Established in 1903 by Frederick Carder in Corning, New York. A leader in art glass, the company was purchased by the Corning Glass Works in 1918. Corning continues to produce some of the finest crystal in the world.

Stevens & Williams Glassmaking firm that produced art glass and developed a cheaper method of making cameo glass. It operated through the Brierly Hill Glassworks in Stourbridge, England, from the 1830s to the 1920s.

Stippling A decorating technique in which shallow dots are produced by striking a diamond or steel point against a glass object. Image highlights are produced by the dots, while the untouched finished glass leaves a shadowy background.

Straus & Sons Established by German immigrant Lazarus Straus in 1872 in New York City; it began as a retailer of china and glass products but later began cutting glass in 1888. As the demand for cut glass declined, the company returned to the retail market.

Striped glass An American art glass from the late 19th century characterized by wavy bands of contrasting colors.

Sugar A small cuplike vessel that may or may not have handles and that is used for serving sugar (often paired with a creamer for serving tea).

Sugar and lemon tray A two-tiered object used for serving lemons and sugar. Cut lemons are placed on the bottom level, while sugar in a bowl is kept on the top level.

Sugar shaker A small upright container, usually cylindrical or angular in shape and with a metal or plastic cover with holes, used for sprinkling sugar on various foods (larger than typical salt and pepper shakers).

Sulphide A ceramic relief in a clear glass paperweight, usually a portrait of a historical figure. (Sometimes spelled "sulfide.")

Sunset-glow glass An 18th-century European milk or opalescent white colored glass.

Superimposed decoration A glass decoration separate from the object to which it is applied.

Sweetmeat dish or compote A small flat or shallow tray or bowl-like object used for serving sweetmeat hors d'oeuvres.

Swizzle stick A thin glass rod with an enlarged end that is used to stir liquids (swizzle originally was a sweetened alcoholic beverage made with rum).

Syrup pitcher A small, wide-mouthed vessel with a spout, a handle, and a hinged metal lid that is used for pouring syrup.

Tank A large holding vessel constructed in a furnace for melting a batch of glass. Tanks replaced pots in large glass factories in the later 19th century.

Tankard A large drinking vessel somewhat straight-edged with a single handle that may or may not contain a hinged lid (as in steins, the lid and handle may be made of metal).

Taylor Brothers Established in 1902 in Philadelphia, Pennsylvania, by Albert and Lafayette Taylor. The company produced cut glass until 1915.

Tazza An unusually wide dessert cup or serving plate with or without handles mounted on a stemmed foot.

Tea caddy A large, wide-mouthed glass canister with cover used for storing tea bags or loose tea.

Teal A bluish-green glass (stronger blue coloring than ultramarine).

Teapot A vessel with handle, spout, and lid used to serve tea. Glass teapots typically are found in children's tea sets.

Tear A bubble of air trapped in glass that is sometimes purposefully created for a decorative effect.

Tempered opal A heat-resistant, translucent milk glass that was developed during World War II by the Corning Glass Works. Tempered opal is the basis for colored Pyrex kitchenware products.

Tempering A technique that increases the strength of glass by heating it slightly below the softening point, then suddenly cooling it with a blast of cold air.

Tendrils Slender, coiling, stemlike glass trailings, that resemble a plant's tendrils.

Thatcher Brothers Established by George and Richard Thatcher in 1891 in New Bedford, Massachusetts; the company produced cut glass until 1907.

Thread circuit A decorative pattern applied with ropelike strings or twists of glass. The strings or threads are often colored and applied in concentric circles or other symmetrical patterns.

Thumbprint A decorative style usually made by pressing in the form of oval-shaped shallow depressions arranged in rows. Several variations of the basic thumbprint pattern exist (e.g., almond thumbprint, diamond thumbprint).

Tidbit Tray A tiered dish with a pole connecting two or more levels. The pole usually runs through the center and the sizes of the levels gradually decrease from bottom to top.

Tiffany, Louis Comfort The most celebrated leader of the Art Nouveau style of the 19th century. Tiffany established a glass factory on Long Island, New York, in 1885 and was noted for several famous designs, including Favrile. His designs were used for lamps, windows, and decorative objects.

Tiffin Glass Co. Established in 1888 in Tiffin, Ohio. It became part of the U.S. Glass Company in 1891 and was later purchased by employees in 1963. The company closed in 1980. Tiffin is noted for table, bar, and decorative glassware.

Tobacco jar A large, canisterlike glass container with cover used for storing tobacco.

Toddy jar A tall, wide-mouthed glass receptacle used for serving hot toddies (alcoholic beverages consisting of liquor, water, sugar, and spices).

Toilet water bottle A glass receptacle with a narrow neck and a stopper used on dressing tables and vanities for holding water (larger than a cologne bottle).

Toothbrush bottle A tall, narrow, cylindrical glass container with a cap used to store a single toothbrush.

Toothpick holder A small glass or ceramic receptacle designed to hold toothpicks; usually cut or patterned to taper inward at the top.

Toothpowder jar A small glass receptacle with a cover used for holding toothpowder.

Topaz A mineral used as a coloring agent to produce a bright yellow color in glass.

Toy mug A miniature glass vessel in the shape of a mug. Normal capacity is 1 to $1^1/_2$ ounces.

Toy whiskey taster A small glass tumbler first made in America around 1840 for the tasting, sampling, or consuming of whiskey in small amounts.

Trailing The process of pulling out a thread of glass and applying it to the surface of a glass object in spiral or other string designs.

Transfer A complete design printed on a paper backing that is removed from the backing, applied to glassware, then fired on in a special enameling lehr.

Translucent Glass that transmits or diffuses light so that objects cannot be seen clearly through it.

Transparent Glass that transmits light without appreciable scattering so that objects are clearly visible.

Tray A flat glass object, usually oval or rectangular in shape, used for holding or serving various items.

Trivet A glass plate, usually trifooted, used under a hot dish to protect a surface.

Tumble-up An inverted glass set for a dresser or nightstand that usually includes a water bottle and other items such as a tray and tumblers.

Tumbler A drinking vessel ordinarily without a foot, stem, or handle, featuring a pointed or convex base.

Tuthill Cut Glass Co. Established in 1900 by Charles G. Tuthill, James F. Tuthill, and Susan Tuthill in Middletown, New York. The company, noted for cut glass and some intaglio engraving, closed in 1923.

Twist See **Air twist**.

Ultramarine A bluish-green aqua color produced by the mineral lazulite or from a mixture of kaolin, soda ash, sulfur, and charcoal.

Undercutting A technique of decorating glass in relief by cutting away part of the glass between the body of the object and its decoration.

Unger Brothers Established in 1901 in Newark, New Jersey; the company began as a silver manufacturer of household items and added cut glass products shortly afterward. It later switched to cheaper pressed blanks before closing in 1918.

Union Glass Co. Established in 1851 by Amory Houghton in Somerville, Massachusetts. The firm operated as a cut glass operation. Houghton later sold his interest to Julian de Cordova (whose initials are sometimes found on the liners of certain objects). The company closed in 1927.

U.S. Glass Co. An American glass conglomerate that was established in 1891 when 18 separate companies from the Glass Belt (Ohio, Pennsylvania, West Virginia, etc.) merged.

Uranium glass A brilliant yellowish-green glass produced by the addition of uranium oxide. Uranium glass is mildly radioactive (not harmful) and glows brightly under a black light. It was first made in the 1830s.

Urn An ornamental glass vase with or without pedestal (may or may not have handles); also a closed glass vessel with spigot used for serving liquids.

Val St. Lambert Cristalleries A Belgium factory established in 1825 by Messieurs Kemlin and Lelievre. It is still in operation today and is noted for engraved cameo art glass styles.

Variant A glass item that differs slightly from the original form or standard version of a particular item or pattern.

Vasa murrhina An American 19th-century art glass characterized by an inner layer of colored glass with powdered metals or mica added for decoration.

Vase A round or angled glass vessel, usually with a depth that is greater than its width, used for holding flowers.

Vaseline glass Glass made with a small amount of uranium, which imparts a light greenish-yellow color (a greasy appearance like Vaseline). Vaseline glass usually glows under black light.

Venetian glass Clear and colored glassware produced in Venice, Italy, and the surrounding area (especially the island of Murano) from the 13th century to the present.

Venini & Company Founded in 1921 by Paolo Venini in Murano, Italy. The company is noted for a revival of filigree techniques and innovative use of canes and murrhine. Venini is the most recognizable name in modern Venetian glassmaking and continues to operate today.

Verre-de-soie An art glass first produced by Steuben characterized by a smooth translucent iridescent finish.

Vial A small glass bottle used for ointments, medicines, and perfumes.

Victorian glass English-made glass from about the 1820s through the 1940s characterized by colors, opalescence, opaqueness, art glass, and unusual designs and shapes (named for Queen Victoria).

Viking Glass Co. Viking purchased New Martinsville in 1944 and continued using some of New Martinsville's original molds. In 1991 Viking was purchased by Kenneth Dalzell (former president of Fostoria) to become Dalzell-Viking. The company is still in operation today.

Wafer dish A small flat or shallow dish, usually square or rectangular in shape, used for serving crackers or wafers.

Waisted A vessel (usually a vase) that has a smaller diameter in the middle than at the top and bottom. The sides form a continuous inward curve.

Watch box A small rectangular or circular glass vessel, with or without a cover, used for storing a single wristwatch.

Water bottle A glass container with a narrow neck and mouth and usually without handle, used for drinking water or other liquids.

Waterford The first Waterford Glass Company was established in Waterford, Ireland, in 1783 by the Penrose family and sold to the Gatchell family in 1799. The company specialized in handmade crystal that featured a bluish tint and heavy cuts. The factory closed in 1851. A new Waterford factory was built in 1951. Since then Waterford has become the world's largest manufacturer of handmade crystal. Today, it operates as Waterford Wedgwood PLC.

Wear marks Tiny, barely visible scratches on the base, foot, or rim that indicate normal wear and tear through years of use. Glass with wear marks is usually not considered in mint condition, but it holds much more value than damaged glass.

Weathering The harmful effects of age, moisture, and chemical action on glass.

Webb, Thomas & Sons Established in 1837 by Thomas Webb in Stourbridge, England; the company has been in continuous operation since and is noted for several art glass styles (cameo, peach blow, alexandrite, Burmese, etc.).

Westmoreland Specialty Co. Established in Grapeville, Pennsylvania, in 1889; it was noted most for English Hobnail patterned glassware. The company closed in 1985.

Wheeling glass Glass made in Wheeling, Virginia, in the 19th century (before West Virginia became a state).

Wheels Cutting wheels developed from lapidary equipment. Large stone wheels are used for deep cuts and smaller copper wheels for finer engraving.

Whimsey A small decorative glass object made to display a particular glassmaker's skill (sometimes called a "frigger").

Whiskey jug A large glass vessel or decanter used for serving whiskey. It has a small mouth, a cover or stopper, and usually a small handle.

Whiskey sample glass Small whiskey tumbler or cordial with a capacity of up to 4 ounces for sampling whiskey or other distilled spirits. Sample glasses were produced in the late 19th century until Prohibition (1919). Most glasses featured advertising of a distiller or brand of whiskey (also referred to as "pre-Prohibition advertising glass").

Whiskey tumbler A small shot glass usually without a foot, stem, or handle; it features a pointed or convex base and is used for drinking distilled spirits in small amounts.

Whitney glass An early-18th-century American glass consisting of bottles and flasks.

Wine glass A tall footed glass with a long stem and deep bowl. The most common capacity is 4 ounces.

Wine set A decanter with matching wine glasses (may or may not include a matching tray).

Witch ball A spherical glass globe, usually 3″ to 7″ in diameter, dating from the early 18th century. It was used in England to ward off evil.

Wrything ornamentation A decoration consisting of swirled ribbing or fluting.

Yellow glass Chromate of lead and silver act as the primary coloring agents in producing a deep yellow color within glass (see **Canary yellow**).

Zanesville glass An American art glass produced in Ohio in the mid 19th century.

Zwischengoldglas An 18th-century Bohemian or German glass characterized by gilding and inlaid decoration within another straight-sided glass.

MANUFACTURER'S MARKS

Abraham & Straus Inc.

Akro Agate Company

C.G. Alford & Company

C.G. Alford and Co.

Almay & Thomas

American Wholesale
Corp.

Anchor-Hocking
Glass Corp.

Anchor-Hocking
Fire-King

M.J. Averback

Baccarat Glass Co.

Bartlett-Collins Co.

J.D. Bergen Co.

J.D. Bergen Co.

BIRKS

House of Birks
Montreal, Canada

Blenko Glass Co.

George L. Borden & Co.

George Borgfeldt
& Company

Boyd Art Glass
1978–1983

Boyd Art Glass
1983–1988

Boyd Art Glass
1989–

Bradley & Hubbard

Buffalo Cut Glass Co.

Burley & Tyrrell Co.

Cambridge Glass Co.

T.B. Clark & Co.

Conlow-Dorworth Co.

Corona Cut Glass Co.

Crown Cut Glass Co.

Crystal Cut Glass Co.

Crystolyne Cut Glass Co.

Czechoslovakia
20th Century

Daum Glass
Nancy, France

De Vilbiss Co.

SILVART

Deidrick Glass Co.

Diamond Cut
Glass Works

Dominion Glass Co.
Montreal, Canada

C. Dorflinger & Sons

George Drake
Cut Glass Co.

G.W. Drake & Co.

Duffner & Kimberly

FLORAL CRYSTAL

Duncan Dithridge

Durand Art
Glass Co.

O.F. Egginton
Company

Empire Cut Glass Co.

VESTALIA

Eska Mfg. Co.

Federal Glass Co.

Fenton Glass Co.
1969–1970

Fenton Glass Co.
1980s (with 8)

Fenton Glass Co.
1985–

Fenton Paper Labels

1920

Fostoria Paper Label
1924–1957

"Iris" Fostoria
Glass Co. Paper
Labels

1920 to 1957

Fostoria Paper Label

FRY

H.C. Fry Glass Co.

Emile Gallé

Gibson Glass

GILLINDER

Gillinder & Sons

Gowans, Kent & Co.,
Ltd., Toronto, Canada

Gundy-Clapperton Co.,
Toronto, Canada

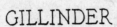

Handel and Co.

T.G. Hawkes
& Company

Hazel-Atlas Glass Co.

A. H. Heisey Glass Co.

L. Hinsberger Cut Glass

J. Hoare & Co.

Hobbs Glass Co.

Hobbs, Brocunier & Co.

Hocking Glass Co.

Honesdale
Decorating Co.

Hope Glass Works

Hunt Glass Co.

Imperial Glass Co.
1951–1972

Imperial Glass Co. as
the IGC Liquidating
Corp. 1973–1981

Imperial Glass Co.
under Arthur Lorch
1981–1982

1911

1913

1914

1921

Indiana Glass Co.

Iorio Glass Shop

Imperial Glass Co. 1904–1950

Irving Cut Glass Co.

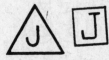

Jeannette Glass Co.

Jewel Cut Glass Co.

PEERLESS

Kelly & Steinman

Keystone Cut
Glass Co., Ltd.

**MARS
STRAND**

Kings Co. Rich Cut
Glass Works

Edward J. Kock
& Company

Kosta

Kosta Boda Limited
Edition Label, 1970s

Kosta Boda Label, 1980s

Krantz, Smith & Co., Inc.

Lackawanna Cut
Glass Co.

R LALIQUE
FRANCE

R LALIQUE
R LALIQUE

R. LALIQUE

LALIQUE

R. Lalique France N:3152

R.LALIQUE

R.LALIQUE   FRANCE

R. LALIQUE
FRANCE

R LALIQUE

R. Lalique

René Lalique

Lansburgh & Bro.

*Lansburgh &
Brother, Inc.*

F Laurel C°

*Laurel Cut
Glass Co.*

Libbey   Libbey   *Libbey* *Libbey*

Libbey

Apr. 16, 1901
(for use on pressed
[figured] blanks)

LIBBEY CUT GLASS
TRADE MARK
TOLEDO, O.

W.L. Libbey & Son

LOCKE
ART
GLASS

LOCKE
ART

Joseph Locke

Ca. Loetz

Loetz Glassworks

Lotus

Lotus Cut Glass Co.

LOWELL CUT GLASS CO.
LOWELL MASS

Lowell Cut Glass Co.

Wm. H. Lum

CUT
LUZERNE
GLASS

Luzerne Cut Glass Co.

LYONS

Lyons Cut Glass Co.

MacBeth-Evans Glass
Co./Corning Glass
Works

Majestic Cut Glass Co.

Maple City Glass Co.

Master
Glass Co.
1970s

McKanna Cut Glass Co.

McKanna Cut Glass Co.

McKee Glass Co.

PRESCUT

*McKee-Jeannette Glass
Works*

Meriden Cut Glass Co.

Millersburg Label

NAKARA

"Nakara"
C.F. Monroe Co.

KELVA

"Kelva"
C.F. Monroe Co.

"Wavecrest"
C.F. Monroe Co.

C.F. M.Cº

C.F. Monroe Co.

Moser Glass Works

Moses, Swan &
McLawee Co.

Mosser Glass Co. 1980s

Mt. Washington
Glass Works
Paper Label

"Crown Milano"
Mt. Washington
Glass Works

"Royal Flemish"
Mt. Washington
Glass Works

Mt. Washington Glass
Works Paper Label

Mt. Washington Glass
Works Paper Label

Richard Murr Co.

A. Douglas Nash
Corporation

National Association of
Cut Glass Manufacturers

Newark Cut Glass Co.

New England Glass
Works Paper Label

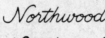

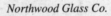

Northwood Glass Co.

J.S. O'Connor Co.

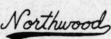

OHIO CUT GLASS COMPANY

NEW YORK SALESROOM, 66 West Broadway.
CHICAGO SALESROOM, Silversmiths' Building.
ST. LOUIS SALESROOM, Holland Building.

Ohio Cut Glass Co.

The Pairpoint Corp'n

Pairpoint Mfg. Company

Pairpoint Mfg. Company

Pairpoint Mfg. Co./Mt. Washington Glass Works

P.X. Parsche & Son Co.

Phoenix Glass Co.

Pilgrim Glass

Pilkington Glass Co.

Pitkin & Brooks

Pope Cut Glass Co., Inc.

U.S.A. Pyrex Corning Glass Works

English Pyrex

Canadian Pyrex

French Pyrex

Pyrex Label

Quaker City
Cut Glass Co.

Quezal Art Glass &
Decorating Co.

Roden Brothers
Toronto, Canada

SABINO   FRANCE

SABINO   PARIS

Sabino Art
Glass Co., France

St. Louis, France

Seattle Cut Glass Co.

Seneca Glass Co.

Signet Glass Co.

H.P. Sinclaire & Co.

Smith Brothers
Decorating Co.

Standard Cut Glass Co.

Sterling Glass Co.

Steuben Glass Works

Steuben Glass Works

**Various Frederick
Carder Signatures,
Steuben Glass Works**

**"Cire Perdue"
Steuben Glass Works**

Steuben Aurene

**Stevens & Williams
England**

L. Straus & Sons

Thatcher Bros. & Co.

TAYLOR

Taylor Brothers Co.

Louis C. Tiffany

furnaces Inc. Favrile

Tiffany Favrile

Tiffin Glass Co.

Tuthill Cut Glass Co.

Unger Bros.

Unger Brothers

"Kew Blas"
Union Glass Co.

United States Glass Co.

United States Glass Co.

Val St. Lambert Belgium

Van Heusen, Charles Co.

E.J.S. Van Houten Co.

Viking Glass Co. 1970s

Viking Glass Co.
Label, 1970s

Venini Murano, Italy

Waterford Glass Co.

THOMAS WEBB & SONS /
GEM CAMEO

THOS. WEBB & SONS, Lᴛᴅ.

Thomas Webb & Sons
England

Westmoreland Glass Co.

Westmoreland Glass Co.
1949–1983

WESTMORELAND

Westmoreland Glass Co.
1983–1985

C.E. Wheelock & Co.

L.G. Wright Glass Co.
1970s

Wright Rich
Cut Glass Co.

BIBLIOGRAPHY

Angus-Butterworth. *British Table and Ornamental Glass.* New York: Arco Publishing Co., 1956.

Archer, Margaret and Douglas. *The Collector's Encyclopedia of Glass Candlesticks.* Paducah, KY: Collector Books, 1983.

———. *Imperial Glass.* Paducah, KY: Collector Books, 1978.

Arwas, Victor. *Art Nouveau to Art Deco.* New York: Rizzoli International Publications Inc., 1977.

Arwas, Victor. *Tiffany.* New York: Rizzoli International Publications Inc., 1977.

Avila, George C. *The Pairpoint Glass Story.* New Bedford, MA: Reynolds-Dewart Printing, Inc., 1968.

Baldwin, Gary, and Lee Carno. *Moser—Artistry in Glass, 1857–1938.* Marietta, OH: Antique Publications, 1988.

Barber, Edwin A. *American Glassware.* Philadelphia: Press of Patterson & White Co., 1990.

Barbour, Harriot Buxton. *Sandwich: The Town That Glass Built.* Boston: Houghton Mifflin Co., 1948.

Barlow, Raymond E., and Joan E. Kaiser. *A Guide to Sandwich Glass.* Windham, NH: Barlow-Kaiser Publishing Co., Inc. 1987.

Barret, Richard Carter. *A Collector's Handbook of American Art Glass.* Manchester, VT: Forward's Color Productions, 1971.

———. *A Collector's Handbook of Blown and Pressed American Glass.* Manchester, VT: Forward's Color Productions, 1971.

———. *Popular American Ruby-Stained Pattern Glass.* Published by Richard Carter Barret and Frank L. Forward, 1968.

Battersby, Martin. *Art Nouveau: The Colour Library of Art.* Middlesex, England: The Hamlyn Publishing Group Ltd., 1969.

Batty, Bob H. *A Complete Guide to Pressed Glass.* Gretna, LA: Pelican Publishing Co., Inc., 1978.

Beard, Geoffrey. *International Modern Glass.* New York: Charles Scribner's Sons, 1976.

Belknap, E. McCamly. *Milk Glass.* New York: Crown Publishers, Inc., 1949.

Bennett, Harold and Judy. *The Cambridge Glass Book.* Des Moines, IA: Wallace-Homestead Book Co., 1970.

Bing, S. *Artistic America, Tiffany Glass and Art Nouveau.* Cambridge, MA: Massachusetts Institute of Technology Press, 1970.

Bishop, Barbara, and Martha Hassell. *Your Obdt. Servt., Deming Jarves.* Sandwich, MA: The Sandwich Historical Society, 1984.

Blount, Berniece and Henry. *French Cameo Glass.* Des Moines, IA: Wallace-Homestead Book Co., 1968.

Blum, John, et al. *The National Experience: A History of the United States.* New York: Harcourt Brace Jovanovich, Inc. 1981.

Boggess, Bill and Louise. *American Brilliant Cut Glass.* New York: Crown Publishers, 1977.

———. *Reflections on American Brilliant Cut Glass.* Atglen, PA: Schiffer Publishing Ltd., 1995.

Bones, Frances. *The Book of Duncan Glass.* Des Moines, IA: Wallace-Homestead Book Co., 1973.

Bossaglia, Rossana. *Art Nouveau.* New York: Crescent Books, 1971.

Boston & Sandwich Glass Co. Boston: Lee Publications, 1968.

Bredehoft, Neila, George Fogg, and Francis Maloney. *Early Duncan Glassware: Geo. Duncan & Sons, 1874–1892.* Boston: Authors, 1987.

Bridgeman, Harriet, and Elizabeth Drury. *The Encyclopedia of Victoriana.* New York: Macmillan Co., 1975.

Brown, Clark W. *A Supplement to Salt Dishes.* Des Moines, IA: Wallace-Homestead Book Co., 1970.

Burns, Carl O. *The Collector's Guide to Northwood's Carnival Glass.* Gas City, IN: L-W Book Sales, 1994.

———. *Imperial Carnival Glass.* Paducah, KY: Collector Books, 1996.

The Cambridge Glass Co. Ohio: National Cambridge Collection Inc., 1978.

Carved and Decorated European Glass. Rutland, Vt: Charles E. Tuttle Co., Inc., 1970.

Charleston, R.J. *English Glass.* London: Allen Unwin. 1984.

Charleston, Robert J. *Masterpieces of Glass: A World History from the Corning Museum of Glass.* New York: Harry N. Abrams, 1980.

Chase, Mark E., and Michael J. Kelly. *Contemporary Fast-Food and Drinking Glass Collectibles.* Radnor, PA: Wallace-Homestead Book Co., 1988.

Cloak, Evelyn Campbell. *Glass Paperweights of the Bergstrom Art Center.* New York: Crown Publishers Inc., 1969.

Collector's Guide to Heisey's Glassware for Your Table. Gas City, IN: L-W Book Sales, 1993.

The Complete Book of McKee. Kansas City, MO: The Tuga Press, 1974.

Conder, Lyle, ed. *Heisey's Collector's Guide to Glassware for Your Table.* Gas City, IN: L-W Book Sales, 1984.

Contemporary Art Glass. New York: Crown Publishers, 1975.

Cosentino Geraldine, and Regina Stewart. *Carnival Glass.* New York: Western Publishing Co., Inc., 1976.

Cousins, Mark. *20th-Century Glass.* Secaucus, NJ: Chartwell Books, 1989.

Cudd, Viola N. *Heisey Glassware.* Brenham, TX: Herrmann Print Shop, 1969.

Curtis, Jean-Louis. *Baccarat.* London, England: Thames & Hudson, Ltd., 1992.

Daniel, Dorothy. *Cut and Engraved Glass, 1771–1905.* New York: M. Barrows & Co., 1950.

―――. *Price Guide to American Cut Glass.* New York: M. Barrows & Co., 1967.

Davis, Derek C., and Keith Middlemas. *Colored Glass.* New York: Clarkson N. Potter Inc., 1967.

―――. *English Bottles and Decanters, 1650–1900.* New York: World Publications Inc., 1972.

Deboni, Franco. *I Vetri Venini.* Torino, Italy: Umberto Allemandi & Co., 1989.

Diamond, Freda. *The Story of Glass.* New York: Harcourt, Brace, and World Inc., 1953.

Dibartolomeo, Robert E., ed. *American Glass Volume II: Pressed and Cut.* New York: Weathervane Books, 1978.

Dorflinger, C., & Sons. *Cut Glass Catalog, 1881–1921.* Hanover, PA: Everybody's Press Inc., 1970.

Doros, Paul E. *The Tiffany Collection of the Chrysler Museum at Norfolk.* Norfolk, VA: Chrysler Museum, 1978.

Drepperd, Carl W. *ABC's of Old Glass.* New York: Doubleday & Company, 1968.

Duncan, Alastair. *Tiffany at Auction.* New York: Rizzoli International Publications, Inc., 1981.

Duncan, Alastair, Martin Eidelberg, and Neil Harris. *Masterworks of Louis Comfort Tiffany.* New York: Harry N. Abrams, Inc., 1989.

Ebbott, Rex. *British Glass of the 17th and 18th Centuries.* London: Oxford University Press, 1972.

Editors of the Pyne Press. *Pennsylvania Glassware, 1870–1904.* Princeton, NJ: Pyne Press, 1972.

Edmonson, Barbara. *Old Advertising Spirits.* Bend, OR: Maverick Publications, 1988.

Edwards, Bill. *Northwood—King of Carnival Glass.* Paducah, KY: Collector Books, 1978.

―――. *The Queen of Carnival Glass.* Paducah, KY: Collector Books, 1976.

————. *Rarities in Carnival Glass.* Paducah, KY: Collector Books, 1978.

————. *The Standard Encyclopedia of Carnival Glass.* Paducah, KY: Collector Books, 1982–1996.

Ehrhardt, Alpha. *Cut Glass Price Guide.* Kansas City, MO: Heart of America Press, 1973.

Eige, Eason, and Rick Wilson. *Blenko Glass, 1930–1953.* Marietta, OH: Antique Publications, Inc., 1987.

Elville, E.M. *English and Irish Cut Glass, 1750–1950.* New York: Charles Scribner's Sons, 1951.

Ericson, Eric E. *A Guide to Colored Steuben* (2 vols.). Colorado: The Lithographic Press, 1963–1965.

Evers, Jo. *The Standard Cut Glass Value Guide.* Paducah, KY: Collector Books, 1975.

Farrar, Estelle Sinclaire, and Jane Shadel Spillman. *The Complete Cut and Engraved Glass of Corning.* New York: Crown Publishers Inc., 1978.

Fauster, Carl U. *Libbey Glass Since 1818.* Toledo, OH: Len Beach Press, 1979.

Feller, John Quentin. *Dorflinger: America's Finest Glass, 1852–1921.* Marietta, OH: Antique Publications, 1988.

Florence, Gene. *The Collector's Encyclopedia of Akro Agate.* Paducah, KY: Collector Books, 1975.

————. *The Collector's Encyclopedia of Depression Glass.* Paducah, KY: Collector Books, 1990–1996.

————. *Collectible Glassware from the 40's, 50's, 60's.* Paducah, KY: Collector Books, 1992.

————. *Kitchen Glassware of the Depression Years.* Paducah, KY: Collector Books, 1981–1995.

Forsythe, Ruth A. *Made in Czechoslovakia.* Marietta, OH: Antique Publications, 1993.

Frantz, Susanne K. *Contemporary Glass: A World Survey from the Corning Museum of Glass.* New York: Harry N. Abrams, Inc., 1989.

Freeman, Larry. *Iridescent Glass.* Watkins Glen, NY: Century House, 1964.

Garage Sale and Flea Market Annual. Paducah, KY: Collector Books, Inc., 1991–1995.

Gardner, Paul F. *Frederick Carder: Portrait of a Glassmaker.* Corning, NY: The Corning Museum of Glass, 1985.

————. *The Glass of Frederick Carder.* New York: Crown Publishers, Inc., 1971.

Garmon, Lee, and Dick Spencer. *Glass Animals of the Depression Era.* Paducah, KY: Collector Books, Inc., 1991.

Grimmer, Elsa H. *Wave Crest Ware.* Des Moines, IA: Wallace-Homestead Book Co., 1979.

Grist, Everett. *Covered Animal Dishes.* Paducah, KY: Collector Books, Inc., 1988.

Grover, Ray and Lee. *Art Glass Nouveau.* Rutland, VT: Charles E. Tuttle Co., 1967.

―――. *Carved and Decorated European Art Glass.* Rutland, VT: Charles E. Tuttle Co., 1967.

―――. *English Cameo Glass.* New York: Crown Publishers, Inc., 1980.

Hand, Sherman. *The Collector's Encyclopedia of Carnival Glass.* Paducah, KY: Collector Books, 1978.

Hardy, Roger and Claudia. *The Complete Line of the Akro Agate Co.* Clarksburg, WV: Clarksburg Publishing Co., 1992.

Harrington, J.C. *Glassmaking at Jamestown: America's First Industry.* Richmond, VA: The Dietz Press Inc., 1952.

Hartung, Marion. *Carnival Glass in Color.* Emporia, KS: Author, 1967.

―――. *Northwood Pattern Glass in Color.* Emporia, KS: Author, 1969.

Haslam, Malcolm. *Marks and Monograms of the Modern Movement, 1875–1930.* New York: Charles Scribner's Sons, 1977.

Hastin, Bud. *Avon Collectibles Price Guide.* Kansas City, MO: Author, 1991.

Heacock, William. *The Encyclopedia of Victorian Colored Pattern Glass.* (Books 1–4, 6–9). Marietta, OH: Antique Publications Inc., 1974–1988.

―――. *Fenton Glass: The First Twenty-five Years.* Marietta, OH: O-Val Advertising Corp., 1978.

―――. *Fenton Glass: The Second Twenty-five Years.* Marietta, OH: O-Val Advertising Corp., 1980.

―――. *Fenton Glass: The Third Twenty-five Years.* Marietta, OH: O-Val Advertising Corp., 1989.

Heacock, William, and Fred Bickenhauser. *The Encyclopedia of Victorian Colored Pattern Glass* (Book 5). Marietta, OH: Antique Publications Inc., 1974–1988.

Heirmans, Marc. *Murano Glass, 1945–1970.* Antwerp: Gallery Novecento, 1989.

Hettes, Karel. "Venetian Trends in Bohemian Glassmaking in the 16th and 17th Centuries." *Journal of Glass Studies,* vol. 5 (1963).

Hollister, Paul, and Dwight Lanmon. *Paperweights.* Corning, NY: The Corning Museum of Glass, 1978.

Hollister, Paul, Jr. *The Encyclopedia of Glass Paperweights.* New York: Clarkson N. Potter Inc., 1969.

Hotchkiss, John F. *Art Glass Handbook.* New York: Hawthorn Books, Inc., 1972.

―――. *Carder's Steuben Glass Handbook and Price Guide.* New York: Hawthorn Books, Inc., 1972.

————. *Cut Glass Handbook and Price Guide.* Des Moines, IA: Wallace-Homestead Book Co., 1970.

House, Caurtman G. *Relative Values of Early American Patterned Glass.* Medina, NY: Author, 1944.

House of Collectibles. *The Official Price Guide to Carnival Glass.* New York: Random House, Inc., 1986.

————. *The Official Price Guide to Depression Glass.* New York: Random House, Inc., 1988.

————. *The Official Price Guide to Glassware.* New York: Random House, Inc., 1987.

Huether, Anne. *Glass and Man.* New York: J.B. Lippincott Co., 1965.

Hughes, G. Bernard. *English Glass for the Collector, 1660–1860.* New York: Macmillan Co., 1968.

Hunter, Frederick William. *Stiegel Glass.* New York: Dover Publications, 1950.

Huxford, Sharon and Bob, eds. *Flea Market Trader.* Paducah, KY: Collector Books, 1993.

Imperial Glass Corp. *The Story of Handmade Glass.* Pamphlet published by Imperial (24 pages), 1941.

Innes, Lowell. *Pittsburgh Glass, 1797–1891: A History and Guide for Collectors.* Boston: Houghton Mifflin Co., 1976.

Jarves, Deming. *Reminiscences of Glassmaking.* Boston: Eastburn's Press, 1854.

Jefferson, Josephine. *Wheeling Glass.* Mount Vernon, OH: The Guide Publishing Co., 1947.

Jenks, Bill, and Jerry Luna. *Early American Pattern Glass, 1850–1910.* Radnor, PA: Wallace-Homestead Book Co., 1990.

Jokelson, Paul. *Sulphides: The Art of Cameo Incrustation.* New York: Thomas Nelson & Sons, 1968.

Kerr, Ann. *Fostoria.* Paducah, KY: Collector Books, Inc., 1994.

Ketchum, William C., Jr. *A Treasury of American Bottles.* New York: The Ridge Press Inc., 1975.

Klamkin, Marian. *The Collector's Guide to Carnival Glass.* New York: Hawthorn Books, Inc., 1976.

————. *The Collector's Guide to Depression Glass.* New York: Hawthorn Books, Inc., 1973.

Klein, Dan, and Ward Lloyd. *The History of Glass.* New York: Crescent Books, 1989.

Koch, Robert. *Louis C. Tiffany: A Rebel in Glass.* New York: Crown Publishers, Inc., 1964.

Kovel, Ralph and Terry. *The Complete Antiques Price List.* New York: Crown Publishers Inc., 1973, 1976, 1980, 1981, 1982, 1985, 1986, 1990.

————. *Kovels' Antique and Collectible Price List.* New York: Crown Publishers Inc., 1990, 1991, 1992, 1993, 1994, 1995, 1996.

————. *Kovels' Bottles Price List.* New York: Crown Publishers Inc., 1992.

————. *Kovels' Depression Glass and American Dinnerware Price List.* New York: Crown Publishers Inc., 1992, 1995.

Krantz, Susan. *Contemporary Glass.* New York: Harry N. Abrams, Inc., 1989.

Krause, Gail. *Duncan Glass.* New York: Exposition Press, 1976.

Lafferty, James R. *The Forties Revisited.* Author, 1968.

Lee, Ruth Webb. *Early American Pressed Glass.* New York: Ferris Printing Co., 1946.

————. *Nineteenth-Century Art Glass.* New York: M. Barrows and Co., 1952.

————. *Sandwich Glass.* New York: Ferris Printing Co., 1947.

Leybourne, Douglas M., Jr. *The Collector's Guide to Old Fruit Jars.* North Muskegon, MI: Author, 1993.

Lindsey, Bessie M. *American Historical Glass.* Rutland, VT: Charles E. Tuttle, 1967.

Mackay, James. *Glass Paperweights.* New York: Facts on File, Inc., 1973.

Madigan, Mary Jean. *Steuben Glass: An American Tradition in Crystal.* New York: Harry N. Abrams, Inc., 1982.

Manley, Cyril. *Decorative Victorian Glass.* New York: Von Nostrand Reinhold Co., 1981.

Mannoni, Edith. *Classic French Paperweights.* Santa Cruz, CA: Paperweight Press, 1984.

Mariacher, G. *Three Centuries of Venetian Glass.* Corning, NY: The Corning Museum of Glass, 1957.

Markowski, Carl and Gene. *Tomart's Price Guide to Character and Promotional Glasses.* Radnor, PA: Wallace-Homestead Book Co., 1990.

Marshall, Jo. *Glass Source Book.* London, England: Quarto Publishing Co., 1990.

McClinton, Katharine Morrison. *Lalique for Collectors.* New York: Charles Scribner's Sons, 1975.

McGee, Marie. *Millersburg Glass.* Marietta, OH: The Glass Press, Inc., 1995.

McKean, Hugh F. *The "Lost" Treasures of Louis Comfort Tiffany.* New York: Doubleday & Co., Inc., 1980.

McKearin, George and Helen. *American Glass.* New York: Crown Publishers, Inc., 1968.

————. *Nineteenth-Century Art Glass.* New York: Crown Publishers, Inc., 1966.

Measell, James. *New Martinsville Glass, 1900–1944.* Marietta, OH: Antique Publications, Inc., 1994.

Mebane, John. *Collecting Brides' Baskets and Other Glass Fancies.* Des Moines, IA: Wallace-Homestead Book Co., 1976.

Melvin, Jean S. *American Glass Paperweights and Their Makers.* New York: Thomas Nelson Publishers, 1970.

Miles, Dori, and Robert W. Miller, eds. *Wallace-Homestead Price Guide to Pattern Glass* (11th ed.). Radnor, PA: Wallace-Homestead Book Co., 1986.

Miller, Robert. *Mary Gregory and Her Glass.* Des Moines, IA: Wallace-Homestead Book Co., 1972.

Miller, Robert, ed. *Wallace-Homestead Price Guide to Antiques and Pattern Glass.* Des Moines, IA: Wallace-Homestead Book Co., 1982.

Miller's International Antiques Price Guide. London: Reed International Books, Ltd., 1996.

Moore, Donald E. *The Complete Guide to Carnival Glass Rarities.* Alameda, CA: Author, 1975.

Moore, N. Hudson. *Old Glass European and American.* New York: Tudor Publishing Co., 1924.

Mortimer, Tony L. *Lalique.* Secaucus, NJ: Chartwell Books, Inc., 1989.

National Cambridge Collector's Inc. *Colors in Cambridge Glass.* Paducah, KY: Collector Books, Inc., 1997.

Neustadt, Egon. *The Lamps of Tiffany.* New York: The Fairfield Press, 1970.

Newark, Tim. *Emile Galle.* London, England: Quintet Publishing Ltd., 1989.

Newbound, Betty and Bill. *Collector's Encyclopedia of Milk Glass.* Paducah, KY: Collector Books, Inc., 1995.

Newman, Harold. *An Illustrated Dictionary of Glass.* London: Thames & Hudson Ltd., 1977.

Nye, Mark. *Cambridge Stemware.* Miami, FL: Author, 1985.

Oliver, Elizabeth. *American Antique Glass.* New York: Golden Press, 1977.

Over, Naomi L. *Ruby Glass of the 20th Century.* Marietta, OH: Antique Publications, 1990.

Padgett, Leonard E. *Pairpoint Glass.* Des Moines, IA: Wallace-Homestead Co., 1979.

Papert, Emma. *The Illustrated Guide to American Glass.* New York: Hawthorn Books, Inc., 1972.

Paul, Tessa. *The Art of Louis Comfort Tiffany.* New York: Exeter Books, 1987.

Pears, Thomas C. III. *Bakewell, Pears & Co. Glass Catalogue.* Pittsburgh, PA: Davis & Warde, Inc., 1977.

Pearson, Michael and Dorothy. *American Cut Glass for the Discriminating Collector.* New York: Vantage Press, 1965.

————. *A Study of American Cut Glass Collections.* Miami, FL: Authors, 1969.

Pesatova, Zuzana. *Bohemian Engraved Glass.* Prague, Czechoslovakia: Knihtisk Publishing, 1968.

Peterson, Arthur G. *400 Trademarks on Glass.* Takoma Park, MD: Washington College Press, 1968.

Phillips, Phoebe, ed. *The Encyclopedia of Glass.* New York: Crown Publishers Inc., 1981.

Pickvet, Mark. *The Definitive Guide to Shot Glasses.* Marietta, OH: Antique Publications Inc., 1992.

————. *The Instant Expert Guide to Collecting Glassware.* New York: Alliance Publishers, Inc., 1996.

————. *Official Price Guide to Glassware.* New York: House of Collectibles, 1995.

————. *Shot Glasses: An American Tradition.* Marietta, OH: Antique Publications Inc., 1989.

Pina, Leslie. *Fifties Glass.* Atglen, PA: Schiffer Publishing, Ltd., 1993.

————. *Fostoria, Serving the American, 1887–1986.* Atglen, PA: Schiffer Publishing, Ltd., 1995.

————. *Popular '50s and '60s Glass.* Atglen, PA: Schiffer Publishing, Ltd., 1995.

Polak, Ada. *Glass, Its Tradition and Its Makers.* New York: G.P. Putnam's Sons, 1975.

Pullin, Anne Geffken. *Signatures, Trademarks and Trade Names.* Radnor, PA: Wallace-Homestead Book Co., 1986.

Rainwater, Dorothy T. *Encyclopedia of American Silver Manufacturers.* New York: Crown Publishers, Inc., 1975.

Revi, Albert Christian. *American Art Nouveau Glass.* New York: Thomas Nelson and Sons, 1968.

————. *American Cut and Engraved Glass.* New York: Thomas Nelson and Sons, 1970.

————. *American Pressed Glass and Figure Bottles.* New York: Thomas Nelson and Sons, 1968.

————. *Nineteenth-Century Glass.* New York: Galahad Books Inc., 1967.

Ring, Carolyn. *For Bitters Only.* Boston: The Nimrod Press Inc., 1980.

Rinker, Harry. *Warman's Americana and Collectibles.* Elkins Park, PA: Warman Publishing Co., 1986.

Rockwell, Robert F. *Frederick Carder and His Steuben Glass, 1903–1933.* West Nyack, NY: Dexter Press, Inc., 1966.

Rogove, Susan Tobier, and Marcia Buan Steinhauer. *Pyrex by Corning.* Marietta, OH: Antique Publications, 1993.

Rose, James H. *The Story of American Pressed Glass of the Lacy Period, 1825–1850.* Corning, NY: The Corning Museum of Glass, 1954.

Ross, Richard and Wilma. *Imperial Glass.* New York: Wallace-Homestead Book Co., 1971.

Rossi, Sara. *A Collector's Guide to Paperweights.* Secaucus, NJ: Wellfleet Books, 1990.

Schmutzler, Robert. *Art Nouveau.* London: Thames & Hudson Ltd., 1978.

Schroeder, Bill. *Cut Glass.* Paducah, KY: Collector Books, Inc., 1977.

Schroeder's Antiques Price Guide. Paducah, KY: Collector Books, Inc., 1993.

Schroy, Ellen. *Warman's Glass.* Radnor, PA: Wallace-Homestead Book Co., 1992.

Schwartz, Marvin D., ed. *American Glass, Volume I: Blown and Molded.* New York: Weathervane Books, 1978.

Scott, Virginia R. *The Collector's Guide to Imperial Candlewick.* Athens, GA: Author, 1980.

Selman, Lawrence H. *The Art of the Paperweight.* Santa Cruz, CA: Paperweight Press, 1988.

Shuman, John III. *American Art Glass.* Paducah, KY: Collector Books, 1988.

———. *Art Glass Sampler.* Des Moines, IA: Wallace-Homestead Book Co., 1978.

Shuman, John III and Susan. *Lion Pattern Glass.* Boston: Branden Press Inc., 1977.

Sichel, Franz. *Glass Drinking Vessels.* San Francisco: Lawton & Alfred Kennedy Printing, 1969.

Spillman, Jane Schadel. *American and European Pressed Glass in the Corning Museum of Glass.* Corning, NY: The Corning Museum of Glass, 1981.

———. *Glass, Tableware, Bowls, and Vases.* New York: Alfred A. Knopf, Inc., 1982.

———. *Glass from World's Fairs, 1851–1904.* Corning, NY: The Corning Museum of Glass, 1986.

Spillman, Jane Schadel, and Susanne K. Frantz. *Masterpieces of American Glass.* Corning, NY: The Corning Museum of Glass, 1990.

Stevens, Gerald. *Canadian Glass.* Toronto, Canada: The Ryerson Press, 1967.

———. *Early Canadian Glass.* Toronto, Canada: The Ryerson Press, 1967.

Stout, Sandra McPhee. *The Complete Book of McKee.* North Kansas City, MO: Trojan Press, 1972.

———. *Depression Glass Price Guide.* Radnor, PA: Wallace-Homestead Book Co., 1975.

———. *Depression Glass III.* Radnor, PA: Wallace-Homestead Book Co., 1976.

Swan, Martha Louise. *American Cut and Engraved Glass of the Brilliant*

Period in Historical Perspective. Des Moines, IA: Wallace-Homestead Book Co., 1986.

Tait, Hugh, ed. *Glass, 5,000 Years.* New York: Harry N. Abrams, Inc., 1991.

The Toledo Museum of Art. *Libbey Glass: A Tradition of 150 Years.* Toledo, OH: The Toledo Museum of Art, 1968.

Toulouse, Julian. *Fruit Jars: A Collector's Manual.* Camden, NJ: Thomas Nelson & Sons, 1969.

Traub, Jules S. *The Glass of Desire Christian.* Chicago: The Art Glass Exchange, 1978.

Truitt, Robert and Deborah. *Collectible Bohemian Glass, 1880–1940.* Kensington, MD: B & D Glass, 1995.

Viking Glass. *Beauty Is Glass from Viking.* New Martinsville, WV: Author, 1967.

Wakefield, Hugh. *19th-Century British Glass.* New York: Thomas Yoseloff Publishing, 1961.

Warman, Edwin G. *American Cut Glass.* Uniontown, PA: E.G. Warman Publishing, Inc., 1954.

Warner, Ian. *Swankyswigs: A Pattern Guide and Check List.* Otisville, MI: Author, 1982.

Warren, Phelps. *Irish Glass.* New York: Charles Scribner's Sons, 1970.

Watkins, Lura Woodside. *Cambridge Glass.* Boston: Marshall Jones Co., 1930.

Weatherman, Hazel Marie. *Colored Glassware of the Depression Era.* Springfield, MO: Weatherman Glass Books, 1974.

―――. *Colored Glassware of the Depression Era II.* Springfield, MO: Weatherman Glass Books, 1974.

―――. *Fostoria: Its First Fifty Years.* Springfield, MO: The Weatherman's Publishers, 1979.

Weatherman, Hazel Marie, and Sue Weatherman. *The Decorated Tumbler.* Springfield, MO: Glassbooks Inc., 1978.

Webber, Norman W. *Collecting Glass.* New York: Arco Publishing Co., 1972.

Weiner, Herbert, and Freda Lipkowitz. *Rarities in American Cut Glass.* Houston, TX: Collectors House of Books Publishing Co., 1975.

Welker, John and Elizabeth. *Pressed Glass in America.* Ivyland, PA: Antique Acres, 1986.

Wheeling Glass, 1829–1939: A Collection of the Oglebay Institute Glass Museum. Wheeling, WV: Oglebay Institute, 1994.

Whitehouse, David. *Glass of the Roman Empire.* Corning, NY: The Corning Museum of Glass, 1988.

Whitmyer, Margaret and Kenn. *Children's Dishes.* Paducah, KY: Collector Books, 1984.

Wilson, Jack D. *Phoenix and Consolidated Art Glass.* Marietta, OH: Antique Publications, 1989.

Wilson, Kenneth M. *New England Glass and Glassmaking.* New York: Thomas Crowell Co., 1972.

Winter, Henry. *The Dynasty of Louis Comfort Tiffany.* Boston: Author, 1971.

Zerwick, Chloe. *A Short History of Glass.* New York: Harry N. Abrams Inc., 1990.

Numerous advertisements, trade catalogs, journals, newsletters, and other publications utilized that are not listed above:

American Antiques
American Carnival Glass Association Newsletters
American Pottery and Glassware Reporter
American Glass Review
Antiques Journal
Antiques Trade Gazette
Antique Trader
M. Bazzett & Co.
A.C. Becken Co.
Butler Brothers
China, Glass, and Lamps
The Connoisseur
The Cosmopolitan
Crockery and Glass Journal
The Crockery Journal
The Daze
Enos' Manual of Old Pattern Glass
Glass Art Society Journal
Glass Line Newsletter
Good Housekeeping
Gordon & Morrison
Harper's
Heart of America Carnival Glass Association
Higgins & Seiter
International Carnival Glass Association Newsletters
The Jeweler's Circular-Weekly
Journal of Glass Studies
Krantz & Smith Company
Marshall Field & Co.
McClure's

Montgomery Ward
S.F. Myers Co.
N. A. & Co.
New Glass Review
Oskamp, Nolting Co.
Pattern Glass Previews
Pottery and Glassware Reporter
The Pottery, Glass & Brass Salesman
R. T. & Co.
Charles Broadway Rouse Wholesale Catalogs
Scribner's
Sears, Roebuck & Co.
William Volker & Co.
Woolworth & Co.
Woman's Day

Company catalogs, brochures, trade journals, and advertisements not included above:

Adams & Company
Akro Agate Company
Alford Cut Glass
Anchor-Hocking Glass Company
Averbeck, M.J.
Baccarat Glass Company
Bakewell, Pears & Company
Bergen Cut Glass Company
Blackmer Cut Glass
Blenko Glass Company
Boston & Sandwich Glass Company
Boyd Art Glass Company
Bryce Brothers
Cambridge Glass Company by National Cambridge Collectors, Inc.
Central Glass Company
T.B. Clark & Company
Consolidated Lamp & Glass Company
Correia Art Glass Company
De Vilbiss Company
Diamond Glass Company
Diamond Glass-Ware Company
Dominion Glass Company
C. Dorflinger & Sons
Dugan Glass Company

Duncan & Miller Glass Company
Durand Art Glass Company
Empire Cut Glass Company
O.F. Egginton Company
Federal Glass Company
Fenton Art Glass Company
Fostoria Art Glass Company
H.C. Fry Glass Company
Gibson Glass Company
T.G. Hawkes & Company
Hazel-Atlas Glass Company
A. H. Heisey & Company
J. Hoare & Company
Hobbs, Brocunier and Company
Hocking Glass Company
Carl Hosch Company
Imperial Glass Company
Indiana Glass Company
Indiana Tumbler & Goblet Company
Jeannette Glass Company
Keystone Cut Glass Company
King, Son, and Company
Lalique
Libbey Glass Company
Loetz Glass
MacBeth-Evans Glass Company
Maple City Glass Company
McKee Brothers
Meriden Cut Glass Company
C.F. Monroe Company
Moser Glass Works
Mt. Washington Glass Works
New England Crystal Company
New England Glass Company
New Martinsville Glass Company
Northwood Glass Company
Orrefors Glasbruck
Paden City Glass Company
Pairpoint Manufacturing Company
Perthshire Paperweights Ltd.
Phoenix Glass Company
Pilgrim Glass Company
Pitkin & Brooks

Quaker City Cut Glass Company
Quezal Art Glass and Decorating Company
Sabino Art Glass Company
H. P. Sinclaire Company
L. E. Smith Company
Steuben Glass Works
L. Straus & Sons
Taylor Brothers
Tiffany
Tipperary Crystal Company
Tuthill Cut Glass Company
Unger Brothers
U.S. Glass Company
Waterford Crystal Ltd.
Thomas Webb & Sons
Westmoreland Glass Company or *Westmoreland Speciality Company*

Auction houses, catalogs, brochures, and advertisements:

Sanford Alderfer Auction Company, Hatfield, PA
Arman Absentee Auctions, Woodstock, CT
Artfact, Inc., Computer Auction Records' Services
James Bakker, Cambridge, MA
Frank H. Boos Gallery, Bloomfield Hills, MI
Ron Bourgeault & Company, Portsmouth, NH
Richard A. Bourne Company, Hyannis, MA
Bullock's Auction House, Flint, MI
Burns Auction Service
Christie's and Christie's East, New York
William Doyle Galleries, New York
Du Mouchelles, Detroit, MI
Dunnings, Elgin, IL
Early Auction Company, Milford, OH
Robert Eldred Company, East Dennis, MA
Emerald Auctions, London, England
Garth's Auction, Inc., Delaware, OH
Glass-Works Auctions, East Greenville, PA
Grogon & Co., Boston, MA
Guerney's, New York
Hanzel Galleries, Chicago, IL
Leslie Hindman, Inc., Chicago, IL
Milwaukee Auction Galleries, Milwaukee, WI
Mordini, Tom & Sharon, Carnival Glass Auction Reports,

Freeport, IL
PK Liquidators, Flint, MI
David Rago, Trenton, NJ
Roan Brothers Auction Gallery, Cogan Station, PA
SGCA Auctions, Flint, MI
Sotheby's, New York

Antique shows and dealers:

AA Ann Arbor Antiques Mall, Ann Arbor, MI
W. D. Adams Antique Mall, Howell, MI
Antique Gallery, Detroit, MI
The Antique Gallery, Flint, MI
The Antique Warehouse, Saginaw, MI
Ark Antiques, New Haven, CT
Bankstreet Antiques Mall, Frankenmuth, MI
Bay City Antiques Center, Bay City, MI
Burton Gallery Antiques, Plymouth, MI
Cherry Street Antique Mall, Flint, MI
Flat River Antique Mall, Lowell, MI
Flushing Antique Emporium, Flushing, MI
Gallery of Antiques, Detroit, MI'
Gilley's Antique Mall, Plainfield, IN
Gene Harris Antiques, Marshalltown, IA
Hemswell Antiques Centre, Gainsborough, England
Hitching Post Antiques Mall, Tecumseh, MI
Indianapolis Antique Mall, Indianapolis, IN
Main Antique Mall, Ardmore, OK
Plymouth Antiques Mall, Plymouth, MI
Reminisce Antique Mall, Flint, MI
Showcase Antique Center, Sturbridge, MA
Water Tower Antiques Mall, Holly, MI
Wolf's Gallery, Cleveland, OH

Special thanks to the many dealers and auction companies who allowed me to snap a few photographs and provided helpful advice on pricing and market trends.

INDEX